# Management Accounting 3

**SECOND EDITION**

ACCT09005

*Compiled by:*
*Abeer Hassan*

**University of the West of Scotland**

ISBN 13: 9781121953024

**McGraw-Hill Custom Publishing**

# www.mcgrawhillcreate.co.uk

Published by McGraw-Hill Education (UK) Ltd an imprint of McGraw-Hill Education, 2 Penn Plaza, New York, NY 10121.

Copyright ©2013 by McGraw-Hill Education (UK) Ltd. All rights reserved. No part of this publication may be reproduced or distributed in any form or by any means, or stored in a database or retrieval system, without prior written permission of the publisher, including, but not limited to, any network or other electronic storage or transmission, or broadcast for distance learning.

This McGraw-Hill Custom text may include materials submitted to McGraw-Hill for publication by the instructor of this course. The instructor is solely responsible for the editorial content of such materials.

**ISBN:** 9781121953024

# Management Accounting 3
## SECOND EDITION

# Contents

- Management Accounting and the Business Environment   1

- Segment Reporting and Decentralization   21

- Pricing and Intra-Company Transfers   69

- Value-Based Management and Strategic Management Accounting   115

- Performance Management, Management Control and Corporate Governance   159

- Business Process Management: Towards the Lean Operation   193

- Strategic Perspectives on Cost Management   243

- Managing in the Global Environment   279

- Managing Organizational Structure and Culture   309

# Credits

- Management accounting and the business environment: *Chapter 1 from Management Accounting, Fourth Edition by Seal, Garrison, Noreen, 2011* 1

- Segment reporting and decentralization: *Chapter 14 from Management Accounting, Fourth Edition by Seal, Garrison, Noreen, 2011* 21

- Pricing and intra-company transfers: *Chapter 15 from Management Accounting, Fourth Edition by Seal, Garrison, Noreen, 2011* 69

- Value-based management and strategic management accounting: *Chapter 16 from Management Accounting, Fourth Edition by Seal, Garrison, Noreen, 2011* 115

- Performance management, management control and corporate governance: *Chapter 17 from Management Accounting, Fourth Edition by Seal, Garrison, Noreen, 2011* 159

- Business process management: towards the lean operation: *Chapter 18 from Management Accounting, Fourth Edition by Seal, Garrison, Noreen, 2011* 193

- Strategic perspectives on cost management: *Chapter 19 from Management Accounting, Fourth Edition by Seal, Garrison, Noreen, 2011* 243

- Managing in the Global Environment: *Chapter 6 from Contemporary Management, Seventh Global Edition by Jones, George, 2011* 279

- Managing Organizational Structure and Culture: *Chapter 10 from Contemporary Management, Seventh Global Edition by Jones, George, 2011* 309

# Management Accounting and the Business Environment

# CHAPTER 1

# Management accounting and the business environment

## LEARNING OBJECTIVES

After studying Chapter 1, you should be able to:

1. Describe what managers do and why they need accounting information
2. Identify the major differences and similarities between financial and management accounting
3. Describe the role of a management accountant in a decentralized organization
4. Discuss the impact of international competition on businesses and on management accounting
5. Review the impact of organizational and technological change on management accounting
6. Identify emerging issues: increasing importance of services, managing for value, the sustainability agenda and corporate governance

## CONCEPTS IN CONTEXT

One of the key changes affecting the finance function (as well as other support services such as human resources) is the increased use of shared service centres. These centres offer lower costs, clearer focus, better information (IT), new location, new people, scaleability, standardization, and so on. There is a fresh challenge for management accountants to become key players in these changes, as managers of the shared services, or as *business partners* acting as intermediaries between the service centres and their business customers. But in order to achieve these roles, management accountants need to adopt an outward-looking, *value-creating* position at the heart of organizational information flows and supply chain relationship with divisions. This new responsibility contrasts with the traditional transaction processing, back office, tasks that accountants might have been used to.

© Jacob Wackerhausen

*Source*: www.shared-services-research.com; Adecco Group 2010, The big shift: value through partnering, CIMA, London

**Management accounting** is concerned with providing information to managers – that is, people inside an organization who direct and control its operations. In contrast, **financial accounting** is concerned with providing information to shareholders, creditors and others who are outside an organization. Management accounting provides the essential data with which organizations are actually run. Financial accounting provides the scorecard by which a company's past performance is judged.

Because it is manager oriented, any study of management accounting must be preceded by some understanding of what managers do, the information managers need, and the general business environment. As the organizations and the business environment changes then the role of management accounting changes. Accordingly, the purpose of this chapter is briefly to examine these subjects.

## The work of management and the need for management accounting information

Every organization – large and small – has managers. Someone must be responsible for making plans, organizing resources, directing personnel and controlling operations. In this chapter, we will use a particular organization – a department store, Happybuy Ltd – to illustrate the work of management. What we have to say about the management of Happybuy Ltd, however, is very general and can be applied to virtually any organization. Managers at Happybuy Ltd, like managers everywhere, carry out three major activities – **planning**, **directing and motivating** and **controlling**. Planning involves selecting a course of action and specifying how the action will be implemented. Directing and motivating involves mobilizing people to carry out plans and run routine operations. Controlling involves ensuring that the plan is actually carried out and is appropriately modified as circumstances change. Management accounting information plays a vital role in these basic management activities – but most particularly in the planning and control functions.

## Planning

The first step in planning is to identify alternatives and then to select from among the alternatives the one that does the best job of furthering the organization's objectives. The basic objective of Happybuy Ltd is to earn profits for the owners of the company by providing superior service at competitive prices in as many markets as possible. To further this objective, every year top management carefully considers a range of options, or alternatives, for expanding into new geographic markets. This year management is considering opening new stores in Shanghai, Helsinki and Milan.

When making this and other choices, management must balance the opportunities against the demands made on the company's resources. Management knows from bitter experience that opening a store in a major new market is a big step that cannot be taken lightly. It requires enormous amounts of time and energy from the company's most experienced, talented and busy professionals. When the company attempted to open stores in both Beijing and Paris in the same year, resources were stretched too thinly. The result was that neither store opened on schedule, and operations in the rest of the company suffered. Therefore, entering new markets is planned very, very carefully.

Among other data, top management looks at the sales volumes, profit margins and costs of the company's established stores in similar markets. These data, supplied by the management accountant, are combined with projected sales volume data at the proposed new locations to estimate the profits that would be generated by the new stores. In general, virtually all important alternatives considered by management in the planning process have some effect on revenues or costs, and management accounting data are essential in estimating those effects.

After considering all of the alternatives, Happybuy Ltd's top management decided to open a store in the burgeoning Shanghai market in the third quarter of the year, but to defer opening any other new stores to another year. As soon as this decision was made, detailed plans were drawn up for all parts of the company that would be involved in the Shanghai opening. For example, the Personnel Department's travel budget was increased, since it would be providing extensive on-site training to the new personnel hired in Shanghai.

As in the Personnel Department example, the plans of management are often expressed formally in **budgets**, and the term budgeting is applied generally to describe this part of the planning process. Typically, budgets are prepared annually and represent management's plans in specific, quantitative terms. In addition to a travel budget, the Personnel Department will be given goals in terms of new hires, courses taught, and detailed breakdowns of expected expenses. Similarly, the manager of each store will be given a target for sales volume, profit, expenses, pilferage losses and employee training. These data will be collected, analysed, and summarized for management use in the form of budgets prepared by management accountants.

## Directing and motivating

In addition to planning for the future, managers must oversee day-to-day activities and keep the organization functioning smoothly. This requires the ability to motivate and effectively direct people. Managers assign tasks to employees, arbitrate disputes, answer questions, solve on-the-spot problems, and make many small decisions that affect customers and employees. In effect, directing is that part of the managers' work that deals with the routine and the here and now. Management accounting data, such as daily sales reports, are often used in this type of day-to-day decision making.

## Controlling

In carrying out the **control** function, managers seek to ensure that the plan is being followed. **Feedback**, which signals whether operations are on track, is the key to effective control. In sophisticated organizations this feedback is provided by detailed reports of various types. One of these reports, which compares budgeted to actual results, is called a **performance report**. Performance reports suggest where operations are not proceeding as planned and where some parts of the organization may require additional attention. For example, before the opening of the new Shanghai store in the third quarter of the year, the store's manager will be given sales volume, profit and expense targets for the fourth quarter of the year. As the fourth quarter progresses, periodic reports will be made in which the actual sales volume, profit and expenses are compared to the targets. If the actual results fall below the targets, top management is alerted that the Shanghai store requires more attention. Experienced personnel can be flown in to help the new manager, or top management may come to the conclusion that plans will have to be revised. As we shall see in following chapters, providing this kind of feedback to managers is one of the central purposes of management accounting.

## The end results of managers' activities

As a customer enters one of the Happybuy stores, the results of management's planning, directing and motivating, and control activities will be evident in the many details that make the difference between a pleasant and an irritating shopping experience. The store will be clean, fashionably decorated and logically laid out. Checkout staff will be alert, friendly and efficient. In short, what the customer experiences does not simply happen; it is the result of the efforts of managers who must visualize and fit together the processes that are needed to get the job done.

## The planning and control cycle

The work of management can be summarized in a model such as the one shown in Exhibit 1.1. The model, which depicts the **planning and control cycle**, illustrates the smooth flow of management activities from planning through directing and motivating, controlling, and then back to planning again. All of these activities involve decision making, so it is depicted as the hub around which the other activities revolve.

## Comparison of financial and management accounting

Financial accounting reports are prepared for the use of external parties such as shareholders and creditors, whereas management accounting reports are prepared for managers inside the organization. This contrast in basic orientation results in a number of major differences between financial and management accounting, even though both financial and management accounting rely on the same underlying financial data. These differences are summarized in Exhibit 1.2.

Part 1 An introduction to management and cost accounting

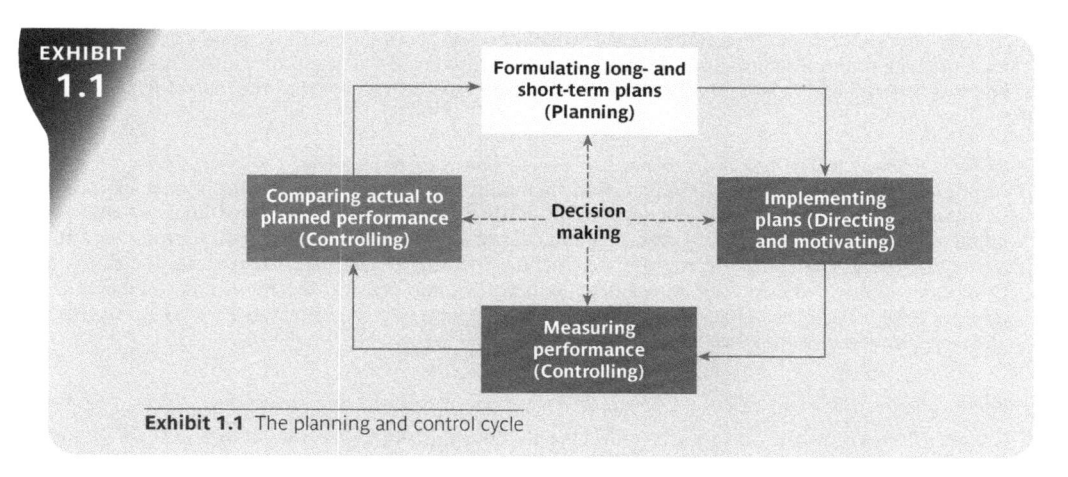

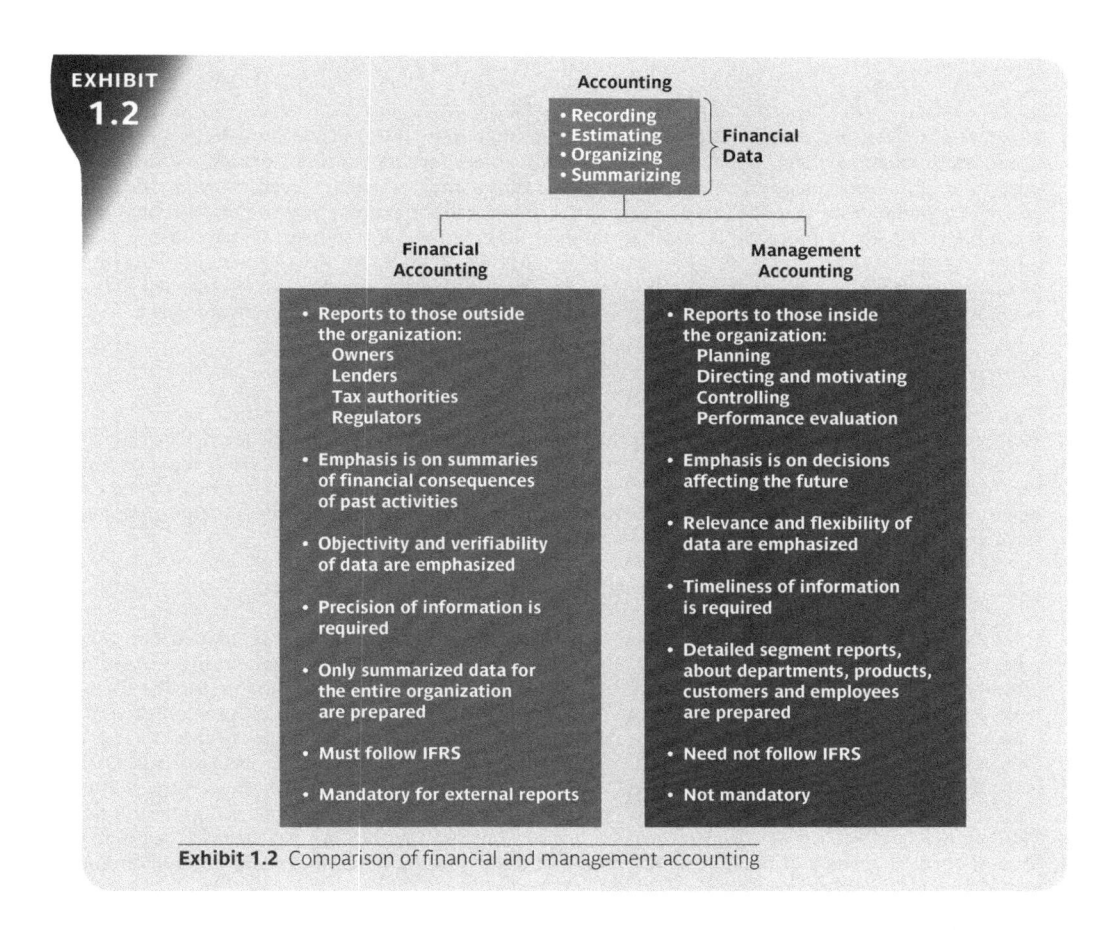

**EXHIBIT 1.1**

```
          Formulating long- and
          short-term plans
          (Planning)
         ↗              ↘
Comparing actual to              Implementing
planned performance  ← Decision →  plans (Directing
(Controlling)          making      and motivating)
         ↖              ↙
          Measuring
          performance
          (Controlling)
```

**Exhibit 1.1** The planning and control cycle

**EXHIBIT 1.2**

Accounting
- Recording
- Estimating
- Organizing
- Summarizing

Financial Data

**Financial Accounting**

- Reports to those outside the organization:
  Owners
  Lenders
  Tax authorities
  Regulators

- Emphasis is on summaries of financial consequences of past activities

- Objectivity and verifiability of data are emphasized

- Precision of information is required

- Only summarized data for the entire organization are prepared

- Must follow IFRS

- Mandatory for external reports

**Management Accounting**

- Reports to those inside the organization:
  Planning
  Directing and motivating
  Controlling
  Performance evaluation

- Emphasis is on decisions affecting the future

- Relevance and flexibility of data are emphasized

- Timeliness of information is required

- Detailed segment reports, about departments, products, customers and employees are prepared

- Need not follow IFRS

- Not mandatory

**Exhibit 1.2** Comparison of financial and management accounting

As shown in Exhibit 1.2, in addition to the difference in who the reports are prepared for, financial and management accounting also differ in their emphasis between the past and the future, in the type of data provided to users and in several other ways. These differences are discussed in the following paragraphs.

## Emphasis on the future

Since planning is such an important part of the manager's job, management accounting has a strong future orientation. In contrast, financial accounting primarily provides summaries of past financial transactions. These summaries may be useful in planning, but only to a point. The difficulty with summaries of the past is that the future is not simply a projection of what has happened in the past. Changes are constantly taking place in economic conditions, customer needs and desires, competitive conditions and so on. All of these changes demand that the manager's planning be based in large part on estimates of what will happen rather than on summaries of what has already happened.

## Relevance and flexibility of data

Financial accounting data are expected to be objective and verifiable. However, for internal uses the manager wants information that is relevant even if it is not completely objective or verifiable. By relevant, we mean appropriate for the problem at hand. For example, it is difficult to verify estimated sales volumes for a proposed new store at Happybuy Ltd, but this is exactly the type of information that is most useful to managers in their decision making. The management accounting information system should be flexible enough to provide whatever data are relevant for a particular decision.

## Less emphasis on precision

Timeliness is often more important than precision to managers. If a decision must be made, a manager would much rather have a good estimate now than wait a week for a more precise answer. A decision involving tens of millions of pounds does not have to be based on estimates that are precise down to the penny, or even to the pound. Estimates that are accurate to the nearest million pounds may be precise enough to make a good decision. Since precision is costly in terms of both time and resources, management accounting places less emphasis on precision than financial accounting. In addition, management accounting places considerable weight on non-monetary data. For example, information about customer satisfaction is of tremendous importance even though it would be difficult to express such data in a monetary form.

## Segments of an organization

Financial accounting is primarily concerned with reporting for the company as a whole. By contrast, management accounting focuses much more on the parts, or **segments**, of a company. These segments may be product lines, sales territories, divisions, departments, or any other categorization of the company's activities that management finds useful. Financial accounting does require some breakdowns of revenues and costs by major segments in external reports, but this is a secondary emphasis. In management accounting, segment reporting is the primary emphasis.

## International Financial Reporting Standards (IFRS)

Financial accounting statements prepared for external users must be prepared in accordance with generally accepted accounting principles such as the International Financial Reporting Standards proposed by the International Accounting Standards Board (IASB). External users must have some assurance that the reports have been prepared in accordance with some common set of ground rules. These common ground rules enhance comparability and help reduce fraud and misrepresentation, but they do not necessarily lead to the type of reports that would be most useful in internal decision making. Management accounting is not bound by generally accepted accounting principles. Managers set their own ground rules concerning the content and form of internal reports. The only constraint is that the expected benefits from using the information should outweigh the costs of collecting, analysing and summarizing the data. Nevertheless, as we shall see in subsequent chapters, it is undeniably true that financial reporting requirements have heavily influenced management accounting practice.

## Management accounting – not mandatory

Financial accounting is mandatory; that is, it must be done. Various outside parties such as the Stock Exchange regulators and the tax authorities require periodic financial statements. Management accounting, on the other hand, is not mandatory. A company is completely free to do as much or as little as it wishes. There are no regulatory bodies or other outside agencies that specify what is to be done, or, for that matter, whether anything is to be done at all. Since management accounting is completely optional, the important question is always, 'Is the information useful?' rather than, 'Is the information required?'

## Basic organizational structure

Since organizations are made up of people, management must accomplish its objectives by working through people. Managing directors of companies like Happybuy Ltd could not possibly execute all of their company's strategies alone; they must rely on other people. This is done by creating an organizational structure that permits **decentralization** of management responsibilities.

### Decentralization

Decentralization is the delegation of decision-making authority throughout an organization by providing managers at various operating levels with the authority to make decisions relating to their area of responsibility. Some organizations are more decentralized than others. Because of Happybuy Ltd's geographic dispersion and the peculiarities of local markets, the company is highly decentralized.

Happybuy Ltd's managing director sets the broad strategy for the company and makes major strategic decisions such as opening stores in new markets, but much of the remaining decision-making authority is delegated to managers on various levels throughout the organization. These levels are as follows: the company has a number of retail stores, each of which has a store manager as well as a separate manager for each section such as women's clothing and household appliance. In addition, the company has support departments such as a central Purchasing Department and a Personnel Department. The organizational structure of the company is depicted in Exhibit 1.3.

The arrangement of boxes shown in Exhibit 1.3 is called an **organization chart**. The purpose of an organization chart is to show how responsibility has been divided among managers and to show formal lines of reporting and communication, or chain of command. Each box depicts an area of management responsibility, and the lines between the boxes show the lines of formal authority between managers. The chart tells us, for example, that the store managers are responsible to the operations manager. In turn, the latter is responsible to the company managing director who, in turn, is responsible to the board of directors. Following the lines of authority and communication on the organization chart, we can see that the manager of the Hong Kong store would ordinarily report to the operations director rather than directly to the managing director of the company.

Informal relationships and channels of communication often develop outside the formal reporting relationships on the organization chart as a result of personal contacts between managers. The informal structure does not appear on the organization chart, but it is often vital to effective operations.

### Line and staff relationships

An organization chart also depicts **line** and **staff** positions in an organization. A person in a line position is directly involved in achieving the basic objectives of the organization. A person in a staff position, by contrast, is only indirectly involved in achieving those basic objectives. Staff positions support or provide assistance to line positions or other parts of the organization, but they do not have direct authority over line positions. Refer again to the organization chart in Exhibit 1.3. Since the basic objective of Happybuy Ltd is to sell recorded merchandise at a profit, those managers whose areas of responsibility are directly related to the sales effort occupy line positions. These positions, which are shown in green in the exhibit, include the managers of the various departments in each store, the store managers, the operations manager and members of top management.

**Exhibit 1.3** Organization chart, Happybuy Ltd

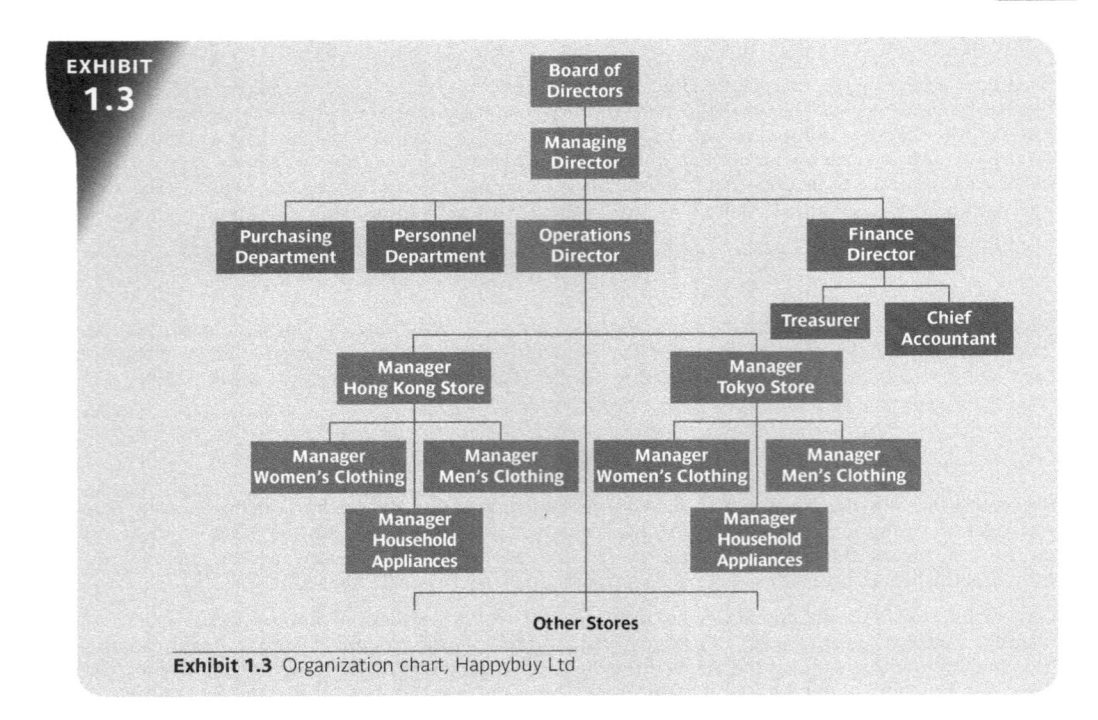

By contrast, the manager of the central Purchasing Department occupies a staff position, since the only function of the Purchasing Department is to support and serve the line departments by doing their purchasing for them. The finance function, which is responsible for the organization's management accounting, is also seen as a staff position. The finance office often combines a number of important functions including the management of the company's computer services and other business information systems.

## Expanding and changing role of management accounting

Management accounting has its roots in the industrial revolution of the 19th century. During this early period, most firms were tightly controlled by a few owner–managers who borrowed based on personal relationships and their personal assets. Since there were no external shareholders and little unsecured debt, there was little need for elaborate financial reports. In contrast, management accounting was relatively sophisticated and provided the essential information needed to manage the early large-scale production of textiles, steel and other products.[1]

After the turn of the 20th century, financial accounting requirements burgeoned because of new pressures placed on companies by capital markets, creditors, regulatory bodies and taxation of income. Johnson and Kaplan state that 'many firms needed to raise funds from increasingly widespread and detached suppliers of capital. To tap these vast reservoirs of outside capital, firms' managers had to supply audited financial reports. And because outside suppliers of capital relied on audited financial statements, independent accountants had a keen interest in establishing well-defined procedures for corporate financial reporting. The inventory costing procedures adopted by public accountants after the turn of the century had a profound effect on management accounting.'[2]

As a consequence, for many decades, management accountants increasingly focused their efforts on ensuring that financial accounting requirements were met and financial reports were released on time. The practice of management accounting stagnated. Johnson and Kaplan's book and their thesis of 'Relevance Lost' stimulated a major debate among both academics and practitioners. Johnson and Kaplan (1987) argued that in the early part of the 20th century, as product lines expanded and operations became more complex, forward-looking companies such as Du Pont, General Motors, and General Electric saw a renewed need for management oriented reports that were separate from financial reports. But, in most companies, management accounting practices up through the mid-1980s were largely indistinguishable from practices that were common prior to the First World War. In recent years, however, new economic forces have led to many important innovations in management accounting. These new practices will be discussed in detail later, and especially in Chapters 16–19. These chapters have been written to compare approaches that accept physical and organizational limitations and optimize subject to given **constraints** with more recent approaches that are based on management practices aimed at shifting constraints. These chapters reflect the way that management accounting practices have evolved since the publication of the 'Relevance Lost' thesis.

## The sources of management accounting knowledge

The practice and principles of management accounting have been developed over many decades, even centuries. In the early days the main source of practice was practitioners such as early industrialists at Josiah Wedgewood's potteries or at Alfred Sloan's General Motors. More recently other inputs have come from business schools, management consultants and even management gurus (Thrift, 2005). In the particular case of accounting other contributors to managerial knowledge production include professional bodies. Managerial and business knowledge may be visualized as being produced via a circulation of ideas and practices.

Yet the processes that impact on the production and circulation of managerial knowledge should not be seen as infallible. Academic theories may be rejected by practitioners on the grounds of 'irrelevance' and practices may develop that weaken rather than enhance long-run business performance (Johnson and Kaplan, 1987). The latest practices may not really be 'best practice' but rather introduced because of managerial fashions and fads (Seal, 2010). One of the aims of this book is to enable the reader to develop a *critical* understanding of the principles behind management accounting so that faulty practices may be recognized even if they cannot always be changed in a particular organizational setting.

## International diversity in management accounting traditions

Management accounting is sometimes presented as a universal tool kit. Yet this image of the subject hides the different traditions in different countries. For example, although we might expect to find basic economic calculations on costs and revenues to be of interest to managers in any system of competitive capitalism, these calculations may be the province of different professional groupings (such as engineers or business economists) in different countries. Although the professional organization of auditors is very widespread throughout the world, the professional organization of management accounting is far less prevalent. The variation in professional organization does not mean that management accounting techniques cannot be applied in different countries but rather that the occupations that control them differ in different countries for all sorts of complex historical[3] and institutional reasons.[4] Indeed, many European countries have problems with the term 'management accounting' because the professions are organized differently and have different rankings in terms of status and technical expertise.[5]

Different traditions mean that historical debates such as the 'Relevance Lost thesis' may have resonance in the US or the UK but not necessarily in Germany or Japan. Indeed, many critics of US (and, by extension, UK) management accounting techniques were partly informed by a historical analysis of the US experience and partly by a perceived competitive weakness compared to the economic successes of Japan in the 1970s and 80s. There is some evidence that management accounting practices are tending to converge under some of the influences such as globalization and new technology, which will be discussed below.[6]

## Globalization and international competition

Over the last few decades, competition has become worldwide in many industries. This has been caused by reductions in tariffs, quotas and other barriers to free trade; improvements in global transportation systems; and increasing sophistication in international markets. These factors work together to reduce the costs of conducting international trade and make it possible for foreign companies to compete on a more

> **FOCUS ON PRACTICE**
>
> *Servitization in manufacturing*
>
> How can manufacturing based in developed countries compete with manufacturing in developing countries such as China which have much lower wage costs and less onerous environmental and social obligations? One response to this global competition has been what is known as *servitization*. Servitization blurs the traditional distinction between manufacturing and services. Companies such as the aero engine manufacturer Rolls Royce 'no longer sells aero engines, it offers a total care package, where customers buy the capability the engines deliver – "power by the hour" with Rolls Royce retaining 'responsibility for risk, maintenance, etc.' With servitization, firms offer services and solutions, associated with their manufactured products in what may be seen as a ProductService System.
>
> **Exercise:** Apply the servitization concept to a company such as IBM in the information technology industry. How has it changed the focus of its business?
>
> *Source:* Neely, A. 2007. Servitization, *Manufacturing Matters*, Winter; http://www.cranfield.ac.uk/sas/pdf/servitization.pdf

equal footing with local firms. As well as continuing expansion of the European Union (EU), competition from rapidly growing countries such as China and India have led to global economic restructuring with new locations for the outsourcing of manufacturing (China) and services (India) by Western and Japanese multinational companies.

Reductions in trade barriers have made it easier for agile and aggressive companies to expand outside of their home markets. As a result, very few firms can afford to be complacent. A company may be very successful today in its local market relative to its local competitors, but tomorrow the competition may come from halfway around the globe. As a matter of survival, even firms that are presently doing very well in their home markets must become world-class competitors. On the bright side, the freer international movement of goods and services presents tremendous export opportunities for those companies that can transform themselves into world-class competitors. And, from the standpoint of consumers, heightened competition promises an even greater variety of goods, at higher quality and lower prices.

What are the implications for management accounting of increased global competition? It would be very difficult for a firm to become world-class if it plans, directs and controls its operations and makes decisions using a second-class management accounting system. An excellent management accounting system will not by itself guarantee success, but a poor management accounting system can stymie the best efforts of people in an organization to make the firm truly competitive.

Throughout this text we will highlight the differences between obsolete management accounting systems that get in the way of success and well-designed management accounting systems that can enhance a firm's performance. It is noteworthy that elements of well-designed management accounting systems have originated in many countries. More and more, management accounting has become a discipline that is worldwide in scope.[7]

## Changes in the business environment and management accounting

### New business processes and technologies

**LEARNING OBJECTIVE 5**

Global competition has been good news for consumers, since intensified competition has generally led to lower prices, higher quality and more choices. However, the last three decades have been a period of wrenching change for many businesses and their employees. Many managers have learned that cherished ways of doing business do not work any more and that major changes must be made in how organizations are managed and in how work gets done. These changes are so great that some observers view them as a second industrial revolution.

This revolution is having a profound effect on the practice of management accounting – as we will see throughout the rest of the text. First, however, it is necessary to have an appreciation of the ways in which organizations are transforming themselves to become more competitive. Since the early 1980s, many companies have gone through several waves of improvement programmes, starting with **just-in-time (JIT)** and passing on to **total quality management (TQM)**, process re-engineering, and various other management programmes often summarized by the term *lean production*. When properly implemented, these improvement programmes can enhance quality, reduce cost, increase output, eliminate delays in responding to customers and ultimately increase profits. They have not, however, always been wisely implemented, and there is considerable controversy concerning the ultimate value of each of these programmes. Nevertheless, the current business environment cannot be properly understood without an appreciation of what each of these approaches attempts to accomplish.

These management approaches have implications for management accounting. In particular, they open up the possibility of managing areas like quality, stock and constraints rather than optimizing a given situation. For example, the traditional optimizing approach for stock management, the economic order quantity (EOQ), has to be placed alongside approaches such as JIT that try to eliminate stock. Later in the book, we contrast a number of optimizing models with more contemporary, active management approaches.

Another significant change that we analyse in later chapters is the influence of new technology, especially in computers and telecommunications. These technologies have not just resulted in the automation of existing manual management accounting systems but have enabled the restructuring of whole industries and economies. Even if some of the hype surrounding the internet has died down a little since the heady days of the late 1990s, the internet has, and is, changing the way business is done. New forms of competition, organization and technologies have implications for management accounting. Some of the more traditional merits of management accounting (such as the idea that businesses plan to make profits!) may have reasserted themselves after the collapse of the 'dotcom' bubble, but the longer lasting changes in **business process** require a response from management accounting if the subject is to remain relevant.

One sector that has changed dramatically in recent years is the airline business, particularly with the success in both Europe and North America of the 'no-frills' airlines such as easyJet, Ryanair and Southwest Airlines. The low-cost airline illustrates many of the features of the combined impact of new organizational forms, business processes, new technology and new personnel approaches.

The low-cost airline example illustrates a combination of new thinking about air travel combined with well-known principles of standardization. The use of new technologies such as databases is combined with older technologies such as the telephone – the essence is the integration of a number of previously separated activities such as booking, ticketing and payment processing.

## Enterprise resource planning systems

Some technological changes have not just affected the environment of management accounting but have had a direct impact on the collection and dissemination of management information.[8] The increasing use of sophisticated real time information systems known as **enterprise resource planning (ERP)** provided by companies such as SAP, Oracle, J.D. Edwards and Baan, has changed the nature of management accounting work and the role of the finance function.[9] One of the emerging implications for the management accountant is that there is more emphasis on business support rather than routine information gathering. Furthermore, not only is there a greater dispersion of finance personnel into process areas, but accounting information itself has become more dispersed throughout the organization as it becomes more accessible to non-accounting personnel. We will explore the impact of ERP in more detail in Chapter 18.

## Deregulation, privatization and re-regulation

It is also worth noting that the increased competition in the airline industry was not possible until the deregulation effects of 'open skies' policies. Deregulation and privatization of former state-owned monopolies had a significant impact in Europe especially in the UK, which pioneered these policies. The changes in ownership and increased competition has not only affected the huge public utilities that were privatized, they also had a knock-on effect on the companies that supplied these giants.

After financial scandals at Enron around the turn of the millennium and the more recent collapse of banking (popularly known as the *credit crunch*), the trend has been towards tighter, rather than lighter, regulation in **corporate governance**. Any companies listed in North America are subject to the Sarbanes–Oxley Act (2002), while UK companies are expected to comply with the Combined Code (2006) on corporate governance. Although it is too early to know the details, the recent problems faced by Western banks, especially in the US and the UK may lead to new banking regulations in the UK as well. Although many of these issues are seen as financial reporting and auditing issues, there is an emerging awareness that corporate governance also involves the aspects of strategic control systems covered in Chapters 16 and 17.[10]

## The increased importance of service sector management

Management accounting has expanded its influence from its traditional base in manufacturing to service sectors, which themselves have become increasing sources of employment and income in many economies. Many traditional management accounting approaches to issues such as costing were developed with manufacturing industry in mind. In comparison with traditional manufacturing, where the product is easy to see and touch, products in service industries are less tangible. A bank may offer a number of different 'products' such as types of account or loans which are defined by dimensions such as accessibility or repayment terms, secured or unsecured and so on. Services cannot be stored in inventory so that managers in banks and other service industries may be less interested in *product* cost but, rather, which *customers* are profitable and which customers are not. Service industries provide new challenges and opportunities for management accounting information, particularly as competitive success is especially dependent on intangible assets such as employee expertise and customer relations.

Not only are service activities becoming more important relative to manufacturing but they are increasingly subject to reorganization in both public and private sectors.[11] In particular, we have seen the emergence of **shared service centres** where the support services of an entire corporation are concentrated in a single geographical location. Other companies have gone a stage further by subcontracting them to independent companies in a practice known as **outsourcing**.[12]

Management accounting's spread into the public sector is driven by government demands for new measures of performance and new delivery systems. Although its precise form and motivation varies in different countries, this phenomenon, often referred to as the 'New Public Management',[13] may be seen as a global movement.[14] These developments are not without controversy, especially where there is an attempt to apply, in the not-for-profit, public sector organizations, the same management philosophies and techniques that were originally developed for private, profit-making organizations.

## Managing for value

Traditionally, accountants were portrayed as 'bean-counters' or 'corporate policemen' with an emphasis on past performance and organizational control. While these functions are still part of an accountant's role, the trend recently has been to emphasize the creation and management of value. Pressures from corporate raiders and new sources of capital, such as private equity, mean that managers have to be increasingly aware of shareholder value. As will be explored in Chapters 14, 16 and 17, there are challenges both to *measure* shareholder value and to discover how to *create* it through the adoption and implementation of corporate strategies. Managers are also aware of the importance of *customer value* and its relationship to shareholder value. Managing for value has to balance the possible gains to short-run profitability arising from cost-cutting exercises to possible long-run damage to shareholder value as costs may be cut at the expense of customer satisfaction. For the management accountant the challenge is not just to devise appropriate financial and non-financial metrics to measure value but to try and understand cause-and-effect relationships.[15]

> ## FOCUS ON PRACTICE
> ### The sustainability of the sustainability agenda
> Was sustainability just a fad, a product of an illusory sense of well-being created in the 'bubble economies' of the affluent West? Will the down turn in those economies after the collapse of Lehman Brothers mean that cost cutting and short-term measures will lead to a neglect of sustainability issues? Not according to a recent survey conducted with leading world business leaders. In the survey, 92 per cent of respondents maintained that their company was addressing sustainability even after the down turn. Although the survey reported that 70 per cent of companies had not developed a 'clear business case for sustainability'…. Once companies begin to act aggressively, they tend to unearth more opportunity, not less, than they expected to find, including tangible bottom-line impacts and new sources of competitive advantage'. In short, being green makes good business sense particularly in terms of consumer opinion of the company's brand.
>
> **Exercise:** Consider the huge negative business impact on company share values associated with environmental disasters such as recent oil spills in the Gulf of Mexico.
>
> *Source:* Berns, M., Townend, A., Khayat, Z., Balagopal, B., Reeves, M., Hopkins, M. and Kruschwitz, N. 2009. The business of sustainability, *MITSloan Management Review Special Report*, Massachusetts Institute of Technology

## Managing for environmental sustainability

Whilst concern about the environment has been around for some decades, the threat of rapid human-induced climate change has raised the profile of a whole range of environmental sustainability issues. A recent survey of accountants in business[16] found that 79% of large companies and 56% of smaller- and medium-sized companies had a formal sustainability strategy. Even managers who focus on shareholder value may be concerned about the environment for three main reasons. First, there is a compliance motive – companies may find that they are forced through regulation and green taxes to manage environmental resources more carefully. Second, eco-efficiency not only may save the planet but reduce the business costs. Finally, there may be strategic reasons – companies may have customers who demand green business policies and who are increasingly suspicious of 'environmental window dressing' through environmental reporting. **Environmental management accounting** is not about reporting. It involves the collection and analysis of *physical* information on flows of energy, water and other materials as well as *monetary* information on environmental costs and benefits in order to make environmentally sensitive decisions.[17]

## Corporate governance, professional and business ethics

A thorough analysis of what makes a profession goes beyond the scope of this book. Technical competence is one part of being professional. Another important aspect is the adherence to a code of ethics. For example, the Chartered Institute of Management Accountants, which is the largest body specifically for management accountants in the UK, have themselves pointed out that being a professional means having responsibilities beyond the narrow pursuit of profit at any cost. In common with other accountancy bodies, they have a code of practice and mechanisms for monitoring and enforcing professional ethics.

If ethical standards were not generally adhered to, there would be undesirable consequences for everyone. Essentially, abandoning ethical standards would lead to a lower standard of living with lower-quality goods and services, less to choose from, and higher prices. In short, following ethical rules is not just a matter of being 'nice'; it is absolutely essential for the smooth functioning of an advanced market economy. For example, one of the short-term consequences of the Enron scandal[18] is that investors have become suspicious about the reliability of reported accounting numbers. Other problems have arisen in other parts of the financial services industry in the UK, where managers offered unsustainable guaranteed returns or incentivized the sales personnel so that they gave faulty investment or pensions advice. Even more dramatically, we have seen how the bonus culture in Western banks encouraged the creation of huge speculative bubbles in property. The consequences of the collapse of these bubbles are still being felt with depressed output, lost jobs and huge public sector deficits. The common theme in so many of these scandals and collapses is that the single-minded emphasis placed on short-term profits in some companies may make it seem as if the only way to get ahead is to act unethically. When top managers say, in effect, that they will only be satisfied with bottom-line results and will accept no excuses, they are asking for trouble. Recent high-profile scandals show that accountants are often placed in difficult ethical positions. Other issues such as transfer pricing practice in multinational companies (which we look at in Chapter 15) and the 'laundering' of illegally obtained money provide particularly pressing challenges to the integrity of all finance professionals.

Although we argued earlier in this chapter that management accounting is mainly concerned with internal reporting, management accountants cannot totally avoid taking responsibility for the integrity of the basic financial data that forms the basis of both financial and management reports (see Exhibit 1.2). Indeed, as we shall learn in the next three chapters, the classification and computation of cost can have a significant impact on reported profit. In Chapter 17 we will look in more detail at the relationships between corporate strategy, risk management and corporate governance.

## Some implications for the roles of management accountants: a first look

The changes in the business environment discussed above have potentially left management accountants with a multitude of roles. The roles may depend on the size of the organization, its line of business and a whole range of issues discussed above and in subsequent chapters. But the role played by the management accountant may also depend on their location in the large corporation. For example, in Exhibit 1.4, we can see that in head office, issues of corporate governance and strategy may be a major concern. In the so-called back office area, the focus will be on more operational matters associated with business processes, organizational structure and information technology. In the front office, the management accountant may be operating outside the designated finance function in multi-functional teams with more direct contact with customers, suppliers and helping to manage frontline processes. In order to fulfil these multiple roles, management accountants need to master a diversity of techniques, concepts and practices which will be elaborated on in the following chapters.[19]

### FOCUS ON PRACTICE

#### New IT and business analysis

Rachel has trained as a management accountant and is now director of divisional finance in a large restaurant and public house chain. The company has an advanced accounting system in which transactions recording and reporting has been automated. Freed up from routine data gathering, Rachel liaises between the regional operational managers and the company's board as she and her team of analysts monitors and manages the financial performance of the many restaurant and pub brands that make up the business.

**Exercise:** Note how advances in IT have automated the 'score-keeping' aspects of accounting and enabled managers not only to have more up to the minute business intelligence but also freeing up their time for value creation.

**Part 1** An introduction to management and cost accounting

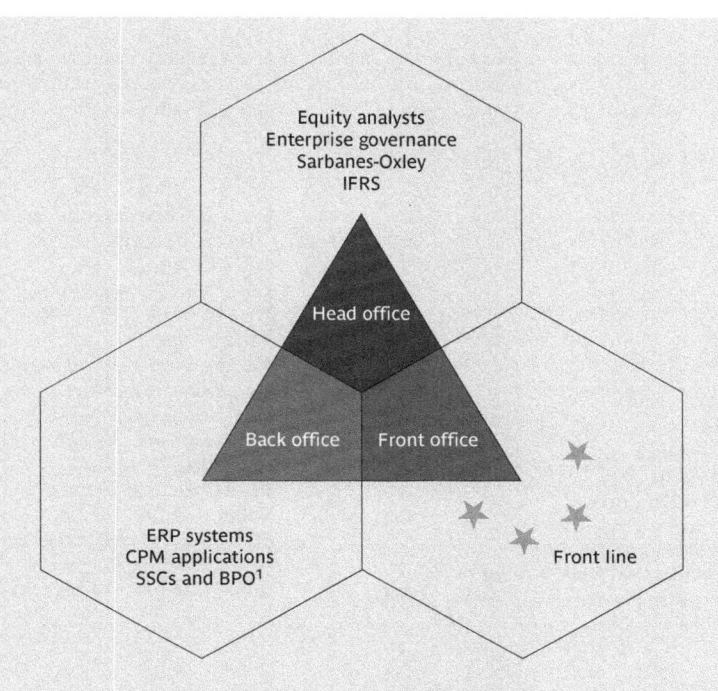

**EXHIBIT 1.4**

Equity analysts
Enterprise governance
Sarbanes-Oxley
IFRS

Head office

Back office    Front office

ERP systems
CPM applications
SSCs and BPO[1]

Front line

[1]Enterprise resource planning (ERP), corporate performance management (CPM), shared service centres (SSCs) and business process outsourcing (BPO).

**Exhibit 1.4** The diverse roles of management accountants within large corporations (reproduced with permission from *Improving decision making in organizations* (2007) CIMA technical report, p.5)

## Summary

- Management accounting assists managers in carrying out their responsibilities, which include planning, directing and motivating, and controlling.
- Since management accounting is geared to the needs of the manager rather than to the needs of outsiders, it differs substantially from financial accounting. Management accounting is oriented more towards the future, places less emphasis on precision, emphasizes segments of an organization (rather than the organization as a whole), is not governed by generally accepted accounting principles, and is not mandatory.
- Most organizations are decentralized to some degree. The organization chart depicts who works for whom in the organization and which units perform staff functions rather than line functions. Accountants perform a staff function – they support and provide assistance to others inside the organization.
- The business environment in recent years has been characterized by increasing competition and a relentless drive for continuous improvement. Several approaches have been developed to assist organizations in meeting these challenges, including just-in-time (JIT), total quality management (TQM), and the theory of constraints (TOC). Organizations have also restructured with outsourcing and relocation of company activities. Reformed public sectors are increasingly applying management accounting techniques.

- Ethical standards serve a very important practical function in an advanced market economy. Without widespread adherence to ethical standards, the economy would slow down dramatically. Ethics are the lubrication that keep a market economy functioning smoothly.

## Key terms for review

At the end of each chapter, a list of key terms for review is given. These terms are highlighted in colour. Full definitions can be found in the glossary at the end of the book. Carefully study each term to be sure you understand its meaning, since these terms are used repeatedly in the chapters that follow. The list for Chapter 1 follows:

**Budgets** (p. 4)
**Business process** (p. 12)
**Constraints** (p. 10)
**Control** (p. 5)
**Controlling** (p. 4)
**Corporate governance** (p. 13)
**Decentralization** (p. 8)
**Directing and motivating** (p. 4)
**Enterprise resource planning (ERP)** (p. 12)
**Environmental management accounting** (p. 14)
**Feedback** (p. 5)
**Financial accounting** (p. 4)
**Just-in-time (JIT)** (p. 12)
**Line** (p. 8)
**Management accounting** (p. 4)
**Organization chart** (p. 8)
**Outsourcing** (p. 13)
**Performance report** (p. 5)
**Planning** (p. 4)
**Planning and control cycle** (p. 5)
**Segments** (p. 7)
**Shared service centres** (p. 13)
**Staff** (p. 8)
**Total quality management (TQM)** (p. 12)

**Level of difficulty:** BASIC  INTERMEDIATE  ADVANCED

## Questions

**1-1** What is the basic difference in orientation between financial and management accounting?

**1-2** What are the three major activities of a manager?

**1-3** Describe the four steps in the planning and control cycle.

**1-4** What function does feedback play in the work of the manager?

**1-5** Distinguish between line and staff positions in an organization.

**1-6** What are the major differences between financial and management accounting?

**1-7** Briefly describe the impact of new technology, globalization and deregulation on the practice of management accounting.

**1-8** Suggest three ways in which management accounting in services may differ from its practice in manufacturing industry.

**1-9** Suggest three reasons why value seeking companies should care about the environment.

**1-10** Why is adherence to ethical standards important for the smooth functioning of an advanced market economy?

**Part 1** An introduction to management and cost accounting

## Exercises

**E1–1** Time allowed: 10 minutes

Listed below are a number of terms that relate to organizations, the work of management and the role of management accounting:

| | | |
|---|---|---|
| Budgets | Chief Accountant | Decentralization |
| Directing and motivating | Feedback | Financial accounting |
| Line | Management accounting | Non-monetary data |
| Performance report | Planning | Precision |
| Staff | | |

Choose the term or terms above that most appropriately complete the following statements:

1. A position on the organization chart that is directly related to achieving the basic objectives of an organization is called a _____ position.
2. When _____, managers oversee day-to-day activities and keep the organization functioning smoothly.
3. The plans of management are expressed formally in _____.
4. _____ consists of identifying alternatives, selecting from among the alternatives the one that is best for the organization, and specifying what actions will be taken to implement the chosen alternative.
5. A _____ position provides service or assistance to other parts of the organization and does not directly achieve the basic objectives of the organization.
6. The delegation of decision-making authority throughout an organization by allowing managers at various operating levels to make key decisions relating to their area of responsibility is called _____.
7. Management accounting places less emphasis on _____ and more emphasis on _____ than financial accounting.
8. _____ is concerned with providing information for the use of those who are inside the organization, whereas _____ is concerned with providing information for the use of those who are outside the organization.
9. The accounting and other reports coming to management that are used in controlling the organization are called _____.
10. The manager in charge of the accounting department is generally known as the _____.
11. A detailed report to management comparing budgeted data against actual data for a specific time period is called a _____.

## Problems

**P1–2** Preparing an organization chart
Time allowed: 30 minutes

Upton University is a large private university located in the Midlands. The university is headed by a vice-chancellor who has five pro-vice chancellors reporting to him. These pro-vice chancellors are responsible for, respectively, auxiliary services, admissions and records, academics, financial services (controller), and physical plant.

In addition, the university has managers over several areas who report to these pro-vice chancellors. These include managers over central purchasing, the university press, and the university bookstore, all of whom report to the pro-vice chancellor for auxiliary services; managers over computer services and over accounting and finance, who report to the pro-vice chancellor for financial services; and managers over grounds and custodial services and over plant and maintenance, who report to the pro-vice chancellor for physical plant.

The university has four colleges – business, humanities, fine arts, and engineering and quantitative methods – and a law school. Each of these units has a dean who is responsible to the academic pro-vice chancellor. Each college has several departments.

### Required

1. Prepare an organization chart for Upton University.
2. Which of the positions on your chart would be line positions? Why would they be line positions? Which would be staff positions? Why?
3. Which of the positions on your chart would have need for accounting information? Explain.

#### P1–3 Ethics and the manager

Richmond plc operates a chain of department stores. The first store began operations in 1965, and the company has steadily grown to its present size of 44 stores. Two years ago, the board of directors of Richmond approved a large-scale remodelling of its stores to attract a more upmarket clientele. Before finalizing these plans, two stores were remodelled as a test. Linda Potter, assistant controller, was asked to oversee the financial reporting for these test stores, and she and other management personnel were offered bonuses based on the sales growth and profitability of these stores. While completing the financial reports, Potter discovered a sizeable stock of outdated goods that should have been discounted for sale or returned to the manufacturer. She discussed the situation with her management colleagues; the consensus was to ignore reporting this stock as obsolete, since reporting it would diminish the financial results and their bonuses.

### Required

1. Would it be ethical for Potter *not* to report the stock as obsolete?
2. Would it be easy for Potter to take the ethical action in this situation?

#### P1–4 Ethics

Suppose all garages routinely followed the practice of attempting to sell customers unnecessary parts and services by recommending unnecessary or expensive repairs.

### Required

1. How would this unethical behaviour affect customers?
2. How might customers attempt to protect themselves against this unethical behaviour?
3. How would this unethical behaviour probably affect profits and employment in the garage industry?

## Group exercise

#### GE1–5 GE1–5 Ethics on the job

Ethical standards are very important in business, but they are not always followed. If you have ever held a job – even a summer job – describe the ethical climate in the organization where you worked. Did employees work a full day or did they arrive late and leave early? Did employees honestly report the hours they worked? Did employees use their employer's resources for their own purposes? Did managers set a good example? Did the organization have a code of ethics and were employees made aware of its existence? If the ethical climate in the organization you worked for was poor, what problems, if any, did it create?

## Cases

#### C1–6 Deregulation, new technology and the reorganization of the finance function
Time allowed: 40 minutes

Megacorp plc is a large international utilities company. The company's business environment has changed rapidly in recent years as a result of the various phases of privatization, deregulation, and the resultant industry restructuring. During the past two years, a shared service centre (SSC) has been established in South Yorkshire, consolidating processes that were formerly dealt with in individual business units (such as power generating stations) in many separate locations. The manager in charge of the finance function explained some of the issues as follows:

> 'We actually run ourselves on process lines – "Purchase-to-Pay" or "Procurement-to-Pay", and "Order-to-Cash". The Sales Ledger is consolidated nationally but the rest is all done locally – we run software systems that these days allow you to have both remote sites and central operations and there is still visibility and transparency across the organization. The same applies to the nominal ledger and other accounting. We do all the statutory accounts centrally now and the main database, the main nominal ledger, is based on a server in this building. But, of course, the data can be accessed anywhere. The accounts are still "owned" by the local Finance Director, Finance Controller and finance teams out in each one of the local business units. The finance people in the local business units need to "own" the statutory accounts even though they don't prepare them these days. If they don't "own" the accounts, then they are signing something without understanding what's there.'

## Required

Discuss how the organization and culture of the finance function in Megacorp has been affected by new information technology, the deregulation of power generation and the more recent post-Enron concerns with financial probity.

You might find it helpful to refer to CIMA (2001b) and May (2002).

## Internet exercise

**IE1-7**

Access the website of the *Association for Accountancy and Business Affairs* (http://visar.csustan.edu/aaba/home.htm), click on one of the issues and follow the links to newspaper cuttings and other sources.

## Endnotes

1. Chandler (1977).
2. Johnson and Kaplan (1987), pp. 129–30.
3. Again see Johnson and Kaplan (1987). See also Loft (1995); Ezzamel, Hoskin and Macve (1990).
4. See, for example, Armstrong (1985) and Armstrong (1987).
5. Bhimani (1996).
6. Granlund and Lukka (1998b).
7. See Granlund and Lukka (1998b).
8. See Scapens, Ezzamel, Burns and Baldvinsdottir (2003).
9. See May (2002).
10. See e.g. Seal (2006).
11. See, for example, Bain and Taylor (2000).
12. Hayward (2002); CIMA (2001a).
13. Hood (1995).
14. Olson, Guthrie and Humphrey (1998).
15. For a historical view on value based management see Ittner and Larker (2001). For a very recent attempt to analyse the cost of customer satisfaction see Cugini, Caru and Zerbini (2007).
16. CIMA (2010).
17. See IFAC (2005).
18. See, for example, Gordon (2002).
19. See Burns and Baldvinsdottir (2007).

When you have read this chapter, log on to the Online Learning Centre for *Management Accounting* at www.mcgraw-hill.co.uk/textbooks/seal, where you'll find multiple choice questions, practice exams and extra study tools for each chapter.

# Segment Reporting and Decentralization

# CHAPTER 14

# Segment reporting and decentralization

## LEARNING OBJECTIVES

After studying Chapter 14, you should be able to:

1. Differentiate between performance measurement in cost centres, profit centres and investment centres
2. Prepare a segmented profit and loss account using the contribution format
3. Identify three business practices that hinder proper cost assignment
4. Compute the return on investment (ROI)
5. Show how changes in sales, expenses and assets affect an organization's ROI
6. Compute residual income and understand its strengths and weaknesses
7. Compute economic value added (EVA) and other value management metrics

## CONCEPTS IN CONTEXT

Quaker Oats provides an example of how use of a specific performance measure can change the way a company operates. Prior to adopting EVA, 'its businesses had one overriding goal – increasing quarterly earnings. To do it, they guzzled capital. They offered sharp price discounts at the end of each quarter, so plants ran overtime turning out huge shipments of Gatorade, Rice-A-Roni, 100 per cent Natural Cereal, and other products. Managers led the late rush, since their bonuses depended on raising operating profits each quarter... Pumping up sales requires many warehouses (capital) to hold vast temporary inventories (more capital). But who cared? Quaker's operating businesses paid no charge for capital in internal accounting, so they barely noticed. It took EVA to spotlight the problem.... One plant has trimmed inventories from $15 million to $9 million, even though it is producing much more, and Quaker has closed five of 15 warehouses, saving $6 million a year in salaries and capital costs.'[1]

© Andriy Petrenko

Once an organization grows beyond a few people, it becomes impossible for the top manager to make decisions about everything. For example, the managing director of the Novotel Hotel chain cannot be expected to decide whether a particular hotel guest at the Novotel in Sheffield should be allowed to check out later than the normal checkout time. To some degree, managers have to delegate decisions to those who are at lower levels in the organization. However, the degree to which decisions are delegated varies from organization to organization.

## Decentralization in organizations

A **decentralized organization** is one in which decision making is not confined to a few top executives but rather is spread throughout the organization, with managers at various levels making *key operating decisions* relating to their sphere of responsibility. Decentralization is a matter of degree, since all organizations are decentralized to some extent out of necessity. At one extreme, a strongly decentralized organization is one in which there are few, if any, constraints on the freedom of even the lowest-level managers and employees to make decisions. At the other extreme, in a strongly centralized organization, lower-level managers have little freedom to make a decision. Although most organizations fall somewhere between these two extremes, there is a pronounced trend toward more and more decentralization.

### Advantages and disadvantages of decentralization

Decentralization has many benefits, including:

1. Top management is relieved of much day-to-day problem solving and is left free to concentrate on strategy, on higher-level decision making, and on co-ordinating activities.
2. Decentralization provides lower-level managers with vital experience in making decisions. Without such experience, they would be ill-prepared to make decisions when they are promoted.
3. Added responsibility and decision-making authority often result in increased job satisfaction. It makes the job more interesting and provides greater incentives for people to put out their best efforts.
4. Lower-level managers generally have more detailed and up-to-date information about conditions in their own area of responsibility than top managers. Therefore, the decisions of lower-level managers are often based on better information.
5. It is difficult to evaluate a manager's performance if the manager is not given much latitude in what he or she can do.

Decentralization has four major disadvantages:

1. Lower-level managers may make decisions without fully understanding the 'big picture'. While top-level managers typically have less detailed information about operations than the lower-level managers, they usually have more information about the company as a whole and may have a better understanding of the company's strategy. This situation can be avoided to some extent with the use of modern management information systems that can, in principle, give every manager at every level the same information that goes to the managing director and other top-level managers.
2. In a truly decentralized organization, there may be a lack of co-ordination among autonomous managers. This problem can be reduced by clearly defining the company's strategy and communicating it effectively throughout the organization.
3. Lower-level managers may have objectives that are different from the objectives of the entire organization. For example, some managers may be more interested in increasing the sizes of their departments than in increasing the profits of the company.[2] To some degree, this problem can be overcome by designing performance evaluation systems that motivate managers to make decisions that are in the best interests of the company.
4. In a strongly decentralized organization, it may be more difficult effectively to spread innovative ideas. Someone in one part of the organization may have a terrific idea that would benefit other parts of the organization, but without strong central direction the idea may not be shared with and adopted by other parts of the organization.

## Decentralization and segment reporting

Effective decentralization requires *segmental reporting*. In addition to the companywide profit and loss account, reports are needed for individual segments of the organization. A **segment** is a part or activity of an organization about which managers would like cost, revenue or profit data. Examples of segments include divisions of a company, sales territories, individual stores, service centres, manufacturing plants, marketing departments, individual customers and product lines. As we shall see, a company's operations can be segmented in many ways. For example, a supermarket chain like Tesco or Sainsbury can segment their businesses by geographic region, by individual store, by the nature of the merchandise (i.e., green groceries, canned goods, paper goods), by brand name, and so on. In this chapter, we learn how to construct profit and loss accounts for such business segments. These segmented profit and loss accounts are useful in analysing the profitability of segments and in measuring the performance of segment managers.

### Cost, profit and investment centres

Decentralized companies typically categorize their business segments into cost centres, profit centres and investment centres – depending on the responsibilities of the managers of the segments.[3]

### Cost centre

A **cost centre** is a business segment whose manager has control over costs but not over revenue or investment funds. Service departments such as accounting, finance, general administration, legal, personnel and so on, are usually considered to be cost centres. In addition, manufacturing facilities are often considered to be cost centres. The managers of cost centres are expected to minimize cost while providing the level of services or the amount of products demanded by other parts of the organization. For example, the manager of a production facility would be evaluated at least in part by comparing actual costs to how much the costs should have been for the actual number of units produced during the period.

### Profit centre

In contrast to a cost centre, a **profit centre** is any business segment whose manager has control over both cost and revenue. Like a cost centre, however, a profit centre generally does not have control over investment funds. For example, the manager in charge of an amusement park would be responsible for both the revenues and costs, and hence the profits, of the amusement park but may not have control over major investments in the park. Profit centre managers are often evaluated by comparing actual profit to targeted or budgeted profit.

### Investment centre

An **investment centre** is any segment of an organization whose manager has control over cost, revenue and investments in operating assets. For example, the managing director of the Truck Division at General Motors (one of the companies that pioneered decentralization in the last century)[4] would have a great deal of discretion over investments in the division. The managing director of the Truck Division would be responsible for initiating investment proposals, such as funding research into more fuel-efficient engines for sport-utility vehicles. Once the proposal has been approved by the top level of managers at General Motors and the board of directors, the managing director of the Truck Division would then be responsible for making sure that the investment pays off. Investment centre managers are usually evaluated using return on investment or residual income measures as discussed later in the chapter.

### Responsibility centres

A **responsibility centre** is broadly defined as any part of an organization whose manager has control over cost, revenue or investment funds. Cost centres, profit centres and investment centres are all known as responsibility centres.

**578** Part 3 Planning and control

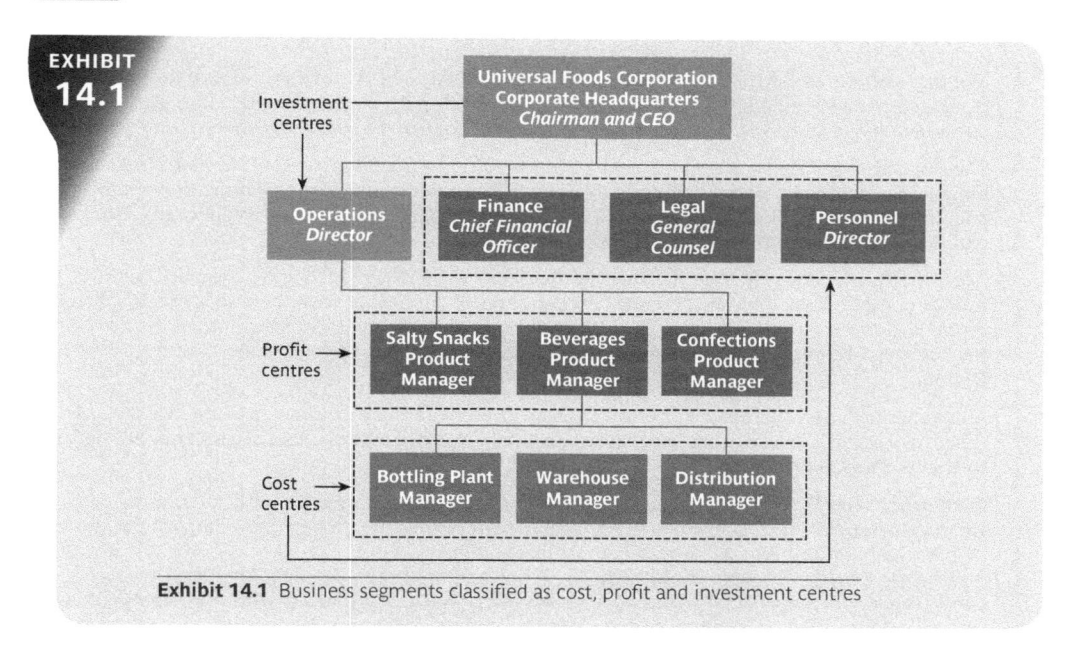

**EXHIBIT 14.1**

**Exhibit 14.1** Business segments classified as cost, profit and investment centres

A partial organization chart for Universal Foods Corporation, a company in the snack food and beverage industry, appears in Exhibit 14.1. This partial organization chart indicates how the various business segments of the company are classified in terms of responsibility. Note that the cost centres are the departments and work centres that do not generate significant revenues by themselves. These are staff departments such as finance, legal and personnel, and operating units such as the bottling plant, warehouse and beverage distribution centre. The profit centres are business segments that generate revenues and include the beverage, salty snacks and confections product segments. The managing director of operations oversees allocation of investment funds across the product segments and is responsible for revenues and costs and so is treated as an investment centre. And finally, corporate headquarters is an investment centre, since it is responsible for all revenues, costs and investments.

## Segment reporting and profitability analysis

As previously discussed, a different kind of profit and loss account is required for evaluating the performance of business segments – a profit and loss account that emphasizes segments rather than the performance of the company as a whole. This point is illustrated in the following discussion.

### MANAGEMENT ACCOUNTING IN ACTION: THE ISSUE

SoftSolutions Ltd is a rapidly growing computer software company founded by Stephanie Evans, who had previously worked in a large software company, and Marjorie Price, who had previously worked in the hotel industry as a general manager. They formed the company to develop and market user-friendly accounting and operations software designed specifically for hotels. They quit their jobs, pooled their savings, hired several programmers, and got down to work.

The first sale was by far the most difficult. No hotel wanted to be the first to use an untested product from an unknown company. After overcoming this obstacle with persistence, good luck, dedication to customer service and a very low introductory price, the company's sales burgeoned.

The company quickly developed similar business software for other specialized markets and then branched out into clip art and computer games. Within four years of its founding, the organization had grown to the point where Evans and Price were no longer able personally to direct all of the company's activities. Decentralization had become a necessity.

Accordingly, the company was split into two divisions – Business Products and Consumer Products. By mutual consent, Price took the title chief executive officer and Evans took the title managing director of the Business Products Division. Chris Worden, a programmer who had spearheaded the drive into the clip art and computer games markets, was designated managing director of the Consumer Products Division.

Almost immediately, the issue arose of how best to evaluate the performance of the divisions. Price called a meeting to consider this issue and asked Evans, Worden and the chief accountant, Bill Carson, to attend. The following discussion took place at that meeting:

***Marjorie Price:*** We need to find a better way to measure the performance of the divisions.
***Chris Worden:*** I agree. Consumer Products has been setting the pace in this company for the last two years, and we should be getting more recognition.
***Stephanie Evans:*** Chris, we are delighted with the success of the Consumer Products Division.
***Chris Worden:*** I know. But it is hard to work out just how successful we are with the present accounting reports. All we have are sales and cost of goods sold figures for the division.
***Bill Carson:*** What's the matter with those figures? They are prepared using internationally accepted accounting principles.
***Chris Worden:*** The sales figures are fine. However, cost of goods sold includes some costs that really aren't the costs of our division, and it excludes some costs that are. Let's take a simple example. Everything we sell in the Consumer Products Division has to pass through the automatic bar-coding machine, which applies a unique bar code to the product.
***Stephanie Evans:*** We know. Every item we ship must have a unique identifying bar code. That's true for items from the Business Products Division as well as for items from the Consumer Products Division.
***Chris Worden:*** That's precisely the point. Whether an item comes from the Business Products Division or the Consumer Products Division, it must pass through the automatic bar-coding machine after the software has been packaged. How much of the cost of the automatic bar coder would be saved if we didn't have any consumer products?
***Marjorie Price:*** Since we have only one automatic bar coder and we would need it anyway to code the business products, I guess none of the cost would be saved.
***Chris Worden:*** That's right. And since none of the cost could be saved even if the entire Consumer Products Division were eliminated, how can we logically say that some of the cost of the automatic bar coder is a cost of the Consumer Products Division?
***Stephanie Evans:*** Just a minute, Chris, are you saying that my Business Products Division should be charged with the entire cost of the automatic bar coder?
***Chris Worden:*** No, that's not what I am saying.
***Marjorie Price:*** But Chris, I don't see how we can have sensible performance reports without making someone responsible for costs like the cost of the automatic bar coder. Bill, as our accounting expert, what do you think?
***Bill Carson:*** I have some ideas for handling issues like the automatic bar coder. The best approach would probably be for me to put together a draft performance report. We can discuss it at the next meeting when everyone has something concrete to look at.
***Marjorie Price:*** Okay, let's see what you come up with.

**Part 3** Planning and control

Bill Carson, the chief accountant of SoftSolutions, realized that segmented profit and loss accounts would be required to evaluate more appropriately the performance of the two divisions. To construct the segmented reports, he would have to segregate carefully costs that are attributable to the two divisions from costs that are not. Since most of the disputes over costs would be about fixed costs such as the automatic bar-coding machine, he knew he would also have to separate fixed from variable costs. Under the conventional absorption costing profit and loss account prepared for the entire company, variable and fixed production costs were being commingled in the cost of goods sold.

Largely for these reasons, Bill Carson decided to use the contribution format profit and loss account discussed in earlier chapters. Recall that when the contribution format is used: (1) the cost of goods sold consists only of the variable manufacturing costs; (2) the variable and fixed costs are listed in separate sections; and (3) a contribution margin is computed. When such a statement is segmented as in this chapter, fixed costs are broken down further into what are called traceable and common costs as discussed later. This breakdown allows a *segment margin* to be computed for each segment of the company. The segment margin is a valuable tool for assessing the long-run profitability of a segment and is also a much better tool for evaluating performance than the usual absorption costing reports.

## Levels of segmented statements

A portion of the segmented report Bill Carson prepared is shown in Exhibit 14.2. The contribution format profit and loss account for the entire company appears at the very top of the exhibit under the column labelled Total company. Immediately to the right of this column are two columns – one for each of the two divisions. We can see that the divisional segment margin is £60,000 for the Business Products Division and £40,000 for the Consumer Products Division. This is the portion of the report that was specifically requested by the company's divisional managers. They wanted to know how much each of their divisions was contributing to the company's profits.

However, segmented profit and loss accounts can be prepared for activities at many levels in a company. To provide more information to the company's divisional managers, Bill Carson has further segmented the divisions according to their *major product lines*. In the case of the Consumer Products Division, the product lines are clip art and computer games. Going even further, Bill Carson has segmented each of the product lines according to how they are sold – in retail computer stores or by catalogue sales. In Exhibit 14.2, this further segmentation is illustrated for the computer games product line. Notice that as we go from one segmented statement to another, we look at smaller and smaller pieces of the company. While not shown in Exhibit 14.2, Bill Carson also prepared segmented profit and loss accounts for the major product lines in the Business Products Division.

Substantial benefits are received from a series of statements such as those contained in Exhibit 14.2. By carefully examining trends and results in each segment, a manager is able to gain considerable insight into the company's operations viewed from many different angles. And advanced computer-based information systems are making it easier and easier to construct such statements and to keep them current.

## Sales and contribution margin

To prepare a profit and loss account for a particular segment, variable expenses are deducted from the sales to yield the contribution margin for the segment. It is important to keep in mind that the contribution margin tells us what happens to profits as volume changes – holding a segment's capacity and fixed costs constant. The contribution margin is especially useful in decisions involving temporary uses of capacity such as special orders. Decisions concerning the most effective uses of existing capacity often involve only variable costs and revenues, which, of course, are the very elements involved in contribution margin. Such decisions were discussed in detail in Chapter 9.

## Traceable and common fixed costs

The most puzzling aspect of Exhibit 14.2 is probably the treatment of fixed costs. The report has two kinds of fixed costs – *traceable* and *common*. Only the *traceable fixed costs* are charged to the segments in the

**EXHIBIT 14.2** Segments defined as divisions

|  | Total company | Divisions Business Products Division | Divisions Consumer Products Division |
|---|---|---|---|
| Sales | £500,000 | £300,000 | £200,000 |
| Less variable expenses: | | | |
|   Variable cost of goods sold | 180,000 | 120,000 | 60,000 |
|   Other variable expenses | 50,000 | 30,000 | 20,000 |
|   Total variable expenses | 230,000 | 150,000 | 80,000 |
| Contribution margin | 270,000 | 150,000 | 120,000 |
| Less traceable fixed expenses | 170,000 | 90,000 | 80,000* |
| Divisional segment margin | 100,000 | £60,000 | £40,000 |
| Less common fixed expenses not traceable to the individual divisions | £85,000 | | |
| Net Profit | £15,000 | | |

Segments defined as product lines of the Consumer Products Division

|  | Consumer Products Division | Product line Clip art | Product line Computer games |
|---|---|---|---|
| Sales | £200,000 | £75,000 | £125,000 |
| Less variable expenses: | | | |
|   Variable cost of goods sold | 60,000 | 20,000 | 40,000 |
|   Other variable expenses | £20,000 | 5,000 | 15,000 |
|   Total variable expenses | £80,000 | £25,000 | £55,000 |
| Contribution margin | 120,000 | 50,000 | 70,000 |
| Less traceable expenses | £70,000 | 30,000 | £40,000 |
| Product-line segment margin | 50,000 | £20,000 | £30,000 |
| Less common fixed expenses not traceable to the individual product lines | £10,000 | | |
| Divisional segment margin | £40,000 | | |

> **EXHIBIT 14.2** Segments defined as sales channels for one product line, computer games, of the Consumer Products Division
>
> |  | Computer games | Sales channels Retail stores | Catalogue sales |
> |---|---|---|---|
> | Sales | £125,000 | £100,000 | £25,000 |
> | Less variable expenses: | | | |
> | Variable cost of goods sold | 40,000 | 32,000 | 8,000 |
> | Other variable expenses | 15,000 | 5,000 | 10,000 |
> | Total variable expenses | 55,000 | 37,000 | 18,000 |
> | Contribution margin | 70,000 | 63,000 | 7,000 |
> | Less traceable expenses | 25,000 | 15,000 | 10,000 |
> | Sales-channel segment margin | 45,000 | £48,000 | £(3,000) |
> | Less common fixed expenses not traceable to the individual sales channels | 15,000 | | |
> | Product-line segment margin | £30,000 | | |
>
> *Notice that this £80,000 in traceable fixed expenses is divided into two parts – £70,000 traceable and £10,000 common – when the Consumer Products Division is broken down into product lines. The reasons for this are discussed later under Traceable costs can become common costs.
>
> **Exhibit 14.2** SoftSolutions Ltd – segmented profit statements in the contribution format

segmented profit and loss accounts in the report. If a cost is not traceable to a segment, then it is not assigned to the segment.

A **traceable fixed cost** of a segment is a fixed cost that is incurred because of the existence of the segment – if the segment had never existed, the fixed cost would not have been incurred; and/or if the segment were eliminated, the fixed cost would disappear. Examples of traceable fixed costs include the following:

- The salary of the Fritos product manager at PepsiCo is a *traceable* fixed cost of the Fritos business segment of PepsiCo.
- The maintenance cost for the building in which Boeing 747s are assembled is a *traceable* fixed cost of the 747 business segment of Boeing.
- The liability insurance at Disney World is a *traceable* fixed cost of the Disney World business segment of the Disney Corporation.

A **common fixed cost** is a fixed cost that supports the operations of more than one segment but is not traceable in whole or in part to any one segment. Even if a segment were entirely eliminated, there would be no change in a true common fixed cost. Note the following:

- The salary of the Managing Director of General Motors is a *common* fixed cost of the various divisions of General Motors.
- The cost of the automatic bar-coding machine at SoftSolutions is a *common* fixed cost of the Consumer Products Division and of the Business Products Division.
- The cost of the receptionist's salary at an office shared by a number of doctors is a *common* fixed cost of the doctors. The cost is traceable to the office, but not to any one of the doctors individually.

### Identifying traceable fixed costs

The distinction between traceable and common fixed costs is crucial in segment reporting, since traceable fixed costs are charged to the segments, whereas common fixed costs are not. In an actual situation, it is sometimes hard to determine whether a cost should be classified as traceable or common.

Chapter 14 Segment reporting and decentralization

The general guideline is to treat as traceable costs *only those costs that would disappear over time if the segment itself disappeared*. For example, if the Consumer Products Division were sold or discontinued, it would no longer be necessary to pay the division manager's salary. Therefore the division manager's salary should be classified as a traceable fixed cost of the division. On the other hand, the managing director of the company undoubtedly would continue to be paid even if the Consumer Products Division were dropped. In fact, he or she might even be paid more if dropping the division was a good idea. Therefore, the managing director's salary is common to both divisions. The same idea can be expressed in another way: *treat as traceable costs only those costs that are added as a result of the creation of a segment*.

### Activity-based costing

Some costs are easy to identify as traceable costs. For example, the costs of advertising Crest toothpaste on television are clearly traceable to Crest. A more difficult situation arises when a building, machine, or other resource is shared by two or more segments. For example, assume that a multi-product company leases warehouse space that is used for storing the full range of its products. Would the lease cost of the warehouse be a traceable or a common cost of the products? Managers familiar with activity-based costing might argue that the lease cost is traceable and should be assigned to the products according to how much space the products use in the warehouse. In like manner, these managers would argue that order processing costs, sales support costs and other *selling, general and administrative (SG&A) expenses* should also be charged to segments according to the segments' consumption of SG&A resources.

To illustrate, consider Holt Corporation, a company that manufactures concrete pipe for industrial uses. The company has three products – 9-centimetre pipe, 12-centimetre pipe and 18-centimetre pipe. Space is leased in a large warehouse on a yearly basis as needed. The lease cost of this space is £4 per square metre per year. The 9-centimetre pipe occupies 1,000 square metres of space, 12-centimetre pipe occupies 4,000 square metres, and 18-centimetre pipe occupies 5,000 square metres. The company also has an order processing department that incurred £150,000 in order processing costs last year. Management believes that order processing costs are driven by the number of orders placed by customers in a year. Last year 2,500 orders were placed, of which 1,200 were for 9-centimetre pipe, 800 were for 12-centimetre pipe, and 500 were for 18-centimetre pipe. Given these data, the following costs would be assigned to each product using the activity-based costing approach:

| | |
|---|---:|
| **Warehouse space cost:** | |
| 9-centimetre pipe: £4 × 1,000 square metres | £4,000 |
| 12-centimetre pipe: £4 × 4,000 square metres | 16,000 |
| 18-centimetre pipe: £4 × 5,000 square metres | 20,000 |
| Total cost assigned | £40,000 |
| **Order processing costs:** | |
| £150,000/2,500 orders = £60 per order | |
| 9-centimetre pipe: £60 × 1,200 orders | £72,000 |
| 12-centimetre pipe: £60 × 800 orders | 48,000 |
| 18-centimetre pipe: £60 × 500 orders | 30,000 |
| Total cost assigned | £150,000 |

This method of assigning costs combines the strength of activity-based costing with the power of the contribution approach and greatly enhances the manager's ability to measure the profitability and performance of segments. However, managers must still ask themselves if the costs would in fact disappear over time if the segment itself disappeared. In the case of Holt Corporation, it is clear that the £20,000 in warehousing costs for the 18-centimetre pipe would be eliminated if they were no longer being produced. The company would simply rent less warehouse space the following year. However, suppose the company owns the warehouse. Then it is not so clear that £20,000 of the cost of the warehouse would really disappear if the 18-centimetre pipes were discontinued as a product. The company might be able to sublease the space, or use it for other products, but then again the space might simply be empty while the costs of the warehouse continue to be incurred.

In assigning costs to segments, the key point is to resist the temptation to allocate costs (such as depreciation of corporate facilities) that are clearly common in nature and that would continue regardless of whether the segment exists or not. *Any allocation of common costs to segments will reduce the value of the segment margin as a guide to long-run segment profitability and segment performance.* This point will be discussed at length later in the chapter.

## Traceable costs can become common costs

Fixed costs that are traceable to one segment may be a common cost of another segment. For example, an airline might want a segmented profit and loss account that shows the segment margin for a particular flight from Los Angeles to Paris, further broken down into first-class, business-class and economy-class *segment margins*. The airline must pay a substantial landing fee at Charles DeGaulle airport in Paris. This fixed landing fee is a traceable cost of the flight, but it is a common cost of the first-class, business-class and economy-class segments. Even if the first-class cabin is empty, the entire landing fee must be paid. So the landing fee is not a traceable cost of the first-class cabin. But on the other hand, paying the fee is necessary in order to have any first-class, business-class, or economy-class passengers. So the landing fee is a common cost of these three classes.

The dual nature of some of the fixed costs can be seen from the diagram in Exhibit 14.3. Notice from the diagram that when segments are defined as divisions, the Consumer Products Division has £80,000 in traceable fixed expenses. Only £70,000 of this amount remains traceable, however, when we narrow the definition of a segment from divisions to product lines. Notice that the other £10,000 then becomes a common cost of the two product lines of the Consumer Products Division.

Why would £10,000 of traceable fixed cost become a common cost when the division is divided into product lines? The £10,000 is the monthly salary of the manager of the Consumer Products Division. This salary is a traceable cost of the division as a whole, but it is a common cost of the division's product lines. The manager's salary is a necessary cost of having the two product lines, but even if one of the product lines were discontinued entirely, the manager's salary would probably not be cut. Therefore, none of the manager's salary can be really traced to the individual products.

**EXHIBIT 14.3**

|  | Total company | Segment Business Products Division | Segment Consumer Products Division |
|---|---|---|---|
| Contribution margin | £270,000 | £150,000 | £120,000 |
| Less traceable fixed expenses | 170,000 | 90,000 | 80,000 |

|  | Consumer Products Division | Segment Clip art | Segment Computer games |
|---|---|---|---|
| Contribution margin | £120,000 | £50,000 | £70,000 |
| Less traceable fixed expenses | 70,000 | 30,000 | 40,000 |
| Product-line segment margin | 50,000 | £20,000 | £30,000 |
| Less common fixed expenses | 10,000 |  |  |
| Divisional segment margin | £40,000 |  |  |

**Exhibit 14.3** Reclassification of traceable fixed expenses from Exhibit 14.2

The £70,000 traceable fixed cost of the product lines consists of the costs of product-specific advertising. A total of £30,000 was spent on advertising clip art and £40,000 was spent on advertising computer games. These costs can clearly be traced to the individual product lines.

### Segment margin

Observe from Exhibit 14.2 that the **segment margin** is obtained by deducting the traceable fixed costs of a segment from the segment's contribution margin. It represents the margin available after a segment has covered all of its own costs. *The segment margin is the best gauge of the long-run profitability of a segment*, since it includes only those costs that are caused by the segment. If a segment cannot cover its own costs, then that segment probably should not be retained (unless it has important side effects on other segments). Notice from Exhibit 14.2, for example, that Catalogue sales has a negative segment margin. This means that the segment is not covering its own costs; it is generating more costs than it collects in revenue.

From a decision-making point of view, the segment margin is most useful in major decisions that affect capacity such as dropping a segment. By contrast, as we noted earlier, the contribution margin is most useful in decisions relating to short-run changes in volume, such as pricing special orders that involve utilization of existing capacity.

## MANAGEMENT ACCOUNTING IN ACTION: THE WRAP-UP

Shortly after Bill Carson, SoftSolutions Ltd's chief accountant, completed the draft segmented profit and loss account, he sent copies to the other managers and scheduled a meeting in which the report could be explained. The meeting was held on the Monday following the first meeting; and Marjorie Price, Stephanie Evans and Chris Worden were all in attendance.

***Stephanie Evans:*** I think these segmented profit and loss accounts are fairly self-explanatory. However, there is one thing I wonder about.
***Bill Carson:*** What's that?
***Stephanie Evans:*** What is this common fixed expense of £85,000 listed under the total company? And who is going to be responsible for it if neither Chris nor I have responsibility?
***Bill Carson:*** The £85,000 of common fixed expenses represents expenses like general administrative salaries and the costs of common production equipment such as the automatic bar-coding machine. Marjorie, do you want to respond to the question about responsibility for these expenses?
***Marjorie Price:*** Sure. Since I'm the managing director of the company, I'm responsible for those costs. Some things can be delegated, others cannot. It wouldn't make any sense for either you or Chris to make decisions about the bar coder, since it affects both of you. That's an important part of my job – Segment making decisions about resources that affect all parts of the organization. This report makes it much clearer who is responsible for what. I like it.
***Chris Worden:*** So do I – my division's segment margin is higher than the net profit for the entire company.
***Marjorie Price:*** Don't get carried away, Chris. Let's not misinterpret what this report means. The segment margins have to be big to cover the common costs of the company. We can't let the big segment margins lull us into a sense of complacency. If we use these reports, we all have to agree that our objective is to increase all of the segment margins over time.
***Stephanie Evans:*** I'm willing to give it a try.
***Chris Worden:*** The reports make sense to me.
***Marjorie Price:*** So be it. Then the first item of business would appear to be a review of catalogue sales of computer games, where we appear to be losing money. Chris, could you brief us on this at our next meeting?
***Chris Worden:*** I'd be happy to. I have been suspecting for some time that our catalogue sales strategy could be improved.
***Marjorie Price:*** We look forward to hearing your analysis. Meeting's adjourned.

**586** Part 3 Planning and control

## There is more than one way to segment a company

SoftSolutions segmented its sales by division, by product line within each division, and by sales channel. An organization can be segmented in many ways. For example, two different ways of segmenting the sales of the General Electric Company are displayed in Exhibit 14.4. In the first diagram, the company's sales are segmented by geographic region. In the second diagram, they are segmented by products. Note that each of the diagrams could be continued, providing progressively more detailed segment data. For example, the sales in France could be broken down by major product line, then by product. Similar breakdowns could be done of General Electric's costs and segment margins, although that would require substantial additional analytical work to identify the segments to which various costs should be assigned.

Segment breakdowns such as those shown in Exhibit 14.4 give a company's managers the ability to look at the company from many different directions. With the increasing availability of companywide databases and sophisticated management information system software, detailed segmental reports of revenues, costs, and margins are becoming much easier to do.

### LEARNING OBJECTIVE 3

## Hindrances to proper cost assignment

For segment reporting to accomplish its intended purposes, costs must be properly assigned to segments. If the purpose is to determine the profits being generated by a particular division, then all of the

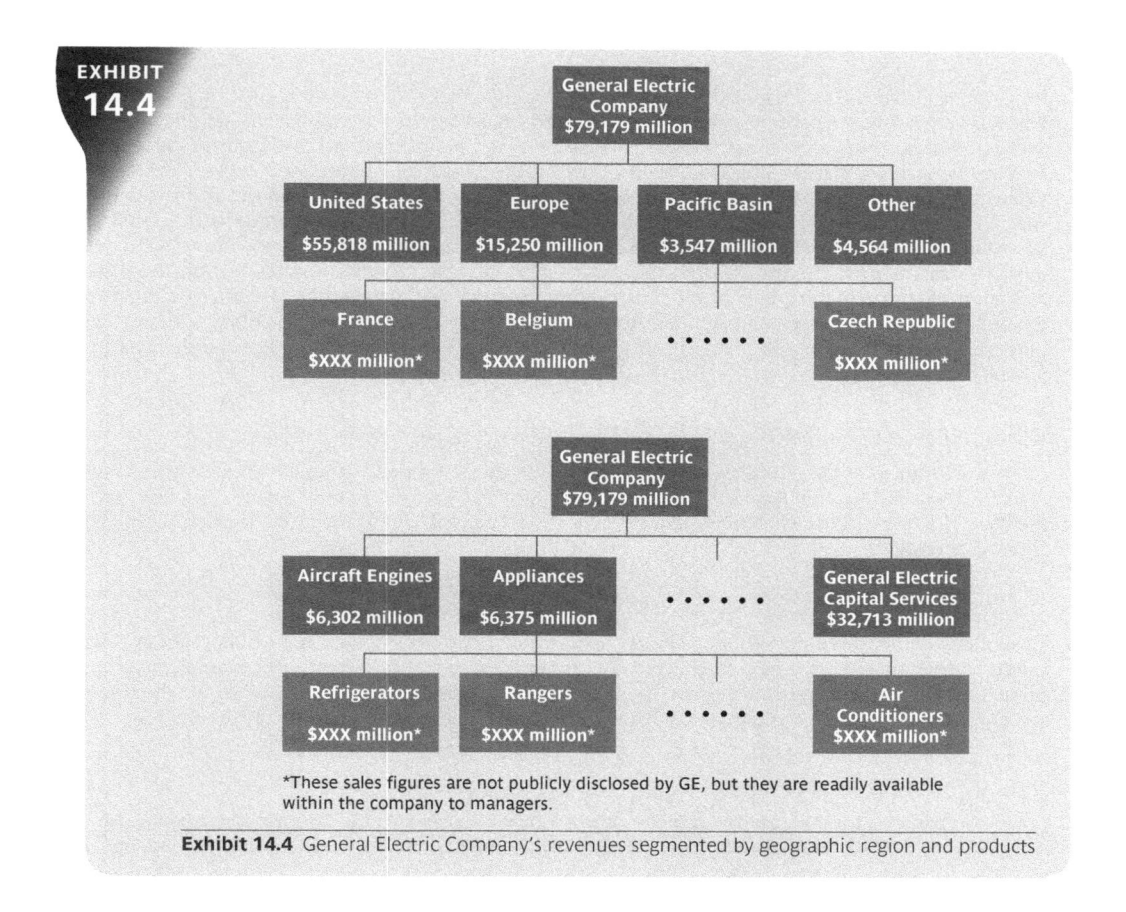

**EXHIBIT 14.4**

General Electric Company
$79,179 million

- United States $55,818 million
  - France $XXX million*
- Europe $15,250 million
  - Belgium $XXX million*
- Pacific Basin $3,547 million
  - ......
- Other $4,564 million
  - Czech Republic $XXX million*

General Electric Company
$79,179 million

- Aircraft Engines $6,302 million
  - Refrigerators $XXX million*
- Appliances $6,375 million
  - Rangers $XXX million*
- ......
  - ......
- General Electric Capital Services $32,713 million
  - Air Conditioners $XXX million*

*These sales figures are not publicly disclosed by GE, but they are readily available within the company to managers.

**Exhibit 14.4** General Electric Company's revenues segmented by geographic region and products

costs attributable to that division – and only those costs – should be assigned to it. Unfortunately, three business practices greatly hinder proper cost assignment: (1) omission of some costs in the assignment process, (2) the use of inappropriate methods for allocating costs among segments of a company, and (3) assignment to segments of costs that are really common costs.

## Omission of costs

The costs assigned to a segment should include all costs attributable to that segment from the company's entire *value chain*. The **value chain**, which is illustrated in Exhibit 14.5, consists of the major business functions that add value to a company's products and services. All of these functions, from research and development, through product design, manufacturing, marketing, distribution and customer service, are required to bring a product or service to the customer and generate revenues.

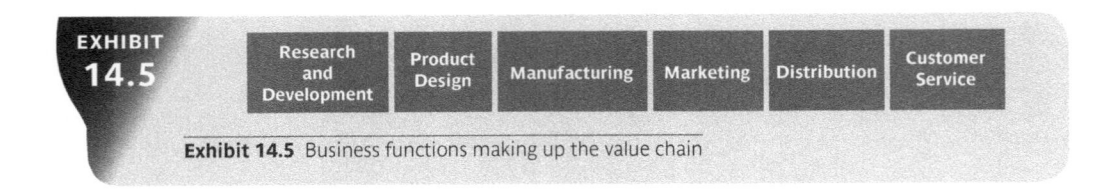

**EXHIBIT 14.5** | Research and Development | Product Design | Manufacturing | Marketing | Distribution | Customer Service

**Exhibit 14.5** Business functions making up the value chain

However, as discussed in Chapters 2, 3 and 6, only manufacturing costs are included in product costs for financial reporting purposes. Consequently, when trying to determine product profitability for internal decision-making purposes, some companies deduct only manufacturing costs from product revenues. As a result, such companies omit from their profitability analysis part or all of the 'upstream' costs in the value chain, which consist of research and development and product design, and the 'downstream' costs, which consist of marketing, distribution and customer service. Yet these non-manufacturing costs are just as essential in determining product profitability as are the manufacturing costs. These upstream and downstream costs, which are usually titled *Selling, General, and Administrative (SG&A)* on the profit and loss account, can represent half or more of the total costs of an organization. If either the upstream or downstream costs are omitted in profitability analysis, then the product is undercosted and management may unwittingly develop and maintain products that in the long run result in losses rather than profits for the company.

## Inappropriate methods for allocating costs among segments

*Cross-subsidization*, or cost distortion, occurs when costs are improperly assigned among a company's segments. Cross-subsidization can occur in two ways; first, when companies fail to trace costs directly to segments in those situations where it is feasible to do so; and second, when companies use inappropriate bases to allocate costs.

### Failure to trace costs directly

Costs that can be traced directly to a specific segment of a company should not be allocated to other segments. Rather, such costs should be charged directly to the responsible segment. For example, the rent for a branch office of an insurance company should be charged directly against the branch to which it relates rather than included in a companywide overhead pool and then spread throughout the company.

### Inappropriate allocation base

Some companies allocate costs to segments using arbitrary bases such as sales or cost of goods sold. For example, under the sales approach, costs are allocated to the various segments according to the percentage of company sales generated by each segment. Thus, if a segment generates 20% of total company sales, it would be allocated 20% of the company's SG&A expenses as its 'fair share'. This same basic procedure is followed if costs of goods sold or some other measure is used as the allocation base.

For this approach to be valid, the allocation base must actually drive the overhead cost. (Or at least the allocation base should be highly correlated with the cost driver of the overhead cost.) For example, when sales are used as the allocation base for SG&A expenses, it is implicitly assumed that SG&A expenses change in proportion to changes in total sales. If that is not true, the SG&A expenses allocated to segments will be misleading.

## Arbitrarily dividing common costs among segments

The third business practice that leads to distorted segment costs is the practice of assigning non-traceable costs to segments. For example, some companies allocate the costs of the corporate headquarters building to products on segment reports. However, in a multi-product company, no single product is likely to be responsible for any significant amount of this cost. Even if a product were eliminated entirely, there would usually be no significant effect on any of the costs of the corporate headquarters building. In short, there is no cause-and-effect relation between the cost of the corporate headquarters building and the existence of any one product. As a consequence, any allocation of the cost of the corporate headquarters building to the products must be arbitrary.

Common costs like the costs of the corporate headquarters building are necessary, of course, to have a functioning organization. The common practice of arbitrarily allocating these costs to segments is often justified on the grounds that 'someone' has to 'cover the common costs'. While it is undeniably true that the common costs must be covered, arbitrarily allocating common costs to segments does not ensure that this will happen. In fact, adding a share of common costs to the real costs of a segment may make an otherwise profitable segment appear to be unprofitable. If a manager erroneously eliminates the segment, the revenues will be lost, the real costs of the segment will be saved, but the common costs will still be there. The net effect will be to reduce the profits of the company as a whole and make it even more difficult to 'cover the common costs'.

In sum, the way many companies handle segment reporting results in *cost distortion*. This distortion results from three practices – the failure to trace costs directly to a specific segment when it is feasible to do so, the use of inappropriate bases for allocating costs and the allocation of common costs to segments. These practices are widespread. One study found that 60% of the companies surveyed made no attempt to assign SG&A costs to segments on a cause-and-effect basis.[5]

## Rate of return for measuring managerial performance

When a company is truly decentralized, segment managers are given a great deal of autonomy. So great is this autonomy that the various profit and investment centres are often viewed as being virtually independent businesses, with their managers having about the same control over decisions as if they were in fact running their own independent firms. With this autonomy, fierce competition often develops among managers, with each striving to make his or her segment the 'best' in the company.

Competition between investment centres is particularly keen for investment funds. How do top managers in corporate headquarters go about deciding who gets new investment funds as they become available, and how do these managers decide which investment centres are most profitably using the funds that have already been entrusted to their care? One of the most popular ways of making these judgements is to measure the rate of return that investment centre managers are able to generate on their assets. This rate of return is called *the return on investment (ROI)*.

### The return on investment (ROI) formula

The **return on investment (ROI)** is defined as net operating profit divided by average operating assets:

$$ROI = \frac{\text{Net operating profit}}{\text{Average operating assets}}$$

Although there are some issues about how to measure net operating profit and average operating assets, this formula seems clear enough. The higher the return on investment of a business segment, the greater the *profit generated per pound invested* in the segment's operating assets.

## Net operating profit and operating assets defined

Note that *net operating profit*, rather than net profit, is used in the ROI formula. **Net operating profit** is profit before interest and taxes and is sometimes referred to as EBIT (earnings before interest and taxes). The reason for using net operating profit in the formula is that the profit figure used should be consistent with the base to which it is applied. Notice that the base (i.e., denominator) consists of *operating assets*. Thus, to be consistent we use net operating profit in the numerator.

**Operating assets** include cash, debtors, inventory, plant and equipment, and all other assets held for productive use in the organization. Examples of assets that would not be included in the operating assets category (i.e., examples of non-operating assets) would include land held for future use, an investment in another company, or a factory building rented to someone else. The operating assets base used in the formula is typically computed as the average of the operating assets between the beginning and the end of the year.

## Plant and equipment: net book value or gross cost?

A major issue in ROI computations is the monetary measure of plant and equipment that should be included in the operating assets base. To illustrate the problem involved, assume that a company reports the following amounts for plant and equipment on its balance sheet:

| | |
|---|---|
| Plant and equipment | £3,000,000 |
| Less accumulated depreciation | 900,000 |
| Net book value | £2,100,000 |

What amount of plant and equipment should the company include with its operating assets in computing ROI? One widely used approach is to include only the plant and equipment's *net book value* – that is, the plant's original cost less accumulated depreciation (£2,100,000 in the example above). A second approach is to ignore depreciation and include the plant's entire *gross cost* in the operating assets base (£3,000,000 in the example above). Both of these approaches are used in actual practice, even though they will obviously yield very different operating asset and ROI figures.

The following arguments can be raised for using *net book value* to measure *operating assets* and for using *gross cost* to measure operating assets in ROI computation.

**Arguments for using net book value to measure operating assets in ROI computations:**

1 The net book value method is consistent with how plant and equipment are reported on the balance sheet (i.e., cost less accumulated depreciation to date).
2 The net book value method is consistent with the computation of operating profit, which includes depreciation as an operating expense.

**Arguments for using gross cost to measure operating assets in ROI computations:**

1 The gross cost method eliminates both the age of equipment and the method of depreciation as factors in ROI computations. (Under the net book value method, ROI will tend to increase over time as net book value declines due to depreciation.)
2 The gross cost method does not discourage replacement of old, worn out equipment. (Under the net book value method, replacing fully depreciated equipment with new equipment can have a dramatic, adverse effect on ROI.)

Managers generally view consistency as the most important of the considerations above. As a result, a majority of companies use the net book value approach in ROI computations. In this text, we will also use the net book value approach unless a specific exercise or problem directs otherwise.

**Part 3** Planning and control

## Controlling the rate of return

When we first defined the return on investment, we used the following formula:

$$\text{ROI} = \frac{\text{Net operating profit}}{\text{Average operating assets}}$$

We can modify this formula slightly by introducing sales as follows:

$$\text{ROI} = \frac{\text{Net operating profit}}{\text{Sales}} \times \frac{\text{Sales}}{\text{Average operating assets}}$$

The first term on the right-hand side of the equation is the *margin*, which is defined as follows:

$$\text{Margin} = \frac{\text{Net operating profit}}{\text{Sales}}$$

The **margin** is a measure of management's ability to control operating expenses in relation to sales. The lower the operating expenses per pound of sales, the higher the margin earned.

The second term on the right-hand side of the preceding equation is *turnover* which is defined as follows:

$$\text{Turnover} = \frac{\text{Sales}}{\text{Average operating assets}}$$

**Turnover** is a measure of the sales that are generated for each pound invested in operating assets.

The following alternative form of the ROI formula, which we will use most frequently, combines margin and turnover:

$$\text{ROI} = \text{Margin} \times \text{Turnover}$$

Which formula for ROI should be used – the original one stated in terms of net operating profit and average operating assets or this one stated in terms of margin and turnover? Either can be used – they will always give the same answer. However, the margin and turnover formulation provides some additional insights.

Some managers tend to focus too much on margin and ignore turnover. To some degree at least, the margin can be a valuable indicator of a manager's performance. Standing alone, however, it overlooks one crucial area of a manager's responsibility – the investment in operating assets. Excessive funds tied up in operating assets, which depresses turnover, can be just as much of a drag on profitability as excessive operating expenses, which depresses margin. One of the advantages of ROI as a performance measure is that it forces the manager to control the investment in operating assets as well as to control expenses and the margin.

Du Pont pioneered the ROI concept and recognized the importance of looking at both margin and turnover in assessing the performance of a manager. The ROI formula is now widely used as the key measure of the performance of an investment centre. The ROI formula blends together many aspects of the manager's responsibilities into a single figure that can be compared to the returns of competing investment centres, the returns of other firms in the industry, and to the past returns of the investment centre itself.

Du Pont also developed the diagram that appears in Exhibit 14.6. This exhibit helps managers understand how they can control ROI. An investment centre manager can increase ROI in basically three ways:

1. Increase sales
2. Reduce expenses
3. Reduce assets.

To illustrate how the rate of return can be improved by each of these three actions, consider how the manager of the Raffles Burger Grill is evaluated. Burger Grill is a small chain of upmarket casual restaurants that

### Exhibit 14.6

**Exhibit 14.6** Elements of return on investment (ROI)

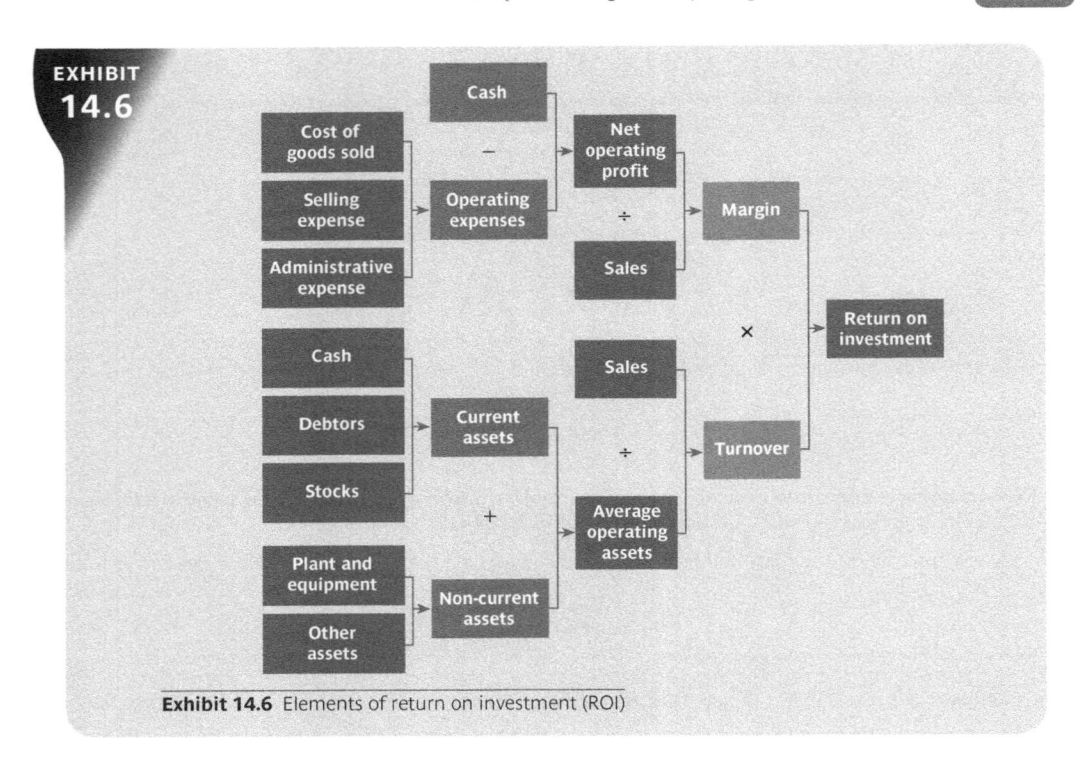

has been rapidly adding outlets via franchising. The Raffles franchise is owned by a group of local surgeons who have little time to devote to management and little expertise in business matters. Therefore, they delegate operating decisions – including decisions concerning investment in operating assets such as inventories – to a professional manager they have hired. The manager is evaluated largely based on the ROI the franchise generates.

The following data represent the results of business activity for the most recent month:

| | |
|---|---|
| Net operating profit | £10,000 |
| Sales | 100,000 |
| Average operating assets | 50,000 |

The rate of return generated by the Raffles Burger Grill investment centre is as follows:

$$\text{ROI} = \text{Margin} \times \text{Turnover}$$

$$= \frac{\text{Net operating profit}}{\text{Sales}} \times \frac{\text{Sales}}{\text{Average operating assets}}$$

$$= \frac{£10,000}{£1,000,000} \times \frac{£100,000}{£50,000}$$

$$= 10\% \times 2 = 20\%$$

As we stated above, to improve the ROI figure, the manager can (1) increase sales, (2) reduce expenses, or (3) reduce the operating assets.

### (1) Increase sales

Assume that the manager of the Raffles Burger Grill is able to increase sales from £100,000 to £110,000. Assume further that either because of good cost control or because some costs in the company are fixed, the net operating profit increases even more rapidly, going from £10,000 to £12,000 per period. The operating assets remain constant.

$$\text{ROI} = \frac{£12,000}{£110,000} \times \frac{£110,000}{£50,000}$$

$$10.91\% \times 2.2 = 24\% \text{ (as compared to 20\% above)}$$

### (2) Reduce expenses

Assume that the manager of the Raffles Burger Grill is able to reduce expenses by £1,000 so that net operating profit increases from £10,000 to £11,000. Both sales and operating assets remain constant.

$$\text{ROI} = \frac{£11,000}{£100,000} \times \frac{£100,000}{£50,000}$$

$$11\% \times 2 = 22\% \text{ (as compared to 20\% above)}$$

### (3) Reduce assets

Assume that the manager of the Raffles Burger Grill is able to reduce operating assets from £50,000 to £40,000. Sales and net operating profit remain unchanged.

$$\text{ROI} = \frac{£10,000}{£100,000} \times \frac{£100,000}{£40,000}$$

$$10\% \times 2.5 = 25\% \text{ (as compared to 20\% above)}$$

A clear understanding of these three approaches to improving the ROI figure is critical to the effective management of an investment centre. We will now look at each approach in more detail.

## Increase sales

In first looking at the ROI formula, one is inclined to think that the sales figure is neutral, since it appears as the denominator in the margin computation and as the numerator in the turnover computation. We *could* cancel out the sales figure, but we do not do so for two reasons. First, this would tend to draw attention away from the fact that the rate of return is a function of *two* variables, margin and turnover. And second, it would tend to conceal the fact that a change in sales can affect both the *margin* and the turnover in an organization. To explain, a change in sales can affect the margin if expenses increase or decrease at a different rate than sales. For example, a company may be able to keep a tight control on its costs as its sales go up, with the result that net operating profit increases more rapidly than sales and increases the margin. Or a company may have fixed expenses that remain constant as sales go up, resulting in an increase in the net operating profit and in the margin. Either (or both) of these factors could have been responsible for the increase in the margin percentage from 10 to 10.91 illustrated in (1) above.

Further, a change in sales can affect the *turnover* if sales either increase or decrease without a proportionate increase or decrease in the operating assets. In the first approach above, for example, sales increased from £100,000 to £110,000, but the operating assets remained unchanged. As a result, the turnover increased from 2 to 2.2 for the period.

## Reduce expenses

Often the easiest route to increased profitability and to a stronger ROI figure is simply to cut the 'fat' out of an organization through a concerted effort to control expenses. When margins begin to be squeezed, this is

### Reduce operating assets

Managers have always been sensitive to the need to control sales, operating expenses and operating margins. However, they have not always been equally sensitive to the need to control investment in operating assets. Firms that have adopted the ROI approach to measuring managerial performance report that one of the first reactions of investment centre managers is to trim their investment in operating assets. The reason, of course, is that these managers soon realize that an excessive investment in operating assets reduces turnover and hurts the ROI. As these managers reduce their investment in operating assets, funds are released that can be used elsewhere in the organization.

How can an investment centre manager control the investment in operating assets? One approach is to eliminate unneeded stock. Just-in-time (JIT) purchasing and JIT manufacturing (see Chapter 18) have been extremely helpful in reducing stocks of all types, with the result that ROI figures have improved dramatically in some companies. Another approach is to devise various methods of speeding up the collection of debtors.

### Criticisms of ROI

Although ROI is widely used in evaluating performance, it is not a perfect tool. The method is subject to the following criticisms:

1. Just telling managers to increase ROI may not be enough. Managers may not know how to increase ROI; they may increase ROI in a way that is inconsistent with the company's strategy; or they may take actions that increase ROI in the short run but harm the company in the long run (such as cutting back on research and development). This is why ROI is best used as part of a balanced scorecard, as we will discuss in Chapter 16. A balanced scorecard can provide concrete guidance to managers, make it more likely that actions taken are consistent with the company's strategy, and reduce the likelihood that short-run performance will be enhanced at the expense of long-term performance.
2. A manager who takes over a business segment typically inherits many committed costs over which the manager has no control. These committed costs may be relevant in assessing the performance of the business segment as an investment but make it difficult fairly to assess the performance of the manager relative to other managers.
3. As discussed in the next section, a manager who is evaluated based on ROI may reject profitable investment opportunities.

## Residual income[6] – another measure of performance

Another approach to measuring an investment centre's performance focuses on a concept known as *residual income*. **Residual income** is the net operating profit that an investment centre earns above the minimum required return on its operating assets. In equation form, residual income is calculated as follows:

Residual = Net operating income − (Average operating assets × Minimum required rate of return)

**Economic value added (EVA)** is a similar concept that differs in some details from residual income.[7] For example, under the economic value added concept, funds used for research and development are treated as investments rather than as expenses.[8] However, for our purposes, we will not draw any distinction between residual income and economic value added.

**Part 3** Planning and control

When residual income or economic value added is used to measure performance, the purpose is to maximize the total amount of residual income or economic value added, not to maximize overall ROI. For purposes of illustration, consider the following data for an investment centre – the Scottish Division of Alaskan Marine Services Corporation.

**Alaskan Marine Services Corporation**
**Scottish Division**
**Basic data for performance evaluation**

| | |
|---|---|
| Average operating assets | £100,000 |
| Net operating profit | £20,000 |
| Minimum required rate of return | 15% |

Alaskan Marine Services Corporation has long had a policy of evaluating investment centre managers based on ROI, but it is considering a switch to residual income. The finance director of the company, who is in favour of the change to residual income, has provided the following table that shows how the performance of the division would be evaluated under each of the two methods:

**Marine Services Corporation**
**Scottish Division**
**Alternative performance measures**

| | ROI | Residual income |
|---|---|---|
| Average operating assets | £100,000 (a) | £100,000 |
| Net operating profit | £20,000 (b) | £20,000 |
| ROI, (b) ÷ (a) | 20% | |
| Minimum required return (15% × £100,000) | | 15,000 |
| Residual income | | £5,000 |

The reasoning underlying the residual income calculation is straightforward. The company is able to earn a rate of return of at least 15% on its investments. Since the company has invested £100,000 in the Scottish Division in the form of operating assets, the company should be able to earn at least £15,000 (15% × £100,000) on this investment. Since the Scottish Division's net operating profit is £20,000, the residual income above and beyond the minimum required return is £5,000. If *residual income* is adopted as the performance measure to replace ROI, the manager of the Scottish Division would be evaluated based on the growth from year to year in residual income.

## Motivation and residual income

One of the primary reasons why the chief accountant of Marine Services Corporation would like to switch from ROI to residual income has to do with how managers view new investments under the two performance measurement schemes. The residual income approach encourages managers to make investments that are profitable for the entire company but that would be rejected by managers who are evaluated by the ROI formula.

To illustrate this problem, suppose that the manager of the Scottish Division is considering purchasing a computerized diagnostic machine to aid in servicing marine diesel engines. The machine would cost £25,000 and is expected to generate additional operating profit of £4,500 a year. From the standpoint of the company, this would be a good investment since it promises a rate of return of 18% (£4,500/£25,000), which is in excess of the company's minimum required rate of return of 15%.

If the manager of the Scottish Division is evaluated based on residual income, she would be in favour of the investment in the diagnostic machine as shown below:

**Marine Services Corporation**
**Scottish Division**
**Performance evaluated using residual income**

|  | Present | New project | Overall |
| --- | --- | --- | --- |
| Average operating assets | £100,000 | £25,000 | £125,000 |
| Net operating profit | £20,000 | £4,500 | £24,500 |
| Minimum required return | 15,000 | 3,750* | 18,750 |
| Residual income | £5,000 | £750 | £5,750 |

*£25,000 × 15% = £3,750.

Since the project would increase the residual income of the Scottish Division, the manager would want to invest in the new diagnostic machine.

Now suppose that the manager of the Scottish Division is evaluated based on ROI. The effect of the diagnostic machine on the division's ROI is computed below:

**Marine Services Corporation**
**Scottish Division**
**Performance evaluated using ROI**

|  | Present | New project | Overall |
| --- | --- | --- | --- |
| Average operating assets (a) | £100,000 | £25,000 | £125,000 |
| Net operating profit (b) | £20,000 | £4,500† |  |
| ROI, (b)/(a) | 20% | 18% | 19.6% |

†£25,000 × 18% = £4,500.

The new project reduces the division's ROI from 20% to 19.6%. This happens because the 18% rate of return on the new diagnostic machine, while above the company's 15% minimum rate of return, is below the division's present ROI of 20%. Therefore, the new diagnostic machine would drag the division's ROI down even though it would be a good investment from the standpoint of the company as a whole. If the manager of the division is evaluated based on ROI, she will be reluctant even to propose such an investment.

Basically, a manager who is evaluated based on ROI will reject any project whose rate of return is below the division's current ROI even if the rate of return on the project is above the minimum required rate of return for the entire company. In contrast, any project whose rate of return is above the minimum required rate of return for the company will result in an increase in residual income. Since it is in the best interests of the company as a whole to accept any project whose rate of return is above the minimum required rate of return, managers who are evaluated based on residual income will tend to make better decisions concerning investment projects than managers who are evaluated based on ROI.

## Divisional comparison and residual income

The residual income approach has one major disadvantage. It cannot be used to compare the performance of divisions of different sizes. You would expect larger divisions to have more residual income

**Part 3** Planning and control

than smaller divisions, not necessarily because they are better managed but simply because of the bigger numbers involved.

As an example, consider the following residual income computations for Division X and Division Y:

|  | Division X | Division Y |
|---|---|---|
| Average operating assets (a) | £1,000,000 | £250,000 |
| Net operating profit | £120,000 | £40,000 |
| Minimum required return: 10% × (a) | 100,000 | 25,000 |
| Residual income | £20,000 | £15,000 |

## FOCUS ON PRACTICE

### Value-based Management at Allianz

At *Allianz*, the company explains the principles behind its use of EVA®. They calculate EVA® as normalized profit minus capital charges, where capital charges are defined as a measure of the company's capital multiplied by the cost of capital. New investment in each division is based on their risk-return profile and their strategic position. Using this process, the divisions can only ensure that they receive growth capital if they:

- operate in a profitable market or business;
- transform their market position into sustainable creation of value and a leading market position;
- maintain an orientation and competency that fits within the long-term strategy of the *Allianz Group*; and
- are able to generate distributable earnings in an amount that is at least equal to their cost of capital.

The requirement to meet the cost of capital is just the minimum. Over the medium term, the objective is to generate a return of 15% or more on the capital employed. Therefore, companies must determine what business activities will increase their value and concentrate their efforts and resources on these activities. Further, new value drivers must be created, for example, through new products, more cost-effective processes and optimized distribution channels. Local management must also prevent value being destroyed along the complete value chain. If value diminishes, countermeasures must be implemented immediately. Because EVA® is an important factor in managing the business, senior management compensation is based on this measurement to a significant extent.

**Exercise:** Consider what issues might be neglected by a company that uses ROI rather than EVA as a key performance metric?

*Source*: adapted from Allianz website; reproduced with permission

Observe that Division X has slightly more residual income than Division Y, but that Division X has £1,000,000 in operating assets as compared to only £250,000 in operating assets for Division Y. Thus, Division X's greater residual income is probably more a result of its size than the quality of its management. In fact, it appears that the smaller division is better managed, since it has been able to generate nearly as much residual income with only a quarter as much in operating assets to work with. This problem can be reduced to some degree by focusing on the percentage change in residual income from year to year rather than on the absolute amount of the residual income.

### The problem of single period metrics: the bonus bank approach

The problem with ROI, RI and EVA is that they are all single period metrics. Thus, although it can be shown that under certain assumptions the capitalized value of residual income equals the net present value of the company,[9] a one-period measure cannot capture the economic value of a division or investment. From this point of view, investment decisions based on these techniques will not be identical to those based on the 'correct' NPV rule.

Advocates of EVA have tried to respond to this problem by basing executive remuneration on a 'bonus bank' system. The aim of this approach is that bonuses are not just based on a single year's performance but may be accumulated over a number of years. The aim is to discourage managers who may be able to boost EVA in the very short term, take a bonus and then leave the company. In fact, one of the distinguishing features of EVA over RI is the great care that is devoted to designing managerial compensation schemes that are aligned with shareholder wealth objectives.[10]

## Summary

- Segment reports can provide information for evaluating the profitability and performance of divisions, product lines, sales territories and other segments of a company. Under the contribution approach to segment reporting, only those costs that are traceable are assigned to a segment. Fixed common costs and other non-traceable costs are not allocated to a segment. A cost is considered to be traceable to a segment only if the cost is caused by the segment and eliminating the segment would result in avoiding the cost.
- Costs that are traceable to a segment are further classified as either variable or fixed. The contribution margin is sales less variable costs. The segment margin is the contribution margin less the traceable fixed costs of the segment.
- For purposes of evaluating the performance of managers, there are at least three kinds of business segments – cost centres, profit centres and investment centres.
- Return on investment (ROI) is widely used to evaluate investment centre performance. However, there is a trend towards using residual income or economic value added instead of ROI.
- The residual income and economic value added approaches encourage profitable investments in many situations where the ROI approach would discourage investment.

## Key terms for review

**Common fixed cost** (p. 582)
**Cost centre** (p. 577)
**Decentralized organization** (p. 576)
**Economic value added (EVA)** (p. 593)
**Investment centre** (p. 577)
**Margin** (p. 590)
**Net operating profit** (p. 589)
**Operating assets** (p. 589)
**Profit centre** (p. 577)

**Residual income** (p. 593)
**Responsibility centre** (p. 577)
**Return on investment (ROI)** (p. 588)
**Segment** (p. 577)
**Segment margin** (p. 585)
**Traceable fixed cost** (p. 582)
**Turnover** (p. 590)
**Value chain** (p. 587)

## Review problem 1: segmented statements

The business staff of the legal firm Frampton, Davis & Smythe has constructed the following report which breaks down the firm's overall results for last month in terms of its two main business segments – family law and commercial law:

|  | Total | Family law | Commercial law |
|---|---|---|---|
| Revenues from clients | £1,000,000 | £400,000 | £600,000 |
| Less variable expenses | 220,000 | 100,000 | 120,000 |
| Contribution margin | 780,000 | 300,000 | 480,000 |
| Less traceable fixed expenses | 670,000 | 280,000 | 390,000 |
| Segment margin | 110,000 | 20,000 | 90,000 |
| Less common fixed expenses | 60,000 | 24,000 | 36,000 |
| Net profit | £50,000 | £(4,000) | £54,000 |

However, this report is not quite correct. The common fixed expenses such as the managing partner's salary, general administrative expenses, and general firm advertising have been allocated to the two segments based on revenues from clients.

### Required

1. Redo the segment report, eliminating the allocation of common fixed expenses. Show both amount and percentage columns for the firm as a whole and for each of the segments. Would the firm be better off financially if the family law segment were dropped? (*Note*: Many of the firm's commercial law clients also use the firm for their family law requirements such as drawing up wills.)
2. The firm's advertising agency has proposed an ad campaign targeted at boosting the revenues of the family law segment. The ad campaign would cost £20,000, and the advertising agency claims that it would increase family law revenues by £100,000. The managing partner of Frampton, Davis & Smythe believes this increase in business could be accommodated without any increase in fixed expenses. What effect would this ad campaign have on the family law segment margin and on overall net profit of the firm?

## Solution to review problem 1: segmented statements

1. The corrected segmented profit and loss account appears below:

|  | Total Amount | % | Family law Amount | % | Commercial law Amount | % |
|---|---|---|---|---|---|---|
| Revenues from clients | £1,000,000 | 100 | £400,000 | 100 | £600,000 | 100 |
| Less variable expenses | 220,000 | 22 | 100,000 | 25 | 120,000 | 20 |
| Contribution margin | 780,000 | 78 | 300,000 | 75 | 480,000 | 80 |
| Less traceable fixed expenses | 670,000 | 67 | 280,000 | 70 | 390,000 | 65 |
| Segment margin | 110,000 | 11 | £20,000 | 5 | £90,000 | 15 |
| Less common fixed expenses | 60,000 | 6 |  |  |  |  |
| Net profit | £50,000 | 5 |  |  |  |  |

No, the firm would not be financially better off if the family law practice were dropped. The family law segment is covering all of its own costs and is contributing £20,000 per month to covering the common fixed expenses of the firm. While the segment margin as a percentage of sales is much lower for family law than for commercial law, it is still profitable; and it is likely that family law is a service that the firm must provide to its commercial clients in order to remain competitive.

2 The ad campaign would be expected to add £55,000 to the family law segment as follows:

| | |
|---|---|
| Increased revenues from clients | £100,000 |
| Family law contribution margin ratio | ×75% |
| Incremental contribution margin | 75,000 |
| Less cost of the ad campaign | 20,000 |
| Increased segment margin | £55,000 |

Since there would be no increase in fixed expenses (including common fixed expenses), the increase in overall net profit should also be £55,000.

## Review problem 2: return on investment (ROI) and residual income

The Magnetic Imaging Division of Medical Diagnostics plc has reported the following results for last year's operations:

| | |
|---|---|
| Sales | £25 million |
| Net operating profit | 3 million |
| Average operating assets | 10 million |

### Required

1 Compute the margin, turnover and ROI for the Magnetic Imaging Division.
2 Top management of Medical Diagnostics plc has set a minimum required rate of return on average operating assets of 25%. What is the Magnetic Imaging Division's residual income for the year?

## Solution to review problem 2: return on investment (ROI) and residual income

1 The required calculations appear below:

$$\text{Margin} = \frac{\text{Net operating profit, £3,000,000}}{\text{Sales, £25,000,000}}$$
$$= 12\%$$

$$\text{Turnover} = \frac{\text{Sales, £25,000,000}}{\text{Average operating assets, £10,000,000}}$$
$$= 2.5\%$$

$$\text{ROI} = \text{Margin} \times \text{Turnover}$$
$$= 12\% \times 2.5$$
$$= 30\%$$

2 The residual income for the Magnetic Imaging Division is computed as follows:

| | |
|---|---|
| Average operating assets | £10,000,000 |
| Net operating income | £3,000,000 |
| Minimum required return (25% × £10,000,000) | 2,500,000 |
| Residual income | £500,000 |

**Level of difficulty:** BASIC  INTERMEDIATE  ADVANCED

## Questions

**14–1** What is meant by the term *decentralization*?
**14–2** What benefits result from decentralization?
**14–3** Distinguish between a cost centre, a profit centre and an investment centre.
**14–4** Define a segment of an organization. Give several examples of segments.
**14–5** How does the contribution approach assign costs to segments of an organization?
**14–6** Distinguish between a traceable cost and a common cost. Give several examples of each.
**14–7** Explain how the segment margin differs from the contribution margin.
**14–8** Why aren't common costs allocated to segments under the contribution approach?
**14–9** How is it possible for a cost that is traceable to a segment to become a common cost if the segment is divided into further segments?
**14–10** What is meant by the terms *margin* and *turnover*?
**14–11** What are the three basic approaches to improving return on investment (ROI)?
**14–12** What is meant by residual income?
**14–13** In what way can the use of ROI as a performance measure for investment centres lead to bad decisions? How does the residual income approach overcome this problem?

## Exercises

**E14–1** Time allowed: 15 minutes

Royal Lawncare Company produces and sells two packaged products, Weedban and Greengrow. Revenue and cost information relating to the products follow:

|  | Product | |
|---|---|---|
|  | Weedban | Greengrow |
| Selling price per unit | £6.00 | £7.50 |
| Variable expenses per unit | 2.40 | 5.25 |
| Traceable fixed expenses per year | 45,000 | 21,000 |

Common fixed expenses in the company total £33,000 annually. Last year the company produced and sold 15,000 units of Weedban and 28,000 units of Greengrow.

### Required

Prepare a profit and loss account segmented by product lines. Show both amount and percentage columns for the company as a whole and for each of the products.

**E14–2** Time allowed: 20 minutes

Raner, Harris & Chan is a consulting firm that specializes in information systems for medical and dental clinics. The firm has two offices – one in Chicago and one in Minneapolis. The firm classifies the direct costs of consulting jobs as variable costs. A segmented profit and loss account for the company's most recent year follows:

|  |  |  | Segment | | | |
|---|---|---|---|---|---|---|
|  | Total company Amount | % | Chicago Amount | % | Minneapolis Amount | % |
| Sales | £450,000 | 100 | £150,000 | 100 | £300,000 | 100 |
| Less variable expenses | 225,000 | 50 | 45,000 | 30 | 180,000 | 60 |
| Contribution margin | 225,000 | 50 | 105,000 | 70 | 120,000 | 40 |
| Less traceable fixed expenses | 126,000 | 28 | 78,000 | 52 | 48,000 | 16 |
| Office segment margin | 99,000 | 22 | £27,000 | 18 | £72,000 | 24 |
| Less common fixed expenses not traceable to segments | 63,000 | 14 |  |  |  |  |
| Net profit | £36,000 | 8 |  |  |  |  |

### Required

1. By how much would the company's net profit increase if Minneapolis increased its sales by £75,000 per year? Assume no change in cost behaviour patterns.
2. Refer to the original data. Assume that sales in Chicago increase by £50,000 next year and that sales in Minneapolis remain unchanged. Assume no change in fixed costs.
   (a) Prepare a new segmented profit and loss account for the company using the format above. Show both amounts and percentages.

**Part 3** Planning and control

(b) Observe from the profit and loss account you have prepared that the contribution margin ratio for Chicago has remained unchanged at 70% (the same as in the data above) but that the segment margin ratio has changed. How do you explain the change in the segment margin ratio?

**E14–3** Time allowed: 15 minutes

Refer to the data in E14–2. Assume that Minneapolis' sales by major market are:

|  | Minneapolis Amount | % | Segment Medical Amount | % | Dental Amount | % |
|---|---|---|---|---|---|---|
| Sales | £300,000 | 100 | £200,000 | 100 | £100,000 | 100 |
| Less variable expenses | 180,000 | 60 | 128,000 | 64 | 52,000 | 52 |
| Contribution margin | 120,000 | 40 | 72,000 | 36 | 48,000 | 48 |
| Less traceable fixed expenses | 33,000 | 11 | 12,000 | 6 | 21,000 | 21 |
| Product-line segment margin | 87,000 | 29 | £60,000 | 30 | £27,000 | 27 |
| Less common fixed expenses not traceable to segments | 15,000 | 5 |  |  |  |  |
| Divisional segment margin | £72,000 | 24 |  |  |  |  |

The company would like to initiate an intensive advertising campaign in one of the two market segments during the next month. The campaign would cost £5,000. Marketing studies indicate that such a campaign would increase sales in the medical market by £40,000 or increase sales in the dental market by £35,000.

### Required

1. In which of the markets would you recommend that the company focus its advertising campaign? Show computations to support your answer.
2. In E14–2, Minneapolis shows £48,000 in traceable fixed expenses. What happened to the £48,000 in this exercise?

**E14–4** Time allowed: 20 minutes

Wingate Company, a wholesale distributor of videotapes, has been experiencing losses for some time, as shown by its most recent monthly profit and loss account below:

| Sales | £1,000,000 |
|---|---|
| Less variable expense | 390,000 |
| Contribution margin | 610,000 |
| Less fixed expenses | 625,000 |
| Net profit (loss) | £(15,000) |

In an effort to isolate the problem, the managing director has asked for a profit and loss account segmented by division. Accordingly, the Accounting Department has developed the following information:

|  | Division East | Central | West |
|---|---|---|---|
| Sales | £250,000 | £400,000 | £350,000 |
| Variable expenses as a percentage of sales | 52% | 30% | 40% |
| Traceable fixed expenses | £160,000 | £200,000 | £175,000 |

### Required

1. Prepare a profit and loss account segmented by divisions, as desired by the managing director. Show both amount and percentage columns for the company as a whole and for each division.
2. As a result of a marketing study, the managing director believes that sales in the West Division could be increased by 20% if advertising in that division was increased by £15,000 each month. Would you recommend the increased advertising? Show computations.

**E14–5**  Time allowed: 15 minutes

You have a client who operates a large upmarket grocery store that has a full range of departments. The management has encountered difficulty in using accounting data as a basis for decisions as to possible changes in departments operated, products, marketing methods, and so forth. List several overhead costs, or costs not applicable to a particular department, and explain how the existence of such costs (sometimes called *common costs*) complicates and limits the use of accounting data in making decisions in such a store.

(*CPA*, adapted)

**E14–6**  Time allowed: 15 minutes

Selected operating data for two divisions of Outback Brewing Ltd of Australia are given below:

|  | Division | |
|---|---|---|
|  | Queensland | New South Wales |
| Sales | £4,000,000 | £7,000,000 |
| Average operating assets | 2,000,000 | 2,000,000 |
| Net operating profit | 360,000 | 420,000 |
| Property, plant, and equipment (net) | 950,000 | 800,000 |

### Required

1. Compute the rate of return for each division using the return on investment (ROI) formula stated in terms of margin and turnover.
2. As far as you can tell from the data, which divisional manager seems to be doing the better job? Why?

**E14–7**  Time allowed: 15 minutes

Provide the missing data in the following tabulation:

|  | Division | | |
|---|---|---|---|
|  | Alpha | Bravo | Charlie |
| Sales | £? | £11,500,000 | £? |
| Net operating profit | ? | 920,000 | 210,000 |
| Average operating assets | 800,000 | ? | ? |
| Margin | 4% | ? | 7% |
| Turnover | 5 | ? | ? |
| Return on investment (ROI) | ? | 20% | 14% |

## Part 3 Planning and control

**E14–8** Time allowed: 20 minutes

Meiji Isetan Corp. of Japan has two regional divisions with headquarters in Osaka and Yokohama. Selected data on the two divisions follow (in millions of yen, denoted by ¥):

|  | Division | |
| --- | --- | --- |
|  | Osaka | Yokohama |
| Sales | ¥3,000,000 | ¥9,000,000 |
| Net operating profit | 210,000 | 720,000 |
| Average operating assets | 1,000,000 | 4,000,000 |

### Required

1. For each division, compute the return on investment (ROI) in terms of margin and turnover. Where necessary, carry computations to two decimal places.
2. Assume that the company evaluates performance by use of residual profit and that the minimum required return for any division is 15%. Compute the residual profit for each division.
3. Is Yokohama's greater amount of residual profit an indication that it is better managed? Explain.

**E14–9** Time allowed: 30 minutes

Selected sales and operating data for three divisions of a multinational structural engineering firm are given below:

|  | Division | | |
| --- | --- | --- | --- |
|  | Asia | Europe | North America |
| Sales | £12,000,000 | £14,000,000 | £25,000,000 |
| Average operating assets | 3,000,000 | 7,000,000 | 5,000,000 |
| Net operating profit | 600,000 | 560,000 | 800,000 |
| Minimum required rate of return | 14% | 10% | 16% |

### Required

1. Compute the return on investment (ROI) for each division using the formula stated in terms of margin and turnover.
2. Compute the residual income for each division.
3. Assume that each division is presented with an investment opportunity that would yield a 15% rate of return.
   (a) If performance is being measured by ROI, which division or divisions will probably accept the opportunity? Reject? Why?
   (b) If performance is being measured by residual income, which division or divisions will probably accept the opportunity? Reject? Why?

## Problems

**P14–10** Segment reporting
Time allowed: 30 minutes

Vulcan Company's profit and loss account for last month is given below:

|  | Vulcan Company<br>Profit and loss account<br>for the month ended 30 June |
|---|---|
| Sales | £750,000 |
| Less variable expenses | 336,000 |
| Contribution margin | 414,000 |
| Less fixed expenses | 378,000 |
| Net profit | £36,000 |

Management is disappointed with the company's performance and is wondering what can be done to improve profits. By examining sales and cost records, you have determined the following:

1. The company is divided into two sales territories – Northern and Southern. The Northern territory recorded £300,000 in sales and £156,000 in variable expenses during June; the remaining sales and variable expenses were recorded in the Southern territory. Fixed expenses of £120,000 and £108,000 are traceable to the Northern and Southern territories, respectively. The rest of the fixed expenses are common to the two territories.

2. The company sells two products – Paks and Tibs. Sales of Paks and Tibs totalled £50,000 and £250,000, respectively, in the Northern territory during June. Variable expenses are 22% of the selling price for Paks and 58% for Tibs. Cost records show that £30,000 of the Northern territory's fixed expenses are traceable to Paks and £40,000 to Tibs, with the remainder common to the two products.

### Required

1. Prepare segmented profit and loss accounts first showing the total company broken down between sales territories and then showing the Northern territory broken down by product line. Show both amount and percentage columns for the company in total and for each segment.
2. Look at the statement you have prepared showing the total company segmented by sales territory. Which points revealed by this statement should be brought to the attention of management?
3. Look at the statement you have prepared showing the Northern territory segmented by product lines. Which points revealed by this statement should be brought to the attention of management?

**P14-11 Return on investment (ROI) and residual income**
Time allowed: 20 minutes

Financial data for Joel de Paris plc for last year follow:

| Joel de Paris plc<br>Balance sheet | | |
|---|---|---|
| Assets | Ending balance | Beginning balance |
| Cash | £120,000 | £140,000 |
| Debtors | 530,000 | 450,000 |
| Stock | 380,000 | 320,000 |
| Plant and equipment, net | 620,000 | 680,000 |
| Investment in Buisson SA | 280,000 | 250,000 |
| Land (undeveloped) | 170,000 | 180,000 |
| Total assets | £2,100,000 | £2,020,000 |

**606** Part 3 Planning and control

| Liabilities and shareholders' equity |  |  |
|---|---|---|
| Creditors | £310,000 | £360,000 |
| Long-term debt | 1,500,000 | 1,500,000 |
| Shareholders' equity | 290,000 | 160,000 |
| Total liabilities and shareholders' equity | £2,100,000 | £2,020,000 |

| Joel de Paris plc<br>Profit and loss account |  |  |
|---|---|---|
| Sales |  | £4,050,000 |
| Less operating expenses |  | 3,645,000 |
| Net operating profit |  | 405,000 |
| Less interest and taxes: |  |  |
|   Interest expense | £150,000 |  |
|   Tax expense | 110,000 | 260,000 |
| Net profit |  | £145,000 |

The company paid dividends of £15,000 last year. The 'Investment in Buisson', on the balance sheet represents an investment in the shares of another company.

### Required

1. Compute the company's margin, turnover and ROI for last year.
2. The board of directors of Joel de Paris Inc has set a minimum required return of 15%. What was the company's residual income last year?

**P14–12** **Restructuring a segmented statement**
Time allowed: 60 minutes

Losses have been incurred in Millard Company for some time. In an effort to isolate the problem and improve the company's performance, management has requested that the monthly profit and loss account be segmented by sales region. The company's first effort at preparing a segmented statement is given below. This statement is for May, the most recent month of activity.

Cost of goods sold and shipping expense are both variable; other costs are all fixed.

Millard Company is a wholesale distributor of office products. It purchases office products from manufacturers and distributes them in the three regions given above. The three regions are about the same size, and each has its own manager and sales staff. The products that the company distributes vary widely in profitability.

### Required

1. List any disadvantages or weaknesses that you see to the statement format illustrated above.
2. Explain the basis that is apparently being used to allocate the corporate expenses to the regions. Do you agree with these allocations? Explain.
3. Prepare a new segmented profit and loss account for May using the contribution approach. Show a Total column as well as data for each region. Include percentages on your statement for all columns.

|  | Sales region |  |  |
|---|---|---|---|
|  | West | Central | East |
| Sales | £450,000 | £800,000 | £750,000 |
| Less regional expenses (traceable): |  |  |  |
| Cost of goods sold | 162,900 | 280,000 | 376,500 |
| Advertising | 108,000 | 200,000 | 210,000 |
| Salaries | 90,000 | 88,000 | 135,000 |
| Utilities | 13,500 | 12,000 | 15,000 |
| Depreciation | 27,000 | 28,000 | 30,000 |
| Shipping expense | 17,100 | 32,000 | 28,500 |
| Total regional expenses | 418,500 | 640,000 | 795,000 |
| Regional profit (loss) before corporate expenses | 31,500 | 160,000 | (45,000) |
| Less corporate expenses: |  |  |  |
| Advertising (general) | 18,000 | 32,000 | 30,000 |
| General administrative expense | 50,000 | 50,000 | 50,000 |
| Total corporate expenses | 68,000 | 82,000 | 80,000 |
| Net profit (loss) | £(36,500) | £78,000 | £(125,000) |

4   Analyse the statement that you prepared in Question 3 above. Which points that might help to improve the company's performance would you be particularly anxious to bring to the attention of management?

**P14-13 Segment reporting; activity-based cost assignment**
⏱ Time allowed: 60 minutes

Diversified Products plc has recently acquired a small publishing company that Diversified Products intends to operate as one of its investment centres. The newly acquired company has three books that it offers for sale – a cookbook, a travel guide and a handy speller. Each book sells for £10. The publishing company's most recent monthly profit and loss account is given below:

|  |  |  | Product line |  |  |
|---|---|---|---|---|---|
|  | Total company |  | Cookbook | Travel guide | Handy speller |
| Sales | £300,000 | 100% | £90,000 | £150,000 | £60,000 |
| Less expenses: |  |  |  |  |  |
| Printing costs | 102,000 | 34% | 27,000 | 63,000 | 12,000 |
| Advertising | 36,000 | 12% | 13,500 | 19,500 | 3,000 |
| General sales | 18,000 | 6% | 5,400 | 9,000 | 3,600 |
| Salaries | 33,000 | 11% | 18,000 | 9,000 | 6,000 |
| Equipment depreciation | 9,000 | 3% | 3,000 | 3,000 | 3,000 |
| Sales commissions | 30,000 | 10% | 9,000 | 15,000 | 6,000 |
| General administration | 42,000 | 14% | 14,000 | 14,000 | 14,000 |
| Warehouse rent | 12,000 | 4% | 3,600 | 6,000 | 2,400 |
| Depreciation – office facilities | 3,000 | 1% | 1,000 | 1,000 | 1,000 |
| Total expenses | 285,000 | 95% | 94,500 | 139,500 | 51,000 |
| Net profit (loss) | £15,000 | 5% | £(4,500) | £10,500 | £9,000 |

**608** Part 3 Planning and control

The following additional information is available about the company:

1. Only printing costs and sales commissions are variable; all other costs are fixed. The printing costs (which include materials, labour and variable overhead) are traceable to the three product lines as shown in the statement above. Sales commissions are 10% of sales for any product.
2. The same equipment is used to produce all three books, so the equipment depreciation cost has been allocated equally among the three product lines. An analysis of the company's activities indicates that the equipment is used 30% of the time to produce cookbooks, 50% of the time to produce travel guides, and 20% of the time to produce handy spellers.
3. The warehouse is used to store finished units of product, so the rental cost has been allocated to the product lines on the basis of sales. The warehouse rental cost is £3 per square metre per year. The warehouse contains 48,000 square metres of space, of which 7,200 square metres is used by the cookbook line, 24,000 square metres by the travel guide line, and 16,800 square metres by the handy speller line.
4. The general sales cost above includes the salary of the sales manager and other sales costs not traceable to any specific product line. This cost has been allocated to the product lines on the basis of sales pounds.
5. The general administration cost and depreciation of office facilities both relate to overall administration of the company as a whole. These costs have been allocated equally to the three product lines.
6. All other costs are traceable to the three product lines in the amounts shown on the statement above.

The management of Diversified Products plc is anxious to improve the new investment centre's 5% return on sales.

## Required

1. Prepare a new segmented profit and loss account for the month using the contribution approach. Show both an amount column and a percentage column for the company as a whole and for each product line. Adjust allocations of equipment depreciation and of warehouse rent as indicated by the additional information provided.
2. After seeing the profit and loss account in the main body of the problem, management has decided to eliminate the cookbook, since it is not returning a profit, and to focus all available resources on promoting the travel guide.
   (a) Based on the statement you have prepared, do you agree with the decision to eliminate the cookbook? Explain.
   (b) Based on the statement you have prepared, do you agree with the decision to focus all available resources on promoting the travel guide? Explain. (You may assume that an ample market is available for all three product lines.)
3. What additional points would you bring to the attention of management that might help to improve profits?

**P14-14** Return on investment (ROI); comparison of company performance
Time allowed: 30 minutes
Comparative data on three companies in the same industry are given below:

|  | Company A | Company B | Company C |
|---|---|---|---|
| Sales | £600,000 | £500,000 | £? |
| Net operating profit | 84,000 | 70,000 | ? |
| Average operating assets | 300,000 | ? | 1,000,000 |
| Margin | ? | ? | 3.5% |
| Turnover | ? | ? | 2 |
| ROI | ? | 7% | ? |

## Required

1. What advantages can you see in breaking down the ROI computation into two separate elements, margin and turnover?
2. Fill in the missing information above, and comment on the relative performance of the three companies in as much detail as the data permit. Make specific recommendations on steps to be taken to improve the return on investment, where needed.

(Adapted from National Association of Accountants, Research Report No. 35, p. 34)

**P14–15** Return on investment (ROI) and residual income
Time allowed: 30 minutes

'I know headquarters wants us to add on that new product line', said Dell Havasi, manager of Billings Company's Office Products Division. 'But I want to see the numbers before I make any move. Our division has led the company for three years, and I don't want any letdown.'

Billings Company is a decentralized organization with five autonomous divisions. The divisions are evaluated on the basis of the return that they are able to generate on invested assets, with year-end bonuses given to the divisional managers who have the highest ROI figures. Operating results for the company's Office Products Division for the most recent year are given below:

| | |
|---|---|
| Sales | £10,000,000 |
| Less variable expenses | 6,000,000 |
| Contribution margin | 4,000,000 |
| Less fixed expenses | 3,200,000 |
| Net operating profit | £800,000 |
| Divisional operating assets | £4,000,000 |

The company had an overall ROI of 15% last year (considering all divisions). The Office Products Division has an opportunity to add a new product line that would require an additional investment in operating assets of £1,000,000. The cost and revenue characteristics of the new product line per year would be:

| | |
|---|---|
| Sales | £2,000,000 |
| Variable expenses | 60% of sales |
| Fixed expenses | £640,000 |

## Required

1. Compute the Office Products Division's ROI for the most recent year; also compute the ROI as it will appear if the new product line is added.
2. If you were in Dell Havasi's position, would you be inclined to accept or reject the new product line? Explain.
3. Why do you suppose headquarters is anxious for the Office Products Division to add the new product line?
4. Suppose that the company views a return of 12% on invested assets as being the minimum that any division should earn and that performance is evaluated by the residual income approach.
   (a) Compute the Office Products Division's residual income for the most recent year; also compute the residual income as it will appear if the new product line is added.
   (b) Under these circumstances, if you were in Dell Havasi's position, would you accept or reject the new product line? Explain.

## 610 Part 3 Planning and control

### P14-16 Activity-based segment reporting
⏱ Time allowed: 60 minutes

'That commercial market has been dragging us down for years,' complained Shanna Reynolds, managing director of Morley Products. 'Just look at that anaemic profit figure for the commercial market. That market had three million pounds more in sales than the home market, but only a few thousand pounds more in profits. What a loser it is!'

The profit and loss account to which Ms Reynolds was referring follows:

|  | Total company |  | Commercial market | Home market | School market |
|---|---|---|---|---|---|
| Sales | £20,000,000 | 100.0% | £8,000,000 | £5,000,000 | £7,000,000 |
| Less expenses: |  |  |  |  |  |
| Cost of goods sold | 9,500,000 | 47.5% | 3,900,000 | 2,400,000 | 3,200,000 |
| Sales support | 3,600,000 | 18.0% | 1,440,000 | 900,000 | 1,260,000 |
| Order processing | 1,720,000 | 8.6% | 688,000 | 430,000 | 602,000 |
| Warehousing | 940,000 | 4.7% | 376,000 | 235,000 | 329,000 |
| Packing and shipping | 520,000 | 42.6% | 208,000 | 130,000 | 182,000 |
| Advertising | 1,690,000 | 8.5% | 676,000 | 422,500 | 591,500 |
| General management | 1,310,000 | 6.6% | 524,000 | 327,500 | 458,500 |
| Total expenses | 19,280,000 | 96.4% | 7,812,000 | 4,845,000 | 6,623,000 |
| Net profit | £720,000 | 3.6% | £188,000 | £155,000 | £377,000 |

'I agree,' said Walt Divot, the company's deputy managing director. 'We need to focus more of our attention on the school market, since it's our best segment. Maybe that will bolster profits and get the shareholders off our backs.'

The following additional information is available about the company:

1. Morley Products is a wholesale distributor of various goods; the cost of goods sold figures above are traceable to the markets in the amounts shown.
2. Sales support, order processing, and packing and shipping are considered by management to be variable costs. Warehousing, general management and advertising are fixed costs. These costs have all been allocated to the markets on the basis of sales pounds – a practice that the company has followed for years.
3. You have compiled the following data:

|  |  | Amount of activity |  |  |  |
|---|---|---|---|---|---|
| Cost pool and allocation base | Total cost | Total | Commercial market | Home market | School market |
| Sales support (number of calls) | £3,600,000 | 24,000 | 8,000 | 5,000 | 11,000 |
| Order processing (number of orders) | 1,720,000 | 8,600 | 1,750 | 5,200 | 1,650 |
| Warehousing (square metres of space) | 940,000 | 117,500 | 35,000 | 65,000 | 17,500 |
| Packing and shipping (kilos shipped) | 520,000 | 104,000 | 24,000 | 16,000 | 64,000 |

4. You have determined the following breakdown of the company's advertising expense and general management expense:

## Chapter 14 Segment reporting and decentralization

|  | Total | Market Commercial | Home | School |
|---|---|---|---|---|
| Advertising: |  |  |  |  |
| Traceable | £1,460,000 | £700,000 | £180,000 | £580,000 |
| Common | 230,000 |  |  |  |
| General management: |  |  |  |  |
| Traceable – salaries | 410,000 | 150,000 | 120,000 | 140,000 |
| Common | 900,000 |  |  |  |

The company is searching for ways to improve profit, and you have suggested that a segmented statement in which costs are assigned on the basis of activities might provide some useful insights for management.

### Required

1 Refer to the data in (3) above. Determine a rate for each cost pool. Then, using this rate, compute the amount of cost assignable to each market.
2 Using the data from Question 1 above and other data from the problem, prepare a revised segmented statement for the company. Use the contribution format. Show an amount column and a percentage column for the company as a whole and for each market segment. Carry percentage figures to one decimal place. (Remember to include warehousing among the fixed expenses.)
3 What, if anything, in your segmented statement should be brought to the attention of management? Explain.

**P14–17 Multiple segmented profit and loss accounts**
⏱ Time allowed: 60 minutes

Companhia Bradesco SA of Brazil has two divisions. The company's profit and loss account segmented by divisions for last year is given below (the currency in Brazil is the real, denoted here by R):

|  | Total company | Division Plastic | Glass |
|---|---|---|---|
| Sales | R1,500,000 | R900,000 | R600,000 |
| Less variable expenses | 700,000 | 400,000 | 300,000 |
| Contribution margin | 800,000 | 500,000 | 300,000 |
| Less traceable fixed expenses: |  |  |  |
| Advertising | 300,000 | 180,000 | 120,000 |
| Depreciation | 140,000 | 92,000 | 48,000 |
| Administration | 220,000 | 118,000 | 102,000 |
| Total | 660,000 | 390,000 | 270,000 |
| Divisional segment margin | 140,000 | R 110,000 | R 30,000 |
| Less common fixed expenses | 100,000 |  |  |
| Net profit | R 40,000 |  |  |

Top management does not understand why the Glass Division has such a low segment margin when its sales are only one-third less than sales in the Plastics Division. Accordingly, management has directed that the Glass Division be further segmented into product lines. The following information is available on the product lines in the Glass Division:

## 612 Part 3 Planning and control

|  | Glass Division product lines |  |  |
| --- | --- | --- | --- |
|  | Flat glass | Auto glass | Speciality glass |
| Sales | R200,000 | R300,000 | R100,000 |
| Traceable fixed expenses: |  |  |  |
| Advertising | 30,000 | 42,000 | 48,000 |
| Depreciation | 10,000 | 24,000 | 14,000 |
| Administration | 14,000 | 21,000 | 7,000 |
| Variable expenses as a percentage of sales | 65% | 40% | 50% |

Analysis shows that R60,000 of the Glass Division's administration expenses are common to the product lines.

### Required

1. Prepare a segmented profit and loss account for the Glass Division with segments defined as product lines. Use the contribution approach. Show both an amount column and a percentage column for the division in total and for each product line.

2. Management is surprised by Speciality Glass's poor showing and would like to have the product line segmented by market. The following information is available about the two markets in which speciality glass is sold:

|  | Speciality glass markets |  |
| --- | --- | --- |
|  | Domestic | Foreign |
| Sales | R60,000 | R40,000 |
| Traceable fixed expenses: |  |  |
| Advertising | 18,000 | 30,000 |
| Variable expenses as a percentage of sales | 50% | 50% |

3. All of Speciality Glass's depreciation and administration expenses are common to the markets in which the product is sold. Prepare a segmented profit and loss account for Speciality Glass with segments defined as markets. Again use the contribution approach and show both amount and percentage columns.

4. Refer to the statement prepared in Question 1 above. The sales manager wants to run a special promotional campaign on one of the products over the next month. A market study indicates that such a campaign would increase sales of Flat Glass by R40,000 or sales of Auto Glass by R30,000. The campaign would cost R8,000. Show computations to determine which product line should be chosen.

**P14-18** Return on investment (ROI) analysis
Time allowed: 30 minutes

The profit and loss account for Huerra Company for last year is given below:

|  | Total | Unit |
| --- | --- | --- |
| Sales | £4,000,000 | £80.00 |
| Less variable expenses | 2,800,000 | 56.00 |
| Contribution margin | 1,200,000 | 24.00 |
| Less fixed expenses | 840,000 | 16.80 |
| Net operating profit | 360,000 | 7.20 |
| Less profit taxes (30%) | 108,000 | 2.16 |
| Net profit | £252,000 | £5.04 |

The company had average operating assets of £2,000,000 during the year.

### Required

1. Compute the company's ROI for the period using the ROI formula stated in terms of margin and turnover.

    For each of the following questions, indicate whether the margin and turnover will increase, decrease, or remain unchanged as a result of the events described, and then compute the new ROI figure. Consider each question separately, starting in each case from the data used to compute the original ROI in Question 1 above.
2. By use of just-in-time (JIT), the company is able to reduce the average level of inventory by £400,000. (The released funds are used to pay off short-term creditors.)
3. The company achieves a cost savings of £32,000 per year by using less costly materials.
4. The company issues bonds and uses the proceeds to purchase £500,000 in machinery and equipment. Interest on the bonds is £60,000 per year. Sales remain unchanged. The new, more efficient equipment reduces production costs by £20,000 per year.
5. As a result of a more intense effort by salespeople, sales are increased by 20%; operating assets remain unchanged.
6. Obsolete items of inventory carried on the records at a cost of £40,000 are scrapped and written off as a loss since they are unsaleable.
7. The company uses £200,000 of cash (received on debtors) to repurchase and retire some of its common stock.

**P14-19 Return on investment (ROI) and residual income**
Time allowed: 30 minutes

Raddington Industries produces tool and die machinery for manufacturers. The company expanded vertically several years ago by acquiring Reigis Steel Company, one of its suppliers of alloy steel plates. Raddington decided to maintain Reigis' separate identity and therefore established the Reigis Steel Division as one of its investment centres.

Raddington evaluates its divisions on the basis of ROI. Management bonuses are also based on ROI. All investments in operating assets are expected to earn a minimum rate of return of 11%.

Reigis' ROI has ranged from 14% to 17% since it was acquired by Raddington. During the past year, Reigis had an investment opportunity that would yield an estimated rate of return of 13%. Reigis' management decided against the investment because it believed the investment would decrease the division's overall ROI.

Last year's profit and loss account for Reigis Steel Division is given below. The division's operating assets employed were £12,960,000 at the end of the year, which represents an 8% increase over the previous year-end balance.

| Reigis Steel Division<br>Divisional profit and loss account<br>for the year ended 31 December | | |
|---|---|---|
| Sales | | £31,200,000 |
| Cost of goods sold | | 16,500,000 |
| Gross margin | | 14,700,000 |
| Less operating expenses: | | |
| Selling expenses | £5,620,000 | |
| Administrative expenses | 7,208,000 | 12,828,000 |
| Net operating profit | | £1,872,000 |

**614** Part 3 Planning and control

### Required

1. Compute the following performance measures for the Reigis Steel Division:
   (a) ROI. (Remember, ROI is based on the average operating assets, computed from the beginning-of-year and end-of-year balances.) State ROI in terms of margin and turnover.
   (b) Residual profit.
2. Would the management of Reigis Steel Division have been more likely to accept the investment opportunity it had last year if residual profit were used as a performance measure instead of ROI? Explain.
3. The Reigis Steel Division is a separate investment centre within Raddington Industries. Identify the items Reigis must be free to control if it is to be evaluated fairly by either the ROI or residual profit performance measures.

(*CMA*, adapted)

**P14–20** Cost-volume-profit analysis; return on investment (ROI); transfer pricing
Time allowed: 45 minutes

The Valve Division of Bendix plc produces a small valve that is used by various companies as a component part in their products. Bendix plc operates its divisions as autonomous units, giving its divisional managers great discretion in pricing and other decisions. Each division is expected to generate a rate of return of at least 14% on its operating assets. The Valve Division has average operating assets of £700,000. The valves are sold for £5 each. Variable costs are £3 per valve, and fixed costs total £462,000 per year. The division has a capacity of 300,000 valves each year.

### Required

1. How many valves must the Valve Division sell each year to generate the desired rate of return on its assets?
   (a) What is the margin earned at this level of sales?
   (b) What is the turnover at this level of sales?
2. Assume that the Valve Division's current ROI is just equal to the minimum required 14%. In order to increase the division's ROI, the divisional manager wants to increase the selling price per valve by 4%. Market studies indicate that an increase in the selling price would cause sales to drop by 20,000 units each year. However, operating assets could be reduced by £50,000 due to decreased needs for debtors and inventory. Compute the margin, turnover and ROI if these changes are made.
3. Refer to the original data. Assume again that the Valve Division's current ROI is just equal to the minimum required 14%. Rather than increase the selling price, the sales manager wants to reduce the selling price per valve by 4%. Market studies indicate that this would fill the plant to capacity. In order to carry the greater level of sales, however, operating assets would increase by £50,000.
   Compute the margin, turnover and ROI if these changes are made.
4. Refer to the original data. Assume that the normal volume of sales is 280,000 valves each year at a price of £5 per valve. Another division of the company is currently purchasing 20,000 valves each year from an overseas supplier, at a price of £4.25 per valve. The manager of the Valve Division has adamantly refused to meet this price, pointing out that it would result in a loss for his division:

| Selling price per valve | | £4.25 |
|---|---|---|
| Cost per valve: | | |
| Variable | | £3.00 |
| Fixed (£462,000 ÷ 300,000 valves) | 1.54 | 4.54 |
| Net loss per valve | | £(0.29) |

The manager of the Valve Division also points out that the normal £5 selling price barely allows his division the required 14% rate of return. 'If we take on some business at only £4.25 per unit, then our ROI is

## Chapter 14 Segment reporting and decentralization

obviously going to suffer', he reasons, 'and maintaining that ROI figure is the key to my future. Besides, taking on these extra units would require us to increase our operating assets by at least £50,000 due to the larger inventories and receivables we would be carrying.' Would you recommend that the Valve Division sell to the other division at £4.25? Show ROI computations to support your answer.

**P14–21 Segmented statements; product-line analysis**
Time allowed: 90 minutes

'At last, I can see some light at the end of the tunnel', said Steve Adams, managing director of Jelco Products. 'Our losses have shrunk from over £75,000 a month at the beginning of the year to only £26,000 for August. If we can just isolate the remaining problems with products A and C, we'll be in the black by the first of next year.'

The company's profit and loss account for the latest month (August) is presented below (absorption costing basis):

### Jelco Products Profit and loss account for August

|  | Total company | Product A | Product B | Product C |
|---|---|---|---|---|
| Sales | £1,500,000 | £600,000 | £400,000 | £500,000 |
| Less cost of goods sold | 922,000 | 372,000 | 220,000 | 330,000 |
| Gross margins | 578,000 | 228,000 | 180,000 | 170,000 |
| Less operating expenses: |  |  |  |  |
| Selling | 424,000 | 162,000 | 112,000 | 150,000 |
| Administrative | 180,000 | 72,000 | 48,000 | 60,000 |
| Total operating expenses | 604,000 | 234,000 | 160,000 | 210,000 |
| Net profit (loss) | £(26,000) | £(6,000) | £20,000 | £(40,000) |

'What recommendations did that business consultant make?' asked Mr Adams. 'We paid the guy £100 an hour; surely he found something wrong.' 'He says our problems are concealed by the way we make up our statements', replied Sally Warren, the deputy managing director. 'He left us some data on what he calls "traceable" and "common" costs that he says we should be isolating in our reports.' The data to which Ms Warren was referring are shown as follows:

|  | Total company | Product A | Product B | Product C |
|---|---|---|---|---|
| Variable costs:* |  |  |  |  |
| Production (materials, labour, and variable overhead) | – | 18% | 32% | 20% |
| Selling | – | 10% | 8% | 10% |
| Traceable fixed costs: |  |  |  |  |
| Production | £376,000 | £180,000 | £36,000 | £160,000 |
| Selling | 282,000 | 102,000 | 80,000 | 100,000 |
| Common fixed costs: |  |  |  |  |
| Production | 210,000 | – | – | – |
| Administrative | 180,000 | – | – | – |

**616** Part 3 Planning and control

'I don't see anything wrong with our statements', said Mr Adams. 'Bill, our chief accountant, says that he has been using this format for over 30 years. He's also very careful to allocate all of our costs to the products.'

'I'll admit that Bill always seems to be on top of things', replied Ms Warren. 'By the way, purchasing says that the X7 chips we use in products A and B are on back order and won't be available for several weeks. From the looks of August's profit and loss account, we had better concentrate our remaining inventory of X7 chips on product B.' (Two X7 chips are used in both product A and product B.)

The following additional information is available on the company:

1 Work in progress and finished goods inventories are negligible and can be ignored.
2 Products A and B each sell for £250 per unit, and product C sells for £125 per unit. Strong market demand exists for all three products.

### Required

1 Prepare a new profit and loss account for August, segmented by product and using the contribution approach. Show both amount and percentage columns for the company in total and for each product.
2 Assume that Mr Adams is considering the elimination of product C due to the losses it is incurring. Based on the statement you prepared in Question 1 above, what points would you make for or against elimination of product C?
3 Do you agree with the company's decision to concentrate the remaining stock of X7 chips on product B? Why or why not?
4 Product C is sold in both a vending and a home market with sales and cost data as follows:

|  | Total | Market Vending | Market Home |
|---|---|---|---|
| Sales | £500,000 | £50,000 | £450,000 |
| Variable costs:* |  |  |  |
| Production | – | 20% | 20% |
| Selling | – | 28% | 8% |
| Traceable fixed costs: |  |  |  |
| Selling | £75,000 | £45,000 | £30,000 |

*As a percentage of sales.

The remainder of product C's fixed selling costs and all of product C's fixed production costs are common to the markets in which product C is sold.

(a) Prepare a profit and loss account showing product C segmented by market. Use the contribution approach and show both amount and percentage columns for the product in total and for each market.
(b) Which points revealed by this statement would you be particularly anxious to bring to the attention of management?

**P14-22 Decentralization**
Time allowed: 50 minutes

PQR is a company that develops bespoke educational computer software. The company is based in Germany. It has recently acquired two companies: W and Z. W is a well-established company that is also based in Germany. It develops educational computer software and was a direct competitor of PQR. Z, which is based in Malaysia, is a new but rapidly growing company that develops off-the-shelf educational software and also produces CD ROMs. Z was acquired so that it could produce CD ROMs for PQR and W.

Chapter 14 Segment reporting and decentralization

The Managing Director of PQR has now realized that the acquisition of these two companies will cause problems for him in terms of planning, control and decision making. He is thinking of implementing a decentralized structure but is unsure of the advantages and disadvantages of such a structure, of how much autonomy to grant the new companies, and also which performance measure to use to appraise their performance. Consequently he has contacted you, the Finance Director of PQR, for help.

### Required

Write a report to the Managing Director which:

(a) explains the advantages and disadvantages that would be experienced by PQR in operating a decentralized structure;
(b) explains which types of responsibility centres you would recommend as being most appropriate for W and Z in a decentralized structure;
(c) critically evaluates the possible use of the financial performance measures 'return on capital employed' and 'residual income' for the decentralized structure of PQR;
(d) discusses the issues that need to be considered in relation to setting transfer prices for transfers made from Z to PQR and W.

*(CIMA Management Accounting – Decision Making, adapted)*

**P14-23** ROI, RI and NPV
Time allowed: 35 minutes

NCL plc, which has a divisionalized structure, undertakes civil engineering and mining activities. All applications by divisional management teams for funds with which to undertake capital projects require the authorization of the board of directors of NCL plc. Once authorization has been granted to a capital application, divisional management teams are allowed to choose the project for investment.

Under the terms of the management incentive plan, which is currently in operation, the managers of each division are eligible to receive annual bonus payments which are calculated by reference to the return on investment (ROI) earned during each of the first two years by new investments. ROI is calculated using the average capital employed during the year. NCL plc depreciates its investments on a straight-line basis.

One of the most profitable divisions during recent years has been the IOA Division, which is engaged in the mining of precious metals. The management of the IOA Division is currently evaluating three projects relating to the extraction of substance 'xxx' from different areas in its country of operation. The management of the IOA Division has been given approval by the board of directors of NCL plc to spend £24 million on one of the three proposals it is considering (i.e. North, East and South projects).

The following net present value (NPV) calculations have been prepared by the management accountant of the IOA Division.

|  | North Project | | East Project | | South Project | |
| --- | --- | --- | --- | --- | --- | --- |
|  | Net cash inflow/ (outflow) £'000 | Present value at 12% £'000 | Net cash inflow/ (outflow) £'000 | Present value at 12% £'000 | Net cash inflow/ (outflow) £'000 | Present value at 12% £'000 |
| Year 0 | (24,000.0) | (24,000.0) | (24,000.0) | (24,000.0) | (24,000.0) | (24,000.0) |
| Year 1 | 6,000.0 | 5,358.0 | 11,500.0 | 10,269.5 | 12,000.0 | 10,716.0 |
| Year 2 | 8,000.0 | 6,376.0 | 11,500.0 | 9,165.5 | 10,000.0 | 7,970.0 |
| Year 3 | 13,500.0 | 9,612.0 | 11,500.0 | 8,188.0 | 9,000.0 | 6,408.0 |
| Year 4 | 10,500.0 | 6,678.0 | – | – | 3,000.0 | 1,908.0 |
| NPV |  | 4,024.0 |  | 3,623.0 |  | 3,002.0 |

**618** Part 3 Planning and control

The following additional information concerning the three projects is available:

1. Each of the above projects has a nil residual value.
2. The life of the East project is three years. The North and South projects are expected to have a life of four years.
3. The three projects have a similar level of risk.
4. Ignore taxation.

### Required

1. Explain (with relevant calculations) why the interests of the management of the IOA Division might conflict with those of the board of directors of NCL plc.
2. Explain how the adoption of residual income (RI) using the annuity method of depreciation might prove to be a superior basis for the management incentive plan operated by NCL plc. (*Note:* No illustrative calculations should be incorporated into your explanation).

   The IOA Division is also considering whether to undertake an investment in the West of the country (the West Project). An initial cash outlay investment of £12 million will be required and a net cash inflow amounting to £5 million is expected to arise in each of the four years of the life of the project.

   The activities involved in the West project will cause the local river to become polluted and discoloured due to the discharge of waste substances from mining operations.

   It is estimated that at the end of year four a cash outlay of £2 million would be required to restore the river to its original colour. This would also clear 90% of the pollution caused as a result of the mining activities of the IOA Division.

   The remaining 10% of the pollution caused as a result of the mining activities of the IOA Division could be cleared up by a further cash outlay of £2 million.

3. Evaluate the West project and, stating your reasons, comment on whether the board of directors of NCL plc should spend the further £2 million in order to eliminate the remaining 10% of pollution.

(Ignore taxation)
(*ACCA Performance Management*, adapted)

## Cases

**C14-24** **Service organization; segment reporting**
  Time allowed: 75 minutes

Music Teachers is an educational association for music teachers that has 20,000 members. The association operates from a central headquarters but has local membership chapters throughout the United States. Monthly meetings are held by the local chapters to discuss recent developments on topics of interest to music teachers. The association's journal, *Teachers' Forum*, is issued monthly with features about recent developments in the field. The association publishes books and reports and also sponsors professional courses that qualify for continuing professional education credit. The association's statement of revenues and expenses for the current year is presented below.

| Music Teachers | |
|---|---|
| Statement of revenues and expenses for the year ended 30 November | |
| Revenues | $3,275,000 |
| Less expenses: | |
| Salaries | 920,000 |
| Personnel costs | 230,000 |
| Occupancy costs | 280,000 |

| | |
|---|---:|
| Reimbursement of member costs to local chapters | 600,000 |
| Other membership services | 500,000 |
| Printing and paper | 320,000 |
| Postage and shipping | 176,000 |
| Instructors' fees | 80,000 |
| General and administrative | 38,000 |
| Total expenses | 3,144,000 |
| Excess of revenues over expenses | $131,000 |

The board of directors of Music Teachers has requested that a segmented statement of operations be prepared showing the contribution of each profit centre to the association. The association has four profit centres: Membership Division, Magazine Subscriptions Division, Books and Reports Division, and Continuing Education Division. Mike Doyle has been assigned responsibility for preparing the segmented statement, and he has gathered the following data prior to its preparation.

1. Membership dues are $100 per year, of which $20 is considered to cover a one-year subscription to the association's journal. Other benefits include membership in the association and chapter affiliation. The portion of the dues covering the magazine subscription ($20) should be assigned to the Magazine Subscription Division.
2. One-year subscriptions to Teachers' Forum were sold to non-members and libraries at $30 per subscription. A total of 2,500 of these subscriptions were sold last year. In addition to subscriptions, the magazine generated $100,000 in advertising revenues. The costs per magazine subscription were $7 for printing and paper and $4 for postage and shipping.
3. A total of 28,000 technical reports and professional texts were sold by the Books and Reports Division at an average unit selling price of $25. Average costs per publication were $4 for printing and paper and $2 for postage and shipping.
4. The association offers a variety of continuing education courses to both members and non-members. The one-day courses had a tuition cost of $75 each and were attended by 2,400 students. A total of 1,760 students took two-day courses at a tuition cost of $125 for each student. Outside instructors were paid to teach some courses.
5. Salary costs and space occupied by division follow:

| | Salaries | Space occupied (square metres) |
|---|---:|---:|
| Membership | 210,000 | 2,000 |
| Magazine Subscriptions | 150,000 | 2,000 |
| Books and Reports | 300,000 | 3,000 |
| Continuing Education | 180,000 | 2,000 |
| Corporate staff | 80,000 | 1,000 |
| Total | $920,000 | 10,000 |

Personnel costs are 25% of salaries in the separate divisions as well as for the corporate staff. The $280,000 in occupancy costs includes $50,000 in rental cost for a warehouse used by the Books and Reports Division for storage purposes.

6. Printing and paper costs other than for magazine subscriptions and for books and reports relate to the Continuing Education Division.

**Part 3** Planning and control

7 General and administrative expenses include costs relating to overall administration of the association as a whole. The company's corporate staff does some mailing of materials for general administrative purposes.

The expenses that can be traced or assigned to the corporate staff, as well as any other expenses that are not traceable to the profit centres, will be treated as common costs. It is not necessary to distinguish between variable and fixed costs.

### Required

1 Prepare a segmented statement of revenues and expenses for Music Teachers. This statement should show the segment margin for each division as well as results for the association as a whole.
2 Give arguments for and against allocating all costs of the association to the four divisions.

*(CMA, adapted)*

## Endnotes

1 Tully (1993).
2 There is a similar problem with top-level managers as well, as we shall see in Chapter 17.
3 Some companies classify business segments that are responsible mainly for generating revenue, such as an insurance sales office, as revenue centres. Other companies would consider this to be just another type of profit centre, since costs of some kind (salaries, rent, utilities) are usually deducted from the revenues in the segment's profit statement.
4 See Johnson and Kaplan (1987).
5 Emore and Ness (1991) p. 39.
6 Since residual income was developed in the United States, the term 'income' rather than 'profit' is used.
7 The basic idea underlying residual income and economic value added has been around for over 100 years. In recent years, economic value added has been popularized and trademarked by the consulting firm Stern, Stewart & Co.
8 Over 100 different adjustments could be made for deferred taxes, LIFO reserves, provisions for future liabilities, mergers and acquisitions, gains or losses due to changes in accounting rules, operating leases, and other accounts, but most companies make only a few. For further details, see Young and O'Byrne (2001).
9 O'Hanlon and Peasnell (1998).
10 See, for example, Young and O'Byrne (2001)

When you have read this chapter, log on to the Online Learning Centre for *Management Accounting* at www.mcgraw-hill.co.uk/textbooks/seal, where you'll find multiple choice questions, practice exams and extra study tools for each chapter.

# Pricing and Intra-Company Transfers

# CHAPTER 15

# Pricing and intra-company transfers

## LEARNING OBJECTIVES

After studying Chapter 15, you should be able to:

1. Compute the profit-maximizing price using the price elasticity of demand and variable cost
2. Compute the selling price of a product using the absorption costing approach
3. Compute the mark-up percentage under the absorption costing approach
4. Compute the target cost for a new product or service
5. Compute and use the billing rates used in time and material pricing
6. Understand the basics of revenue management in capacity constrained businesses
7. Understand the main issues in transfer pricing in decentralized companies

## CONCEPTS IN CONTEXT

Airlines and hotels are industries with very high fixed costs and 'perishable products'. Since an unfilled seat or empty bedroom is a lost contribution, these industries make use of revenue-maximizing models whereby the price of an airline ticket or a room is altered according to the time of booking relative to departure time or hotel stay. These sectors have learned the importance of altering prices in order to operate at much higher capacities than they would if prices remained fixed.[1]

© Sieto Verver

**Part 3** Planning and control

Some businesses have no pricing problems. They make a product that is in competition with other, identical products for which a market price already exists. Customers will not pay more than this price, and there is no reason for any company to charge less. Under these circumstances, the company simply charges the prevailing market price. Markets for basic raw materials such as farm products and minerals follow this pattern.

In this chapter, we are concerned with the more common situation in which a company is faced with the problem of setting its own prices. Clearly, the pricing decision can be critical. If the price is set too high, customers will avoid purchasing the company's products. If the price is set too low, the company's costs may not be covered.

The usual approach in pricing is to *mark up* cost. A product's **mark-up** is the difference between its selling price and its cost. The mark-up is usually expressed as a percentage of cost. This approach is called **cost-plus pricing** because the predetermined mark-up percentage is applied to the cost base to determine a target selling price.

$$\text{Selling price} = \text{Cost} + (\text{Mark-up percentage} \times \text{Cost})$$

For example, if a company uses a mark-up of 50%, it adds 50% to the costs of its products to determine the selling price. If a product costs £10, then it would charge £15 for the product.

There are two key issues when the cost-plus approach to pricing is used. First, what cost should be used? Second, how should the mark-up be determined? Several alternative approaches are considered in this chapter, starting with the approach generally favoured by economists.

## The economists' approach to pricing

If a company raises the price of a product, unit sales ordinarily fall. Because of this, pricing is a delicate balancing act in which the benefits of higher revenues per unit are traded off against the lower volume that results from charging higher prices. The sensitivity of unit sales to changes in price is called the *price elasticity of demand*.

### Elasticity of demand

A product's price elasticity should be a key element in setting its price. The **price elasticity of demand** measures the degree to which the volume of unit sales for a product or service is affected by a change in price. Demand for a product is said to be *inelastic* if a change in price has little effect on the number of units sold. The demand for designer perfumes sold by trained personnel at cosmetic counters in department stores is relatively inelastic. Lowering prices on these luxury goods has little effect on sales volume; factors other than price are more important in generating sales. On the other hand, demand for a product is said to be *elastic* if a change in price has a substantial effect on the volume of units sold. An example of a product whose demand is elastic is petrol. If a petrol station raises its price for petrol, there will usually be a substantial drop in volume as customers seek lower prices elsewhere.

Price elasticity is very important in determining prices. Managers should set higher mark-ups over cost when customers are relatively insensitive to price (i.e., demand is inelastic) and lower mark-ups when customers are relatively sensitive to price (i.e., demand is elastic). This principle is followed in department stores. Merchandise sold in the bargain basement has a much lower mark-up than merchandise sold elsewhere in the store because customers who shop in the bargain basement are much more sensitive to price (i.e., demand is elastic).

The price elasticity of demand for a product or service, $\varepsilon_d$, can be estimated using the following formula.[2]

$$\varepsilon_d = \frac{\ln(1 + \%\,\text{change in quantity sold})}{\ln(1 + \%\,\text{change in price})}$$

For example, suppose that the managers of Nature's Garden believe that every 10% increase in the selling price of their apple-almond shampoo would result in a 15% decrease in the number of bottles of shampoo sold.[3] The price elasticity of demand for this product would be computed as follows:

$$\varepsilon_d = \frac{\ln(1 + (-0.15))}{\ln(1 + (0.10))} = \frac{\ln(0.85)}{\ln(1.10)} = -1.71$$

For comparison purposes, the managers of Nature's Garden believe that another product, strawberry glycerine soap, would experience a 20% drop in unit sales if its price were increased by 10%. (Purchasers of this product are more sensitive to price than the purchasers of the apple-almond shampoo.) The price elasticity of demand for the strawberry glycerine soap is:

$$\varepsilon_d = \frac{\ln(1 + (-0.20))}{\ln(1 + (0.10))} = \frac{\ln(0.80)}{\ln(1.10)} = -2.34$$

Both of these products, like other products, have a price elasticity that is less than –1. Note also that the price elasticity of demand for the strawberry glycerine soap is larger (in absolute value) than the price elasticity of demand for the apple-almond shampoo. The more sensitive customers are to price, the larger (in absolute value) is the price elasticity of demand. In other words, a larger (in absolute value) price elasticity of demand indicates a product whose demand is more elastic.

In the next subsection, the price elasticity of demand will be used to compute the selling price that maximizes the profits of the company.

## The profit-maximizing price

Under certain conditions, it can be shown that the *profit-maximizing price* can be determined by marking up *variable cost* using the following formula:[4]

$$\text{Profit-maximizing mark-up on variable cost} = \left(\frac{\varepsilon_d}{1 + \varepsilon_d}\right) - 1$$

Using the above mark-up is equivalent to setting the selling price using this formula:

$$\text{Profit-maximizing price on variable cost} = \left(\frac{\varepsilon_d}{1 + \varepsilon_d}\right) \text{Variable cost per unit}$$

The profit-maximizing prices for the two Nature's Garden products are computed below using these formulas:

|  | Apple-almond shampoo | Strawberry glycerine soap |
|---|---|---|
| Price elasticity of demand ($\varepsilon_d$) | –1.71 | –2.34 |
| Profit-maximizing mark-up on variable cost (a) | $\left(\frac{-1.71}{-1.71+1}\right) - 1$ | $\left(\frac{-2.34}{-2.34+1}\right) - 1$ |
|  | = 2.41 – 1 = 1.41 | = 1.75 – 1 = 0.75 |
|  | or 141% | or 75% |
| Variable cost per unit – given (b) | £2.00 | £0.40 |
| Mark-up, (a) × (b) | 2.82 | 0.30 |
| Profit-maximizing price | £4.82 | £0.70 |

Note that the 75% mark-up for the strawberry glycerine soap is lower than the 141% mark-up for the apple-almond shampoo. The reason for this is that purchasers of strawberry glycerine soap are more sensitive to

### 624 Part 3 Planning and control

price than the purchasers of apple-almond shampoo. This could be because strawberry glycerine soap is a relatively common product with close substitutes available in nearly every grocery store.

Exhibit 15.1 shows how the profit-maximizing mark-up is affected by how sensitive unit sales are to price. For example, if a 10% increase in price leads to a 20% decrease in unit sales, then the optimal mark-up on variable cost according to the exhibit is 75% – the figure computed above for the strawberry glycerine soap. Note that the optimal mark-up drops as unit sales become more sensitive to price.

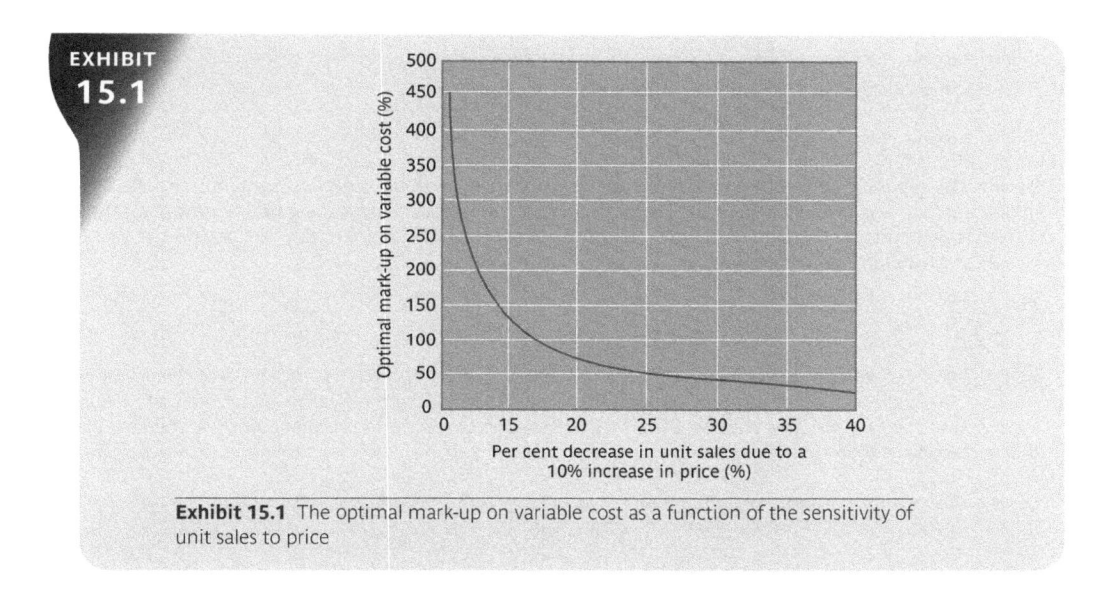

**EXHIBIT 15.1**

[Graph: Optimal mark-up on variable cost (%) on y-axis from 0 to 500; Per cent decrease in unit sales due to a 10% increase in price (%) on x-axis from 0 to 40, showing a decreasing curve.]

**Exhibit 15.1** The optimal mark-up on variable cost as a function of the sensitivity of unit sales to price

Caution is advised when using these formulas to establish a selling price. The assumptions underlying the formulas are probably not completely true, and the estimate of the percentage change in unit sales that would result from a given percentage change in price is likely to be inexact. Nevertheless, the formulas can provide valuable clues regarding whether prices should be increased or decreased. Suppose, for example, that the strawberry glycerine soap is currently being sold for £0.60 per bar. The formula indicates that the profit-maximizing price is £0.70 per bar. Rather than increasing the price by £0.10, it would be prudent to increase the price by a more modest amount to observe what happens to unit sales and to profits.

The formula for the profit-maximizing price also conveys a very important lesson. The optimal selling price should depend on two factors – the variable cost per unit and how sensitive unit sales are to changes in price. In particular, fixed costs play no role in setting the optimal price. If the total fixed costs are the same whether the company charges £0.60 or £0.70, they cannot be relevant in the decision of which price to charge for the soap. Fixed costs are relevant when deciding whether to offer a product but are not relevant when deciding how much to charge for the product.

Incidentally, we can directly verify that an increase in selling price for the strawberry glycerine soap from the current price of £0.60 per bar is warranted, based just on the forecast that a 10% increase in selling price would lead to a 20% decrease in unit sales. Suppose, for example, that Nature's Garden is currently selling 200,000 bars of the soap per year at the price of £0.60 a bar. If the change in price has no effect on the company's fixed costs or on other products, the effect on profits of increasing the price by 10% can be computed as follows:

|  | Present price | Higher price |
| --- | --- | --- |
| Selling price | £0.60 | £0.60 + (0.10 × £0.60) |
|  |  | = £0.66 |
| Unit sales | 200,000 | 200,000 − (0.20 × 200,000) |
|  |  | = 160,000 |
| Sales | £120,000 | £105,600 |
| Variable cost | 80,000 | 64,000 |
| Contribution margin | £40,000 | £41,600 |

Despite the apparent optimality of prices based on marking up variable costs according to the price elasticity of demand, surveys consistently reveal that most managers approach the pricing problem from a completely different perspective. They prefer to mark up some version of full, not variable, costs, and the mark-up is based on desired profits rather than on factors related to demand.

## LEARNING OBJECTIVE 2: The absorption costing approach to cost-plus pricing

The absorption costing approach to cost-plus pricing differs from the economists' approach both in what costs are marked up and in how the mark-up is determined. Under the absorption approach to cost-plus pricing, the cost base is the absorption costing unit product cost as defined in Chapters 2, 3 and 4 rather than variable cost.

---

### FOCUS ON PRACTICE

#### Dynamic pricing in the hospitality industry

In a recent CIMA funded study on management accounting practices in the hospitality industry in which one of the authors participated, the researchers noted that most of the management accounting innovation revolved around *revenue* management rather than *cost* management. The cases illustrated some issues. First, dynamic pricing can conflict with good customer relationship practice as prices depend on *when* you book rather than 'who you are'. Secondly, new businesses may have difficulty in setting up a yield management model because newcomers lack the historical data on which to forecast demand. Thirdly, in contrast to the received wisdom, practitioners were familiar with and drew upon economic concepts such as price elasticities. New information management systems which analysed bookings and related them to rate control, as well as the availability of price data from the internet and benchmarking organizations, enabled managers to derive optimal benefit from yield management.

**Exercise**: The influence of the internet in the hotel industry is double-edged – customers find it easier to compare prices and products – at the same time, managers can access rich real time data sets on which to base their room rates. Discuss.

---

### Setting a target selling price using the absorption costing approach

To illustrate, let us assume that the management of Ritter Company wants to set the selling price on a product that has just undergone some design modifications. The Accounting Department has provided cost estimates for the redesigned product as shown below:

**Part 3** Planning and control

|  | Per unit | Total |
|---|---|---|
| Direct materials | £6 |  |
| Direct labour | 4 |  |
| Variable manufacturing overhead | 3 |  |
| Fixed manufacturing overhead | – | £70,000 |
| Variable selling, general and administrative expenses | 2 |  |
| Fixed selling, general and administrative expenses | – | 60,000 |

The first step in the absorption costing approach to cost-plus pricing is to compute the unit product cost. For Ritter Company, this amounts to £20 per unit at a volume of 10,000 units, as computed below:

| | |
|---|---|
| Direct materials | £6 |
| Direct labour | 4 |
| Variable manufacturing overhead | 3 |
| Fixed manufacturing overhead (£70,000 ÷ 10,000 units) | 7 |
| Unit product cost | £20 |

Ritter Company has a general policy of marking up unit product costs by 50%. A price quotation sheet for the company prepared using the absorption approach is presented in Exhibit 15.2. Note that selling, general and administrative (SG&A) costs are not included in the cost base. Instead, the mark-up is supposed to cover these expenses. Let us see how some companies compute these mark-up percentages.

**EXHIBIT 15.2**

| | |
|---|---|
| Direct materials | £6 |
| Direct labour | 4 |
| Variable manufacturing overhead | 3 |
| Fixed manufacturing overhead (£70,000 ÷ 10,000 units) | 7 |
| Unit product cost | 20 |
| Mark-up to cover selling, general and administrative expenses and desired profit – 50% of unit manufacturing costs | 10 |
| Target selling price | £30 |

**Exhibit 15.2** Price quotation sheet – absorption basis (10,000 units)

## Determining the mark-up percentage

**LEARNING OBJECTIVE 3**

How did Ritter Company arrive at its mark-up percentage of 50%? This figure could be a widely used rule of thumb in the industry or just a company tradition that seems to work. The mark-up percentage may also be the result of an explicit computation.

As we have discussed, the mark-up over cost ideally should be largely determined by market conditions. However, a popular approach is to at least start with a mark-up based on cost and desired profit. The reasoning

## Chapter 15 Pricing and intra-company transfers

goes like this. The mark-up must be large enough to cover SG&A expenses and provide an adequate return on investment (ROI). Given the forecasted unit sales, the mark-up can be computed as follows:

$$\text{Mark-up percentage on absorption cost} = \frac{(\text{Required ROI} \times \text{Investment}) + \text{SG \& A expenses}}{\text{Unit sales} \times \text{Unit product cost}}$$

To show how the formula above is applied, assume Ritter Company must invest £100,000 to produce and market 10,000 units of the product each year. The £100,000 investment covers purchase of equipment and funds needed to carry stocks and debtors. If Ritter Company requires a 20% ROI, then the mark-up for the product would be determined as follows:

$$\text{Mark-up percentage on absorption cost} = \frac{(20\% \times 100,000) + (£2 \times 10,000 + £60,000)}{10,000 \times £20}$$

$$\text{Mark-up percentage on absorption cost} = \frac{(£20,000) + (£80,000)}{£200,000} = 50\%$$

As shown earlier, this mark-up of 50% leads to a target selling price of £30 for Ritter Company. As shown in Exhibit 15.3, *if the company actually sells 10,000 units* of the product at this price, the company's ROI on this product will indeed be 20%. If it turns out that more than 10,000 units are sold at this price, the ROI will be greater than 20%. If less than 10,000 units are sold, the ROI will be less than 20%. *The required ROI will be attained only if the forecasted unit sales volume is attained.*

### EXHIBIT 15.3

| | |
|---|---:|
| Direct materials | £6 |
| Direct labour | 4 |
| Variable manufacturing overhead | 3 |
| Fixed manufacturing overhead (£70,000 ÷ 10,000 units) | 7 |
| Unit product cost | £20 |

**Ritter Company Absorption costing profit statement**

| | |
|---|---:|
| Sales (£30 × 10,000 units) | £300,000 |
| Less cost of goods sold (£20 × 10,000 units) | 200,000 |
| Gross margin | 100,000 |
| Less selling, general and administration expenses (£2 × 10,000 units + £60,000) | 80,000 |
| Net operating profit | £20,000 |

ROI

$$\text{ROI} = \frac{\text{Net operating profit}}{\text{Average operating assets}}$$

$$= \frac{£20,000}{£100,000}$$

$$= 20\%$$

**Exhibit 15.3** Profit statement and ROI analysis – Ritter Company actual unit sales = 10,000 units; selling price = £30

**Part 3** Planning and control

## Problems with the absorption costing approach

Using the absorption costing approach, the pricing problem looks deceptively simple. All you have to do is compute your unit product cost, decide how much profit you want, and then set your price. It appears that you can ignore demand and arrive at a price that will safely yield whatever profit you want. However, as noted above, the absorption costing approach relies on a forecast of unit sales. Neither the mark-up nor the unit product cost can be computed without such a forecast.

The absorption costing approach essentially assumes that customers *need* the forecasted unit sales and will pay whatever price the company decides to charge. However, customers have a choice. If the price is too high, they can buy from a competitor or they may choose not to buy at all. Suppose, for example, that when Ritter Company sets its price at £30, it sells only 7,000 units rather than the 10,000 units forecasted. As shown in Exhibit 15.4, the company would then have a loss of £25,000 on the product instead of a profit of £20,000. Some managers believe that the absorption costing approach to pricing is safe. This is an illusion. The absorption costing approach is safe only as long as customers choose to buy at least as many units as managers forecasted they would buy.

**EXHIBIT 15.4**

| | |
|---|---:|
| Direct materials | £6 |
| Direct labour | 4 |
| Variable manufacturing overhead | 3 |
| Fixed manufacturing overhead (£70,000 ÷ 7,000 units) | 10 |
| Unit product cost | £23 |

**Ritter Company Absorption costing profit statement**

| | |
|---|---:|
| Sales (£30 × 7,000 units) | £210,000 |
| Less cost of goods sold (£23 × 7,000 units) | 161,000 |
| Gross margin | 49,000 |
| Less selling, general and administration expenses (£2 × 10,000 units + £60,000) | 74,000 |
| Net operating profit | £(25,000) |

ROI

$$ROI = \frac{\text{Net operating profit}}{\text{Average operating assets}}$$

$$= \frac{(£25,000)}{£100,000}$$

$$= -25\%$$

**Exhibit 15.4** Profit statement and ROI analysis – Ritter Company actual unit sales = 7,000 units; selling price = £30

## Target costing

Our discussion thus far has presumed that a product has already been developed, has been costed, and is ready to be marketed as soon as a price is set. In many cases, the sequence of events is just the reverse. That is, the company will already *know* what price should be charged, and the problem will be to *develop* a product that can be marketed profitably at the desired price. Even in this situation, where the normal sequence of events is reversed, cost is still a crucial factor. The company's approach will be to employ *target costing*. **Target costing** is the process of determining the maximum allowable cost for a new product and then developing a prototype that can be profitably made for that maximum target cost figure. Many companies use target costing, including Compaq, Cummins Engine, Daihatsu Motors, Ford, Isuzu Motors, ITT Automotive, Komatsu, Matsushita Electric, Mitsubishi Kasei, NEC, Nippondenso, Nissan, Olympus, Sharp, Texas Instruments and Toyota.

The target costing approach was developed in recognition that many companies have less control over price than they would like to think. The market (i.e., supply and demand) really determines prices, and a company that attempts to ignore this does so at its peril. Therefore, the anticipated market price is taken as a given in target costing. Second, as we shall see in Chapters 16 and 19, target costing is more than just an approach to pricing – it takes a *strategic approach to cost management* by linking a whole series of organizational functions such as marketing, design, production and procurement.

The target cost for a product is computed by starting with the product's anticipated selling price and then deducting the desired profit, as follows:

$$\text{Target cost} = \text{Anticipated selling price} - \text{Desired profit}$$

The product development team is given the responsibility of designing the product so that it can be made for no more than the target cost.

### An example of target costing

To provide a simple numerical example of target costing, assume the following situation: Handy Appliance Company feels that there is a market niche for a hand mixer with certain new features. Surveying the features and prices of hand mixers already on the market, the Marketing Department believes that a price of £30 would be about right for the new mixer. At that price, Marketing estimates that 40,000 of the new mixers could be sold annually. To design, develop, and produce these new mixers, an investment of £2,000,000 would be required. The company desires a 15% ROI. Given these data, the target cost to manufacture, sell, distribute, and service one mixer is £22.50 as shown below.

| | |
|---|---:|
| Projected sales (40,000 mixers × £30) | £1,200,000 |
| Less desired profit (15% × £2,000,000) | 300,000 |
| Target cost for 40,000 mixers | £900,000 |
| Target cost per mixer (£900,000/40,000 mixers) | £22.50 |

This £22.50 target cost would be broken down into target costs for the various functions: manufacturing, marketing, distribution, after-sales service, and so on. Each functional area would be responsible for keeping its actual costs within target.

## Service companies – time and material pricing

**LEARNING OBJECTIVE 5**

Some companies – particularly in service industries – use a variation on cost-plus pricing called **time and material pricing**. Under this method, two pricing rates are established – one based on direct labour time and the other based on the cost of direct material used. This pricing method is widely used in repair shops, in printing shops, and by many professionals such as doctors and dentists. The time and material rates are usually market-determined. In other words, the rates are determined by the interplay of supply and demand and by competitive conditions in the industry. However, some companies set the rates using a process similar to the process followed in the absorption costing approach to cost-plus pricing. In this case, the rates include allowances for selling, general and administrative expenses; for other direct and indirect costs; and for a desired profit. This section will show how the rates might be set using the cost-plus approach.

### Time component

The time component is typically expressed as a rate per hour of labour. The rate is computed by adding together three elements: (1) the direct costs of the employee, including salary and fringe benefits; (2) a pro rata allowance for selling, general and administrative expenses of the organization; and (3) an allowance for a desired profit per hour of employee time. In some organizations (such as a repair shop), the same hourly

## Material component

The material component is determined by adding a **material loading charge** to the invoice price of any materials used on the job. The material loading charge is designed to cover the costs of ordering, handling and carrying materials in stock, plus a profit margin on the materials themselves.

## An example of time and material pricing

To provide a numerical example of time and material pricing, assume the following data.

The Quality Auto Shop uses time and material pricing for all of its repair work. The following costs have been budgeted for the coming year:

|  | Repairs | Parts |
|---|---|---|
| Mechanics' wages | £300,000 | £ – |
| Service manager – salary | 40,000 | – |
| Parts manager – salary | – | 36,000 |
| Clerical assistant – salary | 18,000 | 15,000 |
| Pensions and insurance – 16% of salaries and wages | 57,280 | 8,160 |
| Supplies | 720 | 540 |
| Utilities | 36,000 | 20,800 |
| Property taxes | 8,400 | 1,900 |
| Depreciation | 91,600 | 37,600 |
| Invoice cost of parts used | – | 400,000 |
| Total budgeted cost | £552,000 | £520,000 |

The company expects to bill customers for 24,000 hours of repair time. A profit of £7 per hour of repair time is considered to be feasible, given the competitive conditions in the market. For parts, the competitive mark-up on the invoice cost of parts used is 15%.

Exhibit 15.5 shows the computation of the billing rate and the material loading charge to be used over the next year. Note that the billing rate, or time component, is £30 per hour of repair time and the material loading charge is 45% of the invoice cost of parts used. Using these rates, a repair job that requires 4.5 hours of mechanics time and £200 in parts would be billed as follows:

| | | |
|---|---:|---:|
| Labour time: 4.5 hours × £30 | | £135 |
| Parts used: | | |
|   Invoice cost | £200 | |
|   Material loading charge: 45% × £200 | 90 | 290 |
| Total price of the job | | £425 |

## EXHIBIT 15.5

| | Time component: repairs | | Parts: material loading charge | |
|---|---|---|---|---|
| | Total | Per hour* | Total | Percent† |
| Cost of mechanics' time: | | | | |
|   Mechanics' wages | £300,000 | | | |
|   Retirement and insurance (16% of wages) | 48,000 | | | |
|   Total cost | 348,000 | £14.50 | | |
| For repairs – other cost of repair service. | | | | |
| For parts – costs of ordering, handling and storing parts: | | | | |
|   Repairs service manager – salary | 40,000 | | £– | |
|   Parts manager – salary | – | | 36,000 | |
|   Clerical assistant – salary | 18,000 | | 15,000 | |
|   Retirement and insurance (16% of salaries) | 9,280 | | 8,160 | |
|   Supplies | 720 | | 540 | |
|   Utilities | 36,000 | | 20,800 | |
|   Property taxes | 8,400 | | 1,900 | |
|   Depreciation | 91,600 | | 37,600 | |
|   Total cost | 204,000 | 8.50 | 120,000 | 30% |
| Desired profit: | | | | |
|   24,000 hours × £7 | 168,000 | 7.00 | | |
|   15% × £400,000 | – | | 60,000 | 15% |
| Total amount to be billed | £720,000 | £30.00 | £180,000 | 45% |

*Based on 24,000 hours.
†Based on £400,000 invoice cost of parts. The charge for ordering, handling and storing parts, for example, is computed as follows: £120,000 cost ÷ £400,000 invoice cost = 30%.

**Exhibit 15.5** Time and material pricing

Rather than using labour-hours as the basis for computing the time rate, a machine shop, a printing shop or a similar organization might use machine-hours.

This method of setting prices is a variation of the absorption costing approach. As such, it is not surprising that it suffers from the same problem. Customers may not be willing to pay the rates that have been computed. If actual business is less than the forecasted 24,000 hours and £400,000 worth of parts, the profit objectives will not be met and the company may not even break even.

### LEARNING OBJECTIVE 6

## Revenue and yield management

Some industries such as hotels and airlines are characterized by high fixed costs and perishability. The capacity of a plane or a hotel is fixed in the short run. Furthermore, an empty bedroom at night or an empty seat in a plane that has taken off represent a sale that is lost forever. Ideally, hotel managers would like to sell all rooms at the highest (rack) rate but they know that there is a trade-off between high occupancy and high room rates. The problem becomes one of determining how much to sell, at what price

## Part 3 Planning and control

and to which market segment, so as to maximize revenue. The resolution lies in control over rates (being price restrictive if demand is high and more flexible if it low) and restrictions to occupancy (blocking of rooms in advance) in order to maximize overall gross revenue per period of time. These are the principles behind the technique of *yield management*. **Yield management (YM)** is a practice of achieving high capacity utilization through varying prices according to market segments and time of booking.[5]

To use YM, a hotel must know its market segments and why guests need to stay and develop appropriate marketing strategies for each market segment. To ensure the optimization of the total revenues from the room stock of a group of hotels, for example, and to allow access to its demand history, a centralized reservations system is needed. There should be some return from linking YM systems to marketing expenditure plans. For example, predicted periods of low demand from YM team meetings can trigger the need to advertise short-break packages. The overall effectiveness of a YM system is dependent on the implementation of the following market-focused principles: identification of a customer base using a detailed segmentation strategy; developing an awareness of customers' changing needs and expectations; estimating the price elasticity of demand per market segment; responsiveness of management to cope with changing market conditions; and accurate historical demand analysis, combined with a reliable forecasting method. The key performance metric in this model is the *yield percentage*:

$$\text{Yield percentage} = \frac{\text{Actual revenue}}{\text{Maximum potential revenue}} \times 100$$

The **yield percentage** will depend on the average price × the number of units sold (hotel rooms, airline seats). The maximum potential revenue is a full hotel or plane charging the maximum price.[6]

## Transfer pricing

There are special problems in evaluating pricing goods or services transferred from one division/segment of a company to another. The problems revolve around the question of what transfer price to charge between the segments. A **transfer price** is the price charged when one segment of a company provides goods or services to another segment of the company. For example, most companies in the oil industry, such as BP, Exxon, Shell and Texaco, have petroleum refining and retail sales divisions that are evaluated on the basis of ROI or residual income. The petroleum refining division processes crude oil into petrol, kerosene, lubricants and other end products. The retail sales division takes petrol and other products from the refining division and sells them through the company's chain of service stations. Each product has a price for transfers within the company. Suppose the transfer price for petrol is £0.80 a litre. Then the refining division gets credit for £0.80 a litre of revenue on its segment report and the retailing division must deduct £0.80 a litre as an expense on its segment report. Clearly, the refining division would like the transfer price to be as high as possible, whereas the retailing division would like the transfer price to be as low as possible. However, the transaction has no direct effect on the entire company's reported profit. It is like taking money out of one pocket and putting it into the other.

Managers are intensely interested in how transfer prices are set, since they can have a dramatic effect on the apparent profitability of a division. Three common approaches are used to set transfer prices:

1. Allow the managers involved in the transfer to negotiate their own transfer price.
2. Set transfer prices at cost using:
   (a) Variable cost.
   (b) Full (absorption) cost.
3. Set transfer prices at the market price.

We will consider each of these transfer pricing methods in turn, beginning with negotiated transfer prices. Throughout the discussion we should keep in mind that *the fundamental objective in setting transfer prices is to motivate the managers to act in the best interests of the overall company*. In contrast, **sub-optimization** occurs when managers do not act in the best interests of the overall company or even in the best interests of their own segment.

## Negotiated transfer prices

A **negotiated transfer price** is a transfer price that is agreed on between the selling and purchasing divisions. Negotiated transfer prices have several important advantages. First, this approach preserves the autonomy of the divisions and is consistent with the spirit of decentralization. Second, the managers of the divisions are likely to have much better information about the potential costs and benefits of the transfer than others in the company.

When negotiated transfer prices are used, the managers who are involved in a proposed transfer within the company meet to discuss the terms and conditions of the transfer. They may decide not to go through with the transfer, but if they do, they must agree to a transfer price. Generally speaking, we cannot predict the exact transfer price they will agree to. However, we can confidently predict two things: (1) the selling division will agree to the transfer only if the profits of the selling division increase as a result of the transfer, and (2) the purchasing division will agree to the transfer only if the profits of the purchasing division also increase as a result of the transfer. This may seem obvious, but it is an important point.

Clearly, if the transfer price is below the selling division's cost, a loss will occur on the transaction and the selling division will refuse to agree to the transfer. Likewise, if the transfer price is set too high, it will be impossible for the purchasing division to make any profit on the transferred item. For any given proposed transfer, the transfer price has both a lower limit (determined by the situation of the selling division) and an upper limit (determined by the situation of the purchasing division). The actual transfer price agreed to by the two division managers can fall anywhere between those two limits. These limits determine the **range of acceptable transfer prices** – the range of transfer prices within which the profits of both divisions participating in a transfer would increase.

An example will help us to understand negotiated transfer prices. Harris & Louder Ltd owns fast-food restaurants and snack food and beverage manufacturers in the United Kingdom. One of the restaurants, Pizza Maven, serves a variety of beverages along with pizzas. One of the beverages is ginger beer, which is served on tap. Harris & Louder has just purchased a new division, Imperial Beverages, that produces ginger beer. The managing director of Imperial Beverages has approached the managing director of Pizza Maven about purchasing Imperial Beverages' ginger beer for sale at Pizza Maven restaurants rather than its usual brand of ginger beer. Managers at Pizza Maven agree that the quality of Imperial Beverages' ginger beer is comparable to the quality of their regular brand. It is just a question of price. The basic facts are listed below:

| Imperial Beverages: | |
|---|---|
| Ginger beer production capacity per month | 10,000 barrels |
| Variable cost per barrel of ginger beer | £8 per barrel |
| Fixed costs per month | £70,000 |
| Selling price of Imperial Beverages' ginger beer on outside market | £20 per barrel |
| Pizza Maven: | |
| Purchase price of regular brand of ginger beer | £18 per barrel |
| Monthly consumption of ginger beer | 2,000 barrels |

### The selling division's lowest acceptable transfer price

The selling division, Imperial Beverages, will be interested in a proposed transfer only if its profit increases. Clearly, the transfer price must not fall below the variable cost per barrel of £8. In addition, if Imperial Beverages has insufficient capacity to fill the Pizza Maven order, then it would have to give up some of its regular sales. Imperial Beverages would expect to be compensated for the contribution margin on these lost sales. In sum, if the transfer has no effect on fixed costs, then from the selling division's standpoint, the transfer price must cover both the variable costs of producing the transferred units and any opportunity costs from lost sales.

**Seller's perspective:**

$$\text{Transfer price} \geq \text{Variable cost per unit} + \frac{\text{Total contribution margin on lost sales}}{\text{Number of units transferred}}$$

### The purchasing division's highest acceptable transfer price

The purchasing division, Pizza Maven, will be interested in the proposal only if its profit increases. In cases like this where a purchasing division has an outside supplier, the purchasing division's decision is simple. Buy from the inside supplier if the price is less than the price offered by the outside supplier.

**Purchaser's perspective:**

$$\text{Transfer price} \leq \text{Cost of buying from outside supplier}$$

We will consider several different hypothetical situations and see what the range of acceptable transfer prices would be in each situation.

### Selling division with idle capacity

Suppose that Imperial Beverages has sufficient idle capacity to satisfy the demand for ginger beer from Pizza Maven without cutting into sales of ginger beer to its regular customers. To be specific, let's suppose that Imperial Beverages is selling only 7,000 barrels of ginger beer a month on the outside market. That leaves unused capacity of 3,000 barrels a month – more than enough to satisfy Pizza Maven's requirement of 2,000 barrels a month. What range of transfer prices, if any, would make both divisions better off with the transfer of 2,000 barrels a month?

1. The selling division, Imperial Beverages, will be interested in the proposal only if:

$$\text{Transfer price} \geq \text{Variable cost per unit} + \frac{\text{Total contribution margin on lost sales}}{\text{Number of units transferred}}$$

   Since Imperial Beverages has ample idle capacity, there are no lost outside sales. And since the variable cost per unit is £8, the lowest acceptable transfer price as far as the selling division is concerned is also £8.

$$\text{Transfer price} \geq £8 + \frac{£0}{2,000} = £8$$

2. The purchasing division, Pizza Maven, can buy similar ginger beer from an outside vendor for £18. Therefore, Pizza Maven would be unwilling to pay more than £18 per barrel for Imperial Beverages' ginger beer.

$$\text{Transfer price} \leq \text{Cost of buying from outside supplier} = £18$$

3. Combining the requirements of both the selling division and the purchasing division, the acceptable range of transfer prices in this situation is:

$$£8 \leq \text{Transfer price} \leq £18$$

Assuming that the managers understand their own businesses and that they are co-operative, they should be able to agree on a transfer price within this range.

### Selling division with no idle capacity

Suppose that Imperial Beverages has no idle capacity; it is selling 10,000 barrels of ginger beer a month on the outside market at £20 per barrel. To fill the order from Pizza Maven, Imperial Beverages would have to divert 2,000 barrels from its regular customers. What range of transfer prices, if any, would make both divisions better off transferring the 2,000 barrels within the company?

1. The selling division, Imperial Beverage, will be interested in the proposal only if:

$$\text{Transfer price} \geq \text{Variable cost per unit} + \frac{\text{Total contribution margin on lost sales}}{\text{Number of units transferred}}$$

Since Imperial Beverage has no idle capacity, there *are* lost outside sales. The contribution margin per barrel on these outside sales is £12 (£20 – £8).

$$\text{Transfer price} \geq £8 + \frac{(20 - £8) \times 2{,}000}{2{,}000} = £8 + (£20 - £8) = £20$$

Thus, as far as the selling division is concerned, the transfer price must at least cover the revenue on the lost sales, which is £20 per barrel. This makes sense since the cost of producing the 2,000 barrels is the same whether they are sold on the inside market or on the outside. The only difference is that the selling division loses the revenue of £20 per barrel if it transfers the barrels to Pizza Maven.

2. As before, the purchasing division, Pizza Maven, would be unwilling to pay more than the £18 per barrel it is already paying for similar ginger beer from its regular supplier.

$$\text{Transfer price} \leq \text{Cost of buying from outside supplier} = £18$$

3. Therefore, the selling division would insist on a transfer price of at least £20. But the purchasing division would refuse any transfer price above £18. It is impossible to satisfy both division managers simultaneously; there can be no agreement on a transfer price and no transfer will take place. Is this good? The answer is yes. From the standpoint of the entire company, the transfer doesn't make sense. Why give up sales of £20 to save £18?

Basically, the transfer price is a mechanism for dividing between the two divisions any profit the entire company earns as a result of the transfer. If the company loses money on the transfer, there will be no profit to divide up, and it will be impossible for the two divisions to come to an agreement. On the other hand, if the company makes money on the transfer, there will be a potential profit to share, and it will always be possible for the two divisions to find a mutually agreeable transfer price that increases the profits of both divisions. If the pie is bigger, it is always possible to divide it up in such a way that everyone has a bigger piece.

### Selling division has some idle capacity

Suppose now that Imperial Beverages is selling 9,000 barrels of ginger beer a month on the outside market. Pizza Maven can only sell one kind of ginger beer on tap. They cannot buy 1,000 barrels from Imperial Beverages and 1,000 barrels from their regular supplier; they must buy all their ginger beer from one source.

To fill the entire 2,000-barrel a month order from Pizza Maven, Imperial Beverages would have to divert 1,000 barrels from its regular customers who are paying £20 per barrel. The other 1,000 barrels can be made using idle capacity. What range of transfer prices, if any, would make both divisions better off transferring the 2,000 barrels within the company?

1. As before, the selling division, Imperial Beverage, will insist on a transfer price that at least covers their variable cost and opportunity cost:

$$\text{Transfer price} \geq \text{Variable cost per unit} + \frac{\text{Total contribution margin on lost sales}}{\text{Number of units transferred}}$$

**Part 3** Planning and control

Since Imperial Beverage does not have enough idle capacity to fill the entire order for 2,000 barrels, there are lost outside sales. The contribution margin per barrel on the 1,000 barrels of lost outside sales is £12 (£20 − £8).

$$\text{Transfer price} \geq £8 + \frac{(£20 - £8) \times 1{,}000}{2{,}000} = £8 + £6 = £14$$

Thus, as far as the selling division is concerned, the transfer price must cover the variable cost of £8 plus the average opportunity cost of lost sales of £6.

2   As before, the purchasing division, Pizza Maven, would be unwilling to pay more than the £18 per barrel it pays its regular supplier.

$$\text{Transfer price} \leq \text{Cost of buying from outside suppliers} = £18$$

3   Combining the requirements for both the selling and purchasing divisions, the range of acceptable transfer prices is:

$$£14 \leq \text{Transfer price} \leq £18$$

Again, assuming that the managers understand their own businesses and that they are co-operative, they should be able to agree on a transfer price within this range.

### No outside supplier

If Pizza Maven has no outside supplier for the ginger beer, the highest price the purchasing division would be willing to pay depends on how much the purchasing division expects to make on the transferred units – excluding the transfer price. If, for example, Pizza Maven expects to earn £30 per barrel of ginger beer after paying its own expenses, then it should be willing to pay up to £30 per barrel to Imperial Beverages. Remember, however, that this assumes Pizza Maven cannot buy ginger beer from other sources.

### Evaluation of negotiated transfer prices

As discussed earlier, if a transfer within the company would result in higher overall profits for the company, there is always a range of transfer prices within which both the selling and purchasing division would also have higher profits if they agree to the transfer. Therefore, if the managers understand their own businesses and are co-operative, then they should always be able to agree on a transfer price if it is in the best interests of the company that they do so.

The difficulty is that not all managers understand their own businesses and not all managers are co-operative. As a result, negotiations often break down even when it would be in the managers' own best interests to come to an agreement. Sometimes that is the fault of the way managers are evaluated. If managers are pitted against each other rather than against their own past performance or reasonable benchmarks, a non-cooperative atmosphere is almost guaranteed. Nevertheless, it must be admitted that even with the best performance evaluation system, some people by nature are not co-operative.

Possibly because of the fruitless and protracted bickering that often accompanies disputes over transfer prices, most companies rely on some other means of setting transfer prices. Unfortunately, as we will see below, all the alternatives to negotiated transfer prices have their own serious drawbacks.

### Transfers at the cost to the selling division

Many companies set transfer prices at either the variable cost or full (absorption) cost incurred by the selling division. Although the cost approach to setting transfer prices is relatively simple to apply, it has some major defects.

First, the use of cost – particularly full cost – as a transfer price can lead to bad decisions and thus suboptimization. Return to the example involving the ginger beer. The full cost of ginger beer can never be less than

£15 per barrel (£8 per barrel variable cost + £7 per barrel fixed cost at capacity). What if the cost of buying the ginger beer from an outside supplier is less than £15 – for example, £14 per barrel? If the transfer price were bureaucratically set at full cost, then Pizza Maven would never want to buy ginger beer from Imperial Beverages, since it could buy its ginger beer from the outside supplier at less cost. However, from the standpoint of the company as a whole, ginger beer should be transferred from Imperial Beverages to Pizza Maven whenever Imperial Beverages has idle capacity. Why? Because when Imperial Beverage has idle capacity, it only costs the company £8 in variable cost to produce a barrel of ginger beer, but it costs £14 per barrel to buy from outside suppliers.

Secondly, if cost is used as the transfer price, the selling division will never show a profit on any internal transfer. The only division that shows a profit is the division that makes the final sale to an outside party.

A third problem with cost-based prices is that they do not provide incentives to control costs. If the costs of one division are simply passed on to the next, then there is little incentive for anyone to work to reduce costs. This problem can be overcome to some extent by using standard costs rather than actual costs for transfer prices.

Despite these shortcomings, cost-based transfer prices are commonly used in practice. Advocates argue that they are easily understood and convenient to use.

## Transfers at market price

Some form of competitive **market price** (i.e., the price charged for an item on the open market) is often regarded as the best approach to the transfer pricing problem – particularly if transfer price negotiations routinely become bogged down.

The market price approach is designed for situations in which there is an *intermediate market* for the transferred product or service. By **intermediate market**, we mean a market in which the product or service is sold in its present form to outside customers. If the selling division has no idle capacity, the market price in the intermediate market is the perfect choice for the transfer price. The reason for this is that if the selling division can sell a transferred item on the outside market instead, then the real cost of the transfer as far as the company is concerned is the opportunity cost of the lost revenue on the outside sale. Whether the item is transferred internally or sold on the outside intermediate market, the production costs are exactly the same. If the market price is used as the transfer price, the selling division manager will not lose anything by making the transfer, and the purchasing division manager will get the correct signal about how much it really costs the company for the transfer to take place.

While the market price works beautifully when there is no idle capacity, difficulties occur when the selling division has idle capacity. Recalling once again the ginger beer example, the outside market price for the ginger beer produced by Imperial Beverages is £20 per barrel. However, Pizza Maven can purchase all of the ginger beer it wants from outside suppliers for £18 per barrel. Why would Pizza Maven ever buy from Imperial Beverages if Pizza Maven is forced to pay Imperial Beverages' market price? In some market price-based transfer pricing schemes, the transfer price would be lowered to £18, the outside vendor's market price, and Pizza Maven would be directed to buy from Imperial Beverages as long as Imperial Beverages is willing to sell. This scheme can work reasonably well, but a drawback is that managers at Pizza Maven will regard the cost of ginger beer as £18 rather than the £8, which is the real cost to the company when the selling division has idle capacity. Consequently, the managers of Pizza Maven will make pricing and other decisions based on an incorrect cost.

Unfortunately, none of the possible solutions to the transfer pricing problem are perfect – not even market-based transfer prices.

## Divisional autonomy and sub-optimization

A question often arises as to how much autonomy should be granted to divisions in setting their own transfer prices and in making decisions concerning whether to sell internally or to sell outside. Should the divisional heads have complete authority to make these decisions, or should top corporate management step in if it appears that a decision is about to be made that would result in sub-optimization? For example, if the selling division has idle capacity and divisional managers are unable to agree on a transfer price, should top corporate management step in and *force* a settlement?

Efforts should always be made, of course, to bring disputing managers together. But the almost unanimous feeling among top corporate executives is that divisional heads should not be forced into an agreement over a transfer price. That is, if a manager flatly refuses to change his or her position in a dispute, *then this decision should be respected even if it results in sub-optimization*. This is simply the price that is paid for divisional autonomy. If top corporate management steps in and forces the decisions in difficult situations, then the purposes of decentralization are defeated and the company simply becomes a centralized operation with decentralization of only minor decisions and responsibilities. In short, if a division is to be viewed as an autonomous unit with independent profit responsibility, then it must have control over its own destiny – even to the extent of having the right to make bad decisions.

We should note, however, that if a division consistently makes bad decisions, the results will sooner or later reduce its profit and rate of return, and the divisional manager may find that he or she has to defend the division's performance. Even so, the manager's right to get into an embarrassing situation must be respected if decentralization is to operate successfully. Divisional autonomy and independent profit responsibility generally lead to much greater success and profitability than do closely controlled, centrally administered operations. Part of the price of this success is occasional sub-optimization due to pettiness, bickering or just plain stubbornness.

Furthermore, one of the major reasons for decentralizing is that top managers cannot know enough about every detail of operations to make every decision themselves. To impose the correct transfer price, top managers would have to know details about the intermediate market, variable costs and capacity utilization. If top managers have all of this information, it is not clear why they decentralized in the first place.

## International aspects of transfer pricing

The objectives of transfer pricing change when a multinational corporation (MNC) is involved and the goods and services being transferred cross international borders. The objectives of international transfer pricing, as compared to domestic transfer pricing, are summarized in Exhibit 15.6.[7]

As shown in the exhibit, the objectives of international transfer pricing focus on minimizing taxes, duties and foreign exchange risks, along with enhancing a company's competitive position and improving its relations with foreign governments. Although domestic objectives such as managerial motivation and divisional autonomy are always important, they often become secondary when international transfers are involved. Companies will focus instead on charging a transfer price that will slash its total tax bill or that will strengthen a foreign subsidiary.

For example, charging a low transfer price for parts shipped to a foreign subsidiary may reduce customs duty payments as the parts cross international borders, or it may help the subsidiary to compete in foreign markets by keeping the subsidiary's costs low. On the other hand, charging a high transfer price may help an MNC draw profits out of a country that has stringent controls on foreign remittances, or it may allow an MNC to shift income from a country that has high income tax rates to a country that has low rates.

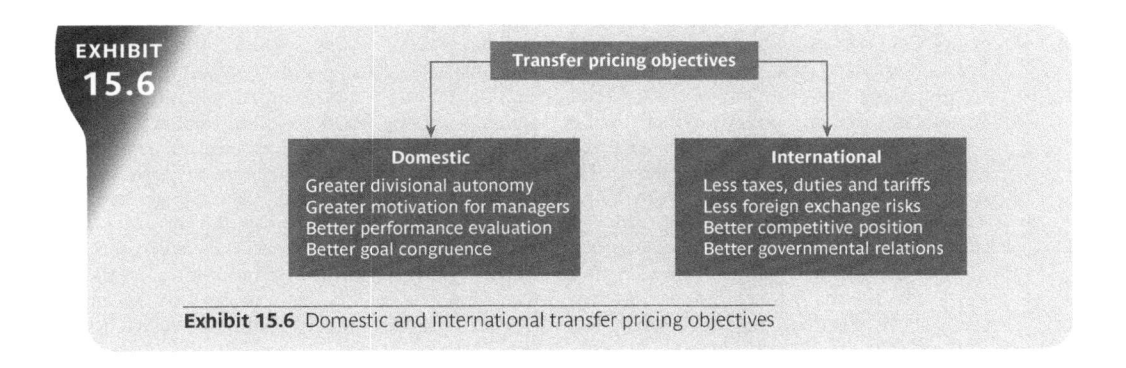

**EXHIBIT 15.6**

Transfer pricing objectives

**Domestic**
Greater divisional autonomy
Greater motivation for managers
Better performance evaluation
Better goal congruence

**International**
Less taxes, duties and tariffs
Less foreign exchange risks
Better competitive position
Better governmental relations

**Exhibit 15.6** Domestic and international transfer pricing objectives

## FOCUS ON PRACTICE

### Transfer pricing and tax avoidance

There is a potential clash of interest between national tax authorities who want to raise revenue and multinational companies who wish to pay as little tax as possible. International transfer pricing may be used to reduce a company's tax burden in at least one country. Even more dramatically, profits from a high tax regime may be shifted to a zero tax regime in an offshore tax haven. The Organization for Economic Co-operation and Development (OECD) has calculated that 60% of world trade consists of transfers within multinationals which effectively result in profits being made by anonymous subsidiaries in tax-free jurisdictions.[8] Oxfam estimates that offshore tax havens cost the United Kingdom nearly £85 billion in lost tax revenue every year.[9]

In an attempt to curb the abuse of such international transfer pricing, legislation tries to ensure that 'arm's-length' prices are charged in transactions between related parties. An arm's-length relationship between two related parties should exhibit the characteristics that would be found if the same relationship existed between two unrelated parties. Taxation authorities ask themselves 'Would the transaction have been entered into between comparable independent enterprises?' If so, then the next question is: 'Is the price charged compatible with the arm's-length principle?'[10]

**Exercise**: Drawing on earlier treatment of transfer pricing, identify situations where the 'arm's-length' principle may conflict with the optimal transfer price.

## Summary

- Pricing involves a delicate balancing act. Higher prices result in more revenue per unit sold but drive down unit sales. Exactly where to set prices to maximize profit is a difficult problem, but, in general, the mark-up over cost should be highest for those products where customers are least sensitive to price. The demand for such products is said to be price inelastic.
- Managers often rely on cost-plus formulas to set target prices. In the absorption costing approach, the cost base is absorption costing unit product cost and the mark-up is computed to cover both non-manufacturing costs and to provide an adequate return on investment. However, costs will not be covered and there will not be an adequate return on investment unless the unit sales forecast used in the cost-plus formula is accurate. If applying the cost-plus formula results in a price that is too high, the unit sales forecast will not be attained.
- Some companies take a different approach to pricing. Instead of starting with costs and then determining prices, they start with prices and then determine allowable costs. Companies that use target costing estimate what a new product's market price is likely to be, based on its anticipated features and prices of products already on the market. They subtract desired profit from the estimated market price to arrive at the product's target cost. The design and development team is then given the responsibility of ensuring that the actual cost of the new product does not exceed the target cost.
- A special approach to pricing is required when goods or services are being transferred between segments or divisions of the same company. The theoretically optimal market price may not be appropriate if the company has spare capacity. Overall the aim should be to determine a price that maximizes the profit for the whole company. International transfer prices in multinational companies raise important taxation issues where the interests of the company and national taxation authorities may be in conflict.

## Key terms for review

**Cost-plus pricing** (p. 622)
**Intermediate market** (p. 637)
**Market price** (p. 637)
**Mark-up** (p. 622)
**Material loading charge** (p. 630)
**Negotiated transfer price** (p. 633)
**Price elasticity of demand** (p. 622)
**Range of acceptable transfer prices** (p. 633)
**Sub-optimization** (p. 632)
**Target costing** (p. 628)
**Time and material pricing** (p. 629)
**Transfer price** (p. 632)
**Yield management (YM)** (p. 632)
**Yield percentage** (p. 632)

## Review problem: transfer pricing

### Situation A

Collyer Products plc has a Valve Division that manufactures and sells a standard valve as follows:

| | |
|---|---|
| Capacity in units | 100,000 |
| Selling price to outside customers on the intermediate market | £30 |
| Variable costs per unit | 16 |
| Fixed costs per unit (based on capacity) | 9 |

The company has a Pump Division that could use this valve in the manufacture of one of its pumps. The Pump Division is currently purchasing 10,000 valves per year from an overseas supplier at a cost of £29 per valve.

### Required

1. Assume that the Valve Division has ample idle capacity to handle all of the Pump Division's needs. What is the acceptable range, if any, for the transfer price between the two divisions?
2. Assume that the Valve Division is selling all that it can produce to outside customers on the intermediate market. What is the acceptable range, if any, for the transfer price between the two divisions?
3. Assume again that the Valve Division is selling all that it can produce to outside customers on the intermediate market. Also assume that £3 in variable expenses can be avoided on transfers within the company, due to reduced selling costs. What is the acceptable range, if any, for the transfer price between the two divisions?

## Solution to situation A

**1** Since the Valve Division has idle capacity, it does not have to give up any outside sales to take on the Pump Division's business. Applying the formula for the lowest acceptable transfer price from the viewpoint of the selling division, we get:

$$\text{Transfer price} \geq \text{Variable cost per unit} + \frac{\text{Total contribution margin on lost sales}}{\text{Number of units transferred}}$$

$$\text{Transfer price} \geq £16 + \frac{£0}{10,000} = £16$$

The Pump Division would be unwilling to pay more that £29, the price it is currently paying an outside supplier for its valves. Therefore, the transfer price must fall within the range:

$$£16 \leq \text{Transfer price} \leq £29$$

**2** Since the Valve Division is selling all that it can produce on the intermediate market, it would have to give up some of these outside sales to take on the Pump Division's business. Thus, the Valve Division has an opportunity cost that is the total contribution margin on lost sales:

$$\text{Transfer price} \geq \text{Variable cost per unit} + \frac{\text{Total contribution margin on lost sales}}{\text{Number of units transferred}}$$

$$\text{Transfer price} \geq £16 + \frac{(£30 - £16) \times 10,000}{10,000} = £16 + £14 = £30$$

Since the Pump Division can purchase valves from an outside supplier at only £29 per unit, no transfers will be made between the two divisions.

**3** Applying the formula for the lowest acceptable price from the viewpoint of the selling division, we get:

$$\text{Transfer price} \geq \text{Variable cost per unit} + \frac{\text{Total contribution margin on lost sales}}{\text{Number of units transferred}}$$

$$\text{Transfer price} \geq (£16 - £3) + \frac{(30 - £16) \times 10,000}{10,000} = £13 + £14 = £27$$

In this case, the transfer price must fall within the range:

$$£27 \leq \text{Transfer price} \leq £29.$$

## Situation B

Refer to the original data in situation A above. Assume that the Pump Division needs 20,000 special high-pressure valves per year. The Valve Division's variable costs to manufacture and ship the special valve would be £20 per unit. To produce these special valves, the Valve Division would have to reduce its production and sales of regular valves from 100,000 units per year to 70,000 units per year.

### Required

As far as the Valve Division is concerned, what is the lowest acceptable transfer price?

## Solution to situation B

To produce the 20,000 special valves, the Valve Division will have to give up sales of 30,000 regular valves to outside customers. Applying the formula for the lowest acceptable price from the viewpoint of the selling division, we get:

$$\text{Transfer price} \geq \text{Variable cost per unit} + \frac{\text{Total contribution margin on lost sales}}{\text{Number of units transferred}}$$

$$\text{Transfer price} \geq (£20) + \frac{(30 - £16) \times 30,000}{20,000} = £20 + £21 = £41$$

**Level of difficulty:** BASIC  INTERMEDIATE  ADVANCED

## Questions

**15-1** What is meant by cost-plus pricing?

**15-2** What does the price elasticity of demand measure? What is meant by inelastic demand? What is meant by elastic demand?

**15-3** According to the economists' approach to setting prices, the profit-maximizing price should depend on which two factors?

**15-4** Which product should have a larger mark-up over variable cost, a product whose demand is elastic or a product whose demand is inelastic?

**15-5** When the absorption costing approach to cost-plus pricing is used, what is the mark-up supposed to cover?

**15-6** What assumption does the absorption costing approach make about how consumers react to prices?

**15-7** Discuss the following statement: 'Full cost can be viewed as a floor of protection. If a firm always sets its prices above full cost, it will never have to worry about operating at a loss.'

**15-8** What is target costing? How do target costs enter into the pricing decision?

**15-9** What is time and material pricing?

**15-10** From the standpoint of a selling division that has idle capacity, what is the minimum acceptable transfer price for an item?

**15-11** From the standpoint of a selling division that has no idle capacity, what is the minimum acceptable transfer price for an item?

**15-12** What are the advantages and disadvantages of cost-based transfer prices?

**15-13** If a market price for a product can be determined, why isn't it always the best transfer price?

Chapter 15 Pricing and intra-company transfers

## Exercises

**E15-1** Time allowed: 15 minutes

Maria Lorenzi owns an ice cream stand that she operates during the summer months in West Yellowstone, Montana. Her store caters primarily to tourists passing through town on their way to Yellowstone National Park.

Maria is unsure of how she should price her ice cream cones and has experimented with two prices in successive weeks during the busy August season. The number of people who entered the store was roughly the same in the two weeks. During the first week, she priced the cones at $1.89 and 1,500 cones were sold. During the second week, she priced the cones at $1.49 and 2,340 cones were sold. The variable cost of a cone is $0.43 and consists solely of the costs of the ice cream and of the cone itself. The fixed expenses of the ice cream stand are $675 per week.

### Required

1. Did Maria make more money selling the cones for $1.89 or for $1.49?
2. Estimate the price elasticity of demand for the ice cream cones.
3. Estimate the profit-maximizing price for ice cream cones.

**E15-2** Time allowed: 10 minutes

Martin Company is considering the introduction of a new product. To determine a target selling price, the company has gathered the following information:

| | |
|---|---:|
| Number of units to be produced and sold each year | 14,000 |
| Unit product cost | £25 |
| Projected annual selling, general, and administrative expenses | 50,000 |
| Estimated investment required by the company | 750,000 |
| Desired return on investment (ROI) | 12% |

### Required

The company uses the absorption costing approach to cost-plus pricing.

1. Compute the mark-up the company will have to use to achieve the desired ROI.
2. Compute the target selling price per unit.

**E15-3** Time allowed: 5 minutes

Shimada Products Corporation of Japan is anxious to enter the electronic calculator market. Management believes that in order to be competitive in world markets, the electronic calculator that the company is developing cannot be priced at more than £15. Shimada requires a minimum return of 12% on all investments. An investment of £5,000,000 would be required to acquire the equipment needed to produce the 300,000 calculators that management believes can be sold each year at the £15 price.

### Required

Compute the target cost of one calculator.

**E15-4** Time allowed: 30 minutes

Sako Company's Audio Division produces a speaker that is widely used by manufacturers of various audio products. Sales and cost data on the speaker follow:

| | |
|---|---:|
| Selling price per unit on the intermediate market | £60 |
| Variable costs per unit | 42 |
| Fixed costs per unit (based on capacity) | 8 |
| Capacity in units | 25,000 |

Sako Company has just organized a Hi-Fi Division that could use this speaker in one of its products. The Hi-Fi Division will need 5,000 speakers per year. It has received a quote of £57 per speaker from another manufacturer. Sako Company evaluates divisional managers on the basis of divisional profits.

### Required

1. Assume that the Audio Division is now selling only 20,000 speakers per year to outside customers on the intermediate market.
   (a) From the standpoint of the Audio Division, what is the lowest acceptable transfer price for speakers sold to the Hi-Fi Division?
   (b) From the standpoint of the Hi-Fi Division, what is the highest acceptable transfer price for speakers purchased from the Audio Division?
   (c) If left free to negotiate without interference, would you expect the division managers to voluntarily agree to the transfer of 5,000 speakers from the Audio Division to the Hi-Fi Division? Why or why not?
   (d) From the standpoint of the entire company, should the transfer take place? Why or why not?
2. Assume that the Audio Division is selling all of the speakers it can produce to outside customers on the intermediate market.
   (a) From the standpoint of the Audio Division, what is the lowest acceptable transfer price for speakers sold to the Hi-Fi Division?
   (b) From the standpoint of the Hi-Fi Division, what is the highest acceptable transfer price for speakers purchased from the Audio Division?
   (c) If left free to negotiate without interference, would you expect the division managers to voluntarily agree to the transfer of 5,000 speakers from the Audio Division to the Hi-Fi Division? Why or why not?
   (d) From the standpoint of the entire company, should the transfer take place? Why or why not?

**E15-5** Time allowed: 15 minutes

The Reliable TV Repair Shop had budgeted the following costs for next year:

| | |
|---|---:|
| Repair technicians: | |
|    Wages | £120,000 |
|    Fringe benefits | 30,000 |
|      Repairs operation per year | 90,000 |
| Materials: | |
|    Costs of ordering, handling, and storing parts | 20% of invoice cost |

In total, the company expects 10,000 hours of repair time it can bill to customers. According to competitive conditions, the company believes it should aim for a profit of £6 per hour of repair time. The competitive mark-up on materials is 40% of invoice cost. The company uses time and material pricing.

### Required

1. Compute the time rate and the material loading charge that would be used to bill jobs.
2. One of the company's repair technicians has just completed a repair job that required 2.5 hours of time and £80 in parts (invoice cost). Compute the amount that would be billed for the job.

Chapter 15 Pricing and intra-company transfers

**E15-6** Time allowed: 20 minutes

In each of the cases below, assume that Division X has a product that can be sold either to outside customers on an intermediate market or to Division Y of the same company for use in its production process. The managers of the divisions are evaluated based on their divisional profits.

|  | Case A | Case B |
|---|---|---|
| **Division X:** |  |  |
| Capacity in units | 200,000 | 200,000 |
| Number of units being sold on the intermediate market | 200,000 | 160,000 |
| Selling price per unit on the intermediate market | £90 | £75 |
| Variable costs per unit | 70 | 60 |
| Fixed costs per unit (based on capacity) | 13 | 8 |
| **Division Y:** |  |  |
| Number of units needed for production | 40,000 | 40,000 |
| Purchase price per unit now being paid to an outside supplier | £86 | £74 |

### Required

1. Refer to the data in case A above. Assume in this case that £3 per unit in variable costs can be avoided on intra-company sales. If the managers are free to negotiate and make decisions on their own, will a transfer take place? If so, within what range will the transfer price fall? Explain.

2. Refer to the data in case B above. In this case there will be no savings in variable costs on intra-company sales. If the managers are free to negotiate and make decisions on their own, will a transfer take place? If so, within what range will the transfer price fall? Explain.

**E15-7** Time allowed: 15 minutes

Division A manufactures electronic circuit boards. The boards can be sold either to Division B of the same company or to outside customers. Last year, the following activity occurred in Division A:

| Selling price per circuit board | £125 |
|---|---|
| Production cost per circuit board | 90 |
| Number of circuit boards: |  |
| Produced during the year | 20,000 |
| Sold to outside customers | 16,000 |
| Sold to Division B | 4,000 |

Sales to Division B were at the same price as sales to outside customers. The circuit boards purchased by Division B were used in an electronic instrument manufactured by that division (one board per instrument). Division B incurred £100 in additional cost per instrument and then sold the instruments for £300 each.

### Required

1. Prepare profit statements for Division A, Division B, and the company as a whole.

2. Assume that Division A's manufacturing capacity is 20,000 circuit boards. Next year, Division B wants to purchase 5,000 circuit boards from Division A rather than 4,000. (Circuit boards of this type are not available from outside sources.) From the standpoint of the company as a whole, should Division A sell the 1,000 additional circuit boards to Division B or continue to sell them to outside customers? Explain.

## Problems

### P15–8 Economists' approach to pricing
*Time allowed: 30 minutes*

The postal service of St Vincent, an island in the West Indies, obtains a significant portion of its revenues from sales of special souvenir sheets to stamp collectors. The souvenir sheets usually contain several high-value St Vincent stamps depicting a common theme, such as the life of Princess Diana. The souvenir sheets are designed and printed for the postal service by Imperial Printing, a stamp agency service company in the United Kingdom. The souvenir sheets cost the postal service $0.80 each. (The currency in St Vincent is the East Caribbean dollar.) St Vincent has been selling these souvenir sheets for $7.00 each and ordinarily sells about 100,000 units. To test the market, the postal service recently priced a new souvenir sheet at $8.00 and sales dropped to 85,000 units.

#### Required

1. Does the postal service of St Vincent make more money selling souvenir sheets for $7.00 each or $8.00 each?
2. Estimate the price elasticity of demand for the souvenir sheets.
3. Estimate the profit-maximizing price for souvenir sheets.
4. If Imperial Printing increases the price it charges to the St Vincent postal service for souvenir sheets to $1.00 each, how much should the St Vincent postal service charge its customers for the souvenir sheets?

### P15–9 Standard costs; mark-up computations; pricing decisions
*Time allowed: 30 minutes*

Wilderness Products plc has designed a self-inflating sleeping pad for use by backpackers and campers. The following information is available about the new product:

1. An investment of £1,350,000 will be necessary to carry stocks and debtors and to purchase some new equipment needed in the manufacturing process. The company requires a 24% return on investment for new products.

2. A standard cost card has been prepared for the sleeping pad, as shown below:

|  | Standard quantity or hours | Standard price or rate | Standard cost |
|---|---|---|---|
| Direct materials | 4.0 metres | £2.70 per metre | £10.80 |
| Direct labour | 2.4 hours | 8.00 per hour | 19.20 |
| Manufacturing overhead (1/5 variable) | 2.4 hours | 12.50 per hour | 30.00 |
| Total standard cost per pad |  |  | £60.00 |

3. The only variable selling, general and administrative expenses on the pads will be £9 per pad sales commission. Fixed selling, general and administrative expenses will be (per year):

| Salaries | £82,000 |
|---|---|
| Warehouse rent | 50,000 |
| Advertising and other | 600,000 |
| Total | £732,000 |

4 Since the company manufactures many products, it is felt that no more than 38,400 hours of direct labour time per year can be devoted to production of the new sleeping pads.
5 Manufacturing overhead costs are allocated to products on the basis of direct labour-hours.

### Required

1. Assume that the company uses the absorption approach to cost-plus pricing.
   (a) Compute the mark-up that the company needs on the pads to achieve a 24% return on investment (ROI) if it sells all of the pads it can produce.
   (b) Using the mark-up you have computed, prepare a price quotation sheet for a single sleeping pad.
   (c) Assume that the company is able to sell all of the pads that it can produce. Prepare an income statement for the first year of activity and compute the company's ROI for the year on the pads.
2. After marketing the sleeping pads for several years, the company is experiencing a fall-off in demand due to an economic recession. A large retail outlet will make a bulk purchase of pads if its label is sewn in and if an acceptable price can be worked out. What is the absolute minimum price that would be acceptable for this special order?

### P15–10 Pricing
Time allowed: 30 minutes

A small company is engaged in the production of plastic tools for the garden. Subtotals on the spreadsheet of budgeted overheads for a year reveal:

|  | Moulding Department | Finishing Department | General factory overhead |
| --- | --- | --- | --- |
| Variable overhead (£000) | 1,600 | 500 | 1,050 |
| Fixed overhead (£000) | 2,500 | 850 | 1,750 |
| Budgeted activity |  |  |  |
| Machine-hours (000) | 800 | 600 |  |
| Practical capacity |  |  |  |
| Machine-hours (000) | 1,200 | 800 |  |

For the purposes of reallocation of general factory overhead it is agreed that the variable overheads accrue in line with the machine-hours worked in each department. General factory fixed overhead is to be reallocated on the basis of the practical machine-hour capacity of the two departments.

It has been a long-standing company practice to establish selling prices by applying a mark-up on full manufacturing cost of between 25% and 35%.

A possible price is sought for one new product which is in a final development stage. The total market for this product is estimated at 200,000 units per annum. Market research indicates that the company could expect to obtain and hold about 10% of the market. It is hoped the product will offer some improvement over competitors' products, which are currently marketed at between £90 and £100 each.

The product development department has determined that the direct material content is £9 per unit. Each unit of the product will take two labour-hours (four machine-hours) in the moulding department and three labour-hours (three machine-hours) in finishing. Hourly labour rates are £5.00 and £5.50 respectively.

Management estimate that the annual fixed costs which would be specifically incurred in relation to the product are: supervision £20,000, depreciation of a recently acquired machine £120,000 and advertising £27,000. It may be assumed that these costs are included in the budget given above. Given the state of development of this new product, management do not consider it necessary to make revisions, to the budgeted activity levels given above, for any possible extra machine-hours involved in its manufacture.

**Part 3** Planning and control

### Required

1. Briefly explain the role of costs in pricing.
2. Prepare full cost and marginal cost information which may help with the pricing decision.
3. Comment on the cost information and suggest a price range which should be considered.

*(ACCA Managerial Finance, adapted)*

**P15-11 Transfer pricing; divisional performance**
Time allowed: 45 minutes

Stanco plc is a decentralized organization with five divisions. The company's Electronics Division produces a variety of electronics items, including an XL5 circuit board. The division (which is operating at capacity) sells the XL5 circuit board to regular customers for £12.50 each. The circuit boards have a variable production cost of £8.25 each.

The company's Clock Division has asked the Electronics Division to supply it with a large quantity of XL5 circuit boards for only £9 each. The Clock Division, which is operating at only 60% of capacity, will put the circuit boards into a timing device that it will produce and sell to a large oven manufacturer. The cost of the timing device being manufactured by the Clock Division follows:

| | |
|---|---|
| XL5 circuit board (desired cost) | £9.00 |
| Other purchased parts (from outside vendors) | 30.00 |
| Other variable costs | 20.75 |
| Fixed overhead and administrative costs | 10.00 |
| Total cost per timing device | £69.75 |

The manager of the Clock Division feels that she can't quote a price greater than £70 per timing device to the oven manufacturer if her division is to get the job. As shown above, in order to keep the price at £70 or less, she can't pay more than £9 per unit to the Electronics Division for the XL5 circuit boards. Although the £9 price for the XL5 circuit boards represents a substantial discount from the normal £12.50 price, she feels that the price concession is necessary for her division to get the oven manufacturer contract and thereby keep its core of highly trained people.

The company uses return on investment (ROI) to measure divisional performance.

### Required

1. Assume that you are the manager of the Electronics Division. Would you recommend that your division supply the XL5 circuit boards to the Clock Division for £9 each as requested? Why or why not? Show all computations.
2. Would it be profitable for the company as a whole for the Electronics Division to supply the Clock Division with the circuit boards for £9 each? Explain your answer.
3. In principle, should it be possible for the two managers to agree to a transfer price in this particular situation? If so, within what range would that transfer price lie?
4. Discuss the organizational and manager behaviour problems, if any, inherent in this situation. What would you advise the company's CEO to do in this situation?

**P15-12 Transfer pricing, divisional performance**
Time allowed: 45 minutes

Division A, which is part of the ACF Group, manufactures only one type of product, a Bit, which it sells to external customers and also to division C, another member of the group. ACF Group's policy is that divisions have the freedom to set transfer prices and choose their suppliers.

Chapter 15 Pricing and intra-company transfers

The ACF Group uses residual income (RI) to assess divisional performance and each year it sets each division a target RI. The group's cost of capital is 12% a year.

**Division A**

Budgeted information for the coming year is:

| | |
|---|---|
| Maximum capacity | 150,000 Bits |
| External sales | 110,000 Bits |
| External selling price | £35 per Bit |
| Variable cost | £22 per Bit |
| Fixed costs | £1,080,000 |
| Capital employed | £3,200,000 |
| Target residual income | £180,000 |

**Division C**

Division C has found two other companies willing to supply Bits:

X could supply at £28 per Bit, but only for annual orders in excess of 50,000 Bits.

Z could supply at £33 per Bit for any quantity ordered.

Required

(*Note:* Ignore tax for parts a and b.)

1. Division C provisionally requests a quotation for 60,000 Bits from division A for the coming year.
   (a) Calculate the transfer price per Bit that division A should quote in order to meet its residual income target.
   (b) Calculate the two prices division A would have to quote to division C, if it became group policy to quote transfer prices based on opportunity costs.
2. Evaluate and discuss the impact of the group's current and proposed policies on the profits of divisions A and C, and on group profit. Illustrate your answer with calculations.
3. Assume that divisions A and C are based in different countries and consequently pay taxes at different rates: division A at 55% and division C at 25%. Division A has now quoted a transfer price of £30 per Bit for 60,000 Bits. Calculate whether it is better for the group if division C purchases 60,000 Bits from division A or from supplier X.

(*CIMA Management Accounting – Decision Making*, adapted)

**P15–13** Transfer pricing
Time allowed: 30 minutes

1. Alpha division has an external market for product A which fully utilizes its production capacity.
   (a) Explain the principle which would suggest that Alpha division should transfer product A to Beta division of the same group of companies at the existing market price.
   (b) Explain circumstances in which Alpha division may offer to transfer product A to Beta division at less than the external market price and yet report the same total profit.
2. The transfer pricing method to be used for an intermediate product between two divisions in a group is under debate. The supplying division wishes to use actual cost plus a 25% profit mark-up. The receiving

## Part 3 Planning and control

division suggests the use of standard cost plus a 25% profit mark-up. A suggested compromise is to use revised standard cost plus 25% profit mark-up. The revised standard cost is arrived at after taking into account the appropriate elements of a planning and operational variance analysis at the supplying division.

Discuss the impact of EACH of the above transfer pricing methods and their acceptability to the supplying and receiving divisions.

3  An intermediate product is manufactured in limited quantities at three divisions of a group and is available in limited quantities from an external source. The intermediate product is required by four divisions in the group as an input for products to be sold externally. The total quantity of intermediate product which is available is insufficient to satisfy demand at the four user divisions.

Explain the procedure which should lead to a transfer pricing and deployment policy which will result in group profit maximization.

*(ACCA Information for Control and Decision Making, adapted)*

### P15–14 Target costing
Time allowed: 45 minutes

National Restaurant Supply Inc sells restaurant equipment and supplies throughout most of the United States. Management of the company is considering adding a machine that makes sorbet to its line of ice cream making machines. Management is preparing to enter into negotiations with the Swedish manufacturer of the sorbet machine concerning the price at which the machine would be sold to National Restaurant Supply.

Management of National Restaurant Supply believes the sorbet machine can be sold to its customers in the United States for $4,950. At that price, annual sales of the sorbet machine should be 100 units. If the sorbet machine is added to National Restaurant Supply's product lines, the company will have to invest $600,000 in inventories and special warehouse fixtures. The variable cost of selling the sorbet machines would be $650 per machine.

### Required

1  If National Restaurant Supply requires a 15% return on investment (ROI), what is the maximum amount the company would be willing to pay the Swedish manufacturer for the sorbet machines?

2  The manager who is flying to Sweden to negotiate the purchase price of the machines would like to know how the purchase price of the machines would affect National Restaurant Supply's ROI. Construct a chart that shows National Restaurant Supply's ROI as a function of the purchase price of the sorbet machine. Put the purchase price on the X-axis and the resulting ROI on the Y-axis. Plot the ROI for purchase prices between $3,000 and $4,000 per machine.

3  After many hours of negotiations, management has concluded that the Swedish manufacturer is unwilling to sell the sorbet machine at a low enough price so that National Restaurant Supply is able to earn its 15% required ROI. Apart from simply giving up on the idea of adding the sorbet machine to National Restaurant Supply's product lines, what could management do?

### P15–15 Time and material pricing
Time allowed: 45 minutes

City Appliance Ltd operates an appliance service business with a fleet of trucks dispatched by radio in response to calls from customers. The company's profit margin has dropped steadily over the last two years, and management is concerned that pricing rates for time and material may be out of date. According to industry trade magazines, the company should be earning £8.50 per hour of repair service time, and a profit of 10% of the invoice cost of parts used. The company maintains a large parts inventory in order to give prompt repair service to customers.

Costs associated with repair work and with the parts inventory over the past year are provided below:

Chapter 15 Pricing and intra-company transfers

|  | Repairs | Parts |
|---|---:|---:|
| Repair service manager – salary | £25,000 | £– |
| Parts manager – salary | – | 20,000 |
| Repair technicians – wages | 180,000 | – |
| Office assistant – salary | 9,000 | 3,000 |
| Depreciation – trucks and equipment | 15,400 | – |
| Depreciation – buildings and fixtures | 6,000 | 17,500 |
| Retirement benefits (15% of salaries and wages) | 32,100 | 3,450 |
| Health insurance (5% of salaries and wages) | 10,700 | 1,150 |
| Utilities | 2,600 | 12,000 |
| Truck operating costs | 36,000 | – |
| Property taxes | 900 | 3,400 |
| Liability and fire insurance | 1,500 | 1,900 |
| Supplies | 800 | 600 |
| Invoice cost of parts used | – | 210,000 |
| Total cost | £320,000 | £273,000 |

During the past year, customers were billed for 20,000 hours of repair time.

### Required

1. Using the data above, compute the following:
   (a) The rate that would be charged per hour of repair service time using time and material pricing.
   (b) The material loading charge that would be used in billing jobs. The material loading charge should be expressed as a percentage of the invoice cost of parts.
2. Assume that the company adopts the rates that you have computed in Question 1 above. What would be the total price charged on a repair that requires 112 hours of service time and £108 in parts?
3. During the past year, the company billed repair service time at £20 per hour and added a material loading charge of 35% to parts. If the company adopts the rates that you have computed in Question 1 above, would you expect the company's profits to improve? Explain.

**P15–16** Missing data; mark-up computations: return on investment (ROI); pricing
⏱ Time allowed: 45 minutes

South Seas Products plc has designed a new surfboard to replace its old surfboard line. Because of the unique design of the new surfboard, the company anticipates that it will be able to sell all the boards that it can produce. On this basis, the following incomplete budgeted profit statement for the first year of activity is available:

| | |
|---|---:|
| Sales (? boards at ? per board) | £? |
| Less cost of goods sold (? boards at ? per board) | 1,600,000 |
| Gross margin | ? |
| Less selling, general, and administrative expenses | 1,130,000 |
| Profit | £? |

**Part 3** Planning and control

Additional information on the new surfboard is given below:

1. An investment of £1,500,000 will be necessary to carry stocks and debtors and to purchase some new equipment needed in the manufacturing process. The company requires an 18% return on investment for all products.
2. A partially completed standard cost card for the new surfboard follows:

|  | Standard quantity or hours | Standard price | Standard cost |
|---|---|---|---|
| Direct materials | 6 feet | £4.50 per foot | £27 |
| Direct labour | 2 hours | ? per hour | ? |
| Manufacturing overhead | ? | ? per hour | ? |
| Total standard cost per surfboard |  |  | £? |

3. The company will employ 20 workers in the manufacture of the new surfboards. Each will work a 40-hour week, 50 weeks a year.
4. Other information relating to production and costs follows:

| Variable manufacturing overhead cost (per board) | £5 |
|---|---|
| Variable selling cost (per board) | 10 |
| Fixed manufacturing overhead cost (total) | 600,000 |
| Fixed selling, general, and administrative cost (total) | ? |
| Number of boards produced and sold (per year) | ? |

5. Overhead costs are allocated to production on the basis of direct labour-hours.

### Required

1. Complete the standard cost card for a single surfboard.
2. Assume that the company uses the absorption costing approach to cost-plus pricing.
   (a) Compute the mark-up that the company needs on the surfboards to achieve an 18% ROI.
   (b) Using the mark-up you have computed, prepare a price quotation sheet for a single surfboard.
   (c) Assume, as stated, that the company is able to sell all of the surfboards that it can produce. Complete the profit statement for the first year of activity, and then compute the company's ROI for the year.
3. Assuming that direct labour is a variable cost, how many units would the company have to sell at the price you computed in Question 2 above to achieve the 18% ROI? How many units would have to be sold to just break even without achieving the 18% ROI?

**P15–17** **Economist's model of cost/volume price**
Time allowed: 45 minutes

The per unit average revenue (AR) and average cost (AC) functions for a business have been determined as follows:

$$AR = -x/100 + 29$$

$$AC = 15 + 3{,}000/x$$

where $x$ is the level of output in units (between 200 and 1,200 units).

### Required

1. Determine the functions for total revenue (TR) and total costs (TC), and demonstrate that the total profit function (TP) is given by:

$$TP = -x^2/100 + 14x - 3{,}000$$

2. Using the total profit function (TP) in Question 1 above, draw a graph of the function (plotting units in 250 unit intervals between 200 and 1,200).
3. By equation, establish the roots of the total profit function.
4. Using differential calculus, establish the profit maximizing output.
5. Explain briefly the relationship between the roots of the total profit function and the profit maximizing output. Use the results to Questions 3 and 4 to demonstrate this relationship.

*(ACCA Management Information, adapted)*

**P15–18** Economists' approach to pricing; absorption costing approach to costplus pricing

Time allowed: 60 minutes

Software Solutions plc was started by two young software engineers to market SpamBlocker, a software application they had written that screens incoming email messages and eliminates unsolicited mass mailings. Sales of the software have been good at 50,000 units a month, but the company has been losing money as shown below:

| | |
|---|---:|
| Sales (50,000 units × £25 per unit) | £1,250,000 |
| Variable cost (50,000 units × £6 per unit) | 300,000 |
| Contribution margin | 950,000 |
| Fixed expenses | 960,000 |
| Net operating profit (loss) | £(10,000) |

The company's only variable cost is the £6 fee it pays to another company to reproduce the software on CDs, print manuals, and package the result in an attractive box for sale to consumers. Monthly fixed selling, general and administrative expenses total £960,000.

The company's marketing manager has been arguing for some time that the software is priced too high. She estimates that every 5% decrease in price will yield an 8% increase in unit sales. The marketing manager would like your help in preparing a presentation to the company's owners concerning the pricing issue.

### Required

1. To help the marketing manager prepare for her presentation, she has asked you to fill in the blanks in the following table. The selling prices in the table were computed by successively decreasing the selling price by 5%. The estimated unit sales were computed by successively increasing the unit sales by 8%. For example, £23.75 is 5% less than £25.00 and 54,000 units is 8% more than 50,000 units.

**Part 3** Planning and control

| Selling price | Estimated unit sales | Sales | Variable Cost | Fixed expenses | Net operating |
|---|---|---|---|---|---|
| £25.00 | 50,000 | £1,250,000 | £300,000 | £960,000 | £(10,000) |
| £23.75 | 54,000 | £1,282,500 | £324,000 | £960,000 | £(1,500) |
| £22.56 | 58,320 | ? | ? | ? | ? |
| £21.43 | 62,986 | ? | ? | ? | ? |
| £20.36 | 68,025 | ? | ? | ? | ? |
| £19.34 | 73,467 | ? | ? | ? | ? |
| £18.37 | 79,344 | ? | ? | ? | ? |
| £17.45 | 85,692 | ? | ? | ? | ? |
| £16.58 | 92,547 | ? | ? | ? | ? |
| £15.75 | 99,951 | ? | ? | ? | ? |

2  Using the data from the table, construct a chart that shows the net operating profit as a function of the selling price. Put the selling price on the x-axis and the net operating profit on the y-axis. Using the chart, determine the approximate selling price at which net operating profit is maximized.

3  Compute the price elasticity of demand for the SpamBlocker software. Based on this calculation, what is the profit-maximizing price?

4  The owners have invested £400,000 in the company and feel that they should be earning at least 10% on these funds. If the absorption costing approach to pricing were used, what would be the target selling price based on the current sales of 50,000 units? What do you think would happen to the net operating profit of the company if this price were charged?

5  If the owners of the company are dissatisfied with the net operating profit and return on investment at the selling price you computed in Question 3 above, should they increase the selling price? Explain.

**P15–19** Transfer price; well-defined intermediate market
Time allowed: 45 minutes

Hrubec Products plc operates a Pulp Division that manufactures wood pulp for use in the production of various paper goods. Revenue and costs associated with a ton of pulp follow:

| | | |
|---|---:|---:|
| Selling price | | £70 |
| Less expenses: | | |
|   Variable | £42 | |
|   Fixed (based on a capacity of 50,000 tons per year) | 18 | 60 |
| Net profit | | £10 |

Hrubec Products has just acquired a small company that manufactures paper cartons. This company will be treated as a division of Hrubec with full profit responsibility. The newly formed Carton Division is currently purchasing 5,000 tons of pulp per year from a supplier at a cost of £70 per ton, less a 10% quantity discount. Hrubec's managing director is anxious for the Carton Division to begin purchasing its pulp from the Pulp Division if an acceptable transfer price can be worked out.

### Required

For Questions 1 and 2 below, assume that the Pulp Division can sell all its pulp to outside customers at the normal £70 price.

1. Are the managers of the Carton and Pulp Divisions likely to agree to a transfer price for 5,000 tons of pulp next year? Why or why not?
2. If the Pulp Division meets the price that the Carton Division is currently paying to its supplier and sells 5,000 tons of pulp to the Carton Division each year, what will be the effect on the profits of the Pulp Division, the Carton Division, and the company as a whole?

For Questions 3–6 below, assume that the Pulp Division is currently selling only 30,000 tons of pulp each year to outside customers at the stated £70 price.

3. Are the managers of the Carton and Pulp Divisions likely to agree to a transfer price for 5,000 tons of pulp next year? Why or why not?
4. Suppose that the Carton Division's outside supplier drops its price (net of the quantity discount) to only £59 per ton. Should the Pulp Division meet this price? Explain. If the Pulp Division does not meet the £59 price, what will be the effect on the profits of the company as a whole?
5. Refer to Question 4 above. If the Pulp Division refuses to meet the £59 price, should the Carton Division be required to purchase from the Pulp Division at a higher price for the good of the company as a whole?
6. Refer to Question 4 above. Assume that due to inflexible management policies, the Carton Division is required to purchase 5,000 tons of pulp each year from the Pulp Division at £70 per ton. What will be the effect on the profits of the company as a whole?

**P15–20 Basic transfer pricing**
Time allowed: 60 minutes

Alpha and Beta are divisions within the same company. The managers of both divisions are evaluated based on their own division's return on investment (ROI). Assume the following information relative to the two divisions:

|  | Case 1 | Case 2 | Case 3 | Case 4 |
| --- | --- | --- | --- | --- |
| **Alpha Division:** |  |  |  |  |
| Capacity in units | 80,000 | 400,000 | 150,000 | 300,000 |
| Number of units now being sold to outside customers on the intermediate market | 80,000 | 400,000 | 100,000 | 300,000 |
| Selling price per unit on the intermediate market | £30 | £90 | £75 | £50 |
| Variable costs per unit | 18 | 65 | 40 | 26 |
| Fixed costs per unit (based on capacity) | 6 | 15 | 20 | 9 |
| **Beta Division:** |  |  |  |  |
| Number of units needed annually | 5,000 | 30,000 | 20,000 | 120,000 |
| Purchase price now being paid to an outside supplier | £27 | £89 | £75* | – |

*Before any quantity discount.

Managers are free to decide if they will participate in any internal transfers. All transfer prices are negotiated.

## 656 Part 3 Planning and control

### Required

1. Refer to Case 1 above. Alpha Division can avoid £2 per unit in commissions on any sales to Beta Division. Will the managers agree to a transfer and if so, within what range will the transfer price be? Explain.

2. Refer to Case 2 above. A study indicates that Alpha Division can avoid £5 per unit in shipping costs on any sales to Beta Division.
   (a) Would you expect any disagreement between the two divisional managers over what the transfer price should be? Explain.
   (b) Assume that Alpha Division offers to sell 30,000 units to Beta Division for £88 per unit and that Beta Division refuses this price. What will be the loss in potential profits for the company as a whole?

3. Refer to Case 3 above. Assume that Beta Division is now receiving an 8% quantity discount from the outside supplier.
   (a) Will the managers agree to a transfer? If so, what is the range within which the transfer price would be?
   (b) Assume that Beta Division offers to purchase 20,000 units from Alpha Division at £60 per unit. If Alpha Division accepts this price, would you expect its ROI to increase, decrease, or remain unchanged? Why?

4. Refer to Case 4 above. Assume that Beta Division wants Alpha Division to provide it with 120,000 units of a different product from the one that Alpha Division is now producing. The new product would require £21 per unit in variable costs and would require that Alpha Division cut back production of its present product by 45,000 units annually. What is the lowest acceptable transfer price from Alpha Division's perspective?

### P15–21 Pricing
*Time allowed: 45 minutes*

Just over two years ago, R Ltd was the first company to produce specific 'off-the-shelf' accounting software packages. The pricing strategy, decided on by the Managing Director, for the packages was to add a 50% mark-up to the budgeted full cost of the packages. The company achieved and maintained a significant market share and high profits for the first two years.

Budgeted information for the current year (Year 3) was as follows:

| | |
|---|---|
| Production and sales | 15,000 packages |
| Full cost | £400 per package |

At a recent Board meeting, the Finance Director reported that although costs were in line with the budget for the current year, profits were declining. He explained that the full cost included £80 for fixed overheads. This figure had been calculated by using an overhead absorption rate based on labour-hours and the budgeted level of production which, he pointed out, was much lower than the current capacity of 25,000 packages.

The Marketing Director stated that competitors were beginning to increase their market share. He also reported the results of a recent competitor analysis which showed that when R Ltd announced its prices for the current year, the competitors responded by undercutting them by 15%. Consequently, he commissioned an investigation of the market. He informed the Board that the market research showed that at a price of £750 there would be no demand for the packages but for every £10 reduction in price the demand would increase by 1,000 packages. The Managing Director appeared to be unconcerned about the loss of market share and argued that profits could be restored to their former level by increasing the mark-up.

*Note:* If price = $a - bx$ then marginal revenue = $a - 2bx$

### Required

1. Discuss the Managing Director's pricing strategy in the circumstances described above. Your appraisal must include a discussion of the alternative strategies that could have been implemented at the launch of the packages.

2. (a) Based on the data supplied by the market research, calculate the maximum annual profit that canbe earned from the sale of the packages from Year 3 onwards.

   (b) A German computer software distribution company, L, which is interested in becoming the sole distributor of the accounting software packages, has now approached R Ltd. It has offered to purchase 25,000 accounting packages per annum at a fixed price of £930 per package. If R Ltd were to sell the packages to L, then the variable costs would be £300 per package. The current exchange rate is £1 = £0.60.

   Draw a diagram to illustrate the sensitivity of the proposal from the German company to changes in the exchange rate and then state and comment on the minimum exchange rate needed for the proposal to be worth while.

3. R Ltd has signed a contract with L to supply the accounting packages. However, there has been a fire in one of the software manufacturing departments and a machine has been seriously damaged and requires urgent replacement.

   The replacement machine will cost £1 million and R Ltd is considering whether to lease or buy the machine. A lease could be arranged under which R Ltd would pay £300,000 per annum for four years with each payment being made annually in advance. The lease payments would be an allowable expense for taxation purposes.

   Corporation tax is payable at the rate of 30% per annum in two equal instalments: one in the year that profits are earned and the other in the following year. Writing-down allowances are allowed at 25% each year on a reducing balance basis. It is anticipated that the machine will have a useful economic life of four years, at the end of which there will be no residual value.

   The after-tax cost of capital is 12%.

   Evaluate the acquisition of the new machine from a financial viewpoint.

   (*CIMA Management Accounting – Decision Making*, adapted)

**P15–22 Pricing and transfer pricing**
Time allowed: 45 minutes

### Part (a)

The Premier Cycle Company has two divisions: the Frame Division and the Assembly Division. One type of frame produced by the Frame Division is a high-quality carbon frame for racing bicycles. The Frame Division can sell the frames directly to external customers as 'frame only' or the frames can be transferred to the Assembly Division where they are assembled into complete racing bicycles.

*Company policy*
It is current company policy for the managers of each division to seek to maximize their own divisional profits. Consequently, the transfer price of a carbon frame is set by the manager of the Frame Division to be the same as the external selling price.

*Frame Division*
The relationship between the selling price of carbon frames and the annual quantity demanded by external customers is such that at a price of £4,000 there will be no demand, but demand will increase by 500 frames for every £250 decrease in price. The variable cost of producing a carbon frame is £1,000. The division has a maximum annual output of 10,000 frames and fixed costs of £2 million each year.

*Assembly Division*

## 658 Part 3 Planning and control

The relationship between selling price and annual demand for a complete bicycle is such that at a price of £7,000 there will be no demand, but demand will increase by 300 bicycles for every £100 decrease in price. The Assembly Division has a maximum annual capacity of 30,000 assemblies and fixed costs of £1.2 million each year. The total variable costs of additional parts and assembling are £1,750 for each bicycle.

*Note:* If the relationship between Price ($P$) and quantity demanded ($x$) is represented by the equation $Pa - bx$ then Marginal Revenue ($MR$) will be given by $MR = a - 2bx$.

### Required

1. Calculate the unit selling price of an assembled bicycle and the quantity that would be demanded given the current company policy.
2. Calculate the unit selling price, and quantity demanded, of an assembled bicycle that would maximize the profit of the Premier Cycle Company.

### Part (b)

Freezer Foods Ltd is a divisionalized company that specializes in the production of frozen foods. Each division is a profit centre. The Pizza Division produces frozen pizzas. In order to ensure a regular supply of suitable packaging, Freezer Foods Ltd recently acquired a company that produces high-quality packaging. This company is now the Box Division.

*Bonus scheme*
Freezer Foods Ltd will pay a fixed bonus to each Divisional Manager next year if he/she earns a minimum profit equivalent to at least 12% of his/her division's fixed costs.

*Pizza Division*
The manager of the Pizza Division has just won a fixed price contract to supply 7 million pizzas to a chain of food shops. This contract will fully utilize all of the capacity of the Pizza Division for the next year.

Budget details for the next year are:

| Variable cost per pizza | £0.89 (this does *not* include the box) |
| Fixed costs | £4.50 million |
| Revenue | £11.55 million |
| Capacity | 7 million pizzas |

*Box Division*
Budget details for the Box Division for the next year are:

| Variable production cost | £0.025 per box |
| Fixed costs | £1 million |
| External market demand | 32 million boxes |

### Required

1. Calculate the price per box that the Box Division will want to charge the Pizza Division if this is to equal the budgeted external selling price.
2. Calculate the maximum price per box that the Pizza Division would be willing to pay.
3. Discuss the validity of using relevant costs as a basis to set transfer prices for internal performance measurement. You should use data from Freezer Foods Ltd to illustrate your answer.

(*CIMA Management Accounting – Decision Making*, adapted)

## Cases

**C15-23**  Time allowed: 50 minutes

X manufactures and sells audio-visual products. Over the last two years it has developed a DVD recorder (the DVDR). The company is currently deciding whether it should manufacture the DVDR itself or sell the design to another manufacturer for $3 million net of tax. Information relating to the in-house manufacture and sale of the DVDR is as follows.

### Investment

The equipment needed to manufacture the DVDR would cost $5.12 million and could be sold for $1.12 million at the end of Year four. The equipment would be depreciated in equal amounts over four years.

Working capital of $1.2 million will be needed.

### Sales

The Managing Director of X thinks that a target-costing-based approach should be adopted. As a result of a market research survey that has already been conducted at a cost of $750,000, it has been decided that the selling price of the DVDR will be set, and held, at $180 per unit. It is thought that this price will be lower than that charged by competitors.

The annual unit sales forecasts for the DVDR are:

| Year | Unit sales |
| --- | --- |
| 1 | 190,000 |
| 2 | 200,000 |
| 3 | 150,000 |
| 4 | 100,000 |

It is thought that the DVDR will be obsolete in Year 5 due to further advances in audio-visual technology.

### Costs

The Management Accountant expects that the variable costs will reduce as a result of the impact of a learning curve. She has forecast the following relationship between the unit variable cost of a DVDR and the selling price:

| Year | Variable cost/Selling price |
| --- | --- |
| 1 | 105% |
| 2 | 85% |
| 3 | 60% |
| 4 | 60% |

The annual fixed costs directly attributable to the DVDR project are forecast to be:

| | |
| --- | --- |
| Depreciation | $1.00 million |
| Manufacturing overhead | $0.90 million |
| Administration overhead | $0.10 million |
| Marketing and distribution overhead | $0.35 million |

**660** Part 3 Planning and control

## Taxation

X pays tax at 30%. This is payable at the end of the year after that in which profits are earned. An annual writing down allowance of 25% on a reducing balance basis will be available on the manufacturing equipment. The company has sufficient profits from other activities to offset any losses that may arise on the DVDR project.

## Cost of capital

X has an after-tax cost of capital of 14% per year.

## Required

1. Prepare calculations that show, from a financial perspective, whether X should manufacture the DVDR. State clearly your recommendation based upon your calculations.
2. Discuss any other factors that the management of X should consider before making the decision.
3. (a) Briefly explain 'target costing'.
   (b) Identify and explain evidence from the scenario that X has adopted 'target costing'.

(*CIMA Management Accounting – Decision Making*, adapted)

### C15-24 Transfer pricing; divisional performance
Time allowed: 45 minutes

Weller Industries is a decentralized organization with six divisions. The company's Electrical Division produces a variety of electrical items, including an X52 electrical fitting. The Electrical Division (which is operating at capacity) sells this fitting to its regular customers for £7.50 each; the fitting has a variable manufacturing cost of £4.25.

The company's Brake Division has asked the Electrical Division to supply it with a large quantity of X52 fittings for only £5 each. The Brake Division, which is operating at 50% of capacity, will put the fitting into a brake unit that it will produce and sell to a large commercial airline manufacturer. The cost of the brake unit being built by the Brake Division follows:

| | |
|---|---|
| Purchased parts (from outside vendors) | £22.50 |
| Electrical fitting X52 | 5.00 |
| Other variable costs | 14.00 |
| Fixed overhead and administration | 8.00 |
| Total cost per brake unit | £49.50 |

Although the £5 price for the X52 fitting represents a substantial discount from the regular £7.50 price, the manager of the Brake Division believes that the price concession is necessary if his division is to get the contract for the airplane brake units. He has heard 'through the grapevine' that the airplane manufacturer plans to reject his bid if it is more than £50 per brake unit. Thus, if the Brake Division is forced to pay the regular £7.50 price for the X52 fitting, it will either not get the contract or it will suffer a substantial loss at a time when it is already operating at only 50% of capacity. The manager of the Brake Division argues that the price concession is imperative to the well-being of both his division and the company as a whole.

Weller Industries uses return on investment (ROI) and profits in measuring divisional performance.

## Chapter 15 Pricing and intra-company transfers

### Required

1. Assume that you are the manager of the Electrical Division. Would you recommend that your division supply the X52 fitting to the Brake Division for £5 each as requested? Why or why not? Show all computations.
2. Would it be to the economic advantage of the company as a whole for the Electrical Division to supply the fittings to the Brake Division if the airplane brakes can be sold for £50? Show all computations, and explain your answer.
3. In principle, should it be possible for the two managers to agree to a transfer price in this particular situation? If so, within what range would that transfer price lie?
4. Discuss the organizational and manager behaviour problems, if any, inherent in this situation. What would you advise the company's managing director to do in this situation?

*(CMA, adapted)*

**C15–25 Pricing, experience curve**
Time allowed: 50 minutes

VI plc produces a number of mobile telephone products. It is an established company with a good reputation that has been built on well-engineered, reliable and good quality products. It is currently developing a product called Computel and has spent £1.5 million on development so far. The company has to decide whether it should proceed further and launch the product in one year's time.

If VI plc decides to continue with the project, it will incur further development costs of £0.75 million straight away. Assets worth £3.5 million will be required immediately prior to the product launch, and working capital of £1.5 million would be required. VI plc expects that it could sell Computel for three years before the product becomes out of date.

It is estimated that the first 500 Computels produced and sold would cost an average of £675 each unit, for production, marketing and distribution costs. The fixed costs associated with the project are expected to amount to £2.4 million (cash out flow) for each year the product is in production.

Because of the cost estimates, the Chief Executive expected the selling price to be in the region of £950. However, the Marketing Director is against this pricing strategy; he says that this price is far too high for this type of product and that he could sell only 6,000 units in each year at this price. He suggests a different strategy: setting a price of £425, at which price he expects sales to be 15,000 units each year.

VI plc has found from past experience that a 70% experience curve applies to production, marketing and distribution costs. The company's cost of capital is 7% a year.

### Required

1. The Chief Executive has asked you to help sort out the pricing dilemma. Prepare calculations that demonstrate:
   (a) which of the two suggestions is the better pricing strategy;
   (b) the financial viability of the better strategy.
2. Discuss other issues that VI plc should consider in relation to the two pricing strategies.
3. Calculate and comment on the sensitivity of the financially better pricing strategy to changes in the selling price.

*(CIMA Management Accounting – Decision Making, adapted)*

**C15–26 Divisional performance and transfer pricing**
Time allowed: 60 minutes

G&P plc (hereafter G&P) is a manufacturer of chemical-based products and is a major listed company on the London Stock Exchange. It has two separate operating divisions: the *retailing division* which sells a range of chemical-based cleaning products to supermarkets and the *industrial division* which sells bulk chemicals to other chemical companies for further processing. These divisions are both operated as investment centres.

The company also has three service divisions: marketing, information technology, and research and development. The service divisions charge their services to the two main operating divisions at full standard operating cost, thereby aiming to break even. The service divisions do not currently generate any revenue from other companies.

## The Marketing Division

The directors of G&P have been pleased by the growth in company sales in recent years but they are unsure how much of this is due to the marketing division and how much is due to other factors, such as new products. Two further concerns have now arisen:

- The directors are uncertain how to measure the performance of the marketing division
- A number of key marketing personnel have left the company recently complaining of a lack of performance-based motivation and incentives.

## Strategic solutions

The following two strategies have been proposed to the directors of G&P with respect to the marketing division:

| | |
|---|---|
| Strategy 1 | A change in the transfer pricing system would be introduced to make the marketing division a profit centre as a means of measuring performance and providing incentives. |
| Strategy 2 | The marketing division would become a separate company, Marketo Ltd, with G&P holding a controlling equity stake. The new company would then be operated independently and thus be free to offer its services at commercial prices not only to G&P, but also to external clients. The G&P operating divisions would similarly be free to purchase marketing services from outside the company. |

Under the existing transfer pricing system the budgeted summary profit and loss account for the year to 30 June 2010 for the marketing division would be as follows:

| | £m | £m |
|---|---|---|
| Revenue | | 36 |
| Variable costs | 30 | |
| Fixed costs | | |
| Use of G&P premises | 2 | |
| Fixed overheads | 4 | |
| Profit | | 36 |
| | | Nil |

The company is considering measuring performance using residual income. In this case the divisional capital employed would be £20 million and the annual rate of interest 10%. Interest has not been included in the above summary profit and loss account.

## Required

1. Assess, and critically appraise, how performance measures can be used in respect of the marketing division in each of the following circumstances:
    (a) The current system

(b) Strategy 1
(c) Strategy 2.

2  Evaluate the incentives that can be given to marketing division managers under each of the performance measures identified in Question 1.

3  Assume that Strategy 2 is implemented and that external sales of £10 million per year are expected by Marketo Ltd, priced on the basis of variable cost plus 25%.

Calculate the annual revenue that must be generated from sales with G&P to achieve an overall residual income for Marketo Ltd of £3 million. Assume for this purpose that fixed costs are £6 million and that the mark-up on variable costs in respect of sales to G&P is as per the original budget.

(*ICAEW Business Management*, adapted)

**C15–27 Integrative case: relevant costs; pricing**
⏲ Time allowed: 50 minutes

Jenco Ltd's only product is a combination fertilizer-weed killer called Fertikil. Fertikil is sold nationwide through normal marketing channels to retail nurseries and garden stores.

Taylor Nursery plans to sell a similar fertilizer-weed killer compound through its regional nursery chain under its own private label. Taylor does not have manufacturing facilities of its own, so it has asked Jenco (and several other companies) to submit a bid for manufacturing and delivering a 25,000-kilo order of the private brand compound to Taylor. While the chemical composition of the Taylor compound differs from that of Fertikil, the manufacturing processes are very similar.

The Taylor compound would be produced in 1,000 kilo lots. Each lot would require 30 direct labour-hours and the following chemicals:

| Chemicals | Quantity in kilos |
| --- | --- |
| CW–3 | 400 |
| JX–6 | 300 |
| MZ–8 | 200 |
| BE–7 | 100 |

The first three chemicals (CW–3, JX–6, and MZ–8) are all used in the production of Fertikil. BE–7 was used in another compound that Jenco discontinued several months ago. The supply of BE–7 that Jenco had on hand when the other compound was discontinued was not discarded. Jenco could sell its supply of BE–7 at the prevailing market price less £0.10 per kilo selling and handling expenses.

Jenco also has on hand a chemical called CN–5, which was manufactured for use in another product that is no longer produced. CN–5, which cannot be used in Fertikil, can be substituted for CW–3 on a one-for-one basis without affecting the quality of the Taylor compound. The CN–5 in inventory has a salvage value of £500.

Inventory and cost data for the chemicals that can be used to produce the Taylor compound are as shown below:

| Raw material | Kilos in inventory | Actual price per kilo when purchased | Current market price per kilo |
| --- | --- | --- | --- |
| CW–3 | 22,000 | £0.80 | £0.90 |
| JX–6 | 5,000 | 0.55 | 0.60 |
| MZ–8 | 8,000 | 1.40 | 1.60 |
| BE–7 | 4,000 | 0.60 | 0.65 |
| CN–5 | 5,500 | 0.75 | (Salvage) |

**664** Part 3 Planning and control

The current direct labour rate is £14 per hour. The predetermined overhead rate is based on direct labour-hours (DLH). The predetermined overhead rate for the current year, based on a two-shift capacity of 400,000 total DLH with no overtime, is as follows:

| Variable manufacturing overhead | £4.50 per DLH |
| Fixed manufacturing overhead | 7.50 per DLH |
| Combined rate | £12.00 per DLH |

Jenco's production manager reports that the present equipment and facilities are adequate to manufacture the Taylor compound. Therefore, the order would have no effect on total fixed manufacturing overhead costs. However, Jenco is within 400 hours of its two-shift capacity this month. Any additional hours beyond 400 hours must be done in overtime. If need be, the Taylor compound could be produced on regular time by shifting a portion of Fertikil production to overtime. Jenco's rate for overtime hours is one and a half times the regular pay rate, or £21 per hour. There is no allowance for any overtime premium in the predetermined overhead rate.

### Required:

1 Jenco, has decided to submit a bid for a 25,000-kilo order of Taylor Nursery's new compound. The order must be delivered by the end of the current month. Taylor Nursery has indicated that this is a one-time order that will not be repeated. Calculate the lowest price that Jenco could bid for the order without reducing its net operating income.

2 Refer to the original data. Assume that Taylor Nursery plans to place regular orders for 25,000-kilo lots of the new compound during the coming year. Jenco expects the demand for Fertikil to remain strong. Therefore, the recurring orders from Taylor Nursery would put Jenco over its two-shift capacity. However, production could be scheduled so that 60% of each Taylor Nursery order could be completed during regular hours. As another option, some Fertikil production could be shifted temporarily to overtime so that the Taylor Nursery orders could be produced on regular time. Current market prices are the best available estimates of future market prices.

Jenco's standard mark-up policy for new products is 40% of the full manufacturing cost, including fixed manufacturing overhead. Calculate the price that Jenco would quote Taylor Nursery for each 25,000-kilo lot of the new compound, assuming that it is to be treated as a new product and this pricing policy is followed.

**C15–28 Transfer pricing; divisional performance**
⏱ Time allowed: 50 minutes

Stanco Plc is a decentralized organization with five divisions. The company's Electronics Division produces a variety of electronics items, including an XL5 circuit board. The division (which is operating at capacity) sells the XL5 circuit board to regular customers for £12.50 each. The circuit boards have a variable production cost of £8.25 each.

The company's Clock Division has asked the Electronics Division to supply it with a large quantity of XL5 circuit boards for only £9 each. The Clock Division, which is operating at only 60% of capacity, will put the circuit boards into a timing device that it will produce and sell to a large oven manufacturer. The cost of the timing device being manufactured by the Clock Division follows:

| XL5 circuit board (desired cost) | £9.00 |
| Other purchased parts (from outside vendors) | 30.00 |
| Other variable costs | 20.75 |
| Fixed overhead and administrative costs | 10.00 |
| Total cost per timing device | £69.75 |

The manager of the Clock Division feels that she can't quote a price greater than £70 per timing device to the oven manufacturer if her division is to get the job. As shown above, in order to keep the price at £70 or less, she can't pay more than £9 per unit to the Electronics Division for the XL5 circuit boards. Although the £9 price for the XL5 circuit boards represents a substantial discount from the normal £12.50 price, she feels that the price concession is necessary for her division to get the oven manufacturer contract and thereby keep its core of highly trained people.

The company uses return on investment (ROI) to measure divisional performance.

### Required

1. Assume that you are the manager of the Electronics Division. Would you recommend that your division supply the XL5 circuit boards to the Clock Division for £9 each as requested? Why or why not? Show all computations.
2. Would it be profitable for the company as a whole for the Electronics Division to supply the Clock Division with the circuit boards for £9 each? Explain your answer.
3. In principle, should it be possible for the two managers to agree to a transfer price in this particular situation? If so, within what range would that transfer price lie?
4. Discuss the organizational and manager behaviour problems, if any, inherent in this situation. What would you advise the company's CEO to do in this situation?

## Endnotes

1. Harris (1999).
2. The term 'ln()' is the natural log function. You can compute the natural log of any number using the LN or lnx key on your calculator. For example, ln(0.85) = 20.1625.
   This formula assumes that the price elasticity of demand is constant. This occurs when the relation between the selling price, $p$, and the unit sales, $q$, can be expressed in the following form: $\ln(q) = a = \varepsilon_d \ln(p)$. Even if this is not precisely true, the formula provides a useful way to estimate a product's real price elasticity.
3. The estimated change in unit sales should take into account competitors' responses to a price change.
4. The formula assumes that (a) the price elasticity of demand is constant; (b) Total cost = Total fixed cost = Variable cost per unit $\times q$; and (c) the price of the product has no effect on the sales or costs of any other product. The formula can be derived using calculus.
5. Kimes (1989).
6. Harris (1999).
7. The exhibit is adapted from Abdallah (1988).
8. Davies (2002).
9. Sikka (2002). For other examples, see AABA website, www.visar.csustan.edu/aaba/home.htm
10. Brick (2001).

When you have read this chapter, log on to the Online Learning Centre for *Management Accounting* at www.mcgraw-hill.co.uk/textbooks/seal, where you'll find multiple choice questions, practice exams and extra study tools for each chapter.

# Value-Based Management and Strategic Management Accounting

# CHAPTER 16

# Value-based management and strategic management accounting

## LEARNING OBJECTIVES

After studying Chapter 16, you should be able to:

1. Define the concepts of strategy and strategic management accounting
2. Understand the impact of corporate strategy on management accounting
3. Understand the relationship between profit-planning and value-based management
4. Understand some basic strategic models and their relationship with management accounting techniques
5. Examine the impact of lean technologies
6. Understand how a balanced scorecard fits together and how it supports a company's strategy
7. Consider the impact of emergent strategies and organizational learning on management accounting

## CONCEPTS IN CONTEXT

Some commentators have argued that the recent Credit Crunch represents a 'structural break' in the business environment. In the US and UK and in parts of Europe, the fast growing sectors of finance and construction are unlikely to grow and may even contract. Western consumers cannot plausibly live off Chinese or Japanese savers for ever. These changes mean that it is no longer possible just to extrapolate from the past. Budgets cannot just be based on a few percentage changes from previous years – a company's whole strategic position may need reassessment. Strategic management accounting provides tools, concepts and practices that can help managers choose and implement new strategies appropriate to a post-Credit Crunch world.

© Pali Rao

*Source*: Rumelt, R. 2008. Strategy in a 'structural break', *McKinsey Quarterly*, December

Part 4 Value metrics and performance management in a strategic context

**LEARNING OBJECTIVE 1**

The term 'strategic management accounting' (SMA) has been used to describe the process of 'provision and analysis of management accounting data about a business and its competitors for use in developing and monitoring business strategy'.[1] We may illustrate the basic ideas of SMA by looking at one of the leading retailers in the United Kingdom, Tesco, which has tailored its key performance indicators to the economics of its business. For example, rather than maximize EVA, Tesco has realized that its main fixed assets are its stores. With this type of asset base, the company aims to reduce the cost of building good quality new stores through strategic partnering with construction companies. In order to check its market positioning, the company is constantly monitoring the prices of its merchandise relative to the prices charged by its main competitors. As well as promoting customer loyalty, it uses its store card as a database for targeting the specific needs of individual customers as revealed through their purchase patterns. It also keeps a close eye on non-financial indicators such as the length of queues at the checkouts.

**LEARNING OBJECTIVE 2**

In this chapter we will review both short- and long-term financial planning but in the context of *strategic choice*. **Strategic choice** means that companies can *choose* which industries and products they want to compete in but it also means that different companies in the *same* industry may decide to adopt different strategies with quite different implications for management accounting and control. For example, a company's strategy may determine whether management will be concentrating on a tight control of costs, maintaining quality or generating new product ideas.

As more and more reliance is placed on bought-in goods and services, a higher proportion of costs are generated by a firm's suppliers, which suggests that major improvements in cost, quality and innovation are potentially available through the effective management of the firm's supply chain. In *strategic* as opposed to *traditional* management accounting, there is a recognition that managers may have some freedom to choose which industry they operate in, which technology is used and how the organization is structured. Thus, rather than passively adapting to given competitive, technological and organizational circumstances, **strategic management accounting (SMA)** helps managers make choices through information support. Strategic management accounting is also concerned with the *implementation* of strategies by setting up control systems that drive through the chosen strategies. For example, if a company wishes to pursue a low-cost strategy then traditional budgetary control may help implementation. However, few companies compete on price alone so additional performance measures may be non-financial, such as delivery or queueing time.

As described above, Tesco's approach in linking its goals and its management information systems demonstrates many of the principles of SMA. The company has decided how it is going to compete, reviewed its internal and external operations and chosen key performance indicators that enable it to monitor the development of its chosen business model. The search for data is driven by decision needs rather than by what is simply easily available.

Finally, in some businesses, strategy is seen as involving **organizational learning** rather than as a top-down, centralized process. In this business model, management accounting may be used as part of an interactive communication process both within the organization and between the organization and its customers and suppliers.

The chapter begins by showing how the techniques developed in Chapters 2–15 can be used to plan and control profit and shareholder value. We will then consider the limitations of this framework and argue that these techniques can be further enhanced by putting them in a strategic context. While traditional management accounting focuses on the analysis of existing activities, with SMA there is a concern with the analysis of data about the organization in relation to its competitors in order to monitor and develop business options. Performance indicators should be relative, with a continuous recognition of *rivalry* with competitors. For example, market share has intrinsic value because a high market share may reflect weaker competition. As in a game of chess, there is a need not only to develop your own strategy but also to understand the strategy of your opponent. In many instances, strategic management accounting may involve new applications of existing approaches rather than new techniques. For example, strategic management accounting that attempts to measure competitors' or suppliers' costs may well use the same sort of techniques that we have already covered in the earlier parts of the book. Yet the context of the cost analysis will be different because strategic management seeks to establish *relative* market positions and *relative* costs.

## Profit planning with a given industry and product: cost structure and business orientation

**LEARNING OBJECTIVE 3**

Traditionally, management accounting is presented as a matter of fitting cost systems to particular business environments and technological tasks. As we saw in Chapters 3 and 4, process or job costing systems are applied according to batch sizes and the nature of the product. We may decide that a given cost structure of a business will help to determine its profit planning orientation as discussed in our work on flexible budgeting in Chapter 13. The first steps to profit planning can be based on a combination of the techniques introduced in earlier chapters – particularly, *cost behaviour, CVP analysis, flexible budgeting* and *pricing* as shown in Exhibit 16.1. Thus cost behaviour analysis may help determine whether a business is 'market-oriented' or 'cost-oriented'.[2] If, for example, the business has a high proportion of fixed costs relative to variable costs, then it may be seen as being 'market-oriented' because, as CVP analysis indicates, it has to achieve high levels of capacity utilization in order to break even.

Profit planning techniques not only may help the choice of business orientation but they also lend themselves to the possibility of 'what-if' sensitivity exercises. For example, given a firm's cost and revenue structure, how would the firm's profits change with a 10% cut in price or 10% cut in fixed costs? As shown in Chapter 15, techniques such as *yield management* may also be used as they are in the airline and hotel industries, to segment the market and offer different prices to different segments at different booking times. Finally, the practice of flexible budgeting ensures that variance analysis is based on variable levels of activity rather than a single estimate as with static budgeting.

## Value-based management

Useful as they are for short-term decision making there are a number of limitations to the techniques in the basic profit planning model. First, short-term profit increases may be made at the expense of long-term profit.[3] Second, there is no analysis of the use of capital resources. Indeed, from a *shareholder perspective*, a 'company only makes a real or economic profit after it has repaid the cost of capital that was used to generate it'.[4] Third, the approach is inward- rather than outward-looking – for example, how would the firm's competitors react to a 10% cut in price? Is it realistic to just assume that they will not also respond with similar cuts? Finally, a focus on profit by definition limits the applicability of the approach to for-profit organizations and neglects the interests of other *stakeholders* such as consumers, employees or regulators.

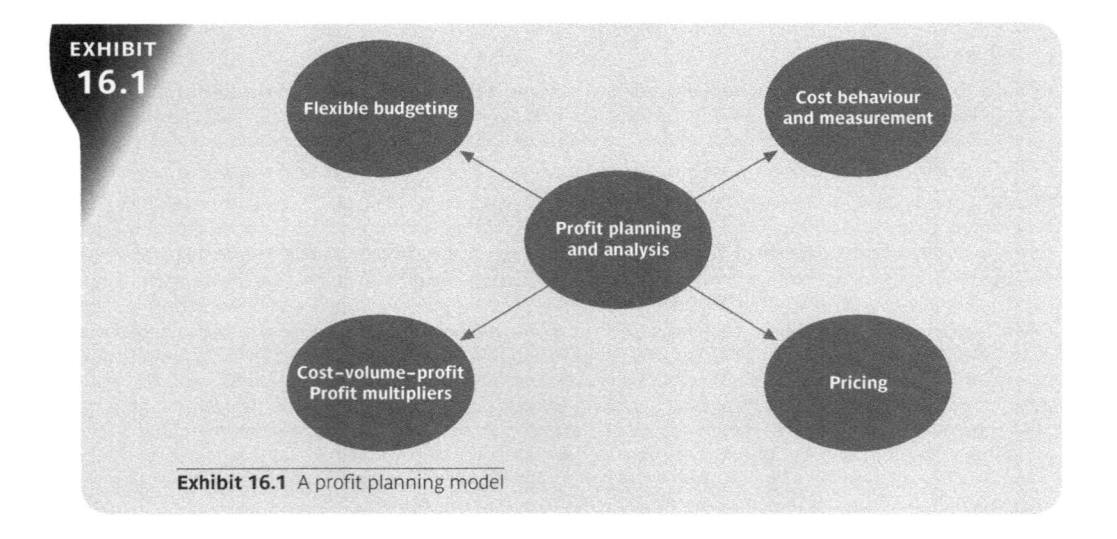

**EXHIBIT 16.1**

- Flexible budgeting
- Cost behaviour and measurement
- Profit planning and analysis
- Cost–volume–profit Profit multipliers
- Pricing

**Exhibit 16.1** A profit planning model

The criticisms that profit-seeking is short-termist and ignores the cost and allocation of capital have been explicitly addressed in for-profit firms by focusing on the goal of increasing shareholder wealth through the application of *value-based management*. In its narrowest form, **value-based management (VBM)** focuses on how to increase a shareholder wealth metric such as *residual income* (see Chapter 14) or *net present value* (see Chapter 10) through the identification and management of value-drivers.[5] In its wider form, value-based management is 'an integrated framework for measuring and managing businesses, with the explicit objective of creating superior long-term value for shareholders'.[6] In this chapter, we prefer to adopt the narrower definition of VBM as it enables us to distinguish between VBM and SMA with the latter emphasizing the importance of *competitor analysis*. Indeed, as our *Management accounting in action* section illustrates below, companies that have embraced VBM have not always analysed their competitors' actions very carefully.

## MANAGEMENT ACCOUNTING IN ACTION: A LESSON FROM BUSINESS HISTORY

Arnold Weinstock became GEC's Managing Director in 1963 and was behind a big expansion and diversification with the take-over of Associated Electrical Industries (AEI) in 1967 and, in 1968, with the merger with English Electric. At this point, GEC was the fourth largest industrial company in the UK and the second largest electrical company in the world outside the USA. GEC continued to expand and diversify with the acquisition of Yarrow Shipbuilders in 1974 and Avery in 1979. The late 1980s witnessed further mergers and joint ventures, with the creation of GPT by GEC and Plessey in 1988, and the joint acquisition of Plessey by GEC and Siemens the following year. An equal investment by GEC and Compagnie General d'Electricitie (CGE) formed the power generation and transport arm, GEC ALSTHOM, in 1989.

### Accounting ratios and control routines in GEC

Copying some aspects of the pioneers of divisionalization such as General Motors and Du Pont, GEC sought to control a large number of generally unrelated business units (sometimes as many as 140). Never designed to fit a particular product-market environment, GEC managed diversity through a *financial control style*.[7] Financial control companies create standalone business units, do not formally intervene in the companies' strategies but monitor results through financial targets. GEC seemed to fit the model perfectly because while strategy was the responsibility of the various investment centres, Weinstock monitored their financial performance frequently and personally. In GEC's case, the financial links between the centre and the business units were particularly tight. Business units had to submit a monthly report, which would be analysed by Weinstock. The format was rigid. The first page contained a number of figures, such as the ratio of sales and profit to capital employed, debtors' ratios and a cumulative record of sales per employee. Subsequent pages would include further details of significance in a *financial accounting* perspective, such as a breakdown of provisions and capital employed. In the latter analysis, cash was identified as negative funding – the property of the parent rather than the subsidiary! There was relatively little emphasis on profit and loss and no attempt to consolidate results until the year-end. In short, accounting ratios were a central part of GEC's *routines* of management and internal reporting. While the growth of GEC may sometimes have seemed haphazard and opportunistic, there was nothing haphazard about the 'Weinstock system' based on financial ratios and a monthly internal reporting system.

### Marconi (1996–2001) boom...

The retirement of Weinstock and changes in some major customers in the defence and telecom industries plus an emerging preference in the City for focused companies led to a change in management style that affected both the nature and corporate role of its management accounting. The appointment of George Simpson as Chief Executive together with a number of other strategic appointments

Chapter 16 Value-based management and strategic management accounting

was accompanied by a new management ethos of 'GEC to be no. 1 or no. 2 in the world in particular industries'. As a symbol of the policy of focus, GEC changed its name to Marconi, a name reminiscent of the pioneer of radio.[8]

The new strategic direction involved different ways of working. In particular, the old source of expansion through largely unrelated acquisition had been abandoned. The company was seeking organic growth and acquisition that would enhance its market and technological capability. Acquisitions were intended to be integrated to fully exploit cross-selling and technological synergies.

Other changes were:

- Globalization, with acquisitions in Europe, North America and the Asia–Pacific region.
- Integration of acquisitions. Financial reports that were sent to the group finance office were arrayed in a matrix structure so that items such as sales, profit and loss, and so on, could be viewed from both product and regional perspectives.
- The introduction of an EVA-style value management system that signalled a continuous awareness of the company's stock market performance.
- More outsourcing, with a new emphasis on process and multi-functional teams in supply chain management.
- More diversity in reporting and decision-making innovations. In particular, non-financial performance indicators were reported directly to the finance group by a specially designated Performance Improvement function.

### . . . and bust!

Marconi's rise and fall was not untypical of many companies in the global telecom sector. From a share price that peaked at over £12 in 2000, a series of profit warnings culminated in huge losses and a collapse in the share price to a few pence in 2002. The difference between Marconi and many other high-tech bubble companies was its transformation from a cash-rich conglomerate as GEC to a company that is now non-existent as an independent business entity.

There are a number of points to note in this case. It could be argued that it illustrates the limitations of the narrow view of value-based management which focuses on a shareholder value metric such as residual income but does little to indicate how value is to be created or sustained. GEC/Marconi *did* change from ROI to value-based management and it *did* introduce some improved operational innovations in its business processes and supply chain. But as the case demonstrates so dramatically, it is no good being world class at producing a product when the market for that product is so overcrowded with competitors! With the benefit of hindsight, the company's adoption of management innovations was incomplete. In particular, the *strategic management accounting information* that could monitor developments in the industry as a whole was either not collected or was not analysed in a systematic way.

The next section of the chapter will show how SMA can be used to help to *choose*, *implement* and *monitor* a company's strategy. It will introduce a number of ways of developing strategy and some new metrics, non-financial as well as financial, in order to implement and monitor strategy. As will be shown in Chapter 17, the basic ideas of SMA and scorecards can also be applied to not-for-profit organizations and accommodate social and environmental objectives.

## Some basic techniques of strategic management accounting

SMA has an orientation towards the firm's environment. The relevant environment may be in its value chain, that is, its 'upstream' relations with suppliers and 'downstream' relations with its customers. The other relevant environment is its competitive position relative to both existing and potential competitors. Its competitive position will not just depend on price but on a **marketing mix**.

**Part 4** Value metrics and performance management in a strategic context

> ### FOCUS ON PRACTICE
> #### GEC – right metric, wrong strategy?
> GEC was an example of a company that seemed to thrive while it used ROI but then collapsed as it adopted value-based management/residual income. Yet a more sophisticated analysis might suggest that it was the choice of strategy rather than the adoption of a particular metric that led to problems. The company focused on telecoms just at the height of the so-called Dotcom bubble when many other companies also decided to focus on that industry. As a consequence, there was overcapacity in that industry and a fall in profitability.
>
> **Exercise**: Perhaps GEC should have paid more attention to actions of its competitors as suggested by the principles of SMA? Discuss.
>
> *Source*: Seal, W.B. 2010. Managerial discourse and the link between theory and practice: from ROI to value-based management, *Management Accounting Research*, 21, pp. 95–109

Sometimes SMA will use existing information and sometimes new information will be sought. For example, the increased emphasis on marketing may involve the use of techniques such as **attribute costing** that costs product attributes that appeal to customers, using brand value as a basis for managerial decisions and measuring the costs of quality. The competitive position is monitored through competitor cost assessment through estimates of competitors' costs based on an appraisal of facilities, technology, economies of scale, market share, volume, unit costs and return on sales. Strategic management accounting is also concerned with the long run through the use of target and **life-cycle costing**[9] that looks at the costs incurred throughout the life of a product as it goes through various stages such as development and full production.

## SMA and the concept of strategic positioning

Both the choice of strategic options and the ongoing search for strategic information may be informed by a variety of corporate strategy models. In short, a further development of SMA integrates the more outward and forward-looking aspects of the strategic intelligence approach with some well-known models of strategic choice.

Some strategic choice models involve deciding on a company's *strategic position*. For example, following Miles and Snow,[10] should the company be a **defender** concentrating on reducing costs and/or improving quality, a **prospector** continually searching for market opportunities or an analyser which combines the defender and prospector positions? Or, following Michael Porter,[11] should the company concentrate on **cost leadership** (aiming to be the lowest-cost producer in an industry) or **product differentiation** (maintain a price premium based on superior product quality)? Porter argues that: '(T)he worst strategic error is to be *stuck in the middle* or to try simultaneously to pursue all the strategies. This is a recipe for strategic mediocrity and below-average performance, because pursuing all strategies simultaneously means that a firm is not able to achieve any of them because of their inherent contradictions.'[12]

The implications for management accounting of these positional strategies could be that a company that seeks cost leadership may use standard costing with flexible budgets for manufacturing cost control. With product cost being the key input to pricing decisions, it may also analyse costs of competitors in order to review its positioning. If the company is a differentiator then traditional costing may be less important, and more attention is paid to new product development and marketing expenditures.

Porter's generic strategy model may be linked to another of his innovations, the concept of the value chain. The **value chain**,[13] which is illustrated in Exhibit 16.2, consists of the major business functions that add value to a company's products and services. All these functions, from research and development through product design, manufacturing, marketing, distribution and customer service, are required to bring a product or service to the customer and generate revenues.

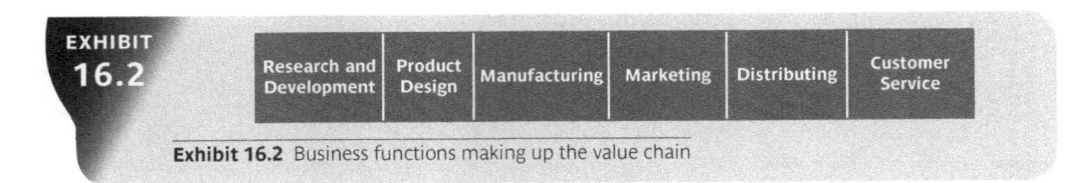

Chapter 16 Value-based management and strategic management accounting

**EXHIBIT 16.2**

| Research and Development | Product Design | Manufacturing | Marketing | Distributing | Customer Service |

**Exhibit 16.2** Business functions making up the value chain

With value-chain analysis, the aim is to find linkages between value-creating activities, which result in lower costs and/or enhanced differentiation. John Shank's *strategic cost management*[14] approach shows how Porter's ideas on strategic positioning and gaining competitive advantage can have an impact on management accounting. Shank advocates a cost-driver analysis, which suggests that costs are driven by *structural* and *executional* factors. **Structural drivers** consider factors such as scale, scope, experience, technology and complexity, while **executional drivers** include factors such as work force involvement, quality management capacity utilization, plant lay-out efficiency, product configuration effectiveness, and exploitation of linkages.

## Strategic investment appraisal: investment appraisal with strategic 'bolt-ons'?

In Chapter 10, we considered the various techniques of investment appraisal such as net present value and internal rate of return. In principle, many strategic decisions, such as acquisitions or major marketing initiatives, could be analysed using these techniques by estimating and discounting future net cash flows and choosing the option that seems to give the highest return or largest NPV. As we also saw in Chapter 10, the risks attached to the various options may also be analysed using mathematical techniques. Yet some advocates of more strategic approaches have argued that the conventional investment appraisal approach may set up business problems in a misleading way with an overemphasis on financial calculation leaving strategic issues either neglected or treated in an *ad hoc*, 'bolt-on' manner. John Shank argues that the NPV model follows four steps:

Step 1    Identifying spending proposals
Step 2    Quantitative analysis of incremental cash flows
Step 3    Qualitative issues that cannot be fitted into NPV are then treated in an *ad hoc* manner
Step 4    Decision – *Yes/No*.

According to Shank, in conventional capital budgeting/investment appraisals, *Step 1* is hardly analysed since the investment proposals just appear out of thin air. *Step 2*, in contrast, gets a great deal of attention with elaborate considerations of relevant cash flows and sophisticated treatments of risk. *Step 3* is a 'step-child' concerned with 'soft-issues' that cannot be handled in *Step 2*. *Step 4*, the decision, *then generally flows out of Step 2*.

Shank[15] argues that the finance framework sets up strategic problems in a misleading way and argues that pure NPV analysis misses the richness of real business problems and is often merely set up to rationalize a prior decision. He illustrates the point with a case study, *Mavis Machines*.

### The Mavis Machines case

Mavis Machine shop is a small metal working company producing drill bits for oil exploration. At present, the shop has four large manual lathes each operated by a skilled worker. The question facing the Managing Director of Mavis Machines is whether the company should install a numerically controlled lathe to replace all manual lathes. The numerical lathe would require only one operator but with different skills in computerized automation.

**Part 4** Value metrics and performance management in a strategic context

The decision can be set up using an NPV model and produces a very high rate of internal rate of return, as shown in Exhibit 16.3.

The main cash savings stem from the need for fewer workers. However, other significant savings can be made in the net cost of the initial investment because of the healthy trade-in value of the relatively modern manual lathes. Indeed, 60% of the attractiveness of the project comes from the scrap value of the old machines, which suggests that the previous replacement decision might have been faulty. In an NPV approach other factors such as *flexibility, marketing* and *corporate image* are treated in rather an *ad hoc* manner.

An alternative strategic approach suggests a different perspective on the choice. Indeed when explicit strategic models are used to explore the issues the emphasis on a positive NPV in the financial analysis is eclipsed

---

**EXHIBIT 16.3**

**Net Investment**

| | | |
|---|---|---|
| Purchase price | | $680,000 |
| Less: | | |
| Trade-in value of old machines | | (240,000) |
| Tax saving from trade-in (46%) | | (108,000) |
| Book value | 476,000 | |
| Selling price | 240,000 | |
| Loss on resale | 236,000 | |
| Investment tax credit (10%) | | (68,000) |
| **Net** | | **($263,400)** |

**Annual cash savings**

| | | |
|---|---|---|
| Labour – six operators (3/shift × 2 shifts) × $20,800 each | | ($124,800) |
| Factory space savings (no difference in cash flows) | | 0 |
| Other cash savings (supplies, maintenance and power) | | 20,000 |
| Total, pre-tax | | $144,800 |
| Less additional taxes (46%) | | (60,600) |
| Cash saved – pre-tax | 144,800 | |
| Additional depreciation | (13,000)* | |
| Additional taxable income | 131,800 | |
| Annual after tax cash savings | | $84,200 |
| (ignoring inflation in savings in future years) | | |

*Old depreciation = $590 – $20/15 = $38,000
New depreciation = $680 – $68/12 = $51,000
Difference = $13,000

Summary of cash flows*
Period 0 (263,400) 12 year IRR = 32 + %, real

**Periods 1–12 $84,200**

*Ignoring the minor impact from the lost salvage values in year 12.

*Source*: Shank, J. 1996. 'Analyzing technology investments – from NPV to Strategic Cost Management', *Management Accounting Research*, 7, 185–97.

**Exhibit 16.3** Summary of the quantitative analysis of the automation project in Mavis Machines

by other factors. *Competitive analysis* suggests that as a small machine shop, Mavis is best positioned as a *niche* player rather than a cost leader. The manual lathes and the skilled operators give it more product flexibility and greater security than one numerical lathe. Its strength lies in its flexibility to vary its products and sources of raw material. *Value chain analysis* suggested that it would lose both buyer and seller power because it would be more dependent only on those suppliers that could meet stringent quality requirements and would be more dependent on a single customer. There were also questions concerning the ease of maintenance of the new machine and the likely impact that firing eight workers out of a small work force would have on morale and the firm's local reputation.

## Strategic investment appraisal: an iterative model

Does the criticism of NPV by Shank and others mean that the material in Chapter 10 is of limited relevance for strategic decisions? Not according to Tomkins and Carr,[16] who suggest that strategic investment decisions may be modelled to include both financial and strategic analysis as shown in Exhibit 16.4. They suggest that a three-stage approach is followed:

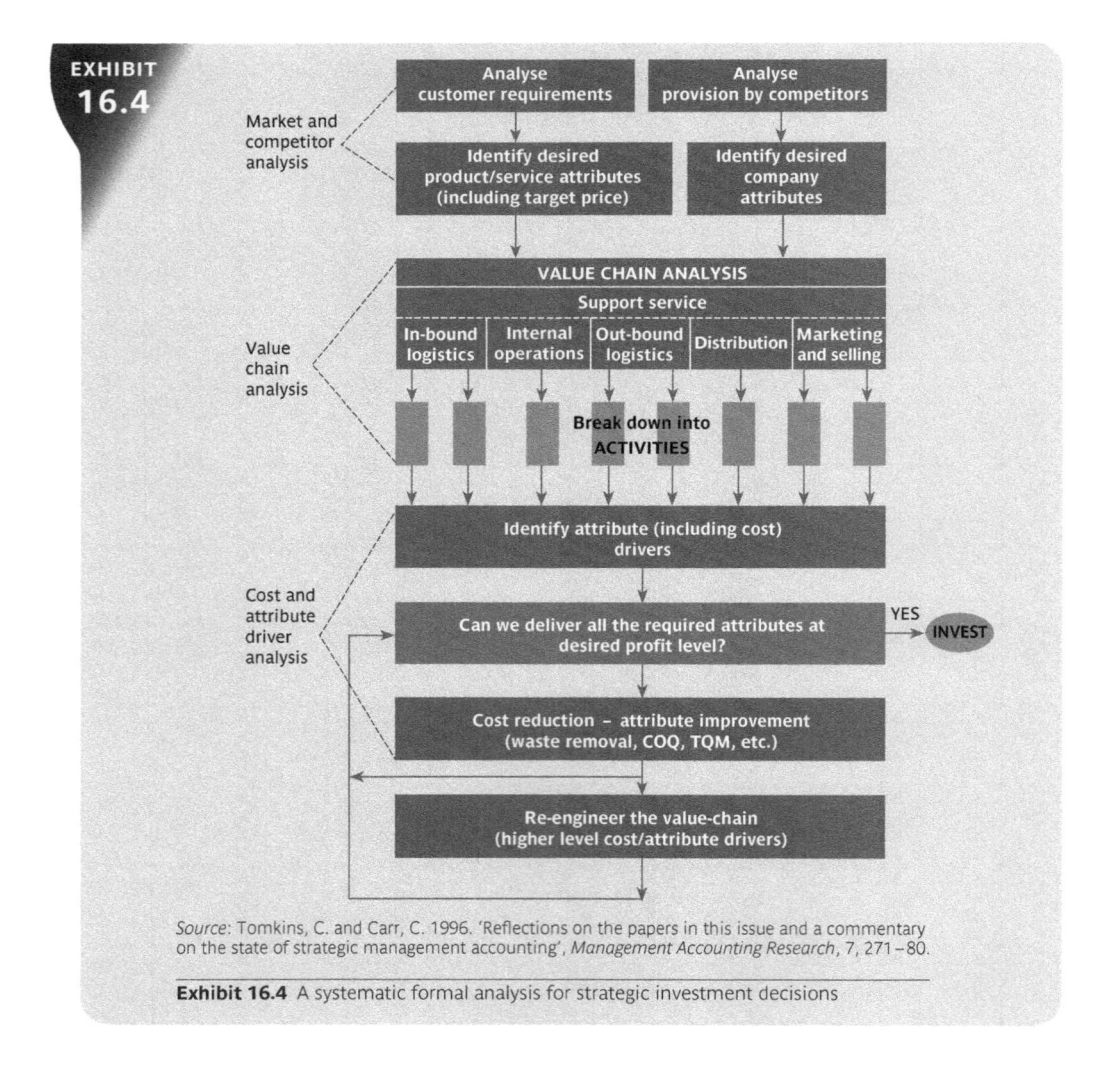

**EXHIBIT 16.4**

```
Market and competitor analysis:
    Analyse customer requirements  →  Analyse provision by competitors
           ↓                                    ↓
    Identify desired product/service         Identify desired
    attributes (including target price)      company attributes
           ↓                                    ↓

Value chain analysis:
    VALUE CHAIN ANALYSIS
    Support service
    In-bound logistics | Internal operations | Out-bound logistics | Distribution | Marketing and selling
                            Break down into ACTIVITIES

Cost and attribute driver analysis:
    Identify attribute (including cost) drivers
           ↓
    Can we deliver all the required attributes at desired profit level?  — YES →  INVEST
           ↓ (No)
    Cost reduction – attribute improvement
    (waste removal, COQ, TQM, etc.)
           ↓
    Re-engineer the value-chain
    (higher level cost/attribute drivers)
```

*Source*: Tomkins, C. and Carr, C. 1996. 'Reflections on the papers in this issue and a commentary on the state of strategic management accounting', *Management Accounting Research*, 7, 271–80.

**Exhibit 16.4** A systematic formal analysis for strategic investment decisions

**Part 4** Value metrics and performance management in a strategic context

1. The firm decides which markets to be in, by assessing both customer requirements and the relative ability of rivals to meet them. The firm will generate a number of investment possibilities based on product attributes related to volume of sales.
2. Analysis of the value chain assesses the means by which the attributes of the product can be delivered. This analysis will review possible suppliers and distributors as part of an iterative process to check on performance throughout the whole product life cycle.
3. The first two steps may then be modelled in terms of a cost and attribute driver analysis to see if the attributes can be delivered at an acceptable profit. The process is iterative in that a first assessment may suggest unacceptable low levels of profitability. The next assessment may then consider whether the profitability can be improved through piecemeal cost savings or whether existing delivery systems must be changed more radically through process re-engineering. Tomkins and Carr call this search for improvement, a process of 'probing' that uses discounted cash flow analysis but which also draws on an array of market, technological and other data.[17]

## Strategy as collision: lean enterprises and business process re-engineering

There have been some criticisms of the strategic positioning models by those who argue that some companies seem to have done quite well by being 'stuck-in-the-middle' and that firms that have failed were not stuck in the middle but just bad at what they were doing.[18] It has also been argued that strategic positioning models were appropriate in the 1970s and 80s but that recently firms face a more hectic form of competition where they cannot choose a generic strategy that tries to avoid head-on competition. According to Cooper[19] the emerging **lean enterprises** do not just compete, they *collide*. Lean enterprises are faced with increasingly sophisticated *lean customers* who can shop around to get the best package. The worldwide web has increased the power of the consumer to acquire product knowledge and search for the best deal. New technology also means customers can 'do it for themselves' whether it is buying air tickets or choosing a new car. Many products such as cars, refrigerators, computers and DVD players have matured. Competition between firms has increased due to falling trade barriers. It is easier to enter a market and easier to start up with new forms of venture capital and more accessible technology.

Lean enterprises have to be technologically up to date and must have a full product line. Differentiation and cost leadership strategies are less viable because costs are already very low and new products can be introduced very quickly. Lean enterprises do not have a chance to create sustainable competitive advantage but can only seek repeatedly to create *temporary* advantages. Rather than avoiding competition by strategic positioning, they seek it out, working on the *survival triplet* based on product *price*, *quality* (conformance), and *functionality* (meeting customer specifications). Lean enterprises are also able to cope with low volume production and attack niche producers.

Lean enterprises rely on close relations with innovating suppliers who all work in regional clusters that increase the overall rate of technological diffusion. Quality becomes a hygiene factor and the firms' survival zones are very narrow.

In the lean company, cost management is vital but it must include feed forward features such as *target costing* and *value engineering* (see Chapters 15 and 19) as well as feedback features such as *kaizen costing* (see Chapter 12). Cost management depends on competitive environment (affects product mix), the maturity of technology (managing the cost of future products) and the length of the product life cycle (managing the cost of existing products). The lean enterprise may be created from scratch or a re-engineered version from an existing company. In Chapter 18, we will look at the process of re-engineering and the lean enterprise in more detail.

## Modelling and monitoring strategy: the balanced scorecard and other non-financial measures

So far in this chapter although we have discussed strategic choice, our focus on *financial metrics* of various sorts is arguably inappropriate for strategic decision making. We will now consider a very influential model, the *balanced scorecard*, which may be used by organizations to develop, implement and control strategy through a balanced use of financial and *non-financial* indicators. Rather than focus on an individual strategic investment, the balanced scorecard is concerned with the maintenance of an outward and forward-looking stance on a continuous and routine basis through a systematic process of monitoring and reporting on a variety of different performance dimensions.

A **balanced scorecard (BSC)** consists of an integrated set of performance measures that are derived from the company's strategy and that support the company's strategy throughout the organization.[20] A strategy is essentially a theory about how to achieve the organization's goals. For example, low-cost European carriers such as easyJet, Ryanair and Go have copied Southwestern Airlines' strategy of offering passengers low prices on short-haul jet service. The low prices result from the absence of costly frills such as meals, assigned seating and interline baggage checking.

Under the balanced scorecard approach, top management translates its strategy into performance measures that employees can understand and can do something about. For example, the amount of time passengers have to wait in line to have their baggage checked might be a performance measure for a supervisor in charge of the check-in counter at an airport. This performance measure is easily understood by the supervisor, and can be improved by the supervisor's actions.

## Divisional performance measures and the balanced scorecard

In Chapter 14 we considered various financial measures of divisional performance such as ROI and RI. The great advantage of the balanced scorecard is that it can provide managers with guidance on how to improve these metrics. Generally speaking, ROI can be increased by increasing sales, decreasing costs, and/or decreasing investments in operating assets. However, it may not be obvious to managers how they are supposed to increase sales, decrease costs and decrease investments in a way that is consistent with the company's strategy. For example, a manager who is given inadequate guidance may cut back on investments that are critical to implementing the company's strategy.

For that reason, when managers are evaluated based on ROI, a *balanced scorecard* approach is advised. And indeed, ROI, or residual income, is typically included as one of the financial performance measures on a company's balanced scorecard. The balanced scorecard provides a way of communicating a company's strategy to managers throughout the organization. The scorecard indicates how the company intends to improve its financial performance. A well-constructed balanced scorecard should answer questions such as: 'What internal business processes should be improved?' and 'Which customer should be targeted and how will they be attracted and retained at a profit?' In short, a well-constructed balanced scorecard can provide managers with a road map that indicates how the company intends to increase its ROI. In the absence of such a road map of the company's strategy, managers may have difficulty understanding what they are supposed to do to increase ROI and they may work at cross-purposes rather than in harmony with the overall strategy of the company. Other critics of EVA are also concerned that a single top-down metric will not be enough to guide the generation of corporate wealth.[21]

## Common characteristics of balanced scorecards

Performance measures used in the balanced scorecard approach tend to fall into the four groups illustrated in Exhibit 16.5: financial, customer, internal business processes, and learning and growth. Internal business processes are what the company does in an attempt to satisfy customers. For example, in a manufacturing company, assembling a product is an internal business process. In an airline, handling baggage is an internal business process. The basic idea is that learning is necessary to improve internal business processes; improving business processes is necessary to improve customer satisfaction; and improving customer satisfaction is necessary to improve financial results.

Note that the emphasis in Exhibit 16.5 is on *improvement* – not on just attaining some specific objective such as profits of £10 million. In the balanced scorecard approach, continual improvement is encouraged. In many industries, this is a matter of survival. If an organization does not continually improve, it will eventually lose out to competitors that do.

Financial performance measures appear at the top of Exhibit 16.5. Ultimately, most companies exist to provide financial rewards to owners. There are exceptions. Some companies – for example, The Body Shop – may

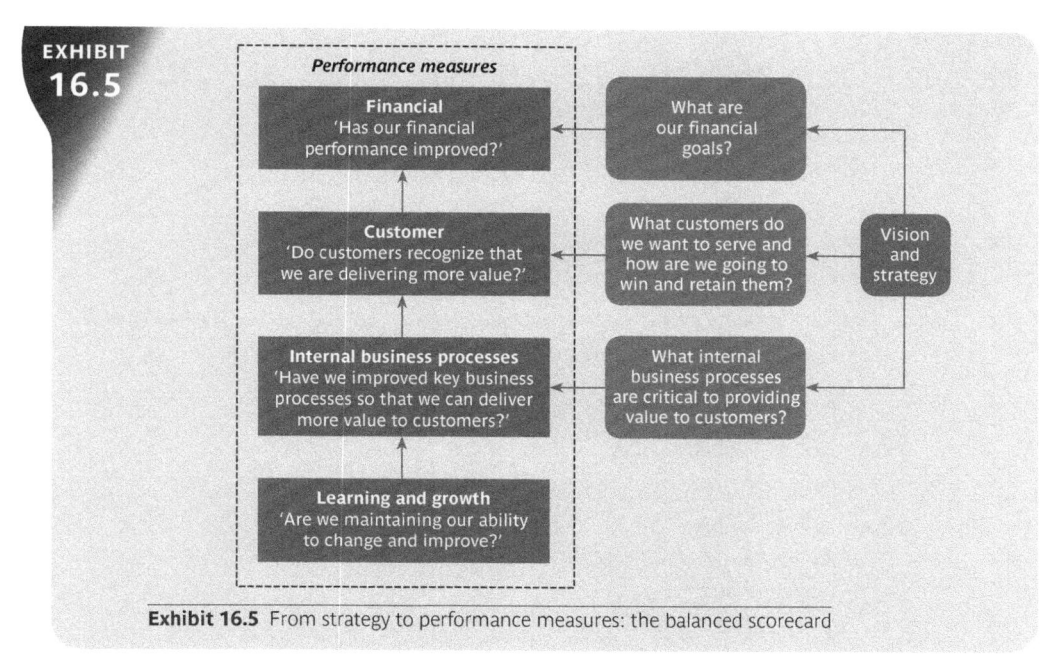

**EXHIBIT 16.5**

**Performance measures**

- **Financial** — 'Has our financial performance improved?'
- **Customer** — 'Do customers recognize that we are delivering more value?'
- **Internal business processes** — 'Have we improved key business processes so that we can deliver more value to customers?'
- **Learning and growth** — 'Are we maintaining our ability to change and improve?'

- What are our financial goals?
- What customers do we want to serve and how are we going to win and retain them?
- What internal business processes are critical to providing value to customers?

**Vision and strategy**

**Exhibit 16.5** From strategy to performance measures: the balanced scorecard

---

have loftier goals, such as providing environmentally friendly products to consumers. However, even non-profit organizations must generate enough financial resources to stay in operation.

Ordinarily, top managers are responsible for the financial performance measures – not lower level managers. The supervisor in charge of checking in passengers can be held responsible for how long passengers have to queue. However, this supervisor cannot reasonably be held responsible for the entire company's profit. That is the responsibility of the airline's top managers.

Exhibit 16.6 lists some examples of performance measures that can be found on the balanced scorecards of companies. However, few companies, if any, would use all of these performance measures, and almost all companies would add other performance measures. Managers should carefully select the performance measures for their company's balanced scorecard, keeping the following points in mind. First and foremost, the performance measures should be consistent with, and follow from, the company's strategy. If the performance measures are not consistent with the company's strategy, people will find themselves working at cross-purposes. Second, the scorecard should not have too many performance measures. This can lead to a lack of focus and confusion.

While the entire organization will have an overall balanced scorecard, each responsible individual will have his or her own personal scorecard as well. This scorecard should consist of items the individual can personally influence that relate directly to the performance measures on the overall balanced scorecard. The performance measures on this personal scorecard should not be overly influenced by actions taken by others in the company or by events that are outside of the individual's control.

With those broad principles in mind, we will now take a look at how a company's strategy affects its balanced scorecard.

## A company's strategy and the balanced scorecard

Returning to the performance measures in Exhibit 16.6, each company must decide which customers to target and what internal business processes are crucial to attracting and retaining those customers. Different companies, having different strategies, will target different customers with different kinds of products and

## EXHIBIT 16.6

| Customer perspective Performance measure | Desired change |
|---|---|
| Customer satisfaction as measured by survey results | + |
| Number of customer complaints | − |
| Market share | + |
| Product returns as a percentage of sales | − |
| Percentage of customers retained from last period | + |
| Number of new customers | + |

| Internal business processes perspective Performance measure | Desired change |
|---|---|
| Percentage of sales from new products | + |
| Time to introduce new products to market | − |
| Percentage of customer calls answered within 20 seconds | + |
| On-time deliveries as a percentage of all deliveries | + |
| Work in progress inventory as a percentage of sales | − |
| Unfavourable standard cost variances | − |
| Defect-free units as a percentage of completed units | + |
| Delivery cycle time* | − |
| Throughput time* | − |
| Manufacturing cycle efficiency* | + |
| Quality costs† | − |
| Set-up time | − |
| Time from call by customer to repair of product | − |
| Percentage of customer complaints settled on first contact | + |
| Time to settle a customer claim | − |

| Learning and growth perspective Performance measure | Desired change |
|---|---|
| Suggestions per employee | + |
| Value-added employee‡ | + |
| Employee turnover | − |
| Hours of in-house training per employee | + |

*Explained later in this chapter.
†See cost of quality in Chapter 18.
‡Value-added is revenue less externally purchased materials, supplies and services

**Exhibit 16.6** Examples of performance measures for balanced scorecards

services. Take the car industry as an example. BMW stresses engineering and handling; Volvo, safety; Jaguar, luxury detailing; and Toyota, reliability. Because of these differences in emphases, a one-size-fits-all approach to performance measurement will not work even within this one industry. Performance measures must be tailored to the specific strategy of each company.

Suppose, for example, that Jaguar's strategy is to offer distinctive, richly finished luxury automobiles to wealthy individuals who prize handcrafted, individualized products. Part of Jaguar's strategy might be to create such a large number of options for details, such as leather seats, interior and exterior colour combinations, and wooden dashboards, that each car becomes virtually one of a kind. For example, instead of just offering tan or blue leather seats in standard cowhide, the company may offer customers the choice of an almost infinite palate of colours in any of a number of different exotic leathers. For such a system to work effectively, Jaguar would have to be able to deliver a completely customized car within a reasonable amount of time – and without incurring more cost for this customization than the customer is willing to pay. Exhibit 16.7 suggests how Jaguar might reflect this strategy in its balanced scorecard.

If the balanced scorecard is correctly constructed, the performance measures should be linked together on a cause-and-effect basis. Each link can then be read as a hypothesis in the form 'If we improve this performance measure, then this other performance measure should also improve.' Starting from the bottom of Exhibit 16.7, we can read the links between performance measures as follows. If employees acquire the skills to install new options more effectively, then the company can offer more options and the options can be installed in less time. If more options are available and they are installed in less time, then customer surveys should show greater satisfaction with the range of options available. If customer satisfaction improves, then the number of cars sold should increase. In addition, if customer satisfaction improves, the company should be able to maintain or increase its selling prices, and if the time to install options decreases, the costs of installing the options should decrease. Together, this should result in an increase in the contribution margin per car. If the contribution margin per car increases and more cars are sold, the result should be an increase in profits.

In essence, the balanced scorecard articulates a theory of how the company can attain its desired outcomes (financial, in this case) by taking concrete actions. While the strategy laid out in Exhibit 16.7 seems plausible, it should be regarded as only a theory that should be discarded if it proves to be invalid. For example, if the company succeeds in increasing the number of options available and in decreasing the time required to install options and yet there is no increase in customer satisfaction, the number of cars sold, the contribution margin per car, or profits, the strategy would have to be reconsidered. One of the advantages of the

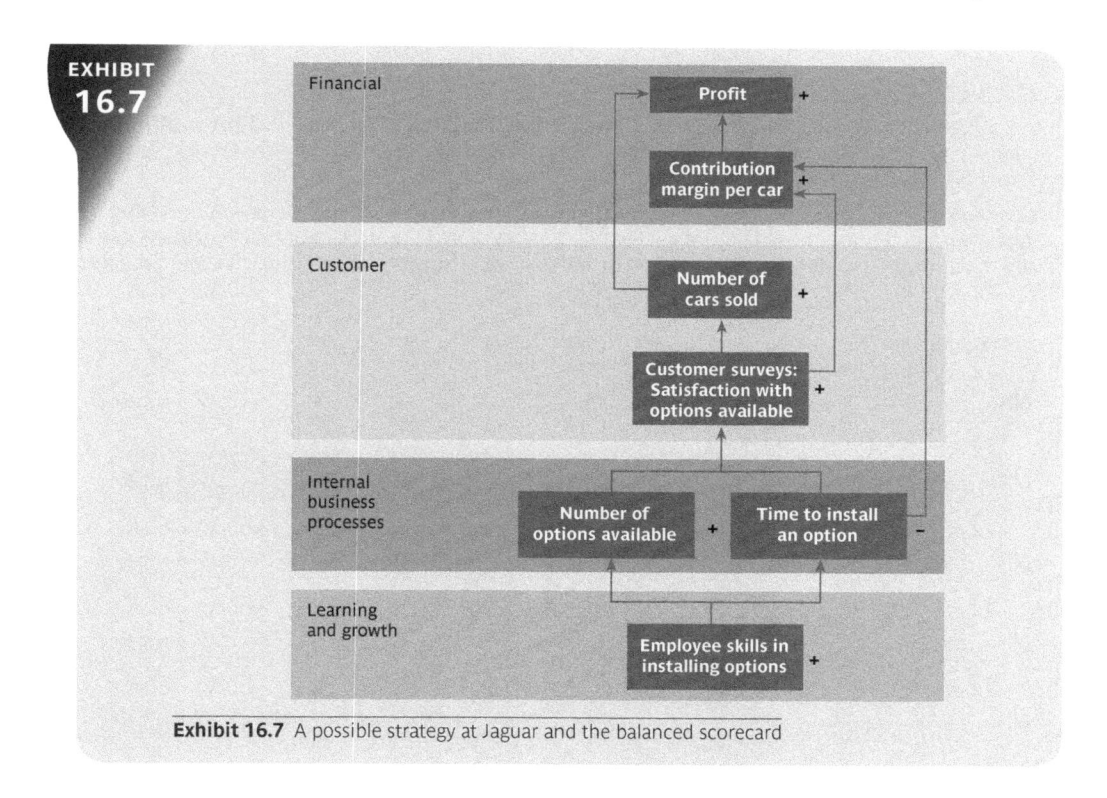

**EXHIBIT 16.7**

**Exhibit 16.7** A possible strategy at Jaguar and the balanced scorecard

balanced scorecard is that it continually tests the theories underlying management's strategy. If a strategy is not working, it should become evident when some of the predicted effects (i.e. more car sales) do not occur. Without this feedback, management may drift on indefinitely with an ineffective strategy based on faulty assumptions.

### Advantages of timely feedback

Whatever performance measures are used, they should be reported on a frequent and timely basis. For example, data about defects should be reported to the responsible managers at least once a day so that action can quickly be taken if an unusual number of defects occurs. In the most advanced companies, any defect is reported *immediately*, and its cause is tracked down before any more defects can occur. Another common characteristic of the performance measures under the balanced scorecard approach is that managers focus on trends in the performance measures over time. The emphasis is on progress and *improvement* rather than on meeting any specific standard.

### Some measures of internal business process performance

Most of the performance measures listed in Exhibit 16.6 are self-explanatory. However, three are not – *delivery cycle time, throughput time* and *manufacturing cycle efficiency* (MCE). These three important performance measures are discussed next.

### Delivery cycle time

The amount of time between when an order is received from a customer to when the completed order is shipped is called **delivery cycle time**. This time is clearly a key concern to many customers, who would like the delivery cycle time to be as short as possible. Cutting the delivery cycle time may give a company a key competitive advantage – and may be necessary for survival – and therefore many companies would include this performance measure on their balanced scorecard.

### Throughput (manufacturing cycle) time

The amount of time required to turn raw materials into completed products is called **throughput time**, or manufacturing cycle time. The relationship between the delivery cycle time and the throughput (manufacturing cycle) time is illustrated in Exhibit 16.8.

Note that, as shown in Exhibit 16.8, the throughput time, or manufacturing cycle time, is made up of process time, inspection time, move time and queue time. Process time is the amount of time in which work is actually done on the product. Inspection time is the amount of time spent ensuring that the product is not

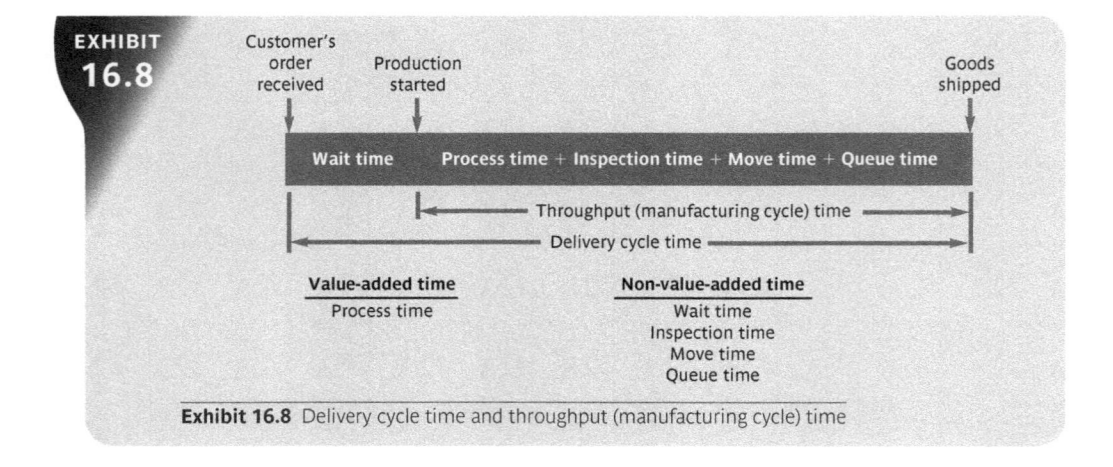

**EXHIBIT 16.8**

| Customer's order received | Production started | | Goods shipped |
|---|---|---|---|
| Wait time | Process time + Inspection time + Move time + Queue time | | |

Throughput (manufacturing cycle) time
Delivery cycle time

| Value-added time | Non-value-added time |
|---|---|
| Process time | Wait time |
| | Inspection time |
| | Move time |
| | Queue time |

**Exhibit 16.8** Delivery cycle time and throughput (manufacturing cycle) time

**Part 4** Value metrics and performance management in a strategic context

defective. Move time is the time required to move materials or partially completed products from workstation to workstation. Queue time is the amount of time a product spends waiting to be worked on, to be moved, to be inspected, or in storage waiting to be shipped.

As shown at the bottom of Exhibit 16.8, the only one of these four activities that adds value to the product is process time. The other three activities – inspecting, moving and queueing – add no value and should be eliminated as much as possible.

### Manufacturing cycle efficiency (MCE)

Through concerted efforts to eliminate the non-value-added activities of inspecting, moving and queueing, some companies have reduced their throughput time to only a fraction of previous levels. In turn, this has helped to reduce the delivery cycle time from months to only weeks or hours. The throughput time, which is considered to be a key measure in delivery performance, can be put into better perspective by computing the **manufacturing cycle efficiency (MCE)**. The MCE is computed by relating the value-added time to the throughput time. The formula is as follows:

$$\text{MCE} = \frac{\text{Value-added time}}{\text{Throughput (manufacturing cycle) time}}$$

If the MCE is less than 1, then non-value-added time is present in the production process. An MCE of 0.5, for example, would mean that half of the total production time consisted of inspection, moving and similar non-value-added activities. In many manufacturing companies, the MCE is less than 0.1 (10%), which means that 90% of the time a unit is in process is spent on activities that do not add value to the product. By monitoring the MCE, companies are able to reduce non-value-added activities and thus get products into the hands of customers more quickly and at a lower cost.

To provide a numeric example of these measures, assume the following data for Novex Company.

Novex Company keeps careful track of the time relating to orders and their production. During the most recent quarter, the following average times were recorded for each unit or order:

|  | **Days** |
|---|---|
| Wait time | 17.0 |
| Inspection time | 0.4 |
| Process time | 2.0 |
| Move time | 0.6 |
| Queue time | 5.0 |

Goods are shipped as soon as production is completed.

### Required

1. Compute the throughput time, or velocity of production.
2. Compute the manufacturing cycle efficiency (MCE).
3. What percentage of the production time is spent in non-value-added activities?
4. Compute the delivery cycle time.

## Solution

1. Throughput time = Process time + Inspection time + Move time + Queue time

    = 2.0 days + 0.4 days + 0.6 days + 5.0 days

    = 8.0 days

**Chapter 16** Value-based management and strategic management accounting

2. Only process time represents value-added time; therefore, the computation of the MCE would be as follows:

$$\text{MCE} = \frac{\text{Value-added time, 2.0 days}}{\text{Throughput time, 8.0 days}}$$
$$= 0.25$$

Thus, once put into production, a typical unit is actually being worked on only 25% of the time.

3. Since the MCE is 25%, the complement of this figure, or 75% of the total production time, is spent in non-value-added activities.

Delivery cycle time = Wait time + Throughput time
= 17.0 days + 8.0 days
= 25.0 days.

### FOCUS ON PRACTICE
#### Using the balanced scorecard in an economic downturn

The balanced scorecard (BSC) can be very useful for organizations facing hard times. For example, *Vita Liquid Polymers*, a medium-sized manufacturer of industrial polymers and plastics, used its balanced scorecard in order to review its strategy in the face of falling demand from new products, changes in consumer tastes and new, off-shore sources of supply. It then used the BSC to identify and measure new critical success factors appropriate to the new strategy. Advocates of the scorecard point out that whilst the scorecard might produce unpalatable measures during a downturn, this is no reason to abandon it ('shooting the messenger?').

**Exercise**: Strategic thinkers call on organizations to be 'agile'. How can the BSC support the agility of organizations?

*Source*: Scopes, J. 2009. Can a balanced scorecard help in a recession? *Finance & Management*, November, www.icaew.com/fmfac

We would like to emphasize a few points concerning the balanced scorecard. First, the balanced scorecard should be tailored to the company's strategy; each company's balanced scorecard should be unique. The examples given in this chapter are just that – examples. They should not be interpreted as general templates to be fitted to each company. Second, the balanced scorecard reflects a particular strategy, or theory, about how a company can further its objectives by taking specific actions. The theory should be viewed as tentative and subject to change if the actions do not in fact lead to attaining the company's financial and other goals. If the theory (i.e. strategy) changes, then the performance measures on the balanced scorecard should also change. For example, as will be seen in Chapter 17, companies may use the score card to embed sustainability strategies. The balanced scorecard should be viewed as a dynamic system that evolves as the company's strategy evolves.[22,23]

The balanced scorecard should not be seen just as a 'four bucket' model[24] with four boxes that must be filled. Organizations may choose to have five main dimensions. As we see in the Focus on Practice example, banks may wish to have an extra box labelled 'risk management'. As we have seen recently with the worldwide credit crunch, banks that have failed to manage risk have suffered financially or even gone out of business completely. As will be further explored in Chapter 17 and in the Focus on Practice example below, scorecard models may be used by non-profit making, public sector bodies.

## FOCUS ON PRACTICE
### Risk and the balanced scorecard*

One of the authors was recently involved in a research project looking at the implementation of the balanced scorecard in a major European bank. The bank had 'customized' the scorecard by including 'Risk' as a major objective. Relative to some of its competitors, this bank did seem to better prepared for the credit crunch with a much less riskier approach to lending. Another interesting feature of the bank was the way that each employee had a personal scorecard which was aligned to the local business unit through to corporate objectives. The scorecard implementation had a board level corporate champion and was 'owned' by both human resource and finance functions.

**Exercise**: Not all performance indicators in the balanced scorecard are positively related. Consider in this example the potential trade-off between risk and financial return?

Source: *Ye, L. and Seal, W. 2009. The balanced scorecard, *Financial Management*, September, pp. 27–28.

## FOCUS ON PRACTICE
### A health service scorecard

Many business and services used a balanced scorecard type system to report on key operating statistics and performance indicators. The Health Service Executive (HSE) is the state agency responsible for the running of the public health service in Ireland. It has over 100,000 employees and an annual budget of approximately £15 billion. The HSE uses a reporting system called HealthStat to monitor its performance in delivering health and care services.

HealthStat is described by the HSE as 'a comprehensive databank of performance information for Irish public health services'. To provide a comprehensive view of how services are delivered, HealthStat groups performance indicators under three headings: (1) Access – measuring waiting time for services; (2) Integration – checks that patients receive the correct services, in the right location and are informed about their treatment; and (3) Resources – whether a hospital or care facility is making best use of its financial and human resources. In total, 18 performance metrics across these three headings are reported on a monthly basis. Each metric is compared to a national target – these targets have been set against best international practice and are regularly reviewed. Each month, a traffic-light type dashboard (green = better than target, amber = below target, but improving, red = well below target) is compiled and reported to clinical managers, hospitals and the HSE's board. The data is also released to the public via the HSE's website – see example above. According to the HSE, HealthStat, being the first unified reporting systems used by the HSE, provides all staff and managers with a platform to monitor and improve service delivery.

**Exercise**: Looking at the example given, do you think these performance metrics take into account factors like quality of care received, willingness of medical professionals to communicate to patients, and so on? Should such things be included in performance measurements?

Source: http://www.hse.ie/eng/staff/Healthstat/about/

## Some criticisms of the balanced scorecard

Although the balanced scorecard has many merits, there have been some criticisms, particularly from academics. Some researchers have questioned whether the alleged cause-and-effect relationship between non-financial and financial indicators can be supported. In particular, customer satisfaction 'does not necessarily yield good financial results'.[25] Furthermore, the score card does not have an explicit way of monitoring competitor actions and does not propose a specific remuneration system (as with EVA, for example).[26] The widespread adoption of the balanced scorecard may, in part, be explained by the effective rhetoric deployed by its advocates.[27] Perhaps, as we will see in Chapter 17, it is the way that the scorecard is implemented and the way that different control systems *interact* that help to determine their effectiveness. Whatever its limitations, the balanced scorecard can fit in with a more sophisticated view of management that sees strategy as an *emergent process* and which takes a less 'top-down', 'keep-on-track' approach to organizational control. The balanced scorecard can facilitate this learning process as can other techniques such as **benchmarking** (see Chapter 18) through a consciously interactive relationship between performance indicators and management action.[28] We will develop these ideas more fully in Chapter 17 when we look at the relationship between strategy and organizational control.

## Strategy as an emergent process: interactive control systems and the learning organization

When strategy is viewed as an emergent process, the organization is seen as engaged in a learning both through internal communication and through contact with its customers and suppliers. Strategy can evolve through the input not just of senior managers but through the actions of front-line staff. In a learning system, information is used to encourage debate up and down organizations. Rather than being the product of a 'central plan', strategy is seen as a more emergent process[29] linking up strategy with tactics. The aim of management accounting in this approach to strategy is to aid the development of **double-loop learning**. In contrast with a single-loop control model such as standard costing, which simply requires conformance to existing policies, double-loop learning constantly questions both standards and policies. Another source of learning comes from benchmarking against the best practices in other organizations. Benchmarking may be based on cost performance (see Chapter 18 for ABM examples) or on processes to improve quality (see Chapter 18). The key to successful benchmarking is to adopt a learning orientation rather than the blame culture that can sometimes develop from a league-table approach. Sometimes a company will change its strategy unintentionally, whereby successive adaptations to changing markets, competitive position and technology leads to a new organizational identity, a new realization of where the company's core competences[30] actually lie.

## Some obstacles to SMA

Strategic management accounting has not become a branded technique widely marketed by consultants in the same way as ABC,[31] EVA and the BSC. One obstacle to the development of an SMA perspective by accountants may be that, traditionally, accountants have a *performance* rather than a *learning* orientation. Thus, rather than look for new data (outside the organization and traditional accounting systems) and fearing failure, accountants stick to the familiar.[32] To accountants, the familiar usually means financial data.[33] Furthermore, although the data for SMA may be held in different functional areas of the organization (such as marketing), there may be a reluctance to share with other functional areas such as management accounting.

Some sceptical commentators have suggested that companies may actually respond to business challenges by following the principles that comprise SMA but without a conscious adoption of an SMA package. Identifying the key principles of SMA as the *collection of competitor information, the exploitation of cost reduction opportunities* and *the matching of accounting emphasis with strategic position*, Lord[34] argues that:

> ... the characteristics that have been ascribed to strategic management accounting are likely to be already operating in many firms. However, it appears that the management accountant does not need to be involved in their operation, nor do they need to be quantified in accounting figures. Perhaps the widely touted 'strategic management accounting' is but a figment of academic imagination.

In short, the data for SMA are usually available somewhere, the difficulty is pulling them together in an organizational context. Indeed, the advantage of the BSC is that it offers a neat format for integrating financial and non-financial data into organizational reporting systems. As we shall see in the next chapter, scorecard models in general may be used to enhance corporate accountability from both shareholder and wider stakeholder perspectives.

## Summary

- Profit and shareholder value metrics may be used for business planning but they may not provide sufficient information for developing and implementing strategies.
- Strategic management accounting has evolved from the collection of competitor information to attempts to match management accounting systems with an organization's strategic position.
- As competition has become tougher and strategic positions seem harder to sustain, the managerial emphasis has shifted to supporting the lean enterprise.
- A balanced scorecard consists of an integrated system of performance measures that are derived from and support the company's strategy. Different companies will have different balanced scorecards because they have different strategies. A well-constructed balanced scorecard provides a means for guiding the company and also provides feedback concerning the effectiveness of the company's strategy.
- As competitive advantage becomes based on the development of corporate knowledge rather than the simple ownership of tangible assets, we may use the balanced scorecard as a flexible model that can help the organization learn from its customers and suppliers.

## Key terms for review

**Attribute costing** (p. 674)
**Balanced scorecard (BSC)** (p. 679)
**Benchmarking** (p. 687)
**Cost leadership** (p. 674)
**Defender** (p. 674)
**Delivery cycle time** (p. 683)
**Double-loop learning** (p. 687)
**Executional drivers** (p. 675)
**Lean enterprises** (p. 678)
**Life-cycle costing** (p. 674)
**Manufacturing cycle efficiency (MCE)** (p. 684)
**Marketing mix** (p. 673)
**Organizational learning** (p. 670)
**Product differentiation** (p. 674)
**Prospector** (p. 674)
**Strategic choice** (p. 670)
**Strategic management accounting (SMA)** (p. 670)
**Structural drivers** (p. 675)
**Throughput time** (p. 683)
**Value-based management (VBM)** (p. 672)
**Value chain** (p. 674)

Level of difficulty: BASIC  INTERMEDIATE  ADVANCED

## Questions

**16-1** Why is market share an important indicator to monitor?
**16-2** What aspects of a competitor's costs should be analysed in a strategic assessment?
**16-3** What sources are useful for strategic intelligence gathering?
**16-4** What is the difference between a prospector and a defender company?
**16-5** What is the difference between a cost leader and a product differentiator?
**16-6** What are the three steps/dimensions that combine financial and strategic analysis as proposed by Tomkins and Carr?
**16-7** What are the implications of the 'strategy as collision' model?
**16-8** Why does the balanced scorecard include financial performance measures as well as measures of how well internal business processes are doing?

## Chapter 16 Value-based management and strategic management accounting

**16-9** What is the difference between the delivery cycle time and the throughput time? What four elements make up the throughput time? Into what two classes can these four elements be placed?

**16-10** If a company has a manufacturing cycle efficiency (MCE) of less than 1, what does it mean? How would you interpret an MCE of 0.40?

**16-11** How can a balanced scorecard aid organizational learning?

**16-12** Why does the balanced scorecard differ from company to company?

**16-13** Which views of strategy would you expect to provoke the most resistance from the 'traditional' management accountants?

## Exercises

**E16-1** Time allowed: 20 minutes

Management of Mittel Rhein AG of Köln, Germany, would like to reduce the amount of time between when a customer places an order and when the order is shipped. For the first quarter of operations during the current year the following data were reported:

|  | Days |
|---|---|
| Inspection time | 0.3 |
| Wait time (from order to start of production) | 14.0 |
| Process time | 2.7 |
| Move time | 1.0 |
| Queue time | 5.0 |

### Required

1. Compute the throughput time, or velocity of production.
2. Compute the manufacturing cycle efficiency (MCE) for the quarter.
3. What percentage of the throughput time was spent in non-value-added activities?
4. Compute the delivery cycle time.
5. If by use of just-in-time (JIT) all queue time during production is eliminated, what will be the new MCE?

## Problems

**P16-2 Perverse effects of some performance measures**
Time allowed: 30 minutes

There is often more than one way to improve a performance measure. Unfortunately, some of the actions taken by managers to make their performance look better may actually harm the organization. For example, suppose the marketing department is held responsible only for increasing the performance measure 'total revenues'. Increases in total revenues may be achieved by working harder and smarter, but they can also usually be achieved by simply cutting prices. The increase in volume from cutting prices almost always results in greater total revenues; however, it does not always lead to greater total profits. Those who design performance measurement systems need to keep in mind that managers who are under pressure to perform may take actions to improve performance measures that have negative consequences elsewhere.

### Required

For each of the following situations, describe actions that managers might take to show improvement in the performance measure but which do not actually lead to improvement in the organization's overall performance.

1. Concerned with the slow rate at which new products are brought to market, top management of a consumer electronics company introduces a new performance measure – speed-to-market. The research and development department is given responsibility for this performance measure, which measures the average amount of time a product is in development before it is released to the market for sale.

**Part 4** Value metrics and performance management in a strategic context

2  The Chief Executive of a telephone company has been under public pressure from city officials to fix the large number of public pay phones that do not work. The company's repair people complain that the problem is vandalism and damage caused by theft of coins from coin boxes – particularly in high crime areas in the city. The Chief Executive says she wants the problem solved and has pledged to city officials that there will be substantial improvement by the end of the year. To ensure that this is done, she makes the managers in charge of installing and maintaining pay phones responsible for increasing the percentage of public pay phones that are fully functional.

3  A manufacturing company has been plagued by the chronic failure to ship orders to customers by the promised date. To solve this problem, the production manager has been given the responsibility of increasing the percentage of orders shipped on time. When a customer calls in an order, the production manager and the customer agree to a delivery date. If the order is not completed by that date, it is counted as a late shipment.

4  Concerned with the productivity of employees, the board of directors of a large multinational corporation has dictated that the manager of each subsidiary will be held responsible for increasing the revenue per employee of his or her subsidiary.

**P16–3** Use of quantitative techniques and non-financial indicators
Time allowed: 45 minutes

PMF plc is a long-established public transport operator that provides a commuter transit link between an airport and the centre of a large city.

The following data has been taken from the sales records of PMF plc for the last two years:

| Quarter | Number of passengers carried | |
|---|---|---|
| | Year 1 | Year 2 |
| 1 | 15,620 | 34,100 |
| 2 | 15,640 | 29,920 |
| 3 | 16,950 | 29,550 |
| 4 | 34,840 | 56,680 |

The trend equation for the number of passengers carried has been found to be:

$$x = 10{,}000 + 4{,}200q$$

where $x$ = number of passengers carried per quarter

and $q$ = time period (year 1 quarter 1: $q = 1$)
(year 1 quarter 2: $q = 2$)
(year 2 quarter 1: $q = 5$).

Based on data collected over the last two years, PMF plc has found that its quarterly costs have the following relationships with the number of passengers carried:

| Cost item | Relationship |
|---|---|
| Premises costs | $y = 260{,}000$ |
| Premises staff | $y = 65{,}000 + 0.5x$ |
| Power | $y = 13{,}000 + 4x$ |
| Transit staff | $y = 32{,}000 + 3x$ |
| Other | $y = 9{,}100 + x$ |

where $y$ = the cost per quarter (£)
and $x$ = number of passengers per quarter.

## Chapter 16 Value-based management and strategic management accounting

### Required

1. Using the trend equation for the number of passengers carried and the multiplicative (proportional) time series model, determine the expected number of passengers to be carried in the third quarter of Year 3.
2. Explain why you think that the equation for the Transit staff cost is in the form $y = 32,000 + 3x$.
3. Using your answer to Question 1 and the cost relationships equations, calculate for each cost item and in total, the costs expected to be incurred in the third quarter of Year 3.
4. Explain briefly why there may be differences between the actual data for the third quarter of year 3 and the values you have predicted.
5. Prepare a report, addressed to the Board of Directors of PMF plc, that briefly explains the following in the context of measuring the *effectiveness* of the transport service:
   - Why the company should consider the use of non-financial performance measures;
   - Three non-financial performance measures that could be used.

*(CIMA Management Accounting – Performance Management)*

**P16–4 Strategic analysis**
Time allowed: 45 minutes

M-HK provides a passenger ferry service between two large cities separated by the mouth of a major river. The ferries are frequent, well supported by passengers and cover the distance between the cities in one hour. M-HK also transports passengers and goods by water ferry to other cities located on the river mouth. There are other ferry operators providing services between each of these locations besides M-HK.

### Required

1. Explain what strategic information is required by M-HK's management in respect of customer demand, competition, competitiveness, and finance in order to plan its future ferry services.
2. Using the information in your answer to Question 1, discuss how M-HK's Chartered Management Accountant should provide reports to M-HK's senior management for operational and strategic planning purposes.

*(CIMA Management Accounting – Business Strategy)*

**P16–5 Strategic analysis**
Time allowed: 45 minutes

R is a large high-class hotel situated in a thriving city. It is part of a worldwide hotel group owned by a large number of shareholders. The majority of the shares are held by individuals, each holding a small number; the rest are owned by financial institutions. The hotel provides full amenities, including a heated swimming pool, as well as the normal facilities of bars, restaurants and good-quality accommodation. There are many other hotels in the city which all compete with R. The city in which R is situated is old and attracts many foreign visitors, particularly in its summer season.

### Required

1. State the main stakeholders with whom relationships need to be established and maintained by the management of R. Explain why it is important that relationships are developed and maintained with each of these stakeholders.
2. Explain how the management of R should carry out a benchmarking exercise on its services, and recommend ways in which the outcomes should be evaluated.

*Note:* Do NOT describe different methods of benchmarking in answering this question.

*(CIMA Management Accounting – Business Strategy)*

**P16–6 Strategic management accounting**
Time allowed: 60 minutes

The Y Corporation is based in the USA. It was founded in the early part of the last century when Mr Y produced cartoon films. These soon proved very popular as a form of family entertainment and the characters in the films became household names. The Corporation established a theme park (based around the film characters) in southern USA, where there was a warm and mainly dry climate. The theme park, known as Yland, proved to be an immediate success, attracting millions of visitors each year. A whole range of family entertainment flourished, based on the original theme of the cartoon characters. These included shops, restaurants, hotels and amusement rides.

Following the success of Y-land in the USA, the directors of the Corporation established another Y theme park based in northern Europe. The rationale behind this was that although many Europeans visited Y-land in the USA, the cost of travel made visiting the attraction very expensive. The directors believed that establishing a Y-land in northern Europe would enable European people to visit the attraction without incurring high travel expenses. Y-land Europe was built in a highly populated area of northern Europe which is easily accessible. A factor which differentiates Y-land Europe from the theme park in the USA is that it is located in a region which is frequently affected by rain and it does not enjoy a guaranteed warm climate.

Y-land Europe did not in fact attract the volume of visitors that were expected and almost went bankrupt before receiving a massive cash injection from a wealthy donor who took part shares in the theme park.

## Further strategic development

The Y Corporation is now considering building another theme park, this time in a tropical area in the Far East. Y-land FE will be part-funded by the host government in the Far East, which will take a 60% share in the park. The Y Corporation will fund the remaining 40%. Profits and losses will be shared in direct proportion to the shareholding of each of the joint venture partners. It is believed that local tourism and related sectors of the entertainment industry will benefit from the development as the theme park will attract more visitors to the region. Similar to the other two Y-land theme parks, the development will include many facilities such as hotels, bars and restaurants as well as the entertainment attractions.

It will take two years to build Y-land FE before any paying visitors enter the park. The Y Corporation has based its estimates of visitors in the first year of operation (that is, after the two years of construction) on the following probabilities:

|  | Visitors | Probability |
| --- | --- | --- |
| Optimistic | 8 million | 0.25 |
| Most likely | 3 million | 0.50 |
| Pessimistic | 2 million | 0.25 |

After the first year of operation, it is expected that the number of visitors will increase by 50% in the next year. The Y Corporation directors consider that this number of visitors will be the maximum and after that the theme park will suffer a reduction in the number of visitors (marketing decay) of 5% compounded each year for the next two years. After two years, the directors expect the number of visitors each year to remain constant at this level. The host government believes that the theme park will create about 15,000 new jobs in the area through servicing the facilities. It expects the construction of the park to create about 5,000 jobs in addition to the 8,000 who will be employed in land reclamation and other necessary infrastructural work associated with the project.

## Cost and revenue estimates

It is expected that the overall capital cost of the theme park will be $2,200 million. This sum will be spread evenly over the construction period and, for the purposes of calculation, the actual cash outflow may be assumed to arise at the end of each of the two years. The Y Corporation will be responsible for raising 40% of this sum.

In any year, the visitors are expected to be in the proportion of 40% adults and 60% children or people who will obtain a concession (reduction) on their entrance fees. For simplicity, the entrance charges will be set at a flat rate of $50 for each adult and $30 for each child or concession. There will be no further fees for entertainment after the entrance charge has been made to the visitor.

### Chapter 16 Value-based management and strategic management accounting

Past experience has shown that running expenses of the theme park show a certain level of consistency. In terms of labour, the costs follow the pattern of a 90% learning curve which applies on average to every million visitors. This lasts for the first two years, after which the labour costs for each visitor become constant. The cost of labour at the time the park will open is expected to be $3 for each visitor. The effects of this are that the cumulative average direct labour costs in the first year of operation (that is, Year 3 of the project) are estimated to be $972 million (after being multiplied by the number of expected visitors in that year). The cumulative average labour costs for both the first and second years of operation (that is, Years 3 and 4 of the project) are expected to be $2,114 million (after being multiplied by the total number of visitors for the first two years of operation). After this point the learning effect is expected to cease.

The other direct costs, which are not subject to learning, can be assumed to be incurred at the rate of $2 for each visitor. Attributable fixed running expenses are estimated to be $100 million each year in cash terms. In addition, the Y Corporation expects that its joint venture with the host government will earn average net contribution of $10 from the sale of souvenirs and refreshments and $100 from accommodation charges for each adult, child or concessionary visitor each year.

The cost of capital for the whole project is expected to be 15%.

### Shareholder value

The Y Corporation believes that its main objective is to increase the wealth of its owners. The corporation requires a gross return on investment of 22% after eight years of income generated from the venture. It has been recommended to the directors of the Y Corporation that the return is calculated by taking the net present value of the project after eight years of operation and dividing this by the gross initial undiscounted capital outlay of $2,200 million.

*Ignore taxation, inflation and variations due to exchange rates.*

### Required

1. Produce a discounted cash flow (DCF) calculation for Y-land FE from the start of building work in the first year until eight years of cash inflows have been generated (that is, ten years in total), and calculate the return on investment in accordance with the method recommended.
2. Analyse and critically appraise the DCF calculation and the resulting return on investment as defined by the method recommended to the directors of the Y Corporation, and advise the directors as to whether they should proceed with Y-land FE. You should consider financial and non-financial factors in providing your advice.

(Abbreviated version from *CIMA Management Accounting – Business Strategy*)

**P16-7 Uncertainty, strategic management accounting**
Time allowed: 50 minutes

Lipo plc ('Lipo') manufactures labels for consumer goods. The company obtained a listing on the Alternative Investment Market in 1998, having been established in 1955.

### Basic labels

Lipo's sole manufacturing site is in Newcastle in the north-east of England. For many years the company produced only basic, low technology labels ('basic labels') for a range of consumer goods. It has a market share in the UK of about 3%. These are mainly stick-on labels for plastic containers including those for soft drinks, detergents and food products. In common with its competitors, which are of similar size to Lipo, manufacturing takes place using low-tech machinery and a standardized process.

Historically, about half of the basic labels were sold in the UK and half overseas, mainly to the Far East. Selling prices are determined in sterling and are the same in all markets. The strength of sterling in recent years relative to most Far Eastern currencies, however, has caused the overseas market to decline significantly to around 25% of total sales and, as a consequence, company profitability also fell.

Within the UK, sales have remained stable, being strongest in northern England and southern Scotland. Good relations have been developed with a wide ranging and loyal customer base.

**Part 4** Value metrics and performance management in a strategic context

### Hi-tech labels

The significant decline in Far Eastern markets forced the company to search for an additional product market. After some internal debate it was decided in 1998 to set up a separate division and heavily invest in new machinery to make high-tech security labels ('hi-tech labels') with embedded microchips. These could be used with a wide range of goods (including electrical goods, motor vehicles and, even, animals) to prevent theft, but also to enable police to identify ownership if stolen goods are subsequently recovered.

Large-scale investment was required as it is necessary to make large volumes for the production of hi-tech labels to be viable. The new investment is financed by borrowing and, as a result, the company has reached its debt capacity. Raising further equity finance is not currently feasible.

Lipo sells hi-tech labels only in the UK market. In contrast with basic labels, however, it competes against both small and large competitors.

Microchips are imported from a major international company based in Japan, as few other manufacturers can match their price. Recently, however, the Japanese company patented, and commenced production of, a second generation microchip for security labels. This new microchip significantly improves performance, but it also costs much more than the first generation microchip.

### The industry background

The labels industry has a number of small companies similar to Lipo, but there are also a few high volume producers, and some consumer goods manufacturers make their own labels in-house. The market tends to segment with the smaller companies making basic labels and selling to smaller manufacturers. Conversely, the large labelling companies sell good quality basic labels, but also high-tech labels, targeting larger manufacturers in each case.

The market for high-tech labels has grown very significantly in recent years at about 75% per annum, as new applications and new technology have been developed. While the prices were initially high, greater production volumes have lowered both costs and prices over the past year. The increase in demand has also drawn in many new entrants to the industry. This means that the customers of high-tech labelling companies are constantly switching suppliers as competitive conditions change.

| Draft profit and loss accounts for the year to 30 September 2001 | | | | |
|---|---|---|---|---|
| | Basic labels | | Hi-tech labels | |
| | £000 | | £000 | |
| Turnover | | 15,000 | | 22,000 |
| Variable manufacturing costs | 4,500 | | 5,000 | |
| Fixed manufacturing costs | 2,000 | | 10,000 | |
| Administration | 3,000 | | 4,000 | |
| Selling costs | 1,000 | | 2,750 | |
| | | 10,500 | | 21,750 |
| Operating profit | | 4,500 | | 250 |

### The board meeting

A board meeting was held to review the strategic direction of the company, and particularly to review hi-tech label production.

The director in charge of the Hi-Tech Division was enthusiastic. 'This division is the future. We started from nothing four years ago and we now have a much greater turnover than the Basic Labels Division. What is more, we have achieved 50% growth in each of the last two years, and this year we won some major contracts at the expense of much larger competitors.'

## Chapter 16 Value-based management and strategic management accounting

The finance director commented 'Hi-Tech Division is certainly achieving growth and market share, but it is not generating any profit. It has cut prices to win contracts but winning a contract and making a profit on it are two different things.'

The director in charge of basic labels agreed: 'Hi-Tech Division has had all the investment recently. My division has had nothing. In short, the core business is being squeezed in favour of a new technique which can only compete in the market by cutting prices with the result that it makes no profit. In contrast, since the disastrous few years following currency devaluations in the Far East, our division has been quite stable in terms of both turnover and operating profit.'

### Required

1. So far as the information permits, evaluate the causes and consequences of environmental uncertainty in the labelling industry for:
   (a) Basic labels
   (b) Hi-tech labels.
2. As a strategic consultant write a memorandum to the board of Lipo which assesses each of the following issues in determining the future direction of the company:
   (a) Future development of Basic Labels Division
   (b) Hi-tech security labels:
       Competitor analysis
       Pricing policy
       Viability.

*(ICAEW Business Management)*

**P16–8 Balanced scorecard**
Time allowed: 45 minutes

The Royal Hotel Ltd is privately owned and situated in Keswick, an inland resort in the English Lake District. It is a medium-sized hotel with 50 bedrooms. Whilst high standards of building maintenance exist, the hotel has been conservatively managed by William Wordsworth, who owns 100% of its share capital. The hotel currently offers accommodation and restaurant facilities only, and has experienced little innovation in services offered during recent years.

William Wordsworth intends to retire in five years' time, so he has invited Pam Ayres to join him in partnership, with a view to her taking a controlling interest in the hotel on his retirement. She has recently qualified with a Masters Degree from the University of Birmingham, and has some knowledge of the latest approaches to the measurement of business performance. She has conducted a preliminary investigation of the hotel's performance over the past two years, to form a basis for taking a decision on joining William in partnership. The data she has gathered, based on the balanced scorecard approach to performance measurement, is presented in Appendix 1 and Appendix 2.

### Appendix 1: Financial data

|  | Current year | Previous year |
| --- | --- | --- |
| Estimated market value of the business | £2,000,000 | £2,000,000 |
| Turnover | £1,000,000 | £950,000 |
| Net profit | £200,000 | £188,000 |
| Current assets (cash, stock and credit card debtors) | £30,000 | £25,000 |
| Current liabilities (trade creditors) | £7,000 | £10,000 |

**Part 4** Value metrics and performance management in a strategic context

### Appendix 2: Non-financial data

*Customer perspective*

|  | Current year | Previous year |
|---|---|---|
| Room occupancy (during the 300 days the hotel is open each year) | 55% | 65% |
| Market share of overnight hotel accommodation in Keswick | 4.33% | 3.67% |
| Customer satisfaction rating (score maximum 100%) | 55% | 65% |
| Customers indicating they would return to the Royal Hotel if visiting Keswick again | 25% | 45% |

*Internal business processes*

|  | Current year | Previous year |
|---|---|---|
| Audited percentage of procedures done according to job specification | 75% | 85% |
| Year on year employee retention rate | 30% | 50% |
| Customer rating of staff responsiveness (score maximum 100%) | 60% | 85% |
| Customer rating of staff competence (score maximum 100%) | 50% | 90% |
| Customer rating of staff courtesy (score maximum 100%) | 60% | 78% |

*Learning and growth perspective*

|  | Current year | Previous year |
|---|---|---|
| Royal Hotel percentage of revenue from accommodation and restaurant | 100% | 100% |
| Keswick hotels industry average percentage of revenue from accommodation and restaurants | 65% | 75% |
| Average percentage of staff with hotel and restaurant qualifications | 55% | 65% |

### Required

1. Assess the financial performance of the Royal Hotel based only on the information provided in Appendix 1.
2. Explain why the information in Appendix 2 is likely to give a better indication of future success than the information in Appendix 1.
3. Using all the information at your disposal, assess the future prospects of the Royal Hotel, and advise Pam Ayres on the desirability of becoming a partner in the business.

*(Thanks to Alan Coad, University of Birmingham)*

## Cases

**C16–9 The balanced scorecard**
Time allowed: 60 minutes

Weierman Department Store is located in the downtown area of a medium-sized city in the American Midwest. While the store had been profitable for many years, it is facing increasing competition from large national chains that have set up stores in the city's suburbs. Recently the downtown area has been undergoing revitalization, and the owners of Weierman Department Store are somewhat optimistic that profitability can be restored.

In an attempt to accelerate the return to profitability, the management of Weierman Department Store is in the process of designing a balanced scorecard for the company. Management believes the company should

Chapter 16 Value-based management and strategic management accounting

focus on two key problems. First, customers are taking longer and longer to pay the bills they incur on the department store's charge card and they have far more bad debts than are normal for the industry. If this problem were solved, the company would have more cash to make much needed renovations. Investigation has revealed that much of the problem with late payments and unpaid bills is apparently due to disputed bills that are the result of incorrect charges on the customer bills. These incorrect charges usually occur because sales assistants enter data incorrectly on the charge account slip. Secondly, the company has been incurring large losses on unsold seasonal apparel. Such items are ordinarily resold at a loss to discount stores that specialize in such distress items.

The meeting in which the balanced scorecard approach was discussed was disorganized and ineffectively led – possibly because no one other than one of the vice presidents had read anything about how to put a balanced scorecard together. Nevertheless, a number of potential performance measures were suggested by various managers. These potential performance measures are listed below:

- Total sales revenue
- Percentage of sales clerks trained to correctly enter data on charge account slips
- Customer satisfaction with accuracy of charge account bills from monthly customer survey
- Sales per employee
- Travel expenses for buyers for trips to fashion shows
- Average age of debtors
- Courtesy shown by junior staff members to senior staff members based on surveys of senior staff
- Unsold inventory at the end of the season as a percentage of total cost of sales
- Sales per square metre of floor space
- Percentage of suppliers making just-in-time deliveries
- Quality of food in the staff cafeteria based on staff surveys
- Written-off debtors (bad debts) as a percentage of sales
- Percentage of charge account bills containing errors
- Percentage of employees who have attended the city's cultural diversity workshop
- Total profit
- Profit per employee.

### Required

1. As someone with more knowledge of the balanced scorecard than almost anyone else in the company, you have been asked to build an integrated balanced scorecard. In your scorecard, use only performance measures suggested by the managers above. You do not have to use them all, but you should build a balanced scorecard that reveals a strategy for dealing with the problems with accounts receivable and with unsold merchandise. Construct the balanced scorecard following the format used in Exhibit 16.7. Do not be particularly concerned with whether a specific performance measure falls within the learning and growth, internal business process, customer or financial perspective. However, clearly show the causal links between the performance measures with arrows and whether the performance measures should show increases or decreases.

2. Assume that the company adopts your balanced scorecard. After operating for a year, there are improvements in some performance measures but not in others. What should management do next?

3. (a) Suppose that customers express greater satisfaction with the accuracy of their charge account bills but the performance measures for the average age of receivables and for bad debts do not improve. Explain why this might happen.

   (b) Suppose that the performance measures for the average age of accounts receivable, bad debts, and unsold inventory improve, but total profits do not. Explain why this might happen. Assume in your answer that the explanation lies within the company.

**C16–10** Strategic management accounting
Time allowed: 90 minutes

Bernard Mason has just been appointed as Commercial Manager of the Salchester Theatre. The theatre has just completed a disappointing year with low attendances, culminating in a loss of £57,000. Details of the financial position of Salchester Theatre are given in Table 16.1. The current Artistic Director had, until now,

**698**  Part 4 Value metrics and performance management in a strategic context

been responsible for both the commercial and creative activities of the theatre. Mason has been brought in to improve the financial health of the theatre. His previous experience has been in the financial function within the manufacturing industry, and more recently as a finance manager at the town's university. Bernard considers himself to be a man of culture and not just a hard, bottom-line oriented businessman. He has welcomed this challenge to improve the fortunes of Salchester Theatre. Salchester is situated about 50 miles from London, has a population of about 200,000 people, and is home to one of the newer universities. The main sources of employment are in the commercial sector, including the headquarters of a large insurance company, and in the computing industry. There are also a significant number of commuters who travel daily to work in London. The theatre is reasonably modern, built in the early 1980s, and is located in the centre of town, having a seating capacity of 350. There is also a restaurant/coffee shop which is open throughout the day. However, this facility is poorly supported and is only ever busy for pre-theatre meals in the evening. There is also a rehearsal stage which is adjacent to the theatre. The theatre employs 20 full-time actors and actresses and a stage crew of twelve – which includes set designers and builders, carpenters, electricians and painters. Ticket sales and administration are handled by two full-time employees. Much of the work done during performances is by the 'Friends of Salchester Theatre' – a small group of active volunteers, many of whom are retired. These people act as bar and restaurant staff. They deal with mailing lists and also collect tickets, show people to their seats, and sell ice cream and confectionery to the audience at the interval. The 20 actors and actresses are usually divided into two groups, each performing a play for three weeks. While one group is performing, the other group is rehearsing for its next three-week commitment. Occasionally when a larger cast is required, such as for a performance of Shakespeare, members of one group will supplement the other. In fact when requirements are for a large number of actors they are helped by volunteers from the drama department of the university. The theatre company operates for 42 weeks in a year. The theatre is closed for one week each year for refurbishment and decoration. The remaining nine weeks are used by touring companies for shows such as opera, ballet and musicals, the Christmas show targeted at young children for the holiday period, and by the local choral society for its concerts.

The funding of the theatre is typical of many regional theatres. The Arts Council (a central government-funded body to support cultural activities throughout the country) provides an annual grant of £180,000,

**Table 16.1 Financial Details of Salchester Theatre (financial year September – August) (£000)**

|  | 1996/97 | 1997/98 | 1998/99 |
|---|---|---|---|
| Income |  |  |  |
| Theatre Group | 410.00 | 390.00 | 340.00 |
| Touring Companies | 118.00 | 120.00 | 140.00 |
| Restaurant | 31.00 | 36.00 | 32.00 |
| Arts Council | 180.00 | 180.00 | 180.00 |
| Local Authority | 130.00 | 130.00 | 130.00 |
| University | 5.00 | 5.00 | 5.00 |
| Hire to Local Choral Groups | 3.50 | 3.50 | 4.00 |
| Total Income | 877.50 | 864.50 | 831.00 |
| Expenditure |  |  |  |
| Wages and Salaries | 500.00 | 520.00 | 550.00 |
| Materials and Other Costs | 100.00 | 103.00 | 120.00 |
| Restaurant (food etc.) | 28.50 | 30.00 | 35.00 |
| Fixed Costs (rent, lighting, heating) | 30.00 | 33.00 | 38.00 |
| Cost of Touring Companies | 110.00 | 115.00 | 145.00 |
| Total Expenditure | 768.50 | 801.00 | 888.00 |
| Surplus/Deficit | 109.00 | 63.50 | – 57.00 |

subject to the programme being artistically acceptable. The Arts Council aims to encourage both artistic and cultural development. The town council in Salchester provides another subsidy of £130,000 each year. They believe that the existence of a theatre in Salchester is valuable for a number of reasons. It provides both culture and entertainment for the population of Salchester. Furthermore it enhances the reputation of the town. This is thought to be particularly important in attracting students. The university has 8,000 students who provide valuable income to the town, including shopkeepers and providers of student accommodation. With increasing competition for students Salchester does not want to lose a potential attraction. In addition, the university has a drama department and the theatre provides both resources and support to this department. Although there is only a nominal charge for this (about £5,000 a year) the theatre does receive help from the graphics and advertising department of the university in the form of posters and publicity material, as well as tapes for local radio advertising. The rest of the income has to be generated by the theatre itself. Box office receipts have been falling over the past three years and in the financial year just completed amounted to only £340,000. Until last year ticket prices had been £8 for weekday performances (Monday–Thursday) and £10 for weekends (Fridays and Saturdays). In order to cut the deficit the prices have been increased to £10 for midweek and £12.50 for weekends. The strategy does not appear to have worked and the receipts have continued to fall.

Mason has decided that there must be a review of the theatre's operations. Attendances are continuing to fall. He has reviewed the productions over the past year and has discovered that on average attendances were less than a third of capacity. There were few shows which could be considered to be financially successful. The twice-yearly Shakespeare productions are always popular because the management wisely choose to perform the plays which are being used as the examination texts by the local schools. Naturally the local students take the opportunity to see these plays. The Christmas show is successful for about two weeks but unfortunately the performances are scheduled for three weeks. Some of the touring groups for opera and ballet are well supported but the cost of attracting these companies is very high and although the attendance is almost at capacity the revenue does not cover the operating costs. However, the main problem appears to be with the resident theatre group. Their costs are escalating but they do not appear to be attracting the public to their productions.

Mason called a meeting with the various groups who have an interest in the theatre's future to look at alternative approaches for improving the situation. The outcome of this meeting has not resulted in an agreed plan of action for the future. The actors and actresses who are looking for challenging modern plays are suggesting that future programmes be more adventurous and modern. One of them said 'We need to educate the audience to accept more creative material. The old favourites are boring and provide no interest for us.' However, this view has been totally rejected by the theatre supporters club who do most of the voluntary work. They are looking for an increase in established and popular plays with which the audience are familiar. They want comedies and easy-to-understand detective plays. This request has met with total opposition from the performers, who have said that this type of material is both uninteresting and unacceptable to them. Finally, the members of the local council, who appear to enjoy the privilege of free entry to the theatre as a result of their patronage, seem more concerned with attracting outside companies to the theatre. The presence of nationally known theatre groups and performers apparently enhances the town's reputation.

Bernard Mason is unhappy at this inability to agree a way to resolve the current unacceptable position. There has to be some agreed strategy if the theatre is to survive and yet most of the groups, who have a stake in the theatre, cannot reach an understanding. Unless a viable solution can be found and agreed upon, Salchester Theatre will have to close, just as have many other regional theatres. This job is going to be more difficult and challenging than Mason originally had thought.

### Required

1. It appears that the stakeholders in the theatre cannot agree on a strategic direction to solve the financial problems. Mason believes that a mission statement for the theatre could draw the conflicting parties closer together. With reference to the problems of Salchester Theatre, identify the major characteristics of a good mission statement, and comment on the problems which Mason may experience in drawing up such a statement.
2. Evaluate the current position at Salchester Theatre and critically review the solutions which the various parties have suggested might improve the financial position of the theatre.

**Part 4** Value metrics and performance management in a strategic context

3   Discuss what actions Mason might take in order to correct the worrying deterioration in the financial position.

*(ACCA Management and Strategy)*

### C16–11  Strategic management accounting
Time allowed: 75 minutes

Sports & Leisure Ltd (SL) is a private company which operates two private health and fitness clubs in Yorkshire.

## The company history

SL was formed in 1986 by its two shareholders and directors, Mike Conn and Archie Moon, who opened the first fitness club in Toddmartin. This is a prosperous commuter town of about 25,000 people just outside Leeds. Mike and Archie had been physiotherapists with a major football club and had used savings and mortgaged their houses to finance their shares in the company. They took an active role in supervising club members and advertised their previous professional experience.

The Toddmartin leisure club prospered with growth stabilizing over the past three years at the current level of about 1,000 members. Each member currently pays an annual subscription fee of £500. This has risen in excess of inflation for a number of years.

The success of the business was due to a number of factors. First, it is the only fitness club in the town; second, it has the personal day-to-day involvement of the owners, both of whom have a good local reputation; and, third, the staff has a good knowledge of health and fitness and is paid premium rates.

In order to expand further, SL opened a second fitness club in 1999 in Dingledown, a town near Sheffield, of some 45,000 people, mainly in the low to middle income groups. It is about 30 miles from the Toddmartin club and adopted the same general approach and level of fees as in Toddmartin. Dingledown has no other fitness clubs.

## The fitness club industry

Health and fitness has experienced a significant increase in demand in the UK, with annual membership growth figures of over 10% over recent years, despite an average increase in fees above inflation. Currently, it is estimated that some 5% of the UK population are members of fitness clubs, but membership is more concentrated in the higher income group.

On the supply side there are several major health and fitness chains which have a national reputation and are operated by subsidiaries of the major brewing and hotel groups. These tend to have the best equipment, largest memberships and highest fees. They are usually located in major cities.

There are also many smaller chains or single club organizations around the country. Market surveys suggest that there is still an undersupply with a potential to attain the US level of fitness club membership of 7% of the total population.

## Strategic issues

The shareholders are concerned about two issues which developed this year.

*Issue 1: Rival competition at Toddmartin*
A rival, medium-sized company, Premier Leisure Ltd, has announced that it is to open a new fitness club in Toddmartin in six months' time. It will use the latest equipment, in contrast to SL's facilities which are in need of some updating.

Premier Leisure Ltd will offer discounted membership fees for the first three months, but the long-term annual fees charged by Premier Leisure Ltd at existing clubs are around £450. This is possible as they operate with fewer and less qualified staff than SL.

*Issue 2: Establishing the Dingledown Club*
The performance of the Dingledown Club is disappointing. The membership is growing, but more slowly than had been anticipated. The manager originally employed to run the club had focused more on operational

Chapter 16 Value-based management and strategic management accounting

activities and less on marketing and expanding membership. A replacement manager has recently been appointed. His remuneration package is yet to be decided but some incentive to expand membership, while maintaining the long-term reputation, is being considered. Additionally, an approach has been made by a large industrial company, Filochem plc. It is offering to pay a lump sum of £50,000 if SL offers half-price membership to any of its employees and ex-employees joining over the next year. Initial estimates are that 250 people would join the club under this scheme. Filochem plc provides a significant amount of employment in the town, but recently it received adverse publicity having made some employees redundant.

## Draft accounts

The directors prepared the following draft accounts for the year to 31 March 2001.

|  | Toddmartin £000 | Dingledown £000 | Total £000 |
| --- | --- | --- | --- |
| Fitness Activities |  |  |  |
| Fees | 500 | 100 | 600 |
| Fitness salaries | 230 | 90 | 320 |
| Net income | 270 | 10 | 280 |
| Overheads |  |  |  |
| Lease rentals – building | 50 | 50 | 100 |
| Depreciation | 15 | 20 | 35 |
| Other | 20 | 25 | 45 |
| Net profit/(loss) | 185 | (85) | 100 |

## Required

1 Analyse and justify the strategic position of each of SL's two fitness clubs according to their positions in the product life cycle and in the Boston Consulting Group Matrix.
2 Write a memorandum to the directors, as an external adviser, which assesses and advises upon each of the two strategic issues. In so doing use the following headings:

*Issue 1 Competition at Toddmartin*
(a) Competitive strategy, market segmentation and pricing
(b) Long-term viability of two fitness clubs in Toddmartin
(c) Determining the circumstances under which SL should exit the Toddmartin market

*Issue 2 Establishing the Dingledown Club*
(a) The relationship between costs, revenues and profitability
(b) The Filochem contract
(c) Marketing strategy and incentives (excluding Filochem)
(d) Long-term viability.

*(ICAEW Business Management)*

**C16–12 Strategic management accounting**
Time allowed: 80 minutes

Saxex plc (hereafter Saxex) is listed on the London Stock Exchange and is the largest jewellery retailer in the UK.

## Company profile

Saxex operates some 600 jewellery outlets in the UK. Products include: traditional jewellery of gold and gem stones, costume jewellery, watches, clocks and silverware. Saxex's turnover makes up about 17% of the UK jewellery market which is valued at around £2.7 billion per year. Its brand name, used in all outlets, is 'Jewel in the Crown' and is well recognized as a sign of good value and reasonable quality.

The company currently manufactures some jewellery from gold and rough gem stones, but it also buys in jewellery ready for sale. Given the volume of its purchases it obtains significant discounts from all types of supplier.

While the company is profitable, its rate of growth has slowed significantly in recent years. The major reasons for this are:

1. There is an outlet in every city and most major towns in the UK and Saxex has thus reached the point of market saturation.
2. The 'Jewel in the Crown' stores are essentially mid-market and this has not been a growth area for the industry in recent years. It is particularly susceptible to a downturn in the economy.

## An industry profile

Jewellery in the UK is retailed through a variety of outlets including shops, mail order, jewellery counters in department stores, market stalls and catalogue showrooms.

Retailers include large listed companies with many branches, smaller private companies (normally with a limited number of branches in a particular region) and independent single outlets. There is also a very wide range of quality and prices in the industry.

## Strategies for growth

The board of Saxex is considering two strategies to return the business to higher growth. The company does not have significant liquid resources and thus intends to use debt to finance strategic development.

*Strategy A – Open a new, up-market jewellery division*

The board is considering opening shops under a new name to sell up-market jewellery at a higher price and at a much greater profit margin than the existing business. As yet it is unsure whether to buy retailing space and create a new brand or to buy an existing up-market jewellery chain.

*Strategy B – Expand Overseas*

Saxex is considering opening up further outlets in Europe under its existing brand name and selling its existing product range. It is unsure whether to buy existing overseas companies and re-brand them with the 'Jewel in the Crown' label or merely to buy retailing space.

## Required

1. Assume the following with respect to an existing outlet and a new outlet under *Strategy A*.

|  | Existing | Up-market |
| --- | --- | --- |
| Annual Fixed Costs | £240,000 | £360,000 |
| Expected sales volume | 37,500 | 24,000 |
| Average variable cost per item | £24 | £36 |

Assume that existing outlets generate a contribution margin (i.e. contribution divided by sales) of 25%.

Calculate the average price that the new up-market outlet must charge per item in order to earn the same overall profit as the existing outlet.

2. Evaluate each of the proposed development strategies under the following headings:
   (a) Marketing strategy
   (b) Risk
   (c) Growth by acquisition or by internal development; and conclusions.

Where appropriate, refer to relevant strategic models.

*(ICAEW Business Management)*

**Chapter 16** Value-based management and strategic management accounting

### C16-13 Strategic management accounting
⏱ Time allowed: 90 minutes

Alexander Simmonds is the founder and Managing Director of Playwell Ltd, a privately owned UK company specializing in making educational toys for young children and for children with special educational needs. These toys are robust and of simple construction made from high-quality materials, mainly wood, acquired from a local supplier. The main selling lines are building blocks of different shapes, sizes and colours, and toy trains and carriages (with no mechanical or electrical components). These simple toys are intended to stimulate the imagination of young children and to help them develop their visual and co-ordination abilities.

Alexander started the company in the early 1980s. He had initially made toys in his garage for his own children. He was soon persuaded to expand his activities and he had a ready demand for his products from friends and neighbours. In 1983 he was made redundant from his full-time job and he decided to put his redundancy money into setting up his own company. To his surprise the demand for his products grew at a faster rate than he had expected. There was an obvious gap in the market for simple, high-quality toys. Young children did not appear to want the complex and high-technology products which were expensively promoted on television and in magazines. The early success of the company was helped by being a low-cost operation. At the start, Alexander's sales were made on a direct basis, using no intermediaries. He promoted his products within a fifty mile radius using local newspapers; orders were shipped directly to the customers. Additionally the supplier of the materials provided Playwell with extended and low-cost credit until the final payment was made to the company for the completed toys. This arrangement has continued to the present time.

Between 1983 and 1988 sales grew from a figure of £30,000 to almost £700,000. Net profit after tax was about 12%. Alexander's policy had been to reinvest these profits into the business. By 1988 he had moved out of his garage and had taken over a small factory in an industrial development area in a nearby town. Skilled labour was relatively easy to acquire. There was high unemployment in the area as a result of recent factory closures. By 1988 Alexander employed nearly 30 people in a range of jobs from design, manufacturing, sales, invoicing and distribution. Labour turnover was, unsurprisingly, very low. The workers were very loyal and Alexander paid them competitive wages and provided them with above-average benefits, particularly attractive in an area where unemployment was still high. The firm continued to grow at a rate of about 20% a year during the late 1980s and early 1990s. Although most of the sales were still marketed directly to the customer a significant proportion of sales were now made through one retailer who had a group of fifteen shops. This retailer sells products for young children, ranging through clothing, cots and prams as well as toys, and even in 1999, this retailer still relied on Playwell for a significant amount of its toy purchases. About 40% of the UK sales (excluding those to the special educational needs market) are currently made to this retailer. The target market for these shops is professional and middle-class parents who generally value quality above price.

As in any growing organization Alexander now found himself moving away from a hands-on operation and becoming more concerned with future growth and strategy. By the end of 1994 Alexander decided to look at another market to generate increased growth in sales. Although sales were now almost £1.5 million a year and there were nearly 50 employees, the company now had the capacity to double its output. Fixed costs, including labour, accounted for 60% of total costs and any future increase in sales ought to generate improved profit margins. This was important if the company was to prosper and grow and provide security for the workers in an area where employment opportunities were limited. The company was then looking for sales to increase by about 30% a year. However, such an increase could not easily be funded out of retained earnings. Playwell's past performance and conservative financial record was sufficiently attractive for the company's bank to be more than willing to extend its credit lines to provide the necessary working capital.

The new area that Playwell was interested in was the development of toys designed for the 'special education needs' market. This term is generally used to refer to the education of children who have one or more physical, mental or emotional disabilities. Toys such as shaped building blocks, sponge balls, pegboards and three-dimensional puzzles can all help children with disabilities to improve their visual perception, spatial awareness, memory and muscle control. In addition there were other products such as balance boards and beams and disks, all made from high quality wood, which can help to co-ordinate mental and muscular activities. However, it was likely that the method of marketing and distribution might have to

**Part 4** Value metrics and performance management in a strategic context

be adapted. The new market segment was much more easily identifiable and accessible. Databases of parents of children with special educational needs were readily available and it was possible to access the parents of these children via the specialist schools which these children attended. These schools were enthusiastic about Playwell's products but they alone could not support this new range of products. In fact part of Playwell's strategy was to distribute its products to these schools at very low prices in the hope that parents would then purchase these specialist toys for home use. This proved less easy than had been anticipated. First, parents of these children with special educational needs incurred many other expenses such as the additional costs of care. Furthermore, because of the increased care which these children usually required, one of the parents often had to stay at home or could only take on part-time work. Consequently the parents' discretionary income was significantly less. In addition, whereas the company had hoped that the teachers would recommend its products to the parents, it became apparent that teachers were not doing so, being worried that the parents would not have the expertise to use some of the equipment properly. As a result the revenues from this market were not as large as had been anticipated, particularly as the products' placement in the schools was seen initially as a loss-leader. Nevertheless sales of Playwell's core products (the non-specialist toys) were still gradually increasing (8% a year), but the momentum of earlier years was now not being maintained. By the beginning of 1997 Alexander decided that any future market expansion should be focused overseas, although he still intended to persevere with the 'special education' venture.

The company had acquired a good reputation within the United Kingdom and was operating in a growing niche market, in which Playwell was a significant participant. However, the company now decided that exports were to be the favoured means of growth. In an effort to avoid high risks Alexander decided to concentrate his activities in Western Europe. There were a number of advantages to this strategy – the purchasing processes of both parents and children were thought to be similar to that of the domestic market, transportation costs were likely to be lower than sales to America or Asia, and being part of the European Union there would be no trade barriers. However after an initial period of success Playwell discovered that sales were not as easily achieved as they had been in the UK. First the major European countries of France, Germany and Italy were at different stages in the business cycle to the UK. Whilst the British economy was growing the continental ones were suffering from recession. Consequently the demand for products such as toys was not buoyant. Furthermore high interest rates within the UK resulted in a high level of the pound sterling against the euro and other continental currencies, so making any exporting from the UK an expensive option. It appeared that price was now becoming a serious consideration in the customer's purchasing decision, particularly for a company with no strong overseas reputation. (Table 16.2 provides financial data for Playwell between 1994–1999.)

**Table 16.2 Financial data for Playwell between 1994–1999**

|  | £ million | | | | | |
|---|---|---|---|---|---|---|
|  | 1994 | 1995 | 1996 | 1997 | 1998 | 1999 (forecast) |
| Sales to general toy retailers – UK | 1.50 | 1.62 | 1.75 | 1.89 | 2.04 | 2.20 |
| Cost of sales | 0.53 | 0.57 | 0.62 | 0.67 | 0.72 | 0.78 |
| UK special needs toys sales |  | 0.30 | 0.30 | 0.25 | 0.25 | 0.15 |
| Cost of sales |  | 0.14 | 0.14 | 0.11 | 0.11 | 0.07 |
| Overseas sales |  |  |  | 0.50 | 0.55 | 0.55 |
| Cost of sales |  |  |  | 0.30 | 0.33 | 0.33 |
| Total sales | 1.50 | 1.92 | 2.05 | 2.64 | 2.84 | 2.90 |
| Fixed costs | 0.65 | 0.95 | 1.00 | 1.25 | 1.40 | 1.40 |

Chapter 16 Value-based management and strategic management accounting

Alexander had now made two efforts to expand his business, neither of which could be judged as successful and he was now anxious to determine the future progress of the company.

### Required

1. Alexander Simmonds appears to be the only person who is determining the objectives and strategic direction of Playwell plc. Identify any other parties who could have an interest in the success of this company. How might their goals be different to those of Alexander and to what extent would these differences be relevant?

2. You have been retained as a business consultant by Alexander to provide impartial advice as to the future strategy which the company should adopt. Given its relative failure in its last two ventures provide a briefing paper recommending a strategy which Playwell should pursue in the next two to three years. You should support your recommendation with appropriate financial analysis and the use of suitable analytical models.

3. The exporting venture appears to have failed because of an inadequate knowledge of the market. Identify the main types of information concerning the company's business environment you would consider to be essential before committing the company to an export strategy, giving reasons to justify your selection.

(*ACCA Management and Strategy*, adapted)

**C16-14** Time allowed: 90 minutes

Sam and Annabelle Burns own and manage the firm Hair Care Ltd, based in the UK. The firm was formed in 1998 when Sam and his wife remortgaged their house and borrowed heavily from the bank to buy out the company from a conglomerate organization who were disposing of non-core businesses. Sam had been a senior salesman with the hair-care subsidiary of the conglomerate. This subsidiary bought hair-care products, mainly small value items and consumables – scissors, brushes, combs, hair nets, curlers and hair-dryers – from manufacturers and resold them to wholesalers and large retail chemist chains within the UK, mainly for use in hairdressing salons. The new business has continued in this direction. The manufacturers are almost entirely non-UK suppliers, many based in Hong Kong but with manufacturing facilities in mainland China, Taiwan and Malaysia. However, about 30% of the products are sourced in Europe – Italy and Germany predominantly.

The company has met with success very quickly and the initial loans have already been repaid ahead of schedule. The company now owns the freehold of a large warehouse/distribution centre which is five times the size of the original depot, leased when the company first started trading five years ago. Sales turnover, now in excess of £5 million, has increased by more than 50% each year and shows little signs of slowing down. Despite this apparent rapid growth Hair Care Ltd only accounts for about half of the current market, leaving some potential for growth. The company is run cost effectively, with minimum staffing. Sam, as Managing Director, is solely concerned with the marketing side of the business. He spends most of his time in the selling role and in customer care, which he rates as a major contributor to the company's success. The only other key manager is his wife who is responsible for managing the warehouse staff, arranging distribution, general administration and financial management. The company started with six employees, in addition to Sam and Annabelle, and now has 15. Staff rarely leave the company. The staff is almost entirely employed in the distribution and packaging function, although there are two other sales people apart from Sam, but they only deal with the smaller buyers. With the continued growth in turnover it is inevitable that the number of employees will have to increase. It is expected that there will have to be a total of about 30 staff, all non-managerial, in two years if sales continue to increase at the current rate.

The success of Hair Care Ltd can be accounted for by a number of factors. Sam is a very good salesman who is responsible for looking after all the major accounts. He is popular and much of the business is built on his personal relationship with the key clients. There is a considerable amount of customer loyalty which is mainly attributable to Sam, and both he and his wife are always accessible to customers and they go out of their way to provide a first-class service. Even on vacation the two owners are in daily contact with the office. The company has been able to manage its purchases wisely. Most of the products, being purchased abroad, require payment in a foreign currency. Hair Care Ltd has been able to benefit from the relative weakness of the euro as against sterling for its European supplies. Although most of the products sourced in the Far East are priced in US dollars, the relative strength of that currency has enabled Hair Care Ltd to negotiate lower purchasing prices. However, it is questionable as to how long this situation concerning foreign exchange can be held. The situation may change should the UK join the euro in the near future and much, of course, will depend upon the level at which sterling enters the euro exchange.

Sam has also developed strong links with his suppliers and he has, until recently, attempted to trade with only a few so that his lines of communication and control are kept as simple as possible. Most of his current suppliers have been with him since the start of the company in 1998. This has provided the company with reliable and good quality products. In fact Hair Care Ltd often has exclusive access to certain products. For example, it has the sole rights to distribute an Italian hair-dryer which is generally recognized to be the best on the market. This product strength has enabled the company to build on the customer loyalty. However, it is inevitable that as demand has increased, existing suppliers have not been able to keep up with the necessary volumes and Sam has had to look for, and buy from new manufacturers.

The company has benefited from a period of relatively steady growth in the economy and even in the current economic downturn Sam has argued that demand for hair-care products is usually recession-proof. Furthermore, Hair Care Ltd has currently no near competitors. Many of the small competitors in the wholesale market place have chosen to concentrate on other areas of the hair-care business – salon furnishings and the supply of cheap, low-value items such as towels, razors, and so on – leaving much of this basic business (sales of other relatively low-value and mainly disposable products) to Sam's company. Additionally quite a number of the small firms have even left the market. All this has helped to contribute to the overall growth rate of Hair Care Ltd. There are some major international companies who make shampoos, conditioners and other cosmetic type products who also buy in consumer hairdressing products such as the ones sold by Hair Care Ltd. They then sell these mainly to the retail trade for domestic use by consumers and not directly to the hairdressing salons as does Hair Care Ltd. Furthermore, these are large companies and Sam believes that they do not currently see his company as a major threat.

The company has registered a brand name for its main products which it repackages, rather than using the individual brands of the original manufacturers. This has enabled Hair Care Ltd to generate even greater loyalty from its customers and often to obtain a price premium from these products.

Sam believes that part of the company's success stems from the fact that he has an organization with minimal administrative overheads. He outsources all of his products, adding value mainly through branding and the maintenance of customer care. He believes that strategy is not mainly about beating the competition but in serving the real needs of the customer. The company has also been able to develop a strong relationship with the country's leading retail chemist chain, providing it with good quality, low-cost disposable products such as hair nets and brushes to be sold under an own-brand label. Although the margins are inevitably small, the volumes involved more than compensate for this.

The company has had to incur increased investment as a result of the large growth in turnover. The building of the warehouse, the increased stock-holding costs, capital expenditure on items such as computing systems, fork-lift trucks and automated stock control and retrieval systems could not be financed out of current earnings, but the company's bank was only too ready to lend the company the necessary money considering that the original loan had been repaid ahead of schedule.

All the success which Hair Care Ltd has achieved has not diminished Sam's appetite for growth. He now seems to be driven more by seeking power and influence than acquiring wealth. He questions the ability of the company to continue its current growth in the prevailing environment and therefore he is looking for ideas which may facilitate corporate expansion. He has asked his accountant to provide some options for him to consider (see Table 16.3).

### Required

1. Assuming the role of Sam's accountant, prepare a report for Sam, evaluating the current position of Hair Care Ltd and highlighting any financial and strategic issues concerning future developments which you feel should be brought to his attention.
2. As his accountant, prepare a short report for Sam, identifying and assessing the strategies which he could consider in attempting to further the company's development.

Chapter 16 Value-based management and strategic management accounting

3  Sam seems preoccupied with growth. Identify reasons for potential corporate decline and suggest ways that Sam could avoid them in the context of the case study scenario.
4  Sam currently appears to have a successful formula for growth. Using the concept of the value chain, demonstrate how he has been able to achieve this success.

*(CIMA Strategic Business Planning and Development)*

Table 16.3 Details of performance of Hair Care Ltd: 2000–2003 (unless otherwise stated, figures are in £'000)

|  | 2000 £'000 | 2001 £'000 | 2002 £'000 | 2003 forecast £'000 |
|---|---|---|---|---|
| Sales | 2,300 | 3,500 | 5,010 | 7,500 |
| Cost of sales | 1,450 | 2,380 | 3,507 | 5,250 |
| Marketing costs | 200 | 250 | 290 | 350 |
| Distribution costs | 300 | 400 | 430 | 500 |
| Administration | 50 | 55 | 80 | 120 |
| Interest payments | 0 | 80 | 220 | 700 |
| Operating profit | 300 | 335 | 483 | 580 |
| Loans | 0 | 850 | 2,400 | 5,000 |
| Number of suppliers (actual) | 15 | 20 | 30 | 50 |
| Range of products (actual) | 35 | 85 | 110 | 130 |
| Total staff including Sam and Annabelle | 12 | 14 | 15 | 23 |
| Stocks | 230 | 400 | 700 | 1,400 |
| Fixed assets | 500 | 1,500 | 2,700 | 6,300 |
| Return on sales (%) | 13.0 | 9.6 | 9.6 | 7.7 |

### C16–15 Strategy and performance
Time allowed: 60 minutes

#### Introduction
The island of Oceania attracts thousands of tourists every year. They come to enjoy the beaches, the climate and to explore the architecture and history of this ancient island. Oceania is also an important trading nation in the region and it enjoys close economic links with neighbouring countries. Oceania has four main airports and until 1997 had two airlines, one based in the west (OceaniaAir) and one based in the east (Transport Oceania) of the island. However, in 1997 these two airlines merged into one airline – Oceania National Airlines (ONA) with the intention of exploiting the booming growth in business and leisure travel to and from Oceania.

#### Market sectors
ONA serves two main sectors. The first sector is a network of routes to the major cities of neighbouring countries. ONA management refer to this as the regional sector. The average flight time in this sector is one and a half hours and most flights are timed to allow business people to arrive in time to attend a meeting and then to return to their homes in the evening. Twenty five major cities are served in the regional sector with, on average, three return flights per day. There is also significant leisure travel, with many families visiting relatives in the region. The second sector is what ONA management refer to as the international sector. This is a network of flights to continental capitals. The average flight time in this sector is four hours. These flights attract both business and leisure travellers. The leisure travellers are primarily holiday-makers from the continent. Twenty cities are served in this sector with, on average, one return flight per day to each city.

### Image, service and employment

ONA is the airline of choice for most of the citizens of Oceania. A recent survey suggested that 90% of people preferred to travel ONA for regional flights and 70% preferred to travel with ONA for international flights. 85% of the respondents were proud of their airline and felt that it projected a positive image of Oceania. The company also has an excellent safety record, with no fatal accident recorded since the merging of the airlines in 1997. The customer service of ONA has also been recognized by the airline industry itself. In 2005 it was voted Regional Airline of the Year by the International Passenger Group (IPG) and one year later the IPG awarded the ONA catering department the prestigious Golden Bowl as provider of the best airline food in the world. The courtesy and motivation of its employees (mainly Oceanic residents) is recognized throughout the region. 95% of ONA employees belong to recognized trade unions. ONA is perceived as an excellent employer. It pays above industry average salaries, offers excellent benefits (such as free health care) and has a generous non-contributory pension scheme. In 2004 ONA employed 5400 people, rising to 5600 in 2005 and 5800 in 2006.

### Fleet

Fleet details are given in Table 16.4. Nineteen of the Boeing 737s were originally in the fleet of OceaniaAir. Boeing 737s are primarily used in the international sector. Twenty-three of the Airbus A320s were originally

**Table 16.4 Fleet details**

|  | Boeing 737 | Airbus A320 | Embraer RJ145 |
|---|---|---|---|
| Total aircraft in service |  |  |  |
| 2006 | 21 | 27 | 3 |
| 2005 | 21 | 27 | 3 |
| 2004 | 20 | 26 | 2 |
| Capacity (passengers) | 147 | 149 | 50 |
| Introduced | October 1991 | November 1988 | January 1999 |
| Average age | 12.1 years | 12.9 years | 6.5 years |
| Utilization (hrs per day) | 8.70 | 7.41 | 7.50 |

part of the Transport Oceania fleet. Airbuses are primarily used in the regional sector. ONA also used three Embraer RJ145 jets in the regional sector.

### Performance

Since 2004 ONA has begun to experience significant competition from 'no frills' low-cost budget airlines, particularly in the international sector. Established continental operators now each offer, on average, three low fares flights to Oceania every day. 'No frills' low-cost budget airlines are also having some impact on the regional sector. A number of very small airlines (some with only one aircraft) have been established in some regional capitals and a few of these are offering low-cost flights to Oceania. A recent survey for ONA showed that its average international fare was double that of its low-cost competitors. Some of the key operational statistics for 2006 are summarized in Table 16.5.

ONA have made a number of operational changes in the last few years. Their website, for example, now allows passengers to book over the internet and to either have their tickets posted to them or to pick them up at the airport prior to travelling. Special promotional fares are also available for customers who book online. However, the website does not currently allow passengers to check in online, a facility provided by some competitors. Furthermore, as Table 16.5 shows, a large percentage of sales are still commission sales made through travel agents. Direct sales are those sales made over the telephone or at the airport itself. Most

### Table 16.5 Key operational statistics for ONA in 2006

|  | Regional | International | Low-cost Competitor Average |
|---|---|---|---|
| *Contribution to revenue ($m)* | | | |
| Passenger | 400 | 280 | Not applicable |
| Cargo | 35 | 15 | Not applicable |
| *Passenger load factor* | | | |
| Standard Class | 73% | 67% | 87% |
| Business Class | 90% | 74% | 75% |
| Average annual pilot salary | $106,700 | $112,500 | $96,500 |
| *Source of revenue* | | | |
| On-line sales | 40% | 60% | 84% |
| Direct sales | 10% | 5% | 12% |
| Commission sales | 50% | 35% | 4% |
| Average age of aircraft | See Table 1 | | 4.5 years |
| Utilization (hrs per day) | See Table 1 | | 9·10 |

leisure travellers pay standard or economy fares and travel in the standard class section of the plane. Although many business travellers also travel in standard class, some of them choose to travel business class for which they pay a price premium.

In the last three years, the financial performance of ONA has not matched its operational success. The main financial indicators have been extracted and are presented in Table 16.6. In a period (2004–2006) when world-wide passenger air travel revenue increased by 12% (and revenue from air travel to Oceania by 15%) and cargo revenue by 10%, ONA only recorded a 4.6% increase in passenger revenue.

### Future strategy

The management team at ONA are keen to develop a strategy to address the airline's financial and operational weaknesses. One suggestion has been to reposition ONA itself as a 'no frills' low-cost budget airline. However, this has been angrily dismissed by the CEO as likely to lead 'to an unnecessary and bloody revolution that could cause the death of the airline itself'.

### Required

(a) Using the information provided in the scenario, evaluate the strengths and weaknesses of ONA and their impact on its performance. Please note that opportunities and threats are NOT required in your evaluation.

(b) The CEO of Oceania National Airways (ONA) has already strongly rejected the re-positioning of ONA as a 'no frills' low-cost budget airline.
 (i) Explain the key features of a 'no frills' low-cost strategy.
 (ii) Analyse why moving to a 'no frills' low-cost strategy would be inappropriate for ONA.

(c) Identify and evaluate other strategic options ONA could consider to address the airline's current financial and operational weaknesses.

*(ACCA Business Analysis)*

**Part 4** Value metrics and performance management in a strategic context

Table 16.6 Extracted Financial Information all figures in $m

| Extracted from the Balance Sheet | | | |
|---|---|---|---|
| *Non-current assets* | 2006 | 2005 | 2004 |
| Property, plant and equipment | 788 | 785 | 775 |
| Other non-current assets | 60 | 56 | 64 |
| Total | 848 | 841 | 839 |
| *Current assets* | | | |
| Inventories | 8 | 7 | 7 |
| Trade receivables | 68 | 71 | 69 |
| Cash and cash equivalents | 289 | 291 | 299 |
| Total | 365 | 369 | 375 |
| Total assets | 1213 | 1210 | 1214 |
| *Total shareholders' equity* | 250 | 259 | 264 |
| *Non-current liabilities* | | | |
| Interest bearing long-term loans | 310 | 325 | 335 |
| Employee benefit obligations | 180 | 178 | 170 |
| Other provisions | 126 | 145 | 143 |
| Total non-current liabilities | 616 | 648 | 648 |
| *Current liabilities* | | | |
| Trade payables | 282 | 265 | 255 |
| Current tax payable | 9 | 12 | 12 |
| Other current liabilities | 56 | 26 | 35 |
| Total current liabilities | 347 | 303 | 302 |
| **Total equity and liabilities** | **1213** | **1210** | **1214** |
| Extracted from the Balance Sheet | | | |
| *Revenue* | | | |
| Passenger | 680 | 675 | 650 |
| Cargo | 50 | 48 | 45 |
| Other revenue | 119 | 112 | 115 |
| Total | 849 | 835 | 810 |
| *Cost of Sales* | | | |
| Purchases | 535 | 525 | 510 |
| Total | 535 | 525 | 510 |
| **Gross Profit** | 314 | 310 | 300 |
| Wages & Salaries | 215 | 198 | 187 |
| Directors' Salaries | 17 | 16 | 15 |
| Interest payable | 22 | 21 | 18 |
| Total | 254 | 235 | 220 |
| **Net Profit before tax** | 60 | 75 | 80 |
| Tax Expense | 18 | 23 | 24 |
| Net Profit after tax | 42 | 52 | 56 |

## Endnotes

1. Simmonds (1981).
2. Graham and Harris (1999).
3. See Kaplan (1984) and Johnson and Kaplan (1987) for a critique of short-term accounting measures.
4. CIMA (2004), p. 5.
5. Rappaport (1999).
6. Ittner and Larcker (2003).
7. Goold and Campbell (1987).
8. Seal (2001).
9. See Chapter 19 for a more detailed treatment of life-cycle costing.
10. Miles and Snow (1978).
11. Porter (1980).
12. Porter (1990), p. 40.
13. Porter (1985).
14. Shank (1996).
15. Shank (1996).
16. Tomkins and Carr (1996).
17. For a discussion of strategic investment appraisal see also Northcott and Alkaraan (2007).
18. For example, see Cronshaw, Davis and Kay (1994).
19. Cooper (1996).
20. The balanced scorecard concept was developed by Robert Kaplan and David Norton. For further details, see their articles Kaplan and Norton (1992), (1996a), (1996b), (1997) and (2004). In the 1960s, the French developed a concept similar to the balanced scorecard called Tableau de Bord or 'dashboard'. For details see Lebas (1994).
21. Mouritsen (1998).
22. Kaplan and Norton (1996b).
23. For a critical evaluation of the BSC see Norreklit (2000).
24. Ittner and Larcker (2003).
25. Norreklit (2000), p. 82.
26. Otley (1999)
27. Norreklit (2003).
28. See, especially, Simons (1995).
29. Emergent strategy is especially associated with the work of Mintzberg (1978).
30. See Prahalad and Hamel (1990).
31. Bromwich and Bhimani (1994).
32. Coad (1996).
33. Wilson (1995).
34. Lord (1996), p. 364. See also Roslender and Hart (2003) and Shank (2006).

When you have read this chapter, log on to the Online Learning Centre for *Management Accounting* at www.mcgraw-hill.co.uk/textbooks/seal, where you'll find multiple choice questions, practice exams and extra study tools for each chapter.

# Performance Management, Management Control and Corporate Governance

# CHAPTER 17
# Performance management, management control and corporate governance

## LEARNING OBJECTIVES

After studying Chapter 17, you should be able to:

1. Consider some criticisms of budgeting as a performance management system
2. Understand some generic features of performance measurement and management control
3. Analyse the 'levers of control' approach to strategy implementation
4. Reappraise the role of management accounting in corporate governance
5. Review the relationship between corporate governance and risk management
6. Appreciate the importance of the environment and the role of environmental management accounting
7. Critically examine performance management and social responsiveness in the public sector

## CONCEPTS IN CONTEXT

The recent credit crunch which has seen the collapse of banks and substantial write-downs in many European and US banks has a number of complex causes. One major problem seemed to be related to the measurement and management of risk. In this chapter, we suggest that risk management is part of a wider issue of corporate governance. We also argue that risk management and other corporate governance matters have a management accounting dimension – well-governed organizations need to have their own systems to measure and manage risk. Furthermore, if non-executive directors are to make a real contribution to the monitoring of corporate strategy and risk then they need to have appropriate financial and non-financial information.[1]

© Frank van den Bergh

In Chapter 1, management accounting techniques were introduced as being part of a cycle of control (see especially Exhibit 1.1). In addition to budgeting, we have also analysed a number of organizational control systems such as the *balanced scorecard* (BSC), *return on investment* (ROI) and *residual income/economic value added* (EVA). In this chapter we develop some of the ideas introduced in Chapter 1 where we described the basic functions of management by reviewing the role of management accounting within *performance management* and *management control systems*. In addition, we consider how and whether managers' decisions can be made accountable to other stakeholders in the organization such as shareholders, debtors, customers, employees and so on. These concerns are often dealt with in emerging topics such as *corporate governance* and *corporate social responsiveness*. **Corporate governance** may be interpreted quite narrowly as being concerned with protecting the interests of the suppliers of capital[2] while **corporate social responsiveness**[3] **(or responsibility)** refers to the capacity of the organization to respond to the demand of society as a whole. While these concepts can be linked to our earlier discussion on the importance of business and professional ethics in Chapter 1, this chapter shows how ethical behaviour may be located in wider organizational frameworks where appropriate internal governance mechanisms are designed to support rather than penalize ethical decision making.

We have already seen how management accounting techniques such as budgeting and balanced scorecards help managers plan, make decisions and control activities. Yet although it is clear that such techniques help to operationalize organizational objectives and measure whether the *actual* have matched the *planned* outcomes, there has been little discussion of how or indeed, whether, such techniques can drive human behaviour in organizations. In short, target setting and measurement are only parts of wider organizational control systems which may involve the analysis of reward systems and the impact of *informal controls* based on conformance to organizational and social norms.

Developments in management accounting, especially the non-financial performance measures and strategic management accounting techniques that we covered in Chapter 16, *can* be used to enhance corporate responsiveness towards shareholders, employees, customers, government and the physical environment. But if corporate social responsibility is going to be more than 'window-dressing' and actually *change* corporate behaviour, then specific performance indicators and processes may need to be embedded alongside the more familiar, financially oriented management control systems.[4]

## FOCUS ON PRACTICE

### Bank bonuses and performance management

The issues of bankers' bonuses is very topical. Understandably, the public ask why it was that managers who ran banks that have had to be rescued by the taxpayer were entitled to huge bonuses in the past. Even more scandalously, they seem to continue to expect them! The profits on which they based their bonuses seemed to be unrelated to the huge risks they were taking on non-performing loans, especially sub-prime mortgages in an overblown property market. As the Bank of England put it: 'banks' profits have been flattered by the mismeasurement of risk' this decade, and profitability has been 'as much mirage as miracle'. The proposal is that bankers' performance should be based against returns on risk-weighted assets.

**Exercise**: Consider how the required return in the residual income model could be adjusted to allow for risk.

*Source*: Aldrick, P. 2011. Bold reform needed if capitalism's heart to beat more strongly, *Daily Telegraph*, 8 January.

## Some criticisms of budgeting as a performance management system

In earlier chapters we covered the technical aspects of budgeting and profit planning in some detail. Such detailed coverage is understandable as for many if not most businesses, the budget is a key planning and control mechanism with many desirable characteristics (see Chapters 11 and 13 especially). Yet, as we noted at the end of Chapter 11, budgeting has come in for much criticism in recent years. It has been described by Jan Wallander as 'an unnecessary evil' and Jack Welch as the 'bane of corporate America'.[5] Such criticisms of budgeting are easier to appreciate when looked at in the wider context of performance management systems. Furthermore, not only may we consider some organizational problems caused by budgeting but we can see that there are alternative, or at least supplementary, control models suggested by the performance management perspective.

One common criticism is that budgets produce a particular type of **constrained management style**, they concentrate on easy to measure events and they are *too historically based*. The last point is often linked to the view that budgets tend to be *incrementalist*. Particularly in not-for-profit organizations in the public sector, discussions about changes to budgets concentrate on marginal or incremental increases or decreases in particular departmental budgets. The problem with incrementalism is that activities become institutionalized through the budget and there is a reluctance to ask questions about fundamental purposes.[6]

Another criticism is that budgeting makes organizations *inflexible* and *unable to respond to uncertainty*. Budgeting is seen as being *mechanistic* with *rigid, formalized* and *tightly coupled* systems. Budgeting-led organizations may be slow to recognize changes in the market and also slow to react to changes even when they have been noticed. Other criticisms of budgeting are that it is *too time consuming*, it tends to *focus on cost control* rather than value creation, it tends to be *top down*, it encourages *gaming* and *opportunism*, it reinforces departmental *barriers* and it *hinders knowledge sharing*. Overall it makes *people feel undervalued*.[7]

Much of the criticism of budgeting is driven by a changing business environment, especially the belief that competition in modern markets has increased the importance of *intellectual capital* relative to physical or tangible capital.[8] In order to respond to this new competitive challenge, it is argued that companies need to adopt a *network* rather than a hierarchical, departmental structure. A network model may still use budgets for cash forecasting but not for cost control. The aim is to avoid 'actual versus budget' reports and concentrate on *relative performance*. These alternative approaches draw on other forms of management control such as benchmarking and the mix of financial and non-financial measures found in approaches such as the balanced scorecard.

## Reform or abandon budgeting?

Given the criticisms of budgeting, what is the appropriate response? Currently, there seems to be two main practice-led approaches. One approach is to improving budgeting and the other is to abandon it.[9] If we review the criticisms of budgeting there seems to be two main issues. One issue concerns the question of *predictability*. It could be argued that budgets work well if managers' predictions are reliable because the budget can then represent a viable plan. Conversely, budgets tend to work badly in conditions of great uncertainty and turbulent environments.[10] The other issue concerns *organizational* and *time-frame problems*. It is argued that budgeting fosters a centralizing and stifling atmosphere as well as a possible mismatch between operational strategies and annual reporting cycles. These organizational problems tend to reduce the ability of units and employees to use their initiative.

## The beyond budgeting round table

Some of the criticism and proposals for reform of budgeting have come from the *beyond budgeting* round table of practitioners and academics.[11] This group argue that as well as critiquing budgeting, it is important to propose viable alternatives. They suggest a number of principles and practices. Arguing that in a globalized economy which increasingly rewards innovation and intellectual capital, the stifling effect of budgeting may damage shareholder interests. With respect to shareholder interests, the round table proposes that targets should be aimed at maximizing long-term value and that resources management should be over the lifetime of an investment and not on the basis of short-term budget allocations. The round table emphasizes the principle of delegation of responsibility with an approach to strategy development that involves the front line as well as the head office. A beyond budgeting corporate culture aims to encourage radical thinking which analyses whether activities (and the costs that they incur) add value. Radical thinking helps the organization to break away from budgetary models of planning characterized by incrementalism (see

Chapter 11). Overall, the emphasis is on an organizational culture that encourages worker and management empowerment.

When it is advocated that organizations abandon budgeting, it may mean that budgets are still used for cash management and other financial purposes but, crucially, not for *performance evaluation*. The aim is to avoid the annual performance trap associated with budgeting by working with what have been called 'relative performance contracts with hindsight'.[12] The significance of the term 'relative' is that performance is benchmarked against *internal* or *external comparators* rather than against historical standards such as last year's results. The term 'with hindsight' means that rather than referring to fixed targets set at the *beginning* of the period, 'targets are adjusted by looking back and incorporating the actual operating and economic circumstances during the period'.[13] Managerial and employee rewards tend to be based on subjective and group criteria with an 'objective to engender a philosophy doing what is best for the firm in the light of current circumstance and to promote teamwork'.[14] These issues will be developed further below where it is argued that alternative control systems or reforms to budgeting are best studied as part of a more general review of possible approaches to organizational control.

## FOCUS ON PRACTICE
### Beyond budgeting? Some survey evidence

The critics of budgeting can sometimes present a rather simplified view of how budgets are actually used. A recent survey suggested that the actual application of budgets is more subtle than the critics allow and that the problems (such as short-termism and inflexibility) are dealt with via adaptations to the budgeting control system. In particular, companies use subjective evaluations and non-financial systems based on human resource management. The budgets are revised frequently and are linked to long-term strategic plans. The budgets are supplemented by cultures of information sharing and managing for the long term.

**Exercise**: The survey found that budgets were used *interactively* rather than *diagnostically*. Which management model are these terms associated with?

*Source:* Libby, T. and Lindsay, R. 2010. Beyond budgeting or budgeting reconsidered? A survey of North American budgeting practice, *Management Accounting Research*, 21: 56–75.

## General models of performance measurement and management control

The concept of control may be introduced by considering a simple thermostat where the system maintains a pre-specified temperature by switching a boiler on and off. More sophisticated models include the use of feedforward information and **double loop learning**. **Feedforward control** relies on a predictive model of processes so that errors can be anticipated and corrected for. As we saw in Chapter 16, *double loop learning* concerns the use of information to learn from past performance in order to change processes, change inputs or alter objectives.[15] The basic control model illustrated in Exhibit 17.1 indicates in very general terms the characteristics of a process control system.

In order to operationalize process control systems for human organizations, we need to be more specific about objectives, motivation, culture and other organizational issues. If it is true that 'What you measure is what you get',[16] then a key feature of a performance management framework is a **performance measurement system** with the following desirable features:[17]

- The performance measures must be consistent with the strategy and objectives of the organization.
- There must be a system of feedback and review to ensure that the information flows enable the organization to learn and adapt from its experience.

**Exhibit 17.1** Process control: single loop, feedforward and learning loops

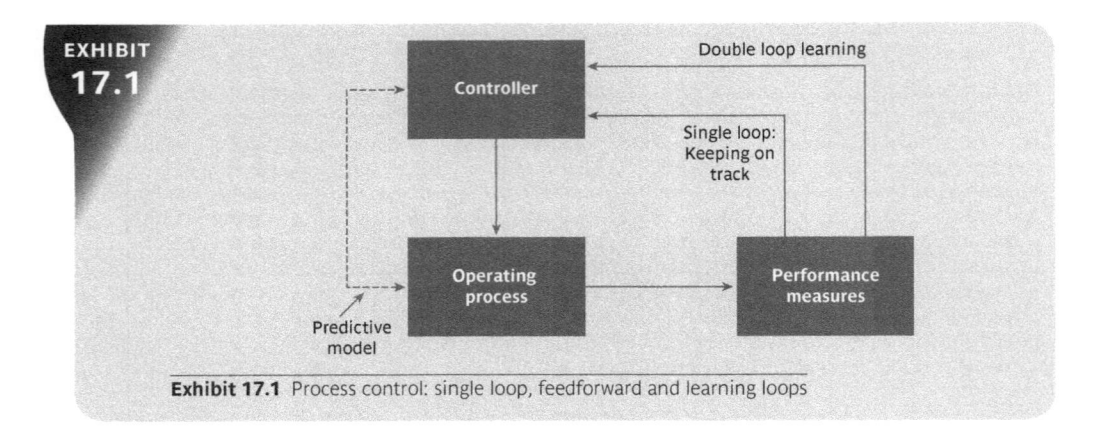

- The performance measurement system must be comprehensive, including non-financial as well as financial indicators.
- Although comprehensive, the measurements system needs to be simple, clear and understandable focusing on **key performance indicators (KPIs)**.
- The performance measurement system must be owned and supported throughout the organization and be aligned with the rewards/penalties that managers and other employees receive for achieving performance targets.

With the above elements in place, we can construct a **performance management** or **management control** framework where organizational behaviour is based on formal, information-based systems. As we shall see below, such systems may then form a part of an overall model of strategy implementation.

## The levers of control approach to strategy implementation

In Chapter 16 we began to explore emergent strategies and organizational learning and other issues that we have developed in this chapter.[18] These aspects of strategy have informed an influential approach to strategy implementation known as the *levers of control*[19] model. One of the characteristics of this more sophisticated approach to strategy and performance management is the recognition that *tensions are inevitable*. For example, there are tensions between performance measures that seem to contradict each other (such as employee morale versus control of wage costs). Furthermore, there are tensions between strategic objectives that encourage creativity and innovation, on the one hand, and the objectives that emphasize a more cautious, risk management approach. The **levers of control model** suggests ways by which these tensions can be managed. Simons[20] criticizes what he terms 'Old style strategy' which he characterizes as being very rational, very analytical and top down. Furthermore, in the old style, the implementation of strategy is either neglected or based on a hierarchical single loop approach to control. In contrast, the 'New style strategy' is more an emergent process in a decentralized, *learning*/flexible firm strategy which is characterized by employee empowerment and responding to customer needs. In practice, intended and emergent strategies tend to operate *simultaneously* with a need to balance both control and learning aspects.

Simons suggests that there are four basic levers of control:

- *belief systems* that inspire and direct;
- *boundary systems* that limit opportunism;
- *diagnostic control systems* that are used to motivate and monitor;
- and *interactive control systems* that stimulate organizational learning.

The search for strategic opportunities is guided by **belief systems** that motivate search behaviour and **boundary systems** that constrain search and innovation. Belief systems are deliberately broad with the aim of fostering inspiration and not simply checking against pre-set standards. Belief systems should increase commitment, provide a core of stability and reinforce the distinctiveness of organization. In contrast, boundary systems are concerned with dos and don'ts such as ethical codes, business association rules and professional norms. It would be wrong to think of risks as simply being associated with fraud or regulatory issues. Thus some of the boundaries set by the firm are of a strategic nature, such as capital budgeting systems with their hurdle rates and positive present value rules.

As Simons points out, his third lever, **diagnostic control systems**, are generally well known as they consist of the sort of cybernetic, feedback-based models that dominate the conventional management control literature. Indeed, they may be summed up by a definition of management control as '[T]he formal, information-based routines and procedures that managers use to maintain or alter patterns in organizational activities'.[21] These diagnostic systems incorporate practices such as budgeting, standard costing, balanced scorecard, and so on. The aim of these systems is that measures should be objective, complete and responsive to actions/effort. Even here tensions may exist. For example, completeness may conflict with responsiveness (e.g. profit). The wrong choice of measures could lead to disasters or at the very least dysfunctional behaviour. For example, there may be a neglect or negative impact on teamwork and a failure to recognize problems of output ambiguity.

Simons' fourth lever is **interactive control systems** where the aim is to use information to encourage debate up and down organizations and to foster an emergent process that links strategy with tactics. The aim here is to develop double-loop learning that questions existing standards/policies. In this area, we need management information that picks up patterns of change but is relatively simple and usable by junior managers. The information should trigger revised action plans and develop an awareness of strategic uncertainties.

While the conflicting objectives shown in Exhibit 17.2 have to be managed, management, itself, is a scarce resource since managers face problems of *unlimited choice* and *limited attention*. Given the scarcity of management resources, the **return-on-management** is optimized by balancing and reconciling the tensions between attention and opportunity.

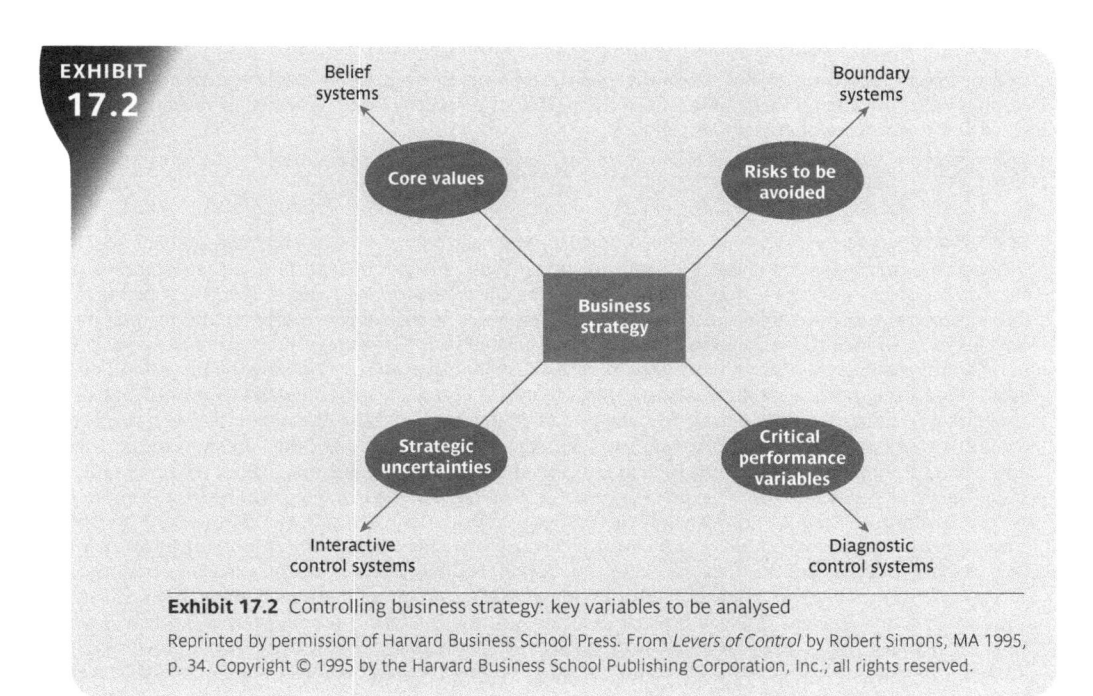

**Exhibit 17.2** Controlling business strategy: key variables to be analysed

Reprinted by permission of Harvard Business School Press. From *Levers of Control* by Robert Simons, MA 1995, p. 34. Copyright © 1995 by the Harvard Business School Publishing Corporation, Inc.; all rights reserved.

## FOCUS ON PRACTICE

### Interactive use of control levers at ABB

In a case study in a subsidiary of the giant multinational company, ABB, the researcher noted that the company used its score card set of financial and non-financial indicators in the interactive way suggested by the levers of control model. This mode of management control seemed to improve the company's strategic management and increase the commitment to strategic targets. However, there were instances where the increased visibility of actions that came out of the interactive discussion of specific performance metrics actually led to resistance against the system. For example, the sales director had been happier with a diagnostic implementation of budgetary control rather than with a score card that exposed the activities of the sales staff. Furthermore, managers complained that the interactive use of performance measures could be time consuming both in the collection of data and in the discussion of results.

**Exercise**: The resistance described in the case did not seem to be helping the attainment of organizational effectiveness. But what sort of 'resistance' might be considered both expected and even encouraged in the levers of the control model?

*Source*: Tuomela, T. (2005) The interplay of different levers of control: a case study of introducing a new performance measurement system, *Management Accounting Research*, 16: 293–320.

With respect to organizational motivation, Simons tries to avoid a **reductionist model of humanity** arguing that humans have creative and achievement orientations as well as material goals. Good management, therefore, is about mobilizing creative human traits rather than just ensuring 'conformance to plan'. Yet, with the emergent problems of the dotcom bubble and financial scandals, the conformance to plan suddenly seems more appealing and less boring than it must have seemed in the more gung-ho days when Simons first proposed his model. As we shall see below, a tougher regulatory environment and an increased emphasis on risk management have raised the profile of boundary systems aimed at restraining both the greed and exuberance of senior executives.

## Corporate governance: a financial perspective

In Chapter 1, we discussed the distinction between financial and management accounting which was summarized in Exhibit 1.2. From a learning perspective, it is important to understand the different aspects of accounting for *reporting* and accounting for *decision making* and *control*. On a practical level, these distinctions may be maintained by using 'different costs for different purposes'. In this chapter we point out that even though they should make distinctions between costs for external reporting and costs for decision making, management accountants generally also have a responsibility to ensure the integrity of financial data for reporting purposes.[22] In this respect, we are moving on to a more complex view on the role of management accounting than the one we initially presented in Chapter 1. The distinction between management accounting and financial accounting was justified in the historical context of the latter part of the 20th century when prominent commentators such as Johnson and Kaplan were concerned about the potentially damaging effect of financial reporting practices on the internal decision making. However, the most recent evidence from the US, UK and elsewhere, is that wealth has been destroyed, not by a lack of creativity or entrepreneurship but by reckless, greedy and sometimes fraudulent behaviour by executives at the highest level of giant corporations. In these instances, the boundary between internal and external decision making becomes more blurred as does our earlier distinction between the roles of management and financial accounting. Just as strategies need to be embedded in an organization's control systems and may involve tensions between expansive belief systems and a more constraining boundary system, there can be tensions between the free-wheeling spirit associated with entrepreneurship and the more constraining values associated with financial probity and integrity.[23]

In corporate disasters that have stemmed from mismanagement rather than obvious fraud, the scandal here is that too often the senior executives who were responsible for the poor decisions were able to walk away from the mess of wrecked livelihoods and pensions with their own wealth and financial security unharmed. The 'reward for failure syndrome' means that the supposed morality tale of capitalism, that business failure leads to financial penalty, seems to have broken down for the very people who bear the greatest decision making responsibility.[24] The fashionable term for analysing these issues is *corporate governance*.

## FOCUS ON PRACTICE

### Corporate remuneration and the 'reward for failure' syndrome

The 'reward for failure' syndrome may easily be observed in high-profile companies such as the retail giant, Sainsbury's. Over his four years at the top of Sainsbury's, the ousted chairman, Sir Peter Davis, received about £11 million. Over the same period, the company fell behind main rivals, Tesco and Asda, and profits fell to a 15-year low. Even without corporate disasters, chief executives have been awarded remuneration packages that pay bonuses even if performance goes down.[25] In the past decade, the *average* remuneration package of FTSE100 directors rose in spite of flat and falling stock market returns. Cohen argues that '(F)ree market economics can't explain the runaway growth in incomes. Try as hard as they might, conventional economists can't find a link between executive pay and performance.'[26]

Another indicator of executive excess is the ratio of CEO pay to average worker pay. In the UK the multiplicand of CEO pay to full-time manual worker pay has increased from 10 times in 1980 to 80 times in 2002. In the US, the multiplicand reached 516 in 1999![27]

A large number of examples of corporate malfeasance involving tax evasion, false accounting, money laundering and other dubious practices may be found on the website of the *Association for Accountancy and Business Affairs*, www.visar.csustan.edu/aaba/home.htm.

**Exercise**: Review how the proposed *bonus bank* system in EVA can, at least in principle, address one of the weaknesses of executive remuneration whereby bonuses are too often linked to *short-run* performance.

Corporate governance has several implications for the study and practice of management accounting. In particular, one assumption generally implicit in management accounting is that decision makers are profit maximizers because this is the goal that serves the owners of the firm. The assumption of profit maximization has been questioned on both theoretical and empirical grounds. Empirically, the evident suspicion of directors and senior managers in the City pages of even the most conservative of newspapers suggests that the notion that managers may pursue their own rather than shareholders' interests is accepted as a stylized fact of mainstream corporate life. A special theory called agency theory, which is beyond the scope of this book, addresses the difficulties of monitoring and linking managerial behaviour to the interests of shareholders.[28] With respect to theory, the adherence to the profit maximization assumption seems to ignore a financial accounting literature that deals with activities such as earnings management[29] and the various *managerialist* models of the firm that have been derived from standard neoclassical economics.[30] Managerialist theories of the firm may themselves be related to a finance view of corporate governance where the key questions are:

> ... How do the suppliers of finance get managers to return some of the profits to them? How do they make sure that managers do not steal the capital they supply or invest in bad projects? How do suppliers of finance control managers?[31]

Although corporate governance issues have long been the subject matter of related subjects such as financial reporting and auditing, the question that has been addressed less thoroughly is the contribution of *organizational/internal* accounting to corporate governance. Certainly, if internal accounting *does* play a role assuring outside suppliers of capital then the criterion of *relevance* becomes a much more complex issue. From an agency perspective, the apparent domination of financial reporting conventions over 'correct' decision-making rules may not be a mistake but rather a rational response to the increasing separation of ownership and control. We will now explore this issue further by looking at some examples of the links between financial and management accounting.

## Management accounting and the integrity of financial information

Easily buried by the avalanche of articles and books debating the then emerging relevance lost thesis, a relatively neglected piece of research[32] explicitly explored the tension between the accountant as a member of a management team and the management accountant (or controller) as the guardian of the integrity of the externally reported financial information. In the latter role, the management accountant must exhibit a degree of independence from the business decision-making process.

## Management accounting and regulatory approaches to corporate governance

The integrity of corporate reporting has been made the subject of intense regulatory and legal scrutiny. In the US, the emphasis has been on increased judicial enforcement of financial reporting standards in the Sarbanes–Oxley Act (2002). These regulatory innovations seem to suggest that the suppliers of capital no longer trust their most immediate agents, the senior executives of large corporations. In the UK with the publication of the Higgs Report (2003), one of the ways that management accounting can contribute to improving corporate governance is to advocate new performance measures that are designed to enhance the ability of non-executive directors to monitor their fellow executive directors.[33]

But how can non-executive directors make a difference if they do not know what is going on in the company? From this perspective, it is a short step to see a potential role for management accounting to provide non-executives with information with which to assess risk, check on strategy and monitor the behaviour of executive board members. Indeed many of the criticisms of conventional reporting and the proposed remedies will be unsurprising to academic management accountants. If conventional transaction-based financial accounting data is too late and too backward looking, then many of the key trends and key performance drivers will be driven by approaches such as the balanced scorecard and strategic management accounting.

The response from the management accounting profession to the corporate governance debate has been articulated in a CIMA technical report,[34] which outlines the sort of board reporting practices that are deemed necessary for good market performance and sound corporate governance. Drawing on previous reports on governance such as the Cadbury Report, Starovic builds on the Combined Code on Corporate Governance.[35] Along with the usual admonitions that good quality information should be relevant, focused, forward looking and so on, Starovic also argues for integrated information systems and processes. The role of management accountants in the financial perspective on corporate governance is summarized in Exhibit 17.3.

Yet such an ambitious proposal begs some obvious questions. Why should non-executive directors be provided with strategic management accounting (SMA) data when even senior accounting officials seem reluctant to collect such information?[36] Guilding *et al.* (2000) found that respondents scored SMA higher on *merit* than in actual usage. One interpretation of this finding is that however desirable it may be in principle, there are few incentives for the extra information to be collected. More generally, why should managers who perhaps own very little of the stock of the company care about shareholders let alone other stakeholders? Taking an even more sceptical view, if managers are rewarded through stock options and compensated for loss of office, why should they worry too much about the possible downside of their chosen strategies? Although they may be concerned about their reputations, *these are most likely to be damaged not by strategies that fail but which are different.*

If we consider the *Management accounting in action* example in Chapter 16, senior executives at Marconi claimed that they were only doing what everyone else is doing (focusing and internationalizing in the telecom industry). So how can they blamed if the result is corporate meltdown?[37] Yet strategic management accounting techniques *should* enable managers to develop a *unique* company strategy based on an appraisal of how actual and potential competitors will react. Adopting a unique strategy is probably the only way that

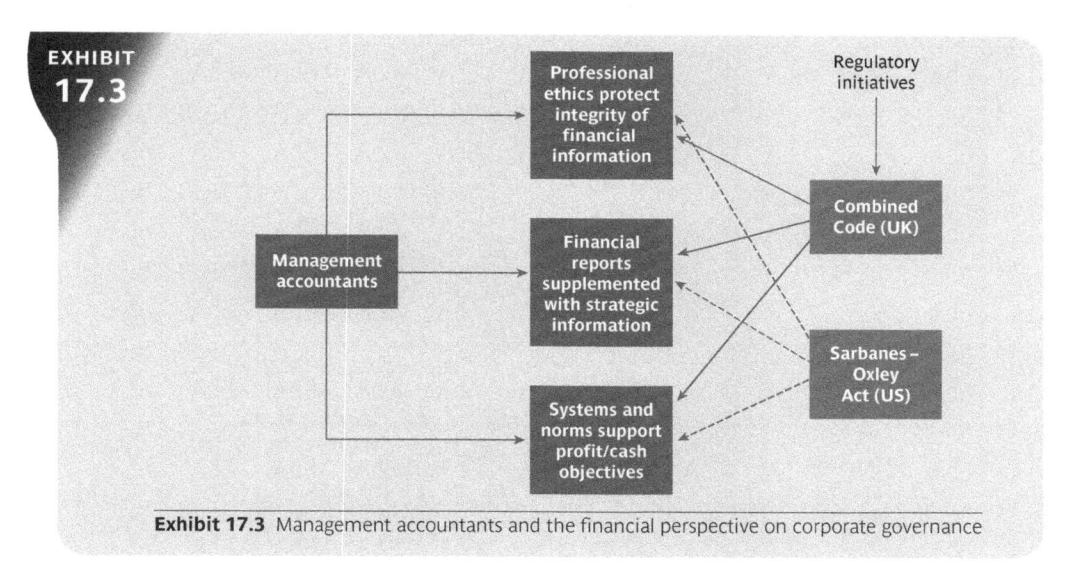

**Exhibit 17.3** Management accountants and the financial perspective on corporate governance

a company may obtain a competitive advantage and thus a higher return.[38] If a company just does what all its competitors are doing, then at best the company will just match the industry return. At worst, as in the Marconi case described in Chapter 16, if all companies try to expand in one industry, then a huge surplus of capacity and low returns are very likely. In short, institutional theory suggests that strategic management accounting is unlikely to be adopted by managers driven by mimetic behaviour.

Another way of looking at the corporate governance crisis at the turn of the century is to see it as a problem of *risk management*. In the next section, we will look at a particular version of risk management that is associated with improving corporate governance that ties in with our earlier review of the importance of boundary systems.[39]

## Corporate governance and risk management

In Chapter 10, we looked at a number of techniques for modelling risk using probability theory and decision trees. We also argued that other approaches to controlling risk involved policies of diversification and organizational design that enabled a flexible response to changing circumstances. Another approach to risk sees the establishment of effective internal controls as so important that company boards have a specific responsibility for **risk management**. In the UK, the Turnbull Report[40] offered guidance for boards so that they followed 'a risk-based approach to establishing a sound system of internal control and reviewing its effectiveness'. According to Gould a 'robust' risk management system means that a company will have:

- 'understood the nature of the risks facing it;
- decided the extent and categories of risk which it regards as acceptable for it to bear;
- considered the likelihood of the risks materializing;
- judged its ability to reduce the incidence and impact on the business of risks that do materialize; *and*
- estimated the costs of operating particular controls relative to the benefit thereby obtained in managing the related risks'.[41]

As may be seen in Exhibit 17.4, Turnbull was concerned with a very extensive list of possible risks that have to be managed at board level. Some of these risks are clearly concerned with reporting and compliance issues but others are operational and strategic issues that should be informed by many of the techniques and measures that we introduced in this book. Exhibit 17.5 shows a wheel of action approach to risk management that may easily be related to our generic control models with both elements of keeping

## Exhibit 17.4

| Business | Operational and other |
|---|---|
| Wrong business strategy | Business processes not aligned to strategic goals |
| Competitive pressure on price/market share | Failure of major change initiative |
| General economic problems | Loss of entrepreneurial spirit |
| Regional economic problems | Stock-out of raw materials |
| Political risks | Skills shortage |
| Obsolescence of technology | Physical disasters (including fire and explosion) |
| Substitute products | Failure to create and exploit intangible assets |
| Adverse government policy | Loss of intangible assets |
| Industry sector in decline | Breach of confidentiality |
| Take-over target | Loss of physical assets |
| Inability to obtain further capital | Lack of business continuity |
| Bad acquisition | Succession problems |
| Too slow to innovate | Year 2000 problems |
| **Financial** | Loss of key people |
| Liquidity risk | Inability to reduce cost base |
| Market risk | Major customers impose tough contract obligations |
| Going concern problems | Over-reliance on key suppliers or customers |
| Overtrading | Failure of new products or services |
| Credit risk | Poor service levels |
| Interest risk | Failure to satisfy customers |
| Currency risk | Quality problems |
| High cost of capital | Lack of orders |
| Treasury risk | Failure of major project |
| Misuse of financial resources | Loss of key contracts |
| Occurrence of types of fraud to which the business is susceptible | Inability to make use of the internet |
| Misstatement risk related to published financial information | Failure of outsource provider to deliver |
| Breakdown of accounting system | Industrial action |
| Unrecorded liabilities | Failure of big technology related project |
| Unreliable accounting records | Lack of employee motivation or efficiency |
| Penetration and attack of IT systems by hackers | Inability to implement change |
| Decisions based on incomplete or faulty Information | Inefficient/ineffective processing of documents |
| Too much data and not enough analysis | Poor brand management |
| Unfulfilled promises to investors | Product liability |
| **Compliance** | Inefficient/ineffective management process |
| Breach of Listing Rules | Problems arising from exploiting employees in developing countries |
| Breach of financial regulations | Other business probity issues |
| Breach of Companies Act requirements | Other issues giving rise to reputational problems |
| Litigation risk | Missed business opportunities |
| Breach of competition laws | |
| VAT problems | |
| Breach of other regulations and laws | |
| Tax penalties | |
| Health and safety risks | |
| Environmental problems | |

**Exhibit 17.4** Possible risks according to Turnbull

**Part 4** Value metrics and performance management in a strategic context

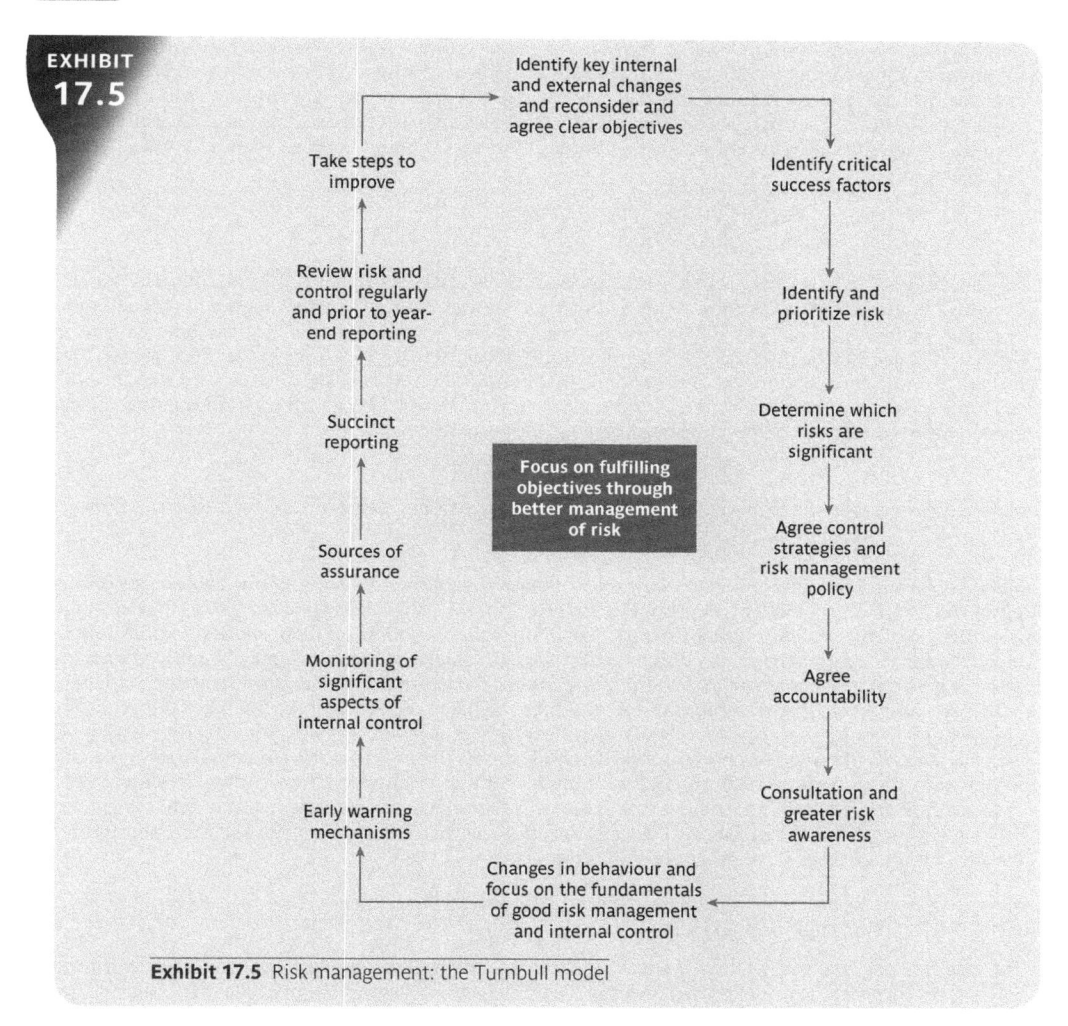

**EXHIBIT 17.5**

```
                    Identify key internal
                    and external changes
                    and reconsider and
                    agree clear objectives
     Take steps to                          Identify critical
      improve                               success factors

     Review risk and                        Identify and
     control regularly                      prioritize risk
     and prior to year-
     end reporting

     Succinct                               Determine which
     reporting                              risks are
                     ┌──────────────┐       significant
                     │Focus on fulfilling│
                     │objectives through │
     Sources of      │better management │  Agree control
     assurance       │of risk           │  strategies and
                     └──────────────┘       risk management
                                            policy

     Monitoring of                          Agree
     significant                            accountability
     aspects of
     internal control

     Early warning                          Consultation and
     mechanisms                             greater risk
                                            awareness
                    Changes in behaviour and
                    focus on the fundamentals
                    of good risk management
                    and internal control
```

**Exhibit 17.5** Risk management: the Turnbull model

on track, searching for early warning indicators and organizational learning with a constant review of objectives and critical success factors.

## Wealth creation and good corporate governance: the role of boundary systems

Although we have suggested that strategic management accounting techniques can make a contribution to corporate governance by informing both executive and non-executive directors, the usual assumption is that strategic information is concerned with adding value and wealth creation. Compliance systems in contrast are sometimes seen as being constraining and even inimical to the sort of enterprising decisions and behaviour that generate wealth. Yet some constraints or boundary systems actually enable organizational freedom and flexibility. As Simons puts it: 'Ask yourself why there are brakes in a car. Is their function to slow the car down or to allow it to go fast? Boundary systems are like brakes on a car: without them, cars (or organizations) cannot operate at high speeds.[42] Boundary systems may be driven by external codes such as those on corporate governance and company law, professional ethics or even the result of commercial prudence. Simons argues that business conduct boundaries are particularly important when uncertainty is high or when internal trust is low. In this arena, boundary systems may be seen as a vital part of risk management.

## Enterprise governance

A recently developed concept, **enterprise governance**, stresses the duty of both company boards and executive managements to provide strategic direction, manage risks and verify that the organization uses its resources in a responsible way.[43] The enterprise governance model argues that a balance must be struck between the goals of conformance and accountability assurance (the corporate governance strand) and performance and value creation (the business governance strand). In this respect, we can see that, post-Enron, the profession is recognizing the tensions discussed in this chapter and which were originally identified by academics such as Sathe (1982) and Simons (1995).

## A broader view on corporate governance: stakeholders, social and environmental responsiveness

So far we have taken a rather narrow view on corporate governance by focusing on the interests of the suppliers of capital. In a broader perspective, we are concerned with issues that are often covered under the heading of *corporate responsiveness* with a particular emphasis on *social* and *environmental* responsibility. This broader view recognizes that many obstacles to corporate social responsiveness may be caused by an organization's performance management system. For example, the normal divisionalized structures of large companies are designed to achieve economic rather than social goals especially if the usual ROI/EVA type metrics are adopted. In general, the conventional accounting system is biased towards financial data with a neglect of social data. Furthermore, in profit-oriented organizations, the incentive system tends to reward economic rather than social performance. In short, although many firms now specify some social objectives, they often fail to reinforce their attainment through their performance measurement and reward system. Ethical problems arise within organizations because ethical goals that reflect corporate social responsibility may conflict with *material* goals of profit and staff bonuses.

### The Performance Prism

The general principles of effective organizational control are similar whether we are concerned with the narrow view of corporate governance that prioritizes the interests of the suppliers of capital or a broader approach that considers corporate social responsiveness and the interests of a diversity of **stakeholders**,[44] which includes customers, employees, suppliers, regulators and pressure groups as well as shareholders and other suppliers of capital.

A good example of a management control model that incorporates a broad view of corporate governance, we may consider the **Performance Prism** which includes five facets of business performance – *stakeholder contribution, stakeholder satisfaction, strategies, processes* and *capabilities*. Rather than derive performance measures from strategy, the performance measurement system is built up by initially asking: *who* are the stakeholders and *what* do they want? The next step then considers the strategies that should be adopted in order to satisfy stakeholders.

But as well as having wants, stakeholders also make contributions to the organization, as shown in Exhibit 17.6. The dual relationship between wants and contributions can be illustrated by customers who want quality products at low prices but potentially offer profitability to the organization through customer loyalty. Similarly, suppliers want prompt payment and advance warnings of product changes but potentially offer on-time delivery of quality product.

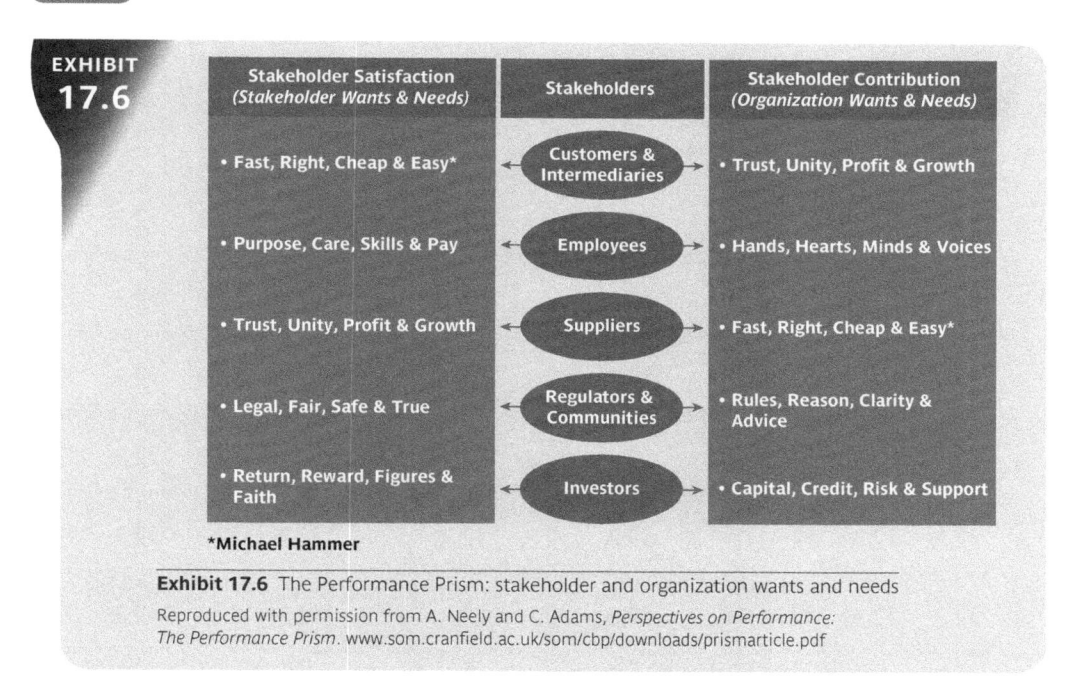

**EXHIBIT 17.6**

| Stakeholder Satisfaction (Stakeholder Wants & Needs) | Stakeholders | Stakeholder Contribution (Organization Wants & Needs) |
|---|---|---|
| • Fast, Right, Cheap & Easy* | Customers & Intermediaries | • Trust, Unity, Profit & Growth |
| • Purpose, Care, Skills & Pay | Employees | • Hands, Hearts, Minds & Voices |
| • Trust, Unity, Profit & Growth | Suppliers | • Fast, Right, Cheap & Easy* |
| • Legal, Fair, Safe & True | Regulators & Communities | • Rules, Reason, Clarity & Advice |
| • Return, Reward, Figures & Faith | Investors | • Capital, Credit, Risk & Support |

*Michael Hammer

**Exhibit 17.6** The Performance Prism: stakeholder and organization wants and needs

Reproduced with permission from A. Neely and C. Adams, *Perspectives on Performance: The Performance Prism*. www.som.cranfield.ac.uk/som/cbp/downloads/prismarticle.pdf

The Performance Prism has been applied in a number of commercial and non-profit making organizations. In order to illustrate the latter, we have reproduced the outline success map for a non-profit making organization, London Youth, in Exhibit 17.7. London Youth is a charity with a membership of youth clubs, groups and projects that involve about 75,000 young and 5,000 adult leaders and committee members. Its main mission is to assist the development of children and young people in the Greater London area but its subsidiary goals are to grow membership; improve the range of products offered; provide affordable residential experience; raise its profile; raise funds and ensure efficient and effective governance. These strategies are clearly linked because donors do not like to give funds to corrupt, ineffective or unaccountable organizations.

Models like the Performance Prism show that there is no conceptual reason why performance management systems may not be used to drive the attainment of social objectives. Although the general principles of the formal control model are the same, the objectives, measurement systems and tangible rewards are explicitly designed to include social objectives as well as the more conventional financial goals. Such models do not mean that conflicts between objectives disappear just because a broader view of corporate governance is accepted. For example, compliance with environmental regulations usually increases business costs and involves more complex decision making which we may analyse under the umbrella term of **environmental management accounting**.

## Environmental management accounting

Profit-oriented firms have a number of reasons why they should take environmental issues seriously. At its most basic, they have little choice as in many countries strong environmental regulatory regimes generate extra pollution and compliance costs which feed directly into their bottom line (the *compliance motive*). They may also find that the bottom line may be improved because more efficiency in the use of energy, water and other raw materials may actually reduce costs and boost profits (the *eco-efficiency motive*). From a more strategic perspective many firms have also realized that there is an increasing market for green products and green business practices (the *strategic motive*). Finally, as we argued in Chapter 1, businesses have ethical responsibilities to the wider community and, even more fundamentally, their common home, 'Planet Earth'.

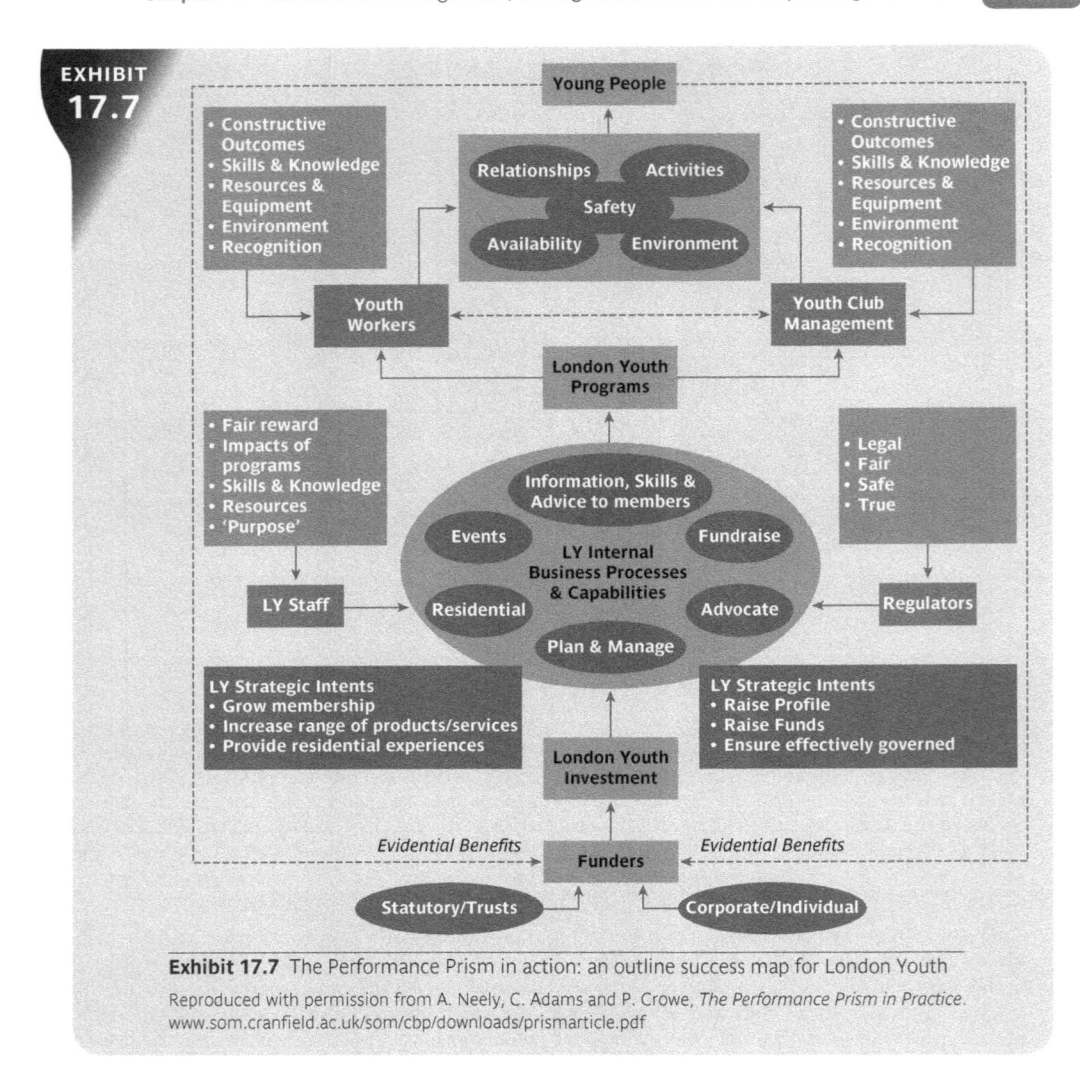

**Exhibit 17.7** The Performance Prism in action: an outline success map for London Youth

Reproduced with permission from A. Neely, C. Adams and P. Crowe, *The Performance Prism in Practice*. www.som.cranfield.ac.uk/som/cbp/downloads/prismarticle.pdf

Environmental Management Accounting (EMA) may be defined as 'the identification, collection, analysis and use of two types of information for internal decision making:

- physical information on the use, flows and destinies of energy, water and materials (including wastes) and
- monetary information on environment-related costs, earnings and savings.'[45]

The EMA agenda is summarized in Exhibit 17.8 which traces and elaborates on the three themes of compliance, eco-efficiency and strategic position. As we saw in earlier chapters, a decision analysis can be flawed by incorrectly including irrelevant costs such as sunk costs and future costs that do not differ between alternatives. It can also be flawed by omitting future costs that *do* differ between alternatives. This is particularly a problem with **environmental costs** that have dramatically increased in recent years and about which many managers have little knowledge. Environmental costs for a company are the costs of complying with environmental regulations. For the wider society, they are costs generated by human activities and may or may not be measured in monetary terms.

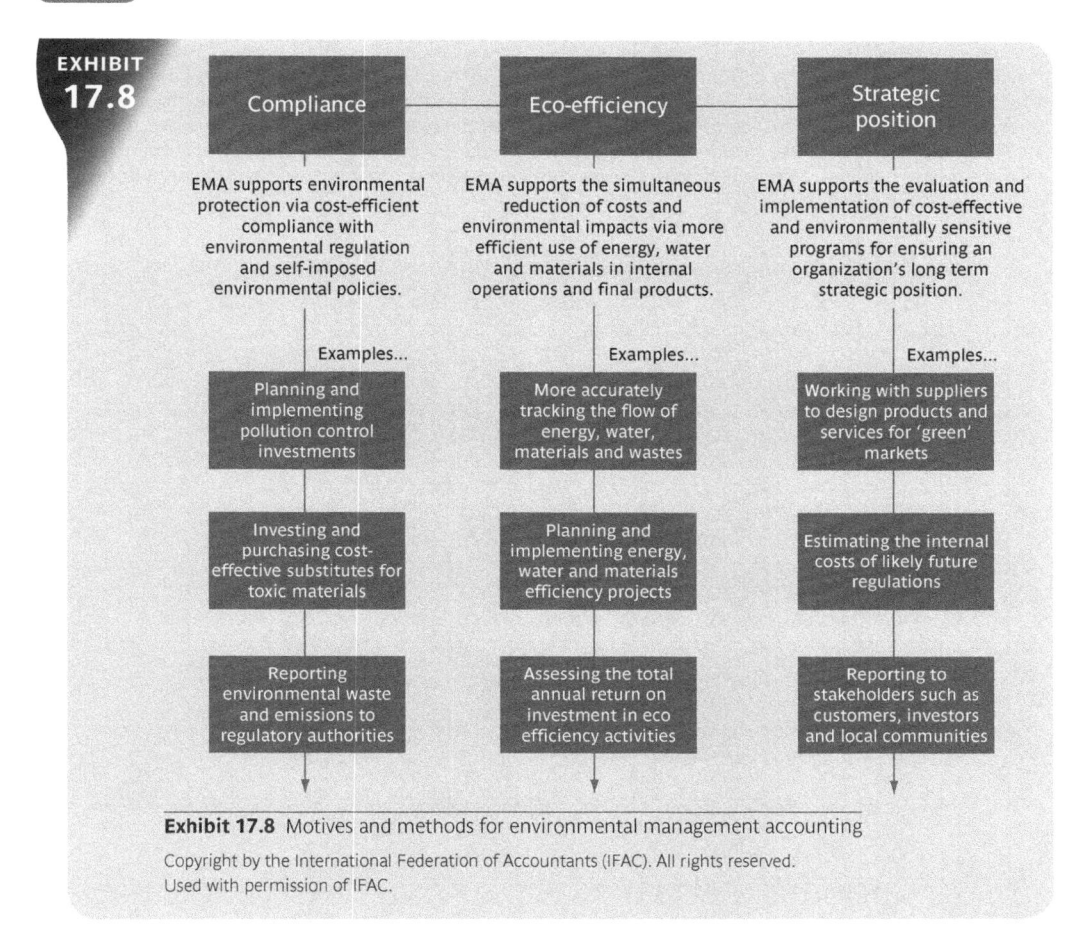

**Exhibit 17.8**

| Compliance | Eco-efficiency | Strategic position |
|---|---|---|
| EMA supports environmental protection via cost-efficient compliance with environmental regulation and self-imposed environmental policies. | EMA supports the simultaneous reduction of costs and environmental impacts via more efficient use of energy, water and materials in internal operations and final products. | EMA supports the evaluation and implementation of cost-effective and environmentally sensitive programs for ensuring an organization's long term strategic position. |

Examples...

| Compliance | Eco-efficiency | Strategic position |
|---|---|---|
| Planning and implementing pollution control investments | More accurately tracking the flow of energy, water, materials and wastes | Working with suppliers to design products and services for 'green' markets |
| Investing and purchasing cost-effective substitutes for toxic materials | Planning and implementing energy, water and materials efficiency projects | Estimating the internal costs of likely future regulations |
| Reporting environmental waste and emissions to regulatory authorities | Assessing the total annual return on investment in eco efficiency activities | Reporting to stakeholders such as customers, investors and local communities |

**Exhibit 17.8** Motives and methods for environmental management accounting

Copyright by the International Federation of Accountants (IFAC). All rights reserved. Used with permission of IFAC.

## An example of environmental management accounting

Consider the environmental complications posed by a decision of whether to install a solvent-based or powder-based system for spray-painting parts. In a solvent painting system, parts are sprayed as they move along a conveyor. The paint that misses the part is swept away by a wall of water, called a water curtain. The excess paint accumulates in a pit as sludge that must be removed each month. Environmental regulations classify this sludge as hazardous waste. As a result, the company must obtain a permit to produce the waste and must maintain meticulous records of how the waste is transported, stored and disposed of. The annual costs of complying with these regulations can easily exceed £140,000 in total for a painting facility that initially cost only £400,000 to build. The costs of complying with environmental regulations include the following:

- The waste sludge must be hauled to a special disposal site. The typical disposal fee is about £300 per barrel or £55,000 per year for a modest solvent-based painting system.
- Workers must be specially trained to handle the paint sludge.
- The company must carry special insurance.
- The company must pay substantial fees to the state for releasing pollutants (i.e., the solvent) into the air.
- The water in the water curtain must be specially treated to remove contaminants. This cost can run into tens of thousands of pounds per year.

In contrast, a powder-based painting system avoids almost all of these environmental costs. Excess powder used in the painting process can be recovered and reused without creating a hazardous waste. Additionally, the powder-based system does not release contaminants into the atmosphere. Therefore, even though the cost of building a powder-based system may be higher than the cost of building a solvent-based system, over the long run the costs of the powder-based system may be far lower due to the high environmental costs of a solvent-based system. Managers need to be aware of such environmental costs and take them fully into account when making decisions.

> ## FOCUS ON PRACTICE
> ### Embedding and evaluating sustainability
>
> Some companies have adapted the balanced scorecard framework in order to specify environmental objectives and measures. For example, Bristol-Myers record cost savings from accident reduction (financial perspective), consumer education (customer perspective), water use (Internal Process) and Training hours (Learning & Growth) as well as other financial and non-financial measures of sustainability. Other researchers argue that these sort of measures can be used by fund managers looking to select socially responsible investments (SRI). These approaches demonstrate a commitment by the organization and aim to change behaviour. In the Finnish case study, the researchers found the score card being used in an environmental management system.
>
> **Exercise**: Using the balanced scorecard model suggest other possible financial and non-financial measures which could guide sustainable actions
>
> *Source*: Tsai1,W., Chou1,W-C. and Hsu1, W. 2009. The sustainability balanced scorecard as a framework for selecting socially responsible investment: an effective MCDM model, *Journal of the Operational Research Society*, 60: 1396–1410; Lansiluoto, A. and Jarvenpaa, M. 2008. Environmental and performance management forces: integrating 'greenness' into balanced scorecard, *Qualitative Research in Accounting & Management*, 5(3): 184–206

## Organizational control and service delivery in the public sector: beyond incrementalism?

The primacy of the shareholder in most discussions of corporate governance is understandable given the origins and legal structures of the private sector, for-profit organization. We should expect that, in principle at least, social responsiveness *should* be better in not-for-profit organizations in the public sector whose structures and objectives are overtly designed to serve the public interest. Yet even here, social responsiveness has a technical dimension as public policies need to be implemented and managed in order to ensure that appropriate strategies and public services are delivered. Indeed, the problems of budgeting in the public sector, especially *incrementalism*, may be even more serious than in the private sector where companies have more choice over how binding their budgets are.

**Incrementalism** is associated with a tendency to increase or decrease existing budgets by small amounts without asking whether the underlying local services that are being financed are still necessary or are being provided in the most effective way. In the traditional approach to public sector budgeting, the budget holder starts with last year's budget and adds to it (or subtracts from it), according to anticipated needs. In an incremental approach to budgeting, the previous year's budget is taken for granted as a baseline.

**Zero-based budgeting** is an alternative approach that is sometimes used in the public sector.[46] Under a zero-based budget, managers are required to justify all budgeted expenditures, not just changes in the budget from the previous year. The baseline is zero rather than last year's budget. A zero-based budget requires considerable documentation. In addition to all the schedules in the usual master budget, the manager must prepare a series of 'decision packages' in which all the activities of the department are ranked according to their relative importance and the cost of each activity is identified. Higher-level managers can then review the decision packages and cut back in those areas that appear to be less critical or whose costs do not appear to be justified.

Under zero-based budgeting, the review is performed every year. Critics of zero-based budgeting charge that properly executed zero-based budgeting is too time consuming and too costly to justify on an annual basis. In addition, it is argued that annual reviews soon become mechanical and that the whole purpose of zero-based budgeting is then lost. Whether or not an organization should use an annual review is a matter of judgement. In some situations annual zero-based reviews may be justified; in other situations they may not because of the time and cost involved. However, most managers would at least agree that on occasion zero-based reviews can be very helpful.

The rigidity of the budgeting system in public sector organizations is often understandable given that public bodies have a special responsibility to account for the taxpayers' funds that support their activities. Historically, the emphasis in public sector organizations like local authorities has been on **financial stewardship** – demonstrating to citizens and other tiers of government that monies have been handled with probity and prudence. Indeed, it is only a relatively recent development that has seen public sectors throughout the world applying more sophisticated systems that combine performance management with financial management. New public corporate structures, performance indicators systems and budgeting can be used to try to make the public sector more responsive to the needs of citizens. We cannot cover all the changes that have been introduced in the UK public sector over the last 20 years but an example based on recent fieldwork (1997–2003) shows how attempts have been made to reform corporate governance, financial management and service delivery in the local public sector. The field study follows the experience of two local authorities, Southshire and Eastmet.[47]

## New political and management structures

Certain types of traditional organizational structures of UK local government were almost inevitably incrementalist. Services were managed by big specialist departments in areas such as education, housing and social services that were accountable to specialized committees of elected counsellors (known as 'members'). In common with many English local authorities, Eastmet and Southshire abolished the old departmental structures and adopted small 'cabinets' with senior members holding portfolios. The portfolios were designed to reflect a cross-cutting perspective so that, for example, a single organizational structure and budget for children's services replaced the original education and social service departments.

## The introduction of policy-led budgeting

Both Eastmet and Southshire developed long- and medium-term plans that were intended to indicate the councils' priorities and guide long-term financial strategies. In order to operationalize the plans, both authorities made an increased use of *non-financial performance indicators in conjunction with financial measures*. New reporting systems were developed that not only picked up the traditional budgetary variances but also monitored non-financial performance. Both authorities adopted three-year financial strategies with special mechanisms to allow investment in services and promote changes in service provision. An example of how service performance and financial management data may be combined is illustrated in Exhibit 17.9. The exhibit demonstrates how the general control principles developed earlier in the chapter can be applied to the management of a public service such as education with its emphasis on social goals and objectives.

In an attempt to combat incrementalism, services (and their budgets) were subject to periodic (but not annual) fundamental reviews. Although there was both a commitment and an increased managerial capacity to base budgets on medium- to long-term priorities and move funds around, it could not be claimed that incrementalist practices had been abolished. The political and organizational issues that make incrementalism so compelling and rational management so difficult that were identified so brilliantly[48] more than 30 years ago were still prevalent after successive waves of modernizing initiatives.

Many of the reforms of the public sector, sometimes known as the **New Public Management**,[49] have been extremely controversial. Although it is beyond the scope of this book to do full justice to ongoing debates, at least some of the potential problems relate to the use of performance indicators in the public sector.

## Key Performance Indicators and Targets

| Indicator | Actual Result 2000/1 | Target for 01/02 | Actual performance 2001/2 | Sun, cloud or lightning | Target 02/03 | Long term target 2006/7 | Comments on our performance |
|---|---|---|---|---|---|---|---|
| To increase the resources going into schools | £5m added to schools budget | To add another £3m to schools budget | Achieved | ☀ | To add further £3m to Schools Budget | N/A | The objective to add £11m to schools budget will have been achieved by 2002/3 |
| Percentage infant classes with more than 30 pupils per teacher | 2.3% | 0% | 0.7% | ☀ | 0% | 0% | Some legitimate exceptions push the percentage above 0% |
| % Unauthorized absence: secondary schools | 2.6% | 1.1% | 2.6% | ☁ | 1.0% | 0.8% | Performance was affected by reorganization but is improving again |
| GCSE: Percentage with 5 + A* – C grades | 32.8% | 36.5% | 34.3% | ☁ | 39.5% | 55% | Results went up but not by as much as hoped. The year group had not come through reorganized schools but through the old system |
| GCSE: Percentage with 1 + A* – G grades | 91.6% | 94.5% | 92.3% | ☁ | 97% | 99% | Performance on this indicator is sensitive to the absence rate |
| GCSE: Average Points score | 30.9 | 33.5 | 31.3 | ☁ | 36.0 | 45.0 | The average points score did not improve as was hoped |
| Key Stage 2 Maths: Percentage at Level 4+ | 59.9% | 66% | 59.7% | ☁ | 73% | 95% | Test results improved but not by as much as the targets required. Steady improvement is expected now that the Direct Service Provider is in place |
| Key Stage 2 English: Percentage at Level 4+ | 65.9% | 72% | 66.6% | ☁ | 76% | 100% | The maths comment applies equally to the English test results |
| To complement successfully all activities set out in the Ofsted Action Plan | N/A | 75% | 90% | ☀ | 100% | N/A | Scheduled for completion by August 2002 |

**Exhibit 17.9** Combining performance planning and financial management in the public sector: an example of Best Value in UK local government

Exhibit 17.10 summarizes many of the distorting effects on managerial behaviour that can result from an excessive use of performance indicators.[50] Although some of these same problems may be found in for-profit organizations, it is generally claimed that because profits and share prices are outcomes that aggregate the effects of a variety of organizational behaviours and decisions, many of the distortions identified in Exhibit 17.10 are less pressing. But of course, if financial indicators such as profit can summarize organizational performance then it is clearly very important to be vigilant about the last potential problem of misrepresentation!

## FOCUS ON PRACTICE

### Cost reduction in the public sector: three levels of change

Many Western governments face huge fiscal deficits and have begun to cut public expenditure. Cuts are inevitably controversial and subject to political debate. From a technical/management perspective, it is possible to identify three levels of change: improving efficiency using existing methods and organizations; considering whether existing programmes could be delivered in totally new ways to improve efficiency; reviewing policies and priorities. Politicians hope that option three can be avoided and argue that savings can be achieved through savings in the 'back office'.

**Exercise**: Suggest some reasons why politicians prefer changes in the first two levels.

*Source*: Deloittes (2010) Reducing costs in public organizations in an age of austerity

### EXHIBIT 17.10

| | | |
|---|---|---|
| Tunnel vision | Excessive focus on achieving indicators | Input indicators may be easier to create and manage |
| Suboptimization | Neglect of wider goals of organization | Problem of the lack of a 'Profit-type' indicator that can capture wider goals of the organization |
| Myopia | Concentration on short-term results | Non-financial indicators may fail to encourage long-term, investment type activity |
| Convergence | Avoiding exposure as exceptional either in good or bad performance | Public sector organizations are often more exposed to media scrutiny |
| Ossification | Reluctance to innovate or take risks | Hard to reward risk taking in public sector; easier to penalize non-conformance |
| Gaming | See budgeting – e.g. keep hidden reserves | Problem in public sector is that it can be hard to develop an independent basis for checking on the claims made by subordinate units |
| Misrepresentation | Creative accounting and fraud | Clearly a potential problem in both public and for-profit organizations! |

**Exhibit 17.10** Possible distortions of management control through the use of performance indicators in the public sector

*Based on Smith, P. 1993. 'Outcome-related performance indicators and organizational control in the public sector', British Journal of Management, 4: 135–151.

## Informal versus formal control systems

Traditional management accounting control systems tend to emphasize formal control based on techniques such as budgets and investment appraisal techniques based on written procedures and motivated by physical rewards such as bonuses and promotion. Yet informal systems of control based on shared values, beliefs and traditions may be very important, particularly when output measures are ambiguous and knowledge on the technical relationship between inputs and outputs is vague.[51] Indeed, in the 1980s, the success of the Japanese corporate model was often attributed to the apparent reliance on *clan* rather than bureaucratic control. In the **clan model**, control of the organization is motivated by a desire for peer approval and an avoidance of deviance from group ideals. Although we have introduced social control in the context of corporate governance and social responsibility, the socialization processes advocated to build a clan corporation in the 1980s were aimed to reinforce the commercial competitiveness rather than improve social responsiveness.[52]

Most of the corporate social responsibility literature focuses on external reporting, which is beyond the scope of this book. Yet the adoption of social responsibility reporting may have a positive impact on the issues of *internal* governance covered in this chapter. The process of producing reports may help mobilize the examples of socially responsible practices that the corporation will generally emphasize.[53] The act of narrating, visualizing and numbering has the effect of making socially responsible activities manageable in the same way that intellectual capital statements may make knowledge more manageable.

## Summary

- In this chapter we have looked at questions of organizational control and performance management including the problems and possible solutions associated with budgeting.
- We have reviewed a number of models of organizational control that aim to embed strategy and foster organizational learning.
- We have also discussed the importance of boundary systems and risk management in the particular context of corporate governance.
- More rigorous regulation of financial reporting may lead to a change of emphasis in organizational accounting practices with a renewed concern with the integrity of financial and non-financial information.
- Management accounting *can* provide key information for non-executive directors on issues such as the strategic direction of the firm.
- We have introduced a number of broader issues related to corporate social responsibility.
- We have shown how attempts are being made to use management accounting practices to improve the accountability and service delivery in the public sector.

## Key terms for review

**Belief systems** (p. 717)
**Boundary systems** (p. 717)
**Clan model** (p. 733)
**Constrained management style** (p. 715)
**Corporate governance** (p. 714)
**Corporate social responsiveness (or responsibility)** (p. 714)
**Diagnostic control systems** (p. 718)
**Double loop learning** (p. 716)
**Enterprise governance** (p. 725)
**Environmental costs** (p. 727)
**Environmental management accounting** (p. 726)
**Feedforward control** (p. 716)
**Financial stewardship** (p. 730)

**Incrementalism** (p. 729)
**Interactive control systems** (p. 718)
**Key performance indicators (KPIs)** (p. 717)
**Levers of control model** (p. 717)
**Management control** (p. 717)
**New Public Management** (p. 730)
**Performance management** (p. 717)
**Performance measurement system** (p. 716)
**Performance Prism** (p. 725)
**Reductionist model of humanity** (p. 719)
**Return-on-management** (p. 718)
**Risk management** (p. 722)
**Stakeholders** (p. 725)
**Zero-based budgeting** (p. 729)

**Level of difficulty:** BASIC  INTERMEDIATE  ADVANCED

## Problems

**P17-1 Ethics; just-in-time (JIT) purchasing**
Time allowed: 30 minutes

WIW is a publicly owned company that makes various control devices used in the manufacture of mechanical equipment. B.J. is the president of WIW, Tony is the purchasing agent, and Diane is J.B.'s executive assistant. All three have been with WIW for about five years. Charlie is WIW's controller and has been with the company for two years.

**J.B.:** Hi, Charlie, come on in. Diane said you had a confidential matter to discuss. What's on your mind?

**Charlie:** J.B., I was reviewing our increased purchases from A-1 Warehouse Sales last week and wondered why our volume has tripled in the past year. When I discussed this with Tony he seemed a bit evasive and tried to dismiss the issue by stating that A-1 can give us one-day delivery on our orders.

**J.B.:** Well, Tony is right. You know we have been trying to implement just-in-time and have been trying to get our inventory down.

**Charlie:** We still have to look at the overall cost. A-1 is more of a jobber than a warehouse. After investigating orders placed with them, I found that only 10% are delivered from their warehouse and the other 90% are drop-shipped from the manufacturers. The average markup by A-1 is 30%, which amounted to about £600,000 on our orders for the past year. If we had ordered directly from the manufacturers when A-1 didn't have an item in stock, we could have saved about £540,000 (£600,000 × 90%). In addition, some of the orders were late and not complete.

**J.B.:** Now look, Charlie, we get quick delivery on most items, and who knows how much we are saving by not having to stock this stuff in advance or worry about it becoming obsolete. Is there anything else on your mind?

**Charlie:** Well, J.B., as a matter of fact, there is. I ordered a Dun & Bradstreet credit report on A-1 and discovered that Mike Bell is the principal owner. Isn't he your brother-in-law?

**J.B.:** Sure he is. But don't worry about Mike. He understands this JIT approach. Besides, he's looking out for our interests.

**Charlie:** (to himself) This conversation has been enlightening, but it doesn't really respond to my concerns. Can I legally or ethically ignore this apparent conflict of interests?

### Required

1. Would Charlie be justified in ignoring this situation, particularly since he is not the purchasing agent?
2. State the specific steps Charlie should follow to resolve this matter.

**P17-2 Performance indicators/social responsiveness**
Time allowed: 45 minutes

The Royal Botanical Gardens has been established for more than 120 years and has the following mission statement:

> The Royal Botanical Gardens belongs to the Nation. Our mission is to increase knowledge and appreciation of plants, their importance and their conservation, by managing and displaying living and preserved collections and through botanical and horticultural research.

Located towards the edge of the city, the Gardens are regularly visited throughout the year by many local families and are an internationally well-known tourist attraction. Despite charging admission it is one of the top five visitor attractions in the country. Every year it answers many thousands of enquiries from universities and research establishments, including pharmaceutical companies from all over the world and charges for advice and access to its collection. Enquiries can range from access to the plant collection for horticultural work, seeds for propagation or samples for chemical analysis to seek novel pharmaceutical compounds for commercial exploitation. It receives an annual grant in aid from Central Government, which is fixed once every five years. The grant in aid is due for review in three years' time.

The Finance Director has decided that, to strengthen its case when meeting the Government representatives to negotiate the grant, the Management Board should be able to present a balanced scorecard demonstrating the performance of the Gardens. He has asked you, the Senior Management Accountant, to assist him in taking this idea forward. Many members of the board, which consists of eminent scientists, are unfamiliar with the concept of a balanced scorecard.

### Required

1. For the benefit of the Management Board, prepare a briefing on the concept of a balanced scorecard, which also analyses its usefulness for The Royal Botanical Gardens.
2. Discuss the process you would employ to develop a suitable balanced scorecard for The Royal Botanical Gardens and give examples of measures that would be incorporated within it.

*(CIMA Pilot Paper Management Accounting – Business Strategy)*

**P17-3 Corporate governance**
Time allowed: 45 minutes

You have recently been appointed as Head of the Internal Audit function for a large UK listed company that trades internationally, having worked within its finance function for two years prior to your new appointment. Your company has also appointed a new Chief Executive, headhunted from a large US corporation where she had held the post of Vice President, Finance.

### Required

As part of the new Chief Executive's orientation programme, you have been asked to prepare a detailed report which provides key information on the principles of good corporate governance for UK listed companies. You should address the following in your report, remembering that her background is in US governance and procedures.

1. The role and responsibilities of the Board of Directors.
2. The role and responsibilities of the audit committee.
3. Disclosure of corporate governance arrangements.

*(CIMA Pilot Paper Management Accounting – Risk and Control Strategy)*

**P17-4** Time allowed: 45 minutes

The NLE organization sells a range of leisure products on the Internet including books, CDs, DVDs and computer games. The organization's mission statement is to be the most reliable and cost efficient supplier of books and CDs on the Internet. It was formed six years ago, and has grown quickly. Two years ago it became one of the first Internet companies to report a net operating profit. NLE is recognized as being one of the market leaders on the Internet, and its share price is increasing at 20% per annum. In a recent market survey, 80% of people between the ages of 20 and 45 identified the NLE brand name as one they would use when ordering goods from the Internet.

The company now has a positive cash flow, with no outstanding loans. The directors are investigating alternative investments. One possibility is the purchase of 25 bookshops located in major cities in one country. These shops would be re-branded with the NLE name, and offer a similar range of products to the NLE Internet site. However, as no shop could hold the 2.5 million items currently available on the NLE site, a next-day 'collect from shop' option would be made available. This means that customers could order goods from the Internet, or by visiting an NLE bookshop and then collect those goods on the next working day. Goods would be despatched overnight from NLE's main warehouse to fulfil these orders.

### Required

1. Assuming that the Board of NLE decides to purchase the bookshops, advise them on the Information Strategy issues that they should consider, clearly explaining the information required when considering each issue.
   *Note:* You are not required to advise on alternative sources of finance.
2. Identify and explain two critical success factors and their supporting performance indicators that can be used to determine the success or otherwise of the purchase of the bookshops, should this acquisition go ahead.

*(CIMA Management Accounting – Information Systems)*

## Cases

### C17-5 Ethics and the manager
Time allowed: 40 minutes

Terri Ronsin had recently been transferred to the Home Security Systems Division of National Home Products. Shortly after taking over her new position as divisional controller, she was asked to develop the division's predetermined overhead rate for the upcoming year. The accuracy of the rate is of some importance, since it is used throughout the year and any overapplied or underapplied overhead is closed out to Cost of Goods Sold only at the end of the year. National Home Products uses direct labour-hours in all of its divisions as the allocation base for manufacturing overhead.

To compute the predetermined overhead rate, Terri divided her estimate of the total manufacturing overhead for the coming year by the production manager's estimate of the total direct labour-hours for the coming year. She took her computations to the division's general manager for approval but was quite surprised when he suggested a modification in the base. Her conversation with the general manager of the Home Security Systems Division, Harry Irving, went like this:

**Ronsin:** Here are my calculations for next year's predetermined overhead rate. If you approve, we can enter the rate into the computer on January 1 and be up and running in the job-order costing system right away this year.

**Irving:** Thanks for coming up with the calculations so quickly, and they look just fine. There is, however, one slight modification I would like to see. Your estimate of the total direct labour-hours for the year is 440,000 hours. How about cutting that to about 420,000 hours?

**Ronsin:** I don't know if I can do that. The production manager says she will need about 440,000 direct labour-hours to meet the sales projections for the year. Besides, there are going to be over 430,000 direct labour-hours during the current year and sales are projected to be higher next year.

**Irving:** Terri, I know all of that. I would still like to reduce the direct labour-hours in the base to something like 420,000 hours. You probably don't know that I had an agreement with your predecessor as divisional controller to shave 5% or so off the estimated direct labour-hours every year. That way, we kept a reserve that usually resulted in a big boost to net income at the end of the fiscal year in December. We called it our Christmas bonus. Corporate headquarters always seemed as pleased as punch that we could pull off such a miracle at the end of the year. This system has worked well for many years, and I don't want to change it now.

### Required

1. Explain how shaving 5% off the estimated direct labour-hours in the base for the predetermined overhead rate usually results in a big boost in net income at the end of the fiscal year.
2. Should Terri Ronsin go along with the general manager's request to reduce the direct labour-hours in the predetermined overhead rate computation to 420,000 direct labour hours?

### C17-6 Ethics and the manager
Time allowed: 30 minutes

Stacy Cummins, the newly hired controller at Merced Home Products plc, was disturbed by what she had discovered about the standard costs at the Home Security Division. In looking over the past several years of quarterly earnings reports at the Home Security Division, she noticed that the first-quarter earnings were always poor, the second-quarter earnings were slightly better, the third-quarter earnings were again slightly better, and then the fourth quarter and the year always ended with a spectacular performance in which the Home Security Division always managed to meet or exceed its target profit for the year. She was also concerned to find letters from the company's external auditors to top management warning about an unusual use of standard costs at the Home Security Division.

When Ms Cummins ran across these letters, she asked the assistant controller, Gary Farber, if he knew what was going on at the Home Security Division. Gary said that it was common knowledge in the company that the vice president in charge of the Home Security Division, Preston Lansing, had rigged the standards at the Home Security Division in order to produce the same quarterly earnings pattern every year. According to company policy, variances are taken directly to the profit statement as an adjustment to cost of goods sold.

Favourable variances have the effect of increasing profit and unfavourable variances have the effect of decreasing profit. Lansing had rigged the standards so that there were always large favourable variances. Company policy was a little vague about when these variances have to be reported on the divisional profit statements. While the intent was clearly to recognize variances on the profit statement in the period in which they arise, nothing in the company's accounting manuals actually explicitly required this. So for many years Lansing had followed a practice of saving up the favourable variances and using them to create a nice smooth pattern of earnings growth in the first three quarters, followed by a big 'Christmas present' of an extremely good fourth quarter. (Financial reporting regulations forbid carrying variances forward from one year to the next on the annual audited financial statements, so all of the variances must appear on the divisional profit statement by the end of the year.)

Ms Cummins was concerned about these revelations and attempted to bring up the subject with the president of Merced Home Products but was told that 'we all know what Lansing's doing, but as long as he continues to turn in such good reports, don't bother him.' When Ms Cummins asked if the board of directors was aware of the situation, the chairman somewhat testily replied, 'Of course they are aware.'

### Required

1. How did Preston Lansing probably 'rig' the standard costs – are the standards set too high or too low? Explain.
2. Should Preston Lansing be permitted to continue his practice of managing reported earnings?
3. What should Stacy Cummins do in this situation?

#### C17-7 Metroshire Blues
Time allowed: 35 minutes

'Improving our schools is a central part of our agenda that sees education as the key to greater prosperity and social inclusion'. These words, which she had spoken only a few hours ago in the House of Commons, were still giving Toni Cherry a warm feeling. What a great sound bite, she thought, as she sat in the back of her chauffeur-driven ministerial car as it sped through her constituency in Metroshire. She was due to meet with some local public officials and counsellors but, as she was early for that appointment, she asked her driver to pull in at a local secondary school where she knew the head teacher, Mary Brown, from their own school days.

Mary was excited to be meeting her old, high flying friend who had phoned her just a few minutes ago. She showed Toni into her office and they began to chat over a cup of coffee.

'So, Mary how are you spending all the extra resources that our government has put into the school system?' said Toni.

'Extra resources!' exclaimed Mary. 'What extra resources? We have just introduced a freeze on new appointments, laid off our temporary staff and pulled out of the local project that offered extra tuition to pupils receiving free school meals. We have also asked parents to pay for their children's textbooks.'

'But we have increased spending on education by over 20% in the last two years. Isn't the money getting through to you? Don't you have the freedom to manage your own budgets these days?', exclaimed Toni.

'Yes, of course we can set our own budgets – we have already set a deficit budget for next year that forecasts that we will have to dip into our reserves just to keep going. The increases in our costs such as the extra national insurance payments and the need to raise staff salaries have more than eaten up the extra money. Remember, this is a very expensive area to live in and we have to pay our teachers extra increments to stop them from moving to schools where housing is cheaper.'

After this exchange, Toni made her excuses and left in a bad temper. When she arrived at her appointment she accused the local authority officials of not passing on the extra funding that they had received for

**Part 4** Value metrics and performance management in a strategic context

educational spending in the schools. A major row broke out when the head of the council, Alderman Alf Roberts protested:

'Of course, we passed on the extra money but schools manage their own budgets now and we don't have the detailed knowledge of the cost drivers that we had when the local authority managed school budgets.'

Toni responded: 'But couldn't you see that they were in trouble when they sent in an indicative deficit budget?'

'But they do that every year! Partly they are "crying wolf" and partly we are all erring on the side of caution when we don't know what the government is going to give to us from one year to the next.'

At the end of the day, a rather less complacent Toni Cherry was glad to back in London and chat with her life style guru about which outfits to wear on her forthcoming trip to the Far East. *Postscript*: Parliament gave schools some extra funds and, additionally, the projected budgetary deficits were lower than predicted by the schools.

### Required

Explain the origins of the budgeting problems in the local schools in Metroshire and suggest some possible improvements to overall budgeting practices.

**C17–8 Ethics and the manager; absorption costing profit and loss statements**
Time allowed: 120 minutes

Guochang Li was hired as chief executive officer (CEO) in late November by the board of directors of ContactGlobal, a company that produces an advanced global positioning system (GPS) device that pinpoints the user's location anywhere on earth to within a hundred metres. The previous CEO had been fired by the board of directors due to a series of shady business practices including shipping defective GPS devices to dealers.

Guochang felt that his first priority was to restore employee morale – which had suffered during the previous CEO's reign. He was particularly anxious to build a sense of trust between himself and the company's employees. His second priority was to prepare the budget for the coming year, which the board of directors wanted to review in their 15 December meeting.

After hammering out the details in meetings with key managers, Guochang was able to put together a budget that he felt the company could realistically meet during the coming year. That budget appears below:

| Basic budget data | |
|---|---|
| Units in beginning inventory | 0 |
| Units produced | 400,000 |
| Units sold | 400,000 |
| Units in ending inventory | 0 |
| Variable costs per unit: | |
| Direct materials | £57.20 |
| Direct labour | 15.00 |
| Variable manufacturing overhead | 5.00 |
| Variable selling and administrative | 10.00 |
| Total variable cost per unit | £87.20 |
| Fixed costs: | |
| Fixed manufacturing overhead | £6,888,000 |
| Fixed selling and administrative | 4,560,000 |
| Total fixed costs | £11,448,000 |

### Chapter 17 Performance management, management control and corporate governance

|  | Contact Global<br>Budgeted profit and loss statement<br>(absorption method) |  |
|---|---|---|
| Sales (400,000 units × £120 per unit) |  | £48,000,000 |
| Less cost of goods sold: |  |  |
| Beginning inventory | £0 |  |
| Add cost of goods manufactured |  |  |
| (400,000 units × £94.42 per unit) | 37,768,000 |  |
| Goods available for sale | 37,768,000 |  |
| Less ending inventory | 0 | 37,768,000 |
| Gross margin |  | 10,232,000 |
| Less selling and administrative expenses: |  |  |
| Variable selling and administrative |  |  |
| (400,000 units × £10 per unit) | 4,000,000 |  |
| Fixed selling and administrative | 4,560,000 | 8,560,000 |
| Profit |  | £1,672,000 |

The board of directors made it clear that this budget was not as ambitious as they had hoped. The most influential member of the board stated that 'managers should have to really stretch to meet profit goals'. After some discussion, the board decided to set a profit goal of £2,000,000 for the coming year. To provide strong incentives, the board agreed to pay out very substantial bonuses to top managers of £10,000 to £25,000 each if this profit goal were met. The bonus would be all-or-nothing. If actual profit turned out to be £2,000,000 or more, the bonus would be paid. Otherwise, no bonus would be paid.

### Required

1 Assuming that the company does not build up its inventory (i.e., production equals sales) and its selling price and cost structure remain the same, how many units of the GPS device would have to be sold in order to meet the profit goal of £2,000,000?

2 Verify your answer to (1) above by constructing a revised budget and budgeted profit statement that yields a profit of £2,000,000. Use the absorption costing method.

3 Unfortunately, by October of the next year it had become clear that the company would not be able to make the £2,000,000 target profit. In fact, it looked like the company would wind up the year as originally planned, with sales of 400,000 units, no ending inventories, and a profit of £1,672,000.

Several managers who were reluctant to lose their year-end bonuses approached Guochang and suggested that the company could still show a profit of £2,000,000. The managers pointed out that at the present rate of sales, there was enough capacity to produce tens of thousands of additional GPS devices for the warehouse and thereby shift fixed manufacturing costs to another year. If sales are 400,000 units for the year and the selling price and cost structure remains the same, how many units would have to be produced in order to show a profit of at least £2,000,000 under absorption costing?

4 Verify your answer to (3) above by constructing a profit statement. Use the absorption costing method.

5 Do you think Guochang Li should approve the plan to build ending inventories in order to attain the target profit?

6 What advice would you give to the board of directors concerning how they determine bonuses in the future?

**C17-9** Ethics and the manager; shut down or continue operations
Time allowed: 75 minutes

Haley Platt had just been appointed CEO of the North Region of the Bank Services Corporation (BSC). The company provides cheque processing services for European banks. The banks send cheques presented for

**740** Part 4 Value metrics and performance management in a strategic context

deposit or payment to BSC, which records the data on each cheque in a computerized database. BSC then sends the data electronically to the nearest bank cheque-clearing centre where the appropriate transfers of funds are made between banks. The North Region has three cheque processing centres, which are located in Billingham, Grantham and Cleethorpes. Prior to her promotion to CEO, Ms Platt had been the manager of a cheque processing centre in Mansfield.

Immediately upon assuming her new position, Ms Platt requested a complete financial report for the just-ended fiscal year from the region's controller, John Littlebear. Ms Platt specified that the financial report should follow the standardized format required by corporate headquarters for all regional performance reports. That report follows:

**Bank Services Corporation (BSC)**
**North Region**
**Financial performance**

|  | Total | Billingham | Grantham | Cleethorpes |
|---|---|---|---|---|
| Sales | £50,000,000 | £20,000,000 | £18,000,000 | £12,000,000 |
| Operating expenses: | | | | |
| Direct labour | 32,000,000 | 12,500,000 | 11,000,000 | 8,500,000 |
| Variable overhead | 850,000 | 350,000 | 310,000 | 190,000 |
| Equipment depreciation | 3,900,000 | 1,300,000 | 1,400,000 | 1,200,000 |
| Facility expense | 2,800,000 | 900,000 | 800,000 | 1,100,000 |
| Local administrative expense* | 450,000 | 140,000 | 160,000 | 150,000 |
| Regional administrative expense† | 1,500,000 | 600,000 | 540,000 | 360,000 |
| Corporate administrative expense‡ | 4,750,000 | 1,900,000 | 1,710,000 | 1,140,000 |
| Total operating expense | 46,250,000 | 17,690,000 | 15,920,000 | 12,640,000 |
| Operating profit | £3,750,000 | £2,310,000 | £2,080,000 | £(640,000) |

*Local administrative expenses are the administrative expenses incurred at the cheque processing centres.
†Regional administrative expenses are allocated to the cheque processing centres based on sales.
‡Corporate administrative expenses are charged to segments of the company such as the North Region and the cheque processing centres at the rate of 9.5% of their sales.

Upon seeing this report, Ms Platt summoned John Littlebear for an explanation.

***Platt:*** What's the story on Cleethorpes? It didn't have a loss the previous year did it?
***Littlebear:*** No, the Cleethorpes facility has had a nice profit every year since it was opened six years ago, but Cleethorpes lost a big contract this year.
***Platt:*** Why?
***Littlebear:*** One of our national competitors entered the local market and bid very aggressively on the contract. We couldn't afford to meet the bid. Cleethorpes's costs – particularly their facility expenses – are just too high. When Cleethorpes lost the contract, we had to lay off a lot of employees, but we could not reduce the fixed costs of the Cleethorpes facility.
***Platt:*** Why is Cleethorpes's facility expense so high? It's a smaller facility than either Billingham and Grantham and yet its facility expense is higher.
***Littlebear:*** The problem is that we are able to rent suitable facilities very cheaply at Billingham and Grantham. No such facilities were available at Cleethorpes, we had them built. Unfortunately, there were big cost overruns. The contractor we hired was inexperienced at this kind of work and in fact went bankrupt before the project was completed. After hiring another contractor to finish the work, we were way over budget. The large depreciation charges on the facility didn't matter at first because we didn't have much competition at the time and could charge premium prices.

**Chapter 17** Performance management, management control and corporate governance

*Platt:* Well we can't do that anymore. The Cleethorpes facility will obviously have to be shut down. Its business can be shifted to the other two cheque processing centres in the region.

*Littlebear:* I would advise against that. The £1,200,000 in depreciation at the Cleethorpes facility is misleading. That facility should last indefinitely with proper maintenance. And it has no resale value; there is no other commercial activity around Cleethorpes.

*Platt:* What about the other costs at Cleethorpes?

*Littlebear:* If we shifted Cleethorpes's business over to the other two processing centres in the region, we wouldn't save anything on direct labour or variable overhead costs. We might save £90,000 or so in local administrative expense, but we would not save any regional administrative expense and corporate headquarters would still charge us 9.5% of our sales as corporate administrative expense.

In addition, we would have to rent more space in Billingham and Grantham in order to handle the work transferred from Cleethorpes; that would probably cost us at least £600,000 a year. And don't forget that it will cost us something to move the equipment from Cleethorpes to Billingham and Grantham. And the move will disrupt service to customers.

*Platt:* I understand all of that, but a money-losing processing centre on my performance report is completely unacceptable.

*Littlebear:* And if you shut down Cleethorpes, you are going to throw some loyal employees out of work.

*Platt:* That's unfortunate, but we have to face hard business realities.

*Littlebear:* And you would have to write off the investment in the facilities at Cleethorpes.

*Platt:* I can explain a write-off to corporate headquarters; hiring an inexperienced contractor to build the Cleethorpes facility was my predecessor's mistake. But they'll have my head at headquarters if I show operating losses every year at one of my processing centres. Cleethorpes has to go. At the next corporate board meeting, I am going to recommend that the Cleethorpes facility be closed.

### Required

1. From the standpoint of the company as a whole, should the Cleethorpes processing centre be shut down and its work redistributed to other processing centres in the region? Explain.
2. Do you think Haley Platt's decision to shut down the Cleethorpes facility is ethical? Explain.
3. What influence should the depreciation on the facilities at Cleethorpes have on prices charged by Cleethorpes for its services?

**C17-10 Management control of risk**

Time allowed: 90 minutes

Crashcarts IT Consultancy is a £100 million turnover business listed on the Stock Exchange with a reputation for providing world class IT consultancy services to blue chip clients, predominantly in the retail sector. In 2000, Crashcarts acquired a new subsidiary for £2 million based on a P/E ratio of 8, which it renamed Crashcarts Call Centre. The call centre subsidiary leased all of its hardware, software and telecommunications equipment over a five-year term. The infrastructure provides the capacity to process three million orders and ten million line items per annum. In addition, maintenance contracts were signed for the full five-year period. These contracts include the provision of a daily back-up facility in an off-site location.

Crashcarts Call Centre provides two major services for its clients. First, it holds databases, primarily for large retail chains' catalogue sales, connected in real time to clients' inventory control systems. Second, its call centre operation allows its clients' customers to place orders by telephone. The real-time system determines whether there is stock available and, if so, a shipment is requested. The sophisticated technology in use by the call centre also incorporates a secure payment facility for credit and debit card payments, details of which are transferred to the retail stores' own computer system. The call centre charges each retail client a lump sum each year for the IT and communications infrastructure it provides. There is a 12 month contract in place for each client. In addition, Crashcarts earns a fixed sum for every order it processes, plus an additional amount for every line item. If items are not in stock, Crashcarts earns no processing fee. Crashcarts Call Centre is staffed by call centre operators (there were 70 in 2001 and 80 in each of 2002 and 2003). In addition, a management team, training staff and administrative personnel are employed. Like other call centres, there is a high turnover of call centre operators (over 100% per annum) and this requires an almost continuous process of staff training and detailed supervision and monitoring.

**742** Part 4 Value metrics and performance management in a strategic context

A summary of Crashcarts Call Centre's financial performance for the last three years is as follows:

|  | 2001 £000 | 2002 £000 | 2003 £000 |
|---|---|---|---|
| Revenue |  |  |  |
| Contract fixed fee | 400 | 385 | 385 |
| Order processing fees | 2,500 | 3,025 | 3,450 |
| Line item processing fees | 600 | 480 | 390 |
| Total revenue | £3,500 | £3,890 | £4,225 |
| Expenses |  |  |  |
| Office rent and expenses | 200 | 205 | 210 |
| Operator salaries and salary-related costs | 1,550 | 1,920 | 2,180 |
| Management, administration and training salaries | 1,020 | 1,070 | 1,120 |
| IT and telecomms lease and maintenance expenses | 300 | 310 | 330 |
| Other expenses | 150 | 200 | 220 |
| Total expenses | £3,220 | £3,705 | £4,060 |
| Operating profit | £280 | £185 | £165 |

Non-financial performance information for the same period is as follows:

|  | 2001 | 2002 | 2003 |
|---|---|---|---|
| Number of incoming calls received | 1,200,000 | 1,300,000 | 1,350,000 |
| Number of orders processed | 1,000,000 | 1,100,000 | 1,150,000 |
| Order strike rate (orders/calls) | 83.3% | 84.6% | 85.2% |
| Number of line items processed | 3,000,000 | 3,200,000 | 3,250,000 |
| Average number of line items per order | 3.0 | 2.9 | 2.8 |
| Number of retail clients | 8 | 7 | 7 |
| Fixed contract income per client | £50,000 | £55,000 | £55,000 |
| Income per order processed | £2.50 | £2.75 | £3.00 |
| Income per line item processed | £0.20 | £0.15 | £0.12 |
| Average number of orders per operator | 15,000 | 15,000 | 15,000 |
| Number of operators required | 66.7 | 73.3 | 76.7 |
| Actual number of operators employed | 70.0 | 80.0 | 80.0 |

### Required

1 Discuss the increase in importance of risk management to all businesses (with an emphasis on listed ones) over the last few years and the role of management accountants in risk management.
2 Advise the Crashcarts Call Centre on methods for analysing its risks.

3 Apply appropriate methods to identify and quantify the major risks facing Crashcarts at both parent level and subsidiary level.
4 Categorize the components of a management control system and recommend the main controls that would be appropriate for the Crashcarts Call Centre.

*(CIMA Pilot Paper Management Accounting – Risk and Control Strategy)*

## Internet exercises

**IE17-11 Corporate social responsibility**

1 Discuss the questions posed on the website on corporate social responsibility www.goodbusiness.co.uk.
2 Follow up some of the cases introduced by Mouritsen *et al.* (2001b) on the company websites in order to update yourself on some approaches to these issues (see e.g. Systematic (www.systematic.dk) and Carl Bro (www.carlbro.dk).
3 Access the Environmental Management Accounting website (www.emawebsite.org) and compare its approach with that proposed by Boyce (2000).

**IE17-12 Public sector performance management**

Access a local government website (e.g. www.Birmingham.gov.uk) and critically review the authority's performance plan.

## Endnotes

1. Seal (2006).
2. See, e.g., Shleifer and Vishny (1997), p. 737.
3. See, e.g., Norris and O'Dwyer (2004).
4. Norris and O'Dwyer (2004).
5. Hope and Hope (1997).
6. Wildavsky (1975).
7. Neely, Sutcliff and Heyns (2001).
8. Hope and Hope (1997).
9. Hansen, Otley and Van der Stede (2003).
10. See. e.g., Hope and Fraser, (1997; 2003).
11. Wallander (1999).
12. Hansen *et al.* (2003), p. 101.
13. Hansen *et al.* (2003), p. 101.
14. Hansen *et al.* (2003), p. 102.
15. See Otley and Berry (1980).
16. Kaplan and Norton (1992).
17. These features are based on Otley (1999) and CIMA (2002).
18. The authors would like to thank Alan Coad and Sharzad Uddin for their comments on this chapter.
19. Simons (1995).
20. This section draws heavily on Simons (1995).
21. Simons (1995).
22. Sathe (1982).
23. Sathe (1982).
24. Schwartz (2004).
25. Dyson (2004).
26. Cohen (2004).
27. Erturk, Froud, Johal and Williams (2003).

28 There is a huge literature on agency theory. For an introductory approach in a corporate governance context see Mallin (2003).
29 Healy and Wahlen (1999).
30 See, e.g., Baumol (1959); Marris (1964); Williamson (1964).
31 Shleifer and Vishny (1997), p. 737.
32 Sathe (1982).
33 Higgs (2003); Seal (2006).
34 Starovic (2002).
35 The latest version of the *Combined Code on Corporate Governance* was published in 2006. See www.frc.org.uk/documents/pagemanager/frc/combined%20Code%20June%202006.pdf
36 Guilding, Cravens and Tayles (2000).
37 Mayo (2001).
38 Porter (1980).
39 As this edition was being prepared, there were emerging examples of companies (especially banks) in the financial sector which were suffering the effects of poor risk management.
40 Institute of Chartered Accountants in England and Wales (1999), p. 4.
41 Gould (2002), p. 53.
42 Simons (1995), p. 41.
43 IFAC/CIMA, 2004.
44 Norris and O'Dwyer (2004).
45 IFAC, p. 19.
46 See, e.g., Hofstede (1981). For a more detailed treatment of zero-based budgeting see Jones and Pendlebury (2000).
47 Although these authorities are real, we have deliberately anonymized them. See Seal and Ball (2004).
48 Wildavsky (1975).
49 See, e.g., Hood (1995); Humphrey, Miller and Scapens (1993); Humphrey, Miller and Smith (1998); Pollock (2004).
50 This list is taken from Smith (1993).
51 Ouchi (1977).
52 Ouchi (1980).
53 Hilton (2004).

When you have read this chapter, log on to the Online Learning Centre for *Management Accounting* at www.mcgraw-hill.co.uk/textbooks/seal, where you'll find multiple choice questions, practice exams and extra study tools for each chapter.

# Business Process Management: Towards the Lean Operation

# CHAPTER 18

# Business process management: towards the lean operation

## LEARNING OBJECTIVES

After studying Chapter 18, you should be able to:

1. Appreciate the business process and lean approach to the management of organizations
2. Determine the reorder point using the EOQ model
3. Consider the impact of JIT approaches to stock management
4. Review the role of management accounting in business models that minimize working capital
5. Evaluate the contribution of ERP models
6. Review the role of management accounting in e-commerce
7. Measure the costs of quality
8. Review the relationship between management accounting and TQM systems
9. Understand the technique of benchmarking
10. Understand the contribution of business process re-engineering and ABM
11. Appreciate the contribution of Six Sigma and lean production

## CONCEPTS IN CONTEXT

A good example of a business that has used the internet is provided by Cheshire ironmonger, Cooksons. The weakness of their old business was that they only had a single outlet in Stockport which was vulnerable to out-of-town DIY superstores. The strength of the old business was a good reputation with specialist customers and a good supply chain. With the establishment of www.cooksonhardware.com, these advantages could be made available to a wider customer base. 'The business itself holds no stock; its suppliers meet the online orders.'[1]

© Siniša Botaš/istock

In this chapter, we take a more operations management perspective. From an operations perspective, the organization is visualized as procuring, transforming and delivering a flow of products or services to customers. Thus, in contrast to some earlier chapters (see especially Chapter 14), the focus is on the management of *business processes* rather than organizational structures such as departments or divisions. In Exhibit 18.1, there is a contrast between a business process perspective and a departmental or divisional perspective. The latter is sometimes visualized as tending to produce a 'silo mentality' with some flows up and down the silo but little communication between individual 'silos'. In the previous chapter, we saw how the management of departments with budgets may contribute to the development of a 'silo mentality'. The business process perspective challenges managers to find metrics which monitor the processes *across* the organization which serve customers and thus generate value.

Over the last few years, new technology, especially *enterprise resource planning* (ERP) packages have generated improved operations management information which may enable the integration of 'end-to-end' business processes from procurement through to final delivery and payment. Even more recently, the internet has created whole new business models with cost and revenue streams that are only just beginning to be understood. In some of these businesses such as online retailers, a company's ability to hold huge stocks and offer an immense choice is a source of commercial strength – in this type of business stock has to be managed but it cannot be eliminated. Thus although we acknowledge the impact of philosophies such as just-in-time (JIT) that aim at the elimination of stocks, we also review some of the more traditional, **optimizing**, approaches to inventory management such as the *economic order quantity* (EOQ) model. As we shall see, JIT required an uncompromising attitude to quality as stocks had previously been used to hide the effects of low quality and poor business flow management. Indeed, the JIT approach combined with wider competitive pressures have challenged the traditional, *cost of quality* (COQ) model approach through the practice of *total quality management* (TQM) with its zero defects philosophy. Later on in the chapter we will be looking at techniques that seek to improve business processes, such as *benchmarking*, and practices, such as *activity-based management* (ABM) and *business process re-engineering* (BPR), that aim to identify and eliminate non-value adding activities.[2]

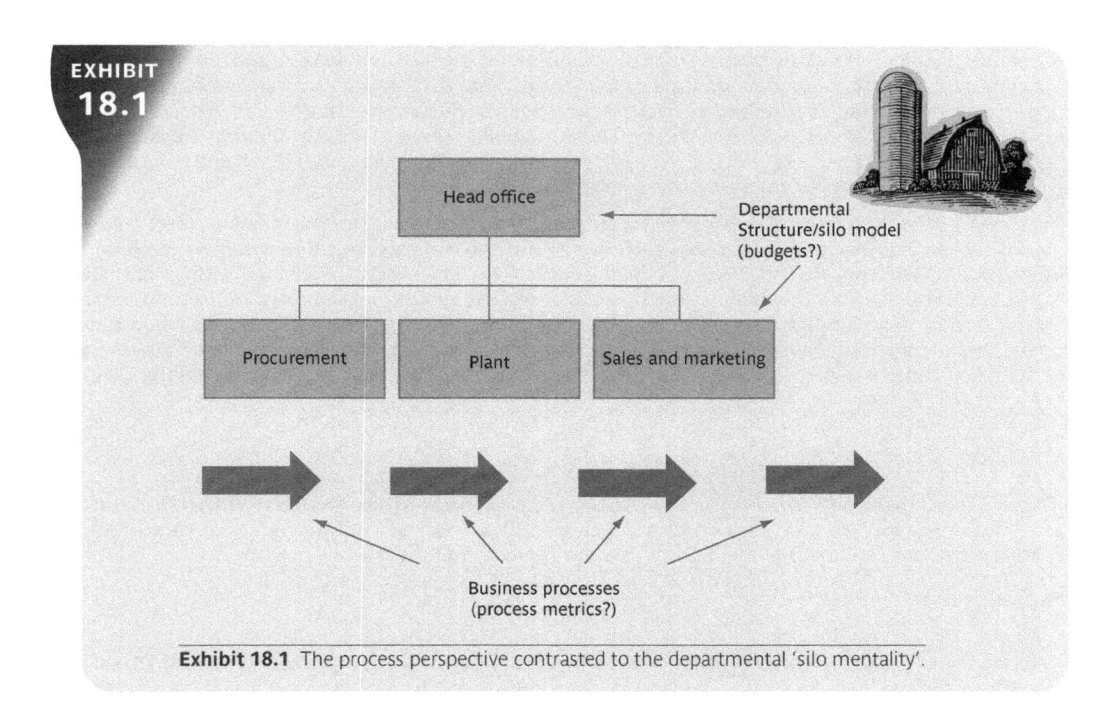

**EXHIBIT 18.1**

**Exhibit 18.1** The process perspective contrasted to the departmental 'silo mentality'.

Chapter 18 Business process management: towards the lean operation

Many of these business process improvement techniques are associated with the philosophy of the *lean enterprise* or *lean production*, a strategy that was proposed as an alternative to a market positioning (see Chapter 16). **Lean production** techniques were first introduced in manufacturing (especially by Toyota) but are increasingly being applied in service sectors, including not-for-profit organizations in the public sector.[3] Indeed, there are some similarities between inventories in manufacturing and queues of customers in services particularly since both are the result of failing to match supply and demand. Lean principles also involve other focuses such as the reduction of waste and virtual elimination of defects. Such objectives are now part of management orthodoxy but were seen as revolutionary only a few years ago when the philosophy of *optimization* epitomized by the EOQ model dominated thinking in many business schools.[4]

## Optimizing stock: the economic order quantity (EOQ) and the reorder point

In the optimization model of stock management, selecting the 'right' level of stock involves balancing three groups of costs: *stock ordering costs*, *stock carrying costs*, and the *costs of not carrying sufficient stock*. These costs are discussed in this section.

### Costs associated with stock

**Stock ordering costs** are incurred each time a stock item is ordered. These costs may include clerical costs associated with ordering stock, and some handling and transportation costs. They are triggered by the act of ordering stock and are essentially the same whether 1 unit or 10,000 units are ordered; these costs are driven by the number of orders placed – not by the size of the orders. If stock ordering costs are large, a manager may want to place small numbers of big orders on an infrequent basis rather than large numbers of small orders.

**Stock carrying costs** are incurred to keep units in stock. These costs include storage costs, handling costs, property taxes, insurance and the interest on the funds invested in stock. These costs are driven by the amount and value of stock that is held by the company. In addition to these costs, work in progress creates operating problems. Work in progress may physically get in the way and make it difficult to keep track of operations. Moreover, work in progress tends to hide problems that are not discovered until it is too late to take corrective action. This results in erratic production, inefficient operations, 'lost' orders, high defect rates, and substantial risks of obsolescence. These intangible costs of work in progress stock are largely responsible for the movement to JIT. If stock carrying costs are high, managers will want to reduce the overall level of stock and to place frequent orders in small quantities.

The **costs of not carrying sufficient stock** result from not having enough stock to meet customers' needs. These costs include lost sales, customer ill will, and the costs of expediting orders for goods not held in stock. If these costs are high, managers will want to hold large stock. Conceptually, the 'right' level of stock to carry is the level that will minimize the total of these three groups of costs. In the following pages we show how to accomplish this task. The problem is broken down into two dimensions – how much to order (or how much to produce in a single production run or batch) and how often to do it. These two decisions – how much to order and how often to order – determine the average level of stock and the likelihood of being out of stock.

### Computing the economic order quantity (EOQ)

The question 'How much to order?' is answered by the **economic order quantity (EOQ)**. It is the order size that minimizes the sum of the costs of ordering stock and the costs of carrying stock. We will consider two approaches to computing the EOQ – the *tabular approach* and the *formula approach*.

#### The tabular approach

Suppose that 12,000 units of a particular item are required each year. Managers could order all 12,000 units at once or they could order smaller numbers of units spread over the year – perhaps 1,000 units per month.

**Part 4** Value metrics and performance management in a strategic context

Placing only one order would minimize the total costs of ordering stock but would result in high stock carrying costs, since the average stock level would be very large. On the other hand, placing many small orders would result in high ordering costs but in low stock carrying costs, since the average stock level would be reduced. As stated above, the EOQ is the order size that will optimally balance these two costs – stock ordering costs and stock holding costs.

To show how EOQ is computed, assume that a manufacturer uses 3,000 sub-assemblies in the manufacturing process each year. The sub-assemblies are purchased from a supplier at a cost of £20 each. Other cost data are given below:

| | |
|---|---|
| Stock carrying costs, per unit, per year | £0.80 |
| Cost of placing a purchase order | 10.00 |

Exhibit 18.2 contains a tabulation of the total costs associated with various order sizes for the sub-assemblies. Most of this table is straightforward, but the average stock requires some explanation. If 50 units are ordered at a time and the items are ordered only when the stock gets down to zero, then the size of the stock will vary from 50 units to 0 units. Thus, on average, there will be 25 units in stock. Notice that total annual cost is lowest (and is equal) at the 250- and 300-unit order sizes. The EOQ will lie somewhere between these two points. We could locate it precisely by adding more columns to the tabulation, and we would eventually zero in on 274 units as being the exact EOQ.

The cost relationships from this tabulation are shown graphically in Exhibit 18.3. The EOQ is indicated on the graph. Notice that the EOQ minimizes the total annual costs. It also is the point where annual carrying costs and annual ordering costs are equal. At the EOQ, these two costs are exactly balanced.

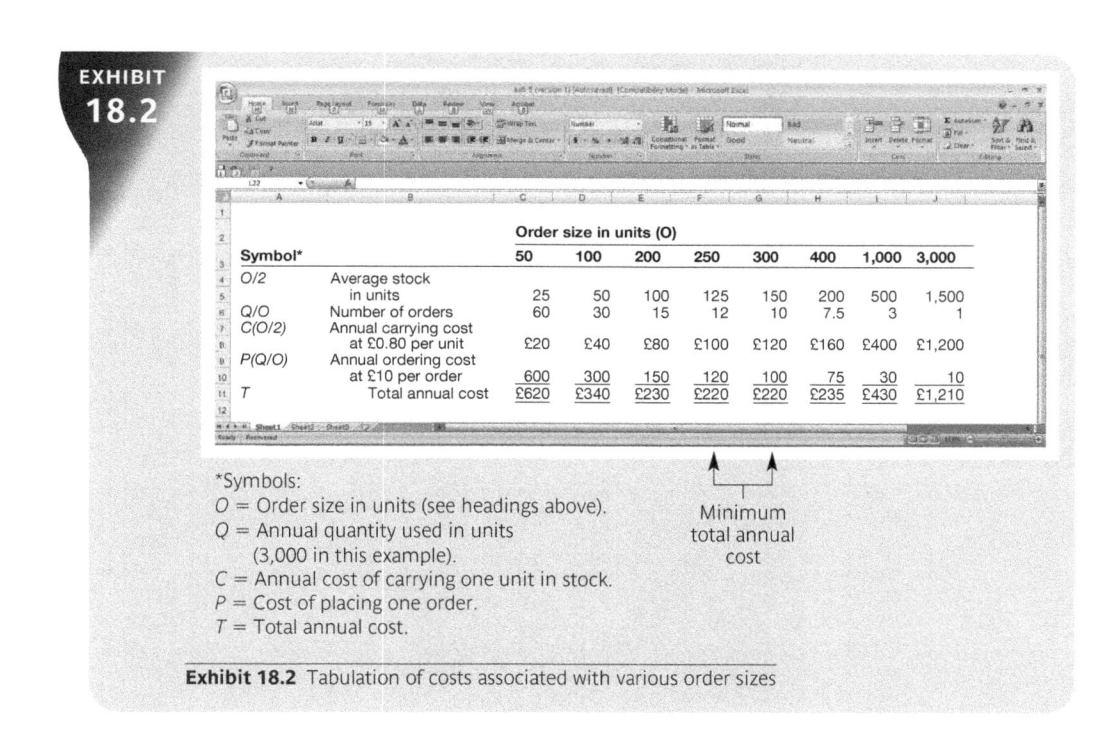

**EXHIBIT 18.2**

| Symbol* | | Order size in units (O) | | | | | | | |
|---|---|---|---|---|---|---|---|---|---|
| | | 50 | 100 | 200 | 250 | 300 | 400 | 1,000 | 3,000 |
| O/2 | Average stock in units | 25 | 50 | 100 | 125 | 150 | 200 | 500 | 1,500 |
| Q/O | Number of orders | 60 | 30 | 15 | 12 | 10 | 7.5 | 3 | 1 |
| C(O/2) | Annual carrying cost at £0.80 per unit | £20 | £40 | £80 | £100 | £120 | £160 | £400 | £1,200 |
| P(Q/O) | Annual ordering cost at £10 per order | 600 | 300 | 150 | 120 | 100 | 75 | 30 | 10 |
| T | Total annual cost | £620 | £340 | £230 | £220 | £220 | £235 | £430 | £1,210 |

Minimum total annual cost

*Symbols:
$O$ = Order size in units (see headings above).
$Q$ = Annual quantity used in units (3,000 in this example).
$C$ = Annual cost of carrying one unit in stock.
$P$ = Cost of placing one order.
$T$ = Total annual cost.

**Exhibit 18.2** Tabulation of costs associated with various order sizes

**Chapter 18** Business process management: towards the lean operation

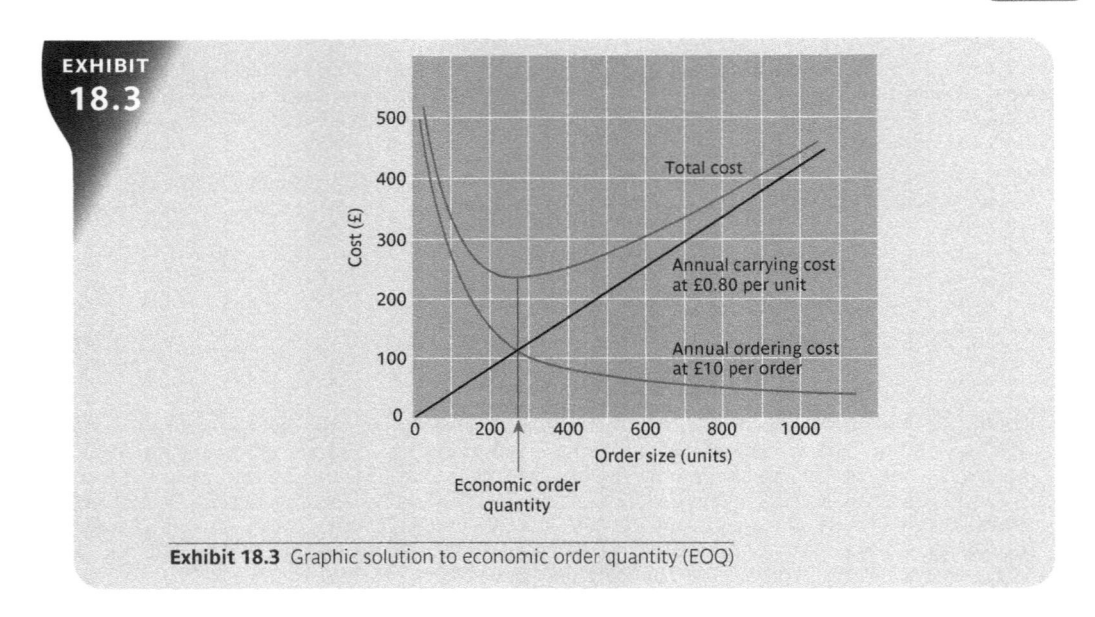

**EXHIBIT 18.3**

**Exhibit 18.3** Graphic solution to economic order quantity (EOQ)

Observe from the graph that total cost shows a tendency to flatten out between 200 and 400 units. Most firms look for this minimum cost range and choose an order size that falls within it, rather than choosing the exact EOQ. The primary reason is that suppliers will often ship goods only in round-lot sizes.

### The formula approach

The EOQ can also be found by means of a formula that can be derived using calculus:

$$E = \sqrt{\frac{2QP}{C}}$$

where:

$E$ = economic order quantity (EOQ)
$Q$ = annual quantity used in units
$P$ = cost of placing one order
$C$ = annual cost of carrying one unit in stock.

Using the data from the preceding example, we can directly compute the EOQ as follows:

$Q$ = 3,000 sub-assemblies used per year
$P$ = £10 cost to place one order
$C$ = £0.80 cost to carry one sub-assembly in stock for one year

$$E = \sqrt{\frac{2QP}{C}} = \sqrt{\frac{2(3,000)(£10)}{£0.80}} = \sqrt{\frac{£60,000}{£0.80}} = \sqrt{£75,000}$$
$$E = 274 \text{ units}$$

## Just-in-time (JIT) and the economic order quantity (EOQ)

By examining the EOQ formula, you can see that the economic order quantity, $E$, will decrease if:

1. The cost of placing an order, P, decreases, or
2. The cost of carrying stock in stock, C, increases.

As we shall see below, proponents of JIT argue that the cost of carrying stock in stock is much greater than generally realized because of the waste and inefficiency that stock create. They also argue that following JIT procedures, such as concentrating all orders on a few high quality suppliers, will dramatically reduce the cost of placing an order. As a consequence, JIT advocates argue that companies should purchase more frequently in smaller amounts. Assume, for example, that a company has used the following data to compute its EOQ:

$Q$ = 4,800 units needed each year

$P$ = £75 cost to place one order

$C$ = £4.50 cost to carry one unit in stock for one year.

Given these data, the EOQ would be as follows:

$$E = \sqrt{\frac{2QP}{C}} = \sqrt{\frac{2(4,800)(£15)}{(£4.50)}} = \sqrt{£160,000}$$

$$E = 400 \text{ units}$$

Now assume that as a result of JIT purchasing, the company is able to decrease the cost of placing an order to only £3. Also assume that due to the waste and inefficiency caused by stock, the true cost of carrying a unit in stock is £8 per year. The revised EOQ would be as follows:

$$E = \sqrt{\frac{2QP}{C}} = \sqrt{\frac{2(4,800)(£3)}{£8}} = \sqrt{£3,600}$$

$$E = 60 \text{ units}$$

Under JIT purchasing, the company would not necessarily order in 60-unit lots, since purchases would be geared to current demand. Nevertheless, this example shows quite dramatically the economics behind reducing order sizes.

## Production lot size

The EOQ concept can also be applied to the problem of determining the **economic lot size**. When companies manufacture a variety of products, they must decide how many units of one product should be manufactured before switching over to another product. The number of units in a lot, or production run, is referred to as the *lot size* or *batch size*. For example, Nintendo must decide how many units of a particular video game are to be produced in one lot before switching over to production of a different video game. This is a problem because switching from one product to another requires changing settings on machines, changing tools, and getting different materials ready for processing. Making these changes requires time and may involve substantial out-of-pocket costs. These **set-up costs** are analogous to the order costs discussed above, and they can be used in the EOQ formula in place of the order costs to determine the optimal lot size.

To illustrate, Chittenden Company has determined that the following costs are associated with one of its products:

$Q$ = 15,000 units produced each year

$P$ = £150 set-up costs to switch production from one product to another

$C$ = £2 to carry one unit in stock for one year.

What is the optimal production lot size for this product? It can be determined by using the EOQ formula:

$$E = \sqrt{\frac{2QP}{C}} = \sqrt{\frac{2(15,000)(£150)}{£2}} = \sqrt{£2,250,000}$$
$$E = 1,500 \text{ units (economics lot size)}$$

Chittenden Company will minimize its overall costs by producing in lots of 1,500 units each.

In computing the economic lot size, note again the impact of modern manufacturing methods. First, managers now realize that the costs of holding stock are far higher than previously assumed. Excess work in progress stock make it very difficult to operate efficiently and hence generate many unnecessary costs. Second, managers and workers are cutting set-up times from many hours to a few minutes by cleverly applying techniques such as *single-minute-exchange-of-dies* (see page 755). The benefit of reducing *set-up time* is that it makes it economically feasible for the company to produce in smaller lots and to respond much more quickly to the market. Indeed, reducing set-ups to the barest minimum is an essential step in any successful implementation of JIT.

To illustrate how these aspects of modern manufacturing methods affect the economic lot size, consider the Chittenden Company data. Suppose that the company has been able to reduce the cost of a set-up to only £3. Further, suppose that the company realizes, after more careful analysis of all of the costs of holding stock, that the true cost of carrying a unit in stock is £36 per year. The new economic lot size would be as follows:

$$E = \sqrt{\frac{2QP}{C}} = \sqrt{\frac{2(15,000)(£3)}{£36}} = \sqrt{£2,500}$$
$$E = 50 \text{ units (economic lot size)}$$

Thus, the company's economic lot size has been reduced from 1,500 units to only 50 units – a reduction of nearly 97%.

## Activity-based costing (ABC) and the production lot size

Managers should be extremely cautious when applying the results of ABC analyses to computation of the economic lot size. Typically, one of the results of an ABC analysis is a dramatic increase in the apparent costs of set-ups. The reason for this is that under conventional costing systems, many of the costs that might be attributed to switching over from one product to another are lumped into the general manufacturing overhead cost pool and distributed to products based on direct labour-hours or some other measure of volume. When an ABC analysis is done, these costs are separately identified as set-up costs. As a consequence, set-up costs appear to increase, and this would seem to imply that the economic lot size should be increased. However, a close examination of the costs attributed to set-ups in the ABC analysis will usually reveal that most of the costs cannot actually be avoided by reducing the number of set-ups. For example, machinery depreciation may be included in set-up costs. However, reducing the number of set-ups may have no impact at all on the amount of machinery depreciation actually incurred.

## Reorder point and safety stock

We stated that the stock problem has two dimensions – how much to order and how often to do it. The 'how often to do it' involves what are commonly termed the *reorder point* and the *safety stock*. The basic idea is to minimize the costs of holding stock while ensuring that there will be no stockouts (i.e., situations in which there are insufficient stock to satisfy current production requirements or customer demand). First, we will discuss the reorder point and then we will discuss the safety stock.

The **reorder point** tells the manager when to place an order or when to initiate production to replenish depleted stocks. It is dependent on three factors – the EOQ (or economic production-run size), the *lead time*, and the rate of usage during the lead time. The **lead time** can be defined as the interval between the time that an order is placed and the time when the order is finally received from the supplier or from the production line.

## Constant usage during the lead time

If the rate of usage during the lead time is known with certainty, the reorder point can be determined by the following formula:

Reorder point = Lead time × Average daily or weekly usage

To illustrate the formula's use, assume that a company's EOQ is 500 units, that the lead time is three weeks, and that the average weekly usage is 50 units.

Reorder point = 3 weeks × 50 units per week = 150 units

The reorder point would be 150 units. That is, the company will automatically place a new order for 500 units when stocks drop to a level of 150 units, or three weeks' supply, left on hand.

## Variable usage during the lead time

The previous example assumed that the 50 units per week usage rate was constant and was known with certainty. Although some firms enjoy the luxury of certainty, the more common situation is to find considerable variation in the rate of usage of stock items from period to period. If usage varies from period to period, the firm that reorders in the way computed above may soon find itself out of stock. A sudden spurt in demand, a delay in delivery, or a snag in processing an order may cause stock levels to be depleted before a new shipment arrives.

Companies that experience problems in demand, delivery, or processing of orders have found that they need some type of buffer to guard against stockouts. Such a buffer is called a **safety stock**. A safety stock serves as a kind of insurance against greater than usual demand and against problems in the ordering and delivery of goods. Its size is determined by deducting *average usage* from the *maximum usage* that can reasonably be expected during a period. For example, if the firm in the preceding example was faced with variable demand for its product, it would compute a safety stock as follows:

| | |
|---|---|
| Maximum expected usage per week | 65 units |
| Average usage per week | 50 units |
| Excess | 15 units |
| Lead time | × 3 weeks |
| Safety stock | 45 units |

The reorder point is then determined by *adding the safety stock to the average usage during the lead time*. In formula form, the reorder point is:

Reorder point = (Lead time × Average daily or weekly usage) + Safety stock

Computation of the reorder point is shown both numerically and graphically in Exhibit 18.4. As shown in the exhibit, the company will place a new order for 500 units when stocks drop to a level of 195 units left on hand.

## Reducing stock: just-in-time (JIT)

When companies use the **just-in-time (JIT)** production and stock control system, they purchase materials and produce units only as needed to meet actual customer demand. In a JIT system, stocks are reduced to the minimum and in some cases to zero. The JIT approach can be used in both merchandising and manufacturing companies. It has the most profound effects, however, on the operations of manufacturing companies, which maintain three classes of stock – *raw materials, work in progress* and *finished goods*.

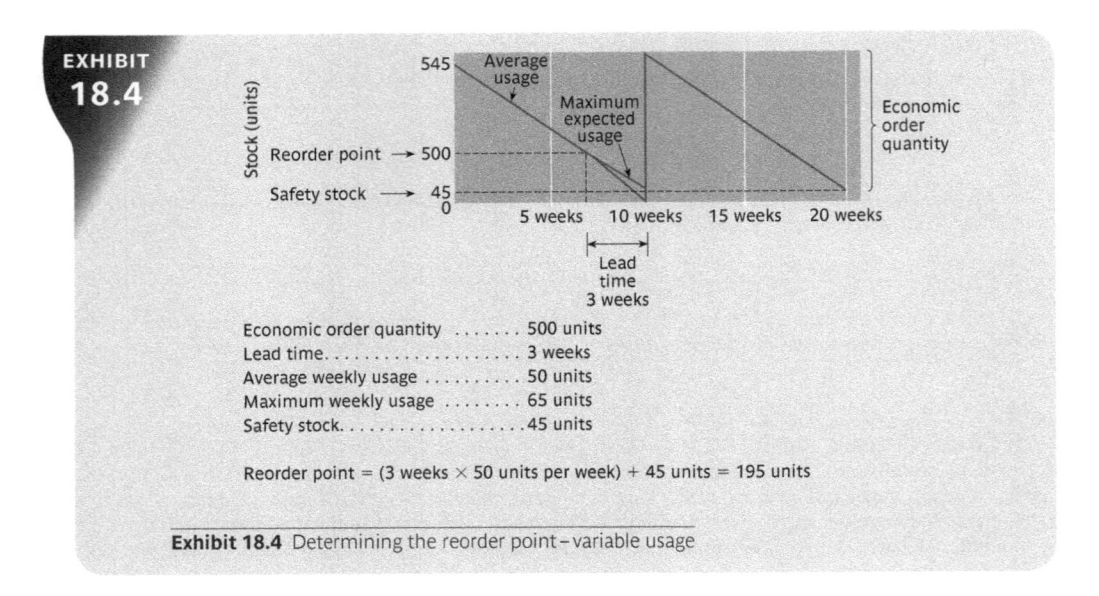

**Chapter 18** Business process management: towards the lean operation     **753**

> **EXHIBIT 18.4**
>
> [Graph showing stock depletion over 20 weeks with reorder point at 500 units, safety stock at 45 units, average usage line, maximum expected usage, lead time of 3 weeks, and economic order quantity of 545 units.]
>
> Economic order quantity ....... 500 units
> Lead time. . . . . . . . . . . . . . . . . . . 3 weeks
> Average weekly usage . . . . . . . . . 50 units
> Maximum weekly usage . . . . . . . . 65 units
> Safety stock. . . . . . . . . . . . . . . . . . 45 units
>
> Reorder point = (3 weeks × 50 units per week) + 45 units = 195 units
>
> **Exhibit 18.4** Determining the reorder point – variable usage

Traditionally, manufacturing companies have maintained large amounts of all three kinds of stock to act as buffers so that operations can proceed smoothly even if there are unanticipated disruptions. Raw materials stock provide insurance in case suppliers are late with deliveries. Work in progress stock are maintained in case a workstation is unable to operate due to a breakdown or other reason. Finished goods stock are maintained to accommodate unanticipated fluctuations in demand.

While these stock provide buffers against unforeseen events, they have a cost. In addition to the money tied up in the stock, experts argue that the presence of stock encourages inefficient and sloppy work, results in too many defects, and dramatically increases the amount of time required to complete a product. None of this is obvious – if it were, companies would have long ago reduced their stocks. Managers at Toyota are credited with the insight that large stocks often create more problems than they solve and Toyota pioneered the JIT approach.

### LEARNING OBJECTIVE 4

## The JIT concept

Under ideal conditions, a company operating a JIT system would purchase *only* enough materials each day to meet that day's needs. Moreover, the company would have no goods still in progress at the end of the day, and all goods completed during the day would have been shipped immediately to customers. As this sequence suggests, 'just-in-time' means that raw materials are received just in time to go into production, manufactured parts are completed *just in time* to be assembled into products, and products are completed *just in time* to be shipped to customers.

Although few companies have been able to reach this ideal, many companies have been able to reduce stock to only a fraction of their previous levels. The result has been a substantial reduction in ordering and warehousing costs, and much more effective operations.

How does a company avoid a build-up of parts and materials at various workstations and still ensure a smooth flow of goods when JIT is in use? In a JIT environment, the flow of goods is controlled by a *pull approach*. The pull approach can be explained as follows: At the final assembly stage, a signal is sent to the preceding workstation as to the exact amount of parts and materials that will be needed *over the next few hours* to assemble products to fill customer orders, and only that amount of parts and materials is provided. The same signal is sent back through each preceding workstation so that a smooth flow of parts and materials is maintained with no appreciable stock build-up at any point. Thus, all workstations respond to the pull

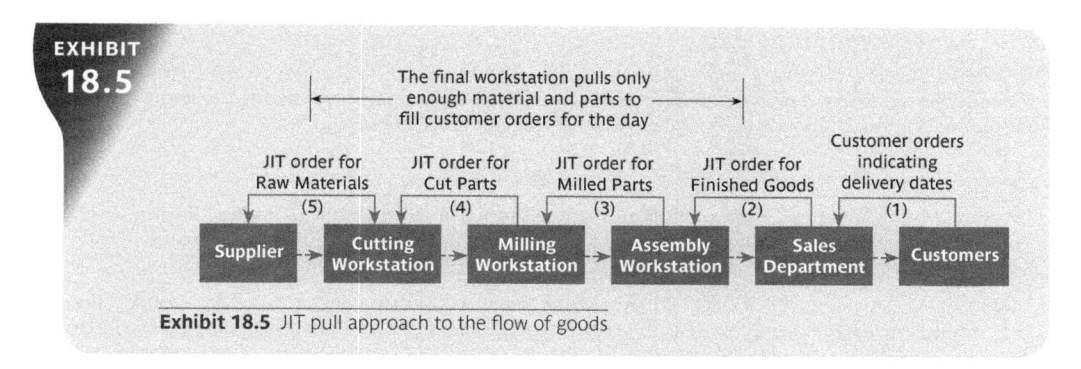

**Exhibit 18.5**

```
                The final workstation pulls only
        ←——    enough material and parts to    ——→
                fill customer orders for the day
                                                                    Customer orders
                                                                     indicating
    JIT order for    JIT order for    JIT order for    JIT order for    delivery dates
    Raw Materials    Cut Parts        Milled Parts    Finished Goods
        (5)              (4)              (3)              (2)              (1)

    Supplier  →  Cutting      →  Milling      →  Assembly     →  Sales        →  Customers
                 Workstation     Workstation     Workstation     Department
```

**Exhibit 18.5** JIT pull approach to the flow of goods

exerted by the final assembly stage, which in turn responds to customer orders. As one worker explained, 'Under a JIT system you don't produce anything, anywhere, for anybody unless they ask for it somewhere downstream. Stocks are an evil that we're taught to avoid.' The pull approach is illustrated in Exhibit 18.5.

The pull approach described above can be contrasted to the *push approach* used in conventional manufacturing systems. In conventional systems, when a workstation completes its work, the partially completed goods are 'pushed' forward to the next workstation regardless of whether that workstation is ready to receive them. The result is an unintentional stockpiling of partially completed goods that may not be completed for days or even weeks. This ties up funds and also results in operating inefficiencies. For one thing, it becomes very difficult to keep track of where everything is when so much is scattered all over the factory floor.

Another characteristic of conventional manufacturing systems is an emphasis on 'keeping everyone busy' as an end in itself. This inevitably leads to excess stock – particularly work in progress stock – for reasons that will be more fully explored in a later section on the theory of constraints. In JIT, the traditional emphasis on keeping everyone busy is abandoned in favour of producing only what customers actually want – even if that means some workers are idle.

## JIT purchasing

Any organization with stock – retail, wholesale, distribution, service, or manufacturing – can use *JIT purchasing*. Under JIT purchasing:

1. *A company relies on a few ultra reliable suppliers.* IBM, for example, eliminated 95% of the suppliers from one of its plants, reducing the number from 640 to only 32. Rather than soliciting bids from suppliers each year and going with the low bidder, the dependable suppliers are rewarded with long-term contracts.
2. *Suppliers make frequent deliveries in small lots just before the goods are needed.* Rather than deliver a week's (or a month's) supply of an item at one time, suppliers must be willing to make deliveries as often as several times a day, and in the exact quantities specified by the buyer. Undependable suppliers who do not meet delivery schedules are weeded out. Dependability is essential, since a JIT system is highly vulnerable to any interruption in supply. If a single part is unavailable, the entire assembly operation may have to be shut down. Or, in the case of a merchandising company, if the supplier allows stock to get down to zero, customers may be turned away unsatisfied.
3. *Suppliers must deliver defect-free goods.* Because of the vulnerability of a JIT system to disruptions, defects cannot be tolerated. Indeed, suppliers must become so reliable that incoming goods do not have to be inspected.

Companies that adopt JIT purchasing often realize substantial savings from streamlined operations. Note that a company does not have to eliminate all stock to use the JIT approach. Indeed, retail organizations must maintain some stock or they could not operate. But the amount of time a product spends on a shelf or in a warehouse can be greatly reduced.

### Key elements in a JIT system

In addition to JIT purchasing, four key elements are usually required for the successful operation of a JIT manufacturing system. These elements include improving the plant layout, reducing the set-up time needed for production runs, striving for zero defects, and developing a flexible workforce.

### Improving plant layout

Properly to implement JIT, a company typically must improve the manufacturing *flow lines* in its plant. A flow line is the physical path taken by a product as it moves through the manufacturing process as it is transformed from raw materials to completed goods.

Traditionally, companies have designed their plant floors so that similar machines are grouped together. Such a functional layout results in all drill presses in one place, all lathes in another place, and so forth. This approach to plant layout requires that work in progress be moved from one group of machines to another – frequently across the plant or even to another building. The result is extensive material-handling costs, large work in progress stock, and unnecessary delays.

In a JIT system, all machines needed to make a particular product are often brought together in one location. This approach to plant layout creates an individual 'mini' factory for each separate product, frequently referred to as a *focused factory* or as a 'factory within a factory'. The flow line for a product can be straight, as shown earlier in Exhibit 18.4, or it can be in a U-shaped configuration. The key point is that all machines in a *product flow line* are tightly grouped together so that partially completed units are not shifted from place to place all over the factory. *Manufacturing cells* are also often part of a JIT product flow line. In a *cell*, a single worker operates several machines.

The *focused factory approach* allows workers to focus all their efforts on a product from start to finish and minimizes handling and moving. After one large manufacturing company rearranged its plant layout and organized its products into individual flow lines, the company determined that the distance travelled by one product had been decreased from 3 miles to just 100 metres. Apart from reductions in handling, this more compact layout makes it much easier to keep track of where a particular job is in the production process.

An improved plant layout can dramatically increase *throughput*, which is the total volume of production through a facility during a period, and it can dramatically reduce **throughput time** (also known as *cycle time*), which is the time required to make a product.

### Reduced set-up time

*Set-ups* involve activities – such as moving materials, changing machine settings, setting up equipment, and running tests – that must be performed whenever production is switched over from making one type of item to another. For example, it may not be a simple matter to switch over from making 1.25 cm brass screws to making 2 cm brass screws on a manually controlled milling machine. Many preparatory steps must be performed, and these steps can take hours. Because of the time and expense involved in such set-ups, many managers believe set-ups should be avoided and therefore items should be produced in large batches. For example, one batch of 400 units requires only one set-up, whereas four batches of 100 units each would require four set-ups. The problem with big batches is that they create large amounts of stock that must wait for days, weeks, or even months before further processing at the next workstation or before they are sold.

One advantage of a dedicated flow line is that it requires fewer set-ups. If equipment is dedicated to a single product, set-ups are largely eliminated and the product can be produced in any batch size desired. Even when dedicated flow lines are not used, it is often possible to slash set-up time by using techniques such as single-minute-exchange-of-dies. A *die* is a device used for cutting out, forming or stamping material. For example, a die is used to produce the stamped metal door panels on a car. A die must be changed when it wears out or when production is switched to a different product. This changeover can be time consuming. The goal with *single-minute-exchange-of-dies* is to reduce the amount of time required to change a die to a minute or less. This can be done by simple techniques such as doing as much of the changeover work in advance as possible rather than waiting until production is shut down.[5] When such techniques are followed, batch sizes can be very small.

Smaller batches reduce the level of stock, make it easier to respond quickly to the market, reduce cycle times, and generally make it much easier to spot manufacturing problems before they result in a large number of defective units.

### Zero defects and JIT

Defective units create big problems in a JIT environment. If a completed order contains a defective unit, the company must ship the order with less than the promised quantity or it must restart the whole production process to make just one unit. At minimum, this creates a delay in shipping the order and may generate a ripple effect that delays other orders. For this and other reasons, defects cannot be tolerated in a JIT system. Companies that are deeply involved in JIT tend to become zealously committed to a goal of *zero defects*. Even though it may be next to impossible to attain the zero defect goal, companies have found that they can come very close. For example, Motorola, Allied Signal, and many other companies now measure defects in terms of the number of defects per million units of product.

In a traditional company, parts and materials are inspected for defects when they are received from suppliers, and quality inspectors inspect units as they progress along the production line. In a JIT system, the company's suppliers are responsible for the quality of incoming parts and materials. And instead of using quality inspectors, the company's production workers are directly responsible for spotting defective units.

A worker who discovers a defect is supposed to punch an alarm button that stops the production flow line and sets off flashing lights. Supervisors and other workers then descend on the workstation to determine the cause of the defect and correct it before any further defective units are produced. This procedure ensures that problems are quickly identified and corrected, but it does require that defects are rare – otherwise there would be constant disruptions to the production process.

### Flexible workforce

Workers on a JIT line must be multiskilled and flexible. Workers are often expected to operate all of the equipment on a JIT product flow line. Moreover, workers are expected to perform minor repairs and do maintenance work when they would otherwise be idle. In contrast, on a conventional assembly line a worker performs a single task all the time every day and all maintenance work is done by a specialized maintenance crew.

### Benefits of a JIT system

The main benefits of JIT are the following:

1 Working capital is bolstered by the recovery of funds that were tied up in stock
2 Areas previously used to store stock are made available for other, more productive uses
3 Throughput time is reduced, resulting in greater potential output and quicker response to customers
4 Defect rates are reduced, resulting in less waste and greater customer satisfaction.

As a result of benefits such as those cited above, more companies are embracing JIT each year. Most companies find, however, that simply reducing stock is not enough. To remain competitive in an ever changing and ever more competitive business environment, companies must strive for continuous improvement.

## Stock control and enterprise resource planning (ERP)

Systems of stock control such as JIT have been helped by developments in information technology. The most sophisticated example involves the automation of management information systems through the **enterprise resource planning (ERP)** software offered by companies such as SAP, Oracle, Baan and J.D. Edwards. Stock control is only part of an integrated system, which tracks transactions across the company.

The main characteristics, costs and benefits of ERPs are:[6]

- Systems are based on integrated client-server technology
- All data are entered only once where the data originate
- The implementation of such a total system is typically costly and time consuming

Chapter 18 Business process management: towards the lean operation

- But, updating the old heterogeneous system platform (e.g., for euro-currency) is costly as well
- Firms may also aim at business model improvements via the adoption of ERPs (e.g., ABC[7])
- ERP represents a *process-oriented information system* based on *value chain thinking*
- The installation of an ERP may result in a lack of flexibility when a company operates in different countries.[8]

Given the theoretical benefits of a single *IT driven management information system*, it seems strange that for many years companies have been disappointed with the returns from their huge investments in new IT systems.[9] One problem with ERP models is that the benefits of the new systems are not so much in the 'hard returns' of reduced *headcounts* as in 'soft returns' such as revenue or employee gains that are harder to identify.[10] Many of the gains are so-called '*back-door*' gains such as agreeing common data with the same vocabulary and format. Not only are business processes standardized but the implementation process helps to inculcate a more learning, improving culture. Part of the problem with early computer applications was that companies were automating *existing* organizational and production systems. The really significant benefits come when the new technology is used to fundamentally reconfigure business practices.[11] Indeed, some businesses argue that the bulk of benefits come from the organizational changes rather than the new technology.[12]

## LEARNING OBJECTIVE 6 E-commerce: new challenges for management accounting

A lot of hype has been generated by the internet. Yet many of the breakthroughs in inter-personal and inter-organizational communication rely on older technologies such as **electronic data interchange (EDI)** and telephones. The power of the telephone has been massively increased because the teleworker can be linked to the company's database via a personal computer. Thus the huge reduction in paper, floor space, queueing and so on, in an operation such as telephone banking or a ticketless airline, does not necessarily require internet technology. But for these operations, the internet is cheaper than both telephone and EDI as well as opening up the possibility of real-time screen communication for both consumers and smaller companies.

### FOCUS ON PRACTICE

#### Performance measurement of internet sites

In the early days, few internet companies could measure their sites' performance or whether their sites were becoming more effective over time. Internet companies attracted visitors to their sites but were less successful at making sales or retaining customers. If anything, the more visitors the sites drew, the more money they lost. As in any business, long-term profitability is based on lifetime customer value: the revenue customers generate over their lives, less the cost of acquiring, converting and retaining them. New site performance indicators are being developed that measure attraction, conversion and retention plus other factors such as the rate at which the number of customers increases, and customer gross margins.[13] Paradoxically, it would be wrong to think that internet companies are the most likely candidates for stock elimination. For example, part of the success of one of the more established dot-com companies, Amazon.com, is that its stocks of books, CDs, videos are far larger than local retailers.

More direct relations between customers and producers (disintermediation) means that huge chains of dedicated high street branches are assets of doubtful value. But as companies become more virtual there are new challenges for management accounting. In a virtual company 'assets are not only tangible but also include intangible assets such as brand value, intellectual property, human capital (people), virtual integration, information management, quality of service and customer relations, they need to be factored into performance measurement exercises. Otherwise a company may end up with a distorted picture of its overall economic value, market position and future potential.'[14] Distorted pictures were certainly a feature of the

**Part 4** Value metrics and performance management in a strategic context

dotcom boom when many internet start-ups attracted both media and investor attention. With inflated stock market values bearing no relation to traditional indicators of value, there was vague talk of a 'new economic model'.

The hype of the dotcom boom has now passed. Many of the dotcom start-ups have either disappeared or are struggling to make profits. In retrospect, some of these companies may have benefited from more traditional business plans that showed how an internet site could generate profits. The approach to evaluating site performance is becoming more rigorous as the nature of internet commerce is better understood.[15]

## Quality and business processes: measurement and management

Earlier we saw how a JIT system is based on defect-free production and inputs. Yet there are more general motives for measuring and managing quality even, or, especially, in service companies that do not have inventory. Companies that develop a reputation for low-quality products generally lose market share and face declining profits. It doesn't do much good to have a product with a high-quality design that is made with high-quality materials if the product falls apart on the first use. One very important aspect of quality is the absence of defects. Defective products result in high warranty costs, but more importantly, they result in dissatisfied customers. People who are dissatisfied with a product are unlikely to buy the product again. They are also likely to tell others about their bad experiences. One study found that '[c]ustomers who have bad experiences tell approximately 11 people about it'.[16] This is the worst possible sort of advertising. To prevent such problems, companies have been expending a great deal of effort to reduce defects. The objective is to have high *quality of conformance*.

### The cost of quality model

A product that meets or exceeds its design specifications and is free of defects that mar its appearance or degrade its performance is said to have high quality of conformance. Note that if an economy car is free of defects, it can have a **quality of conformance** that is just as high as a defect-free luxury car. The purchasers of economy cars cannot expect their cars to be as opulently equipped as luxury cars, but they can and do expect them to be free of defects.

Preventing, detecting and dealing with defects cause costs that are called *quality costs* or the *cost of quality*. The use of the term *quality cost* is confusing to some people. It does not refer to costs such as using a higher-grade leather to make a wallet or using 14K gold instead of gold-plating in jewellery. Instead, the term **quality costs** refers to all of the costs that are incurred to prevent defects or that are incurred as a result of defects occurring.

Quality costs can be broken down into four broad groups. Two of these groups – known as *prevention costs* and *appraisal costs* – are incurred in an effort to keep defective products from falling into the hands of customers. The other two groups of costs – known as *internal failure costs* and *external failure costs* – are incurred because defects are produced despite efforts to prevent them. Examples of specific costs involved in each of these four groups are given in Exhibit 18.6.

Several things should be noted about the quality costs shown in the exhibit. First, note that quality costs do not relate to just manufacturing; rather, they relate to all the activities in a company from initial research and development (R&D) through customer service. Second, note that the number of costs associated with quality is very large; therefore, total quality cost can be quite high unless management gives this area special attention. Finally, note how different the costs are in the four groupings. We will now look at each of these groupings more closely.

### Prevention costs

The most effective way to minimize quality costs while maintaining high-quality output is to avoid having quality problems arise in the first place. This is the purpose of **prevention costs**; such costs relate to any activity that reduces the number of defects in products or services. Companies have learned that it is much

## EXHIBIT 18.6 Typical quality costs

| Prevention costs | Internal failure costs |
|---|---|
| Systems development | Net cost of scrap |
| Quality engineering | Net cost of spoilage |
| Quality training | Rework labour and overhead |
| Quality circles | Reinspection of reworked products |
| Statistical process control activities | Retesting of reworked products |
| Supervision of prevention activities | Downtime caused by quality problems |
| Quality data gathering, analysis, and reporting | Disposal of defective products |
| Quality improvement projects | Analysis of the cause of defects in production |
| Technical support provided to suppliers | Re-entering data because of keying errors |
| Audits of the effectiveness of the quality system | Debugging software errors |
| **Appraisal costs** | **External failure costs** |
| Test and inspection of incoming materials | Cost of field servicing and handling complaints |
| Test and inspection of in-process goods | Warranty repairs and replacements |
| Final product testing and inspection | Repairs and replacements beyond the warranty period |
| Supplies used in testing and inspection | Product recalls |
| Supervision of testing and inspection activities | Liability arising from defective products |
| Depreciation of test equipment | Returns and allowances arising from quality problems |
| Maintenance of test equipment | Lost sales arising from a reputation for poor quality |
| Plant utilities in the inspection area | |
| Field testing and appraisal at customer site | |

less costly to prevent a problem from ever happening than it is to find and correct the problem after it has occurred.

Note from Exhibit 18.6 that prevention costs include activities relating to quality circles and statistical process control. **Quality circles** consist of small groups of employees that meet on a regular basis to discuss ways to improve the quality of output. Both management and workers are included in these circles. Quality circles are widely used and can be found in manufacturing companies, utilities, health care organizations, banks and many other organizations.

**Statistical process control** is a technique that is used to detect whether a process is in or out of control. An out-of-control process results in defective units and may be caused by a miscalibrated machine or some other factor. In statistical process control, workers use charts to monitor the quality of units that pass through their workstations. Using these charts, workers can quickly spot processes that are out of control and that are creating defects. Problems can be immediately corrected and further defects prevented rather than waiting for an inspector to catch the defects later.

Note also from the list of prevention costs in Exhibit 18.6 that some companies provide technical support to their suppliers as a way of preventing defects. Particularly in just-in-time (JIT) systems, such support to suppliers is vital. In a JIT system, parts are delivered from suppliers just in time and in just the correct quantity to fill customer orders. There are no stockpiles of parts. If a defective part is received from a supplier, the part cannot be used and the order for the ultimate customer cannot be filled on time. Hence, every part received from a supplier must be free of defects. Consequently, companies that use JIT often require that their suppliers use sophisticated quality control programmes such as statistical process control and that their suppliers certify that they will deliver parts and materials that are free of defects.

## Appraisal costs

Any defective parts and products should be caught as early as possible. **Appraisal costs**, which are sometimes called *inspection costs*, are incurred to identify defective products *before* the products are shipped to customers. Unfortunately, performing appraisal activities does not keep defects from happening again, and most managers now realize that maintaining an army of inspectors is a costly (and ineffective) approach to quality control.

Professor John K. Shank of Dartmouth College has aptly stated, 'The old-style approach was to say, "We've got great quality. We have 40 quality control inspectors in the factory." Then somebody realized that if you need 40 inspectors, it must be a lousy factory. So now the trick is to run a factory without any quality control inspectors; each employee is his or her own quality control person.'[17]

Employees in both manufacturing and service functions are increasingly being asked to be responsible for their own quality control. This approach, along with designing products to be easy to manufacture properly, allows quality to be built into products rather than relying on inspection to get the defects out.

## Internal failure costs

Failure costs are incurred when a product fails to conform to its design specifications. Failure costs can be either internal or external. **Internal failure costs** result from identification of defects during the appraisal process. Such costs include scrap, rejected products, reworking of defective units, and downtime caused by quality problems. It is crucial that defects be discovered before a product is shipped to customers. Of course, the more effective a company's appraisal activities, the greater the chance of catching defects internally and the greater the level of internal failure costs (as compared to external failure costs). Unfortunately, appraisal activities focus on symptoms rather than on causes and they do nothing to reduce the number of defective items. However, appraisal activities do bring defects to the attention of management, which may lead to efforts to increase prevention activities so that the defects do not happen.

## External failure costs

**External failure costs** result when a defective product is delivered to a customer. As shown in Exhibit 18.6, external failure costs include warranty repairs and replacements, product recalls, liability arising from legal action against a company, and lost sales arising from a reputation for poor quality. Such costs can devastate profits.

In the past, some managers have taken the attitude, 'Let's go ahead and ship everything to customers, and we'll take care of any problems under the warranty.' This attitude generally results in high external failure costs, customer ill will, and declining market share and profits.

## Distribution of quality costs

We stated earlier that a company's total quality cost is likely to be very high unless management gives this area special attention. How does a company reduce its total quality cost? The answer lies in how the quality costs are distributed. Refer to the graph in Exhibit 18.7, which shows total quality costs as a function of the quality of conformance.

The graph shows that when the quality of conformance is low, total quality cost is high and that most of this cost consists of costs of internal and external failure. A low quality of conformance means that a high percentage of units are defective and hence the company must incur high failure costs. However, as a company spends more and more on prevention and appraisal, the percentage of defective units drops (the percentage of defect-free units increases). This results in lower costs of internal and external failure. Ordinarily, total

**Exhibit 18.7**

**Exhibit 18.7** Effect of quality costs on quality of conformance

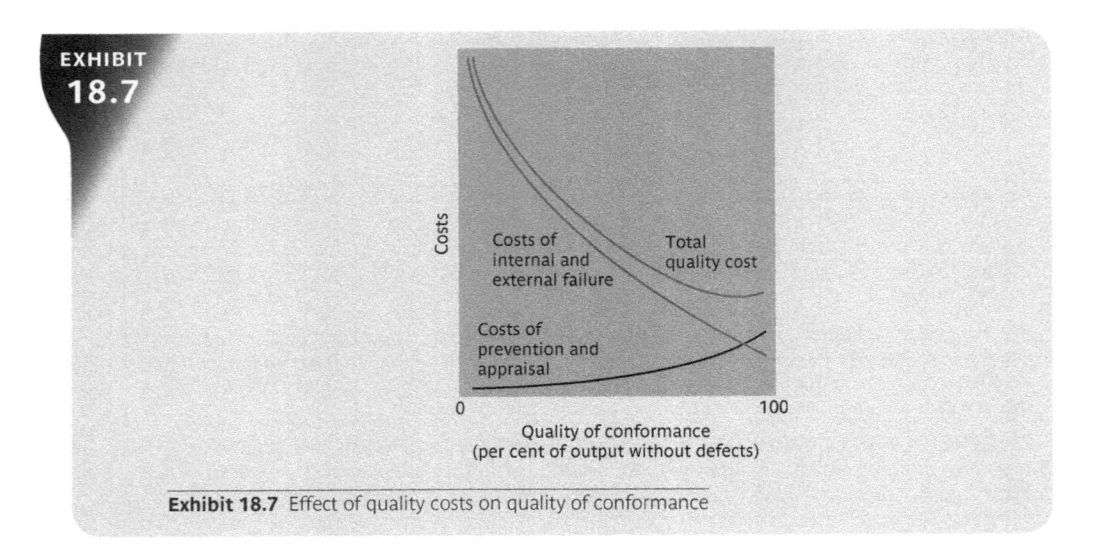

quality cost drops rapidly as the quality of conformance increases. Thus, a company can reduce its total quality cost by focusing its efforts on prevention and appraisal. The cost savings from reduced defects usually swamp the costs of the additional prevention and appraisal efforts.

The graph in Exhibit 18.7 has been drawn so that the total quality cost is minimized when the quality of conformance is less than 100%. However, some experts and managers contend that the total quality cost is not minimized until the quality of conformance is 100% and there are no defects. Indeed, many companies have found that the total quality costs seem to keep dropping even when the quality of conformance approaches 100% and defect rates get as low as one in a million units. Others argue that eventually total quality cost increases as the quality of conformance increases. However, in most companies this does not seem to happen until the quality of conformance is very close to 100% and defect rates are very close to zero.

As a company's quality programme becomes more refined and as its failure costs begin to fall, prevention activities usually become more effective than appraisal activities. Appraisal can only find defects, whereas prevention can eliminate them. The best way to prevent defects from happening is to design processes that reduce the likelihood of defects and to continually monitor processes using statistical process control methods.

## Quality cost reports

As an initial step in quality improvement programmes, companies often construct a *quality cost report* that provides an estimate of the financial consequences of the company's current level of defects. A **quality cost report** details the prevention costs, appraisal costs, and costs of internal and external failures that arise from the company's current level of defective products and services. Managers are often shocked by the magnitude of these costs. A typical quality cost report is shown in Exhibit 18.8.

Several things should be noted from the data in the exhibit. First, note that Ventura Company's quality costs are poorly distributed in both years, with most of the costs being traceable to either internal failure or external failure. The external failure costs are particularly high in Year 1 in comparison to other costs.

Second, note that the company increased its spending on prevention and appraisal activities in Year 2. As a result, internal failure costs go up in that year (from £2 million in Year 1 to £3 million in Year 2), but external failure costs drop sharply (from £5.15 million in Year 1 to only £2 million in Year 2). Because of the increase

**EXHIBIT 18.8**

### Ventura Company Quality cost report for years 1 and 2

|  | Year 2 Amount | Per cent | Year 1 Amount | Per cent |
|---|---|---|---|---|
| **Prevention costs:** |  |  |  |  |
| Systems development | £400,000 | 0.80% | £270,000 | 0.54% |
| Quality training | 210,000 | 0.42% | 130,000 | 0.26% |
| Supervision of prevention activities | 70,000 | 0.14% | 40,000 | 0.08% |
| Quality improvement projects | 320,000 | 0.64% | 210,000 | 0.42% |
| Total | 1,000,000 | 2.00% | 650,000 | 1.30% |
| **Appraisal costs:** |  |  |  |  |
| Inspection | 600,000 | 1.20% | 560,000 | 1.12% |
| Reliability testing | 580,000 | 1.16% | 420,000 | 0.84% |
| Supervision of testing and inspection | 120,000 | 0.24% | 80,000 | 0.16% |
| Depreciation of test equipment | 200,000 | 0.40% | 140,000 | 0.28% |
| Total | 1,500,000 | 3.00% | 1,200,000 | 2.40% |
| **Internal failure costs:** |  |  |  |  |
| Net cost of scrap | 900,000 | 1.80% | 750,000 | 1.50% |
| Rework labour and overhead | 1,430,000 | 2.86% | 810,000 | 1.62% |
| Downtime due to defects in quality | 170,000 | 0.34% | 100,000 | 0.20% |
| Disposal of defective products | 500,000 | 1.00% | 340,000 | 0.68% |
| Total | 3,000,000 | 6.00% | 2,000,000 | 4.00% |
| **External failure costs:** |  |  |  |  |
| Warranty repairs | 400,000 | 0.80% | 900,000 | 1.80% |
| Warranty replacements | 870,000 | 1.74% | 2,300,000 | 4.60% |
| Allowances | 130,000 | 0.26% | 630,000 | 1.26% |
| Cost of field servicing | 600,000 | 1.20% | 1,320,000 | 2.64% |
| Total | 2,000,000 | 4.00% | 5,150,000 | 10.30% |
| **Total quality cost** | **£7,500,000** | **15.00%** | **£9,000,000** | **18.00%** |

*As a percentage of total sales. We assume that in each year sales totalled £50,000,000.

**Exhibit 18.8** Quality cost report

in appraisal activity in Year 2, more defects are being caught inside the company before they are shipped to customers. This results in more cost for scrap, rework and so forth, but saves huge amounts in warranty repairs, warranty replacements and other external failure costs.

Third, note that as a result of greater emphasis on prevention and appraisal, *total* quality cost has decreased in Year 2. As continued emphasis is placed on prevention and appraisal in future years, total quality cost should continue to decrease. That is, future increases in prevention and appraisal costs should be more than offset by decreases in failure costs. Moreover, appraisal costs should also decrease as more effort is placed into prevention.

## Quality cost reports in graphic form

As a supplement to the quality cost report shown in Exhibit 18.8, companies frequently prepare quality cost information in graphic form. Graphic presentations include pie charts, bar graphs, trend lines and so forth. The data for Ventura Company from Exhibit 18.8 are presented in bar graph form in Exhibit 18.9.

The first bar graph in Exhibit 18.9 is scaled in terms of pounds of quality cost, and the second is scaled in terms of quality cost as a percentage of sales. In both graphs, the data are 'stacked' upward. That is, appraisal costs are stacked on top of prevention costs, internal failure costs are stacked on top of the sum of prevention costs plus appraisal costs, and so forth. The percentage figures in the second graph show that total quality cost equals 18% of sales in Year 1 and 15% of sales in Year 2, the same as reported earlier in Exhibit 18.8.

## Uses of quality cost information

The information provided by a quality cost report is used by managers in several ways. First, quality cost information helps managers to see the financial significance of defects. Managers usually are not aware of the magnitude of their quality costs because these costs cut across departmental lines and are not normally tracked and accumulated by the cost system. Thus, when first presented with a quality cost report, managers are often surprised by the amount of cost attributable to poor quality.

Second, quality cost information helps managers to identify the relative importance of the quality problems faced by the firm. For example, the quality cost report may show that scrap is a major quality problem or that the company is incurring huge warranty costs. With this information, managers have a better idea of where to focus efforts.

Third, quality cost information helps managers to see whether their quality costs are poorly distributed. In general, quality costs should be distributed more toward prevention and appraisal activities and less towards failures.

Counterbalancing these uses, three limitations of quality cost information should be recognized. First, simply measuring and reporting quality costs does not solve quality problems. Problems can be solved only by taking action. Second, results usually lag behind quality improvement programmes. Initially, total quality

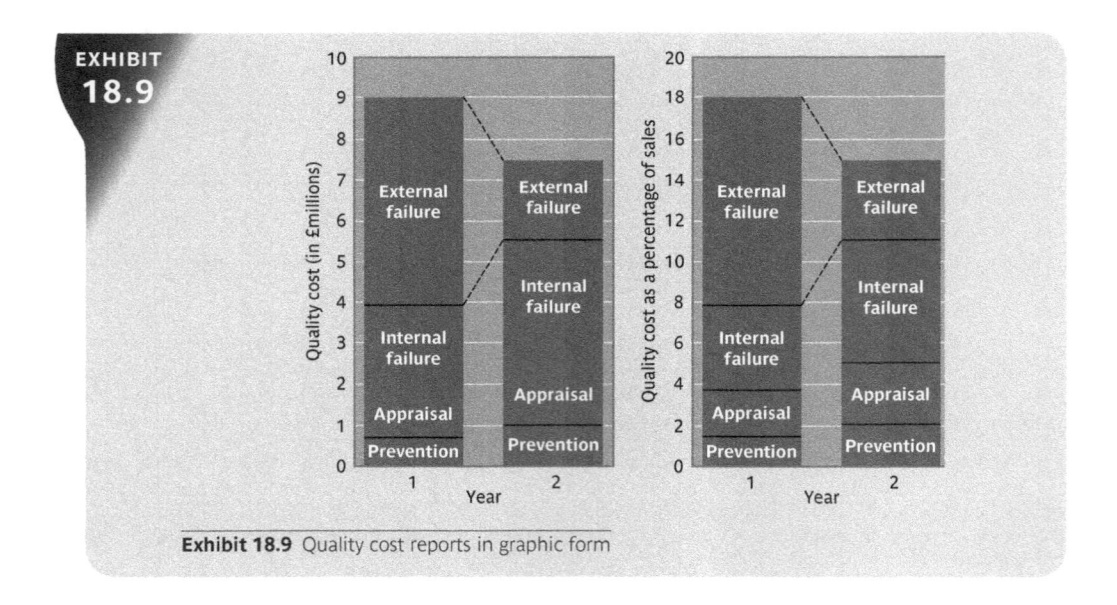

**EXHIBIT 18.9**

**Exhibit 18.9** Quality cost reports in graphic form

cost may even increase as quality control systems are designed and installed. Decreases in these costs may not begin to occur until the quality programme has been in effect for a year or more. And third, the most important quality cost, lost sales arising from customer ill will, is usually omitted from the quality cost report because it is difficult to estimate.

## From modelling the costs of quality to quality management

One way of summarizing and balancing the costs and benefits of quality is to show the trade-offs in a diagram such as that in Exhibit 18.7. The interplay of the various cost functions enable us to identify an optimal level of quality where total costs are minimized. As we saw with the EOQ model and JIT, a cost of quality model can be part of a wider more active management approach that sees quality not as a cost optimizing exercise but as a philosophy that drives the whole organization. Some are more critical of the cost of quality model. For example, Anderson and Sedatole argue that 'accountants' support of quality management is hobbled by a tradition of historical reporting and a focus on one aspect of quality – conformance to design specifications. Conformance quality is a static representation of performance to historical quality standards. A more potent weapon in quality management is the use of performance data to improve new product designs.'[18]

With total quality management the whole organization is called upon to embrace new processes and techniques that strive to make continuous improvements. With continuous improvement, the optimal level of quality as learning-by-doing and further investment push the curves to right over time. Indeed, the dominant ethos of quality management is one of continual improvement rather than static optimization. Typically, during the initial years of a quality improvement programme, the benefits of compiling a quality cost report outweigh the costs and limitations of the reports. As managers gain experience in balancing prevention and appraisal activities, the need for quality cost reports often diminishes.

## Total quality management (TQM)

The most popular approach to continuous improvement is known as **total quality management (TQM)**. There are two major characteristics of TQM: (1) a focus on serving customers and (2) systematic problem solving using teams made up of frontline workers. A variety of specific tools are available to aid teams in their problem solving. One of these tools, **benchmarking**, involves studying organizations that are among the best in the world at performing a particular task. For example, when Xerox wanted to improve its procedures for filling customer orders, it studied how the mail-order company L.L. Bean processes its customer orders.

### The plan-do-check-act cycle

Perhaps the most important and pervasive TQM problem-solving tool is the *plan-do-check-act (PDCA)* cycle, which is also referred to as the Deming Wheel.[19] The **plan-do-check-act cycle (PDCA)** is a systematic, fact-based approach to continuous improvement. The basic elements of the PDCA cycle are illustrated in Exhibit 18.10. The PDCA cycle applies the scientific method to problem solving. In the Plan phase, the problem-solving team analyses data to identify possible causes for the problem and then proposes a solution. In the Do phase, an experiment is conducted. In the Check phase, the results of the experiment are analysed. And in the Act phase, if the results of the experiment are favourable, the plan is implemented. If the results of the experiment are not favourable, the team goes back to the original data and starts all over again.

An important element of TQM is its focus on the customer. The accounting and consulting firm KPMG Peat Marwick periodically surveys its customers' satisfaction with its services. The firm's managing director points out that it costs four times as much to gain a new customer as it does to keep an old customer, and the most satisfied customers are generally the most profitable customers for the firm. 'For each complaint that you hear, there are fifty you don't. If you don't monitor clients' satisfaction, you may find out about their dissatisfaction as they walk out the door.'[20]

**EXHIBIT 18.10**

- Study the current process
- Collect data
- Analyse the data to identify possible causes
- Develop a plan for improvement
- Decide how to measure improvement

Plan → Do → Check → Act

- If successful, make the change permanent
- If the results are not successful, try again

- Implement the plan on a small scale if possible
- Collect data

- Evaluate the data collected during the Do phase
- Did the expected improvement occur?

**Exhibit 18.10** The plan-do-check-act cycle

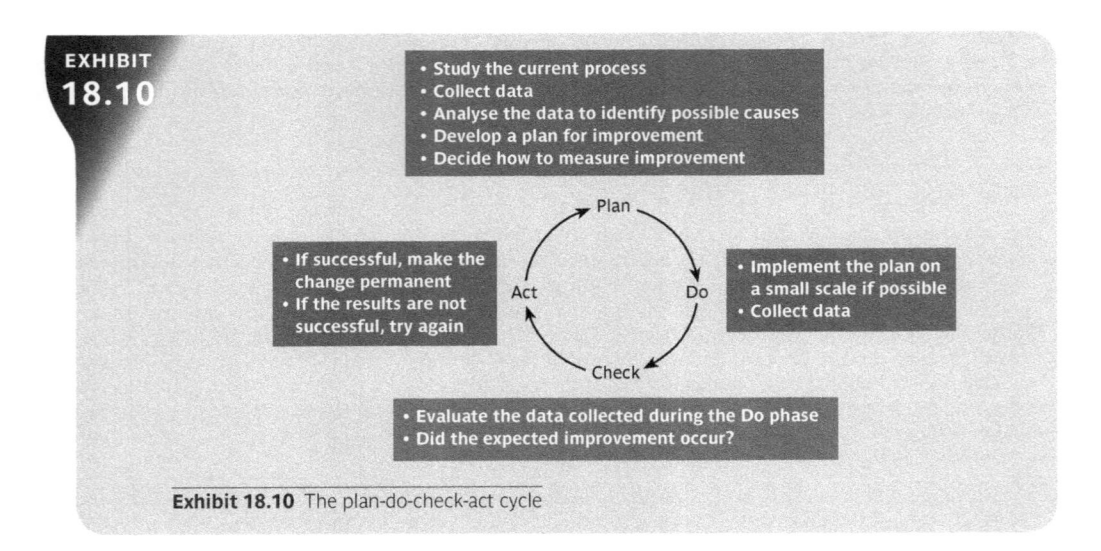

In sum, TQM provides tools and techniques for continuous improvement based on facts and analysis; and if properly implemented, it avoids counterproductive organizational infighting.

## Some criticisms of TQM

There have been a number of criticisms of TQM. They may not always be justified but managers should be aware of possible pitfalls. TQM has been accused of draining innovation from organizations by standardizing internal processes. It is also accused of making organizations more efficient at what they are doing irrespective of whether they should be doing it. The spectre is that TQM results in a finely honed organization that is a world-class producer of wagon wheels or manual typewriters. Like other management change initiatives, TQM suffers from the 'Flavour of the month' syndrome. Typically, organizational members have been bombarded with so many fads that they may merely go through the motions of implementation of TQM hoping that senior managers will soon embrace a new 'three letter acronym'.

## Benchmarking

Much of the data gathered through the introduction of quality management may be used as a basis for comparison with other organizations. In particular, it may be useful to identify organizations that are the best at performing specific activities or producing particular products in order to learn how they achieve their relatively high performance. This process is known as *benchmarking*. With *quality management*, the focus may be on *non-financial* measures as much as financial measures such as costs. Later in the chapter, we can see an example of *cost* benchmarking based on ABC data.

In order to achieve the best result from benchmarking a number of principles should be adhered to. Benchmarking may be seen as an exercise that proceeds according to a sequence of steps.

- *Step 1: Internal and competitive analysis*. At this preliminary stage the organization chooses the areas for analysis and undertakes basic comparisons between internal data and external data. External data may be found in marketing reports, consumer surveys, government statistics. It may not be confined to the firm's industry. For example, the particular part of the organization chosen for benchmarking may involve an activity where the best performers are in a completely different industry. For example, a theatre may study the ticketing procedures used in the airline industry. Although there may be a danger of not comparing like with like such as when a tyre retailer sees a formula one team as an appropriate benchmark for tyre-changing, there may still be lessons that can be learned even from such apparently 'unfair' comparisons.

- *Step 2: Building a benchmarking team.* Changes in practice may involve both radical reorganization and long-term commitment. Thus benchmarking teams must ideally have the backing of senior management, the support of the workforce and a long-term orientation. Typically, teams will be from a number of functional areas representing different professional specialisms and change must be supported by dedicated training programmes.

- *Step 3: Choosing benchmarking partners and sharing information.* This step strikes a balance between the need to *'stretch' performance* and not comparing like with like. Furthermore, if partners are really going to learn from each other then detailed information about operational performance has to be shared, implying an atmosphere of co-operation and trust rather than competition. If trust is absent then information may be shared on the basis of quid pro quo or as part of an industry-wide initiative. Alternatively, information may be gathered on a unilateral basis through activities such as reverse engineering. As we saw in Chapter 16, the collection of data on competitors is an important part of strategic management accounting and may be based wholly on competitive rather than co-operative principles.

- *Step 4: Taking action to meet benchmark.* It is at this stage that the internal implementation of the external analysis may run into difficulties, especially if best practice threatens job security and/or managerial empires. The issues of organizational change take us beyond the material normally found in management accounting books. However, management accountants and others such as politicians and senior managers should be aware of the technical limitations of benchmarking exercises. Organizational resistance is not always based on vested interests.

## Some problems with benchmarking

Using external comparators can lead to criticism on the basis that measures are 'their numbers not ours'. It is therefore important that a consistent set of measures is used with a close match between internal and external indicators. Xerox have overcome this by implementing a structured process based on indicators developed in close collaboration with other people working in industry sectors which have similar operational features. Benchmarking has been described as being a mixed metaphor.[21] On the one hand, we have the language of collaboration with an emphasis on organizational learning. On the other hand, we have descriptions of benchmarking that often convey notions of competition, of being a one-sided attempt by the initiator of the benchmarking exercise to close a perceived performance gap. Even when benchmarking is a public policy initiative, governments often send out a mixed message that both inculcates a 'league table mentality' and tries to nurture a non-blame, learning model.

## Business process re-engineering (BPR)

**Process re-engineering** is a more radical approach to improvement than either TQM or benchmarking. Instead of tweaking the existing system in a series of incremental improvements, a business process is diagrammed in detail, questioned, and then completely redesigned in order to eliminate unnecessary steps, to reduce opportunities for errors, and to reduce costs. A **business process** is any series of steps that is followed in order to carry out some task in a business. For example, the steps followed to make a large seafood pizza at Pizza Hut are a business process. The steps followed by your bank when you deposit a cheque are a business process. While process re-engineering is similar in some respects to TQM, its proponents view it as a more sweeping approach to change. One difference is that while TQM emphasizes a team approach involving people who work directly in the processes, process re-engineering is more likely to be imposed from above and more likely to use outside consultants.

Process re-engineering focuses on *simplification* and *elimination of wasted effort*. A central idea of process re-engineering is that *all activities that do not add value to a product or service should be eliminated*.[22] Activities that do not add value to a product or service that customers are willing to pay for are known as

**non-value-added activities**. For example, moving large batches of work in progress from one workstation to another is a non-value-added activity that can be eliminated by redesigning the factory layout.

The starting point for re-engineering is not 'How do we do something faster or cheaper or better?' but rather 'Why do we do something at all? Is it to meet demands of customers or internal organization?' In short, re-engineering is not piecemeal – it is 'all-or-nothing'.

## What does a re-engineered process look like?

The first step in re-engineering is to look at the underlying process and not at the administrative structure set up to perform it. The aim will be to combine several jobs into one – known as *horizontal compression*. If a process is too much for one person then a case-team will be formed. The aim should be that the workers make decisions. Jobs are vertically compressed through the elimination of hierarchy and checking.

Much re-engineering is enabled through new technology, especially the linkage between a telephone-based customer focused personnel with central databases. Shared databases mean that information can appear simultaneously in as many places as it is needed. *Expert systems* mean that the generalist can do the work of the expert. Telecommunications and portable computers mean that field personnel can send and receive information wherever they are. Paradoxically, organizations are both centralized and decentralized by the new technology. Jobs change from simple tasks to multidimensional work which reduces the work that was created by fragmentation such as checking, reconciling, waiting, monitoring and tracking.

The implications of BPR for management accounting are that management accountants have to be more flexible and work in teams with non-accountants. Accounting work is dispersed and may be done by non-accountants. Non-financial performance measures are more important. The emphasis is on eliminating overhead rather than measuring/allocating it. Organizational structures/departments/budgets are less important than *processes*.

## Some criticisms of re-engineering

In common with other management panaceas, BPR has suffered from over-hyping and from the evangelical language often associated with the management guru. Action that may be easy to write or talk about may be harder to implement in practice. For example, how easy is it for organizations to distinguish between value adding and non-value adding activity? Mistakes have been made where firms took out 'non-value adding' personnel but then subsequently had to re-hire them as they turned out to have created unanticipated value! BPR is likely to face resistance from managers who have been promoted to manage existing structures not take them out!

A recurrent problem in process re-engineering is employee resistance. The cause of much of this resistance is the fear that people may lose their jobs. Workers reason that if process re-engineering succeeds in eliminating non-value-added activities, there will be less work to do and management may be tempted to reduce the payroll. Process re-engineering, if carried out insensitively and without regard to such fears, can undermine morale and will ultimately fail to improve the bottom line (i.e., profits). As with other improvement projects, employees must be convinced that the end result of the improvement will be more secure, rather than less secure, jobs. Real improvement can have this effect if management uses the improvement to generate more business rather than to cut the workforce. If by improving processes the company is able to produce a better product at lower cost, the company will have the competitive strength to prosper. And a prosperous company is a much more secure employer than a company that is in trouble.

## BPR: activity-based management revisited?

In Chapter 8, we saw how ABC has been used to introduce a new rigour into the costing of overheads in both manufacturing and service industries. As **activity-based management (ABM)**, the analysis and costing of processes can be used to identify areas that would benefit from improvements – 'Put simply ABM is ABC in action.'[23] ABM can be combined with benchmarking to provide a systematic approach to identifying the activities with the greatest room for improvement. For example, the Marketing Resources Group of US WEST, the telephone company, performed an ABC analysis of the activities carried out in the Accounting Department.[24] Managers computed the activity rates for the activities of the Accounting Department and then compared these rates to the costs of carrying out the same activities in other companies. Two benchmarks were used: (1) a sample of Fortune 100 companies, which are the largest 100 companies in the United States; and (2) a sample of 'world-class' companies that had been identified by a consultant as having the best accounting practices in the world. These comparisons appear below:

| Activity measure | Activity cost | US WEST | FORTUNE 100 benchmark | World-class benchmark |
|---|---|---|---|---|
| Processing accounts receivable (debtors) | Number of invoices processed | $3.80 per invoice | $15.00 invoice | $4.60 per invoice |
| Processing accounts payable (creditors) | Number of invoices processed | $8.90 per invoice | $7.00 per invoice | $1.80 per invoice |
| Processing payroll cheques | Number of cheques processed | $7.30 per cheque | $5.00 per cheque | $1.72 per cheque |
| Managing customer credit | Number of customer accounts | $12.00 per account | $16.00 account | $5.60 per account |

It is clear from this analysis that US WEST does a good job of processing debtors. Its average cost per invoice is $3.80, whereas the cost in other companies that are considered world class is even higher – $4.60 per invoice. On the other hand, the cost of processing payroll cheques is significantly higher at US WEST than at benchmark companies. The cost per payroll check at US WEST is $7.30 versus $5.00 at Fortune 100 companies and $1.72 at world-class companies. This suggests that it may be possible to wring some waste out of this activity using TQM, process re-engineering or some other method.

## Some problems with ABM

ABM sheds a different interpretation on the true impact of ABC. Beginning with the modest goal of improving the accuracy of the single base absorption system, the ABC/ABM project has expanded into making indirect costs direct. In addition, it has introduced a new 'productivist' agenda to link staff activities to products.[25] Critics of ABM argue that the attempt to count staff functions runs the risk of losing essence of staff functions. Although *some* staff activities may be counted and routinized, both team work and customer relations may suffer because they are hard to measure. Staff may associate most with an accessible, *countable* cost driver so that the volume of activity can be ascertained. The danger then is that the performance of 'activities' will take precedence over original purpose. Both ABM and BPR may mean that *non-routine* staff activity is eliminated even if it creates value for the company.

## Six Sigma

**LEARNING OBJECTIVE 11**

Another approach to business improvement is known as *Six Sigma*. It is a strategic, company-wide, approach that focuses on quality and reliability. The key aims are to:

- Improve quality as perceived by the customer
- Reduce errors (defects) in the process
- Ensure process are capable of producing repeatable outputs
- Reduce the variation in these outputs

## Chapter 18 Business process management: towards the lean operation

- Identify the root causes of quality issues and errors
- Prioritize solution options to make the biggest gain
- Monitor and control processes within defined quality criteria.

The term 'Six Sigma' comes from statistics as the approach focuses on *variation reduction* through statistical analysis. The statistical basis of the approach may be illustrated in Exhibit 18.11 which it is argued that business improvement can come from focusing on *variation from the mean* or rather than average times.

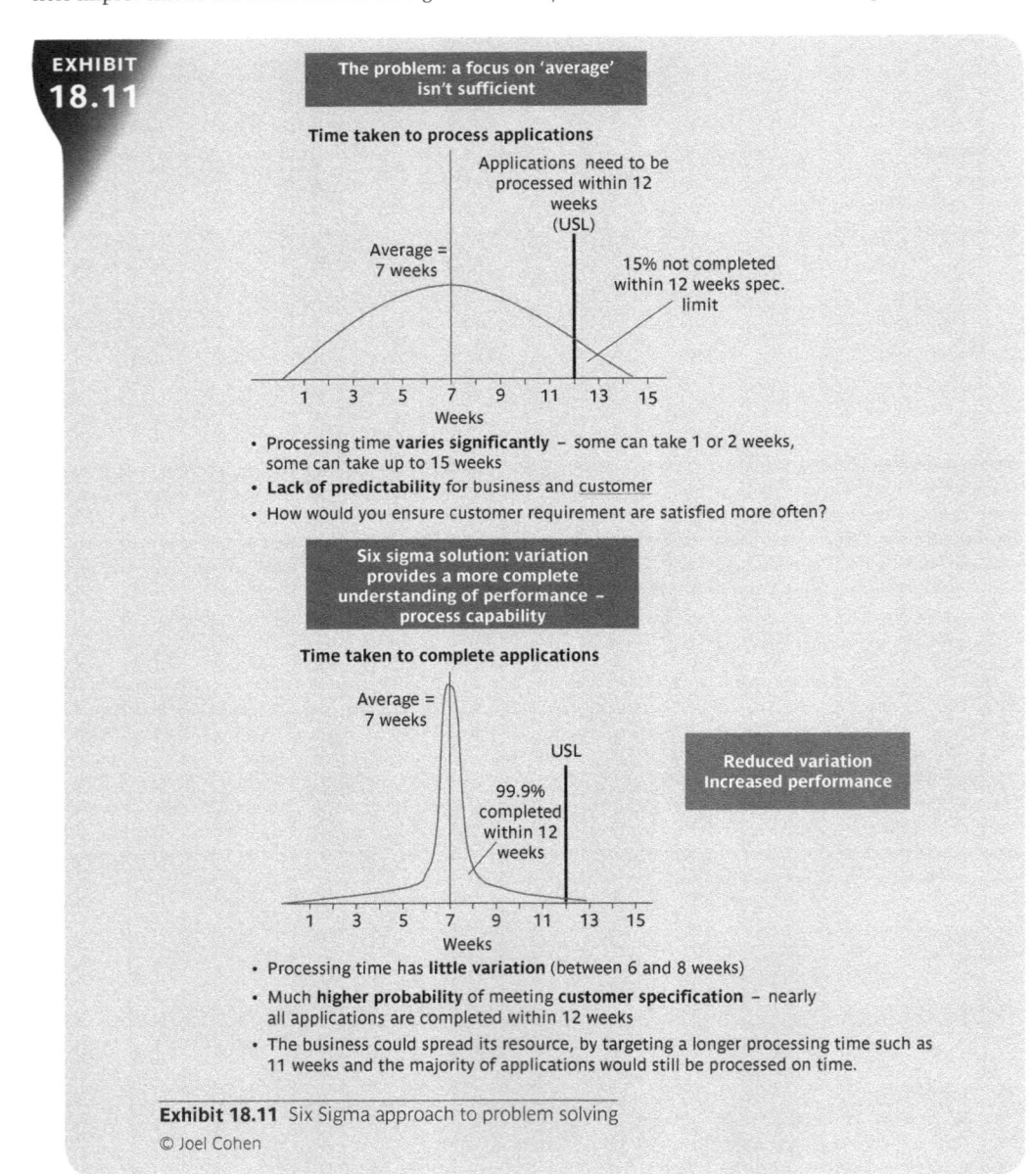

**EXHIBIT 18.11**

**The problem: a focus on 'average' isn't sufficient**

**Time taken to process applications**

Average = 7 weeks

Applications need to be processed within 12 weeks (USL)

15% not completed within 12 weeks spec. limit

Weeks: 1 3 5 7 9 11 13 15

- Processing time **varies significantly** – some can take 1 or 2 weeks, some can take up to 15 weeks
- **Lack of predictability** for business and <u>customer</u>
- How would you ensure customer requirement are satisfied more often?

**Six sigma solution: variation provides a more complete understanding of performance – process capability**

**Time taken to complete applications**

Average = 7 weeks

USL

99.9% completed within 12 weeks

**Reduced variation Increased performance**

Weeks: 1 3 5 7 9 11 13 15

- Processing time has **little variation** (between 6 and 8 weeks)
- Much **higher probability** of meeting **customer specification** – nearly all applications are completed within 12 weeks
- The business could spread its resource, by targeting a longer processing time such as 11 weeks and the majority of applications would still be processed on time.

**Exhibit 18.11** Six Sigma approach to problem solving
© Joel Cohen

## Lean production

Many of the business process improvement tools can be summarized by a very long-standing and robust philosophy known as lean production.[27] Lean enterprises try to organize work around *business processes* rather than on a departmental basis with a traditional emphasis on specialization and a division of labour.

There are five core principles to represent lean production:

1. Specify the *value desired by the customer*
2. Identify the value stream for each product providing that value and challenge all of the *wasted* steps
3. Make the product *flow continuously*
4. Introduce *pull* between all steps where continuous flow is impossible
5. *Manage toward perfection* so that the number of steps and the amount of time and information needed to serve the customer continually falls.

### FOCUS ON PRACTICE

#### Toyota

Many of the business improvement practices introduced in this chapter such as JIT and lean production are associated with the Japanese (and now global) car manufacturer, Toyota. Some well-publicized recalls of recent models do not mean that the business process philosophies and practices are faulty. According to some, Toyota 'remains the benchmark...' and '...stands out for innovating in ways that are likely to shape our future' (Fischer, 2010:12). It has been argued that Toyota 'forgot' some of its principles of quality and knowledge management as it strove for rapid global growth.

In particular, it forgot its 'three nevers' by building a new product, in a new factory with a new workforce.

**Exercise**: Review the important roles played by learning-by-doing/tacit knowledge and attitude of mind for the successful implementation of business process improvement policies.

*Source*: Fischer, B. 2010. That was Kaizen; this is now, *Financial Management*, April, p. 12

## An emphasis on eliminating 'waste'

As can be seen many of the principles of lean may also be found in other approaches to process improvement such as JIT. However, lean production places a great deal of emphasis on the elimination of *waste* where waste is defined as anything that does not add value to the final product or service, in the eyes of the customer; an activity the customer wouldn't want to pay for if they knew it was happening. There are seven possible areas of manufacturing waste: *Transport, Inventory, Motion, Waiting, Overproduction, Over-processing and Defects*. In services, the seven possible areas of waste are: *Delay, Duplication, Unnecessary Movement, Unclear Communication, Incorrect Inventory, Opportunity Lost and Errors*.

> **FOCUS ON PRACTICE**
>
> *Lean in public services*
>
> Although it began in manufacturing, lean thinking has spread to the service sector. In recent years it has also been introduced in the public services. The same principles of focusing on meeting customer needs, streamlining flows along process lines and reducing waste are very relevant. Lean offers potential not only for cost savings but for improving the service offered to citizens and even improving staff morale. All these issues are becoming increasingly important as governments seek to reduce public spending in the post-credit crunch era.
>
> **Exercise**: Consider an organization that you are familiar with. How does that organization generate value for its customers? Are there some areas of the organization that do not seem to be part of that value adding process?
>
> *Source*: In the hot seat: Reducing costs in public sector organizations in an age of austerity, Deloitte Research paper, http://www.deloitte.com/view/en_GB/uk/industries/government-public-sector/, 12 April, 2010

## Lean accounting

In order to support a lean approach to creating value, accounting measures have to be used selectively and supplemented with non-financial performance measures. The key emphasis should be on measuring flow through the whole process rather than on the more traditional approach of local machine or labour utilization. Such measures include production by the hour, cycle times, and so on. The emphasis is on measuring and minimizing stock, work in progress and other forms of working capital such as accounts receivables. Managers need to understand the capacity of the process and constantly seek ways that will increase throughput. Financial information should be timely and relevant. In practice that means providing management information in real time or at least so that operations can be supported as they take place rather than 'after the event'. The emphasis will probably be on contribution costing rather than the more complicated and time-consuming standard costing. Revenues will be based on actual deliveries to customers rather than production for stock. In short, lean synthesizes the key insights of JIT, TQM and TOC. Finally, the philosophy of the accounting system should be on continuous improvement with information that is both forward- and outward-looking data.

## Obstacles to organizational change and the advantages of a fresh start

As we discussed in connection with TQM and benchmarking, whatever the technical strengths of the techniques or whatever the potential improvements identified, there may be significant implementation problems. For this reason, it may be easier to start up an entirely new organization rather than re-engineer an existing one. As the example of low-cost airlines such as easyJet and Ryanair illustrate, radical changes have been achieved by new entrants to the airline industry. Although they are low cost, these carriers generally meet the quality standards that their customers expect from a no-frills service.

## Summary

- This chapter focuses on business processes which may cut across an organization's departments and/or divisions.
- Stock management is an area that has evolved from the optimizing approach of the EOQ model to the sophistication of the build-to-order company. JIT emphasizes the importance of reducing stocks to the barest minimum possible. This reduces working capital requirements, frees up space, reduces throughput time, reduces defects and eliminates waste.
- New information technology such as ERP and the internet offer new ways to optimize not just on stock but on other areas of working capital management.
- Quality costs are summarized on a quality cost report. This report shows the type of quality costs being incurred and their significance and trends. The report helps managers to understand the importance of quality costs, spot problem areas, and assess the way in which the quality costs are distributed.
- The measurement of quality costs may be used as part of a more comprehensive approach – TQM – which involves the use of a number of non-financial as well as financial measures. TQM involves focusing on the customer, and it employs systematic problem solving using teams made up of frontline workers. Specific TQM tools include benchmarking and the plan-do-check-act (PDCA) cycle.
- BPR, a related but generally more radical approach to organizational change, aims to push the analysis and optimization of business processes to higher levels. Process re-engineering involves completely redesigning a business process in order to eliminate non-value-added activities and to reduce opportunities for errors.
- Measures may be used to monitor internal processes, supplier and customer perceptions. Organizations may use these measures as a way of comparing or benchmarking themselves against best practice.
- The techniques of work measurement of BPR and ABM can be seen as job- and cost-cutting exercises. Furthermore, there may be technical difficulties in distinguishing between value- and non-value-adding activities.
- Many of the practices in this chapter are associated with the philosophy of lean production.

## Key terms for review

**Activity-based management (ABM)** (p. 767)
**Appraisal costs** (p. 760)
**Benchmarking** (p. 764)
**Business process** (p. 766)
**Costs of not carrying sufficient stock** (p. 747)
**Economic lot size** (p. 750)
**Economic order quantity (EOQ)** (p. 747)
**Electronic data interchange (EDI)** (p. 757)
**Enterprise resource planning (ERP)** (p. 756)
**External failure costs** (p. 760)
**Internal failure costs** (p. 760)
**Just-in-time (JIT)** (p. 752)
**Lead time** (p. 751)
**Lean production** (p. 747)
**Non-value-added activities** (p. 767)
**Optimizing** (p. 746)
**Plan-do-check-act (PDCA) cycle** (p. 764)
**Prevention costs** (p. 758)
**Process re-engineering** (p. 766)
**Quality circles** (p. 759)
**Quality cost report** (p. 761)
**Quality costs** (p. 758)
**Quality of conformance** (p. 758)
**Reorder point** (p. 751)
**Safety stock** (p. 752)
**Set-up costs** (p. 750)
**Statistical process control** (p. 759)
**Stock carrying costs** (p. 747)
**Stock ordering costs** (p. 747)
**Throughput time** (p. 755)
**Total quality management (TQM)** (p. 764)

## Chapter 18 Business process management: towards the lean operation

**Level of difficulty:** BASIC · INTERMEDIATE · ADVANCED

### Questions

**18-1** What are the three groups of costs associated with the economic order quantity (EOQ) model?
**18-2** What is the potential impact of just-in-time (JIT) purchasing on the EOQ?
**18-3** What trade-offs in costs are involved in computing the EOQ (economic order quantity)?
**18-4** Define lead time and safety stock.
**18-5** In a just-in-time system, what is meant by the pull approach to the flow of goods, as compared to the push approach used in conventional systems?
**18-6** How does the plant layout differ in a company using JIT as compared to a company that uses a more conventional approach to manufacturing? What benefits accrue from a JIT layout?
**18-7** Identify the benefits that can result from reducing the set-up time for a product.
**18-8** How does a workforce in a JIT facility differ from the workforce in a conventional facility?
**18-9** What are the major benefits of a JIT system?
**18-10** What are three benefits and three costs of installing an ERP system?
**18-11** Is there a difference between a virtual company and a dotcom company?
**18-12** Costs associated with the quality of conformance can be broken down into four broad groups. What are these four groups and how do they differ?
**18-13** In their efforts to reduce the total cost of quality, should companies generally focus on decreasing prevention costs and appraisal costs?
**18-14** What is probably the most effective way to reduce a company's total quality costs?
**18-15** What are the main uses of quality cost reports?
**18-16** Why are managers often unaware of the magnitude of quality costs?
**18-17** Explain how the plan-do-check-act cycle applies the scientific method to problem solving.
**18-18** Why is process re-engineering a more radical approach to improvement than total quality management?
**18-19** How can process re-engineering undermine employee morale?
**18-20** Does activity-based costing always precede activity-based management (ABM)?
**18-21** What are the problems in the application of ABM to service areas?

### Exercises

**E18-1** Time allowed: 10 minutes

Listed below are a number of costs that are incurred in connection with a company's quality control system.

(a) Product testing
(b) Product recalls
(c) Rework labour and overhead
(d) Quality circles
(e) Downtime caused by defects
(f) Cost of field servicing
(g) Inspection of goods
(h) Quality engineering

**Part 4** Value metrics and performance management in a strategic context

(i) Warranty repairs
(j) Statistical process control
(k) Net cost of scrap
(l) Depreciation of test equipment
(m) Returns and allowances arising from poor quality
(n) Disposal of defective products
(o) Technical support to suppliers
(p) Systems development
(q) Warranty replacements
(r) Field testing at customer site
(s) Product design

## Required

1 Classify each of the costs above into one of the following categories: prevention cost, appraisal cost, internal failure cost, or external failure cost.
2 Which of the costs in Question 1 above are incurred in an effort to keep poor quality of conformance from occurring? Which of the costs in Question 1 above are incurred because poor quality of conformance has occurred?

### E18–2  Time allowed: 10 minutes

Listed below are a number of terms relating to quality management:

| | |
|---|---|
| Appraisal costs | Quality circles |
| Quality cost report | Prevention costs |
| Quality of conformance | External failure costs |
| Internal failure costs | Quality costs |

## Required

Choose the term or terms that most appropriately complete the following statements. The terms can be used more than once. (A fill-in blank can hold more than one word.)

1 A product that has a high rate of defects is said to have a low _____.
2 All of the costs associated with preventing and dealing with defects once they occur are known as _____.
3 In many companies, small groups of employees, known as _____, meet on a regular basis to discuss ways to improve quality.
4 A company incurs _____ and _____ in an effort to keep defects from occurring.
5 A company incurs _____ and _____ because defects have occurred.
6 Of the four groups of costs associated with quality of conformance, _____ are generally the most damaging to a company.
7 Inspection, testing, and other costs incurred to keep defective products from being shipped to customers are known as _____.
8 _____ are incurred in an effort to eliminate poor product design, defective manufacturing practices, and the providing of substandard service.
9 The costs relating to defects, rejected products, and downtime caused by quality problems are known as _____.

Chapter 18 Business process management: towards the lean operation

10 When a product that is defective in some way is delivered to a customer, _____ are incurred.
11 Over time a company's total quality costs should decrease if it redistributes its quality costs by placing its greatest emphasis on _____ and _____.
12 One way to ensure that management is aware of the costs associated with quality is to summarize such costs on a _____.

**E18–3** Time allowed: 30 minutes

The management at Megafilters Ltd has been discussing the possible implementation of a just-in-time (JIT) production system at its Sheffield plant, where oil and air filters are manufactured. The Metal Stamping Department at the Sheffield plant has already instituted a JIT system for controlling raw materials inventory, but the remainder of the plant is still discussing how to proceed with the implementation of this concept. The Metal Stamping Department implemented JIT with no advance planning, and some of the other department managers have become uneasy about adopting JIT after hearing about the problems that have arisen.

Robert Goertz, manager of the Sheffield plant, is a strong proponent of the JIT approach. He recently made the following statement at a meeting of all departmental managers:

We will all have to make many changes in the way we think about our employees, our suppliers and our customers if we are going to be successful in using JIT procedures. Rather than dwelling on some of the negative things you have heard from the Metal Stamping Department, I want each of you to prepare a list of things we can do to make a smooth transition to the JIT approach for the rest of the plant.

### Required

1 The JIT approach has several characteristics that distinguish it from conventional production systems. Describe these characteristics.
2 For the JIT approach to be successful, Megafilters Ltd must establish appropriate relationships with its suppliers. Describe these relationships under JIT.

(*CMA*, adapted)

**E18–4** Time allowed: 15 minutes

Kaufheim AG of Dresden, Germany, distributes medical supplies throughout Germany. Selected information relating to a quick-developing X-ray film carried by the company is given below:

| Economic order quantity (EOQ) | 700 units |
| Maximum weekly usage | 60 units |
| Lead time | 4 weeks |
| Average weekly usage | 50 units |

Management is trying to determine the proper safety stock to carry on this item and to determine the proper reorder point.

### Required

1 Assume that no safety stock is to be carried. What is the reorder point?
2 Assume that a full safety stock is to be carried.
   (a) What would be the size of the safety stock in units?
   (b) What would be the reorder point?

**E18–5** Time allowed: 20 minutes

Flint Company uses 9,000 units of part AK-4 each year. To get better control over its stock, the company is anxious to determine the economic order quantity (EOQ) for this part.

Part 4 Value metrics and performance management in a strategic context

## Required

1. The company has determined that the cost to place an order for the part is £30, and it has determined that the cost to carry one part in stock for one year is £1.50. Compute the EOQ for the part.
2. Assume that the cost to place an order increases from £30 to £40 per order. What will be the effect on the EOQ? Show computations.
3. Assume that the cost to carry a part in stock increases from £1.50 to £2.00 per part. (Ordering costs remain unchanged at £30 per order.) What will be the effect on the EOQ? Show computations.
4. In Questions 2 and 3 above, why does an increase in cost cause the EOQ to go up in one case and to go down in the other?

## Problems

**P18–6** JIT; process re-engineering
Time allowed: 30 minutes

Snedden Products manufactures athletic equipment, including footballs. The footballs are manufactured in several steps, which are listed below:

1. Leather and other materials are received at a centrally located dock where the materials are checked to be sure they conform to exacting company standards. Rejected materials are returned to the supplier.
2. Acceptable materials are transported to a stores warehouse pending use in production.
3. A materials requisition form is issued, and materials are transferred from the stores warehouse to the Cutting Department where all cutting equipment is located.
4. Since the Cutting Department cuts materials for a variety of products, the leather is placed on large pallets and stationed by the appropriate machines.
5. The leather and other materials are cut to proper shape, with the operator taking care to cut all sections of a football from a single piece of leather. Waste materials are placed in a bin, and at the end of each day the materials are sorted to reclaim the items that can be used in manufacturing other products.
6. Each cut item of material is examined by one of three checkers to ensure uniformity of cut, thickness of the leather, and direction of the grain. Rejected pieces are tossed in the scrap bin.
7. Cut materials are placed on pallets and transferred to the Centralized Sewing Department, where the pallets are placed in a staging area.
8. Materials are taken from the pallets, the company's name and logo are stamped into one section of each set of cut pieces, and the pieces are then sewed together.
9. The sewn pieces are placed in bins, which are then transferred to the staging area of the Assembly Department.
10. An operator in the Assembly Department installs a lining in the football, stitches the ball closed with a stitching machine, and then inflates it.
11. The completed footballs are placed on a conveyor belt that passes by another set of checkers. Each ball is checked for uniformity of shape and for other potential defects.
12. Completed footballs are boxed and transferred to the finished goods warehouse.

## Required

Assume that the company adopts JIT inventory practices and establishes individual product flow lines. Explain what changes would have to be made in manufacturing procedures and prepare a sketch of how the football product flow line would be arranged.

**P18–7** EOQ
Time allowed: 30 minutes

A company uses Material Z (cost £3.50 per kg) in the manufacture of Products A and B. The following forecast information is provided for the year ahead:

Chapter 18 Business process management: towards the lean operation

|  | Product A | Product B |
|---|---|---|
| Sales (units) | 24,600 | 9,720 |
| Finished goods stock increase by year end (units) | 447 | 178 |
| Post-production rejection rate (%) | 1% | 2% |
| Material Z usage (kg per completed unit, net of wastage) | 1.8 | 3.0 |
| Material Z wastage (%) | 5% | 11% |

Additional information:

- Average purchasing lead time for Material Z is two weeks.
- Usage of Material Z is expected to be even over the year.
- Annual stock holding costs are 18% of the material cost.
- The cost of placing orders is £30 per order.
- The reorder level for Material Z is set at the average usage in average lead time, plus 1,000 kg of safety (buffer) stock.

Required

1 State two items that would be regarded as 'stock holding costs' and explain how they may be controlled effectively.
2 Calculate for the year ahead:
    (a) the required production of Products A and B (in units)
    (b) the total requirement for Material Z (in kgs)
    (c) the economic order quantity for Material Z (in kgs).
3 Calculate the average stock investment (£) and the annual stock holding costs (£) for Material Z.

*(ACCA Management Information)*

**P18-8 Stock management**
Time allowed: 25 minutes

A traditional view of the environment in which goods are manufactured and sold is where stocks of materials and components are held. Such stocks are then used to manufacture products to agreed standard specifications, aiming at maximizing the use of production capacity. Finished goods are held in stock to satisfy steady demand for the product range at agreed prices.

Required

1 Discuss aspects of the operation of the management accounting function which are likely to apply in the above system.
2 Describe an alternative sequence from purchasing to the satisfaction of customer demand, which may be more applicable in the current business environment. Your answer should refer to the current 'techniques or philosophies' which are likely to be in use.
3 Name specific ways in which changes suggested in Question 2 will affect the operation of the management accounting function.

*(ACCA Information for Control and Decision Making)*

**P18-9 Economic order quantity (EOQ); safety stock**
Time allowed: 30 minutes

Myron Metal Works uses a small casting in one of its finished products. The castings are purchased from a foundry located in another state. In total, Myron Metal Works purchases 54,000 castings per year at a cost of £8 per casting. The castings are used evenly throughout the year in the production process on a 360-day-per-year basis. The company estimates that it costs £90 to place a single purchase order and about £3 to carry one casting in inventory for a year. The high carrying costs result from the need to keep the castings in carefully controlled temperature and humidity conditions, and from the high cost of insurance. Delivery from the foundry generally takes 6 days, but it can take as much as 10 days. The days of delivery time and the percentage of their occurrence are shown in the following tabulation:

| Delivery time (days) | Percentage of occurrence |
|---|---|
| 1–6 | 75% |
| 7 | 10% |
| 8 | 5% |
| 9 | 5% |
| 10 | 5% |
|  | 100% |

### Required

1. Compute the economic order quantity (EOQ).
2. Assume that the company is willing to assume a 15% risk of being out of stock. What would be the safety stock? The reorder point?
3. Assume that the company is willing to assume only a 5% risk of being out of stock. What would be the safety stock? The reorder point?
4. Assume a 5% stockout risk as stated in (3) above. What would be the total cost of ordering and carrying inventory for one year?
5. Refer to the original data. Assume that using process re-engineering the company reduces its cost of placing a purchase order to only £6. Also, the company estimates that when the waste and inefficiency caused by inventories are considered, the true cost of carrying a unit in stock is £7.20 per year.
   (a) Compute the new EOQ.
   (b) How frequently would the company be placing an order, as compared to the old purchasing policy?

**P18-10** Time allowed: 45 minutes

The management team of WZX is about to start preparing the budgets for the year ending 31 December 2010. Relevant information is given below:

### Sales

The predicted sales for 2010 are as follows:

|  | Quarter |  |  |  |  |
|---|---|---|---|---|---|
|  | 1 | 2 | 3 | 4 | Total |
| Sales (units) | 25,799 | 24,078 | 34,763 | 39,820 | 124,460 |

Sales demand is the principal budget factor.

### Costs

The production costs have been predicted to be:

| Materials | £15 per unit, but if production exceeds 30,000 units in a quarter a discount of 5% will be allowed on all units in the quarter. |
|---|---|
| Labour | £25 per unit in normal time. However, if production exceeds 30,000 units in a quarter, overtime will have to be worked and costs will rise to £38 per unit for those in excess of 30,000 in the quarter. |
| *Overheads* | |
| Variable | £10 per unit at all levels of activity. |
| Fixed | £100,000 per quarter for up to 30,000 units produced, but rising by 20% if output exceeds 30,000 units. |

### Stocks

WZX uses a just-in-time (JIT) system for raw materials.

It is company policy that there should be no stock of finished goods at the start of any year. Finished goods are valued at the budgeted average annual marginal production cost per unit.

### Production schedule

The total annual production requirement will be scheduled to be produced in equal amounts in the four quarters.

### Costing system

WZX uses a marginal costing system based on the budgeted average annual cost per unit.

### Required

1. Prepare the production cost of sales budget for WZX for 2010 on the basis of its current purchasing, production and stock holding policies and its use of marginal costing. You should show the costs of each quarter and the total for the year.
2. The management of WZX is thinking of extending its use of a JIT approach to include finished goods and production.
   Prepare the production cost of sales budget for 2010 on the basis of this policy change. You should show the costs of each quarter and the total for the year.
3. Explain the reasons for the differences in materials, labour and fixed overhead costs in your answers to parts (a) and (b) above.
4. Sales demand in 2011 is expected to be subject to seasonal fluctuations, as it has been in previous years. These seasonal variations are expected to be as follows:

| Quarter | 1 | 2 | 3 | 4 |
|---|---|---|---|---|
| % variation | − 10 | − 20 | + 10 | + 20 |

Assume that sales for Quarter 3 of 2010 will be 34,763 units and will continue to show an underlying growth of 5% per quarter. This trend of underlying growth is expected to continue throughout 2011.

Prepare a forecast of the sales volumes expected for each quarter of 2011.

(CIMA *Performance Management*, adapted)

**P18-11 Quality cost report**
Time allowed: 60 minutes

In response to intensive foreign competition, the management of Florex Company has attempted over the past year to improve the quality of its products. A statistical process control system has been installed and

**780** Part 4 Value metrics and performance management in a strategic context

other steps have been taken to decrease the amount of warranty and other field costs, which have been trending upward over the past several years. Costs relating to quality and quality control over the last two years are given below:

|  | This year | Last year |
| --- | --- | --- |
| Inspection | £900,000 | £750,000 |
| Quality engineering | 570,000 | 420,000 |
| Depreciation of test equipment | 240,000 | 210,000 |
| Rework labour | 1,500,000 | 1,050,000 |
| Statistical process control | 180,000 | – |
| Cost of field servicing | 900,000 | 1,200,000 |
| Supplies used in testing | 60,000 | 30,000 |
| Systems development | 750,000 | 480,000 |
| Warranty repairs | 1,050,000 | 3,600,000 |
| Net cost of scrap | 1,125,000 | 630,000 |
| Product testing | 1,200,000 | 810,000 |
| Product recalls | 750,000 | 2,100,000 |
| Disposal of defective products | 975,000 | 720,000 |

Sales have been flat over the past few years, at £75,000,000 per year. A great deal of money has been spent in the effort to upgrade quality, and management is anxious to see whether or not the effort has been effective.

### Required

1 Prepare a quality cost report that contains data for both this year and last year. Carry percentage computations to two decimal places.
2 Prepare a bar graph showing the distribution of the various quality costs by category.
3 Prepare a written evaluation to accompany the reports you have prepared in Questions 1 and 2 above. This evaluation should discuss the distribution of quality costs in the company, changes in this distribution that you see taking place, the reasons for changes in costs in the various categories, and any other information that would be of value to management.

**P18–12 Quality cost report**
Time allowed: 60 minutes

'Maybe the emphasis we've placed on upgrading our quality control system will pay off in the long run, but it doesn't seem to be helping us much right now,' said Renee Penretti, managing director of Halogen Products. 'I thought improved quality would give a real boost to sales, but sales have remained flat at £50,000,000 for the last two years.'

Halogen Products has seen its market share decline in recent years due to increased foreign competition. An intensive effort to strengthen the quality control system was initiated at the beginning of the current year in the hope that better quality would strengthen the company's competitive position and also reduce warranty and servicing costs. Costs relating to quality and quality control over the last two years are given below:

## Chapter 18 Business process management: towards the lean operation

|  | This year | Last year |
|---|---|---|
| Product testing | £800,000 | £490,000 |
| Rework labour | 1,000,000 | 700,000 |
| Systems development | 530,000 | 320,000 |
| Warranty repairs | 700,000 | 2,100,000 |
| Net cost of scrap | 620,000 | 430,000 |
| Supplies used in testing | 30,000 | 20,000 |
| Field servicing | 600,000 | 900,000 |
| Quality engineering | 400,000 | 280,000 |
| Warranty replacements | 90,000 | 300,000 |
| Inspection | 600,000 | 380,000 |
| Product recalls | 410,000 | 1,700,000 |
| Statistical process control | 370,000 | – |
| Disposal of defective products | 380,000 | 270,000 |
| Depreciation of testing equipment | 170,000 | 110,000 |

### Required

1. Prepare a quality cost report that contains data for both years. Carry percentage computations to two decimal places.
2. Prepare a bar graph showing the distribution of the various quality costs by category.
3. Prepare a written evaluation to accompany the reports you have prepared in Questions 1 and 2 above. This evaluation should discuss the distribution of quality costs in the company, changes in this distribution that you detect have taken place over the last year, and any other information you believe would be useful to management.

**P18–13 Analysing a quality cost report**
Time allowed: 45 minutes

Mercury Ltd produces pagers at its plant in Essex. In recent years, the company's market share has been eroded by stiff competition from overseas competitors. Price and product quality are the two key areas in which companies compete in this market.

A year ago, the company's pagers had been ranked low in product quality in a consumer survey. Shocked by this result, Steve Davis, Mercury's managing director, initiated a crash effort to improve product quality. Davis set up a task force to implement a formal quality improvement programme. Included on this task force were representatives from the Engineering, Marketing, Customer Service, Production, and Accounting departments. The broad representation was needed because Davis believed that this was a company-wide programme and that all employees should share the responsibility for its success.

After the first meeting of the task force, Holly Elsoe, manager of the Marketing Department, asked John Tran, production manager, what he thought of the proposed programme. Tran replied, 'I have reservations. Quality is too abstract to be attaching costs to it and then to be holding you and me responsible for cost improvements. I like to work with goals that I can see and count! I'm nervous about having my annual bonus based on a decrease in quality costs; there are too many variables that we have no control over.'

Mercury's quality improvement programme has now been in operation for one year. The company's most recent quality cost report is shown below.

**Part 4** Value metrics and performance management in a strategic context

| Mercury Ltd Quality cost report (in thousands) | | |
|---|---|---|
| | **This year** | **Last year** |
| Prevention costs: | | |
| Machine maintenance | £120 | £70 |
| Training suppliers | 10 | – |
| Quality circles | 20 | – |
| Total | 150 | 70 |
| Appraisal costs: | | |
| Incoming inspection | 40 | 20 |
| Final testing | 90 | 80 |
| Total | 130 | 100 |
| Internal failure costs: | | |
| Rework | 130 | 50 |
| Scrap | 70 | 40 |
| Total | 200 | 90 |
| External failure costs: | | |
| Warranty repairs | 30 | 90 |
| Customer returns | 80 | 320 |
| Total | 110 | 410 |
| Total quality cost | £590 | £670 |
| Total production cost | £4,800 | £4,200 |

As they were reviewing the report, Elsoe asked Tran what he now thought of the quality improvement programme. Tran replied. 'I'm relieved that the new quality improvement programme hasn't hurt our bonuses, but the programme has increased the workload in the Production Department. It is true that customer returns are way down, but the pagers that were returned by customers to retail outlets were rarely sent back to us for rework.'

### Required

1 Expand the company's quality cost report by showing the costs in both years as percentages of both total production cost and total quality cost. Carry all computations to one decimal place. By analysing the report, determine if Mercury's quality improvement programme has been successful. List specific evidence to support your answer.
2 Do you expect the improvement programme as it progresses to continue to increase the workload in the Production Department?
3 Steve Davis believed that the quality improvement programme was essential and that Mercury, could no longer afford to ignore the importance of product quality. Discuss how Mercury could measure the cost of not implementing the quality improvement programme.

(*CMA*, adapted)

**P18–14** **ABC and ABM internet**
Time allowed: 60 minutes

S & P Products plc purchases a range of good quality gift and household products from around the world; it then sells these products through 'mail order' or retail outlets. The company receives 'mail orders' by post, telephone and internet. Retail outlets are either department stores or S & P Products plc's own small shops. The company started to set up its own shops after a recession in the early 1990s and regards them as the

Chapter 18 Business process management: towards the lean operation

flagship of its business; sales revenue has gradually built up over the last 10 years. There are now 50 department stores and 10 shops.

The company has made good profits over the last few years but recently trading has been difficult. As a consequence, the management team has decided that a fundamental reappraisal of the business is now necessary if the company is to continue trading.

Meanwhile the budgeting process for the coming year is proceeding. S & P Products plc uses an activity-based costing (ABC) system and the following estimated cost information for the coming year is available:

| | Retail outlet costs | | | |
|---|---|---|---|---|
| | | | Number each year for | |
| Activity | Cost driver | Rate per cost driver | Department store | Own shop |
| Telephone queries and requests to S & P | Calls | 15 | 40 | 350 |
| Sales visits to shops and stores by S & P sales staff | Visits | 250 | 2 | 4 |
| Shop orders | Orders | 20 | 25 | 150 |
| Packaging deliveries | | 100 | 28 | 150 |
| Delivery to shops | Deliveries | 150 | 28 | 150 |

Staffing, rental and service costs for each of S & P Products plc's own shops cost on average £300,000 a year.

| | Mail order costs | | | |
|---|---|---|---|---|
| | | Rate per cost driver | | |
| Activity | Cost driver | Post £ | Telephone £ | Internet £ |
| Processing 'mail orders' | Orders | 5 | 6 | 3 |
| Dealing with 'mail order' queries | Orders | 4 | 4 | 1 |
| | | Number of packages per order | | |
| Packaging and deliveries for 'mail orders' – cost per package £10 | Packages | 2 | 2 | 1 |

The total number of orders through the whole 'mail order' business for the coming year is expected to be 80,000. The maintenance of the internet link is estimated to cost £80,000 for the coming year.

The following additional information for the coming year has been prepared:

| | Department store | Own shop | Post | Telephone | Internet |
|---|---|---|---|---|---|
| Sales revenue per outlet | £50,000 | £1,000,000 | | | |
| Sales revenue per order | | | £150 | £300 | £100 |
| Gross margin: mark-up on purchase cost | 30% | 40% | 40% | 40% | 40% |
| Number of outlets | 50 | 10 | | | |
| Percentage of 'mail orders' | | | 30% | 60% | 10% |

## Part 4 Value metrics and performance management in a strategic context

Expected Head Office and warehousing costs for the coming year:

|  | £ |
|---|---|
| Warehouse | 2,750,000 |
| IT | 550,000 |
| Administration | 750,000 |
| Personnel | 300,000 |
|  | 4,350,000 |

### Required

1. (a) Prepare calculations that will show the expected profitability of the different types of sales outlet for the coming year.
   (b) Comment briefly on the results of the figures you have prepared.
2. In relation to the company's fundamental reappraisal of its business,
   (a) discuss how helpful the information you have prepared in Question 1 is for this purpose and how it might be revised or expanded so that it is of more assistance;
   (b) advise what other information is needed in order to make a more informed judgement.

*(CIMA Management Accounting – Decision Making)*

### P18–15 ABC/ABM
Time allowed: 50 minutes

FF plc is a bank that offers a variety of banking services to its clients. One of the services offered is aimed at high net worth individuals and the bank is currently reviewing the performance of its client base. The high net worth clients are classified into four groups based on the value of their individual liquid assets deposited in FF plc. The following annual budgeted information has been prepared:

| Group | W | X | Y | Z |
|---|---|---|---|---|
| Individual value (000s) | $500–$999 | $1,000–$2,999 | $3,000–$5,999 | $6,000–$9,999 |
| Number of clients | 1,000 | 1,500 | 2,000 | 1,800 |
|  | $000 | $000 | $000 | $000 | Total $000 |
| Total contribution | 500 | 900 | 1,400 | 2,500 | 5,300 |
| Overheads: |  |  |  |  |  |
| Share of support costs | 285 | 760 | 790 | 1,165 | 3,000 |
| Share of facility costs | 100 | 160 | 240 | 500 | 1,000 |
| Profit/(loss) | 115 | (20) | 370 | 835 | 1,300 |

FF plc is about to implement an activity-based costing (ABC) system. The implementation team recently completed an analysis of the support costs. The analysis revealed that these costs were variable in relation to certain drivers. The details of the analysis are shown below.

| Group<br>Activity | W<br>000s | X<br>000s | Y<br>000s | Z<br>000s | Total<br>000s |
|---|---|---|---|---|---|
| Number of telephone enquiries | 200 | 150 | 220 | 300 | 870 |
| Number of statements prepared | 120 | 120 | 240 | 480 | 960 |
| Number of client meetings | 60 | 100 | 110 | 200 | 470 |

| Activity | Support costs/Overheads $000 |
|---|---|
| Telephone enquiries | 1,000 |
| Statements prepared | 250 |
| Client meetings | 1,750 |
| Total | 3,000 |

The Bank Manager feels that the low profitability from client Group W and the losses from client Group X need to be investigated further and that consideration should be given to discontinuing these services and concentrating the marketing and sales effort on increasing the number of clients within Group Y and Group Z. He has outlined two proposals, as follows:

### Proposal 1

Discontinue both of Groups W and X in order to concentrate on Groups Y and Z (so that the bank would have only two client groups). If this option were implemented, it is expected that the facility costs would increase by 10%.

The Marketing Manager has calculated the probability of the number of clients the bank would serve to be as shown below.

| Projected revised numbers of clients in Groups Y and Z |||| 
|---|---|---|---|
| [Group Y] || [Group Z] ||
| Client numbers | Probability | Client numbers | Probability |
| 2,250 | 0.30 | 2,000 | 0.20 |
| 2,500 | 0.40 | 2,200 | 0.50 |
| 2,750 | 0.30 | 2,500 | 0.30 |

### Proposal 2

Discontinue either Group W or Group X in order to concentrate on Groups Y and Z (so that the bank would have three client groups). If this option were implemented, it is expected that the facility costs would increase by 8%.

If this proposal is implemented, the Marketing Manager estimates that the increase in client numbers in Groups Y and Z would be reduced by 75%, compared with proposal 1.

### Required

1. Prepare a customer profitability statement based on the ABC analysis and comment on your results.
2. Using the ABC details, evaluate the proposal of the Bank Manager (your answer must be supported by calculations).
3. When the bank's annual budget was prepared, it was thought that the bank would have a 25% share of the total market of 10,000 Group Y clients. However, for that year the total market size was 9,500 Group Y clients, of which the bank had 2,750.
   (a) Calculate on a contribution per unit basis the
   - market size variance,
   - market share variance.
   (b) Explain and interpret these variances for the bank.

*(CIMA – Decision Making)*

## P18-16 Process accounting/quality report
⏱ Time allowed: 50 minutes

LMN produces a compound T5, which is used to manufacture tyres. The compound, which earns a contribution of £6 per tonne, is produced by mixing two materials, R1 and R2, in a common process. The process causes the production of a by-product Z, which can be sold without further processing for £5 per tonne. The process is inefficient and large losses occur. The losses can currently only be identified at the completion of the process.

### Process details

In addition to the costs of materials R1 and R2, variable and fixed processing costs are incurred. The expected inputs and outputs of the process are as follows:

| Input: | equal quantities of R1 and R2 |
|---|---|
| Outputs: | T5: 60% of weight of new input |
|  | Z: 10% of weight of new input |
| Loss: | 30% of weight of new input |

### Data for October

Opening work in progress 200 tonnes of T5 fully complete in respect of materials, but only 30% converted. This stock was valued at £450.

| Inputs: | |
|---|---|
| Materials: | 24,000 tonnes of R1 costing £60,480 |
|  | 24,000 tonnes of R2 costing £24,000 |
| Conversion costs: | Variable £36,125 |
| Fixed | £39,015 |
| Outputs | T5: 28,800 tonnes |
| Z: | 4,800 tonnes |

Closing work in progress 200 tonnes of T5 fully complete in respect of materials, but only 80% converted.

*Note*: By-product Z is not considered to be a major source of income and consequently the revenue generated by its sale is credited to the process account.

### Required

1. Prepare the process account for LMN for the month of October using a First In, First Out (FIFO) basis of valuation. Show all your workings.
2. The production director of LMN has been investigating alternative production methods to reduce the loss that arises in the process. Two alternatives have been identified:
   (a) to change the mix of input materials R1 and R2, such that twice as much R1 is used compared to R2. Conversion costs would not be affected and trials have suggested that this would reduce the expected loss to 15% of the materials input during a period with no effect on the output of the by-product.
   (b) to introduce a quality control procedure that would enable any loss to be identified and the units rejected after 60% of the conversion costs had been incurred. It is expected that the quantity of the normal loss will remain at 30% of the input to the process. There would be no capital expenditure costs associated with this quality control procedure, but other costs would comprise £0.20 for every

tonne of input materials processed together with a fixed cost of £1,000 per month. The quantity of the by-product produced and its continued saleability would not be affected by this proposed inspection process.

Evaluate each of the separate alternatives (a) and (b) above and recommend which, if either, should be adopted by LMN. Show all your workings.

3   As a management accountant, prepare a report addressed to the Board of Directors of LMN that explains the costs and benefits that would arise following the adoption of a Quality Control Programme. Your answer should refer to the different quality cost classifications that would be used and also to non-financial factors.

*(CIMA Management Accounting – Performance Management)*

## Cases

### C18–17 Strategy and the internet
Time allowed: 75 minutes

FNJ is a company, which has developed business interests in the very competitive music industry. It produces and sells compact discs (CDs) and traces its history back to when it manufactured vinyl records. It is contracted to produce CDs for many famous recording artists which it is able to distribute through its own worldwide chain of retail music stores.

A new Chief Executive (CJ), who came from an unrelated business, was appointed to run FNJ about 12 months ago. The financial situation for the company has become perilous with falling worldwide sales and difficult trading conditions. The company has issued a number of profit warnings and experienced severe management disputes which have been made public. The result of these factors has been a low share price. CJ implemented cost reductions at FNJ and developed a strategy which focuses the company's attention on the provision of music to customers via the internet, with the eventual aim of replacing CDs with internet sales in the years to come.

WT is a large entertainments group which has growing business interests in producing motion pictures (movies) and retail outlets (trading under its own brand name of WT). The company is well regarded worldwide within its industry. It has augmented the product range with, for example, soft toys (related to its popular movie characters) which are sold through its retail outlets.

### The merger

A merger deal has recently been agreed between the directors of FNJ and WT. This has yet to be ratified by both sets of shareholders, but it is expected to be accepted. The new group (FW) aims to achieve a high market share of total worldwide music sales. Following the merger, it is expected that the two companies will shed jobs throughout the world in the interests of improving efficiency. The contracts for some of the recording artists who are not achieving high sales will not be renewed.

### Financial summary of the merger

The following details highlight the main points relating to the merger:

1   The merger is worth £10 billion in terms of total asset value.
2   WT has 8 seats while FNJ has 7 seats on the new board of FW.
3   CJ will be the Chief Executive of FW.
4   Shares in FW will be allocated in proportion to the current shareholdings. This will result in each company's shareholders holding 50% of the shares.
5   Directors' share options come to fruition on completion of the merger.
6   The share price of FNJ rose by 11% after the merger was announced.

## 788 Part 4 Value metrics and performance management in a strategic context

### Selected details relating to FNJ and WT before the proposed merger

|  | CDs (FNJ) | |
|---|---|---|
|  | Last year | 2 years ago |
| Actual sales | £90 million | £95 million |
| Budgeted sales | £100 million | £100 million |
| Average actual price per CD | £20 | £20 |
| Average actual cost per CD (1/3 of this is variable cost) | £12 | £12 |
| Average budgeted price per CD | £22 | £20 |
| Average budgeted cost per CD (1/3 of this is variable cost) | £15 | £10.5 |

The average annual sales of CDs over the last 5 years were £100 million. The trend of changes in sales levels for CDs which has been apparent over the last two years is expected to continue.

| | Motion pictures (WT) | | | |
|---|---|---|---|---|
| | Last year | 2 years ago | 3 years ago | 4 years ago |
| Total revenue | £2,000 million | £1,800 million | £1,400 million | £1,000 million |
| Total costs | £1,900 million | £1,600 million | £1,100 million | £700 million |
| | Retail music stores (operated by FNJ) | | | |
| | Last year | 2 years ago | 3 years ago | 4 years ago |
| Total revenue | £140 million | £138 million | £136 million | £135 million |
| Total costs | £136 million | £131 million | £134 million | £135 million |

The resale value of FNJ's retail music stores is reducing because of the increasing popularity of alternative methods of shopping.

### Strategic development of FW

CJ has forecast that next year sales of music will be available through the internet with digital downloading to the customer's own personal computer. At the moment, most of the FNJ retail music stores' revenue is generated by the sale of FNJ-produced CDs. He believes that by supplying customers through the internet, overall sales revenue (combining internet sales with CDs), will increase by 20%. The average variable costs for internet sales will reduce by 25% on that currently incurred in CD production. This cost reduction is expected as a result of not needing to employ expensive recording studios which are currently required to produce a CD.

The average selling price and average variable cost of a CD are expected to remain at £20 and £4 respectively throughout next year. The average selling price of each internet sale is also expected to be £20.

Independent research has revealed that the market for digitally downloaded music is forecast to grow next year. Customers will have the opportunity to create their own 'do it yourself' compilation albums.

Some of FW's competitors have already made effective use of the internet to distribute CDs and videos, undercutting high street retailers on price. However, digital download through the internet is still experimental.

### Required

1 Discuss the dynamic nature of the business environment experienced by FNJ and WT, and explain the rationale for the merger.

2  (a)  Analyse the business performance of CDs, motion pictures and FNJ's retail music stores over the period contained in the scenario. Include calculations on the projected change in contribution each year for CD and internet sales if CJ's forecast is accurate.

(b)  Calculate and analyse the contribution volume variance relating to CD sales for last year and two years ago.

(c)  Recommend ways in which the directors of FW should pursue the strategic development of the CD, motion pictures and FNJ's retail music stores businesses.

(Abbreviated version from *CIMA Management Accounting – Business Strategy*)

**C18-18  Stock management and new technology**
Time allowed: 90 minutes

CLB is a profitable manufacturer of clothes with an annual turnover of $650 million. The organization sells by mail order from a paper catalogue sent out to customers and via a website. There are approximately 2.5 million customers on the sales database. Customers spend on average $110 per order.

Clothes are manufactured in 10 different factories, with finished goods being transferred to a central warehouse, where they are placed onto the computerized stock system for internet and catalogue sales. All customer orders are routed to the central warehouse; the factories do not have any sales facilities.

The clothes produced by CLB are fashionable, with most customers being satisfied by the range available. A recent move to sourcing more supplies from overseas has helped to cut costs, although there is increasing competition from some low-cost imports.

### Company aims and mission

The mission of the organization is 'to produce a wide range of reasonably priced clothes that appeal to the majority of the population'. To meet this objective, CLB has three main *critical success factors (CSFs)*:

- Maintain overall gross profit at 40% of sales
- Increase customer satisfaction each year
- Minimize raw material inventory cost.

A 40% gross profit percentage is slightly above the industry standard, but thought to be achievable by the Board of CLB. The organization needs to sell $600 million of clothes each year to break even.

Maintenance of customer satisfaction is essential to selling clothes. However, the directors have had some difficulty in establishing appropriate *performance indicators (PIs)* to measure the CSFs.

Maintaining control over inventory is essential; not only does raw material stock tie up working capital, but any unused raw materials are difficult to dispose of. Changes in fashion mean that raw material stock becomes obsolete very quickly. Finished goods stocks are easier to dispose of – completed garments can normally be sold at cost price or slightly above ensuring that some contribution is made.

### Trends in sales

For a number of years, the Board of CLB has been concerned that the brand awareness of the company's products has been falling. Sales of new product lines have also been less than budgeted, both in absolute terms and in comparison to similar clothes produced by competitors.

(Information on competitor sales is obtained from their published accounts and for some products from the *Clothing Gazette*, a trade journal.) The fall in brand awareness and sales has provided a *decision trigger* to the directors that some amendments may be required to the information systems in CLB. However, they are unclear regarding the information to be obtained to help them make this decision.

### CLB information system

At present, each of the 10 factories of CLB maintains its own information system to provide detail on raw material stocks, production and finished goods ready to transfer to the central warehouse. While this means

**Part 4** Value metrics and performance management in a strategic context

that there is no overall picture of stocks, the benefit of maintaining decentralized control is thought to outweigh this problem. The director of human resources is keen to maintain motivation of individual factory managers by retaining the existing systems.

This strategy has again been queried at board level in the last few months, particularly as manufacturing operations mean that each factory is using similar raw materials. Implementation of a centralized system has been rejected by the HR and IT Directors.

### Required

1  (a) Recommend performance indicators (PIs) that can be used to support the *critical success factors (CSFs)* of CLB, discussing why these PIs are appropriate to the company.
   (b) Explain the information systems that will be required in order to determine whether the PIs suggested in your answer to Question 1(a) have been achieved.
2  With reference to the falling brand awareness, advise the directors on a suitable decision-making process when considering the update of the information systems within CLB. Include relevant examples from the situation in CLB where possible.
3  Describe an information system that can be used to co-ordinate information transfer between the different production factories and between the factories and the central sales warehouse. Explain the business benefits to CLB of such a system and any disadvantages of it.

*(CIMA Management Accounting – Information Strategy)*

**C18–19** Time allowed: 75 minutes

Ochilpark plc has identified and defined a market in which it wishes to operate. This will provide a 'millennium' focus for an existing product range. Ochilpark plc has identified a number of key competitors and intends to focus on close co-operation with its customers in providing products to meet their specific design and quality requirements. Efforts will be made to improve the effectiveness of all aspects of the cycle from product design to after sales service to customers. This will require inputs from a number of departments in the achievement of the specific goals of the 'millennium' product range. Efforts will be made to improve productivity in conjunction with increased flexibility of methods. An analysis of financial and non-financial data relating to the 'millennium' proposal is shown in Schedule 1.1.

**Schedule 1.1**
**'Millennium' proposal – estimated statistics**

|  | 2000 | 2001 | 2002 |
|---|---|---|---|
| Total market size (£m) | 120 | 125 | 130 |
| Ochilpark plc sales (£m) | 15 | 18 | 20 |
| Ochilpark plc – total costs (£m) | 14.1 | 12.72 | 12.55 |
| Ochilpark plc sundry statistics: |  |  |  |
| Production achieving design quality standards (%) | 95 | 97 | 98 |
| Returns from customers as unsuitable (% of deliveries) | 3.0 | 1.5 | 0.5 |
| Cost of after sales service (£m) | 1.5 | 1.25 | 1.0 |
| Sales meeting planned delivery dates (%) | 90 | 95 | 99 |
| Average cycle time (customer enquiry to delivery) (weeks) | 6 | 5.5 | 5 |
| Components scrapped in production (%) | 7.5 | 5.0 | 2.5 |
| Idle machine capacity (%) | 10 | 6 | 2 |

## Chapter 18 Business process management: towards the lean operation

### Required

1. (a) Prepare a table (£m) of the total costs for the 'millennium' proposal for each of years 2000, 2001 and 2002 (as shown in Schedule 1.1), detailing target costs, internal and external failure costs, appraisal costs and prevention costs. The following information should be used in the preparation of the analysis:

|  | 2000 | 2001 | 2002 |
| --- | --- | --- | --- |
| Target costs – variable (as % of sales) | 40% | 40% | 40% |
| Target costs – fixed (total) | £2m | £2m | £2.5m |
| Internal failure costs (% of total target cost) | 20% | 10% | 5% |
| External failure costs (% of total target cost) | 25% | 12% | 5% |
| Appraisal costs | £0.5m | £0.5m | £0.5m |
| Prevention costs | £2m | £1m | £0.5m |

   (b) Explain the meaning of each of the cost classifications in Question 1(a) above and comment on their trend and inter-relationship. You should provide examples of each classification.

2. Prepare an analysis (both discursive and quantitative) of the 'millennium' proposal for the period 2000 to 2002. The analysis should use the information provided in the question, together with the data in Schedule 1.1. The analysis should contain the following:

   (a) A definition of corporate 'vision or mission' and consideration of how the millennium proposal may be seen as identifying and illustrating a specific sub-set of this 'vision or mission'.
   (b) Discussion and quantification of the proposal in both marketing and financial terms.
   (c) Discussion of the external effectiveness of the proposal in the context of ways in which *1. Quality* and *2. Delivery* are expected to affect customer satisfaction and hence the marketing of the product.
   (d) Discussion of the internal efficiency of the proposal in the context of ways in which the management of 1. Cycle Time and 2. Waste are expected to affect productivity and hence the financial aspects of the proposal.
   (e) Discussion of the links between internal and external aspects of the expected trends in performance.

   *(ACCA Information for Decision Making and Control)*

### Endnotes

1. Summers (2002).
2. See Hansen and Mouritsen (2007) for a discussion of the relationship between operations management and management accounting.
3. Radnor, Walley, Stephens and Bucci (2006).
4. See Johnson and Kaplan (1987).
5. Shingo and Robinson (1990).
6. Granlund and Malmi (2001).
7. See, for example, Granlund (2001).
8. Scapens, Jazayeri and Scapens (1998).
9. Currie (2000).
10. Wagle (1998).

11 See, for example, May (2002); Granlund (2001); Scapens, Ezzamel, Burns and Baldvinsdottir (2003).
12 '80% of the benefit that we get from our ERP system comes from changes, such as inventory optimization, which we could have achieved without making the IT investment', Dorien and Wolf (2000), p. 101.
13 Agrawal, Arjona and Lemmens (2001).
14 Currie (2000), p. 117.
15 Barnatt (2004).
16 Hart, Heskett and Sasser (1990).
17 Casey (1990), p. 31.
18 Anderson and Sedatole (1998), p. 214.
19 Dr W. Edwards Deming, a pioneer in TQM, introduced many of the elements of TQM to Japanese industry after the Second World War. TQM was further refined and developed at Japanese companies such as Toyota.
20 Madonna (1992).
21 Cox, Mann and Sampson (1997).
22 Hammer and Champy (1995).
23 CIMA (2001c).
24 Coburn, Gove and Fulcani (1995).
25 Armstrong (2002).
26 See Womack, Jones and Roos (2007).

When you have read this chapter, log on to the Online Learning Centre for *Management Accounting* at www.mcgraw-hill.co.uk/textbooks/seal, where you'll find multiple choice questions, practice exams and extra study tools for each chapter.

# Strategic Perspectives on Cost Management

# CHAPTER 19
# Strategic perspectives on cost management

## LEARNING OBJECTIVES

After studying Chapter 19, you should be able to:
1. Consider the general significance of constraints on managerial decision making
2. Understand the role of linear programming in the case of multiple constraints
3. Review the management accounting issues raised by the theory of constraints
4. Review the long-run impact of constraints through target and life-cycle costing
5. Analyse the make-or-buy decision from a strategic, supply chain management perspective
6. Consider how outsourcing and shared service centres affect the delivery of support services

## CONCEPTS IN CONTEXT

A Dell personal computer (PC) is basically made up of a central processing unit (CPU), an operating system and a memory. The CPU comes from Intel or Advanced Micro Devices; the operating system from Microsoft while the memory has multiple sources. The main direct innovation comes from suppliers with only indirect innovation from the PC manufacturers. The PC has a life cycle of three months to two years with 50% of profits achieved within the first three to six months of the life cycle. The industry typically experiences deep discounting when new processors, operating systems or memory are introduced. Thus older components become obsolete very quickly. In the PC industry, supply chains are no longer linear but networked – 'information moves independently of product at internet speeds'.[1]

© Andrey Volodin/istock

**Part 4** Value metrics and performance management in a strategic context

**LEARNING OBJECTIVE 1**

In the short run, managers can do little to change their basic cost structures. Short-run decisions may be made using models such as the CVP model that we explored in Chapter 7. Furthermore, as we saw in Chapter 9, managers are routinely faced with the problem of deciding how constrained resources are going to be utilized. Because of the constrained resource (also known as a **limiting factor**) the company cannot fully satisfy demand, so the manager must decide how the constrained resource should be used. Fixed costs are usually unaffected by such choices, so the manager should select the course of action that will maximize the firm's total contribution margin.

In Chapter 9, we saw that the total contribution margin will be maximized by promoting those products or accepting those orders that provide the highest unit contribution margin in relation to the constrained resource. We illustrated this principle through the Mountain Goat Cycles example. You should review your understanding of the single constraint problem by referring back to this example. In this chapter, we look at two more approaches to cost management: the multiple constraint problem and the theory of constraints.

Later on, we consider how costs can be managed in the long run with approaches that try to anticipate possible constraints during the design stage of products and processes. As well as taking a more strategic perspective on the make-or-buy decision (see Chapter 9), this approach asks fundamental questions about an organization's core activities. In particular, we analyse the role of cost management when activities are outsourced through partnerships and alliances.

Many of the techniques in this chapter are based on similar philosophies to those introduced in Chapter 18, particularly lean production. Indeed, long-run approaches to cost management that focus on the design stage of products and seek to improve the management of the supply chain are complimentary to the techniques of JIT, TQM and BPR. All these techniques seek to *remove constraints* rather than optimize around them.

## LEARNING OBJECTIVE 2
## The problem of multiple constraints in the short run: linear programming

What does a firm do if it has more than one potential constraint? For example, a firm may have limited raw materials, limited direct labour hours available, limited floor space, and a limited advertising budget to spend on product promotion. How should it proceed to find the right combination of products to produce? The proper combination or 'mix' of products can be found by use of a quantitative method known as linear programming. When there are two products, the main principles of the technique may be illustrated graphically. For simplicity, we have only considered two constraints. The graphical approach can handle more than two constraints but only two products. More complicated examples with more constraints and products may be solved using an iterative mathematical technique known as the **simplex method**. Nowadays there are computer programs that can solve complex linear programming problems at the click of a button.

Colnebank (see Exhibit 19.1) wants to know what output combination of pumps and fans will maximize its profit in the short run. Since there are only two products, we can illustrate and solve the problem graphically. Exhibit 19.2 puts the pumps along the horizontal axis and the fans along the vertical axis. We can build up the diagram by calculating the maximum output of pumps and fans if all the resources were used to produce just one product. For example, if Colnebank decided just to produce pumps then its labour-hours would allow it to produce 6000/22 = 273 pumps. If it decided just to produce fans then its labour-hours would allow it to produce 6000/8 = 750 fans. When we join the two points on each axis, we can trace the labour-hours constraint. If we do the same calculations for material then we have the set of the constraints facing Colnebank as shown in Exhibit 19.2. When both constraints are considered, Colnebank can only produce a combination of the products within the shaded area – the so-called **feasible region**. But which is the best or **optimal combination of product**? The criterion (or **objective function**) is the output that maximizes total contribution. The individual contribution of one unit of each product may be see in Exhibit 19.3.

Graphically, we may plot the objective function by choosing a level of total contribution and plotting an **iso-contribution line**. This line traces all the combinations of P and F that could produce a particular total contribution. In Exhibit 19.4, the iso-contribution line drawn produces a total contribution of £3,000.

## EXHIBIT 19.1

Colnebank Ltd is a medium-sized engineering company and is one of large number of producers in a very competitive market. The company produces two products, pumps and fans that use similar raw materials and labour skills. The market price of a pump is £152 and that of a fan is £118. The resource requirements of producing one unit of each of the two products are:

|      | Material (kg) | Labour hours |
|------|---------------|--------------|
| Pump | 10            | 22           |
| Fan  | 15            | 8            |

Material costs are £4 per kg and labour costs are £3.50 per hour.

During the coming period the company will have the following resources available to it:

4000 kg of material

6000 labour hours

**Exhibit 19.1** The two product, two constraint problem: Colnebank

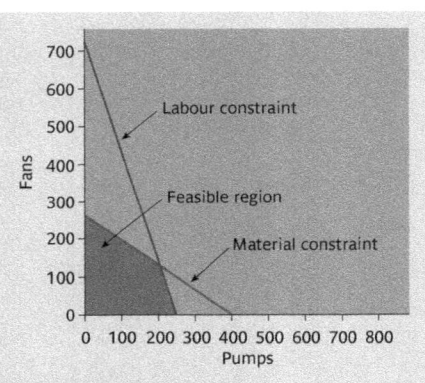

## EXHIBIT 19.2

**Exhibit 19.2** Graphical version of Colnebank

## EXHIBIT 19.3

|                | Pumps £              | Fans £               |
|----------------|----------------------|----------------------|
| Materials      | 40.00 (10 kg at £4)  | 60.00 (15 kg at £4)  |
| Labour         | 77.00 (22 hrs at £3.50) | 28.00 (8 hrs at £3.50) |
|                | 117.00               | 88.00                |
| Selling price  | 152.00               | 118.00               |
| Contribution   | 35.00                | 30.00                |

The linear programming problem is to maximize the total contribution subject to the constraints. If $P$ = units of pumps produced and $F$ = units of fans produced then the problem may be set up as follows.

1 Maximize: £35$P$ + £30$F$

2 Subject to: $10P + 15F \leq 4000$ kg (materials)

3 $22P + 8F \leq 6000$ (labour hours)

**Exhibit 19.3** The linear programming problem

**Part 4** Value metrics and performance management in a strategic context

This level of total contribution is well within the feasible region so we can do better by tracing the highest iso-contribution that is still feasible given the constraints. As we can see in Exhibit 19.4, the highest feasible contribution is at point $X$. Because the model is linear[2] this point is also a **corner point**. We may find the values of $P$ and $F$ at $X$ by inspection or solve for:

$$10P + 15F = 4000$$
$$22P + 8F = 6000$$

This gives:

Pumps = 232    Fans = 112    Total contribution = £11,480.

## Sensitivity analysis

The value of the graphical model is that it illustrates the main principles behind linear programming as well as possible extensions such as *sensitivity analysis*. **Sensitivity analysis** involves asking 'what-if' questions. For example, what happens if the market price of pumps falls to £145? What will be the loss of contribution and will it change the optimal combination? The revised contribution margins are shown in Exhibit 19.5.

Although the total contribution margin has changed, the optimal decision has not. We may change other variables such as the variable cost estimates and see whether they change the optimal decision.

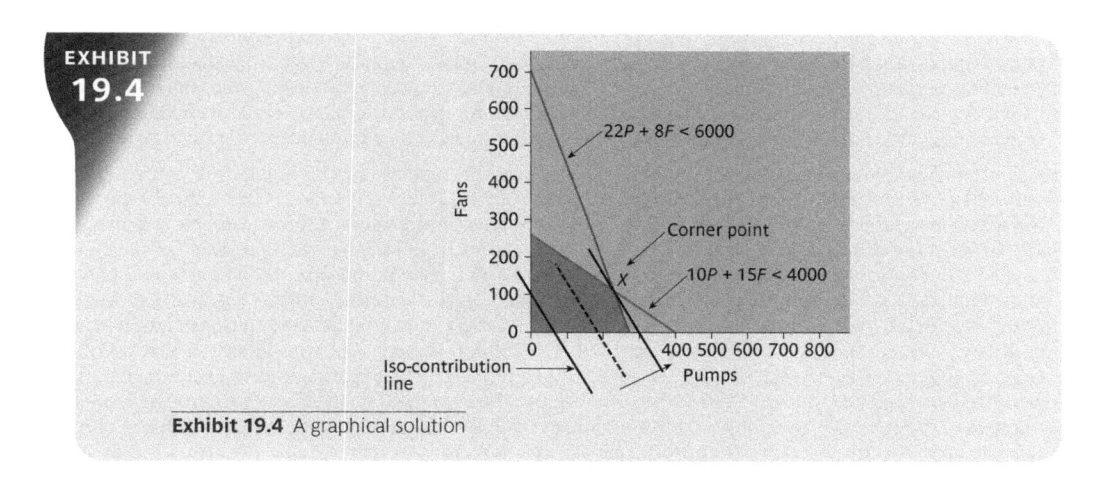

**EXHIBIT 19.4**

**Exhibit 19.4** A graphical solution

**EXHIBIT 19.5**

|  | Pumps<br>£ | Fans<br>£ |
| --- | --- | --- |
| Materials | 40.00 (10 kg at £4) | 60.00 (15 kg at £4) |
| Labour | 77.00 (22 hrs at £3.50) | 28.00 (8 hrs at £3.50) |
|  | 117.00 | 88.00 |
| Selling price | 145.00 | 118.00 |
| Contribution | 28.00 | 30.00 |

**Exhibit 19.5** Sensitivity analysis

## Shadow prices

Each constraint will have an opportunity cost, which is the profit foregone by not having an additional unit of the resource. In linear programming, opportunity costs are known as **shadow prices** and are defined as the increase in value that would be created by having one additional unit of a limiting resource. For example, we could consider what the loss of contribution for Colnebank would be if the available processing hours were reduced by one hour.

## The limitations of the linear programming model as a management accounting technique

There are a number of limitations in using linear programming as a management accounting technique. It ignores marketing considerations and has an excessive focus on the short term. Furthermore, most production resource can be varied even in the short term through overtime and buying-in. More fundamentally, as we saw with both stock control problems and cost of quality decisions in Chapter 18, the alternative to optimizing against given constraints is to concentrate on managing to remove constraints, to eliminate stock or to improve quality.[3]

### Managing constraints

Profits can be increased by effectively managing the organization's constraints. One aspect of managing constraints is to decide how best to utilize them. If the constraint is a bottleneck in the production process, we have seen that the manager should select the product mix that maximizes the total contribution margin. In addition, the manager should take an active role in managing the constraint itself by increasing the efficiency of the bottleneck operation and by increasing its capacity. Such efforts directly increase the output of finished goods and will often pay off in an almost immediate increase in profits.

It is often possible for a manager to effectively increase the capacity of the bottleneck, which is called **relaxing (or elevating) the constraint**. In the case of Mountain Goat Cycles in Chapter 9, the stitching machine operator could be asked to work overtime. This would result in more available stitching time and hence more finished goods that can be sold. The benefits from relaxing the constraint in such a manner are often enormous and can be easily quantified. The manager should first ask, 'What would I do with additional capacity at the bottleneck if it were available?' In the example, if there are unfilled orders for both the touring and mountain panniers, the additional capacity would be used to process more touring panniers, since that would be a better use of the additional capacity. In that situation, the additional capacity would be worth £12 per minute or £720 per hour. This is because adding an hour of capacity would generate an additional £720 of contribution margin if it would be used solely to process more touring panniers. Since overtime pay for the operator is likely to be much less than £720 per hour, running the stitching machine on overtime would be an excellent way to increase the profits of the company while at the same time satisfying customers.

To reinforce this concept, suppose that making touring panniers has already been given top priority and consequently there are only unfilled orders for the mountain pannier. How much would it be worth to the company to run the stitching machine overtime in this situation? Since the additional capacity would be used to make the mountain pannier, the value of that additional capacity would drop to £7.50 per minute or £450 per hour. Nevertheless, the value of relaxing the constraint would still be quite high.

These calculations indicate that managers should pay great attention to bottleneck operations. If a bottleneck machine breaks down or is ineffectively utilized, the losses to the company can be quite large. In our example, for every minute the stitching machine is down due to breakdowns or set-ups, the company loses between £7.50 and £12.00. The losses on an hourly basis are between £450 and £720! In contrast, there is no such loss of contribution margin if time is lost on a machine that is not a bottleneck – such machines have excess capacity anyway.

The implications are clear. Managers should focus much of their attention on managing bottlenecks. As we have discussed, managers should emphasize products that most profitably utilize the constrained resource. They should also make sure that products are processed smoothly through the bottlenecks, with minimal lost time due to breakdowns and set-ups. And they should try to find ways to increase the capacity at the bottlenecks.

The capacity of a bottleneck can be effectively increased in a number of ways, including:

- *Working* overtime on the bottleneck
- *Subcontracting* some of the processing that would be done at the bottleneck
- *Investing in additional machines* at the bottleneck
- *Shifting* workers from processes that are not bottlenecks to the process that is a bottleneck
- *Focusing business process improvement efforts* such as TQM and BPR on the bottleneck
- Reducing *defective units*. Each defective unit that is processed through the bottleneck and subsequently scrapped takes the place of a good unit that could be sold.

The last three methods of increasing the capacity of the bottleneck are particularly attractive, since they are essentially free and may even yield additional cost savings. These somewhat ad hoc examples have been generalized in the *theory of constraints (TOC)*.

## The theory of constraints

A **constraint** is anything that prevents you from getting more of what you want. Every individual and every organization faces at least one constraint, so it is not difficult to find examples of constraints. You may not have enough time to study thoroughly for every subject and to go out with your friends on the weekend, so time is your constraint. Since a constraint prevents you from getting more of what you want, the **theory of constraints (TOC)** maintains that effectively managing the constraint is a key to success.

## TOC and continuous improvement

In TOC, an analogy is often drawn between a business process and a chain. If you want to increase the strength of a chain, what is the most effective way to do this? Should you concentrate your efforts on strengthening the strongest link, the largest link, all the links, or the weakest link? Clearly, focusing effort on the weakest link will bring the biggest benefit.

Continuing with this analogy, the procedure to follow in strengthening the chain is straightforward. First, identify the weakest link, which is the constraint. Second, do not place a greater strain on the system than the weakest link can handle. Third, concentrate improvement efforts on strengthening the weakest link. Fourth, if the improvement efforts are successful, eventually the weakest link will improve to the point where it is no longer the weakest link. At this point, the new weakest link (i.e. the new constraint) must be identified, and improvement efforts must be shifted over to that link. This simple sequential process provides a powerful strategy for continuous improvement. The TOC approach is a perfect complement to TQM, BPR and lean production – it focuses improvement efforts where they are likely to be most effective.

## An example of TOC

A simple example will be used to illustrate the role of a constraint. In Exhibit 19.6, bottlenecks in the National Health Service contribute to the waiting lists that characterize the health care system. The key

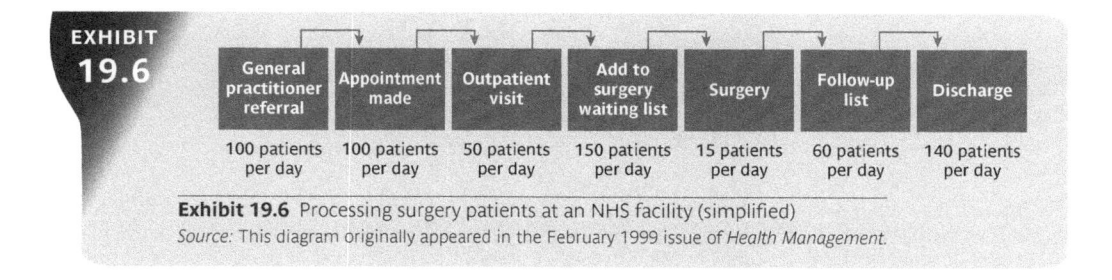

**EXHIBIT 19.6**

| General practitioner referral | Appointment made | Outpatient visit | Add to surgery waiting list | Surgery | Follow-up list | Discharge |
|---|---|---|---|---|---|---|
| 100 patients per day | 100 patients per day | 50 patients per day | 150 patients per day | 15 patients per day | 60 patients per day | 140 patients per day |

**Exhibit 19.6** Processing surgery patients at an NHS facility (simplified)
*Source:* This diagram originally appeared in the February 1999 issue of *Health Management*.

constraint or bottleneck is in Surgery where the maximum number of patients that can be processed is 15 patients a day. Other parts of the systems such as General Practitioners (100 patients per day) and Outpatients (50 patients per day) could process higher numbers. The key to increasing the overall capacity of the system is to improve the capacity in Surgery – improvements in other areas may simply lead to longer waiting lists. If efforts are focused on the first bottleneck in Surgery, subsequent improvements may lead to a situation when another part of the system takes over as the weakest link and hence a focus for management attention.

## The impact of TOC on management accounting

Conventional management accounting has two possible conflicts with TOC. If non-bottleneck machines have a production cut then they begin to look inefficient. Labour efficiency variances may also worsen. Furthermore, a reduction in work in progress may lead to a fall in reported profit. The TOC solution is to change the usual measures by focusing on throughput, stock and operational expense. The theory has its own special definitions:

$$\text{Throughput} = \text{Sales} - \text{Material and purchased services}$$

$$\text{Inventory} = \text{Stock} + \text{Machines and buildings}$$

$$\text{Operating expense} = \text{Non-material conversion costs especially labour costs}$$

$$\text{Net profit} = \text{Throughput} - \text{Operational expense}$$

$$\text{ROI} = \frac{\text{Throughput} - \text{Operational expense}}{\text{Inventory}}$$

Note that direct labour is treated as a fixed cost. Traditional accounting such as standard costing focuses on controlling operational expenses ('cost world'), JIT focuses on cutting stock ('JIT world'). In contrast, 'Throughput world' focuses on throughput even if it means conflicting with JIT by holding buffer stocks or with cost world by tolerating slack labour.

## Throughput accounting[4]

One response to the theory of constraints is a technique that determines the optimum use of bottleneck activity called **throughput accounting (TA)**. The main idea is to rank products by calculating the **throughput accounting ratio**:

$$\text{TA ratio} = \frac{\text{Return per factory hour}}{\text{Cost per factory hour}}$$

where

$$\text{Return per factory hour} = \frac{\text{Sale price} - \text{Material cost}}{\text{Time on key resource}}$$

and

$$\text{Cost per factory hour} = \frac{\text{Total factory cost}}{\text{Total time available on key resource}}$$

Although it incorporates some of the terminology of the theory of constraints, it could be argued that throughput accounting does not reflect the true spirit of the TOC philosophy with its emphasis on the active management of bottlenecks.[5] Indeed, many of the criticisms of accounting approaches to performance measurement

Part 4 Value metrics and performance management in a strategic context

and control raised by advocates of TOC are similar to those raised by advocates of lean production. Readers are advised to refer to the previous chapter in order to review these issues.

## Strategic approaches to cost management: life-cycle costing and the supply chain

**LEARNING OBJECTIVE 4**

The analysis of constraints emphasizes the general point that costs can get 'locked in' by prior decisions. In the long run, the sort of constraints that affect short-term decisions, such as fixed capacity or specific shortages, may be tackled through alternative production configurations. In the even longer run, the boundaries of the organization may be altered so that decisions made to *outsource* activities that were causing bottlenecks or constraining profitable processes are part of a strategic assessment of organizational competence (see Chapter 16). Long-run cost management calls on different techniques, in which costs are controlled through the *anticipation* of specific cost drivers stemming from the design of products or services. Thus there is less emphasis on optimizing a static situation (as with linear programming) and more emphasis on avoiding cost through careful product design and appropriate supply chain strategies.

### Life-cycle costing

Traditional costing sometimes seems to focus too much on costs as they are *incurred* because incurred costs are more visible as they are 'booked' through routine cost accumulation systems. For example, product life-cycle costs may be expressed in the form of a product budget. In Exhibit 19.7, we see that in the early stages of a product life-cycle relatively small spending on research and development may mask the importance of this phase in determining and locking in the huge bulk of production costs. Life-cycle costing draws

**EXHIBIT 19.7**

| | Years | | |
|---|---|---|---|
| | 1 | 2 | 3 |
| **Costs and revenues** | | | |
| Units sold | 20,000 | 210,000 | 200,000 |
| Unit price | £50 | £45 | £40 |
| **Research** | | | |
| R&D costs | £750,000 | £20,000 | – |
| **Manufacturing** | | | |
| Unit variable cost | £16 | £16 | £16 |
| Variable cost per batch | £700 | £700 | £700 |
| Distribution | | | |
| Computers per batch | 400 | 500 | 500 |
| Fixed costs | £200,000 | £600,000 | £600,000 |
| Unit variable costs | £2 | £2 | £2 |
| Computers per batch | 200 | 200 | 200 |
| **Marketing** | | | |
| Fixed costs | £400,000 | £400,000 | £400,000 |
| **Post sales** | | | |
| Fixed costs | £240,000 | £240,000 | £240,000 |
| Unit service costs | £1 | £1 | £1 |

**Exhibit 19.7** A product life-cycle budget: Wise plc – new hand-held computer

extensively on the techniques of target costing, which we introduced in Chapter 15 in connection with pricing decisions. As was argued there, target costing is more than just a pricing technique as it *manages costs* rather than just passively measures them. The aim of target costing is to choose product and process technologies that give an acceptable profit at a planned level of output. Once a product has been designed and has gone into production, not much can be done to significantly reduce its cost. Most of the opportunities to reduce cost come from designing the product so that it is simple to make, uses inexpensive parts, and is robust and reliable. If the company has little control over market price and little control over cost once the product has gone into production, then it follows that the major opportunities for affecting profit come in the design stage where valuable features that customers are willing to pay for can be added and where most of the costs are really determined. So that is where the effort is concentrated – in designing and developing the product. The difference between target costing and other approaches to product development is profound. Instead of designing the product and then finding out how much it costs, the target cost is set first and then the product is designed so that the target cost is attained.

## FOCUS ON PRACTICE

### The £1,300 car

Target costing is widely used in the car industry. For example, at Tata Motors, engineers had to design a car that could be sold for 100,000 rupees (about £1,375)! The target cost for a new model is decomposed into target costs for each of the elements of the car – down to a target cost for each of the individual parts. The designers draft a trial blueprint, and a check is made to see if the estimated cost of the car is within reasonable distance of the target cost. If not, design changes are made, and a new trial blueprint is drawn up. This process continues until there is sufficient confidence in the design to make a prototype car according to the trial blueprint. If there is still a gap between the target cost and estimated cost, the design of the car will be further modified.

After repeating this process a number of times, the final blueprint is drawn up and turned over to the production department. In the first several months of production, the target costs will ordinarily not be achieved due to problems in getting a new model into production. However, after that initial period, target costs are compared to actual costs and discrepancies between the two are investigated with the aim of eliminating the discrepancies and achieving target costs.[6]

**Exercise**: Consider the possibility of target costing in other industries such as food retailing (see, e.g. L. Jack and J. Jones, (2007) Facing up to the new realities: the case for relevant costing and target cost management in agriculture, *Journal of Applied Accounting Research*, 8(3): 116–45.

As up to 90% of cost[7] may be committed or locked in at pre-production stages, management accountants have become more aware of the design and planning phases of the product life-cycle. The distinction between and differential timing of incurred and locked-in costs are illustrated in Exhibit 19.8. The biggest gap is at the research and development stage, where although this function may generate a relatively low proportion of a product's total cost, decisions made here lock in the costs incurred in the manufacturing and marketing phases. In recognition of the importance of the planning phase, *life-cycle* costing tries to estimate a product's costs over its lifetime.

As well as recognizing the importance of the design phase, life-cycle costing also anticipates cost improvements during the manufacturing cycle. This aspect is sometimes known as **kaizen costing** as it is part of the wider philosophy of continuous improvement. Some of the cost improvements will occur through a process of 'learning-by-doing' as workers get more adept at their tasks. Managers may routinize cost reduction through an approach known as **kaizen budgeting**. Rather than devise budgets on standard costs that are based on *past* performance, kaizen budgeting plans for *incremental* improvements in efficiency and reductions in costs.

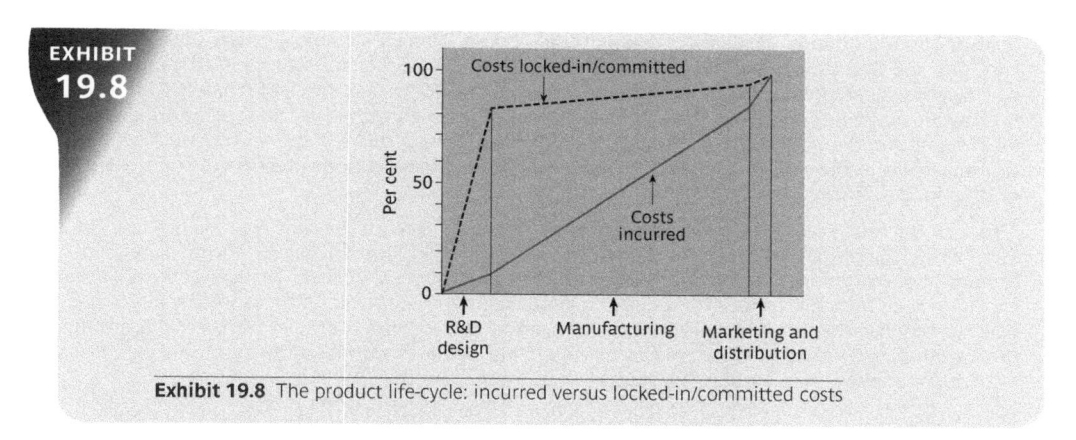

**Exhibit 19.8** The product life-cycle: incurred versus locked-in/committed costs

## Target costing and design

In a competitive market, the design process has to embrace both commercial and technical considerations. Just as management accountants are more aware of design, designers have become increasingly aware of the need to design to cost and quality targets set by competitive conditions. The resulting customer-oriented design is a *team process* with potential inputs from a number of disciplines. Best practice in terms of designing to cost is to assign costs to the functions of product rather than to blocks of components. This technique, which is sometimes known as *attribute costing* (see Chapter 16), aims to encourage creativity rather than continuity in design characteristics.

The creativity of designers may also be guided by techniques such as **value engineering** or **value analysis**. Value in this context may be defined as the ratio of functionality to cost. Thus value may be improved by holding functionality and reducing cost or by increasing functionality while holding cost. Product improvement may stem from innate creativity; it may also emerge from an analysis of competitors' products and processes through techniques associated with target costing such as *teardown analysis, reverse engineering* and *benchmarking*. Although this section has emphasized the cost management aspects of design, we must not forget that design is not just about copying and cost control. As Summers puts it: 'Design, closely allied to innovation, is the key to standing out and maintaining competitiveness'.[8]

## Some problems with target and life-cycle costing

One problem with target costing is that it may reveal an unpalatable view of a company's internal operations, exposing uncompetitive practices and processes that were hidden by more traditional costing techniques. Another problem is that it may be too time-consuming. Thus, while it may be appropriate in the car industry, which is based on relatively mature technologies and lengthy product life cycles, it is less appropriate in industries such as electronics, where the rate of innovation is extremely rapid and time-to-market must be minimized. The other feature of life-cycle costing is that it implicitly assumes a relatively orderly value chain with a dominant customer who can plan the design and delivery of the product. In an industry such as personal computers (PCs), some of the major players are the companies that supply the software (Microsoft) and the microprocessors (Intel). Leading-edge technical innovation is in the hands of these companies rather than the PC assemblers.

## The make or buy decision from a strategic perspective: supply chain management

The PC industry is a particularly advanced example of supply chain management. Many companies and industries are only just beginning to realize the cost management implications of their supply chains. For them, the implementation of a supply chain strategy may begin with the realization of the quantitative importance of bought-in material and services. We have already seen how substantial locked-in costs are, and thus how important product design can be. The importance of supply chain management is dawning on companies as they realize that (apart from the obvious example of retailers who have always been aware of the importance of the purchasing function), bought-in goods and services are quantitatively more significant than internally generated costs. For example, two-thirds of the value of the North American car industry is in the suppliers while 40% of all electronics manufacturers plan to outsource 90% or more of their final product.[9]

Although the historical focus in management accounting has been on the control of *internal* costs, there are areas where traditional management accounting techniques do have an impact on the supply chain. For example, the costs of bought-in materials and services may conventionally be managed through a standard costing system, which identifies variances in material costs and usage. Similarly, as we saw in Chapter 9, the make or buy decision may be viewed as an application of the concept of relevant costs and revenues. Yet these examples themselves illustrate that supply chain management has until recently been a marginal rather than a central concern in management accounting.

In this chapter, we will take a more strategic perspective through the linked concepts of the value chain and supply chain management. The value chain is not just a model of business processes within the firm. Many steps may be involved in getting a finished product into the hands of a consumer and these may involve a number of independently owned companies. First, raw materials have to be obtained through mining, drilling, growing crops, raising animals, and so forth. Second, these raw materials have to be processed to remove impurities and to extract the desirable and usable materials. Third, the usable materials may have to undergo some preliminary fabrication so as to be usable in final products. For example, cotton must be made into thread and textiles before being made into clothing. Fourth, the actual manufacturing of the finished product must take place. And finally, the finished product must be distributed to the ultimate consumer. All of these steps taken together are called an industry *value chain*. Separate companies may carry out each of the steps in the value chain or a single company may carry out several of the steps. When a company owns more than one of these steps in the value chain, it is following a policy of **vertical integration**. Vertical integration is very common. Some firms control all of the activities in the value chain from producing basic raw materials right up to the final distribution of finished goods. Other firms are content to integrate on a smaller scale by purchasing many of the parts and materials that go into their finished products. The value chain illustrated in Exhibit 19.9 shows that horizontal competition may

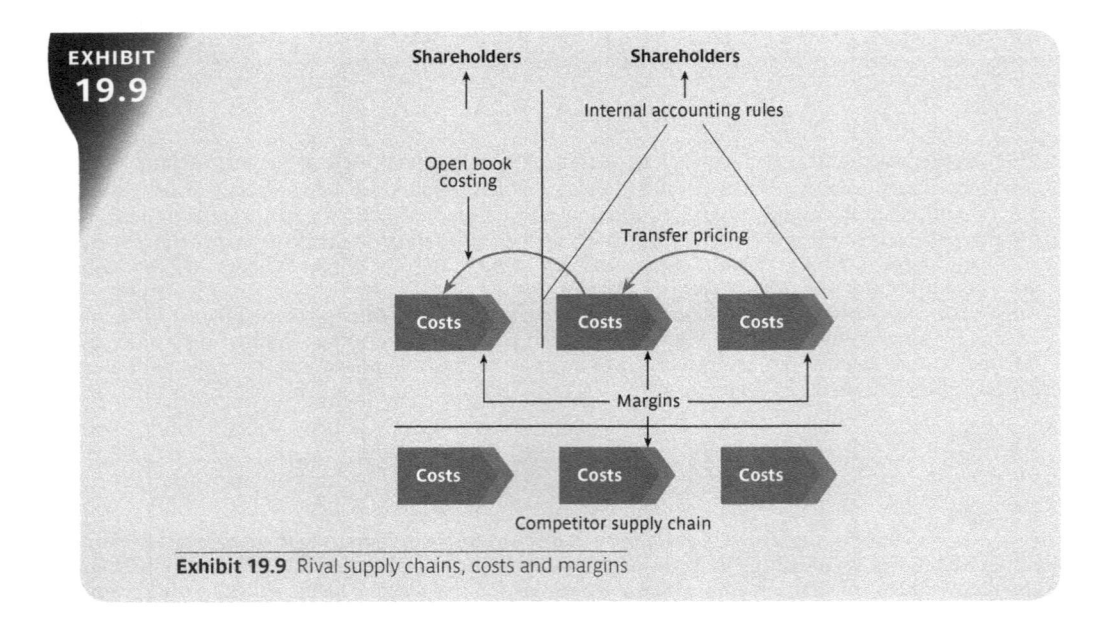

**Exhibit 19.9** Rival supply chains, costs and margins

## Integration versus sub-contracting

Integration provides certain advantages. An integrated firm is less dependent on its suppliers and may be able to ensure a smoother flow of parts and materials for production than a non-integrated firm that uses sub-contracting extensively. For example, a strike against a major parts supplier can interrupt the operations of a non-integrated firm for many months, whereas an integrated firm that is producing its own parts might be able to continue operations. Also, many firms feel that they can control quality better by producing their own parts and materials, rather than by relying on the quality control standards of outside suppliers. In addition, the integrated firm realizes profits from the parts and materials that it is 'making' rather than 'buying', as well as profits from its regular operations.

The advantages of integration are counterbalanced by some advantages of using external suppliers. By pooling demand from a number of firms, a supplier may be able to enjoy economies of scale in research and development and in manufacturing. These economies of scale can result in higher quality and lower costs than would be possible if the firm were to attempt to make the parts on its own. A company must be careful, however, to retain control over activities that are essential to maintaining its competitive position. For example, Hewlett-Packard controls the software for a laser printer that it makes in co-operation with Canon Inc. of Japan to prevent Canon from coming out with a competing product.

The present trend appears to be towards less vertical integration. As firms outsource more and more of their activities, the buy-or-make decision becomes part of an approach known as **supply chain management**. This draws on many of the techniques that we have covered in previous chapters. Supply chain management is an important part of lean production, which, as we saw in Chapter 16, is a feature of new forms of competition. Lean production draws on other management innovations that we have looked at, such as JIT, TQM and BPR and target costing. Most of these new techniques are themselves enabled by new technology such as EDI, ERP and the internet (Chapter 18). However, it would be wrong to see supply chain management as simply a matter of choosing particular management accounting techniques. Some types of supply chain management seek to develop close relationships with suppliers and customers, known as *strategic partnerships*. In these situations, management accounting may play a role in building new forms of collaboration that involve the sharing of information, such as cost data, that is traditionally guarded with great secrecy.[10]

## Traditional supply relationships

The system of supply in a *traditional* tendering process was a game of negotiation. Since both buyers and sellers needed to show year-on-year gains, there was an incentive to keep supply chains slack. As bargaining revolved around the *piece price* of the component, buyers were not interested in the costs *per se* as, at least for non-customized components, they could simply scan the market for the possibility of lower piece prices on offer from other suppliers. On their part, the inbuilt uncertainty of demand meant that suppliers suffered from difficulties in planning production and had an incentive to save costs by shaving quality. In any case, traditional manufacturing was characterized by poor-quality cost accounting information that could not identify cost drivers in *the assemblers' own operations*, let alone in the operations of their suppliers. Not only were internal costs measured in an unsatisfactory way, there was also a failure to understand the 'all-in cost' of bought-in supplies. With long production runs, high levels of vertical integration and tolerance of high rates of defective components, the emphasis in purchasing was on short-term contracts awarded on the basis of lowest price. The lack of awareness of what was driving costs may have meant that the cheapest suppliers, from the point of view of competitive tendering, were not necessarily the best sources if the costs of actually incorporating the bought-in components into a final assembly could be determined. In any case, high levels of vertical integration implied that companies preferred to produce all but the most non-specific components in-house.

Exhibit 19.9 suggests that supply relationships are based on simple linear chains. The aim is to illustrate the difference between transfer pricing and open book costing. It is much more likely that supply relationships will have the characteristics of *networks as shown in Exhibit 19.10*. Here, there are a number of potential suppliers and customers with suppliers possibly supplying competitors and a number of possible customers.

**Exhibit 19.10** Supply networks

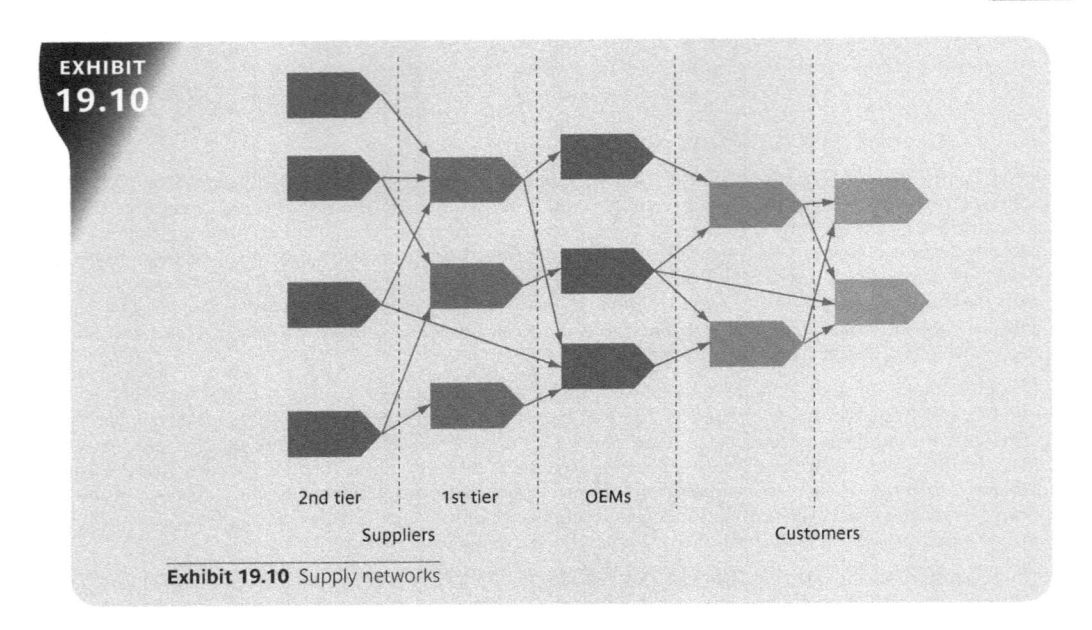

Individual *original equipment manufacturers (OEMs)* may try to rationalize this network by reducing the number of first tier suppliers and giving those suppliers more responsibility over areas such as component innovation and the co-ordination of second tier suppliers. With a smaller number of suppliers to deal with, strategic partnerships may be easier to develop.

## Strategic partnering

Strategic partnership sourcing involves a process of deliberate choice on the basis of current best practice in strategic sourcing. Strategic choice is affected by the competitive drivers that may themselves vary in importance between industries. A number of models have been proposed which try to make the strategic make-or-buy decision more systematic.

Most of these models involve classifying the components or bought-in services and then choosing the type of procurement model. Some approaches classify[11] bought-in items on the criteria of bottleneck, critical, routine and leverage. Other approaches classify components on the criterion of strategic importance.[12] The strategic subsystems may be decomposed into **'families' of components**. Even if the family is non-strategic, it may still be produced in-house if existing capacity is competitive. The long-term aim for non-strategic families, however, is to harvest. If the family is strategic then it will either be produced in-house or through a partnership with a supplier. What might seem strategic or 'core' to a company from an emotional point of view may not be central to a company's competitive advantage and may thus be outsourced to carefully chosen suppliers. This logic is summarized in Exhibit 19.11.

## The implications for management accounting of strategic approaches to make or buy

The concept of all-in cost is sometimes analysed as the **total cost of ownership**. Price may be the most visible cost but it is only part of total cost. Purchasing experts refer to the price/cost 'iceberg', where price is easily seen while costs of delivery, support, defects, stockholding, delays, inspection and handling are hidden below the waterline. Thus negotiations for strategic partnerships may be based on cost rather than price. Partners may even negotiate an 'open-book agreement' where one or both partners reveal costs that are relevant to their specific transactions.

**EXHIBIT 19.11**

|  | Strategic? (Architectural/core) | |
|---|---|---|
| **Competitive?** | **YES** | **NO** |
| **YES** | In-house (invest) | In-house (harvest) |
| **NO** | Outsource via alliance/partnership | Outsource via arm's-length transaction |

**Exhibit 19.11** A strategic approach to make-or-buy

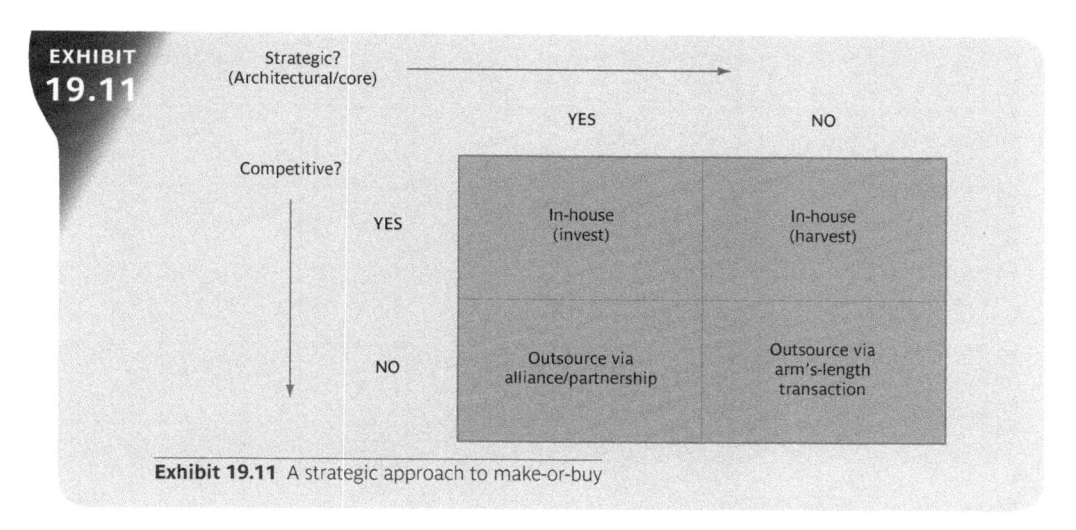

One reason for negotiating on costs is that knowledge of suppliers' costs enable more trusting relations because customers can see the margin that the supplier is making. As can be seen from Exhibit 19.9, suppliers will hope that the focus of improvement will be on taking out cost rather than eroding suppliers' margins. There is no long-term future for a partnership where one of the partners is not making adequate returns. Open-book agreements should reduce the scope for squeezing margins/or suppliers to exploit temporary competitive advantage. Changes may be agreed and the improvement in the transaction atmosphere allows a process of continuous improvement and even the bigger cost reductions that may be identified at the design stage. Open-book relations may not be based on partnership and trust but may be *forced*. Forced open-books may reduce slack in the system in the short run but the increased level of uncertainty and exits from the industry may make it difficult to identify competent suppliers.[13] The 'big stick' approach can work in industries characterized by low levels of concentration and low sophistication in product (such as in much of retailing) but it is a dangerous policy where the supplier has some leverage based on proprietary knowledge.

A summary of the implications for management accounting is shown in Exhibit 19.12. Note that we have already covered the techniques that are relevant to supply chain management. The innovation lies in the way that the techniques may be used in relatively unfamiliar inter-firm relations. The spirit underlying the use of cost data in inter-firm relations is that a 'win–win' situation pervades so that if cost is taken out of the supply chain then the benefits from the savings are shared out between the firms.[14]

## FOCUS ON PRACTICE

### Supply chain management and emergent strategies

Newtech[15] is a small Danish electronics manufacturer specializing in the sale of alarms to a variety of customers in industry and public and private sectors. Its alarms systems are very high-tech and innovative – to such an extent that the firm could determine what customers could expect or what is technically feasible. Newtech's competitive advantage was based on rapid innovation through new technologies such as infrared, thermostatic and molecular sensors. But the rapid rate of technological change created new challenges with much shorter product life-cycles. Furthermore, the firm could not have expertise in all these areas. Their response was to use their suppliers' expertise. They identified two groups of suppliers:

1. Producers of standard components
2. Suppliers with whom they developed new products.

Since the outsourcing led to feelings of loss of control, the company introduced target costing because it seemed to offer a way of regaining control. In addition, Newtech's purchasing budget took on a new prominence: 'The purchasing budget came to play a symbolic role in inter-organizational management controls. Thus, Newtech created a sense of financial urgency in the production and development work. The purchasing budget specified how Newtech drew on other firms' development competences and related them to its own situation.'

Another feature of target costing – functional analysis – encouraged systematic discussion between Newtech and suppliers. There was an unintended outcome to the outsourcing strategy. The functional analysis redefined what Newtech was about in terms of technology, strategy and organization. The company began to see itself as a 'technology co-ordinator' rather than a 'technology developer', as before. Newtech managed at a distance and used the techniques of functional analysis and purchase budgeting to add its specialized market knowledge to the development process.

**Exercise**: Relate this example to the concepts of strategy (especially emergent strategy) covered in Chapter 16.

### EXHIBIT 19.12

| Management accounting technique | Supply chain implications |
|---|---|
| Total cost of ownership | Recognition that the cost of acquiring goods and services includes more than just quoted piece price |
| Life-cycle costing | Locked-in cost issues may affect suppliers |
| Target costing | External sourcing influenced by cost and design specifications set by the market |
| Kaizen costing | Progressive cost cuts required of suppliers |
| Benchmarking | Enables JIT supply and purchasing based on knowledge of suppliers |
| TQM/BPR | Re-engineering/quality affect supplies, for example JIT systems |
| Strategic cost management | Competition is between supply chains rather than individual firms |
| Real-time IT systems (EDI, ERP and the internet) | Synchronization of production plans |
| Open-book accounting | Sharing of cost and output data enables partnership sourcing with sharing benefits of product enhancement, and so on. |

**Exhibit 19.12** Management accounting and supply chain management

## Corporate unbundling: shared service centres and service outsourcing

Some organizations have chosen to reorganize the provision of support services. There are two main types of reorganization: (1) shared service centres; and (2) outsourcing of services. Configuration (1), the shared service centre means that services are not supplied by an independently owned company. However, the shared service centre may be a prelude to configuration (2), full outsourcing, as when services are provided on the basis of a service agreement between the operating departments and the central service centre, it is technically, at least, a relatively short step to move from internal charging to an external contract.

## MANAGEMENT ACCOUNTING IN ACTION
## CASE STUDY: IT TAKES TWO TO TANGO

This case[16] concerns the role of management accounting in the attempted formation of a strategic alliance as part of a supply chain strategy in the automotive engineering industry. There are two main players: an 'Assembler' and a 'Strategic Supplier'. In order to understand the case (and further our understanding of supply chains), it is important to appreciate the point of view of *both* of these parties.

### The Assembler's supply chain management philosophy

The Assembler had a turnover of about £70 million and employed about 1,000 workers. It had recently become a subsidiary of a large US multinational. The company was not a final assembler but produced complex and technologically sophisticated subassemblies both for its parent and for outside customers. The company had begun to recognize the importance of purchasing/procurement by placing it in a focal position within the worldwide management structure. Although the company had a policy of local sourcing, its operations were themselves becoming increasingly global, with subsidiaries in the US, Europe (the former East Germany), India and China. In this context, local sourcing had translated into a global sourcing policy with key suppliers setting up plants close to the Assembler's overseas operations. The company's emerging sourcing policy was based on the logics outlined above in the section on strategic partnership (see especially Exhibit 19.11).

Although they had little experience of the implementation of collaborative agreements, the materials/procurement executives were aware of the underdevelopment of management accounting practices in collaborative agreements. They knew that the companies *should* be exchanging *cost* rather than piece-price data, with expectations that over time they would reduce their suppliers' costs rather than simply squeeze their margins (see Exhibit 19.9). Their problem was to translate these general partnership philosophies into robust practices, which would retain the long-term support of senior corporate management.

### A draft alliance agreement

At the time of the fieldwork, the Strategic Supplier, which was also a subsidiary of a large multinational, was offering an open-book agreement plus rolling cost cuts in return for assurances on demand and participation in research and development. The companies had been doing business for about 25 years but until recently their relationship had been a traditional arm's-length one. The Assembler acknowledged that, at times, they had behaved quite opportunistically towards their suppliers, switching business on a monthly basis to exploit differential pricing agreements.

The initial draft was based on a document drawn up by the Assembler, which stressed the principle of an open and trusting relationship that 'delivers tangible and measurable benefits to both sides over a long period, and allows the sharing of ideas and information'. With an annual cost reduction target of 6% for controllable costs, changes in raw materials prices and exchange rate movements were to be agreed by reference to published data. The document specified areas for continuous improvement, a management review process and a grievance procedure. The alliance proposed that cross-company teams should design mutually beneficial technological projects, which were to be jointly funded but with the Assembler having the first use for a determined period.

### The Strategic Supplier

The Strategic Supplier had an advanced proprietary process with two plants. While the original plant in the UK was quite old, the plant in the US was both new and dedicated to supplying the Assembler in the US. Although controlled from the UK, it served not only as a *technical* exemplar but also as a good model of a supplier/assembler business relationship.

Although the Supplier did want a closer European relationship, it had reservations about the draft alliance document that had been proposed by the assembler. The Supplier was particularly concerned about the clause that specified a 6% annual cost reduction for three years without a clear definition of cost. Their bargaining position was that they *could* reduce the all-in cost to the Assembler *if* they could become the sole supplier in the UK and did more engineering work on the component, as they did in the US. As it stood, they argued that the draft document was not an open-book agreement and lacked mutuality. They argued that knowledge of the Assembler's costs would help them to make replacement decisions on customized machine tools to the mutual benefit of both partners. Open-book agreements may also involve sharing information on rates of return. But returns could vary between industries. Thus while a 5% return was normal in the Assembler's industry in recent years, the parent company of the Supplier expected 9–10%.

## The development of the relationship

Progress was made in the following areas, with the Assembler agreeing:

- To interpret the 6% cost-reduction as a reduction in 'all-in cost'.
- That some of the value-added work on the component could be moved to the Supplier as growth in demand allowed.
- That the shared design approach was aimed primarily to upgrade the performance of the component rather than reduce its cost.

Some problems emerged:

- Difficulties in the measurement of cost reductions and the allocation of the partnership benefits between the parties.
- Difficulties in defining the boundaries of activities, i.e. what information would be shared.
- Difficulties in demonstrating the benefits of the alliance (some of which were quantitative but not necessarily financial) to senior management.

## The evolution of the agreement

At the next meeting between the two senior managers, the discussions proceeded on the basis that the alliance had already agreed on the following matters:

- Single sourcing had been ruled out.
- *Specific* cost-reduction targets were no longer specified in a document but were expected to emerge from detailed discussions between multi-functional teams from both companies.
- The alliance was to be developed through a one-day brainstorming session involving mixed teams from both companies.
- The necessary detail was to be thrashed out through interaction involving a number of inter-company channels and through addressing particular problems and projects.

There are a number of special points to note in this case study:

1 **The role of cost data and other information-sharing in the construction of an agreement**
   The parties seemed to *begin* with a rather specific and detailed document that over time became less specific in detail but broader in terms of general commitment. In particular, with a change in personnel in both companies, the attitude seemed to become that if you knew how to take cost out of a product or process, then this was more important than the precise measurement of existing costs.

**Part 4** Value metrics and performance management in a strategic context

> **2 No open-book agreement**
> Some of the difficulty in developing an open-book agreement seemed to be due to evident weaknesses in both firms' internal cost systems. Significantly, both companies were seeking to improve the management of their supply/distribution chains *at the same time* that they were seeking to make their accounting systems more 'relevant' through innovations such as the balanced scorecard.[17]
>
> **3 Big cost savings were possible through redesign and relocation**
> As engineers, both managers were acutely aware that the really big cost savings were on offer not through incremental improvements to logistics in the supply chain but in *product design* and *locational* issues. Thus, as the Assembler became more cost-conscious in its designs, it would transmit these concerns down the supply chain through an informal form of target costing. On its part, the Supplier knew that dramatic cost savings could be achieved by closing the old UK factory and concentrating production in the modern but underutilized US factory.
>
> **4 Implications for management accounting**
> The ideal role for management accounting would seem to be in an open-book agreement whereby each partner can inspect the revenues and costs of the other party. Although the parties did not achieve a detailed open-book agreement, generic management accounting issues of cost measurement, cost reduction and non-financial performance measurement were still an important part of the looser understanding that was reached.

## The shared service centre model

There are number of different ways that shared service centres (SSC) can be organized and managed. Before we review these issues let us consider two definitions. A **shared service centre** is '(T)he concentration of company resources performing like activities, typically spread across the organization, in order to service multiple internal parties at lower cost and with higher service levels, with the common goal of delighting external customers and enhancing corporate value'.[18] Another source argues that '(S)hared services is a collaborative strategy in which a subset of existing business functions are concentrated in a new, semi-autonomous business unit that has a management structure designed to promote efficiency, value generation, cost savings, and improved service for internal customers of the parent corporation, like a business competing in the open market'.[19] The significance of the SSC can be seen more clearly when it is compared with the alternative multidivisional model in which each division is responsible for providing its own service support. The models are compared in Exhibit 19.13.

There are a number of advantages of the SSC model. Perhaps the most obvious advantage from the point of view of the parent company is that by concentrating service activities in one site, specially chosen for the purpose, the company can reduce costs. Some authors have suggested that an 'easy' 25–30% reduction in costs is possible with the promise of progressive pressure on the SSC as it may itself be threatened by outsourcing to an even lower cost location.[20] But there are more than cost advantages. The SSC should provide better service than the old service departments where there was always a danger that employees in the business units saw themselves as fulfilling low status 'back office functions'. The new SSC culture can 'shake the feeling that they are "low value added employees" performing "cost centre" activities' since the culture of the SSC is affected by the knowledge that providing support service is its core business.[21] The SSC can focus its core competences, standardize processes and apply the best technology appropriate to a service business. The appropriate technology may involve ERP systems combined with other technologies used in call centres which link voice, video and data interaction capability.[22] The standardization and technology may mean that the SSC possibly employ cheaper junior staff but the scale and new focus of the organization should enable it to recruit and concentrate on top experts and professionals. A sophisticated knowledge management perspective may even see the SSC as an opportunity attempt to repackage intellectual capital of company-knowledge management decision about core competences and the management of customer capital, human capital and structural capital.[23] We will explore this approach in more detail later in the chapter when we look at outsourcing. Although SSCs are usually associated with 'back-end processes' like payroll and human resource management and billing, the SSC may be used to provide some strategic services such as market intelligence, marketing, sales and customer support.

## EXHIBIT 19.13

**Conventional divisional structure (support services embedded)**

Head office
- Business Unit 1
  - Operating units
  - Service departments
- Business Unit 2
  - Operating units
  - Service departments
- Business Unit 3
  - Operating units
  - Service departments

↓

**Shared service centre structure**

Head office
- Business Unit 1 — Operating units
- Business Unit 2 — Operating units
- Business Unit 3 — Operating units

Shared service centre

**Exhibit 19.13** Moving to a shared service centre model

---

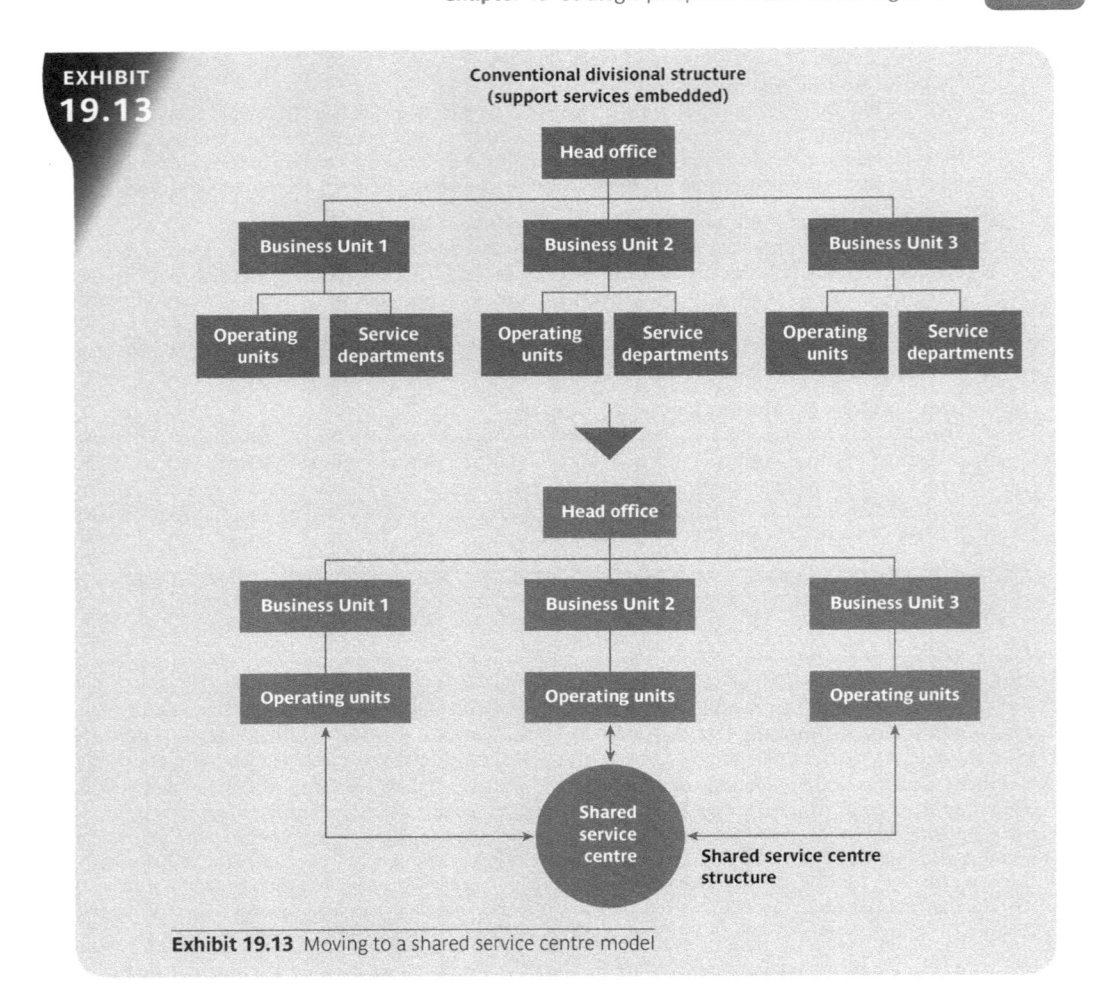

## FOCUS ON PRACTICE

### The logic of the shared service centre

The FSSC was originally conceived to reduce headcount and increase efficiency through using better IT, business process re-engineering and cutting out duplication between divisions. But shared services have a commercial logic that goes beyond cost cutting. If it was just about cost cutting then a third party outsourcing specialist could also do those tasks. Shared service centres define and preserve what a company does for all its stakeholders. The SSC provides accountability, visibility and transparency – all aspects that can lead to improved enterprise governance. By placing the common support services outside of the operating business units, the SSC creates a new visibility of those processes leaving the business units focus on their core competences.

**Exercise**: Discuss the viewpoint that shared services are concerned with what we have earlier defined as overhead costs.

### SSCs: competition and pricing issues

We have already looked at issues of costing service departments in Chapter 15. It is argued that if the SSC is treated like a pure cost centre and costs are allocated then the SSC can concentrate on service provision without worrying about pricing. The disadvantage is that there is less of a break with the old model, it is difficult to obtain costing information for benchmarking and there is little incentive to reduce costs. An intermediate position is to allocate costs by behaviour.

Whenever possible, service department costs should be separated into variable and fixed classifications and allocated separately. This approach is necessary to avoid possible inequities in allocation, as well as to provide more useful data for planning and control of departmental operations.

## Variable costs

Variable costs are the out-of-pocket costs of providing services that vary in total in proportion to fluctuations in the level of service provided. Food cost in a cafeteria would be a variable cost, for example, and one would expect this cost to vary proportionately with the number of persons using the cafeteria.

As a general rule, variable costs should be charged to consuming departments according to whatever activity causes the incurrence of the costs involved. If, for example, the variable costs of a service department such as maintenance are caused by the number of machine-hours worked in the producing departments, then variable maintenance costs should be allocated to the producing departments using machine-hours as the allocation basis. By this means, the departments directly responsible for the incurrence of servicing costs are required to bear them in proportion to their actual usage of the service.

Technically, the assigning of variable servicing costs to consuming departments can more accurately be termed charges than allocations, since the service department is actually charging the consuming departments at some fixed rate per unit of service provided. In effect, the service department is saying, 'I'll charge you X pounds for every unit of my service that you consume. You can consume as much or as little as you desire; the total charge you bear will vary proportionately.'

## Fixed costs

The fixed costs of service departments represent the costs of making capacity available for use. These costs should be allocated to consuming departments in predetermined lump-sum amounts. By predetermined lump-sum amounts we mean that the total amount charged to each consuming department is determined in advance and, once determined, does not change from period to period. The lump-sum amount charged to a department can be based either on the department's peak-period or long-run average servicing needs. The logic behind lump-sum allocations of this type is that when a service department is first established, its capacity will be determined by the needs of the departments that it will service. This capacity may reflect the peak-period needs of the other departments, or it may reflect their long-run average or 'normal' servicing needs. Depending on how much servicing capacity is provided for, it will be necessary to make a commitment of resources to the servicing unit, which will be reflected in its fixed costs. These fixed costs should be borne by the consuming departments in proportion to the amount of capacity each consuming department requires. That is, if available capacity in the service department has been provided to meet the peak-period needs of consuming departments, then the fixed costs of the service department should be allocated in predetermined lump-sum amounts to consuming departments on this basis. If available capacity has been provided only to meet 'normal' or long-run average needs, then the fixed costs should be allocated on this basis.

Once set, allocations should not vary from period to period, since they represent the cost of having a certain level of service capacity available and on line for each consuming department. The fact that a consuming department does not need a peak level or even a 'normal' level of servicing every period is immaterial; if it requires such servicing at certain times, then the capacity to deliver it must be available. It is the responsibility of the consuming departments to bear the cost of that availability.

To illustrate this idea, assume that Novak Company has just organized a Maintenance Department to service all machines in the Cutting, Assembly, and Finishing Departments. In determining the capacity of the newly organized Maintenance Department, the various producing departments estimated that they would have the following peak-period needs for maintenance:

| Department | Peak-period maintenance needs in terms of number of hours of maintenance work required | Percentage of total hours |
|---|---|---|
| Cutting | 900 | 30 |
| Assembly | 1,800 | 60 |
| Finishing | 300 | 10 |
|  | 3,000 | 100 |

Therefore, in allocating the Maintenance Department fixed costs to the producing departments, 30% (i.e., 900/3,000 = 30%) should be allocated to the Cutting Department, 60% to the Assembly Department, and 10% to the Finishing Department. These lump-sum allocations will not change from period to period unless there is some shift in peak-period servicing needs.

## Should actual or budgeted costs be allocated?

Should the actual or budgeted costs of a service department be allocated to operating departments? The answer is that *budgeted* costs should be allocated. What's wrong with allocating actual costs? Allocating actual costs burdens the operating departments with any inefficiencies in the service department. If actual costs are allocated, then any lack of cost control on the part of the service department is simply buried in a routine allocation to other departments.

Any variance over budgeted costs should be retained in the service department and closed out at year end against the company's revenues or against cost of goods sold, along with other variances. Operating department managers justifiably complain bitterly if they are forced to absorb service department inefficiencies.

Yet another approach is to treat the SSC as a profit centre, allow it to charge market prices and even bid for outside contracts. A more intermediate position is to use service level agreements with detailed provisions for fees and delivery clauses. These issues may draw on the principles introduced earlier in this chapter but will also be influenced by the *transfer pricing principles* that we introduced in Chapter 15.

Overall, the great advantage of the SSC when compared with outsourcing is that it should be possible to improve efficiency and effectiveness of service delivery without the loss of control and dependency that may result from full outsourcing. With this warning in mind, we will now consider service outsourcing.

## Service outsourcing

Although we have considered **outsourcing** as a possible response to the problem of constraints, there are usually a number of motives for service outsourcing which are very similar to those reviewed above in connection with SSCs. In comparison with outsourcing, SSCs have high start-up costs and may take time to embed the necessary cultural change. Many companies outsource in order to cut costs, to free up staff to concentrate on core operations, to access specialist expertise in areas like IT, to free up cash and speed up set-up.[24] Companies are making an explicit attempt to review the supply chain and ask where the 'natural ownership'[25] of activities lies. Rather than just look at the product in a strategic version of make-or-buy, managers ask more fundamental questions about *what the company should be doing*. Many companies are actually three businesses – a *customer relationship* business, a *product innovation* business, and an *infrastructure* business.[26] Each business is characterized by different cultures and different economics. For example, the infrastructure business requires economies of scale and an emphasis on cost minimization through standardization, predictability and efficiency. The product innovation business has to be employee-centred, with an emphasis on 'coddling' the company's creative stars. Lower interaction costs allow these competences to be unbundled and reconfigured so that the different economics and cultures can be recognized through increased corporate specialization.

One of the implications of corporate unbundling for management accounting is that increased corporate specialization should make it easier to design appropriate performance measurement systems. While there still needs to be a balance of measures, a customer-focused business will not need the same balance of indicators as an infrastructure business.

From a strategic point of view, the organization can concentrate its attention on its core activities. For example, Boots has outsourced many services such as catering because it is not in business as a caterer. Although as with other forms of outsourcing the main motive for change may be cost management, reorganizations of support services give a considerable impetus to attempts to ascertain the costs of products, jobs and customers more accurately through the use of techniques such as activity-based costing.

### Outsourcing the finance function

Service areas such as human resources, IT, administration and purchasing have been generally leading the way in outsourcing contracts, but there may be a case for outsourcing the finance function. Although it is generally seen as too much of a core business process to outsource, it is possible, in principle, to distinguish between transactional tasks such as payroll, purchase and sales ledgers which can be outsourced and other areas such as *management accounting* which are more contentious.[27] However, this distinction may beg the question as to which tasks are management accounting and which tasks are routine transactions and reporting. For example, local business unit managers need to feel a sense of ownership over the reports that they are signing off, credit control may be a vital part of local customer relations.

SSCs and outsourcing strategies perhaps might force management accountants to reflect on what their unique contribution can be, whether it is as business partners in the business units or as custodians of financial integrity. For example, where should budgeting be located? This function is seen as a particular grey area depending on whether it is routine and mechanical or whether it is closely allied to business strategy and operations. Although the practice of outsourcing and centralization in SSCs is increasing, the amount of academic research in this area is very limited.[28] It is easy to get the consultants' and outsourcers' generally upbeat evaluations of the process. It is much harder to gain access to the business units and the SSCs on a basis that might enable a more balanced and critical approach.

As the trend for outsourcing gathers momentum, there are emerging problems. For example, the outsourcing of the supply chain in the US car industry has been accompanied by a long-term squeeze on suppliers' margins and returns. As suppliers struggle the car manufacturers have begun to face quality problems (Firestone and Ford) and delays in product launches (Daimler Chrysler and its Smart Car).[29] In the UK, the separation of the ownership of track and infrastructure from the ownership of the train operators has led to problems with safety, punctuality and, even more recently, corporate administration for Railtrack. In both these cases, there has been a lack of co-operation between the parties and certainly no attempt to institute a technique such as open-book accounting. Companies sometimes fail to identify their key operations. For example, budget airlines such as Go will not consider outsourcing their cabin staff as these are the areas where they spend time with their customers. The US airline industry has been criticized for outsourcing security before the events of 11 September 2001, as has Railtrack for its outsourcing of line maintenance.[30] In both instances, the industries put a low value on safety with disastrous human and commercial consequences.

### Summary

- In the short run, organizations are faced with resource constraints. Linear programming is a mathematical technique that may be used to find an optimal solution in a multi-product, multi-constraint world.
- The theory of constraints emphasizes the importance of managing the organization's constraints. Since the constraint is whatever is holding back the organization, improvement efforts usually must be focused on the constraint in order to be really effective.
- In the long run, constraints can be anticipated through the design of products and processes. The challenge here is to plan and manage costs throughout the life cycle of a product. The design phase may take cost management into the supply chain.
- A strategic approach to make-or-buy may indicate significant gains to be realized from outsourcing firms' activities. The firm may try to maintain some control over the outsourced activities through partnerships – alliances supported by techniques such as open-book accounting.

- New organizational forms such as shared service centres and outsourcing are having an increasing impact on the delivery of business services. These restructurings raise fundamental questions about the status of sensitive services such as the finance function.

## Key terms for review

**Constraint** (p. 798)
**Corner point** (p. 796)
**'Families' of components** (p. 805)
**Feasible region** (p. 794)
**Iso-contribution line** (p. 794)
**Kaizen budgeting** (p. 801)
**Kaizen costing** (p. 801)
**Limiting factor** (p. 794)
**Objective function** (p. 794)
**Optimal combination of product** (p. 794)
**Outsourcing** (p. 813)
**Relaxing (or elevating) the constraint** (p. 797)
**Sensitivity analysis** (p. 796)
**Shadow prices** (p. 797)
**Shared service centre** (p. 810)
**Simplex method** (p. 794)
**Supply chain management** (p. 804)
**Theory of constraints (TOC)** (p. 798)
**Throughput accounting (TA)** (p. 799)
**Throughput accounting ratio** (p. 799)
**Total cost of ownership** (p. 805)
**Value analysis** (p. 802)
**Value engineering** (p. 802)
**Vertical integration** (p. 803)

**Level of difficulty:** BASIC  INTERMEDIATE  ADVANCED

## Questions

**19-1** Under what circumstances is linear programming appropriate for the analysis of decision making under constraints?

**19-2** Which point defines the optimal output in a linear programming problem?

**19-3** Why might sensitivity analysis be a useful technique in a linear programming problem?

**19-4** Why does the theory of constraints emphasize managing constraints?

**19-5** What are six ways of relaxing a constraint?

**19-6** In what way does throughput accounting misrepresent the theory of constraints?

**19-7** How do you decide whether a component is strategic or non-strategic?

**19-8** Why does supply management emphasize cost rather than price?

**19-9** Suggest some problems that may be encountered in a major outsourcing contract.

## Exercises

**E19-1**  Time allowed: 15 minutes
Listed below are a number of terms that relate to just-in-time, total quality management, process re-engineering, and theory of constraints:

| | | |
|---|---|---|
| Benchmarking | Just-in-time (JIT) | Process re-engineering |
| Business process | Non-constraint | Pull |
| Constraint | Non-value-added activities | Set-up |
| Frequent | Plan-do-check-act cycle | Total quality management |

**816** Part 4 Value metrics and performance management in a strategic context

Choose the term or terms above that most appropriately complete the following statements:

1 To successfully operate a JIT system, a company must learn to rely on a few suppliers who are willing to make _____ deliveries.
2 _____ is an incremental approach to improvement, whereas _____ tends to be a much more radical approach that involves completely redesigning business processes.
3 A production system in which units are produced and materials are purchased only as needed to meet actual customer demand is called _____.
4 In JIT, the flow of goods is controlled by what is described as a _____ approach to manufacturing.
5 Increasing the rate of a _____ as the result of an improvement effort is unlikely to have much effect on profits.
6 _____ involves studying the business processes of companies that are considered among the best in the world at performing a particular task.
7 The activities involved in getting equipment ready to produce a different product are called a _____.
8 The theory of constraints suggests that improvement efforts should be focused on the company's _____.
9 The _____ is a systematic, fact-based approach to continuous improvement that resembles the scientific method.
10 In process re-engineering, two objectives are to simplify and to eliminate _____.
11 A _____ is any series of steps that are followed in order to carry out some task in a business.

## Problems

**P19-2** Pricing/ABC/throughput accounting
Time allowed: 45 minutes

LM Hospital is a private hospital whose management is considering the adoption of an activity-based costing (ABC) system for the year 2010/11. The main reason for its introduction would be to provide more accurate information for pricing purposes. With the adoption of new medical technology, the amount of time that some patients stay in hospital has decreased considerably, and the management feels that the current pricing strategy may no longer reflect the different costs incurred.

Prices are currently calculated by determining the direct costs for the particular type of operation and adding a markup of 135%. With the proposed ABC system, the management expects to use a markup for pricing purposes of 15% on cost. This percentage will be based on all costs except facility sustaining costs. It has been decided that the hospital support activities should be grouped into three categories – admissions and record keeping, caring for patients, and facility sustaining.

The hospital has four operating theatres that are used for 9 hours a day for 300 days a year. It is expected that 7,200 operations will be performed during the coming year. The hospital has 15 consultant surgeons engaged in operating theatre work and consultancy. It is estimated that each consultant surgeon will work at the hospital for 2,000 hours in 2010/11.

The expected costs for 2010/11 are:

|  | £ |
|---|---|
| Nursing services and administration | 9,936,000 |
| Linen and laundry | 920,000 |
| Kitchen and food costs (3 meals a day) | 2,256,000 |
| Consultant surgeons' fees | 5,250,000 |
| Insurance of buildings and general equipment | 60,000 |
| Depreciation of buildings and general equipment | 520,000 |
| Operating theatre | 4,050,000 |
| Pre-operation costs | 1,260,000 |

Chapter 19 Strategic perspectives on cost management    817

| | |
|---|---:|
| Medical supplies – used in the hospital wards | 1,100,000 |
| Pathology laboratory (where blood tests, etc. are carried out) | 920,000 |
| Updating patient records | 590,000 |
| Patient/bed scheduling | 100,000 |
| Invoicing and collections | 160,000 |
| Housekeeping activities, including ward maintenance, window cleaning, and so on | 760,000 |

Other information for 2010/11:

| | |
|---|---:|
| Nursing hours | 480,000 |
| Number of pathology laboratory tests | 8,000 |
| Patient days | 44,000 |
| Number of patients | 9,600 |

Information relating to specific operations for 2010/11:

| | ENT (ear, nose and throat) | Cataract |
|---|---|---|
| Time of stay in hospital | 4 days | 1 day |
| Operation time | 2 hours | 0.5 hour |
| Consultant surgeon's time (which includes time in the operating theatre) | 3 hours | 0.85 hour |

### Required

1. Before making the final decision on the costing/pricing system, management has selected two types of operation for review: an ear, nose and throat (ENT) operation and a cataract operation.
   
   (a) Calculate the prices that would be charged under each method for the two types of operation. (Your answer should include an explanation and calculations of the cost drivers you have used.)
   
   (b) Comment on the results of your calculations and the implications for the proposed pricing policy.

2. Critically assess the method you have used to calculate the ABC prices by selecting two items/categories above which you feel should have been dealt with in a different way.

3. Explain whether the concept of throughput accounting could be used in a hospital.

*(CIMA Management Accounting – Decision Making)*

**P19–3** E-commerce/budgeting/value analysis
Time allowed: 45 minutes

ML plc was formed three years ago to develop e-commerce systems and design websites for clients. The company has expanded rapidly since then and now has a multi-site operation with bases in the UK and overseas.

ML plc has recognized the need to formalize its planning and budgeting procedures and one of its divisional managers has been assigned to co-ordinate the budgets for the year to 31 March 2010. He recently attended a course on Financial Planning and Budgeting and has been puzzled by some of the concepts. In particular, he would like you to explain the following:

- The differences and similarities between zero-based budgeting and activity based budgeting
- The reasons why budget holders should prepare their own budgets

**Part 4** Value metrics and performance management in a strategic context

- The reasons why incremental budgeting may not be appropriate as a basis of budgeting if budget bias is to be minimized.

### Required

1. Prepare a report, addressed to the divisional manager, that explains the issues he has identified above.
2. Techniques that are used in order to improve an organization's performance include:
   - Cost reduction
   - Value analysis.

Explain these techniques and how they may be used by ML plc as part of its planning activities.

*(CIMA Management Accounting – Performance Management)*

**P19–4 Multiple products, life-cycle and target costing**
Time allowed: 45 minutes

'Costing systems attempt to explain how products consume resources but do not indicate the joint benefits of having multiple products.'

### Required

1. Explain the statement above and discuss
   (a) How the addition of a new product to the product range may affect the 'cost' of existing products;
   (b) The consequences, in terms of total profitability, of decisions to increase/decrease the product range.
2. Telmat is a company that manufactures mobile phones. This market is extremely volatile and competitive and achieving adequate product profitability is extremely important. Telmat is a mature company that has been producing electronic equipment for many years and has all the costing systems in place that one would expect in such a company. These include a comprehensive overhead absorption system, annual budgets and monthly variance reports and the balanced scorecard for performance measurement.

The company is considering introducing:
   (a) Target costing
   (b) Life-cycle costing systems.

Discuss the advantages (or otherwise) that this specific company is likely to gain from these two systems.

*(CIMA Management Accounting – Decision Making)*

**P19–5 Cost management/JIT**
Time allowed: 45 minutes

The WYE hotel group operates a chain of 50 hotels. The size of each hotel varies, as do the services that each hotel provides. However, all of the hotels operated by the group provide a restaurant, swimming pool, lounge bar, guest laundry service and accommodation.

Some of the hotels also provide guest entertainment, travel bureaux and shopping facilities. The Managing Director of the group is concerned about the high level of running costs being incurred by the hotels.

### Required

1. Explain how cost reduction, value analysis and zero-based budgeting techniques could be used by the WYE hotel group to improve the profitability of its hotels.
2. M plc is a food manufacturer. It operates a just-in-time (JIT) system with computer-controlled, automated processing and packaging equipment. The focus of M plc's weekly management reports is on the variance analysis that is generated from a standard absorption costing system that uses labour hours as the basis of overhead absorption.

Chapter 19 Strategic perspectives on cost management

3 Explain why standard costing systems based upon absorption costing principles may be inappropriate in the modern manufacturing environment of companies such as M plc.

(*CIMA Management Accounting – Performance Management*)

**P19-6 Linear programming**
Time allowed: 45 minutes

DP plc assembles computers from bought-in components, using a computer controlled robotic assembly line. The assembled computers are then tested by highly qualified computer engineers before they are packaged for despatch to customers. DP plc currently assembles two different types of computer from different combinations of the same components.

The following budgeted details relate to the computers:

|  | Computer X | Computer Y |
| --- | --- | --- |
| Selling price/unit | £800 | £1,200 |
| Component costs per unit | £150 | £310 |
|  | **Minutes per unit** | **Minutes per unit** |
| Assembly time (S1) | 80 | 130 |
| Testing time (S2) | 120 | 180 |
| Packaging time (S3) | 60 | 30 |

The following costs are derived from DP plc's budget for the year to 31 December 2011:

| Assembly | £180/hour |
| --- | --- |
| Testing | £60/hour |
| Packaging | £20/hour |

No cost increases are expected until July 2012.

DP plc is now preparing its detailed plans for the six-month period to 30 June 2012. During this period, it expects that the assembly time available will be limited to 1,000 hours and the testing time available will be limited to 875 hours. The packaging is carried out by part-time workers, and the company believes that there are a number of local residents who would be pleased to undertake this work if the existing packaging staff were unable to complete the level of activity needed.

The maximum levels of demand for each computer will be:

300 units of X (S4)
800 units of Y (S5).

### Required

1 Calculate the contribution per unit for each type of computer.
2 Determine the mix of computers that will maximize DP plc's profits for the six months ending 30 June 2012, using a graphical linear programming solution, and calculate the contribution that will be earned.
3 DP plc now realizes that there may be a limit on the number of packaging hours available. A computer package for linear programming has been used and the following solution determined:

**Part 4** Value metrics and performance management in a strategic context

| Variables | |
|---|---|
| X | 268.75 |
| Y | 112.50 |
| Constraints | |
| S1 | 23,875.00 |
| S2 | 1.46 |
| S3 | 4.75 |
| S4 | 31.25 |
| S5 | 687.50 |
| Contribution | £107,437.50 |

Write a report to the management team that interprets the solution produced by the computer package and makes appropriate recommendations. (*Note:* Do not formulate, or explain the basis of, the computer model.)

4  At the management meeting that discussed the report you produced in Question 3 above, the senior computer engineer responsible for the testing of the computers was surprised at the times per unit being used in your calculations.

'It seems to me', she said, 'that you have used the testing times per unit that were set as the targets when those models of computer were first assembled. We seem to test them much more quickly than this now.'

Explain how the learning effect referred to by the senior computer engineer will affect the calculation of the optimum product mix. Use a 90% learning curve to illustrate your answer but do not determine a revised product mix. (*Note:* The formula for a 90% learning curve is $y = ax^{-0.1520}$.)

(*CIMA Management Accounting – Performance Management*)

### P19–7 Linear programming
Time allowed: 50 minutes

W plc provides two cleaning services for staff uniforms to hotels and similar businesses. One of the services is a laundry service and the other is a dry cleaning service. Both of the services use the same resources, but in different quantities. Details of the expected resource requirements, revenues and costs of each service are shown below:

| | Laundry $ per service | Dry cleaning $ per service |
|---|---|---|
| Selling price | 7.00 | 12.00 |
| Cleaning materials ($10.00 per litre) | 2.00 | 3.00 |
| Direct labour ($6.00 per hour) | 1.20 | 2.00 |
| Variable machine cost ($3.00 per hour) | 0.50 | 1.50 |
| Fixed costs* | 1.15 | 2.25 |
| Profit | 2.15 | 3.25 |

*The fixed costs per service were based on meeting the budget demand for December 2010.

W plc has already prepared its budget for December based on sales and operational activities of 8,000 laundry services and 10,500 dry cleaning services, but it is now revising its plans because of forecast resource problems.

The maximum resources expected to be available in December 2010 are:

| | |
|---|---|
| Cleaning materials | 5,000 litres |
| Direct labour hours | 6,000 hours |
| Machine hours | 5,000 hours |

W plc has one particular contract which it entered into six months ago with a local hotel to guarantee 1,200 laundry services and 2,000 dry cleaning services every month. If W plc does not honour this contract it has to pay substantial financial penalties to the local hotel.

### Required

1 Calculate the mix of services that should be provided by W plc so as to maximize its profit for December 2010.
2 The Sales Director has reviewed the selling prices being used by W plc and has provided the following further information:
   - if the price for laundry were to be reduced to $5.60 per service, this would increase the demand to 14,000 services;
   - if the price for dry cleaning were to be increased to $13.20 per service, this would reduce the demand to 9,975 services.

   Assuming that such selling price changes would apply to *all sales* and that the resource limitations continue to apply, and that a graphical linear programming solution is to be used to maximize profit,

   (a) state the constraints and objective function;
   (b) use a graphical linear programing solution to advise W plc whether it should revise its selling prices.

   (*CIMA Performance Management*)

## Cases

### C19-8 Linear programming
Time allowed: 60 minutes

The Puxi Company manufactures consumer food products, based on soya beans. For convenience purposes the three products can be referred to as Alpha (A), Beta (B) and Cappa (C). The production process is relatively simple. In the Mixing Department, the raw material ingredients are crushed and mixed into a soft paste. This is a machine-intensive rather than labour-intensive process. The 'paste' is then transferred to a Filling Department where the product is bottled, labelled and packaged for distribution. Again, this is a machine-intensive process. Direct labour is a relatively small amount in the overall cost structure. As a result, the company has combined direct labour cost with overhead costs into a 'conversion cost' category.

In recent months, the manager of Puxi Company has become concerned about various 'constraints' facing his company. Perhaps most important was the limited supply of domestically grown soya beans. As a result, the soya beans had to be imported from the US. Unfortunately, most of the soya bean crop grown in the US is genetically modified (GM) and must be tested before use. The practical implication of this is that the supply of soya beans will be limited for the next planning period.

These and other restrictions were discussed at a recent budget meeting of various section managers and are summarized as follows:

1 Supply of soya bean limited to 500,000 kg, equivalent to a total cost of $500,000.
2 Machine hours availability in the Mixing Department restricted to 3,000 hours due to obsolete machinery.

**822**  Part 4 Value metrics and performance management in a strategic context

3 Machine hour availability in the Filling Department restricted to 2,000 hours due to shortage of machine parts.
4 Contracts had already been signed with various customers to supply a minimum of 10,000 units of each of the three products for next year. These minimum units must be produced.
5 Because no increase or decrease in selling price could be made for next year, the maximum demand for the three products was estimated as follows:

| | |
|---|---|
| Alpha (A) = | 60,000 units |
| Beta (B) = | 60,000 units |
| Cappa (C) = | 60,000 units |

The following information is provided regarding the three products:

| Product information | Product A | Product B | Product C |
|---|---|---|---|
| Selling prince per unit | $20 | $26 | $38 |
| Soya bean ingredient cost @ $1 per kg | 3 | 4 | 6 |
| Variable conversion costs* | 6 | 8 | 12 |
| Fixed production overhead costs ** | 6 | 8 | 12 |
| Profit per unit | 5 | 6 | 8 |

| Product information | Product A | Product B | Product C |
|---|---|---|---|
| Machine minutes per unit: | | | |
| Dept. 1 (maximum 3,000 hours) | 1 minute | 1 minute | 2 minutes |
| Dept. 2 (maximum 2,000 hours) | 3/4 minute | 1 minute | 1¼ minutes |

*Variable conversion cost represents variable direct labour and variable overheads but excludes direct material cost.
**The fixed production overhead costs have been absorbed on the basis of direct material, i.e. soya bean cost, using a production level of 40,000 units of each of the three products.

After looking at the information, you quickly present the above data as a linear programming model and solve it using Lindo.

| Computer printout for Puxi Company using LINDO software | |
|---|---|
| 1  Max 11A + 14B + 20C | (Objective function) |
| ST | Subject to (the following restrictions) |
| 2  3A + 4B + 6C < 500,000 | Maximum kgs and spend on Soya ingredients |
| 3  1A + 1B + 2C < 180,000 | Maximum machine mins. In Mixing Department |
| 4  0.75A + 1B 1 +.25C < 120,000 | Maximum machine mins. In Filling Department |
| 5  A > 10,000 | Minimum production units of product A |

| | | |
|---|---|---|
| 6 | B > 10,000 | Minimum production units of product B |
| 7 | C > 10,000 | Minimum production units of product C |
| 8 | A < 60,000 | Maximum sales units of product A |
| 9 | B < 60,000 | Maximum sales units of product B |
| 10 | C < 60,000 | Maximum sales units of product C |
| Objective function value | | $1,760,000 |
| A | | 60,000 (units) |
| B | | 50,000 (units) |
| C | | 20,000 (units) |

| Row | Slack or surplus | Dual (shadow) price |
|---|---|---|
| 2 (Soya) | Nil | 2.50 |
| 3 (Mixing dept) | 30,000 | 0.00 |
| 4 (Filling dept) | Nil | 4.00 |
| 5 Minimum units of A | 50,000 | 0.00 |
| 6 Minimum units of B | 40,000 | 0.00 |
| 7 Minimum units of C | 10,000 | 0.00 |
| 8 Maximum sales units of A | Nil | 0.50 |
| 9 Maximum sales units of B | 10,000 | 0.00 |
| 10 Maximum sales units of C | 40,000 | 0.00 |

**Sensitivity Analysis: Ranges in which the basis remains unchanged**

| Variable $ | Current contribution $ | Allowable increase $ | Allowable decrease |
|---|---|---|---|
| A | 11.00 | Infinity | 0.50 |
| B | 14.00 | 0.66 | 0.66 |
| C | 20.00 | 1.00 | 2.50 |

**Right hand side ranges**

| Row No. | Current RHS | Allowable increase | Allowable decrease |
|---|---|---|---|
| 2 | 500,000 | 32,000 | 8,000 |
| 3 | 180,000 | Infinity | 30,000 |
| 4 | 120,000 | 1,667 | 6,667 |
| 5 | 10,000 | 50,000 | Infinity |
| 6 | 10,000 | 40,000 | Infinity |
| 7 | 10,000 | 10,000 | Infinity |
| 8 | 60,000 | 53,333 | 13,333 |
| 9 | 60,000 | Infinity | 10,000 |
| 10 | 60,000 | Infinity | 40,000 |

## Required

1. Indicate the total sales revenue, the total contribution ($) generated by the optimal production plan and indicate the physical quantities (units) of each of the three products according to the optimal production plan. Also, indicate the net profit for the period based on the optimal plan.
2. Calculate the break-even point (BEP) in $ revenue, assuming the constant product mix of the optimal production plan.
3. Clearly identify the impact, if any, on the optimal production plan and on profit of the following independent events.
   (a) Selling price of product A increased by $1.
   (b) An additional supply of £1,000 of soya beans is available.
   (c) An additional 1,000 minutes of Mixing time becomes available.
   (d) An additional 1,000 minutes in Filling becomes available.
4. Identify and explain what is the opportunity cost, if any, associated with the minimum production of 10,000 units of Product A.
5. What is the maximum price that one would pay for one extra kilogram of soya bean ingredient, bearing in mind that each kilogram currently costs $1 per kg? Briefly explain your answer.
6. Briefly explain three limitations associated with using linear programming as a tool of managerial decision making in this manufacturing company.
7. Some manufacturing companies are currently experiencing a shortage of skilled labour. Suggest three ways in which this constraint could be relaxed, where the company employs a combination of skilled and unskilled labour.

*(Thanks to Peter Clarke of University College Dublin for this case)*

### C19–9 In-house versus outsourcing, business process improvement
Time allowed: 60 minutes

The Country Car Club (3C) was established fifty years ago to offer breakdown assistance to motorists. In return for an annual membership fee, members of 3C are able to phone for immediate assistance if their vehicle breaks down anywhere in the country. Assistance is provided by 'service patrol engineers' who are located throughout the country and who are specialists in vehicle repair and maintenance. If they cannot fix the problem immediately then the vehicle (and its occupants) are transported by a 3C recovery vehicle back to the member's home address free of charge.

Over the last fifteen years 3C has rapidly expanded its services. It now offers vehicle insurance, vehicle history checks (to check for previous accident damage or theft) as well as offering a comprehensive advice centre where trained staff answer a wide range of vehicle-related queries. It also provides route maps, endorses hotels by giving them a 3C starred rating and lobbies the government on issues such as taxation, vehicle emissions and toll road charging. All of these services are provided by permanent 3C employees and all growth has been organic culminating in a listing on the country's stock exchange three years ago. However, since its stock market listing, the company has posted disappointing results and a falling share price has spurred managers to review internal processes and functions. A Business Architecture Committee (BAC) made up of senior managers has been charged with reviewing the scope of the company's business activities. It has been asked to examine the importance of certain activities and to make recommendations on the sourcing of these activities (in-house or outsourced). The BAC has also been asked to identify technological implications or opportunities for the activities that they recommend should remain in-house.

### First review

The BAC's first review included an assessment of the supply and maintenance of 3C's company vehicles. 3C has traditionally purchased its own fleet of vehicles and maintained them in a central garage. When a vehicle needed servicing or maintenance it was returned to this central garage. Last year, 3C had seven hundred vehicles (breakdown recovery vehicles, service patrol engineer vans, company cars for senior staff, etc.)

all maintained by thirty staff permanently employed in this garage. A further three permanent employees were employed at the garage site with responsibility for the purchasing and disposal of vehicles. The garage was in a residential area of a major town, with major parking problems and no room for expansion.

The BAC concluded that the garage was of low strategic importance to the company and, although most of the processes it involved were straightforward, its remoteness from the home base of some vehicles made undertaking such processes unnecessarily complicated. Consequently, it recommended outsourcing vehicle acquisition, disposal and maintenance to a specialist company. Two months ago 3C's existing vehicle fleet was acquired by AutoDirect, a company with service and repair centres nationwide, which currently supplies 45,000 vehicles to companies throughout the country. It now leases vehicles back to 3C for a monthly payment. In the next ten years (the duration of the contract) all vehicles will be leased from AutoDirect on a full maintenance basis that includes the replacement of tyres and exhausts. 3C's garage is now surplus to requirements and all the employees that worked there have been made redundant, except for one employee who has been retained to manage the relationship with AutoDirect.

### Second review

The BAC has now been asked to look at the following activities and their supporting processes. All of these are currently performed in-house by permanent 3C employees.

- *Attendance of repair staff at breakdowns* – currently undertaken by permanent 'service patrol engineers' employed at locations throughout the country from where they attend local breakdowns.
- *Membership renewal* – members must renew every year. Currently renewals are sent out by staff using a bespoke computer system. Receipts are processed when members confirm that they will be renewing for a further year.
- *Vehicle insurance services* providing accident insurance which every motorist legally requires.
- *Membership queries* handled by a call-centre. Members can use the service for a wide range of vehicle-related problems and issues.
- *Vehicle history checks*. These are primarily used to provide 'peace of mind' to a potential purchaser of a vehicle. The vehicle is checked to see if it has ever been in an accident or if it has been stolen. The check also makes sure that the car is not currently part of a loan agreement.

### Required

1. The Business Architecture Committee (BAC) has been asked to make recommendations on the sourcing of activities (in-house or outsourced). The BAC has also been asked to identify technological implications or opportunities for the activities that they recommend should remain in-house.

    Suggest and justify recommendations to the BAC for each of the following major process areas:
    (a) Attendance of repair staff at breakdowns;
    (b) Membership renewal;
    (c) Vehicle insurance services;
    (d) Membership queries; and
    (e) Vehicle history checks.

2. Analyse the advantages that 3C will gain from the decision to outsource the purchase and maintenance of their own vehicles.

*(ACCA Business Analysis)*

## Endnotes

1. Kuglin and Rosenbaum (2001).
2. Students familiar with elementary economics may compare the linear programming model with the curved line called the *production possibility frontier*. While the basic principles are very similar, linear programming enables greater operationality.
3. See Johnson and Kaplan (1987) for an extended justification for managing rather than optimizing.
4. Galloway and Waldron (1988).
5. See Dugdale and Jones (1998); Jones and Dugdale (1998).
6. Monden and Hamada (1991).
7. Tanaka, Yoshikawa, Innes and Mitchell (1994).
8. Summers (2002).
9. Doig, Ritter, Speckhals and Woolson (2001).
10. See Seal, Cullen, Dunlop, Berry and Mirghani (1999).
11. Baily, Farmer, Jessop and Jones (1998).
12. Venkatesan (1992).
13. Lamming (1993).
14. Best practice in supply chain management may not be enough to ensure business survival. See Seal, Berry and Cullen (2004).
15. A real company but the name has been changed. See Mouritsen, Hansen and Hansen (2001a).
16. This is a shorter version of the case study in Seal *et al.* (1999).
17. For more research on open book agreements see Kajüter and Kulmala (2005).
18. Schulman, Dunleavy, Harmer and Lusk (1999), p. 9.
19. Bergeron (2003), p. 3.
20. Quinn, Cooke and Kris (2000).
21. Schulman *et al.* (1999).
22. Schulman *et al.* (1999).
23. Bergeron (2003).
24. Hayward (2002).
25. The term 'natural ownership' was used in Doig *et al.* (2001).
26. Hagel and Singer (1999).
27. Hayward (2003).
28. But see Herman and Brignall (2004).
29. Doig *et al.* (2001).
30. Hayward (2002).

When you have read this chapter, log on to the Online Learning Centre for *Management Accounting* at www.mcgraw-hill.co.uk/textbooks/seal, where you'll find multiple choice questions, practice exams and extra study tools for each chapter.

# Managing in the Global Environment

# CHAPTER 6

# Managing in the Global Environment

## Learning Objectives

*After studying this chapter, you should be able to:*

**LO6-1** Explain why the ability to perceive, interpret, and respond appropriately to the global environment is crucial for managerial success.

**LO6-2** Differentiate between the global task and global general environments.

**LO6-3** Identify the main forces in the global task and general environments, and describe the challenges that each force presents to managers.

**LO6-4** Explain why the global environment is becoming more open and competitive, and identify the forces behind the process of globalization that increase the opportunities, complexities, challenges, and threats managers face.

**LO6-5** Discuss why national cultures differ and why it is important that managers be sensitive to the effects of falling trade barriers and regional trade associations on the political and social systems of nations around the world.

# A MANAGER'S CHALLENGE
## A Turnaround at Sony Is in the Works

**By 2005 Sony was in big trouble; and at this crucial point in their company's history, Sony's Japanese top managers turned to a gaijin, or non-Japanese, executive to lead their company.** Their choice was Sir Howard Stringer, a Welshman, the previous head of Sony's North American operations who had been instrumental in cutting costs and increasing the profits of Sony's U.S. division. Once he became CEO in 2005, Stringer faced the immediate problem of reducing Sony's operating costs, which were double those of its competitors even as it was losing its technological leadership. Stringer had to make many radical strategic decisions.

Japan is a country where large companies traditionally had a policy of lifetime employment, but Stringer made it clear that layoffs were inevitable. Within five years he cut Sony's Japanese workforce by over 25,000 employees and closed 12 factories to reduce costs. Stringer also recognized how the extensive power struggles among the top managers of Sony's different product divisions were hurting the company, and he made it clear that these problems had to stop. Many top divisional managers, including the manager of Sony's successful PlayStation division, ignored Stringer; they were replaced, and he worked steadily to downsize Sony's bloated corporate headquarters staff and to change its culture. In Stringer's own words, the culture or "business of Sony has been management, not making products." In 2009 Stringer announced he would take charge of the Japanese company's struggling core electronics group and would add the title of president to his existing roles as chairman and CEO as he reorganized Sony's divisions. He also replaced four more top executives with

Sir Howard Stringer, flanked by two younger executives, shows off new Sony products. Stringer's embrace of those outside Japan may help turn the flagging multinational around.

young managers who had held positions outside Japan and were "familiar with the digital world." In the future, according to Stringer, managers must prioritize new products and invest in only those with the greatest chance of success so Sony could reduce its out-of-control R&D costs.

Stringer worked hard to bring the realities of global competition to the forefront at Sony—along with the need to deal with them quickly. Beyond his internal problems, he also pushed for major changes in how Sony picked its suppliers. Stringer's goal was to reduce the number of Sony's parts suppliers from 2,500 to 1,200 to cut purchasing costs by over $5 billion or 20%. This would require cooperation between divisions because in the past each division made its own purchasing decisions. In the future Sony will centralize purchasing to negotiate cheaper prices by increasing the amount of business it does with its remaining suppliers.

By 2010 Sony's financial results suggested that Stringer's initiatives were finally paying off; he had stemmed Sony's huge losses, and its products were selling better. For example, PlayStation 3 sales jumped more than 40% after a 25% price cut and continued to outperform Nintendo's Wii. Although Sony still expected to lose money in 2010, Stringer expected Sony to become profitable by 2011. To help ensure this Stringer also took charge of a newly created networked products and services group that included its Vaio computers, Walkman media players, Sony's PlayStation gaming console, and the software and online services to support these products. Stringer's goal was for Sony to regain its global leadership in making the premium, differentiated digital products that command high prices and result in good profit margins. In 2010 Sony announced a major initiative to push into new technologies such as 3D LCD TVs, tablet computers, digital viewers, and action gaming and introduced a new motion controller for its PlayStation.[1] But competitors such as Apple, Samsung, and Panasonic were also competing in these markets, so global rivalry was likely to remain intense.

## Overview

**LO6-1** Explain why the ability to perceive, interpret, and respond appropriately to the global environment is crucial for managerial success.

**LO6-2** Differentiate between the global task and global general environments.

Top managers of a global company like Sony operate in an environment where they compete with other companies for scarce and valuable resources. Managers of companies large and small have found that to survive and prosper in the 21st century, most organizations must become **global organizations** that operate and compete not only domestically, at home, but also globally, in countries around the world. Operating in the global environment is uncertain and unpredictable because it is complex and changes constantly.

If organizations are to adapt successfully to this changing environment, their managers must learn to understand the forces that operate in it and how these forces give rise to opportunities and threats. In this chapter we examine why the environment, both domestically and globally, has become more open, vibrant, and competitive. We examine how forces in the task and general environments affect global organizations and their managers. By the end of this chapter, you will appreciate the changes that are taking place in the environment and understand why it is important

**global organization** An organization that operates and competes in more than one country.

for managers to develop a global perspective as they strive to increase organizational efficiency and effectiveness.

# What Is the Global Environment?

**global environment** The set of global forces and conditions that operate beyond an organization's boundaries but affect a manager's ability to acquire and utilize resources.

The **global environment** is a set of forces and conditions in the world outside an organization's boundary that affect how it operates and shape its behavior.[2] These forces change over time and thus present managers with *opportunities* and *threats*. Some changes in the global environment, such as the development of efficient new production technology, the availability of lower-cost components, or the opening of new global markets, create opportunities for managers to make and sell more products, obtain more resources and capital, and thereby strengthen their organization. In contrast, the rise of new global competitors, a global economic recession, or an oil shortage poses threats that can devastate an organization if managers are unable to sell its products so that revenues and profits plunge. The quality of managers' understanding of forces in the global environment and their ability to respond appropriately to those forces, such as Sony's managers' ability to make and sell the electronic products customers around the world want to buy, are critical factors affecting organizational performance.

In this chapter we explore the nature of these forces and consider how managers can respond to them. To identify opportunities and threats caused by forces in the environment, it is helpful for managers to distinguish between the *task environment* and the more encompassing *general environment* (see Figure 6.1).

**Figure 6.1**
**Forces in the Global Environment**

**task environment** The set of forces and conditions that originate with suppliers, distributors, customers, and competitors and affect an organization's ability to obtain inputs and dispose of its outputs because they influence managers daily.

**general environment** The wide-ranging global, economic, technological, sociocultural, demographic, political, and legal forces that affect an organization and its task environment.

The **task environment** is the set of forces and conditions that originate with global suppliers, distributors, customers, and competitors; these forces and conditions affect an organization's ability to obtain inputs and dispose of its outputs. The task environment contains the forces that have the most *immediate* and *direct* effect on managers because they pressure and influence managers daily. When managers turn on the radio or television, arrive at their offices in the morning, open their mail, or look at their computer screens, they are likely to learn about problems facing them because of changing conditions in their organization's task environment.

The **general environment** includes the wide-ranging global, economic, technological, sociocultural, demographic, political, and legal forces that affect the organization and its task environment. For the individual manager, opportunities and threats resulting from changes in the general environment are often more difficult to identify and respond to than are events in the task environment. However, changes in these forces can have major impacts on managers and their organizations.

## The Task Environment

Forces in the task environment result from the actions of suppliers, distributors, customers, and competitors both at home and abroad (see Figure 6.1). These four groups affect a manager's ability to obtain resources and dispose of outputs daily, weekly, and monthly and thus have a significant impact on short-term decision making.

**LO6-3** Identify the main forces in the global task and general environments, and describe the challenges that each force presents to managers.

### Suppliers

**suppliers** Individuals and organizations that provide an organization with the input resources it needs to produce goods and services.

**Suppliers** are the individuals and companies that provide an organization with the input resources (such as raw materials, component parts, or employees) it needs to produce goods and services. In return, the suppliers receive payment for those goods and services. An important aspect of a manager's job is to ensure a reliable supply of input resources.

Take Acer, for example, one of the world's largest computer makers from Taiwan. Acer has many suppliers of component parts such as microprocessors (Intel and AMD). It also has suppliers of preinstalled software, including operating system and specific applications software (Microsoft). Acer's providers of capital, such as banks and financial institutions, are also important suppliers.

Acer has several suppliers of labor. One source is the educational institutions that train future Acer employees and therefore provide the company with skilled workers. Another is trade unions, organizations that represent employee interests and can control the supply of labor by exercising the right of unionized workers to strike. Unions also can influence the terms and conditions under which labor is employed. Most of Acer's plants are in China where, even if there are unions, they typically are very weak. However, in other settings unions can be very strong. For example, it is the law in Germany that unions are typically represented on the board of directors of publicly traded firms. In organizations and industries where unions are strong, however, such as the transportation industry, an important part of a manager's job is negotiating and administering agreements with unions and their representatives.

Changes in the nature, number, or type of suppliers produce opportunities and threats to which managers must respond if their organizations are to prosper. For example, a major supplier-related threat that confronts managers arises when suppliers' bargaining position is so strong that they can raise the prices of the inputs they supply to the organization. A supplier's bargaining position is especially strong when (1) the supplier is the sole source of an input and (2) the input is vital to the organization.[3] For example, for 17 years G. D. Searle was the sole supplier of NutraSweet, the artificial sweetener used in most diet soft drinks. Not only was NutraSweet an important ingredient in diet soft drinks, but it also was one for which there was no acceptable substitute (saccharin and other artificial sweeteners raised

The purchasing activities of global companies have become increasingly complicated in recent years. More than 700 suppliers around the world produce parts for Boeing's new Dreamliner.

health concerns). Searle earned its privileged position because it invented and held the patent for Nutra-Sweet, and patents prohibit other organizations from introducing competing products for 17 years. As a result Searle was able to demand a high price for Nutra-Sweet, charging twice the price of an equivalent amount of sugar; and paying that price raised the costs of soft drink manufacturers such as Coca-Cola and PepsiCo. When Searle's patent expired many other companies introduced products similar to NutraSweet, and prices fell.[4] In the 2000s Splenda, which was made by McNeil Nutritionals, owned by Tate & Lyle, a British company, replaced NutraSweet as the artificial sweetener of choice, and NutraSweet's price fell further; Splenda began to command a high price from soft drink companies.[5]

In contrast, when an organization has many suppliers for a particular input, it is in a relatively strong bargaining position with those suppliers and can demand low-cost, high-quality inputs from them. Often an organization can use its power with suppliers to force them to reduce their prices, as Acer frequently does. Acer, for example, is constantly searching for low-cost suppliers to keep its PC prices competitive. At a global level, organizations can buy products from suppliers overseas or become their own suppliers by manufacturing their products abroad.

It is important that managers recognize the opportunities and threats associated with managing the global supply chain. On one hand, gaining access to low-cost products made abroad represents an opportunity for companies from mature economies to lower their input costs. On the other hand, managers who fail to use low-cost overseas suppliers create a threat and put their organizations at a competitive disadvantage.[6] Levi Strauss, for example, was slow to realize that it could not compete with the low-priced jeans sold by Walmart and other retailers, and it was eventually forced to close all its U.S. jean factories and outsource manufacturing to low-cost overseas suppliers to cut the price of its jeans to a competitive level. Now it sells its low-priced jeans in Walmart.

A common problem facing managers of large global companies such as Sony and Acer is managing the development of a global supplier network that will allow their companies to keep costs down and quality high. For example, Boeing's 777 jet was originally built using 132,500 engineered components made by 545 global suppliers.[7] Although Boeing made the majority of these parts, eight Japanese suppliers made parts for the 777 fuselage, doors, and wings; a Singapore supplier made the doors for the plane's forward landing gear; and three Italian suppliers produced its wing flaps. Boeing decided to buy so many inputs from global suppliers because these suppliers were the best in the world at performing their particular activities, and Boeing's goal was to produce a high-quality final product—a vital requirement for aircraft safety and reliability.[8]

The purchasing activities of global companies have become increasingly complicated as a result of the development of a whole range of skills and competencies in different countries around the world. It is clearly in companies' interests to search out the lowest-cost, best-quality suppliers. IT and the Internet are continually making it easier for companies to coordinate complicated, long-distance exchanges involving the purchasing of inputs and the disposal of outputs—something Sony has taken advantage of as it trims the number of its suppliers to reduce costs.

**global outsourcing** The purchase or production of inputs or final products from overseas suppliers to lower costs and improve product quality or design.

**Global outsourcing** occurs when a company contracts with suppliers in other countries to make the various inputs or components that go into its products or to assemble the final products to reduce costs. For example, Apple contracts with companies in Taiwan to make inputs such as the chips, batteries, and LCD displays that power its digital devices; then it contracts with Chinese outsourcing companies such as Foxconn to assemble its final products—such as iPods, iPhones, and iPads. Apple outsources the distribution of its products around the world by contracting with companies such as FedEx or DHL. However, one of the costs associated with such supplier networks is that when a supplier does something for which it may be criticized, often the larger and better known firm that is buying the output to sell to consumers receives the negative publicity. For example, Foxconn suffered a number of suicides among employees due to the high work levels expected, but it was Apple that was criticized.

Global outsourcing has grown enormously to take advantage of national differences in the cost and quality of resources such as labor or raw materials that can significantly reduce manufacturing costs or increase product quality or reliability. Today such global exchanges are becoming so complex that some companies specialize in managing other companies' global supply chains. Global companies use the services of overseas intermediaries or brokers, which are located close to potential suppliers, to find the suppliers that can best meet the needs of a particular company. They can design the most efficient supply chain for a company to outsource the component and assembly operations required to produce its final products. Because these suppliers are located in thousands of cities in many countries, finding them is difficult. Li & Fung, based in Hong Kong, is one broker that has helped hundreds of global companies to outsource their component or assembly operations to suitable overseas suppliers, especially suppliers in mainland China.[9]

Although outsourcing to take advantage of low labor costs has helped many companies perform better, in the late 2000s its risks have also become apparent, especially when issues such as reliability, quality, and speed are important. For example, the introduction of Boeing's 787 Dreamliner plane was delayed for over two years because the company, encouraged by the success of its 777 outsourcing program, increased its reliance on companies. To design and make the 787, Boeing turned to its suppliers early in the development process to gain access to foreign ingenuity and cut costs. Boeing uses 50 U.S. suppliers but also 23 suppliers abroad, many of whom had problems in meeting Boeing's delivery requirements.

Design and quality issues arose, such as in 2008 when Boeing announced that an Italian supplier had stopped production of two sections of the fuselage because of structural design problems. The Dreamliner finally took its inaugural flight in 2010.[10] By contrast, in 2010 Hanes Brands (HBI), the underwear maker, announced an agreement to sell its yarn and thread operations to Parkdale, a large-scale yarn manufacturer based in Gastonia, North Carolina. In the future Parkdale will be HBI's yarn supplier in North America; because yarn is a simple product to make, HBI did not need to look outside the United States. Clearly outsourcing decisions need to be carefully considered given the nature of a company's products.[11] On the other hand, some companies do not outsource production; they prefer to establish their own factories in countries around the world, as the example of Nokia in the following "Managing Globally" box suggests.

## Managing Globally

### Why Nokia Makes Cell Phones in Romania

Nokia is still the world's largest cell phone maker, although it has been fighting hard to maintain its lead as the popularity of smartphones has soared and companies like Apple, BlackBerry, Samsung, and now Google and Microsoft are competing for the lucrative smartphone segment of the market. While these other companies outsource their cell phone production to Asian companies, Nokia does not. Indeed, one reason for Nokia's continuing dominance in cell phones is its skills in global supply chain management, which allow it to provide low-cost phones that are customized to the needs of customers in different world regions. To achieve this, Nokia's global strategy is to make its phones in the world region where they are to be sold; so Nokia has built state-of-the-art factories in Germany, Brazil, China, and India, and in 2008 it opened a new plant in Romania to make phones for the expanding eastern European and Russian market.

A major reason for beginning operations in Romania is low labor costs. Skilled Romanian engineers can be hired for a quarter of what they would earn in Finland or Germany, and production line employees can expect to earn about US$450 a month—a fraction of what Nokia's German employees earn. In fact, once Nokia's Romanian factory was running, Nokia closed its factory in Bochum, Germany, in 2008 because it was too expensive to operate in a highly competitive global environment.

Nokia goes global by establishing operations in Romania. The plant has already performed beyond management's expectations, resulting in pay raises and more jobs for the area.

Opening a new factory in a new country is a complex process; and to increase the chances its new factory would operate efficiently, Nokia's managers adopted several strategies. First they worked to create a culture in the factory that is attractive to its new Romanian employees so they will stay with the company and learn the skills required to make it operate more efficiently over time. For example, the factory's cafeteria offers free food, and there are gyms, sports facilities, and (of course) a Finnish sauna. In addition, although managers from other countries run the plant at present, Nokia hopes that within a few years most of the factory's managers and supervisors will be Romanian. Its goal is to create a career ladder that will motivate employees to perform at a high level and so be promoted.

At the same time Nokia is hardheaded about how efficiently it expects its Romanian factory to operate because all its factories are required to operate at the same level of efficiency that its *most* efficient global factory has achieved. Thus Nokia has created a compensation plan for factory managers based on the *collective* performance of all its factories. This means managers in all its factories will see their bonuses reduced if just one factory in any country performs below expectations. This is a tough approach, but its purpose is to encourage all managers to develop more efficient manufacturing techniques, which, when learned in one factory, must be shared with all other factories around the world for managers to obtain their bonuses. Nokia's goal is that efficiency will improve constantly over time as managers are encouraged to find better ways to operate and then share this knowledge across the company.

Just six months after it opened in June 2008 the Romanian plant reached the 1 million handset produced milestone. The plant's efficiency has exceeded Nokia's expectations—so much so that Nokia opened a new cell phone accessory factory next to the plant and has hired hundreds of new workers who received a 9% salary increase in 2010 because of their high productivity. In 2010 Nokia was contemplating opening a plant in Argentina to serve the booming South American market.[12]

## Distributors

**distributors** Organizations that help other organizations sell their goods or services to customers.

**Distributors** are organizations that help other organizations sell their goods or services to customers. The decisions managers make about how to distribute products to customers can have important effects on organizational performance. For example, package delivery companies such as DHL from Germany have become vital distributors for the millions of items bought online and shipped to customers by dot-com companies.

The changing nature of distributors and distribution methods can bring opportunities and threats for managers. If distributors become so large and powerful that they can control customers' access to a particular organization's goods and services, they can threaten the organization by demanding that it reduce the prices of its goods and services.[13] For example, the huge retail distributor Carrefour from France controls its suppliers' access to millions of customers and thus can demand that its suppliers reduce their prices to keep its business. If an organization such as Procter & Gamble refuses to reduce its prices, Carrefour might respond by buying products only from Procter & Gamble's competitors—companies such as Unilever and Colgate.

It is illegal for distributors to collaborate or collude to keep prices high and thus maintain their power over buyers; however, this frequently happens. In the early 2000s several European drug companies conspired to keep the price of vitamins artificially high. In 2005 the three largest global makers of flash memory, including Samsung, were found guilty of price fixing (they collaborated to keep prices high). All these companies paid hundreds of millions of dollars in fines, and many of their top executives were sentenced to jail terms.

## Customers

**customers** Individuals and groups that buy the goods and services an organization produces.

**Customers** are the individuals and groups that buy the goods and services an organization produces. For example, Acer's customers can be segmented into several distinct groups: (1) individuals who purchase PCs for home use, (2) small companies, (3) large companies, and (4) government agencies and educational institutions. Changes in the number and types of customers or in customers' tastes and needs create opportunities and threats. An organization's success depends on its responsiveness to customers—whether it can satisfy their needs. In the PC industry, customers are demanding thinner computers, better graphics and speed, and increased wireless and Internet connections—and lower prices—and PC makers must respond to the changing types and needs of customers, such as by introducing tablet computers. A university, too, must adapt to the changing needs of its customers. For example, if more Mandarin-speaking students enroll, additional classes in English as a second language may need to be scheduled. A manager's ability to identify an organization's main customer groups, and make the products that best satisfy their particular needs, is a crucial factor affecting organizational and managerial success.

Today many products have gained global customer acceptance. This consolidation is occurring both for consumer goods and for business products and has created enormous opportunities for managers. The worldwide acceptance of Coca-Cola, Apple iPods, McDonald's hamburgers, Sony Playstation and Nokia cell phones is a sign that the tastes and preferences of customers in different countries may not be so different after all.[14] Likewise, large global markets exist for business products such as telecommunications equipment, electronic components, and computer and financial services.

## Competitors

**competitors** Organizations that produce goods and services that are similar to a particular organization's goods and services.

One of the most important forces an organization confronts in its task environment is competitors. **Competitors** are organizations that produce goods and services that are similar and comparable to a particular organization's goods and services. In other words, competitors are organizations trying to attract the same customers. In the laptop computer market, Acer competes against Lenovo from China, Hewlett Packard and Dell from the United States, and Toshiba from Japan.

Rivalry between competitors is potentially the most threatening force managers must deal with. A high level of rivalry typically results in price competition, and falling prices reduce customer revenues and profits. In the early 2000s competition in the PC industry became intense as many firms aggressively cut costs and prices to increase their global market share.[15] IBM had to exit the PC business after it lost billions in its battle against low-cost rivals.

Although extensive rivalry between existing competitors is a major threat to profitability, so is the potential for new competitors to enter the task environment. **Potential competitors** are organizations that are not presently in a task environment but have the resources to enter if they so choose. In 2010 Amazon.com, for example, was not in the retail furniture or large appliance business, but it could enter these businesses if its managers decided it could profitably sell such products online. When new competitors enter an industry, competition increases, and prices and profits decrease.

**potential competitors** Organizations that presently are not in a task environment but could enter if they so choose.

**BARRIERS TO ENTRY** In general, the potential for new competitors to enter a task environment (and thus increase competition) is a function of barriers to entry.[16] **Barriers to entry** are factors that make it difficult and costly for a company to enter a particular task environment or industry.[17] In other words, the more difficult and costly it is to enter the task environment, the higher are the barriers to entry. The higher the barriers to entry, the fewer the competitors in an organization's task environment and thus the lower the threat of competition. With fewer competitors, it is easier to obtain customers and keep prices high.

**barriers to entry** Factors that make it difficult and costly for an organization to enter a particular task environment or industry.

Barriers to entry result from three main sources: economies of scale, brand loyalty, and government regulations that impede entry (see Figure 6.2). **Economies of scale** are the cost advantages associated with large operations. Economies of scale result from factors such as manufacturing products in very large quantities, buying inputs in bulk, or making more effective use of organizational resources than do competitors by fully utilizing employees' skills and knowledge. If organizations already in the task environment are large and enjoy significant economies of scale, their costs are lower than the costs that potential entrants will face, and newcomers will find it expensive to enter the industry. Amazon.com, for example, enjoys significant economies of scale relative to most other dot-com companies because of its highly efficient distribution system.[18]

**economies of scale** Cost advantages associated with large operations.

**Brand loyalty** is customers' preference for the products of organizations currently in the task environment. If established organizations enjoy significant brand loyalty, a new entrant will find it difficult and costly to obtain a share of the market. Newcomers must bear huge advertising costs to build customer awareness of the goods or services they intend to provide.[19] Today Google and Amazon.com are worldwide brands that have high levels of loyalty. As a result, these sites have some of the highest Web site hit rates, which allows them to increase their marketing revenues.

**brand loyalty** Customers' preference for the products of organizations currently existing in the task environment.

In some cases, *government regulations* function as a barrier to entry at both the industry and the country levels. Many industries that were deregulated, such as air transport, trucking, utilities, and telecommunications, experienced a high level of new entry after deregulation; this forced existing companies in those industries to operate more efficiently or risk being put out of business. At the national and global

**Figure 6.2**
**Barriers to Entry and Competition**

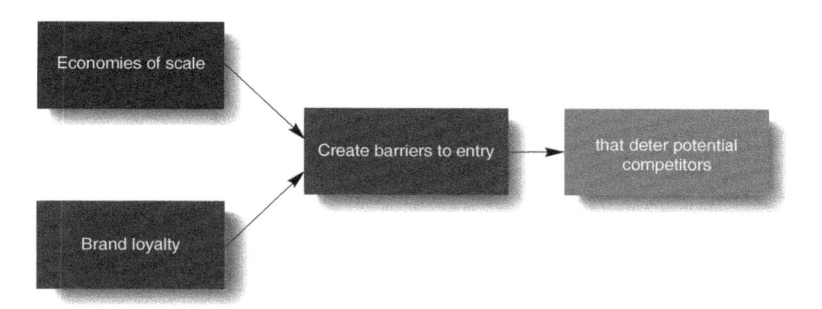

Economies of scale → Create barriers to entry → that deter potential competitors
Brand loyalty →

levels, administrative barriers are government policies that create barriers to entry and limit imports of goods by overseas companies. Japan is well known for the many ways in which it attempts to restrict the entry of overseas competitors or lessen their impact on Japanese firms. Japan has come under intense pressure to relax and abolish regulations such as those governing the import of rice, for example.

The Japanese rice market, like many other Japanese markets, was closed to overseas competitors until 1993 to protect Japan's thousands of high-cost, low-output rice farmers. Rice cultivation is expensive in Japan because of the country's mountainous terrain, and Japanese consumers have always paid high prices for rice. Under overseas pressure, the Japanese government opened the market; but overseas competitors are allowed to export to Japan only 8% of its annual rice consumption to protect its farmers.

In the 2000s, however, an alliance between organic rice grower Lundberg Family Farms of California and the Nippon Restaurant Enterprise Co. found a new way to break into the Japanese rice market. Because there is no tariff on rice used in processed foods, Nippon converts the U.S. organic rice into "O-bento," an organic hot boxed lunch packed with rice, vegetables, chicken, beef, and salmon, all imported from the United States. The lunches, which cost about US$4 compared to a Japanese rice bento that costs about US$9, are sold at railway stations and other outlets throughout Japan and have become very popular. A storm of protest from Japanese rice farmers arose because the entry of U.S. rice growers forced them to leave their rice fields idle or grow less profitable crops. Other overseas companies are increasingly forming alliances with Japanese companies to find new ways to break into the high-priced Japanese market, and little by little, Japan's restrictive trade practices are being whittled away.

In summary, intense rivalry among competitors creates a task environment that is highly threatening and makes it increasingly difficult for managers to gain access to the resources an organization needs to make goods and services. Conversely, low rivalry results in a task environment where competitive pressures are more moderate and managers have greater opportunities to acquire the resources they need to make their organizations effective.

*The tyranny of the lower price. A Japanese businessman purchases a frozen, U.S.-sourced rice O-bento lunch at a Nippon Tokyo store. Nippon's importing practices have angered Japanese rice farmers.*

# The General Environment

Economic, technological, sociocultural, demographic, political, and legal forces in the general environment often have important effects on forces in the task environment that determine an organization's ability to obtain resources—effects that managers may not be aware of. For example, the sudden, dramatic upheavals in the mortgage and banking industry that started in 2007 were brought about by a combination of the development of complex new financial lending instruments called derivatives; a speculative boom in commodities and housing prices; and lax government regulation that allowed unethical bankers and financial managers to exploit the derivatives to make immense short-term profits. These events triggered the economic crisis of 2008–2009 that caused stock markets around the world to plummet, devastating the retirement savings of hundreds of millions of ordinary people, and caused layoffs of millions of employees as companies slashed their workforces because customers reduced their spending.

The implication is clear: Managers must continuously analyze forces in the general environment because these forces affect ongoing decision making and planning. How well managers can perform this task determines how quickly an organization can respond to the changes taking place. Next we discuss the major forces in the general environment and examine their impact on an organization's task environment.

## Economic Forces

**economic forces**
Interest rates, inflation, unemployment, economic growth, and other factors that affect the general health and well-being of a nation or the regional economy of an organization.

**Economic forces** affect the general health and well-being of a country or world region. They include interest rates, inflation, unemployment, and economic growth. Economic forces produce many opportunities and threats for managers. Low levels of unemployment and falling interest rates give people more money to spend, and as a result organizations can sell more goods and services. Good economic times affect the supply of resources that become easier or more inexpensive to acquire, and organizations have an opportunity to flourish. High-tech companies enjoyed this throughout the 1990s as computer and electronics companies like Sony made record profits as the global economy boomed because of advances in IT and growing global trade.

In contrast, worsening macroeconomic conditions, like those in the late 2000s, pose a major threat because they reduce managers' ability to gain access to the resources their organizations need to survive and prosper. Profit-seeking organizations such as hotels and retail stores have fewer customers during economic downturns; hotel rates dropped by 14% in 2009 compared to 2008, for example, just as retail sales plunged. Nonprofits such as charities and colleges also saw donations decline by more than 20% because of the economic downturn.

Poor economic conditions make the environment more complex and managers' jobs more difficult and demanding. Companies often need to reduce the number of their managers and employees, streamline their operations, and identify ways to acquire and use resources more efficiently and effectively. Successful managers realize the important effects that economic forces have on their organizations, and they pay close attention to what is occurring in the economy at the national and regional levels to respond appropriately.

## Technological Forces

**technology** The combination of skills and equipment that managers use in designing, producing, and distributing goods and services.

**technological forces** Outcomes of changes in the technology managers use to design, produce, or distribute goods and services.

**Technology** is the combination of tools, machines, computers, skills, information, and knowledge that managers use to design, produce, and distribute goods and services; **technological forces** are outcomes of changes in that technology. The overall pace of technological change has accelerated greatly in the last decades because technological advances in microprocessors and computer hardware and software have spurred technological advances in most businesses and industries. The effects of changing technological forces are still increasing in magnitude.[20]

Technological forces can have profound implications for managers and organizations. Technological change can make established products obsolete—for example, cathode-ray tube (CRT) computer monitors and televisions (such as Sony's Trinitron), bound sets of encyclopedias, and even newspapers—forcing managers to find new ways to satisfy customer needs. Although technological change can threaten an organization, it also can create a host of new opportunities for designing, making, or distributing new and better kinds of goods and services. Ever more powerful microprocessors developed by Intel and AMD, which now have 8 or 12 processing cores on each chip, are continuing the IT revolution that has spurred demand for all kinds of new digital computing devices and services and has affected the competitive position of all high-tech companies. Will Google devastate Microsoft, for example, just as Microsoft devastated IBM in the 1990s? Managers must move quickly to respond to such changes if their organizations are to survive and prosper.

Changes in IT are altering the nature of work itself within organizations, including that of the manager's job. Today telecommuting, videoconferencing, and text messaging are everyday activities that let managers supervise and coordinate geographically dispersed employees. Salespeople in many companies work from home offices and commute electronically to work. They communicate with other employees through companywide electronic communication networks using PCs and webcams to orchestrate "face-to-face" meetings with coworkers across the country or globe.

# Sociocultural Forces

**sociocultural forces** Pressures emanating from the social structure of a country or society or from the national culture.

**social structure** The traditional system of relationships established between people and groups in a society.

**national culture** The set of values that a society considers important and the norms of behavior that are approved or sanctioned in that society.

**Sociocultural forces** are pressures emanating from the social structure of a country or society or from the national culture, such as the concern for diversity, discussed in the previous chapter. Pressures from both sources can either constrain or facilitate the way organizations operate and managers behave. **Social structure** is the traditional system of relationships established between people and groups in a society. Societies differ substantially in social structure. In societies that have a high degree of social stratification, there are many distinctions among individuals and groups. Caste systems in India and Tibet and the recognition of numerous social classes in Great Britain and France produce a multilayered social structure in each of those countries. In contrast, social stratification is lower in relatively egalitarian New Zealand and in Australia, where the social structure reveals few distinctions among people. Most top managers in France come from the upper classes of French society, but top managers in Australia come from all strata of Australian society.

Societies also differ in the extent to which they emphasize the individual over the group. Such differences may dictate how managers need to motivate and lead employees. **National culture** is the set of values that a society considers important and the norms of behavior that are approved or sanctioned in that society. Societies differ substantially in the values and norms they emphasize. For example, in the United States individualism is highly valued, and in Korea and Japan individuals are expected to conform to group expectations.[21] National culture, discussed at length later in this chapter, also affects how managers motivate and coordinate employees and how organizations do business. Ethics, an important aspect of national culture, were discussed in detail in Chapter 4.

Social structure and national culture not only differ across societies but also change within societies over time. In Germany, attitudes toward the roles of women, sex, marriage, and gays and lesbians changed in each past decade. Many people in Asian countries such as Hong Kong, Singapore, Korea, and even China think the younger generation is far more individualistic than previous generations. Currently, throughout much of eastern Europe, new values that emphasize individualism and entrepreneurship are replacing communist values based on collectivism and obedience to the state. The pace of change is accelerating.

Individual managers and organizations must be responsive to changes in, and differences among, the social structures and national cultures of all the countries in which they operate. In today's increasingly integrated global economy, managers are likely to interact with people from several countries, and many managers live and work abroad. Effective managers are sensitive to differences between societies and adjust their behavior accordingly.

Managers and organizations also must respond to social changes within a society. In the last decades, for example, Europeans have become increasingly interested in their personal health and fitness. Managers who recognized this trend early and took advantage of the opportunities that resulted from it were able to reap significant gains for their organizations such as chains of health clubs. PepsiCo used the opportunity presented by the fitness trend and took market share from archrival Coca-Cola by being the first to introduce diet colas and fruit-based soft drinks. Then Quaker Oats made Gatorade the most popular energy drink, and now others like Red Bull, Monster, and Rockstar are increasing in popularity. The health trend, however, did not offer opportunities to all companies; to some it posed a threat. Tobacco companies came under intense pressure due to consumers' greater awareness of negative health impacts from smoking. The rage for "low-carb" foods in the 2000s increased demand for meat and protein, and bread and pasta companies suffered—until the 2008 recession boosted the sale of inexpensive products such as macaroni and cheese and hamburger helper.

*Pick your poison. The American trend towards fitness has prompted traditional soft drink manufacturers to expand their offerings into a staggering array of energy drinks.*

## Demographic Forces

**demographic forces** Outcomes of changes in, or changing attitudes toward, the characteristics of a population, such as age, gender, ethnic origin, race, sexual orientation, and social class.

**Demographic forces** are outcomes of changes in, or changing attitudes toward, the characteristics of a population, such as age, gender, ethnic origin, race, sexual orientation, and social class. Like the other forces in the general environment, demographic forces present managers with opportunities and threats and can have major implications for organizations. We examined the nature of these challenges in depth in our discussion of diversity in Chapter 5.

Today most industrialized nations are experiencing the aging of their populations as a consequence of falling birth and death rates and the aging of the baby boom generation. Consequently, the absolute number of older people has increased substantially, which has generated opportunities for organizations that cater to older people such as the home health care, recreation, and medical industries, which have seen an upswing in demand for their services. The aging of the population also has several implications for the workplace. Most significant are a relative decline in the number of young people joining the workforce and an increase in the number of active employees who are postponing retirement beyond the traditional age of 65. Indeed, the financial crisis of 2008–2009 has made it impossible for millions of older people to retire because their savings have been decimated. These changes suggest that organizations need to find ways to motivate older employees and use their skills and knowledge—an issue that many Western societies have yet to tackle.

## Political and Legal Forces

**political and legal forces** Outcomes of changes in laws and regulations, such as deregulation of industries, privatization of organizations, and increased emphasis on environmental protection.

**Political and legal forces** are outcomes of changes in laws and regulations. They result from political and legal developments that take place within a nation, within a world region, or across the world and significantly affect managers and organizations everywhere. Political processes shape a nation's laws and the international laws that govern the relationships between nations. Laws constrain the operations of organizations and managers and thus create both opportunities and threats.[22] For example, throughout much of the industrialized world there has been a strong trend toward deregulation of industries previously controlled by the state and privatization of organizations once owned by the state.

Another important political and legal force affecting managers and organizations is the political integration of countries that has been taking place during the past decades.[23] Increasingly, nations are forming political unions that allow free exchange of resources and capital. The growth of the European Union (EU) is one example: Common laws govern trade and commerce between EU member countries, and the European Court has the right to examine the business of any global organization and to approve any proposed mergers between overseas companies that operate inside the EU. For example, Microsoft's anticompetitive business practices came under scrutiny, and it was fined hundreds of millions of euros for its uncompetitive practice of bundling its Internet Explorer Web browser with its software. As part of its agreement with the European Court, Microsoft agreed that from spring 2010 forward it would ship its Windows 7 software with a choice of 10 Web browsers (such as Chrome, Safari, and Mozilla). Also in 2010, after months of delay, the court allowed the merger between Oracle and Sun to proceed providing the companies followed some strict competitive guidelines.

Indeed, international agreements to abolish laws and regulations that restrict and reduce trade between countries have been having profound effects on global organizations. The falling legal trade barriers create enormous opportunities for companies to sell goods and services internationally. But by allowing overseas companies to compete in a nation's domestic market for customers, falling trade barriers also pose a serious threat because they increase competition in the task environment. Between 1980 and 2010, for example, Japanese companies increased their share of the U.S. car market from around 20% to 40%; Taiwanese companies' share grew from 2% to 7%. In essence, removing legal restrictions on global trade has the same effect as deregulating industries and removing restrictions against competition: It increases the intensity of competition in the task environment and forces conservative, slow-moving companies to become more efficient, improve product quality, and learn new values and norms to compete in the global environment.

Deregulation, privatization, and the removal of legal barriers to trade are just a few of the many ways in which changing political and legal forces can challenge organizations and managers. Others include increased emphasis on environmental protection and the preservation of endangered species, increased emphasis on workplace safety, and legal constraints against discrimination on the basis of race, gender, or age. Managers face major challenges when they seek to take advantage of the opportunities created by changing political, legal, and economic forces.

## The Changing Global Environment

The 21st century has banished the idea that the world is composed of distinct national countries and markets that are separated physically, economically, and culturally. Managers need to recognize that companies compete in a truly global marketplace, which is the source of the opportunities and threats they must respond to. Managers continually confront the challenges of global competition such as establishing operations in a country abroad, obtaining inputs from suppliers abroad, or managing in a different national culture.[24] (See Figure 6.3.)

**LO6-4** Explain why the global environment is becoming more open and competitive, and identify the forces behind the process of globalization that increase the opportunities, complexities, challenges, and threats managers face.

In essence, as a result of falling trade barriers, managers view the global environment as open—that is, as an environment in which companies are free to buy goods and services from, and sell goods and services to, whichever companies and countries they choose. They also are free to compete against each other to attract customers around the world. All large companies must establish an international network of operations and subsidiaries to build global competitive advantage. Coca-Cola and PepsiCo, for example, have competed aggressively for decades to develop the strongest global

**Figure 6.3**
**The Global Environment**

soft drink empire, just as Toyota and Honda have built hundreds of car plants around the world to provide the vehicles that global customers like. This is also true in the food processing industry, as the following "Managing Globally" box suggests.

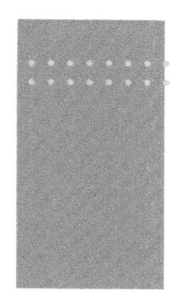

## Managing Globally

### Nestlé's Global Food Empire

Nestlé is the world's largest food company. In 2009 its sales increased by 4%, and it enjoyed record profits of over $100 billion; globally it had over 190,000 employees and 500 factories in 80 countries. It makes and sells over 8,000 food products, including such popular brands as Kit-Kat chocolate bars, Taster's Choice coffee, Carnation Instant milk, and Stouffer's Foods. At its corporate headquarters in Vevey, Switzerland, CEO Peter Brabeck-Latmathe, who has been in charge since 1997, is responsible for Nestlé's improving global performance and has faced and managed many global challenges.[25]

From the beginning Brabeck worked to increase Nestlé's revenues and profits by entering new attractive national markets in both developed and emerging nations as trade barriers fell. He continued the ambitious global expansion that Nestlé began in the 1990s, when, for example, it bought the U.S. food companies Carnation and Buitoni Pasta, the British chocolate maker Rowntree, the French bottled water company Perrier, and the Mexican food maker Ortega. Under Brabeck, Nestlé spent $18 billion to acquire U.S. companies Ralston Purina, Dreyer's Ice Cream, and Chef America. Brabeck's intention was not only to develop these food brands in the United States but also to customize their products to suit the tastes of customers in countries around the world. He was particularly anxious to enter emerging markets such as those in eastern Europe, India, and Asia to take advantage of the enormous numbers of potential new customers in these regions. In this way Nestlé could leverage its well-known brand image and products around the world to drive up its performance.

Increasing global product sale revenues was only the first part of Brabeck's global business model, however. He was also anxious to increase Nestlé's operating efficiency and reduce the cost of managing its global operations. As you can imagine, with over 500 factories the costs of organizing Nestlé's global activities were enormous. Brabeck benchmarked its operating costs to those of competitors such as Kraft Foods and Unilever and found that Nestlé's costs were significantly higher than theirs. Brabeck cut the workforce by 20%, closed 150 factories, and reduced operating costs by over 12%. Nestlé was also using advanced IT both to reduce the number of its global suppliers and to negotiate more favorable supply contracts with them—moves that significantly cut purchasing costs. Brabeck also designed Nestlé's new streamlined operating structure and IT to increase the flow of information between its food products units and all the countries in which it sells its products. His goal was to capitalize on a prime source of its competitive advantage: superior innovation.

Thus Brabeck's global strategy for Nestlé was driven by three main goals: (1) Expand Nestlé's range of products, and offer them to new and existing customers in countries throughout the world; (2) find lower-cost ways to make and sell these products; and (3) speed up Nestlé's product innovation by leveraging its expertise across its

Nescafé anywhere, anytime. Nestlé's expanded operations and benchmarked processes make it a force to be reckoned with.

food businesses to create more attractive food products that would increase its global market share. In addition, many customers around the world have been demanding more nutritious food products. So Brabeck adopted what he called an "organic approach" to developing Nestlé's products. Brabeck claimed his company was engaged in a "transformation" that would lead it to become the "world's leading nutrition, health, and wellness" food company that made consumer health and safety its prime concern.[26]

In the next section we first explain how this open global environment is the result of globalization and the flow of capital around the world. Next we examine how specific economic, political, and legal changes, such as the lowering of barriers to trade and investment, have increased globalization and led to greater interaction and exchanges between organizations and countries. Then we discuss how declining barriers of distance and culture have also increased the pace of globalization, and we consider the specific implications of these changes for managers and organizations. Finally we note that nations still differ widely from each other because they have distinct cultural values and norms and that managers must appreciate these differences to compete successfully across countries.

## The Process of Globalization

**globalization** The set of specific and general forces that work together to integrate and connect economic, political, and social systems *across* countries, cultures, or geographical regions so that nations become increasingly interdependent and similar.

Perhaps the most important reason why the global environment has become more open and competitive is the increase in globalization. **Globalization** is the set of specific and general forces that work together to integrate and connect economic, political, and social systems *across* countries, cultures, or geographic regions. The result of globalization is that nations and peoples become increasingly *interdependent* because the same forces affect them in similar ways. The fates of peoples in different countries become interlinked as the world's markets and businesses become increasingly interconnected. And as nations become more interdependent, they become more similar to one another in the sense that people develop a similar liking for products as diverse as cell phones, iPods, blue jeans, soft drinks, sports teams, Japanese cars, and foods such as curry, green tea, and Colombian coffee. One outcome of globalization is that the world is becoming a "global village": Products, services, or people can become well known throughout the world—something IKEA, with its range of furniture designed to appeal to customers around the world, is taking advantage of, as the following "Managing Globally" box describes.

### Managing Globally

### IKEA Is on Top of the Furniture World

IKEA is the largest furniture chain in the world, and in 2010 the Swedish company operated over 267 stores in 25 countries. In 2009 IKEA sales soared to over US$33 billion, or over 20% of the global furniture market; but to its managers and employees this was just the tip of the iceberg. They believed IKEA was poised for massive growth throughout the world in the coming decade because it could provide what the average customer wanted: well-designed and well-made contemporary furniture at an affordable price. IKEA's ability to provide customers with affordable furniture is the result of its approach to globalization, to how it treats its global employees and operates its global store empire. In a nutshell, IKEA's global approach focuses on simplicity, attention to detail, cost consciousness, and responsiveness in every aspect of its operations and behavior.

Need a new kitchen table? How about a cute rug to go with it, and while you're at it, a cookie sheet, too? Options await you at any one of the thousands of IKEA stores worldwide.

IKEA's global approach derives from the personal values and beliefs of its founder, Ingvar Kamprad, about how companies should treat their employees and customers. Kamprad, who is in his early 80s (and in 2010 ranked as the 11th richest person in the world), was born in Smaland, a poor Swedish province whose citizens are known for being entrepreneurial, frugal, and hardworking. Kamprad definitely absorbed these values—when he entered the furniture business, he made them the core of his management approach. He teaches store managers and employees his values; his beliefs about the need to operate in a no-frills, cost-conscious way; and his view that they are all in business "together," by which he means that every person who works in his global empire plays an essential role and has an obligation to everyone else.

What does Kamprad's approach mean in practice? All IKEA employees fly coach class on business trips, stay in inexpensive hotels, and keep traveling expenses to a minimum. And IKEA stores operate on the simplest rules and procedures possible, with employees expected to cooperate to solve problems and get the job done. Many famous stories circulate about the frugal Kamprad, such as that even he always flies coach class and that when he takes a soda can from the minibar in a hotel room, he replaces it with one bought in a store—despite the fact that he is a multibillionaire.

IKEA's employees see what Kamprad's global approach means as soon as they are recruited to work in a store in one of the many countries in which the company operates. They start learning about IKEA's global corporate culture by performing jobs at the bottom of the ladder, and they are quickly trained to perform all the various jobs involved in store operations. During this process they internalize IKEA's global values and norms, which center on the importance the company attaches to their taking the initiative and responsibility for solving problems and for focusing on customers. Employees are rotated between departments and sometimes stores, and rapid promotion is possible for those who demonstrate the enthusiasm and togetherness that show they have bought into IKEA's global culture.

Most of IKEA's top managers rose from its ranks, and the company holds "breaking the bureaucracy weeks" in which managers are required to work in stores and warehouses for a week each year to make sure they and all employees stay committed to IKEA's global values. No matter which country they operate in, all employees wear informal clothes to work at IKEA—Kamprad has always worn an open-neck shirt—and there are no marks of status such as executive dining rooms or private parking places. Employees believe that if they buy into IKEA's work values, behave in ways that keep its growing global operations streamlined and efficient, and focus on being one step ahead of potential problems, they will share in its success. Promotion, training, above-average pay, a generous store bonus system, and the personal well-being that comes from working in a company where people feel valued are some of the rewards that Kamprad pioneered to build and strengthen IKEA's global approach.

Whenever IKEA enters a new country, it sends its most experienced store managers to establish its global approach in its new stores. When IKEA first entered the United States, the attitude of U.S. employees puzzled its managers. Despite their obvious drive to succeed and good education, employees seemed reluctant to take initiative and assume responsibility. IKEA's managers discovered that their U.S. employees were afraid mistakes would result in the loss of their jobs, so the managers strove to teach employees the "IKEA way." The approach paid off: The United States has become the company's second best country market, and IKEA plans to open many more U.S. stores, as well as stores around the world, over the next decade.[27]

But what drives or spurs globalization? What makes companies like IKEA, Toyota, or Microsoft want to venture into an uncertain global environment? The answer is that the path of globalization is shaped by the ebb and flow of *capital*–valuable wealth-generating assets or resources that people move through companies, countries, and world regions to seek their greatest returns or profits. Managers, employees, and companies like IKEA and Sony are motivated to try to profit or benefit by using their skills to make products customers around the world want to buy. The four principal forms of capital that flow between countries are these:

- *Human capital:* the flow of people around the world through immigration, migration, and emigration.
- *Financial capital:* the flow of money capital across world markets through overseas investment, credit, lending, and aid.
- *Resource capital:* the flow of natural resources, parts, and components between companies and countries, such as metals, minerals, lumber, energy, food products, microprocessors, and auto parts.
- *Political capital:* the flow of power and influence around the world using diplomacy, persuasion, aggression, and force of arms to protect the right or access of a country, world region, or political bloc to the other forms of capital.

Most of the economic advances associated with globalization are the result of these four capital flows and the interactions between them, as nations compete on the world stage to protect and increase their standards of living and to further the political goals and social causes that are espoused by their societies' cultures. The next sections look at the factors that have increased the rate at which capital flows between companies and countries. In a positive sense the faster the flow, the more capital is being utilized where it can create the most value, in the sense of people moving to where their skills earn them more money, or investors switching to the stocks or bonds that give them higher dividends or interest, or companies finding lower-cost sources of inputs. In a negative sense, however, a fast flow of capital also means that individual countries or world regions can find themselves in trouble when companies and investors move their capital to invest it in more productive ways in other countries or world regions—often those with lower labor costs or rapidly expanding markets. When capital leaves a country, the results are higher unemployment, recession, and a lower standard of living for its people.

## Declining Barriers to Trade and Investment

One of the main factors that has speeded globalization by freeing the movement of capital has been the decline in barriers to trade and investment, discussed earlier. During the 1920s and 1930s many countries erected formidable barriers to international trade and investment in the belief that this was the best way to promote their economic well-being. Many of these barriers were high tariffs on imports of manufactured goods. A **tariff** is a tax that a government imposes on goods imported into one country from another. The aim of import tariffs is to protect domestic industries and jobs, such as those in the auto or steel industry, from overseas competition by raising the price of these products from abroad. In 2009, for example, the U.S. government increased the tariffs on vehicle tires imported from China to protect U.S. tire makers from unfair competition; China vigorously protested that the price of its tires was fair and it would retaliate by increasing tariffs on U.S. imports of chicken and other products.

The reason for removing tariffs is that, very often, when one country imposes an import tariff, others follow suit and the result is a series of retaliatory moves as countries progressively raise tariff barriers against each other. In the 1920s this behavior depressed world demand and helped usher in the Great Depression of the 1930s and massive unemployment. During the 2008–2009 economic crisis, the governments of most countries worked hard not to fall into the trap of raising tariffs to protect jobs

**tariff** A tax that a government imposes on imported or, occasionally, exported goods.

and industries in the short run because they knew the long-term consequences of this would be the loss of even more jobs. Governments of countries that resort to raising tariff barriers ultimately reduce employment and undermine the economic growth of their countries because capital and resources will always move to their most highly valued use—wherever that is in the world.[28]

**GATT AND THE RISE OF FREE TRADE** After World War II, advanced Western industrial countries, having learned from the Great Depression, committed themselves to the goal of removing barriers to the free flow of resources and capital between countries. This commitment was reinforced by acceptance of the principle that free trade, rather than tariff barriers, was the best way to foster a healthy domestic economy and low unemployment.[29]

> **free-trade doctrine** The idea that if each country specializes in the production of the goods and services that it can produce most efficiently, this will make the best use of global resources.

The **free-trade doctrine** predicts that if each country agrees to specialize in the production of the goods and services that it can produce most efficiently, this will make the best use of global capital resources and will result in lower prices.[30] For example, if Indian companies are highly efficient in the production of textiles and U.S. companies are highly efficient in the production of computer software, then under a free-trade agreement capital would move to India and be invested there to produce textiles, while capital from around the world would flow to the United States and be invested in its innovative computer software companies. Consequently, prices of both textiles and software should fall because each product is being produced where it can be made at the lowest cost, benefiting consumers and making the best use of scarce capital. This doctrine is also responsible for the increase in global outsourcing and the loss of millions of U.S. jobs in textiles and manufacturing as capital has been invested in factories in Asian countries such as China and Malaysia. However, millions of U.S. jobs have also been created because of new capital investments in the high-tech, IT, and service sectors, which in theory should offset manufacturing job losses in the long run.

Historically countries that accepted this free-trade doctrine set as their goal the removal of barriers to the free flow of goods, services, and capital between countries. They attempted to achieve this through an international treaty known as the General Agreement on Tariffs and Trade (GATT). In the half-century since World War II, there have been eight rounds of GATT negotiations aimed at lowering tariff barriers. The last round, the Uruguay Round, involved 117 countries and was completed in December 1993. This round succeeded in lowering tariffs by over 30% from the previous level. It also led to the dissolving of GATT and its replacement by the World Trade Organization (WTO), which continues the struggle to reduce tariffs and has more power to sanction countries that break global agreements.[31] On average, the tariff barriers among the governments of developed countries declined from over 40% in 1948 to about 3% today, causing a dramatic increase in world trade.[32]

## Declining Barriers of Distance and Culture

Historically, barriers of distance and culture also closed the global environment and kept managers focused on their domestic market. The management problems Unilever, the huge British-based soap and detergent maker, experienced at the turn of the 20th century illustrate the effect of these barriers.

Founded in London during the 1880s by William Lever, Unilever had a worldwide reach by the early 1900s and operated subsidiaries in most major countries of the British Empire, including India, Canada, and Australia. Lever had a very hands-on, autocratic management style and found his far-flung business empire difficult to control. The reason for Lever's control problems was that communication over great distances was difficult. It took six weeks to reach India by ship from England, and international telephone and telegraph services were unreliable.

Another problem Unilever encountered was the difficulty of doing business in societies that were separated from Britain by barriers of language and culture. Different countries have different sets of national beliefs, values, and norms, and Lever found that a management approach that worked in Britain did not necessarily work in India or Persia (now Iran). As a result, management practices had to be tailored to suit each unique national culture. After Lever's death in 1925, top management at Unilever lowered or *decentralized* (see Chapter 10) decision-making authority to the managers of the various national subsidiaries so they could develop a management approach that suited the country in which they were operating. One result of this strategy was that the subsidiaries grew distant and remote from one another, which reduced Unilever's performance.[33]

Since the end of World War II, a continuing stream of advances in communications and transportation technology has worked to reduce the barriers of distance and culture that affected Unilever and all global organizations. Over the last decades, global communication has been revolutionized by developments in satellites, digital technology, the Internet and global computer networks, and video teleconferencing that allow transmission of vast amounts of information and make reliable, secure, and instantaneous communication possible between people and companies anywhere in the world.[34] This revolution has made it possible for a global organization—a tiny garment factory in Li & Fung's network or a huge company such as Sony or Unilever—to do business anywhere, anytime, and to search for customers and suppliers around the world.

One of the most important innovations in transportation technology that has opened the global environment has been the growth of commercial jet travel. New York is now closer in travel time to Tokyo than it was to Philadelphia in the days of the 13 colonies—a fact that makes control of far-flung international businesses much easier today than in William Lever's era. In addition to speeding travel, modern communications and transportation technologies have also helped reduce the cultural distance between countries. The Internet and its millions of Web sites facilitate the development of global communications networks and media that are helping to create a worldwide culture above and beyond unique national cultures. Moreover, television networks such as CNN, MTV, ESPN, BBC, and HBO can now be received in many countries, and Hollywood films are shown throughout the world.

## Effects of Free Trade on Managers

The lowering of barriers to trade and investment and the decline of distance and culture barriers has created enormous opportunities for companies to expand the market for their goods and services through exports and investments in overseas countries. The shift toward a more open global economy has created not only more opportunities to sell goods and services in markets abroad but also the opportunity to buy more from other countries. For example, the success of clothing companies such as Lands' End has been based on its managers' willingness to import low-cost clothing and bedding from overseas manufacturers. Lands' End works closely with manufacturers in Hong Kong, Malaysia, Taiwan, and China to make the clothing that its managers decide has the quality and styling its customers want at a price they will pay.[35] A manager's job is more challenging in a dynamic global environment because of the increased intensity of competition that goes hand in hand with the lowering of barriers to trade and investment.

**REGIONAL TRADE AGREEMENTS** The growth of regional trade agreements such as the North American Free Trade Agreement (NAFTA) also presents opportunities and threats for managers and their organizations. In North America, NAFTA, which became effective in 1994, had the aim of abolishing the tariffs on 99% of the goods traded between Mexico, Canada, and the United States by 2004. Although it did not achieve this lofty goal, NAFTA has removed most barriers on the cross-border flow of resources, giving, for example, financial institutions and retail businesses in Canada and the United States unrestricted access to the Mexican marketplace. After NAFTA was signed, there was a flood of investment into Mexico from the United States, as well as many other countries such as Japan. Similarly major U.S. retail chains have expanded their operations in Mexico; Walmart, for example, is stocking many more products from Mexico in its U.S. stores, and its Mexican store chain is also expanding rapidly. Today, Walmart is the largest retailer in Mexico.

The establishment of free-trade areas creates an opportunity for manufacturing organizations because it lets them reduce their costs. They can do this either by shifting production to the lowest-cost location within the free-trade area (for example, U.S. auto and textile companies shifting production to Mexico) or by serving the whole region from one location rather than establishing separate operations in each country. Some managers, however, view regional free-trade agreements as a threat because they expose a company based in one member country to increased competition from companies based in the other member countries. NAFTA has had this effect; today Mexican managers in some industries face the threat of head-to-head competition against efficient U.S. and Canadian companies. But the opposite is true as well: U.S. and Canadian managers are experiencing threats in labor-intensive industries, such as the flooring tile and textile industries, where Mexican businesses have a cost advantage.

# The Role of National Culture

Despite evidence that countries are becoming more similar because of globalization, and that the world may become "a global village," the cultures of different countries still vary widely because of vital differences in their values, norms, and attitudes. As noted earlier, national culture includes the values, norms, knowledge, beliefs, moral principles, laws, customs, and other practices that unite the citizens of a country.[36] National culture shapes individual behavior by specifying appropriate and inappropriate behavior and interaction with others. People learn national culture in their everyday lives by interacting with those around them. This learning starts at an early age and continues throughout their lives.

## Cultural Values and Norms

**values** Ideas about what a society believes to be good, right, desirable, or beautiful.

The basic building blocks of national culture are values and norms. **Values** are beliefs about what a society considers to be good, right, desirable, or beautiful—or their opposites. They provide the basic underpinnings for notions of individual freedom, democracy, truth, justice, honesty, loyalty, social obligation, collective responsibility, the appropriate roles for men and women, love, sex, marriage, and so on. Values are more than merely abstract concepts; they are invested with considerable emotional significance. People argue, fight, and even die over values such as freedom or dignity.

Although deeply embedded in society, values are not static and change over time; but change is often the result of a slow and painful process. For example, the value systems of many formerly communist states such as Russia and Romania are undergoing significant changes as those countries move away from a value system that emphasizes the state and toward one that emphasizes individual freedom. Social turmoil often results when countries undergo major changes in their values.

**norms** Unwritten, informal codes of conduct that prescribe how people should act in particular situations and are considered important by most members of a group or organization.

**mores** Norms that are considered to be central to the functioning of society and to social life.

**Norms** are unwritten, informal codes of conduct that prescribe appropriate behavior in particular situations and are considered important by most members of a group or organization. They shape the behavior of people toward one another. Two types of norms play a major role in national culture: mores and folkways. **Mores** are norms that are considered to be of central importance to the functioning of society and to social life. Accordingly, the violation of mores brings serious retribution. Mores include proscriptions against murder, theft, adultery, and incest. In many societies mores have been enacted into law. Thus all advanced societies have laws against murder and theft. However, there are many differences in mores from one society to another.[37] In the United States, for example, drinking alcohol is widely accepted; but in Saudi Arabia consumption of alcohol is viewed as a serious violation of social mores and is punishable by imprisonment.

**folkways** The routine social conventions of everyday life.

**Folkways** are the routine social conventions of everyday life. They concern customs and practices such as dressing appropriately for particular situations, good social manners, eating with the correct utensils, and neighborly behavior. Although folkways define how people are expected to behave, violation of folkways is not a serious or moral matter. People who violate folkways are often thought to be eccentric or ill-mannered, but they are not usually considered immoral or wicked. In many countries, strangers are usually excused for violating folkways because they are unaccustomed to local behavior; but if they repeat the violation they are censured because they are expected to learn appropriate behavior. Hence the importance of managers working in countries abroad to gain wide experience.

**LO6-5** Discuss why national cultures differ and why it is important that managers be sensitive to the effects of falling trade barriers and regional trade associations on the political and social systems of nations around the world.

## Hofstede's Model of National Culture

Researchers have spent considerable time and effort identifying similarities and differences in the values and norms of different countries. One model of national culture was developed by Geert Hofstede.[38] As a psychologist for IBM, Hofstede collected data on employee values and norms from more than 100,000 IBM employees in 64 countries. Based on his research, Hofstede developed five dimensions along which national cultures can be placed (see Figure 6.4).[39]

**individualism** A worldview that values individual freedom and self-expression and adherence to the principle that people should be judged by their individual achievements rather than by their social background.

**INDIVIDUALISM VERSUS COLLECTIVISM** The first dimension, which Hofstede labeled "individualism versus collectivism," has a long history in human thought. **Individualism** is a worldview that values individual freedom and self-expression and adherence to the principle that people should be judged by their individual achievements rather than by their social background. In Western countries, individualism usually includes admiration for personal success, a strong belief in individual rights, and high regard for individual entrepreneurs.[40]

**collectivism** A worldview that values subordination of the individual to the goals of the group and adherence to the principle that people should be judged by their contribution to the group.

In contrast, **collectivism** is a worldview that values subordination of the individual to the goals of the group and adherence to the principle that people should be judged by their contribution to the group. Collectivism was widespread in communist countries but has become less prevalent since the collapse of communism in most of those countries. Japan is a noncommunist country where collectivism is highly valued.

Collectivism in Japan traces its roots to the fusion of Confucian, Buddhist, and Shinto thought that occurred during the Tokugawa period in Japanese history (1600–1870s).[41] A central value that emerged during this period was strong attachment

**Figure 6.4**
**Hofstede's Model of National Culture**

| | | |
|---|---|---|
| Individualism | ⟷ | Collectivism |
| Low power distance | ⟷ | High power distance |
| Achievement orientation | ⟷ | Nurturing orientation |
| Low uncertainty avoidance | ⟷ | High uncertainty avoidance |
| Short-term orientation | ⟷ | Long-term orientation |

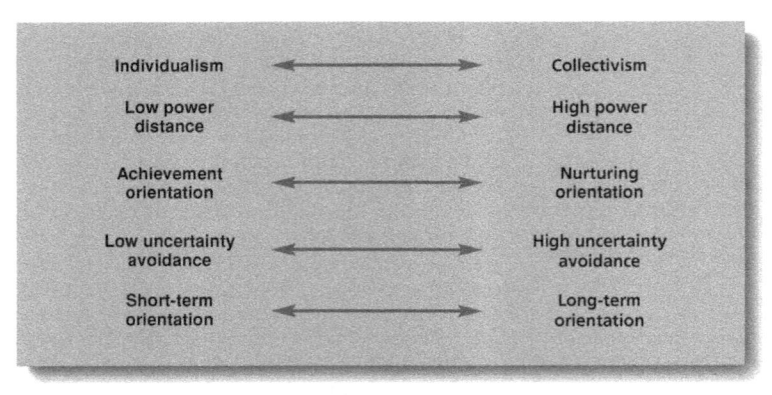

Source: G. Hofstede, B. Nevijen, D. D. Ohayv, and G. Sanders, "Measuring Organizational Cultures: A Qualitative and Quantitative Study across Twenty Cases," *Administrative Science Quarterly* 35, no. 2 (June 1990), pp. 286–316. Approval of request for permission to reprint. © Johnson Graduate School of Management, Cornell University.

to the group—whether a village, a work group, or a company. Strong identification with the group is said to create pressures for collective action in Japan, as well as strong pressure for conformity to group norms and a relative lack of individualism.[42]

Managers must realize that organizations and organizational members reflect their national culture's emphasis on individualism or collectivism. Indeed, one of the major reasons why Japanese and American management practices differ is that Japanese culture values collectivism and U.S. culture values individualism.[43]

**power distance** The degree to which societies accept the idea that inequalities in the power and well-being of their citizens are due to differences in individuals' physical and intellectual capabilities and heritage.

**POWER DISTANCE** By **power distance** Hofstede meant the degree to which societies accept the idea that inequalities in the power and well-being of their citizens are due to differences in individuals' physical and intellectual capabilities and heritage. This concept also encompasses the degree to which societies accept the economic and social differences in wealth, status, and well-being that result from differences in individual capabilities.

Societies in which inequalities are allowed to persist or grow over time have *high power distance*. In high-power-distance societies, workers who are professionally successful amass wealth and pass it on to their children, and, as a result, inequalities may grow over time. In such societies, the gap between rich and poor, with all the attendant political and social consequences, grows very large. In contrast, in societies with *low power distance,* large inequalities between citizens are not allowed to develop. In low-power-distance countries, the government uses taxation and social welfare programs to reduce inequality and improve the welfare of the least fortunate. These societies are more attuned to preventing a large gap between rich and poor and minimizing discord between different classes of citizens.

Advanced Western countries such as the United States, Germany, the Netherlands, and the United Kingdom have relatively low power distance and high individualism. Economically poor Latin American countries such as Guatemala and Panama, and Asian countries such as Malaysia and the Philippines, have high power distance and low individualism.[44] These findings suggest that the cultural values of richer countries emphasize protecting the rights of individuals and, at the same time, provide a fair chance of success to every member of society.

**achievement orientation** A worldview that values assertiveness, performance, success, and competition.

**nurturing orientation** A worldview that values the quality of life, warm personal friendships, and services and care for the weak.

**ACHIEVEMENT VERSUS NURTURING ORIENTATION** Societies that have an **achievement orientation** value assertiveness, performance, success, competition, and results. Societies that have a **nurturing orientation** value the quality of life, warm personal relationships, and services and care for the weak. Japan and the United States tend to be achievement-oriented; the Netherlands, Sweden, and Denmark are more nurturing-oriented.

**uncertainty avoidance** The degree to which societies are willing to tolerate uncertainty and risk.

**UNCERTAINTY AVOIDANCE** Societies as well as individuals differ in their tolerance for uncertainty and risk. Societies low on **uncertainty avoidance** (such as the United States and Hong Kong) are easygoing, value diversity, and tolerate differences in personal beliefs and actions. Societies high on uncertainty avoidance (such as Japan and France) are more rigid and skeptical about people whose behaviors or beliefs differ from the norm. In these societies, conformity to the values of the social and work groups to which a person belongs is the norm, and structured situations are preferred because they provide a sense of security.

**long-term orientation** A worldview that values thrift and persistence in achieving goals.

**short-term orientation** A worldview that values personal stability or happiness and living for the present.

**LONG-TERM VERSUS SHORT-TERM ORIENTATION** The last dimension that Hofstede described is orientation toward life and work.[45] A national culture with a **long-term orientation** rests on values such as thrift (saving) and persistence in achieving goals. A national culture with a **short-term orientation** is concerned with maintaining personal stability or happiness and living for the present. Societies with a long-term orientation include Taiwan and Hong Kong, well known for their high rate of per capita savings. The United States and France have a short-term orientation, and their citizens tend to spend more and save less.

## National Culture and Global Management

Differences among national cultures have important implications for managers. First, because of cultural differences, management practices that are effective in one country might be troublesome in another. General Electric's managers learned this while trying to manage Tungsram, a Hungarian lighting products company GE acquired for $150 million. GE was attracted to Tungsram, widely regarded as one of Hungary's best companies, because of Hungary's low wage rates and the possibility of using the company as a base from which to export lighting products to western Europe. GE transferred some of its best managers to Tungsram and hoped it would soon become a leader in Europe. Unfortunately many problems arose.

One problem resulted from major misunderstandings between the American managers and the Hungarian workers. The Americans complained that the Hungarians were lazy; the Hungarians thought the Americans were pushy. The Americans wanted strong sales and marketing functions that would pamper customers. In the prior command economy, sales and marketing activities were unnecessary. In addition, Hungarians expected GE to deliver Western-style wages, but GE came to Hungary to take advantage of the country's low-wage structure.[46] As Tungsram's losses mounted, GE managers had to admit that, because of differences in basic attitudes between countries, they had underestimated the difficulties they would face in turning Tungsram around. Nevertheless, by 2001 these problems had been solved, and the increased efficiency of GE's Hungarian operations made General Electric a major player in the European lighting market, causing it to invest another US$1 billion.[47]

Often management practices must be tailored to suit the cultural contexts within which an organization operates. An approach effective in Hungary might not work in Japan, the United States, or Mexico because of differences in national culture. For example, U.S.-style pay-for-performance systems that emphasize the performance of individuals might not work well in Japan, where individual performance in pursuit of group goals is the value that receives emphasis.

Managers doing business with individuals from another country must be sensitive to the value systems and norms of that country and behave accordingly. For example, Friday is the Islamic Sabbath. Thus it would be impolite and inappropriate for a U.S. manager to schedule a busy day of activities for Saudi Arabian managers on a Friday.

A culturally diverse management team can be a source of strength for an organization participating in the global marketplace. Compared to organizations with culturally homogeneous management teams, organizations that employ managers from a variety of cultures have a better appreciation of how national cultures differ, and they tailor their management systems and behaviors to the differences.[48] Indeed, one advantage that many Western companies have over their Japanese competitors is greater willingness to create global teams composed of employees from different countries around the world who can draw on and share their different cultural experiences and knowledge to provide service that is customized to the needs of companies in different countries.

## Summary and Review

**LO6-1**

**WHAT IS THE GLOBAL ENVIRONMENT?** The global environment is the set of forces and conditions that operate beyond an organization's boundaries but affect a manager's ability to acquire and use resources. The global environment has two components: the task environment and the general environment.

**LO6-2, 6-3**

**THE TASK ENVIRONMENT** The task environment is the set of forces and conditions that originate with global suppliers, distributors, customers, and competitors and influence managers daily. The opportunities and threats associated with forces in the task environment become more complex as a company expands globally.

LO6-2, 6-3 **THE GENERAL ENVIRONMENT** The general environment comprises wide-ranging global economic, technological, sociocultural, demographic, political, and legal forces that affect an organization and its task environment.

LO6-4, 6-5 **THE CHANGING GLOBAL ENVIRONMENT** In recent years there has been a marked shift toward a more open global environment in which capital flows more freely as people and companies search for new opportunities to create profit and wealth. This has hastened the process of globalization. Globalization is the set of specific and general forces that work together to integrate and connect economic, political, and social systems across countries, cultures, or geographic regions so that nations become increasingly interdependent and similar. The process of globalization has been furthered by declining barriers to international trade and investment and declining barriers of distance and culture.

# Management in Action
## Topics for Discussion and Action

### Discussion

1. Why is it important for managers to understand the forces in the global environment that are acting on them and their organizations? [LO6-1]
2. Which organization is likely to face the most complex task environment—a biotechnology company trying to develop a cure for cancer or a large retailer like Carrefour? Why? [LO6-2, 6-3]
3. The population is aging because of declining birth rates, declining death rates, and the aging of the baby boom generation. What might some of the implications of this demographic trend be for (a) a pharmaceutical company and (b) the home construction industry? [LO6-1, 6-2, 6-3]
4. How do political, legal, and economic forces shape national culture? What characteristics of national culture do you think have the most important effect on how successful a country is in doing business abroad? [LO6-3, 6-5]
5. After the expansion of the EU to Poland many German companies shifted production operations to Poland to take advantage of lower labor costs and worker protection. As a result, they cut their costs and were better able to survive in an increasingly competitive global environment. Was their behavior ethical—that is, did the ends justify the means? [LO6-4]

### Action

6. Choose an organization, and ask a manager in that organization to list the number and strengths of forces in the organization's task environment. Ask the manager to pay particular attention to identifying opportunities and threats that result from pressures and changes in customers, competitors, and suppliers. [LO6-1, 6-2, 6-3]

# Building Management Skills
## Analyzing an Organization's Environment [LO6-1, 6-2, 6-3]

**Pick an organization with which you are familiar. It can be an organization in which you have worked or currently work or one that you interact with regularly as a customer (such as the college you are attending). For this organization do the following:**

1. Describe the main forces in the global task environment that are affecting the organization.
2. Describe the main forces in the global general environment that are affecting the organization.
3. Explain how environmental forces affect the job of an individual manager within this organization. How do they determine the opportunities and threats that its managers must confront?

# Managing Ethically [LO6-4, 6-5]

In recent years the number of European companies that buy their inputs from low-cost overseas suppliers has been growing, and concern about the ethics associated with employing young children in factories has been increasing. In Pakistan and India, children as young as six years old work long hours to make rugs and carpets for export to Western countries or clay bricks for local use. In countries like Malaysia and in Central America, children and teenagers routinely work long hours in factories and sweatshops to produce the clothing that is found in most European discount and department stores.

### Questions

1. Either by yourself or in a group, discuss whether it is ethical to employ children in factories and whether European companies should buy and sell products made by these children. What are some arguments for and against child labor?
2. If child labor is an economic necessity, what methods could be employed to make it as ethical a practice as possible? Or is it simply unethical?

## Small Group Breakout Exercise
### How to Enter the Copying Business [LO6-1, 6-2]

Form groups of three to five people, and appoint one group member as the spokesperson who will communicate your findings to the whole class when called on by the instructor. Then discuss the following scenario:

You and your partners have decided to open a small printing and copying business. Your business will compete with companies like FedEx Kinko's. You know that over 50% of small businesses fail in their first year, so to increase your chances of success, you have decided to perform a detailed analysis of the task environment of the copying business to discover what opportunities and threats you will encounter.

1. Decide what you must know about (a) your future customers, (b) your future competitors, and (c) other critical forces in the task environment if you are to be successful.
2. Evaluate the main barriers to entry into the copying business.
3. Based on this analysis, list some steps you would take to help your new copying business succeed.

## Exploring the World Wide Web [LO6-2, 6-3, 6-4]

Go to Fuji Films' Web site (www.fujifilm.com), click on "About Us," "History," and then "Corporate History," and consider how Fuji's global activities have expanded over time.

1. How would you characterize the way Fuji manages the global environment? For example, how has Fuji responded to the needs of customers in different countries?
2. How have increasing global competition and declining barriers of distance and culture affected Fuji's global operations?

## Be the Manager [LO6-1, 6-2]

### The Changing Environment of Retailing

You are the new manager of a major clothing store that is facing a crisis. This clothing store has been the leader in its market for the last 15 years. In the last three years, however, two other major clothing store chains have opened, and they have steadily been attracting customers away from your store—your sales are down 30%. To find out why, your store surveyed former customers and learned that they perceive your store as not keeping up with changing fashion trends and new forms of customer service. In examining how the store operates, you found out that the 10 purchasing managers who buy the clothing and accessories for the store have been buying from the same clothing suppliers and have become reluctant to try new ones. Moreover, salespeople rarely, if ever, make suggestions for changing how the store operates, and they don't respond to customer requests; the culture of the store has become conservative and risk-averse.

### Questions

1. Analyze the major forces in the task environment of a retail clothing store.
2. Devise a program that will help other managers and employees to better understand and respond to their store's task environment.

# Managing Organizational Structure and Culture

# CHAPTER 10

# Managing Organizational Structure and Culture

## Learning Objectives

*After studying this chapter, you should be able to:*

**LO10-1** Identify the factors that influence managers' choice of an organizational structure.

**LO10-2** Explain how managers group tasks into jobs that are motivating and satisfying for employees.

**LO10-3** Describe the types of organizational structures managers can design, and explain why they choose one structure over another.

**LO10-4** Explain why managers must coordinate jobs, functions, and divisions using the hierarchy of authority and integrating mechanisms.

**LO10-5** List the four sources of organizational culture, and explain why and how a company's culture can lead to competitive advantage.

## part 4

### Organizing and Controlling

# A MANAGER'S CHALLENGE
## Andrea Jung Reorganizes Avon's Global Structure

***How should managers organize to improve performance?*** In 2007 Andrea Jung, CEO of Avon, found that the company's rapid global expansion had given Avon's managers too much autonomy. They had gained so much authority to control operations in their respective countries and world regions that they had made decisions to benefit their own divisions—and these decisions had hurt the performance of the whole company. Avon's country-level managers from Poland to Mexico ran their own factories, made their own product development decisions, and developed their own advertising campaigns. And these decisions were often based on poor marketing knowledge and with little concern for operating costs; their goal was to increase sales as fast as possible. Also, when too much authority is decentralized to managers lower in an organization's hierarchy, these managers often recruit more managers to help them build their country "empires." The result was that Avon's global organizational hierarchy had exploded—it had risen from 7 levels to 15 levels of managers in a decade as tens of thousands of extra managers were hired around the globe.[1] Because Avon's profits were rising fast, Jung had not paid enough attention to the way Avon's organizational structure was becoming taller and taller—just as it was getting wider and wider as it established new divisions in new countries to expand cosmetics sales.

By 2008 Jung realized she had to lay off thousands of Avon's global managers and restructure its organizational hierarchy to reduce costs and increase profitability. She embarked on a program to take away the authority of Avon's country-level managers and to transfer authority to global regional and corporate headquarters managers to

Andrea Jung, here addressing a stellar group of women leaders in the White House, has seen her tough streamlining decisions in the short term begin to pay off over the longer haul.

streamline decision making and reduce costs. She cut out seven levels of management and laid off 25% of Avon's global managers in its 114 worldwide markets. Then, using teams of expert managers from corporate headquarters, she examined all of Avon's functional activities, country by country, to find out why its costs had risen so quickly and what could be done to bring them under control. The duplication of marketing efforts in countries around the world was one source of these high costs. In Mexico one team found that country managers' desire to expand their empires led to the development of a staggering 13,000 different products! Not only had this led product development costs to soar; it had also caused major marketing problems—how could Avon's Mexican sales reps learn about the differences between so many products to help customers choose the right ones for them?

In Avon's new structure, the goal is to centralize all major new product development. Avon still develops over 1,000 new products a year, but in the future while the input from different country managers will be used to customize products to country needs in terms of fragrance, packaging, and so on, R&D will be performed in the United States. Similarly, Avon's present strategy is to develop marketing campaigns targeted toward the average global customer but that can be easily customized to a particular country or world region by, for example, using the appropriate language or nationality of the models. Other initiatives have been to increase the money spent on global marketing, which had not kept pace with Avon's rapid global expansion, and to hire more Avon salespeople in developing nations to attract more customers. Today Avon has recruited over 400,000 reps in China alone![2]

Country-level managers now are responsible for managing this army of Avon reps and for making sure that marketing dollars are directed toward the right channels for maximum impact. However, they no longer have authority to engage in major product development or build new manufacturing capacity—or to hire new managers without the agreement of regional or corporate level managers. The balance of control has changed at Avon, and Jung and all her managers are now firmly focused on making operational decisions in the best interests of the whole company.

Jung's efforts to streamline the company's organizational structure have worked; but the recession necessitated more restructuring, and the company began another program of downsizing. Jung's focus has been on realigning its global value chain operations, particularly in Western Europe and Latin America; and Avon has increased its use of outsourcing, by outsourcing its call centers and transaction processing functions. As a result of these initiatives, approximately 4,000 more global positions will be lost by 2012; but Jung hopes that by then with its new streamlined structure Avon will be able to expand rapidly again when the economy has recovered—analysts claim the prospects for the company in China alone are "outstanding." Avon's share price had recovered by 2010. Clearly, paying attention to organizing is important in determining a company's long-term profitability.

## Overview

**organizational architecture** The organizational structure, control systems, culture, and human resource management systems that together determine how efficiently and effectively organizational resources are used.

**organizational structure** A formal system of task and reporting relationships that coordinates and motivates organizational members so they work together to achieve organizational goals.

As the example of Avon suggests, when the environment changes because, for example, customer tastes change, or because agile competitors have developed new strategies to outperform their rivals, a company often has to change its organizational structure and move to one better suited to its new environment. How an organization is designed also affects employees' behavior and how well the organization operates; and with competition heating up in the cosmetics industry, the challenge facing Avon's Andrea Jung was to identify the best way to organize people and resources to increase efficiency and effectiveness.

In Part 4 of this book, we examine how managers can organize and control human and other resources to create high-performing organizations. To organize and control (two of the four tasks of management identified in Chapter 1), managers must design an organizational architecture that makes the best use of resources to produce the goods and services customers want. **Organizational architecture** is the combination of organizational structure, culture, control systems, and human resource management (HRM) systems that together determine how efficiently and effectively organizational resources are used.

By the end of this chapter, you will be familiar not only with various forms of organizational structures and cultures but also with various factors that determine the organizational design choices that managers make. Then, in Chapters 11 and 12, we examine issues surrounding the design of an organization's control systems and HRM systems.

## Designing Organizational Structure

**LO10-1** Identify the factors that influence managers' choice of an organizational structure.

**organizational design** The process by which managers make specific organizing choices that result in a particular kind of organizational structure.

Organizing is the process by which managers establish the structure of working relationships among employees to allow them to achieve organizational goals efficiently and effectively. **Organizational structure** is the formal system of task and job reporting relationships that determines how employees use resources to achieve organizational goals.[3] *Organizational culture*, discussed in Chapter 3, is the shared set of beliefs, values, and norms that influence how people and groups work together to achieve organizational goals. **Organizational design** is the process by which managers create a specific type of organizational structure and culture so a company can operate in the most efficient and effective way—as Andrea Jung did for Avon.[4]

Once a company decides what kind of work attitudes and behaviors it wants from its employees, managers create a particular arrangement of task and authority relationships, and promote specific cultural values and norms, to obtain these desired attitudes and behaviors. The challenge facing all companies is to design a structure and culture that (1) *motivate* managers and employees to work hard and to develop supportive job behaviors and attitudes and (2) *coordinate* the actions of employees, groups, functions, and divisions to ensure they work together efficiently and effectively.

As noted in Chapter 2, according to contingency theory, managers design organizational structures to fit the factors or circumstances that are affecting the company the most and causing the most uncertainty.[5] Thus there is no one best way to design an organization: Design reflects each organization's specific situation, and researchers have argued that in some situations stable, mechanistic structures may be most appropriate while in others flexible, organic structures might be the most effective. Four factors are important determinants of the type of organizational structure or culture managers select: the nature of the organizational environment, the type of strategy the organization pursues, the technology (and particularly information technology) the organization uses, and the characteristics of the organization's human resources (see Figure 10.1).[6]

### The Organizational Environment

In general, the more quickly the external environment is changing and the greater the uncertainty within it, the greater are the problems managers face in trying to gain access to scarce resources. In this situation, to speed decision making and communication

**Figure 10.1**
**Factors Affecting Organizational Structure**

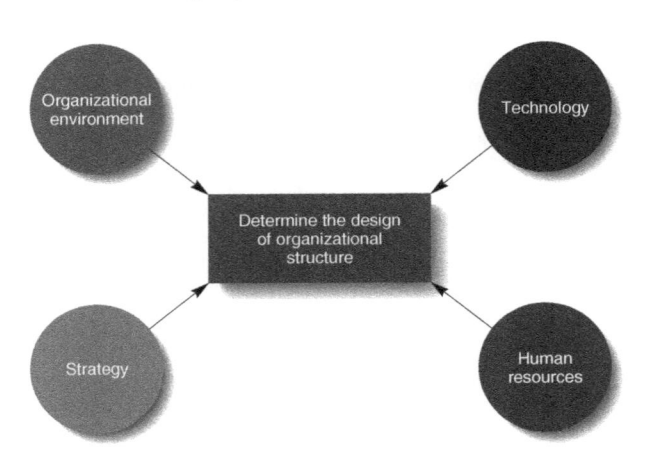

and make it easier to obtain resources, managers typically make organizing choices that result in more flexible structures and entrepreneurial cultures.[7] They are likely to decentralize authority, empower lower-level employees to make important operating decisions, and encourage values and norms that emphasize change and innovation—a more organic from of organizing.

In contrast, if the external environment is stable, resources are readily available, and uncertainty is low, then less coordination and communication among people and functions are needed to obtain resources. Managers can make organizing choices that bring more stability or formality to the organizational structure and can establish values and norms that emphasize obedience and being a team player. Managers in this situation prefer to make decisions within a clearly defined hierarchy of authority and to use detailed rules, standard operating procedures (SOPs), and restrictive norms to guide and govern employees' activities—a more mechanistic form of organizing.

As we discussed in Chapter 6, change is rapid in today's marketplace, and increasing competition both at home and abroad is putting greater pressure on managers to attract customers and increase efficiency and effectiveness. Consequently, interest in finding ways to structure organizations—such as through empowerment and self-managed teams—to allow people and departments to behave flexibly has been increasing.

## Strategy

Chapter 8 suggests that once managers decide on a strategy, they must choose the right means to implement it. Different strategies often call for the use of different organizational structures and cultures. For example, a differentiation strategy aimed at increasing the value customers perceive in an organization's goods and services usually succeeds best in a flexible structure with a culture that values innovation; flexibility facilitates a differentiation strategy because managers can develop new or innovative products quickly—an activity that requires extensive cooperation among functions or departments. In contrast, a low-cost strategy that is aimed at driving down costs in all functions usually fares best in a more formal structure with more conservative norms, which gives managers greater control over the activities of an organization's various departments.[8]

In addition, at the corporate level, when managers decide to expand the scope of organizational activities by vertical integration or diversification, for example, they need to design a flexible structure to provide sufficient coordination among the different business divisions.[9] As discussed in Chapter 8, many companies have been divesting businesses because managers have been unable to create a competitive advantage to keep them up to speed in fast-changing industries. By moving to a more flexible structure, managers gain more control over their different businesses. Finally, expanding internationally and operating in many different countries challenges managers to create organizational structures that allow organizations to be flexible on a global level.[10] As we discuss later, managers can group their departments or divisions in several ways to allow them to effectively pursue an international strategy.

## Technology

Recall that technology is the combination of skills, knowledge, machines, and computers that are used to design, make, and distribute goods and services. As a rule, the more complicated the technology that an organization uses, the more difficult it is to regulate or control it because more unexpected events can arise. Thus the more complicated the technology, the greater is the need for a flexible structure and progressive culture to enhance managers' ability to respond to unexpected situations—and give them the freedom and desire to work out new solutions to the problems they encounter. In contrast, the more routine the technology, the more appropriate is a formal structure because tasks are simple and the steps needed to produce goods and services have been worked out in advance.

What makes a technology routine or complicated? One researcher who investigated this issue, Charles Perrow, argued that two factors determine how complicated or nonroutine technology is: task variety and task analyzability.[11] *Task variety* is the number of new or unexpected problems or situations that a person or function encounters in performing tasks or jobs. *Task analyzability* is the degree to which programmed solutions are available to people or functions to solve the problems they encounter. Nonroutine or complicated technologies are characterized by high task variety and low task analyzability; this means many varied problems occur and solving these problems requires significant nonprogrammed decision making. In contrast, routine technologies are characterized by low task variety and high task analyzability; this means the problems encountered do not vary much and are easily resolved through programmed decision making.

Examples of nonroutine technology are found in the work of scientists in an R&D laboratory who develop new products or discover new drugs, and they are seen in the planning exercises an organization's top management team uses to chart the organization's future strategy. Examples of routine technology include typical mass-production or assembly operations, where workers perform the same task repeatedly and where managers have already identified the programmed solutions necessary to perform a task efficiently. Similarly, in service organizations such as fast-food restaurants, the tasks that crew members perform in making and serving fast food are routine.

**LO10-2** Explain how managers group tasks into jobs that are motivating and satisfying for employees.

## Human Resources

A final important factor affecting an organization's choice of structure and culture is the characteristics of the human resources it employs. In general, the more highly skilled its workforce, and the greater the number of employees who work together in groups or teams, the more likely an organization is to use a flexible, decentralized structure and a professional culture based on values and norms that foster employee autonomy and self-control. Highly skilled employees, or employees who have internalized strong professional values and norms of behavior as part of their training, usually desire greater freedom and autonomy and dislike close supervision.

Flexible structures, characterized by decentralized authority and empowered employees, are well suited to the needs of highly skilled people. Similarly, when people work in teams, they must be allowed to interact freely and develop norms to guide their own work interactions, which also is possible in a flexible organizational structure. Thus, when designing organizational structure and culture, managers must pay close attention to the needs of the workforce and to the complexity and kind of work employees perform.

In summary, an organization's external environment, strategy, technology, and human resources are the factors to be considered by managers seeking to design the best structure and culture for an organization. The greater the level of uncertainty in the organization's environment, the more complex its strategy and technologies, and the more highly qualified and skilled its workforce, the more likely managers are to design a structure and a culture that are flexible, can change quickly, and allow employees to be innovative in their responses to problems, customer needs, and so on. The more stable the organization's environment, the less complex and more well understood its strategy or technology, and the less skilled its workforce, the more likely managers are to design an organizational structure that is formal and controlling and a culture whose values and norms prescribe how employees should act in particular situations.

Later in the chapter we discuss how managers can create different kinds of organizational cultures. First, however, we discuss how managers can design flexible or formal organizational structures. The way an organization's structure works depends on the organizing choices managers make about three issues:

- How to group tasks into individual jobs.
- How to group jobs into functions and divisions.
- How to allocate authority and coordinate or integrate functions and divisions.

## Grouping Tasks into Jobs: Job Design

**job design** The process by which managers decide how to divide tasks into specific jobs.

The first step in organizational design is **job design,** the process by which managers decide how to divide into specific jobs the tasks that have to be performed to provide customers with goods and services. Managers at McDonald's, for example, have decided how best to divide the tasks required to provide customers with fast, cheap food in each McDonald's restaurant. After experimenting with different job arrangements, McDonald's managers decided on a basic division of labor among chefs and food servers. Managers allocated all the tasks involved in actually cooking the food (putting oil in the fat fryers, opening packages of frozen french fries, putting beef patties on the grill, making salads, and so on) to the job of chef. They allocated all the tasks involved in giving the food to customers (such as greeting customers, taking orders, putting fries and burgers into bags, adding salt, pepper, and napkins, and taking money) to food servers. In addition, they created other jobs—the job of dealing with drive-through customers, the job of keeping the restaurant clean, and the job of overseeing employees and responding to unexpected events. The result of the job design process is a *division of labor* among employees, one that McDonald's managers have discovered through experience is most efficient.

Establishing an appropriate division of labor among employees is a critical part of the organizing process, one that is vital to increasing efficiency and effectiveness. At McDonald's, the tasks associated with chef and food server were split into different jobs because managers found that, for the kind of food McDonald's serves, this approach was most efficient. It is efficient because when each employee is given fewer tasks to perform (so that each job becomes more specialized), employees become more productive at performing the tasks that constitute each job.

At Subway, a sandwich shop found in 92 countries, managers chose a different kind of job design. At Subway there is no division of labor among the people who make the sandwiches, wrap the sandwiches, give them to customers, and take the money. The roles of chef and food server are combined into one. This different division of tasks and jobs is efficient for Subway and not for McDonald's because Subway serves a limited menu of mostly submarine-style sandwiches that are prepared to order. Subway's production system is far simpler than McDonald's; McDonald's menu is much more varied, and its chefs must cook many different kinds of foods.

Managers of every organization must analyze the range of tasks to be performed and then create jobs that best allow the organization to give customers the goods and services they want. In deciding how to assign tasks to individual jobs, however, managers must be careful not to take **job simplification,** the process of reducing the number of tasks that each worker performs, too far.[12] Too much job simplification may reduce efficiency rather than increase it if workers find their simplified jobs boring and monotonous, become demotivated and unhappy, and, as a result, perform at a low level.

*At Subway, the roles of chef and server are combined into one, making the job "larger" than the jobs of McDonald's more specialized food servers. The idea behind job enlargement is that increasing the range of tasks performed by the worker will reduce boredom.*

**job simplification** The process of reducing the number of tasks that each worker performs.

## Job Enlargement and Job Enrichment

In an attempt to create a division of labor and design individual jobs to encourage workers to perform at a higher level and be more satisfied with their work, several researchers have proposed ways other than job simplification to group tasks into jobs: job enlargement and job enrichment.

**job enlargement** Increasing the number of different tasks in a given job by changing the division of labor.

**Job enlargement** is increasing the number of different tasks in a given job by changing the division of labor.[13] For example, because Subway food servers make the food as well as serve it, their jobs are "larger" than the jobs of McDonald's food servers. The Subway employee performs the whole process of making the sandwich, including baking the bread. In contrast, the McDonald's employee performs one specific task, such as cooking the hamburgers. The idea behind job enlargement is that increasing the range of tasks performed by a worker will reduce boredom and fatigue and may increase motivation to perform at a high level—increasing both the quantity and the quality of goods and services provided.

**job enrichment** Increasing the degree of responsibility a worker has over his or her job.

**Job enrichment** is increasing the degree of responsibility a worker has over a job by, for example, (1) empowering workers to experiment to find new or better ways of doing the job, (2) encouraging workers to develop new skills, (3) allowing workers to decide how to do the work and giving them the responsibility for deciding how to respond to unexpected situations, and (4) allowing workers to monitor and measure their own performance.[14] The idea behind job enrichment is that increasing workers' responsibility increases their involvement in their jobs and thus improves their interest in the quality of the goods they make or the services they provide.

In general, managers who make design choices that increase job enrichment and job enlargement are likely to increase the degree to which people behave flexibly rather than rigidly or mechanically. Narrow, specialized jobs are likely to lead people to behave in predictable ways; workers who perform a variety of tasks and who are allowed and encouraged to discover new and better ways to perform their jobs are likely to act flexibly and creatively. Thus managers who enlarge and enrich jobs create a flexible organizational structure, and those who simplify jobs create a more formal structure. If workers are grouped into self-managed work teams, the organization is likely to be flexible because team members provide support for each other and can learn from one another.

## The Job Characteristics Model

**LO10-3** Describe the types of organizational structures managers can design, and explain why they choose one structure over another.

J. R. Hackman and G. R. Oldham's job characteristics model is an influential model of job design that explains in detail how managers can make jobs more interesting and motivating.[15] Hackman and Oldham's model (see Figure 10.2) also describes the likely personal and organizational outcomes that will result from enriched and enlarged jobs.

According to Hackman and Oldham, every job has five characteristics that determine how motivating the job is. These characteristics determine how employees react to their work and lead to outcomes such as high performance and satisfaction and low absenteeism and turnover:

- *Skill variety:* The extent to which a job requires that an employee use a wide range of different skills, abilities, or knowledge. Example: The skill variety required by the job of a research scientist is higher than that called for by the job of a McDonald's food server.
- *Task identity:* The extent to which a job requires that a worker perform all the tasks necessary to complete the job, from the beginning to the end of the production process. Example: A craftsworker who takes a piece of wood and transforms it into a custom-made desk has higher task identity than does a worker who performs only one of the numerous operations required to assemble a flat-screen TV.
- *Task significance:* The degree to which a worker feels his or her job is meaningful because of its effect on people inside the organization, such as coworkers, or on people outside the organization, such as customers. Example: A teacher who sees the effect of his or her efforts in a well-educated and well-adjusted student enjoys high task significance compared to a dishwasher who monotonously washes dishes as they come to the kitchen.
- *Autonomy:* The degree to which a job gives an employee the freedom and discretion needed to schedule different tasks and decide how to carry them out. Example: Salespeople who have to plan their schedules and decide how to allocate their time among different customers have relatively high autonomy compared to assembly-line workers, whose actions are determined by the speed of the production line.
- *Feedback:* The extent to which actually doing a job provides a worker with clear and direct information about how well he or she has performed the job. Example: An air traffic controller whose mistakes may result in a midair collision receives

**Figure 10.2**
**The Job Characteristics Model**

| Job characteristics | Psychological states | Outcomes |
|---|---|---|
| Skill variety<br>Task identity<br>Task significance | Experienced meaningfulness of work | High motivation<br>High performance<br>High satisfaction |
| Autonomy | Experienced responsibility for work outcomes | |
| Feedback | Knowledge of results of work | |

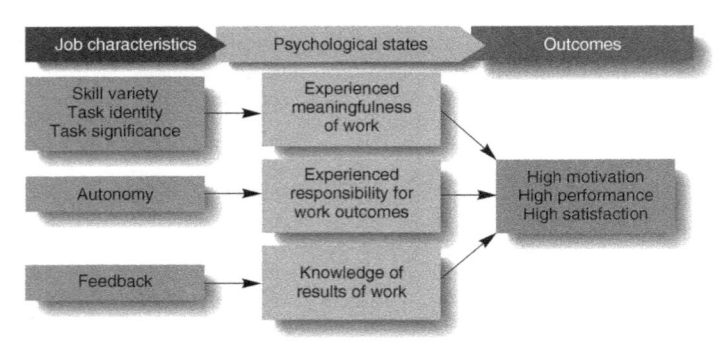

Source: J. Richard Hackman and Greg R. Oldham, *Work Redesign*, 1st edition, © 1980. Reproduced by permission of Pearson Education, Inc., Upper Saddle River, New Jersey.

immediate feedback on job performance; a person who compiles statistics for a business magazine often has little idea of when he or she makes a mistake or does a particularly good job.

Hackman and Oldham argue that these five job characteristics affect an employee's motivation because they affect three critical psychological states (see Figure 10.2). The more employees feel that their work is *meaningful* and that they are *responsible for work outcomes and responsible for knowing how those outcomes affect others*, the more motivating work becomes and the more likely employees are to be satisfied and to perform at a high level. Moreover, employees who have jobs that are highly motivating are called on to use their skills more and to perform more tasks, and they are given more responsibility for doing the job. All of the foregoing are characteristic of jobs and employees in flexible structures where authority is decentralized and where employees commonly work with others and must learn new skills to complete the range of tasks for which their group is responsible.

# Grouping Jobs into Functions and Divisions: Designing Organizational Structure

Once managers have decided which tasks to allocate to which jobs, they face the next organizing decision: how to group jobs together to best match the needs of the organization's environment, strategy, technology, and human resources. Typically managers first decide to group jobs into departments and then design a *functional structure* to use organizational resources effectively. As an organization grows and becomes more difficult to control, managers must choose a more complex organizational design, such as a divisional structure or a matrix or product team structure. The different way in which managers can design organizational structure are discussed next. Selecting and designing an organizational structure to increase efficiency and effectiveness is a significant challenge. As noted in Chapter 8, managers reap the rewards of a well-thought-out strategy only if they choose the right type of structure to implement the strategy. The ability to make the right kinds of organizing choices is often what differentiates effective from ineffective managers and creates a high-performing organization.

## Functional Structure

A *function* is a group of people, working together, who possess similar skills or use the same kind of knowledge, tools, or techniques to perform their jobs. Manufacturing, sales, and research and development are often organized into functional departments. A **functional structure** is an organizational structure composed of all the departments that an organization requires to produce its goods or services. Figure 10.3 shows the functional structure for Affilips N.V., a copper, aluminum, nickel, and lead alloys manufacturer in Belgium. The firm is well known for its use of recycled material.

**functional structure** An organizational structure composed of all the departments that an organization requires to produce its goods or services.

Purchasing, environmental, security, R&D, production, quality, finance, and personnel are the major functions of the firm. Each job inside a function exists because it helps the function perform the activities necessary for high organizational performance.

There are several advantages to grouping jobs according to function. First, when people who perform similar jobs are grouped together, they can learn from observing one another and thus become more specialized and can perform at a higher level. The tasks associated with one job often are related to the tasks associated with another job, which encourages cooperation within a function.

Second, when people who perform similar jobs are grouped together, it is easier for managers to monitor and evaluate their performance.[16] Imagine if marketing experts, purchasing experts, and real estate experts were grouped together in one function and

### Figure 10.3
**The Functional Structure of Affilips N.V. in Tienen, Belgium**

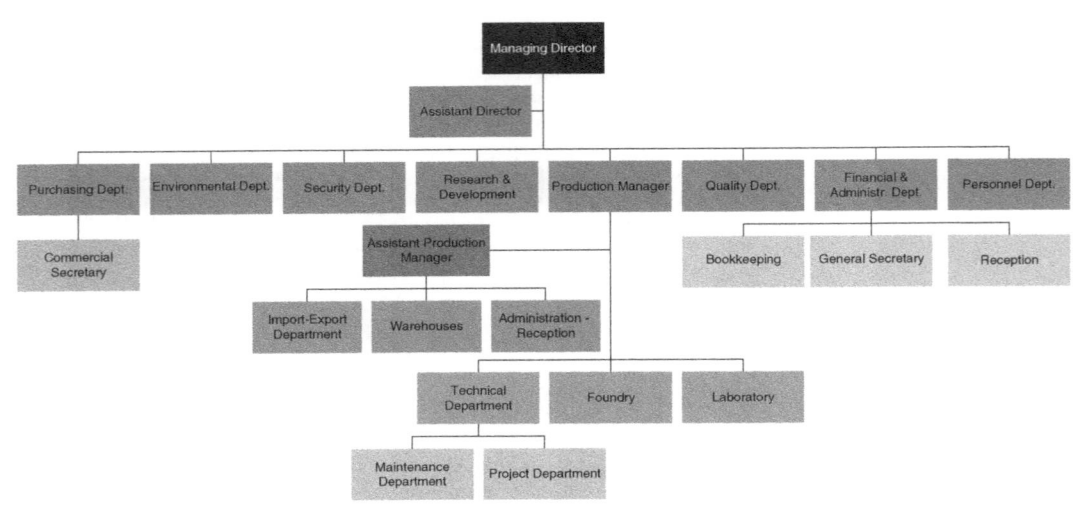

Source: Affilips: Organization Chart, *Welcome to Affilips*, http://www.affilips.com/organization.html, accessed October 19, 2010.

supervised by a manager from merchandising. Obviously the merchandising manager would not have the expertise to evaluate all these different people appropriately. A functional structure allows workers to evaluate how well coworkers are performing their jobs, and if some workers are performing poorly, more experienced workers can help them develop new skills.

Finally, managers appreciate functional structure because it lets them create the set of functions they need to scan and monitor the competitive environment and obtain information about how it is changing.[17] With the right set of functions in place, managers are in a good position to develop a strategy that allows the organization to respond to its changing situation.

As an organization grows, and particularly as its task environment and strategy change because it is beginning to produce a wider range of goods and services for different kinds of customers, several problems can make a functional structure less efficient and effective.[18] First, managers in different functions may find it more difficult to communicate and coordinate with one another when they are responsible for several different kinds of products, especially as the organization grows both domestically and internationally. Second, functional managers may become so preoccupied with supervising their own specific departments and achieving their departmental goals that they lose sight of organizational goals. If that happens, organizational effectiveness will suffer because managers will be viewing issues and problems facing the organization only from their own, relatively narrow, departmental perspectives.[19] Both of these problems can reduce efficiency and effectiveness.

## Divisional Structures: Product, Market, and Geographic

**divisional structure** An organizational structure composed of separate business units within which are the functions that work together to produce a specific product for a specific customer.

As the problems associated with growth and diversification increase over time, managers must search for new ways to organize their activities to overcome the problems associated with a functional structure. Most managers of large organizations choose a **divisional structure** and create a series of business units to produce a specific kind

Affilips N.V., an alloys manufacturer in Belgium, organizes its operations by function, which means that employees can more easily learn from one another and improve the service they provide to customers.

of product for a specific kind of customer. Each *division* is a collection of functions or departments that work together to produce the product. The goal behind the change to a divisional structure is to create smaller, more manageable units within the organization. There are three forms of divisional structure (see Figure 10.4).[20] When managers organize divisions according to the *type of good or service* they provide, they adopt a product structure. When managers organize divisions according to the *area of the country or world* they operate in, they adopt a geographic structure. When managers organize divisions according to *the type of customer* they focus on, they adopt a market structure.

**PRODUCT STRUCTURE** Imagine the problems that managers at Affilips N.V. would encounter if they decided to diversify into producing and selling cars, fast food, and health insurance—in addition to home furnishings—and tried to use their existing set of functional managers to oversee the production of all four kinds of products. No manager would have the necessary skills or abilities to oversee those four products. No individual marketing manager, for example, could effectively market cars, fast food, health insurance, and home furnishings at the same time. To perform a functional activity successfully, managers must have experience in specific markets or industries. Consequently, if managers decide to diversify into new industries or to expand their range of products, they commonly design a product structure to organize their operations (see Figure 10.4a).

Using a **product structure,** managers place each distinct product line or business in its own self-contained division and give divisional managers the responsibility for devising an appropriate business-level strategy to allow the division to compete effectively in its industry or market.[21] Each division is self-contained because it has a complete set of all the functions—marketing, R&D, finance, and so on—that it needs to produce or provide goods or services efficiently and effectively. Functional managers report to divisional managers, and divisional managers report to top or corporate managers.

Grouping functions into divisions focused on particular products has several advantages for managers at all levels in the organization. First, a product structure allows functional managers to specialize in only one product area, so they can build expertise and fine-tune their skills in this particular area. Second, each division's managers

**product structure** An organizational structure in which each product line or business is handled by a self-contained division.

**Figure 10.4**
**Product, Market, and Geographic Structures**

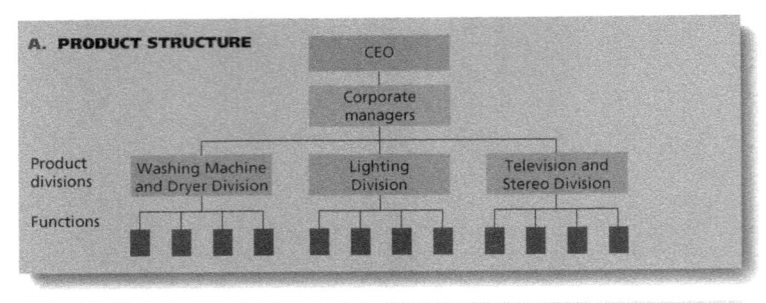

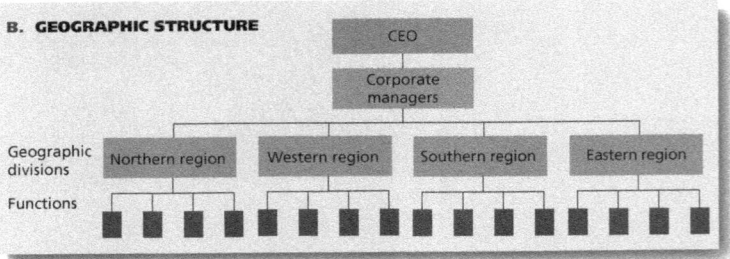

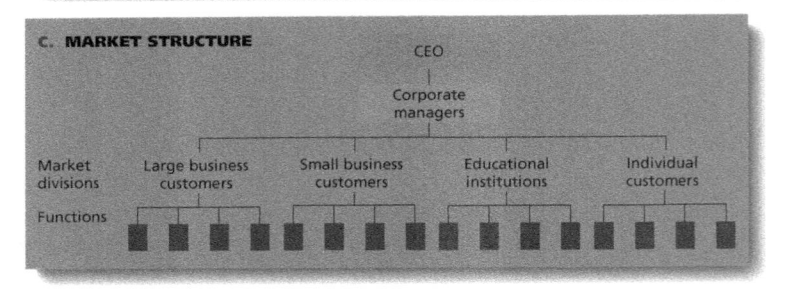

**A. PRODUCT STRUCTURE**

Product divisions: Washing Machine and Dryer Division | Lighting Division | Television and Stereo Division

**B. GEOGRAPHIC STRUCTURE**

Geographic divisions: Northern region | Western region | Southern region | Eastern region

**C. MARKET STRUCTURE**

Market divisions: Large business customers | Small business customers | Educational institutions | Individual customers

can become experts in their industry; this expertise helps them choose and develop a business-level strategy to differentiate their products or lower their costs while meeting the needs of customers. Third, a product structure frees corporate managers from the need to supervise directly each division's day-to-day operations; this latitude lets corporate managers create the best corporate-level strategy to maximize the organization's future growth and ability to create value. Corporate managers are likely to make fewer mistakes about which businesses to diversify into or how to best expand internationally, for example, because they can take an organizationwide view.[22] Corporate managers also are likely to evaluate better how well divisional managers are doing, and they can intervene and take corrective action as needed.

The extra layer of management, the divisional management layer, can improve the use of organizational resources. Moreover, a product structure puts divisional managers close to their customers and lets them respond quickly and appropriately to the changing task environment. One pharmaceutical company that successfully adopted a new product structure to better organize its activities is GlaxoSmithKline, a British pharmaceutical firm. The need to innovate new kinds of prescription drugs to boost performance is a continual battle for pharmaceutical companies. In the

Managing Organizational Structure and Culture

2000s many of these companies have been merging to try to increase their research productivity, and one of them, GlaxoSmithKline, was created from the merger between Glaxo Wellcome and SmithKline Beecham.[23] Prior to the merger, both companies experienced a steep decline in the number of new prescription drugs their scientists were able to invent. The problem facing the new company's top managers was how to best use and combine the talents of the scientists and researchers from both of the former companies to allow them to quickly innovate exciting new drugs.

Top managers realized that after the merger there would be enormous problems associated with coordinating the activities of the thousands of research scientists who were working on hundreds of different kinds of drug research programs. Understanding the problems associated with large size, the top managers decided to group the researchers into eight product divisions to allow them to focus on particular clusters of diseases such as heart disease or viral infections. The members of each product division were told they would be rewarded based on the number of new prescription drugs they were able to invent and the speed with which they could bring these new drugs to the market. GlaxoSmithKline's new product structure worked well; its research productivity doubled after the reorganization, and a record number of new drugs moved into clinical trials.[24]

When Glaxo Wellcome and SmithKline Beecham merged, managers resolved the problem of how to coordinate the activities of thousands of research scientists by organizing them into product divisions focusing on clusters of diseases.

**GEOGRAPHIC STRUCTURE** When organizations expand rapidly both at home and abroad, functional structures can create special problems because managers in one central location may find it increasingly difficult to deal with the different problems and issues that may arise in each region of a country or area of the world. In these cases, a **geographic structure,** in which divisions are broken down by geographic location, is often chosen (see Figure 10.4b).

**geographic structure** An organizational structure in which each region of a country or area of the world is served by a self-contained division.

In adopting a *global geographic structure,* such as shown in Figure 10.5a, managers locate different divisions in each of the world regions where the organization operates. To illustrate, you can see the organizational chart for the Telefónica Group of Argentina in Figure 10.5a. The firm is in 25 countries and these countries are organized into three geographical regions: Spain, Latin America, and Europe. Under each regional group would be a complete set of functional areas. Managers are most likely to do this when they pursue a multidomestic strategy because customer needs vary widely by country or world region. For example, if products that appeal to U.S. customers do not sell in Europe, the Pacific Rim, or South America, managers must customize the products to meet the needs of customers in those different world regions; a global geographic structure with global divisions will allow them to do this.

In contrast, to the degree that customers abroad are willing to buy the same kind of product or slight variations thereof, managers are more likely to pursue a global strategy. In this case they are more likely to use a global product structure. In a *global product structure,* each product division, not the country and regional managers, takes responsibility for deciding where to manufacture its products and how to market them in countries worldwide (see Figure 10.5b). Product division managers manage their own global value chains and decide where to establish foreign subsidiaries to distribute and sell their products to customers in foreign countries. As we noted at the beginning of this chapter, an organization's strategy is a major determinant of its structure both at home and abroad; and in Chapter 6 we discussed how Nokia took a commanding lead in global cell phone sales because of its strategy of customizing phones to the needs of local users and assembling the phones in a factory located in a country within the world region where the phones are to be sold. Nokia's most important function is its design and engineering function, which spearheads its global new product development efforts. And to allow this function, and the company, to

### Figure 10.5
**Global Geographic and Global Product Structures**

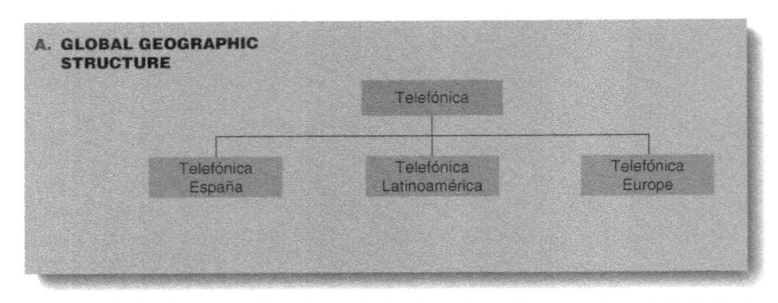

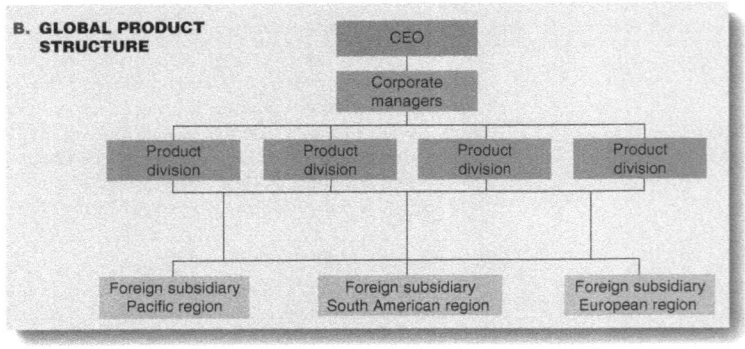

**A. GLOBAL GEOGRAPHIC STRUCTURE**

- Telefónica
  - Telefónica España
  - Telefónica Latinoamérica
  - Telefónica Europe

**B. GLOBAL PRODUCT STRUCTURE**

- CEO
  - Corporate managers
    - Product division
    - Product division
    - Product division
    - Product division
      - Foreign subsidiary Pacific region
      - Foreign subsidiary South American region
      - Foreign subsidiary European region

Source: Telefónica, "About Telefónica, Our Organization, Our Structure," http://www.telefonica.com/en/about_telefonica/html/estrucorganiz/estrucgrupo.shtml, accessed October 20, 2010.

perform most effectively, Nokia adopted a global structure to organize its design activities.

Nokia was the first cell phone manufacturer to recognize that the needs of customers differ markedly in different countries of the world. In Western countries, for example, the style of the phone is paramount, as is its ability to offer users services like e-mail and video downloading, and Nokia is developing advanced smartphones to compete with Apple. In India customers also value style, and they buy a cell phone as a status symbol and so are willing to pay a premium price for it. But in China customers want a bargain—the phone has to be at the right price point if customers are to buy the entry-level version or be enticed to spend more for premium features. How did Nokia discover how much needs diverge among customers in different countries?

Its top managers decided that the engineers in its vast central design studio in Finland should be in charge of basic cell phone R&D and monitoring changing global forces in technology and changing customer demand for services such as video downloads, touch screens, colors, and so forth. However, to get close to customers in different countries, top managers decided to open nine different geographic design studios in various world regions and countries, such as India and China, where Nokia hopes to generate the most sales revenues. Engineers in these geographic studios, aided by marketing experts, determine the most important country-specific customer preferences.[25] These preferences are then transmitted back to Nokia's Finnish design

*Click, click, click. Nokia can pride itself on its forward-thinking momentum, which prompted it to develop regionally based products.*

headquarters, where they are incorporated into the studio's knowledge about changing global preferences for faster Internet service, touch screens, and so on. The result is a range of phones that share much in common but that can be highly customized to the needs of customers in different regions and countries. So Nokia uses a global divisional structure to facilitate its global design and manufacturing competencies as it attempts to remain ahead in the fiercely competitive global cell phone market.

**MARKET STRUCTURE** Sometimes the pressing issue facing managers is to group functions according to the type of customer buying the product in order to tailor the products the organization offers to each customer's unique demands. A PC maker such as Dell, for example, has several kinds of customers, including large businesses (which might demand networks of computers linked to a mainframe computer), small companies (which may need just a few PCs linked together), educational users in schools and universities (which might want thousands of independent PCs for their students), and individual users (who may want a high-quality multimedia PC so they can play the latest video games).

**market structure** An organizational structure in which each kind of customer is served by a self-contained division; also called *customer structure*.

To satisfy the needs of diverse customers, a company might adopt a **market structure,** which groups divisions according to the particular kinds of customers they serve (see Figure 10.4c). A market structure lets managers be responsive to the needs of their customers and allows them to act flexibly in making decisions in response to customers' changing needs. All kinds of organizations need to continually evaluate their structures, as is suggested in the following "Management Insight" box, which examines the concept of business groups.

## Matrix and Product Team Designs

Moving to a product, market, or geographic divisional structure allows managers to respond more quickly and flexibly to the particular circumstances they confront. However, when information technology or customer needs are changing rapidly and the environment is uncertain, even a divisional structure may not give managers enough flexibility to respond to the environment quickly. To operate effectively under these conditions, managers must design the most flexible kind of organizational structure available: a matrix structure or a product team structure (see Figure 10.6).

Management Insight

### Business Groups

Around the world a dominant form of business, not present in North America and limited in Europe, is the business group. Business groups are a set of legally independent entities bound by economic and social ties. These ties lead firms in the group to support one another, for example, by purchasing from each other. In addition they own one another's stock. Thus, rather than widespread stock ownership there is cross ownership within the business group. The best-known business groups are those in Japan, the *keiretsu,* and Korea, the *chaebol.*

To illustrate the keiretsu in Japan, consider the impact of the Mitsubishi group on the Japanese economy. There are over 160 firms in the Mitsubishi group. To begin, Mitsubishi Bank is the largest commercial banking company in the world, with assets of nearly US$820 billion. Next, Meiji Mutual, a Mitsubishi Group member, is the sixth largest mutual life insurance company worldwide, with assets of more than US$90 billion. Mitsubishi Motors is among world's top ten vehicle producers, while Mitsubishi Chemical is among world's top ten chemical companies. Mitsubishi Electric is one of the top ten electronics companies, and one of the fifty largest industrial companies in the world. Mitsubishi Heavy Industries is the largest industrial and farm equipment manufacturer in the world. Other core group members include Mitsubishi Materials (the twelfth largest metals company on earth), Kirin Brewery (the fourth largest beverage company), Mitsubishi Oil (the twenty-eighth petroleum refiner), and Asahi Glass (third in building materials).

This is only a sampling of the Mitsubishi firms. In total the Mitsubishi Group is estimated to contribute about 11% of the Japanese economy.

**Figure 10.6**
**Matrix and Product Team Structures**

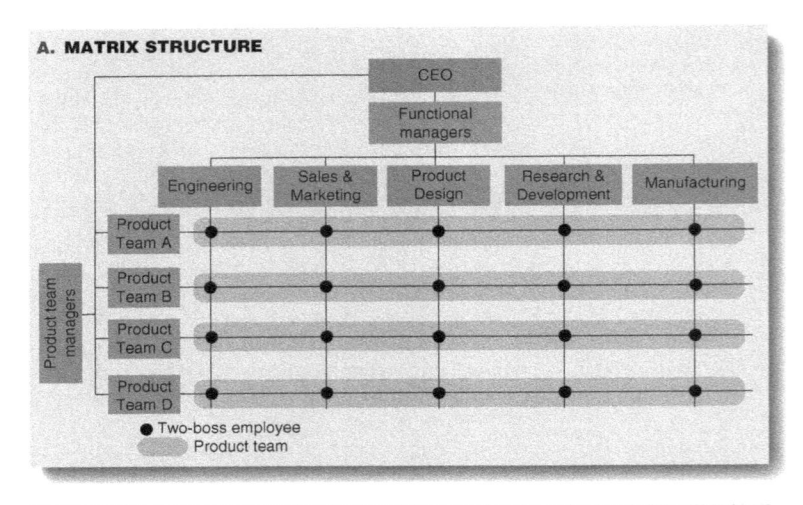

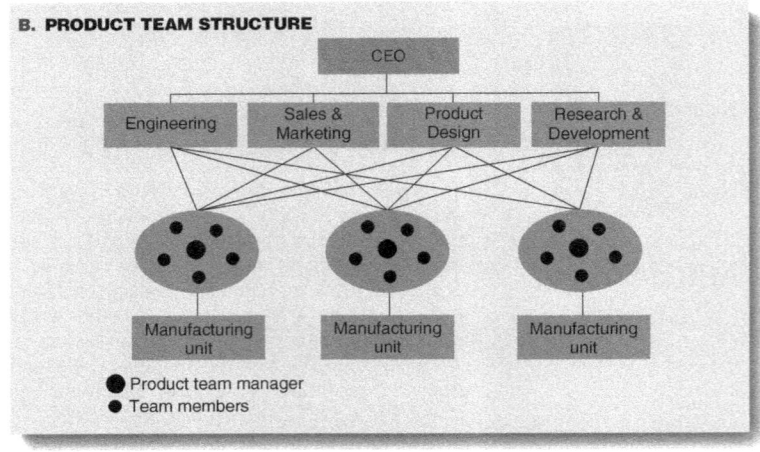

**matrix structure** An organizational structure that simultaneously groups people and resources by function and by product.

**MATRIX STRUCTURE** In a **matrix structure,** managers group people and resources in two ways simultaneously: by function and by product.[26] Employees are grouped by *functions* to allow them to learn from one another and become more skilled and productive. In addition, employees are grouped into *product teams* in which members of different functions work together to develop a specific product. The result is a complex network of reporting relationships among product teams and functions that makes the matrix structure very flexible (see Figure 10.6a). Each person in a product team reports to two managers: (1) a functional boss, who assigns individuals to a team and evaluates their performance from a functional perspective, and (2) the boss of the product team, who evaluates their performance on the team. Thus team members are known as *two-boss employees.* The functional employees assigned to product teams change over time as the specific skills that the team needs change. At the beginning of the product development process, for example, engineers and R&D specialists are assigned to a product team because their skills are needed to develop new products. When a provisional design has been established, marketing experts are assigned to the team to gauge how customers will respond to the new product. Manufacturing personnel join when it is time to find the most efficient way to produce the product. As their specific jobs are completed, team members leave and are reassigned to new teams. In this way the matrix structure makes the most use of human resources.

To keep the matrix structure flexible, product teams are empowered and team members are responsible for making most of the important decisions involved in product development.[27] The product team manager acts as a facilitator, controlling the financial resources and trying to keep the project on time and within budget. The functional managers try to ensure that the product is the best it can be to maximize its differentiated appeal.

High-tech companies that operate in environments where new product development takes place monthly or yearly have used matrix structures successfully for many years, and the need to innovate quickly is vital to the organization's survival. The flexibility afforded by a matrix structure lets managers keep pace with a changing and increasingly complex environment.[28]

**PRODUCT TEAM STRUCTURE** The dual reporting relationships that are at the heart of a matrix structure have always been difficult for managers and employees to deal with. Often the functional boss and the product boss make conflicting demands on team members, who do not know which boss to satisfy first. Also, functional and product team bosses may come into conflict over precisely who is in charge of which team members and for how long. To avoid these problems, managers have devised a way of organizing people and resources that still allows an organization to be flexible but makes its structure easier to operate: a product team structure.

**product team structure** An organizational structure in which employees are permanently assigned to a cross-functional team and report only to the product team manager or to one of his or her direct subordinates.

**cross-functional team** A group of managers brought together from different departments to perform organizational tasks.

The **product team structure** differs from a matrix structure in two ways: (1) It does away with dual reporting relationships and two-boss employees, and (2) functional employees are permanently assigned to a cross-functional team that is empowered to bring a new or redesigned product to market. A **cross-functional team** is a group of managers brought together from different departments to perform organizational tasks. When managers are grouped into cross-functional teams, the artificial boundaries between departments disappear, and a narrow focus on departmental goals is replaced with a general interest in working together to achieve organizational goals. The results of such changes have been dramatic: Ford can introduce a new model of car in two years.

Members of a cross-functional team report only to the product team manager or to one of his or her direct subordinates. The heads of the functions have only an informal, advisory relationship with members of the product teams—the role of functional managers is only to counsel and help team members, share knowledge among teams, and provide new technological developments that can help improve each team's performance (see Figure 10.6b).[29]

Increasingly, organizations are making empowered cross-functional teams an essential part of their organizational architecture to help them gain a competitive advantage in fast-changing organizational environments.

## Coordinating Functions and Divisions

The more complex the structure a company uses to group its activities, the greater are the problems of *linking and coordinating* its different functions and divisions. Coordination becomes a problem because each function or division develops a different orientation toward the other groups that affects how it interacts with them. Each function or division comes to view the problems facing the company from its own perspective; for example, they may develop different views about the major goals, problems, or issues facing a company.

At the functional level, the manufacturing function typically has a short-term view; its major goal is to keep costs under control and get the product out the factory door on time. By contrast, the product development function has a long-term viewpoint because developing a new product is a relatively slow process and high product quality is seen as more important than low costs. Such differences in viewpoint may make manufacturing and product development managers reluctant to cooperate and coordinate their activities to meet company goals. At the divisional level, in a company with a product structure, employees may become concerned more with making *their* division's products a success than with the profitability of the entire company. They may refuse, or simply not see, the need to cooperate and share information or knowledge with other divisions.

The problem of linking and coordinating the activities of different functions and divisions becomes more acute as the number of functions and divisions increases. We look first at how managers design the hierarchy of authority to coordinate functions and divisions so they work together effectively. Then we focus on integration and examine the different integrating mechanisms managers can use to coordinate functions and divisions.

### Allocating Authority

As organizations grow and produce a wider range of goods and services, the size and number of their functions and divisions increase. To coordinate the activities of people, functions, and divisions and to allow them to work together effectively, managers must develop a clear hierarchy of authority.[30] **Authority** is the power vested in a manager to make decisions and use resources to achieve organizational goals by virtue of his or her position in an organization. The **hierarchy of authority** is an organization's *chain of command*—the relative authority that each manager has—extending from the CEO at the top, down through the middle managers and first-line managers, to the nonmanagerial employees who actually make goods or provide services. Every manager, at every level of the hierarchy, supervises one or more subordinates. The term **span of control** refers to the number of subordinates who report directly to a manager.

Figure 10.7 shows a simplified picture of the hierarchy of authority and the span of control of managers in McDonald's in 2008. At the top of the hierarchy is Jim Skinner, CEO and vice chairman of McDonald's board of directors, who took control in 2004.[31] Skinner is the manager who has ultimate responsibility for McDonald's performance, and he has the authority to decide how to use organizational resources to benefit McDonald's stakeholders.[32] Don Thompson, next in line, is president and COO and is responsible for overseeing all of McDonald's global restaurant operations. Thompson reports directly to Skinner, as does chief financial officer Peter Bensen. Unlike the other managers, Bensen is not a line manager, someone in the direct line or chain of command who has formal authority over people and resources. Rather, Bensen is a staff manager, responsible for one of McDonald's specialist

**authority** The power to hold people accountable for their actions and to make decisions concerning the use of organizational resources.

**hierarchy of authority** An organization's chain of command, specifying the relative authority of each manager.

**span of control** The number of subordinates who report directly to a manager.

**Figure 10.7**
**The Hierarchy of Authority and Span of Control at McDonald's Corporation**

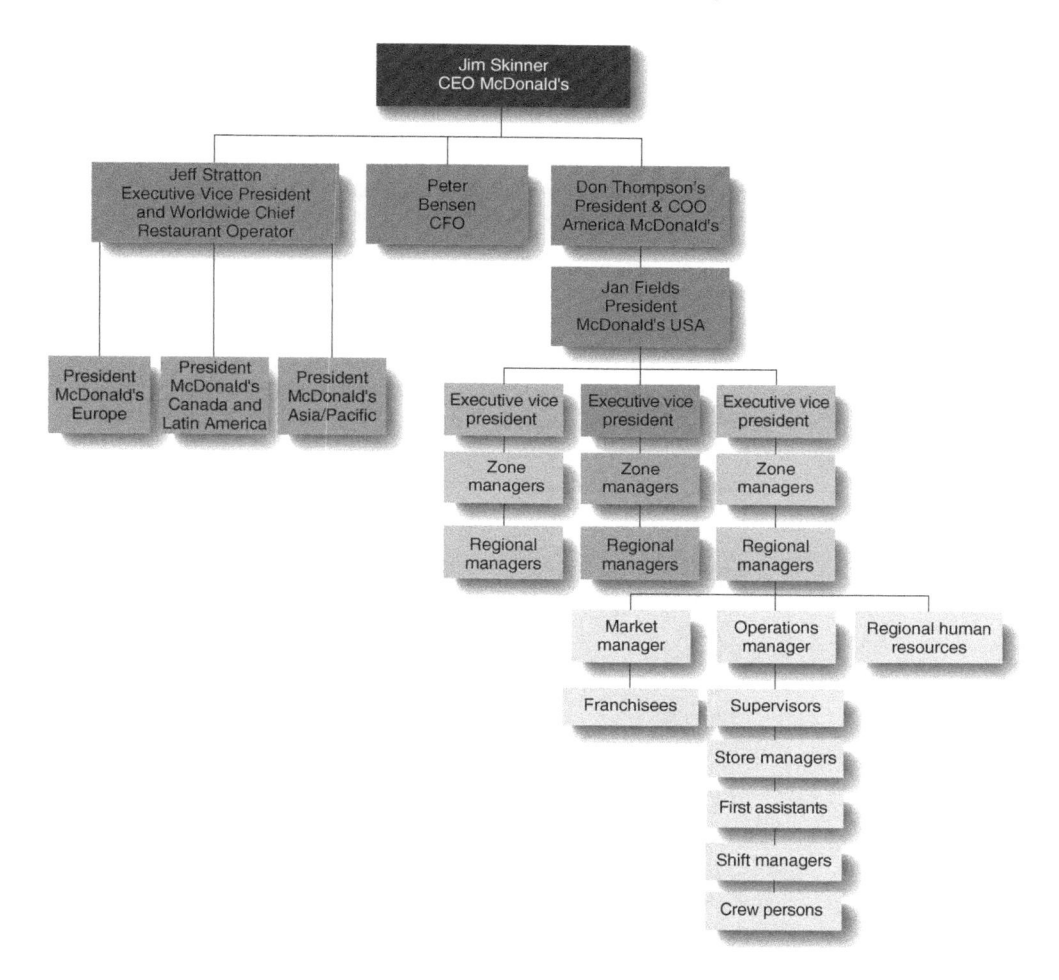

functions, finance. Worldwide chief operations officer Jeff Stratton is responsible for overseeing all functional aspects of McDonald's overseas operations, which are headed by the presidents of world regions: Europe; Canada and Latin America; and Asia/Pacific, Middle East, and Africa. Jan Fields is president of McDonald's U.S. operations and reports to Thompson.

Managers at each level of the hierarchy confer on managers at the next level down the authority to decide how to use organizational resources. Accepting this authority, those lower-level managers are accountable for how well they make those decisions. Managers who make the right decisions are typically promoted, and organizations motivate managers with the prospects of promotion and increased responsibility within the chain of command.

Below Fields are the other main levels or layers in the McDonald's domestic chain of command—executive vice presidents of its West, Central, and East regions, zone managers, regional managers, and supervisors. A hierarchy is also evident in each company-owned McDonald's restaurant. At the top is the store manager; at lower levels are the first assistant, shift managers, and crew personnel. McDonald's managers have decided that this hierarchy of authority best allows the company to pursue its business-level strategy of providing fast food at reasonable prices–and its stock price has exploded in the 2000s as its performance has increased.

**TALL AND FLAT ORGANIZATIONS** As an organization grows in size (normally measured by the number of its managers and employees), its hierarchy of authority normally lengthens, making the organizational structure taller. A *tall* organization has many levels of authority relative to company size; a *flat* organization has fewer levels relative to company size (see Figure 10.8).[33] As a hierarchy becomes taller, problems that make the organization's structure less flexible and slow managers' response to changes in the organizational environment may result.

Communication problems may arise when an organization has many levels in the hierarchy. It can take a long time for the decisions and orders of upper-level managers to reach managers further down in the hierarchy, and it can take a long time for top managers to learn how well their decisions worked. Feeling out of touch, top managers may want to verify that lower-level managers are following

**Figure 10.8**
**Tall and Flat Organizations**

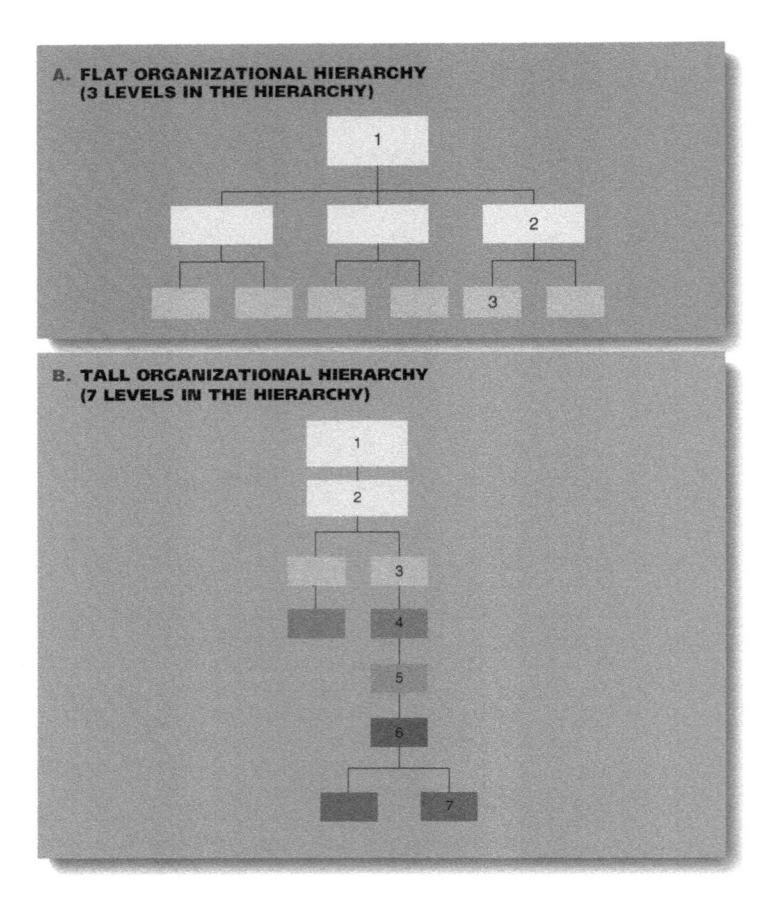

A. FLAT ORGANIZATIONAL HIERARCHY
(3 LEVELS IN THE HIERARCHY)

B. TALL ORGANIZATIONAL HIERARCHY
(7 LEVELS IN THE HIERARCHY)

orders and may require written confirmation from them. Middle managers, who know they will be held strictly accountable for their actions, start devoting too much time to the process of making decisions to improve their chances of being right. They might even try to avoid responsibility by making top managers decide what actions to take.

Another communication problem that can result is the distortion of commands and messages being transmitted up and down the hierarchy, which causes managers at different levels to interpret what is happening differently. Distortion of orders and messages can be accidental, occurring because different managers interpret messages from their own narrow, functional perspectives. Or distortion can be intentional, occurring because managers low in the hierarchy decide to interpret information in a way that increases their own personal advantage.

**THE MINIMUM CHAIN OF COMMAND** To ward off the problems that result when an organization becomes too tall and employs too many managers, top managers need to ascertain whether they are employing the right number of middle and first-line managers and whether they can redesign their organizational architecture to reduce the number of managers. Top managers might well follow a basic organizing principle—the principle of the minimum chain of command—which states that top managers should always construct a hierarchy with the fewest levels of authority necessary to efficiently and effectively use organizational resources. This is something Andrea Jung learned expensively at Avon.

Effective managers constantly scrutinize their hierarchies to see whether the number of levels can be reduced—for example, by eliminating one level and giving the responsibilities of managers at that level to managers above and by empowering employees below. The need to empower workers is increasing as companies work to reduce the number of middle managers to lower costs and to compete with low-cost overseas competitors, as the following "Managing Globally" box suggests.

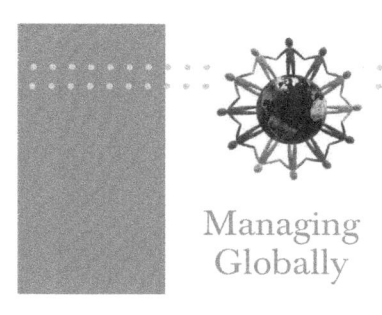

## Managing Globally

### SK Telecom: Restructuring an Organization and Its Impact

SK Telecom is a leading cell phone provider in Korea. However, in recent years the firm faced strong pressure on its revenue as cell phone saturation has grown. In an effort to address this problem, the firm realized it needed to change the organization of the firm and, in turn, the firm's culture. The Korean culture is strongly connected to Confucianism, which stresses hierarchy and respect for order. The firm's organizational structure was consistent with this culture. SK Telecom employed a five-staff-rank system of managers with a rigid top-down structure. The employees typically addressed each other by their title and then last name. In meetings lower-ranking employees were not permitted to question decisions. In October 2006, SK Telecom revamped its organizational structure in hopes of spurring more risk taking and creativity in the firm.

The company's first move was to eliminate five levels of management. Instead, it moved to a flatter organizational structure with greater decentralization of decision making in which there were only three levels of management. In addition, the firm moved to change how employees addressed each other; the firm required employees to simply address each other as "Manager." The firm maintained the very top titles but all levels below vice president were combined into a single category: team leader.

To help change the culture the firm also created new reward mechanisms that reinforced the new structure. One key change was that promotion became based on ability rather than seniority. Before the restructuring it was typical that promotions were based solely on seniority. SK Telecom began to place individuals in their 20s to lead projects for the firm. Previously individuals had to be in their 30s to have such responsibility. Some of the employees also saw their bonus structure change as bonuses are now based on creativity. Other changes that were made to reinforce the new structure included simple things like relaxing the dress code so that a more casual and innovative environment would result. The firm reports over 80% satisfaction by employees in the new environment in anonymous surveys.[34]

**CENTRALIZATION AND DECENTRALIZATION OF AUTHORITY** Another way in which managers can keep the organizational hierarchy flat is by **decentralizing authority**—that is, by giving lower-level managers and nonmanagerial employees the right to make important decisions about how to use organizational resources.[35] If managers at higher levels give lower-level employees the responsibility of making important decisions and only *manage by exception,* then the problems of slow and distorted communication noted previously are kept to a minimum. Moreover, fewer managers are needed because their role is not to make decisions but to act as coach and facilitator and to help other employees make the best decisions. In addition, when decision-making authority is low in the organization and near the customer, employees are better able to recognize and respond to customer needs.

Decentralizing authority allows an organization and its employees to behave in a flexible way even as the organization grows and becomes taller. This is why managers are so interested in empowering employees, creating self-managed work teams, establishing cross-functional teams, and even moving to a product team structure. These design innovations help keep the organizational architecture flexible and responsive to complex task and general environments, complex technologies, and complex strategies.

Although more and more organizations are taking steps to decentralize authority, *too much* decentralization has certain disadvantages. If divisions, functions, or teams are given too much decision-making authority, they may begin to pursue their own goals at the expense of organizational goals. Managers in engineering design or R&D, for example, may become so focused on making the best possible product they fail to realize that the best product may be so expensive few people are willing or able to buy it. Also, too much decentralization can cause lack of communication among functions or divisions; this prevents the synergies of cooperation from ever materializing, and organizational performance suffers.

Top managers must seek the balance between centralization and decentralization of authority that best meets the four major contingencies an organization faces (see Figure 10.1). If managers are in a stable environment, are using well-understood technology, and are producing stable kinds of products (such as cereal, canned soup, or books), there is no pressing need to decentralize authority, and managers at the top can maintain control of much of organizational decision making.[36] However, in uncertain, changing environments where high-tech companies are producing state-of-the-art products, top managers must often empower employees and allow teams to make important strategic decisions so the organization can keep up with the changes taking place. No matter what its environment, a company that fails to control the balance between centralization and decentralization will find its performance suffering. The following "Management Insight" box profiles the organizational structure in a large family business.

**decentralizing authority**
Giving lower-level managers and nonmanagerial employees the right to make important decisions about how to use organizational resources.

## Management Insight

### Organizational Structure in a Large Family Business

The Emami Group is an Indian conglomerate that has an aggregate turnover of about US$170 million. The group owns consumer goods, paper and newsprint, writing instruments, edible oil, agriculture, biodiesel plants, hospitals, pharmaceuticals, cement, coal, real estate, and retail. Emami's founders were two childhood friends, R. S. Agarwal and R. S. Goenka. They have a major concern for the transition to the next generation across two families. Therefore, they have structured the organization to facilitate such a transition.

Agarwal has three children, and Goenka has two. To ensure that the two families work together in all lines of business, they seek to have one child from each family involved in the management of the various lines of business. For example, Aditya, the elder son of Agarwal, and Manish, the younger son of Goenka, together run the hospital, edible oil, biodiesel, and paper businesses. Mohan, Goenka's elder son, and Harsh, Agarwal's youngest child, are spearheading the company's forays into new areas such as cement, power production, and coal. Sureka, Agarwal's daughter, heads new brands in consumer products. Concerns about including both families in the business structure go beyond the children of the founders: Prashant, Goenka's nephew, heads Emami international business.

To reinforce this structure, the families take other actions to ensure that they have strong interconnections so information is shared among all of the members of the two families. Some of these information-sharing methods are formal. For example, they have a family forum each month to ensure that all issues of concern are addressed in a more formal manner. However, there are also informal methods that support the organizational goal of full information sharing. For example, all children of the two families are next to each other at corporate headquarters. Their offices have walls of glass, so no one can hide from the others. The families also still have lunch with each other every day. Both families stay in multi-storied houses on the same lane in their home city. Finally, the two families, the founders and their spouses, their children and spouses, and the founders' grandchildren always take an annual vacation, during the Puja holidays in October.

The founders both have set up a formal structure to support communication in the firm and have also set up informal methods to support that formal structure. Overall, the business group looks well placed to be able to transition to the next generation when the time comes.[37]

## Integrating and Coordinating Mechanisms

**LO10-4** Explain why managers must coordinate jobs, functions, and divisions using the hierarchy of authority and integrating mechanisms.

Much coordination takes place through the hierarchy of authority. However, several problems are associated with establishing contact among managers in different functions or divisions. As discussed earlier, managers from different functions and divisions may have different views about what must be done to achieve organizational goals. But if the managers have equal authority (as functional managers typically do), the only manager who can tell them what to do is the CEO, who has the ultimate authority to resolve conflicts. The need to solve everyday conflicts, however, wastes top management time and slows strategic decision making; indeed, one sign of a poorly performing structure is the number of problems sent up the hierarchy for top managers to solve.

**integrating mechanisms** Organizing tools that managers can use to increase communication and coordination among functions and divisions.

To increase communication and coordination among functions or between divisions and to prevent these problems from emerging, top managers incorporate various **integrating mechanisms** into their organizational architecture. The greater the complexity of an organization's structure, the greater is the need for coordination among people, functions, and divisions to make the organizational structure work efficiently and effectively.[38] Thus when managers adopt a divisional, matrix, or product team structure, they must use complex integrating mechanisms to achieve organizational goals. Several integrating mechanisms are available to managers to increase communication and coordination.[39] Figure 10.9 lists these mechanisms, as well as examples of the individuals or groups who might use them.

**LIAISON ROLES** Managers can increase coordination among functions and divisions by establishing liaison roles. When the volume of contacts between two functions increases, one way to improve coordination is to give one manager in each function or division the responsibility for coordinating with the other. These managers may meet daily, weekly, monthly, or as needed. A liaison role is illustrated in Figure 10.9; the small dot represents the person within a function who has responsibility for coordinating with the other function. Coordinating is part of the liaison's full-time job, and usually an informal relationship develops between the people involved, greatly easing strains between functions. Furthermore, liaison roles provide a way of transmitting information across an organization, which is important in large organizations whose employees may know no one outside their immediate function or division.

**task force** A committee of managers from various functions or divisions who meet to solve a specific, mutual problem; also called *ad hoc committee*.

**TASK FORCES** When more than two functions or divisions share many common problems, direct contact and liaison roles may not provide sufficient coordination. In these cases, a more complex integrating mechanism, a **task force,** may be appropriate (see Figure 10.9). One manager from each relevant function or division is assigned to a task force that meets to solve a specific, mutual problem; members are responsible for reporting to their departments on the issues addressed and the solutions recommended. Task forces are often called *ad hoc committees* because they are temporary; they may meet on a regular basis or only a few times. When the problem or issue is solved, the task force is no longer needed; members return to their normal roles in their departments or are assigned to other task forces. Typically task force members also perform many of their normal duties while serving on the task force.

**Figure 10.9**
**Types and Examples of Integrating Mechanisms**

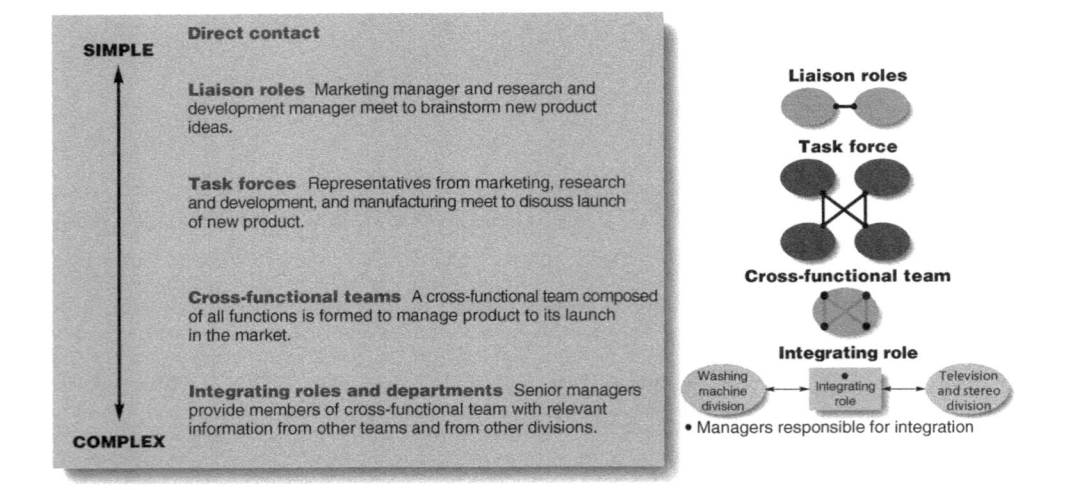

SIMPLE

**Direct contact**

**Liaison roles** Marketing manager and research and development manager meet to brainstorm new product ideas.

**Task forces** Representatives from marketing, research and development, and manufacturing meet to discuss launch of new product.

**Cross-functional teams** A cross-functional team composed of all functions is formed to manage product to its launch in the market.

**Integrating roles and departments** Senior managers provide members of cross-functional team with relevant information from other teams and from other divisions.

COMPLEX

Liaison roles

Task force

Cross-functional team

Integrating role

Washing machine division ↔ Integrating role ↔ Television and stereo division

• Managers responsible for integration

**CROSS-FUNCTIONAL TEAMS** In many cases the issues addressed by a task force are recurring problems, such as the need to develop new products or find new kinds of customers. To address recurring problems effectively, managers are increasingly using permanent integrating mechanisms such as cross-functional teams. An example of a cross-functional team is a new product development committee that is responsible for the choice, design, manufacturing, and marketing of a new product. Such an activity obviously requires a great deal of integration among functions if new products are to be successfully introduced, and using a complex integrating mechanism such as a cross-functional team accomplishes this. As discussed earlier, in a product team structure people and resources are grouped into permanent cross-functional teams to speed products to market. These teams assume long-term responsibility for all aspects of development and making the product.

**INTEGRATING ROLES** An integrating role is a role whose only function is to increase coordination and integration among functions or divisions to achieve performance gains from synergies. Usually managers who perform integrating roles are experienced senior managers who can envisage how to use the resources of the functions or divisions to obtain new synergies. One study found that DuPont, the giant chemical company, had created 160 integrating roles to coordinate the different divisions of the company and improve corporate performance.[40] The more complex an organization and the greater the number of its divisions, the more important integrating roles are.

In summary, to keep an organization responsive to changes in its task and general environments as it grows and becomes more complex, managers must increase coordination among functions and divisions by using complex integrating mechanisms. Managers must decide on the best way to organize their structures—that is, choose the structure that allows them to make the best use of organizational resources.

# Organizational Culture

**organizational culture**
The shared set of beliefs, expectations, values, and norms that influence how members of an organization relate to one another and cooperate to achieve organizational goals.

The second principal issue in organizational design is to create, develop, and maintain an organization's culture. As we discussed in Chapter 3, **organizational culture** is the shared set of beliefs, expectations, values, and norms that influence how members of an organization relate to one another and cooperate to achieve organizational goals. Culture influences the work behaviors and attitudes of individuals and groups in an organization because its members adhere to shared values, norms, and expected standards of behavior. Employees *internalize* organizational values and norms and then let these values and norms guide their decisions and actions.[41]

A company's culture is a result of its pivotal or guiding values and norms. A company's *values* are the shared standards that its members use to evaluate whether they have helped the company achieve its vision and goals. The values a company might adopt include any or all of the following standards: excellence, stability, predictability, profitability, economy, creativity, morality, and usefulness. A company's *norms* specify or prescribe the kinds of shared beliefs, attitudes, and behaviors that its members should observe and follow. Norms are informal, but powerful, rules about how employees should behave or conduct themselves in a company if they are to be accepted and help it to achieve its goals. Norms can be equally as constraining as the formal written rules contained in a company's handbook. Companies might encourage workers to adopt norms such as working hard, respecting traditions and authority, and being courteous to others; being conservative, cautious, and a "team player"; being creative and courageous and taking risks; or being honest and frugal and maintaining high personal standards. Norms may also prescribe certain specific behaviors such as keeping one's desk tidy, cleaning up at the end of the day, taking one's turn to bring doughnuts, and even wearing jeans on Fridays.

Ideally a company's norms help the company achieve its values. For example, a new computer company whose culture is based on values of excellence and innovation may try to attain this high standard by encouraging workers to adopt norms about being creative, taking risks, and working hard now and looking long-term for rewards (this combination of values and norms leads to an *entrepreneurial* culture in a company). On the other hand, a bank or insurance company that has values of stability and predictability may emphasize norms of cautiousness and obedience to authority (the result of adopting these values and norms would be a *stable, conservative* culture in a company).

Over time, members of a company learn from one another how to perceive and interpret various events that happen in the work setting and to respond to them in ways that reflect the company's guiding values and norms. This is why organizational culture is so important: When a strong and cohesive set of organizational values and norms is in place, employees focus on what is best for the organization in the long run—all their decisions and actions become oriented toward helping the organization perform well. For example, a teacher spends personal time after school coaching and counseling students; an R&D scientist works 80 hours a week, evenings, and weekends to help speed up a late project; or a salesclerk at a department store runs after a customer who left a credit card at the cash register. The following "Manager as a Person" box profiles embattled CEO Tony Hayward of British Petroleum, whose decision to streamline management had some unintended consequences.

## Changes in Structure and Unintended Consequences

**Manager as a Person**

British Petroleum (BP) is one of the leading companies in the United Kingdom. In 2007, when Tony Hayward took over as CEO, he restructured the firm's organization with the goal to streamline management. Hayward wanted to eliminate complexity and duplication at every level and to standardize procedures across the company through greater centralization of decision making. The prior structure had multiple interfaces that could be inefficient as there were individual business units that operated big oil fields or other assets. These units enjoyed a large degree of autonomy that often led to waste and business-unit leaders sometimes duplicating each other's initiatives, analysts say. Hayward changed the firm to have two major divisions: exploration & production, and refining & marketing. The firm that previously had major efforts in renewable energy sought to decrease that focus thus folding gas, power, and renewable energy's unit into those two divisions. The number of layers of management between workers and the chief executive was reduced from 11 to 7.

Tony Hayward, BP's former CEO, walks along the beach on the U.S. Gulf Coast during the oil spill crisis. Hayward's decision to reorganize the company's organizational structure may have had a negative impact on the company's ability to make decisions quickly during the environmental disaster.

The market was initially very positive on the change. BP's massive restructuring plan sent its shares to a 52-week high shortly after the change was implemented. However, the firm's structure was questioned following the 2010 oil spill in the Gulf of Mexico. BP's centralized decision making was efficient when there was a normal decision-making environment. However, during the early stages of the oil spill crisis, the local unit looked to Britain for key decisions. The result was delayed decision making and poor public relations during the early stages of the crisis. The firm ultimately rallied and addressed the problem aggressively.[42–44]

# Where Does Organizational Culture Come From?

**LO10-5** List the four sources of organizational culture, and explain why and how a company's culture can lead to competitive advantage.

In managing organizational architecture, some important questions that arise are these: Where does organizational culture come from? Why do different companies have different cultures? Why might a culture that for many years helped an organization achieve its goals suddenly harm the organization?

Organizational culture is shaped by the interaction of four main factors: the personal and professional characteristics of people within the organization, organizational ethics, the nature of the employment relationship, and the design of its organizational structure (see Figure 10.10). These factors work together to produce different cultures in different organizations and cause changes in culture over time.

**CHARACTERISTICS OF ORGANIZATIONAL MEMBERS** The ultimate source of organizational culture is the people who make up the organization. If you want to know why organizational cultures differ, look at how the characteristics of their members differ. Organizations A, B, and C develop distinctly different cultures because they attract, select, and retain people who have different values, personalities, and ethics.[45] Recall the attraction–selection–attrition model from Chapter 3. People may

**Figure 10.10**
**Sources of an Organization's Culture**

be attracted to an organization whose values match theirs; similarly, an organization selects people who share its values. Over time, people who do not fit in leave. The result is that people inside the organization become more similar, the values of the organization become more pronounced and clear-cut, and the culture becomes distinct from those of similar organizations.[46]

The fact that an organization's members become similar over time and come to share the same values may actually hinder their ability to adapt and respond to changes in the environment.[47] This happens when the organization's values and norms become so strong and promote so much cohesiveness in members' attitudes that the members begin to misperceive the environment.[48] Companies such as SAP, Bayer and Toshiba need a strong set of values that emphasize innovation and hard work; they also need to be careful their success doesn't lead members to believe their company is the best in the business. Companies frequently make this mistake. One famous example is the CEO of Digital Equipment, who in the 1990s laughed off the potential threat posed by PCs to his powerful minicomputers, claiming, "Personal computers are just toys." This company no longer exists.

**ORGANIZATIONAL ETHICS** The managers of an organization can set out purposefully to develop specific cultural values and norms to control how its members behave. One important class of values in this category stems from **organizational ethics,** which are the moral values, beliefs, and rules that establish the appropriate way for an organization and its members to deal with each other and with people outside the organization. Recall from Chapter 4 that ethical values rest on principles stressing the importance of treating organizational stakeholders fairly and equitably. Managers and employees are constantly making choices about the right, or ethical, thing to do; and to help them make ethical decisions, top managers purposefully implant ethical values into an organization's culture.[49] Consequently ethical values, and the rules and norms that embody them, become an integral part of an organization's culture and determine how its members will manage situations and make decisions.

**organizational ethics** The moral values, beliefs, and rules that establish the appropriate way for an organization and its members to deal with each other and with people outside the organization.

**THE EMPLOYMENT RELATIONSHIP** A third factor shaping organizational culture is the nature of the employment relationship a company establishes with its employees via its human resource policies and practices. Recall from Chapter 1 our discussion of the changing relationship between organizations and their employees due to the growth of outsourcing and employment of contingent workers. Like a company's hiring, promotion, and layoff policies, human resource policies, along with pay and benefits, can influence how hard employees will work to achieve the organization's goals, how attached they will be to the organization, and whether they will buy into its values and norms.[50] As we discuss in Chapter 12, an organization's human resource policies are a good indicator of the values in its culture concerning its responsibilities to employees. Consider the effects of a company's promotion policy, for example: A company with a policy of promoting from within will fill higher-level positions with employees who already work for the organization. On the other hand, a company with a policy of promotion from without will fill its open positions with qualified outsiders. What does this say about each organization's culture?

Promoting from within will bolster strong values and norms that build loyalty, align employees' goals with the organization, and encourage employees to work hard to advance within the organization. If employees see no prospect of being promoted from within, they are likely to look for better opportunities elsewhere, cultural values and norms result in self-interested behavior, and cooperation and cohesiveness fall. To rebuild their cultures, and make their remaining employees feel like "owners," many companies have HRM pay policies that reward superior performance with bonuses and stock options.[51]

**ORGANIZATIONAL STRUCTURE** We have seen how the values and norms that shape employee work attitudes and behaviors derive from an organization's people, ethics, and HRM policies. A fourth source of cultural values comes from the organization's structure. *Different kinds of structure give rise to different kinds of culture;* so to create a certain culture, managers often need to design a particular type of structure. Tall and highly centralized structures give rise to totally different sets of norms, rules, and cultural values than do structures that are flat and decentralized. In a tall, centralized organization people have little personal autonomy, and norms that focus on being cautious, obeying authority, and respecting traditions emerge because predictability and stability are desired goals. In a flat, decentralized structure people have more freedom to choose and control their own activities, and norms that focus on being creative and courageous and taking risks appear, giving rise to a culture in which innovation and flexibility are desired goals.

Whether a company is centralized or decentralized also leads to the development of different kinds of cultural values. By decentralizing authority and empowering employees, an organization can establish values that encourage and reward creativity or innovation. In doing this, an organization signals employees that it's okay to be innovative and do things their own way—as long as their actions are consistent with the good of the organization. Conversely, in some organizations it is important that employees do not make decisions on their own and that their actions be open to the scrutiny of superiors. In cases like this, centralization can be used to create cultural values that reinforce obedience and accountability. For example, in nuclear power plants, values that promote stability, predictability, and obedience to authority are deliberately fostered to prevent disasters.[52] Through norms and rules, employees are taught the importance of behaving consistently and honestly, and they learn that sharing information with supervisors, especially information about mistakes or errors, is the only acceptable form of behavior.[53]

An organization that seeks to manage and change its culture must take a hard look at all four factors that shape culture: the characteristics of its members, its ethical values, its human resource policies, and its organizational structure. However, changing a culture can be difficult because of the way these factors interact and affect one another.[54] Often a major reorganization is necessary for a cultural change to occur, as we discuss in the next chapter.

## Strong, Adaptive Cultures versus Weak, Inert Cultures

Many researchers and managers believe that employees of some organizations go out of their way to help the organization because it has a strong and cohesive organizational culture—an adaptive culture that controls employee attitudes and behaviors. *Adaptive cultures* are those whose values and norms help an organization to build momentum and to grow and change as needed to achieve its goals and be effective. By contrast, *inert cultures* are those whose values and norms fail to motivate or inspire employees; they lead to stagnation and, often, failure over time. What leads to a strong adaptive culture or one that is inert and hard to change?

Researchers have found that organizations with strong adaptive cultures, like 3M, SAP and Microsoft, invest in their employees. They demonstrate their commitment to their members by, for example, emphasizing the long-term nature of the employment relationship and trying to avoid layoffs. These companies develop long-term career paths for their employees and spend a lot of money on training and development to increase employees' value to the organization. In these ways, terminal and instrumental values pertaining to the worth of human resources encourage the development of supportive work attitudes and behaviors.

In adaptive cultures employees often receive rewards linked directly to their performance and to the performance of the company as a whole. Sometimes employee stock ownership plans (ESOPs) are developed in which workers as a group are allowed to buy a significant percentage of their company's stock. Workers who are owners of the company have additional incentive to develop skills that allow them to perform highly and search actively for ways to improve quality, efficiency, and performance.

Some organizations, however, develop cultures with values that do not include protecting and increasing the worth of their human resources as a major goal. Their employment practices are based on short-term employment according to the needs of the organization and on minimal investment in employees who perform simple, routine tasks. Moreover, employees are not often rewarded on the basis of their performance and thus have little incentive to improve their skills or otherwise invest in the organization to help it achieve goals. If a company has an inert culture, poor working relationships frequently develop between the organization and its employees, and instrumental values of noncooperation, laziness, and loafing and work norms of output restriction are common.

Moreover, an adaptive culture develops an emphasis on entrepreneurship and respect for the employee and allows the use of organizational structures, such as the cross-functional team structure, that empower employees to make decisions and motivate them to succeed. By contrast, in an inert culture, employees are content to be told what to do and have little incentive or motivation to perform beyond minimum work requirements. As you might expect, the emphasis is on close supervision and hierarchical authority, which result in a culture that makes it difficult to adapt to a changing environment.

Nokia, discussed earlier, is a good example of a company in which managers strive to create an adaptive culture.[55] Nokia's top managers have always believed that Nokia's cultural values are based on the Finnish character: Finns are down-to-earth, rational, straightforward people. They are also friendly and democratic people who do not believe in a rigid hierarchy based either on a person's authority or on social class. Nokia's culture reflects these values because innovation and decision making are pushed right down to the bottom line, to teams of employees who take up the challenge of developing the ever-smaller and more sophisticated phones for which the company is known. Bureaucracy is kept to a minimum at Nokia; its adaptive culture is based on informal and personal relationships and norms of cooperation and teamwork.

To help strengthen its culture, Nokia built a futuristic open-plan steel and glass building just outside Helsinki. Here, in an open environment, its R&D employees can work together to innovate new kinds of cell phones focused on Nokia's company mission to produce phones that are more versatile, cheaper, and easier to use than competitor's phones. This is the "Nokia Way"—a system of cultural values and norms that can't be written down but is always present in the values that cement people together and in the language and stories its members use to orient themselves to the company. Yet, as we noted before, Nokia is the cell phone company that is most sensitive to the need to appreciate the values, norms, and tastes of other nations. So the Nokia Way is not just confined to Finland; the company has taken it to every country around the globe in which it operates.

Another company with an adaptive culture is GlaxoSmithKline, the prescription drug maker discussed earlier in the chapter. Much of GSK's success can be attributed to its ability to recruit the best research scientists because its adaptive culture nurtures scientists and emphasizes values and norms of innovation. Scientists are given great freedom to pursue intriguing ideas even if the commercial payoff is questionable. Moreover, researchers are inspired to think of their work as a quest to alleviate human disease and suffering worldwide, and GSK has a reputation as an ethical company whose values put people above profits.

Although the experience of Nokia and GSK suggests that organizational culture can give rise to managerial actions that ultimately benefit the organization, this is not always the case. The cultures of some organizations become dysfunctional, encouraging managerial actions that harm the organization and discouraging actions that might improve performance.[56] For example, Sunflower Electric Power, an electricity generation and transmission cooperative, almost went bankrupt in the early 2000s. A committee of inquiry set up to find the source of the problem put the blame on Sunflower's CEO and decided he had created an abusive culture based on fear and blame that encouraged managers to fight over and protect their turf—an inert culture. The

CEO was fired, and a new CEO was appointed to change the cooperative's culture, which he found hard to do because his top managers were so used to the old values and norms. With the help of consultants, he changed values and norms to emphasize cooperation, teamwork, and respect for others—which involved firing many top managers. Clearly, managers can influence how their organizational culture develops over time.

## Summary and Review

**LO10-1** **DESIGNING ORGANIZATIONAL STRUCTURE** The four main determinants of organizational structure are the external environment, strategy, technology, and human resources. In general, the higher the level of uncertainty associated with these factors, the more appropriate is a flexible, adaptable structure as opposed to a formal, rigid one.

**LO10-2** **GROUPING TASKS INTO JOBS** Job design is the process by which managers group tasks into jobs. To create more interesting jobs, and to get workers to act flexibly, managers can enlarge and enrich jobs. The job characteristics model is a tool that managers can use to measure how motivating or satisfying a particular job is.

**LO10-3** **ORGANIZATIONAL STRUCTURE: GROUPING JOBS INTO FUNCTIONS AND DIVISIONS** Managers can choose from many kinds of organizational structures to make the best use of organizational resources. Depending on the specific organizing problems they face, managers can choose from functional, product, geographic, market, matrix, product team, and hybrid structures.

**LO10-4** **COORDINATING FUNCTIONS AND DIVISIONS** No matter which structure managers choose, they must decide how to distribute authority in the organization, how many levels to have in the hierarchy of authority, and what balance to strike between centralization and decentralization to keep the number of levels in the hierarchy to a minimum. As organizations grow, managers must increase integration and coordination among functions and divisions. Four integrating mechanisms that facilitate this are liaison roles, task forces, cross-functional teams, and integrating roles.

**LO10-5** **ORGANIZATIONAL CULTURE** Organizational culture is the set of values, norms, and standards of behavior that control how individuals and groups in an organization interact with one another and work to achieve organizational goals. The four main sources of organizational culture are member characteristics, organizational ethics, the nature of the employment relationship, and the design of organizational structure. How managers work to influence these four factors determines whether an organization's culture is strong and adaptive or is inert and difficult to change.

## Management in Action

### Topics for Discussion and Action

**Discussion**

1. Would a flexible or a more formal structure be appropriate for these organizations? (a) A large department store, (b) a Big Five accounting firm, (c) a biotechnology company. Explain your reasoning. [LO10-1, 10-2]
2. Using the job characteristics model as a guide, discuss how a manager can enrich or enlarge subordinates' jobs. [LO10-2]
3. How might a salesperson's job or a secretary's job be enlarged or enriched to make it more motivating? [LO10-2, 10-3]
4. When and under what conditions might managers change from a functional to (a) a product, (b) a geographic, or (c) a market structure? [LO10-1, 10-3]
5. How do matrix structure and product team structure differ? Why is product team structure more widely used? [LO10-1, 10-3, 10-4]
6. What is organizational culture, and how does it affect the way employees behave? [LO10-5]

**Action**

7. Find and interview a manager and identify the kind of organizational structure that his or her organization uses to coordinate its people and resources. Why is the organization using that structure? Do you think a different structure would be more appropriate? Which one? [LO10-1, 10-3, 10-4]
8. With the same or another manager, discuss the distribution of authority in the organization. Does the manager think that decentralizing authority and empowering employees is appropriate? [LO10-1, 10-3]
9. Interview some employees of an organization, and ask them about the organization's values and norms, the typical characteristics of employees, and the organization's ethical values and socialization practices. Using this information, try to describe the organization's culture and the way it affects how people and groups behave. [LO10-1, 10-5]

## Building Management Skills

### Understanding Organizing [LO10-1, 10-2, 10-3]

Think of an organization with which you are familiar, perhaps one you have worked for—such as a store, restaurant, office, church, or school. Then answer the following questions:

1. Which contingencies are most important in explaining how the organization is organized? Do you think it is organized in the best way?
2. Do you think national culture will impact these choices?
3. Can you think of any ways in which a typical job could be enlarged or enriched?
4. What kind of organizational structure does the organization use? If it is part of a chain, what kind of structure does the entire organization use? What other structures discussed in the chapter might allow the organization to operate more effectively? For example, would the move to a product team structure lead to greater efficiency or effectiveness? Why or why not?
5. How many levels are there in the organization's hierarchy? Is authority centralized or decentralized? Describe the span of control of the top manager and of middle or first-line managers.
6. Is the distribution of authority appropriate for the organization and its activities? Would it be possible to flatten the hierarchy by decentralizing authority and empowering employees?
7. What are the principal integrating mechanisms used in the organization? Do they provide sufficient coordination among individuals and functions? How might they be improved?
8. Now that you have analyzed the way this organization is structured, what advice would you give its managers to help them improve how it operates?

# Managing Ethically [LO10-1, 10-3, 10-5]

Suppose an organization is downsizing and laying off many of its middle managers. Some top managers charged with deciding whom to terminate might decide to keep the subordinates they like, and who are obedient to them, rather than the ones who are difficult or the best performers. They might also decide to lay off the most highly paid subordinates even if they are high performers. Think of the ethical issues involved in designing a hierarchy, and discuss the following issues.

## Questions

1. What are the laws in your country on layoffs? Can a manager in your home country lay off an employee simply because they choose to?

2. Some people argue that employees who have worked for an organization for many years have a claim on the organization at least as strong as that of its shareholders. What do you think of the ethics of this position—can employees claim to "own" their jobs if they have contributed significantly to the organization's past success? How does a socially responsible organization behave in this situation?

# Small Group Breakout Exercise

## Bob's Appliances [LO10-1, 10-3]

**Form groups of three or four people, and appoint one member as the spokesperson who will communicate your findings to the class when called on by the instructor. Then discuss the following scenario:**

Bob's Appliances sells and services household appliances such as washing machines, dishwashers, ranges, and refrigerators. Over the years, the company has developed a good reputation for the quality of its customer service, and many local builders patronize the store. However, large retailers are also providing an increasing range of appliances. Moreover, to attract more customers these stores also carry a complete range of consumer electronics products—LCD TVs, computers, and digital devices. Bob Lange, the owner of Bob's Appliances, has decided that if he is to stay in business, he must widen his product range and compete directly with the chains.

In 2007 he decided to build a 20,000-square-foot store and service center, and he is now hiring new employees to sell and service the new line of consumer electronics. Because of his company's increased size, Lange is not sure of the best way to organize the employees. Currently he uses a functional structure; employees are divided into sales, purchasing and accounting, and repair. Bob is wondering whether selling and servicing consumer electronics is so different from selling and servicing appliances that he should move to a product structure (see the figure on the next page) and create separate sets of functions for each of his two lines of business.[57]

You are a team of local consultants whom Bob has called in to advise him as he makes this crucial choice. Which structure do you recommend? Why?

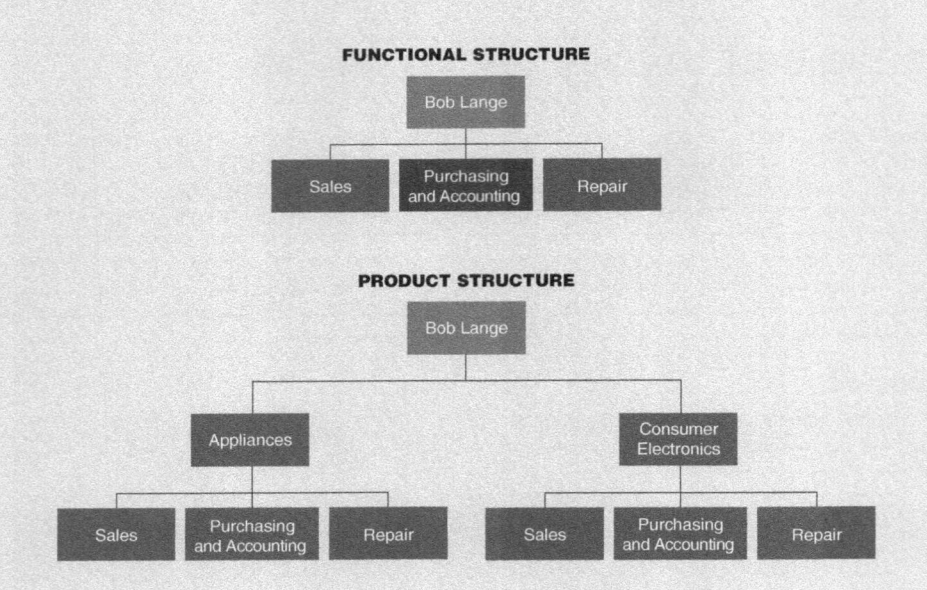

**FUNCTIONAL STRUCTURE**

Bob Lange
- Sales
- Purchasing and Accounting
- Repair

**PRODUCT STRUCTURE**

Bob Lange
- Appliances
  - Sales
  - Purchasing and Accounting
  - Repair
- Consumer Electronics
  - Sales
  - Purchasing and Accounting
  - Repair

## Exploring the World Wide Web [LO10-3]

Go to the Web site of Kraft, the food services company (www.kraft.com). Click on "Corporate Information" and then explore its brands—especially its takeover of Cadbury's.

1. Given the way it describes its brands, what kind of divisional structure do you think Kraft uses? Why do you think it uses this structure?

2. Click on featured brands, and look at products like its Oreo cookies. How is Kraft managing its different brands to increase global sales? What do you think are the main challenges Kraft faces in managing its global food business to improve performance?

## Be the Manager [LO10-1, 10-3, 10-5]

### Speeding Up Web Site Design

You have been hired by a Web site design, production, and hosting company whose new animated Web site designs are attracting a lot of attention and many customers. Currently employees are organized into different functions such as hardware, software design, graphic art, and Web site hosting, as well as functions such as marketing and human resources. Each function takes its turn to work on a new project from initial customer request to final online Web site hosting.

The problem the company is experiencing is that it typically takes one year from the initial idea stage to the time a Web site is up and running; the company wants to shorten this time by half to protect and expand its market niche. In talking to other managers, you discover that they believe the company's current functional structure is the source of the problem—it is not allowing employees to develop Web sites fast enough to satisfy customers' demands. They want you to design a better structure.

### Questions

1. Discuss how you can improve the way the current functional structure operates so it speeds Web site development.

2. Discuss the pros and cons of moving to a (a) multidivisional, (b) matrix, and (c) product team structure to reduce Web site development time.

3. Which of these structures do you think is most appropriate, and why?

4. What kind of culture would you help create to make the company's structure work more effectively?